Blackstone's Statutes on

PLANNING LAW

listed bldg. { publication of list — pp 252
restriction on work affecting listed building } pp 254

Blackstone's Statutes on
PLANNING LAW

Second Edition

Edited by

Victor Moore, LLM, Barrister

Professor of Law Emeritus,
University of Reading

and

David Hughes, LLB (L'pool), LLM (Cantab), FRSA

Professor of Housing and Planning Law
The Environmental Law Institute
De Montfort University, Leicester

First published in Great Britain 1995 by Blackstone Press Limited,
9-15 Aldine Street, London W12 8AW. Telephone 0181-740 1173

© Victor Moore and David Hughes, 1995

ISBN: 1 85431 490 4

First edition, 1995
Second edition, 1995

British Library Cataloguing in Publication Data
A CIP catalogue record for this book is available from the British Library

Typeset by Style Photosetting Ltd, Mayfield, East Sussex
Printed by Ashford Colour Press, Gosport, Hampshire

All rights reserved. No part of this book may be reproduced or transmitted in any form or by any means, electronic or mechanical, including photocopying, recording, or any information storage or retrieval system without prior permission from the publisher.

CONTENTS

Editors' Preface vii

Town and Country Planning Act 1990 1
Planning (Listed Buildings and Conservation Areas) Act 1990 248
Environment Act 1995 304
Town and Country Planning (Environmental Assessment and Permitted Development) Regulations 1995 328
Town and Country Planning (General Permitted Development) Order 1995 .. 332
Town and Country Planning (General Development Procedure) Order 1995 .. 403
Town and Country Planning (Use Classes) Order 1987 441
Town and Country Planning (Assessment of Environmental Effects) Regulations 1988 444
Town and Country Planning (Development Plan) Regulations 1991 461
Town and Country Planning (Inquiries Procedure) Rules 1992 478
Town and Country Planning Appeals (Determination by Inspectors) (Inquiries Procedure) Rules 1992 488
Conservation (Natural Habitats, & c.) Regulations 1994 497
Town and Country Planning (Demolition — Description of Buildings) Direction 1995 507

Index 509

EDITORS' PREFACE

The purpose of this book remains, as it was initially, to provide a portable collection of the primary and secondary legislation most needed by students studying planning law. We believe it will be a most useful addition to the current student textbooks on the subject; and that it will provide an easy reference to the main source material needed by those studying in the field of land use, whether they are following undergraduate or post-graduate courses, be it planning law, town and country planning, land economics or land management, or perhaps courses leading to a professional qualification.

The whole of the main legislation, namely the Town and Country Planning Act 1990 and the Planning (Listed Buildings and Conservation Areas) Act 1990, as amended by the important Planning and Compensation Act 1991, has been published here in full. So too, are the main statutory instruments, which we feel are of crucial importance to a proper understanding of the subject.

We have brought out this second edition, hard on the heels of its predecessor, primarily to take account of the replacement of the former General Development Order 1988 by two new orders, one relating to development control procedure, and the other concerned with permitted development rights. This eighth edition has also given us the opportunity to note the further revision of the Use Classes Order, the substitution of a replacement Direction on the demolition of buildings, and, most importantly, to take account of the changes made by the Environment Act 1995.

It should also be noted that the major changes in the structure of English local government brought about by the Local Government Act 1992 will soon appear 'on the ground', and thus a number of important towns will soon enjoy unitary status, which will have implications for planning. This change will apply, for example, to Milton Keynes, Brighton and Hove, Bournemouth, Durham, Derby, Thamesdown, Portsmouth, Southampton, Luton, Stoke-on-Trent; other places will follow. In the meantime piecemeal change is being made, so far as planning law is concerned, in the structure of Welsh local government under the Local Government (Wales) Act 1994, only parts of which are in force. Some of the modifications potentially brought about by this Act in the body of the 1990 legislation may well be overtaken before coming into force by further change under the Environment Act 1995 as it comes into force. To indicate the current fluid state of the law this edition uses the devices of [—] and underlining to indicate modifications waiting to be brought into effect.

Victor Moore
David Hughes
1995

TOWN AND COUNTRY PLANNING ACT 1990
(1990, c. 8)
(as amended)

PART I
PLANNING AUTHORITIES

Section
1. Local planning authorities: general.
2. Joint planning boards.
3. Joint planning committee for Greater London.
4. National Parks.
4A. National Parks with National Park Authorities
5. The Broads.
6. Enterprise zones.
7. Urban development areas.
8. Housing action areas.
8A. The Urban Regeneration Agency.
9. Power to make consequential and supplementary provision about authorities.

PART II
DEVELOPMENT PLANS
CHAPTER I
UNITARY DEVELOPMENT PLANS: METROPOLITAN AREAS INCLUDING LONDON

Preliminary

10 Application of Chapter I to Greater London and metropolitan counties.

Surveys, etc.

11 Survey of planning areas.

Preparation and adoption of unitary development plans

12. Preparation of unitary development plan.
12A. Urban development corporations.
13. Public participation.
14. Withdrawal of unitary development plan.
15. Adoption of unitary development plan by local planning authority.
16. Local inquiries.

Secretary of State's powers concerning plans

17. Direction to reconsider proposals.
18. Calling in of unitary development plan for approval by Secretary of State.
19. Approval of unitary development plan by Secretary of State.
20. Local inquiry, public examination and consultation by Secretary of State.

Alteration of plans

21. Alteration or replacement of unitary development plan.
22. [Repealed by the Planning and Compensation Act 1991.]

Joint plans

23.	Joint unitary development plans.
23A.	Joint unitary development plans: Wales.
23B.	Unitary development plans for National Parks in Wales.
23C.	Joint unitary development plans for National Parks in Wales.

Supplementary

24.	Disregard of certain representations.
25.	Default powers.
26.	Regulations and directions.
27.	Meaning of 'development plan' in Greater London and metropolitan counties.
27A.	Meaning of 'development plan' in relation to Wales.
28.	Commencement of Chapter I: transitional provisions.

CHAPTER II
STRUCTURE AND LOCAL PLANS: NON-METROPOLITAN AREAS

Preliminary

29.	Application of Chapter II to non-metropolitan areas.

Surveys, etc.

30.	Surveys of planning areas.

Structure plans

31.	Structure plans: continuity, form and content.
32.	Alteration and replacement of structure plans.
33.	Public participation.
34.	Withdrawal of proposals for alteration or replacement of structure plans.
35.	Adoption of proposals.
35A.	Calling in of proposals for approval by Secretary of State.
35B.	Examination in public.
35C.	Duties to notify authorities responsible for local plan.

Local plans

36.	Local plans.
37.	Minerals local plans.
38.	Waste policies.
39.	Alteration and replacement of local plans.
40.	Public participation.
41.	[Repealed by the Planning and Compensation Act 1991.]
42.	Objections: local inquiry or other hearing.
43.	Adoption of proposals.
44.	Calling in of proposals for approval by Secretary of State.
45.	Approval of proposals by Secretary of State.

Conformity between plans

46.	Conformity between plans.
47–48.	[Repealed by the Planning and Compensation Act 1990.]

Supplementary

49.	Disregarding of representations with respect to development authorised by or under other enactments.
50.	Joint structure and local plans.
51.	Default powers.
51A.	Urban development corporations.
52.	Reviews of plans in enterprise zones.
53.	Supplementary provisions as to structure and local plans.
54.	Meaning of 'development plan' outside Greater London and the metropolitan counties.

CHAPTER III
GENERAL

54A. Status of development plans.

PART II
CONTROL OVER DEVELOPMENT

Meaning of development

55. Meaning of 'development'.
56. Time when development begun.

Requirement for planning permission

57. Planning permission required for development.
58. Granting of planning permission: general.

Development orders

59. Development orders: general.
60. Permission granted by development order.
61. Development orders: supplementary provisions.

Applications for planning permission

62. Form and content of applications for planning permission.
63–64. [Repealed by the Planning and Compensation Act 1991.]

Publicity for applications

65. Notice etc. of application for planning permission.
66–68. [Repealed by the Planning and Compensation Act 1991.]
69. Registers of applications, etc.

Determination of applications

70. Determination of applications: general considerations.
70A. Power of local planning authority to decline to determine applications.
71. Consultations in connection with determinations under s. 70.
71A. Assessment of environmental effects.
72. Conditional grant of planning permission.
73. Determination of applications to develop land without compliance with conditions previously attached.
73A. Planning permission for development already carried out.
74. Directions etc. as to method of dealing with applications.
75. Effect of planning permission.
76. Duty to draw attention to certain provisions for benefit of disabled.

Secretary of State's powers as respects planning applications and decisions

77. Reference of applications to Secretary of State.
78. Right to appeal against planning decisions and failure to take such decisions.
79. Determination of appeals.
80–81. [Repealed by the Planning and Compensation Act 1991.]

Simplified planning zones

82. Simplified planning zones.
83. Making of simplified planning zone schemes.
84. Simplified planning zone schemes: conditions and limitations on planning permission.
85. Duration of simplified planning zone scheme.
86. Alteration of simplified planning zone scheme.
87. Exclusion of certain descriptions of land or development.

Enterprise zone schemes

88. Planning permission for development in enterprise zones.
89. Effect on planning permission of modification or termination of scheme.

Deemed planning permission

90. Development with government authorisation.

Duration of planning permission
91. General condition limiting duration of planning permission.
92. Outline planning permission.
93. Provisions supplementary to ss. 91 and 92.
94. Termination of planning permission by reference to time limit: completion notices.
95. Effect of completion notice.
96. Power of Secretary of State to serve completion notices.

Revocation and modification of planning permission
97. Power to revoke or modify planning permission.
98. Procedure for s. 97 orders: opposed cases.
99. Procedure for s. 97 orders: unopposed cases.
100. Revocation and modification of planning permission by the Secretary of State.

References to Planning Inquiry Commission
101. Power to refer certain planning questions to Planning Inquiry Commission.

Other controls over development
102. Orders requiring discontinuance of use or alteration or removal of buildings or works.
103. Confirmation by Secretary of State of s. 102 orders.
104. Power of the Secretary of State to make s. 102 orders.
*105. Reviews by mineral planning authorities.
106. Planning obligations.
106A. Modification and discharge of planning obligations.
106B. Appeals.
*To be repealed as from an appointed day by the Environment Act 1995.

PART IV
COMPENSATION FOR EFFECTS OF CERTAIN ORDERS, NOTICES, ETC.

Compensation for revocation of planning permission, etc.
107. Compensation where planning permission revoked or modified.
108. Compensation for refusal or conditional grant of planning permission formerly granted by development order.
109. Apportionment of compensation for depreciation.
110. Registration of compensation for depreciation.
111. Recovery of compensation under s. 107 on subsequent development.
112. Amount recoverable under s. 111 and provisions for payment or remission of it.
113. [Repealed by the Planning and Compensation Act 1991.]

Compensation for other planning decisions
114. [Repealed by the Planning and Compensation Act 1991.]
115. Compensation in respect of orders under s. 102, etc.
116. Modification of compensation provision in respect of mineral working etc.

General and supplemental provisions
117. General provisions as to compensation for depreciation under Part IV.
118. Determination of claims for compensation.

PART V
119–136. [Repealed by the Planning and Compensation Act 1991.]

PART VI
RIGHTS OF OWNERS ETC. TO REQUIRE PURCHASE OF INTERESTS
CHAPTER I
INTERESTS AFFECTED BY PLANNING DECISIONS OR ORDERS

Service of purchase notices
137. Circumstances in which purchase notices may be served.
138. Circumstances in which land incapable of reasonably beneficial use.

Duties of authorities on service of purchase notice
139. Action by council on whom purchase notice is served.
140. Procedure on reference of purchase notice to Secretary of State.

141.	Action by Secretary of State in relation to purchase notice.
142.	Power to refuse to confirm purchase notice where land has restricted use by virtue of previous planning permission.
143.	Effect of Secretary of State's action in relation to purchase notice.

Compensation

144.	Special provisions as to compensation where purchase notice served.

Special provisions for requiring purchase of whole of partially affected agricultural unit

145.	Counter-notice requiring purchase of remainder of agricultural unit.
146.	Effect of counter-notice under s. 145.
147.	Provisions supplemental to ss. 145 and 146.
147A.	Application of Chapter I to National Parks

Supplemental

148.	Interpretation of Chapter I.

CHAPTER II
INTERESTS AFFECTED BY PLANNING PROPOSALS: BLIGHT

Preliminary

149.	Scope of Chapter II.

Blight notices

150.	Notices requiring purchase of blighted land.
151.	Counter-notices objecting to blight notices.
152.	Further counter-notices where certain proposals have come into force.
153.	Reference of objection to Lands Tribunal: general.
154.	Effect of valid blight notice.
155.	Effect on powers of compulsory acquisition of counter-notice disclaiming intention to acquire.
156.	Withdrawal of blight notice.

Compensation

157.	Special provisions as to compensation for acquisitions in pursuance of blight notices.

Special provisions for requiring purchase of whole of partially affected agricultural unit

158.	Inclusion in blight notices of requiement to purchase parts of agricultural units unaffected by blight.
159.	Objections to s. 158 notices.
160.	Effect of notices served by virtue of s. 158.

Personal representatives, mortgagees and partnerships

161.	Powers of personal representatives in respect of blight notice.
162.	Power of mortgagees to serve blight notice.
163.	Prohibition on service of simultaneous notices under s. 150, 161 and 162.
164.	Special provisions as to partnerships.

Miscellaneous and supplementary provisions

165.	Power of Secretary of State to acquire land affected by orders relating to new towns etc. where blight notice served.
166.	Saving for claimant's right to sell whole hereditament, etc.
167.	No withdrawal of constructive notice to treat.
168.	Meaning of 'owner-occupier' and 'resident owner-occupier'.
169.	'Appropriate authority' for purposes of Chapter II.
170.	'Appropriate enactment' for purposes of Chapter II.
171.	General interpretation of Chapter II.

PART VII
ENFORCEMENT

Introductory

171A.	Expressions used in connection with enforcement.
171B.	Time limits.

Planning contravention notices

171C. Power to require information about activities on land.
171D. Penalties for non-compliance with planning contravention notice.

Enforcement notices

172. Issue of enforcement notice.
173. Contents of enforcement notice.
173A. Variation and withdrawal of enforcement notices.
174. Appeal against enforcement notice.
175. Appeals: supplementary provisions.
176. General provisions relating to determination of appeals.
177. Grant or modification of planning permission on appeals against enforcement notices.
178. Execution and cost of works required by enforcement notice.
179. Offence where enforcement notice not complied with.
180. Effect of planning permission etc., on enforcement or breach of condition notice.
181. Enforcement notice to have effect against subsequent development.
182. Enforcement by the Secretary of State.

Stop notices

183. Stop notices.
184. Stop notices: supplementary provisions.
185. Service of stop notices by Secretary of State.
186. Compensation for loss due to stop notice.
187. Penalties for contravention of stop notice.

Breach of condition

187A. Enforcement of conditions.

Injunctions

187B. Injunctions restraining breaches of planning control.

Registers

188. Register of enforcement and stop notices.

Enforcement of orders for discontinuance of use, etc.

189. Penalties for contravention of orders under s. 102 and Schedule 9.
190. Enforcement of orders under s. 102 and Schedule 9.

Certificate of lawful use or development

191. Certificate of lawfulness of existing use or development.
192. Certificate of lawfulness of proposed use or development.
193. Certificates under sections 191 and 192: supplementary provisions.
194. Offences.
195. Appeals against refusal or failure to give decisions on application.
196. Further provisions as to references and appeals to the Secretary of State.

Rights of entry for enforcement purposes

196A. Rights to enter without warrant.
196B. Rights to enter under warrant.
196C. Rights of entry: supplementary provisions.

PART VIII
SPECIAL CONTROLS
CHAPTER I
TREES

General duty of planning authorities as respects trees

197. Planning permission to include appropriate provision for preservation and planting of trees.

Tree preservation order

198. Power to make tree preservation orders.
199. Form of and procedure applicable to orders.
200. Orders affecting land where Forestry Commissioners interested.

201. Provisional tree preservation orders.
202. Power for Secretary of State to make tree preservation orders.

Compensation for loss or damage caused by orders, etc.

203. Compensation in respect of tree preservation orders.
204. Compensation in respect of requirement as to replanting of trees.
205. Determination of compensation claims.

Consequences of tree removal, etc.

206. Replacement of trees.
207. Enforcement of duties as to replacement of trees.
208. Appeals against s. 207 notices.
209. Execution and cost of works required by s. 207 notice.
210. Penalties for non-compliance with tree preservation order.

Trees in conservation areas

211. Preservation of trees in conservation areas.
212. Power to disapply s. 211.
213. Enforcement of controls as respects trees in conservation areas.
214. Register of s. 211 notices.

Injunctions

214A. Injunctions.

Rights of entry

214B. Rights to enter without warrant.
214C. Right to enter under warrant.
214D. Rights of entry: supplementary provisions.

CHAPTER II
LAND ADVERSELY AFFECTING AMENITY OF NEIGHBOURHOOD

215. Power to require proper maintenance of land.
216. Penalty for non-compliance with s. 215 notice.
217. Appeal to magistrates' court against s. 215 notice.
218. Further appeal to the Crown Court.
219. Execution and cost of works required by s. 215 notice.

CHAPTER III
ADVERTISEMENTS

Advertisement regulations

220. Regulations controlling display of advertisements.
221. Power to make different advertisement regulations for different areas.
222. Planning permission not needed for advertisements complying with regulations.

Repayment of expense of removing prohibited advertisements

223. Repayment of expense of removing prohibited advertisements.

Enforcement of control over advertisements

224. Enforcement of control as to advertisements.
225. Power to remove or obliterate placards and posters.

PART IX
ACQUISITION AND APPROPRIATION OF LAND FOR PLANNING PURPOSES, ETC.

Acquisition for planning and public purposes

226. Compulsory acquisition of land for development and other planning purposes.
227. Acquisition of land by agreement.
228. Compulsory acquisition of land by the Secretary of State for the Environment.
229. Appropriation of land forming part of common, etc.
230. Acquisition of land for purposes of exchange.
231. Power of Secretary of State to require acquisition or development of land.

Appropriation, disposal and development of land held for planning purposes, etc.
232. Appropriation of land held for planning purposes.
233. Disposal by local authorities of land held for planning purposes.
234. Disposal by Secretary of State of land acquired under s. 228.
235. Development of land held for planning purposes.

Extinguishment of certain rights affecting acquired or appropriated land
236. Extinguishment of rights over land compulsorily acquired.
237. Power to override easements and other rights.
238. Use and development of consecrated land.
239. Use and development of burial grounds.
240. Provisions supplemental to ss. 238 and 239.
241. Use and development of open spaces.
242. Overriding of rights of possession.

Constitution of joint body to hold land for planning purposes
243. Constitution of joint body to hold land for planning purposes.

General and supplementary provisions
244. Powers of joint planning boards under Part IX.
244A. Powers of National Park Authorities under Part IX.
245. Modification of incorporated enactments for purposes of Part IX.
246. Interpretation of Part IX.

PART X
HIGHWAYS

Orders made by Secretary of State
247. Highways affected by development: orders by Secretary of State.
248. Highways crossing or entering route of proposed new highway, etc.
249. Order extinguishing right to use vehicles on highway.
250. Compensation for orders under s. 249.
251. Extinguishment of public rights of way over land held for planning purposes.
252. Procedure for making of orders.
253. Procedure in anticipation of planning permission.
254. Compulsory acquisition of land in connection with highways.
255. Concurrent proceedings in connection with highways.
256. Telecommunication apparatus: orders by Secretary of State.

Orders by other authorities
257. Footpaths and bridleways affected by development: orders by other authorities.
258. Extinguishment of public rights of way over land held for planning purposes.
259. Confirmation of orders made by other authorities.
260. Telecommunication apparatus: orders by or on application of other authorities.

Temporary highway orders: mineral workings
261. Temporary stopping up of highways for mineral workings.

PART XI
STATUTORY UNDERTAKERS

Preliminary
262. Meaning of 'statutory undertakers'.
263. Meaning of 'operational land'.
264. Cases in which land is to be treated as not being operational land.
265. Meaning of 'the appropriate Minister'.

Application of Part III to statutory undertakers
266. Applications for planning permission by statutory undertakers.
267. Conditional grants of planning permission.
268. Development requiring authorisation of government department.
269. Revocation or modification of permission to develop operational land.
270. Order requiring discontinuance of use etc. of operational land.

Extinguishment of rights of statutory undertakers, etc.

271. Extinguishment of rights of statutory undertakers: preliminary notices.
272. Extinguishment of rights of telecommunications code system operators: preliminary notices.
273. Notice for same purposes as ss. 271 and 272 but given by undertakers to developing authority.
274. Orders under ss. 271 and 272.

Extension or modification of statutory undertakers' functions

275. Extension or modification of functions of statutory undertakers.
276. Procedure in relation to orders under s. 275.
277. Relief of statutory undertakers from obligations rendered impracticable.
278. Objections to orders under ss. 275 and 277.

Compensation

279. Right to compensation in respect of certain decisions and orders.
280. Measure of compensation to statutory undertakers, etc.
281. Exclusion of s. 280 at option of statutory undertakers.
282. Procedure for assessing compensation.

Advertisements

283. Display of advertisements on operational land.

PART XII
VALIDITY

284. Validity of development plans and certain orders, decisions and directions.
285. Validity of enforcement notices and similar notices.
286. Challenges to validity on ground of authority's powers.
287. Proceedings for questioning validity of development plans and certain schemes and orders.
288. Proceedings for questioning the validity of other orders, decisions and directions.
289. Appeals to High Court relating to enforcement notices and notices under s. 207.
290. [Repealed by the Planning and Compensation Act 1991.]
291. Special provisions as to decisions relating to statutory undertakers.
292. Special provisions as to orders subject to special parliamentary procedure.

PART XIII
APPLICATION OF ACT TO CROWN LAND

Preliminary

293. Preliminary definitions.

Application of Act as respects Crown land

294. Control of development on Crown land: special enforcement notices.
295. Supplementary provisions as to special enforcement notices.
296. Exercise of powers in relation to Crown land.
297. Agreements relating to Crown land.
298. Supplementary provisions as to Crown and Duchy interests.

Provisions relating to anticipated disposal of Crown land

299. Application for planning permission etc. in anticipation of disposal of Crown land.
299A. Crown planning obligations.
300. Tree preservation orders in anticipation of disposal of Crown land.
301. Requirement of planning permission for continuance of use instituted by the Crown.

Enforcement in respect of war-time breaches of planning control by the Crown

302. Enforcement in respect of war-time breaches of planning control by the Crown.

PART XIV
FINANCIAL PROVISIONS

303. Fees for planning applications, etc.
304. Grants for planning applications, etc.

305. Contributions by Ministers towards compensation paid by local authorities.
306. Contributions by local authorities and statutory undertakers.
307. Assistance for acquisition of property where objection made to blight notice in certain cases.
308. Recovery from acquiring authorities of sums paid by way of compensation.
309. [Repealed by the Planning and Compensation Act 1991.]
310. Sums recoverable from acquiring authorities reckonable for purposes of grant.
311. Expenses of government departments.
312. [Repealed by the Planning and Compensation Act 1991.]
313. General provision as to receipts of Secretary of State.
314. Expenses of county councils.

PART XV
MISCELLANEOUS AND GENERAL PROVISIONS

Application of Act in special cases

315. Power to modify Act in relation to minerals.
316. Land of interested planning authorities and development by them.
316A. Local planning authorities as statutory undertakers.
317. [Repealed by the Coal Industry Act 1994.]
318. Ecclesiastical property.
319. Application of Act to Isles of Scilly.

Local inquiries and other hearings

320. Local inquiries.
321. Planning inquiries to be held in public subject to certain exceptions.
322. Orders as to costs of parties where no local inquiry held.
322A. Orders as to costs: supplementary.
323. Procedure on certain appeals and applications.

Rights of entry

324. Rights of entry.
325. Supplementary provisions as to rights of entry.

Miscellaneous and general provisions

326–327. [Repealed by the Planning and Compensation Act 1991.]
328. Settled land and land of universities and colleges.
329. Service of notices.
330. Power to require information as to interests in land.
331. Offences by corporations.
332. Combined applications.
333. Regulations and orders.
334. Licensing planning areas.
335. Act not excluded by special enactments.
336. Interpretation.
337. Short title, commencement and extent.

SCHEDULES
   Schedule 1 — Local planning authorities: distribution of functions.
   Schedule 2 — Development plans: transitional provisions.
      Part I — The metropolitan counties.
      Part II — Greater London.
      Part III — Old development plans.
   Schedule 3 — Development not constituting new development.
      Part I — Development not ranking for compensation under s. 114.
      Part II — Development ranking for compensation under s. 114.
      Part III — Supplementary provisions.
   Schedule 4 — Special provisions as to land use in 1948.
   Schedule 5 — Conditions relating to mineral working.
      Part I — Conditions imposed on grant of permission.
      Part II — Conditions imposed on revocation or modification of permission.

Town and Country Planning Act 1990   11

Schedule 6 — Determination of certain appeals by person appointed by Secretary of State.
Schedule 7 — Simplified planning zones.
Schedule 8 — Planning Inquiry Commissions.
   Part I — Constitution and procedure on references.
   Part II — Meaning of 'the responsible Minister or Ministers'.
Schedule 9 — Requirements relating to discontinuance of mineral working.
Schedule 10 — Condition treated as applicable to rebuilding and alterations.
Schedule 11 — [Repealed by the Planning and Compensation Act 1991.]
Schedule 12 — [Repealed by the Planning and Compensation Act 1991.]
Schedule 13 — Blighted land.
Schedule 14 — Procedure for footpaths and bridleways orders.
   Part I — Confirmation of orders.
   Part II — Publicity for orders after confirmation.
Schedule 15 — Enforcement as respects war-time breaches by the Crown of planning control.
Schedule 16 — Provisions of the planning Acts referred to in sections 314 to 319.
Schedule 17 — Exactments exempted from section 333(6).

An Act to consolidate certain enactments relating to town and country planning (excluding special controls in respect of buildings and areas of special architectural or historic interest and in respect of hazardous substances) with amendments to give effect to recommendations of the Law Commission. [24th May 1990]

PART I
PLANNING AUTHORITIES

1. Local planning authorities: general

(1). In a non-metropolitan county—
   (a) the council of a county is the county planning authority for the county, and
   (b) the council of a district is the district planning authority for the district,
and references in the planning Acts to a local planning authority in relation to a non-metropolitan county shall be construed, subject to any express provision to the contrary, as references to both the county planning authority and the district planning authorities.

[(1A) Subsection (1) does not apply in relation to Wales.
(1B) In Wales—
   (a) the local planning authority for a county is the county council; and
   (b) the local planning authority for a county borough is the county borough council.]

(2) The council of a metropolitan district is the local planning authority for the district and the council of a London borough is the local planning authority for the borough.

(3) In England (exclusive of the metropolitan counties, Greater London and the Isles of Scilly) and in Wales all functions conferred on local planning authorities by or under the planning Acts shall be exercisable both by county planning authorities and district planning authorities.

(4) In this Act 'mineral planning authority' means—
   (a) in respect of a site in a non-metropolitan county, the county planning authority; and
   (b) in respect of a site in a metropolitan district or London borough, the local planning authority.

[(4A) Subsection (4) does not apply in relation to Wales.
(4B) As to any site in Wales, the local planning authority is also the mineral planning authority.]

(5) This section has effect subject to any express provision to the contrary in the planning Acts and, in particular—

(a) subsections (1) to (4) have effect subject to sections 5 to 8A of this Act and Part I of Schedule 17 to the Local Government Act 1972 (National Parks);
(b) subsections (1) and (2) have effect subject to sections 2 and 9; and
(c) subsection (3) has effect subject to section 4 and Schedule 1 (which contains provisions as to the exercise of certain functions under this Act by particular authorities and liaison between them).

[(6) The exercise, in relation to Wales, of functions conferred on local planning authorities is subject to section 4(3) and Schedule 1A.]

[Subsections (1A), (4A) and (6) were inserted by the Local Government (Wales) Act 1994.

The words in Section 1(5)(a) 'and Part I of Schedule 17 to the Local Government Act 1972' will be repealed as from a day to be appointed under the Environment Act 1995, and in Section 1(5)(a) for the underlined words 'sections 5 to' will be substituted 'sections 4A to,' while the words 'subsections (1) to (4)' will be replaced by 'this subsection,' and in Section 1(5)(b) the words '(1) and (2)' will be replaced by '(1) to (2)'. The words underlined in Section 1(6) will be repealed under the Environment Act 1995.]

2. Joint planning boards

(1) If it appears to the Secretary of State that it is expedient that a joint board should be established as the county planning authority for the areas or parts of the areas of any two or more county councils or as the district planning authority for the areas or parts of the areas of any two or more district councils, he may by order—
(a) constitute those areas or parts as a united district for the purposes of this Act; and
(b) constitute a joint board (in this Act referred to as a 'joint planning board') as the county planning authority or, as the case may be, the district planning authority for that united district.

[(1A) Subsection (1) does not apply in relation to Wales.

(1B) If it appears to the Secretary of State that it is expedient that a joint board should be established as the local planning authority for two or more areas, each of which is the whole or part of a Welsh county or county borough, he may by order—
(a) constitute those areas or parts as a united district for the purposes of this Act; and
(b) constitute a joint board as the local planning authority for that united district.

(1C) A joint board constituted under subsection (1) or (1B) shall be known as a 'joint planning board'.

(1D) The areas that may be constituted as a united district for the purposes of this section shall not include the whole or any part of an area which is comprised in a National Park for which there is a National Park authority.]

(2) The Secretary of State shall not make such an order except after holding a local inquiry unless all the councils concerned have consented to the making of the order.

(3) Where a joint planning board is constituted for a united district, references in the planning Acts to the area of a local planning authority—
(a) in relation to the board, shall be construed as references to that district; and
(b) in relation to any local planning authority being the council of a county or district of which part (but not the whole) is included in the united district, shall be construed as references to so much of the county or district as is not so included.

(4) A joint planning board constituted by an order under subsection (1) shall consist of such number of members as may be determined by the order, to be appointed by the constituent councils.

(5) A joint planning board so constituted shall be a body corporate, with perpetual succession and a common seal.

(6) An order constituting a joint planning board and any order amending or revoking any order constituting a joint planning board—
 (a) may, without prejudice to the provisions of section 241 of the Local Government Act 1972 (which authorises the application of the provisions of that Act to joint boards), provide for regulating the appointment, tenure of office and vacation of office of members of the board, for regulating the meetings and proceedings of the board, and for the payment of the expenses of the board by the constituent councils;
 (b) may provide for the transfer and compensation of officers, the transfer of property and liabilities, and the adjustment of accounts and apportionment of liabilities;
 (c) may contain such other provisions as appear to the Secretary of State to be expedient for enabling the board to exercise their functions; and
 (d) may apply to the board, with any necessary modifications and adaptations, any of the provisions of sections 102 and 103 of the Local Government Act 1972.

[(6A) Section 241 of the Local Government Act 1972 shall be taken to authorise the application to a joint planning board, subject to any necessary modifications, of any provisions of Part III (accounts and audit) of the Local Government Finance Act 1982 (as well as of any provisions of the Local Government Act 1972) by such an order as is mentioned in subsection (6) above.]

(7) This section shall have effect subject to sections 5 to 9 of this Act and Part I of Schedule 17 to the Local Government Act 1972 (joint planning boards and special planning boards for National Parks).

[Section 2(1A)–(1C) were inserted by the Local Government (Wales) Act 1994, while subsection (1D) was added by the Environment Act 1995. Section 2(6A) was inserted by, and will be brought into force as from a day appointed under, the Environment Act 1995, while the words underlined in section 2(7) will be repealed as from a day to be appointed under that Act, and the words underlined in Section 2(1)(b) were repealed under the Local Government (Wales) Act 1994 while in Section 2(2) the words underlined 'such an order' will be replaced by 'an order under subsection (1) or (1B)', in Section 2(3) after county in both instances shall be inserted County Borough, while in Section 2(4) after (1) shall be inserted (1B).]

3. Joint planning committee for Greater London

(1) The joint planning committee for Greater London established under section 5 of the Local Government Act 1985 shall continue to discharge the functions mentioned in subsection (2).

(2) The joint planning committee shall—
 (a) consider and advise the local planning authorities in Greater London on matters of common interest relating to the planning and development of Greater London;
 (b) inform the Secretary of State of the views of those authorities concerning such matters including any such matters as to which he has requested their advice;
 (c) inform the local planning authorities for areas in the vicinity of Greater London, or any body on which those authorities and the local planning authorities in Greater London are represented, of the views of the local planning authorities in Greater London concerning any matters of common interest relating to the planning and development of Greater London and those areas;
and the committee may, if it thinks fit, contribute towards the expenses of any such body as is mentioned in paragraph (c).

(3) The expenses of the joint planning committee which have been incurred with the approval of at least two-thirds of the local planning authorities in Greater London

shall be defrayed by those authorities in such proportions as they may decide or, in default of a decision by them, as the Secretary of State may determine.

(4) References in this section to the local planning authorities in Greater London are to the authorities which are local planning authorities for the purposes of Part II.

4. National Parks [To be repealed as from an appointed day by the Environment Act 1995. The words in [ ] inserted by virtue of the Local Government (Wales) Act 1994]

(1) As respects an area in a National Park [in England] outside a metropolitan county all functions conferred by or under the planning Acts on a local planning authority or district planning authority shall, subject to subsections (2) and (3), be functions of the county planning authority and no other authority, and references in those Acts in their application to a National Park outside a metropolitan county to a local planning authority or district planning authority shall be construed accordingly.

(2) The functions conferred on a local planning authority by sections 198 to 201, 206 to 209 and 211 to 215 shall as respects any part of a National Park [in England] outside a metropolitan county be exercisable concurrently with the county planning authority by the district planning authority whose area includes that part of the Park.

(3) Where an order is made under section 7 of the National Parks and Access to the Countryside Act 1949 designating or extending the area of a National Park, the functions exercisable by a local planning authority immediately before the coming into force of the order for any area which under the order becomes part of the Park shall continue to be exercisable by that authority as respects that area unless and until a joint planning board is constituted under section 2 [a special planning board is constituted under paragraph 3A of Schedule 17 to the Local Government Act 1972] or a National Park Committee is appointed under Part I of Schedule 17 to the Local Government Act 1972 for an area co-terminous with or including that area or, as the case may be, is authorised to exercise those functions.

(4) Where a joint planning board for a National Park situated partly in one or more metropolitan counties is the local planning authority as respects the part of the Park situated in that county or those counties, it shall continue to be so.

(5) This section shall have effect subject to section 4A below.

4A. National Parks with National Park authorities

(1) Where a National Park authority has been established for any area, this section, instead of section 4(1) to (4), shall apply, as from such time as may be specified for the purposes of this section in the order establishing that authority, in relation to the Park for which it is the authority.

(2) Subject to subsections (4) and (5) below, the National Park authority for the Park shall be the sole local planning authority for the area of the Park and, accordingly—

    (a) functions conferred by or under the planning Acts on a planning authority of any description (including the functions of a mineral planning authority under those Acts and under the Planning and Compensation Act 1991) shall, in relation to the Park, be functions of the National Park authority, and not of any other authority; and

    (b) so much of the area of any other authority as is included in the Park shall be treated as excluded from any area for which that other authority is a planning authority of any description.

(3) For the purposes of subsection (2) above functions under the planning Acts which (apart from this section) are conferred—

    (a) in relation to some areas on the county or district planning authorities for those areas, and

    (b) in relation to other areas on the councils for those areas,

shall be treated, in relation to those other areas, as conferred on each of those councils as the local planning authority for their area.

Town and Country Planning Act 1990

(4) The functions of a local planning authority by virtue of sections 198 to 201, 206 to 209 and 211 to 215, so far as they are functions of a National Park authority by virtue of this section, shall be exercisable as respects any area which is or is included in an area for which there is a district council, concurrently with the National Park authority, by that council.

(5) For the purposes of any enactment relating to the functions of a district planning authority, the functions of a district council by virtue of subsection (4) above shall be deemed to be conferred on them as a district planning authority and as if the district were the area for which they are such an authority.

[Part III of the Environment Act 1995 which includes this new provision comes into force at the end of two months from the date of that Act's passing, i.e., 19th July 1995. The words underlined in Section 4A(1) will be repealed as from a day to be appointed under the 1995 Act.]

5. The Broads

(1) For the purposes of Chapter I of Part VIII and sections 249, 250 and 300 and any other provision of this Act so far as it has effect for the purposes of those provisions, 'local planning authority', in relation to land in the Broads, includes the Broads Authority.

(2) For the purposes of the provisions mentioned in subsection (3) the Broads Authority shall be the sole district planning authority for the Broads.

(3) The provisions referred to in subsection (2) are Part II, sections 62, 65, 69 to 72, 76 to 79, 91 to 95, 97 to 99, 102, 103, 106 to 106B, 171C, 172, 173, 173A, 178, 183, 184, 187A, 187B, 188, 191 to 197, 211 to 214, 215, 219 to 221, 224, 294, 295, 297, 299, 299A, 301, 316 and 324(1) and (7).

6. Enterprise zones

(1) An order under paragraph 5 of Schedule 32 to the Local Government, Planning and Land Act 1980 (designation of enterprise zone) may provide that the enterprise zone authority shall be the local planning authority for the zone for such purposes of the planning Acts and in relation to such kinds of development as may be specified in the order.

(2) Without prejudice to the generality of paragraph 15(1) of that Schedule (modification of orders by the Secretary of State), an order under that paragraph may provide that the enterprise zone authority shall be the local planning authority for the zone for different purposes of the planning Acts or in relation to different kinds of development.

(3) Where such provision as is mentioned in subsection (1) or (2) is made by an order designating an enterprise zone or, as the case may be, an order modifying such an order, while the zone subsists the enterprise zone authority shall be, to the extent mentioned in the order (as it has effect subject to any such modifications) and to the extent that it is not already, the local planning authority for the zone in place of any authority who would otherwise be the local planning authority for the zone.

(4) The Secretary of State may by regulations make transitional and supplementary provision in relation to a provision of an order under paragraph 5 of that Schedule made by virtue of subsection (1).

(5) Such regulations may modify any provision of the planning Acts or any instrument made under any of them or may apply any such enactment or instrument (with or without modification) in making such transitional or supplementary provision.

7. Urban development areas

(1) Where an order is made under subsection (1) of section 149 of the Local Government, Planning and Land Act 1980 (urban development corporation as

planning authority), the urban development corporation specified in the order shall be the local planning authority for such area as may be so specified in place of any authority who would otherwise be the local planning authority for that area for such purposes and in relation to such kinds of development as may be so specified.

(2) Where an order under subsection (3)(a) of that section confers any functions on an urban development corporation in relation to any area the corporation shall have those functions in place of any authority (except the Secretary of State) who would otherwise have them in that area.

8. Housing action areas

(1) Where an order is made under subsection (1) of section 67 of the Housing Act 1988 (housing action trust as planning authority), the housing action trust specified in the order shall be the local planning authority for such area as may be so specified in place of any authority who would otherwise be the local planning authority for that area for such purposes and in relation to such kinds of development as may be so specified.

(2) Where an order under subsection (3)(a) of that section confers any functions on a housing action trust in relation to any area the trust shall have those functions in place of any authority (except the Secretary of State) who would otherwise have them in that area.

8A. The Urban Regeneration Agency

(1) Where a designation order under section 170 of the Leasehold Reform, Housing and Urban Development Act 1993 (power to make designation orders) makes such provision as is mentioned in subsection (1) of section 171 of that Act (Agency as local planning authority), the Urban Regeneration Agency shall be the local planning authority for such area as may be specified in the order in place of any authority who would otherwise be the local planning authority for that area for such purposes and in relation to such kinds of development as may be so specified.

(2) Where such an order makes such provision as is mentioned in subsection (3)(a) of section 171 of that Act, the Urban Regeneration Agency shall have the functions specified in the order for such area as may be so specified in place of any authority (except the Secretary of State) who would otherwise have them in that area.

9. Power to make consequential and supplementary provision about authorities

Regulations under this Act may make such provision consequential upon or supplementary to the provisions of sections 1 and 2 as appears to the Secretary of State to be necessary or expedient.

PART II
DEVELOPMENT PLANS
CHAPTER 1
UNITARY DEVELOPMENT PLANS: METROPOLITAN AREAS INCLUDING LONDON

Preliminary

10. Application of Chapter 1 to Greater London and metropolitan counties

This Chapter applies, subject to section 28, to the area of any local planning authority in Greater London or a metropolitan county (other than any area in such a county which is part of a National Park).

10A. Application of Chapter I in relation to Wales

(1) This Chapter also applies to the area of any local planning authority in Wales.

(2) Subsections (3) and (4) apply where the area of a local planning authority in Wales includes—
  (a) the whole or any part of an area prescribed under section 23B(2) in relation to a National Park, and
  (b) other land.
(3) The provisions of this Chapter apply separately in relation to—
  (a) the Park area or, if there is more than one, each Park area, and
  (b) the remaining area.
(4) Any reference in any of the following sections of this Chapter to the area of the local planning authority (including any reference which falls to be so construed) shall be construed—
  (a) in its application in relation to any Park area, as a reference to that Park area, and
  (b) in its application in relation to the remaining area, as a reference to that area.
(5) in this section—
  'the Park area' in relation to a National Park, means the part of the local planning authority's area which is within the area prescribed under section 23B(2) in relation to that Park or, where there is more than one such part, those parts taken as a whole;
  'the remaining area' means the part of the local planning authority's area which is not within the area so prescribed in relation to any National Park.
[This section was inserted by, and will come into force on an appointed day under, the Local Government (Wales) Act 1994.]

Surveys etc.

11. Survey of planning areas.
(1) The local planning authority—
  (a) shall keep under review the matters which may be expected to affect the development of their area or the planning of its development; and
  (b) may, if they think fit, institute a survey or surveys of their area or any part of their area for examining those matters.
(2) Without prejudice to the generality of subsection (1), the matters to be kept under review or examined under that subsection shall include—
  (a) the principal physical and economic characteristics of the area of the authority (including the principal purposes for which land is used) and, so far as they may be expected to affect that area, of any neighbouring areas;
  (b) the size, composition and distribution of the population of that area (whether resident or otherwise);
  (c) without prejudice to paragraph (a), the communications, transport system and traffic of that area and, so far as they may be expected to affect that area, of any neighbouring areas;
  (d) any considerations not mentioned in paragraphs (a), (b) and (c) which may be expected to affect any matters mentioned in them;
  (e) such other matters as may be prescribed or as the Secretary of State may in a particular case direct;
  (f) any changes already projected in any of the matters mentioned in any of paragraphs (a) to (e) and the effect which those changes are likely to have on the development of that area or the planning of such development.
(3) A local planning authority shall, for the purpose of discharging their functions under this section of keeping under review and examining any matters relating to the area of another such authority, consult with that other authority about those matters.

Preparation and adoption of unitary development plans

12. Preparation of unitary development plan

(1) The local planning authority shall, within such period (if any) as the Secretary of State may direct, prepare for their area a plan to be known as a unitary development plan.

(2) A unitary development plan shall comprise two parts.

(3) Part I of a unitary development plan shall consist of a written statement formulating the authority's general policies in respect of the development and use of land in their area.

(3A) The policies shall, subject to subsection (3B), include policies in respect of—
  (a) the conservation of the natural beauty and amenity of the land;
  (b) the improvement of the physical environment; and
  (c) the management of traffic.

(3B) Regulations under this section may prescribe the aspects of such development and use with which the general policies in Part I of a unitary development plan are to be concerned, in which case the policies shall be concerned with those aspects and no others.

(4) Part II of a unitary development plan shall consist of—
  (a) a written statement formulating in such detail as the authority think appropriate (and so as to be readily distinguishable from the other contents of the plan) their proposals for the development and use of land in their area;
  (b) a map showing those proposals on a geographical basis;
  (c) a reasoned justification of the general policies in Part I of the plan and of the proposals in Part II of it; and
  (d) such diagrams, illustrations or other descriptive or explanatory matter in respect of the general policies in Part I of the plan or the proposals in Part II of it as the authority think appropriate or as may be prescribed.

(5) A unitary development plan shall also contain such other matters as may be prescribed or as the Secretary of State may in any particular case direct.

(6) In formulating the general policies in Part I of a unitary development plan the authority shall have regard to—
  (a) any regional or strategic planning guidance given by the Secretary of State to assist them in the preparation of the plan;
  (b) current national policies;
  (c) the resources likely to be available; and
  (d) such other matters as the Secretary of State may prescribe or, in a particular case, direct.

(7) The proposals in Part II of a unitary development plan shall be in general conformity with Part I.

(7A) In formulating their proposals in Part II of a unitary development plan, the authority shall have regard to such information and other considerations as the Secretary of State may prescribe or, in a particular case, direct.

(8) Part II of a unitary development plan may designate any part of the authority's area as an action area, that is to say, an area which they have selected for the commencement during a prescribed period of comprehensive treatment by development, redevelopment or improvement (or partly by one and partly by another method) and if an area is so designated that Part of the plan shall contain a description of the treatment proposed by the authority.

(9) In preparing a unitary development plan the authority shall take into account the provisions of any scheme under paragraph 3 of Schedule 32 to the Local Government, Planning and Land Act 1980 relating to land in their area which has been designated under that Schedule as an enterprise zone.

(10) Regulations made under this section may make different provision for different cases and shall be subject to any direction given, in a particular case, by the Secretary of State.

(11) Any provision made by regulations under this section in its application by virtue of section 10 may differ from that made under this section in its application by virtue of section 10A.

[Subsection (11) was added by, and will come into force on an appointed day order under, the Local Government (Wales) Act 1994.]

12A. Urban development corporations

(1) The Secretary of State may direct that a unitary development plan—

   (a) shall not be prepared; or

   (b) shall not operate,

in relation to the area of an urban development corporation.

(2) The Secretary of State may direct that proposals for the alteration or replacement of a unitary development plan shall not be prepared in relation to the area of an urban development corporation.

13. Public participation

(1) When preparing a unitary development plan for their area and before finally determining its contents the local planning authority shall—

   (a) comply with—

      (i) any requirements imposed by regulations made under section 26; and

      (ii) any particular direction given to them by the Secretary of State with respect to a matter falling within any of paragraphs (a) to (c) or (e) of subsection (2) of that section; and

   (b) consider any representations made in accordance with those regulations.

(2) Where the local planning authority have prepared a unitary development plan, before adopting it they shall—

   (a) make copies of it available for inspection at such places as may be prescribed by those regulations;

   (b) send a copy to the Secretary of State; and

   (c) comply with any requirements imposed by those regulations.

(3) Each copy made available for inspection or sent under subsection (2) shall be accompanied by a statement of the prescribed period within which objections may be made to the authority.

(4) In this section 'the prescribed period' means such period as may be prescribed by or determined in accordance with regulations made under section 26 and in this Chapter 'objections made in accordance with the regulations' means objections made—

   (a) in accordance with regulations made under that section; and

   (b) within the prescribed period.

(5) The persons who may make objections in accordance with the regulations include, in particular, the Secretary of State.

(6) A unitary development plan shall not be adopted by the authority under section 15 until—

   (a) after they have considered any objections made in accordance with the regulations; or

   (b) if no such objections are made, after the expiry of the prescribed period.

14. Withdrawal of unitary development plan

(1) A unitary development plan may be withdrawn by the local planning authority at any time before it is adopted by the authority or approved by the Secretary of State and shall be withdrawn by the authority if the Secretary of State so directs.

(2) Where a unitary development plan is withdrawn the authority shall—

(a) withdraw the copies made available for inspection and sent to the Secretary of State under section 13(2); and

(b) give notice that the plan has been withdrawn to every person who has made an objection to it.

(3) [repealed by the Planning and Compensation Act 1991]

(4) Where a unitary development plan is withdrawn the copies of the plan shall be treated as never having been made available under section 13(2).

15. Adoption of unitary development plan by local planning authority

(1) Subject to the following provisions of this section and sections 17 and 18, the local planning authority may by resolution adopt the unitary development plan, either as originally prepared or as modified so as to take account of—

(a) any objections to the plan; or

(b) any other considerations which appear to them to be material.

(2) A unitary development plan shall not be adopted unless Part II of the plan is in general conformity with Part I.

(3) Where an objection to a <u>unitary development plan</u> has been made by the Minister of Agriculture, Fisheries and Food and the local planning authority do not propose to modify the plan to take account of the objection, the authority—

(a) shall send the Secretary of State particulars of the objection and a statement of their reasons for not modifying the plan to take account of it; and

(b) shall not adopt the plan unless the Secretary of State authorises them to do so.

(4) Subject to the following provisions of this Chapter and to section 287, a unitary development plan shall become operative on the date on which it is adopted. [In Section 15(3) after the words 'unitary development plan' will be inserted the words 'for an area in England' on a day appointed under the Local Government (Wales) Act 1994.]

16. Local inquiries

(1) Where any objections have been made, in accordance with the regulations, to proposals for a unitary development plan copies of which have been made available for inspection under section 13(2), the local planning authority shall cause a local inquiry or other hearing to be held for the purpose of considering the objections.

(1A) The local planning authority may cause a local inquiry or other hearing to be held for the purpose of considering any other objections to the proposals.

(1B) The local inquiry or other hearing shall be held by a person appointed by the Secretary of State or, in such cases as may be prescribed, by the authority themselves.

(2) Subsections (2) and (3) of section 250 of the Local Government Act 1972 (power to summon and examine witnesses) shall apply to an inquiry held under this section as they apply to an inquiry under that section.

(3) The Tribunals and Inquiries Act 1971 shall apply to a local inquiry or other hearing held under this section as it applies to a statutory inquiry held by the Secretary of State, but as if in section 12(1) of that Act (statement of reasons for decisions) the reference to any decision taken by the Secretary of State were a reference to a decision taken by a local planning authority.

(4) Regulations made for the purposes of this section may—

(a) make provision with respect to the appointment and qualifications for appointment of persons to hold a local inquiry or other hearing under this section, including provision enabling the Secretary of State to direct a local planning authority to appoint a particular person or one of a specified list or class of persons;

(b) make provision with respect to the remuneration and allowances of a person appointed for that purpose.

(5) No local inquiry or other hearing need be held under this section if all persons who have made objections have indicated in writing that they do not wish to appear.

Secretary of State's powers concerning plans

17. Direction to reconsider proposals

(1) After a copy of a unitary development plan has been sent to the Secretary of State under section 13(2) and before it is adopted by the local planning authority, the Secretary of State may, if it appears to him that the plan is unsatisfactory, direct the authority to modify the proposals in such respects as are indicated in the direction.

(2) An authority to whom a direction is given shall not adopt the plan unless they satisfy the Secretary of State that they have made the modifications necessary to conform with the direction or the direction is withdrawn.

18. Calling in of unitary development plan for approval by Secretary of State

(1) After a copy of a unitary development plan has been sent to the Secretary of State under section 13(2) and before it is adopted by the local planning authority, the Secretary of State may direct that the whole or part of the plan shall be submitted to him for his approval.

(2) If such a direction is given—

(a) the authority shall not take any further steps for the adoption of the plan until the Secretary of State has given his decision on the plan or the relevant part of it; and

(b) the plan or the relevant part of it shall not have effect unless approved by him and shall not require adoption under the previous provisions of this Chapter.

(3) Where particulars of an objection to a <u>unitary development plan</u> have been sent to the Secretary of State under section 15(3), then, unless he is satisfied that the Minister of Agriculture, Fisheries and Food no longer objects to the plan, the Secretary of State must give a direction in respect of it under subsection (1).

(4) Subsection (2)(a) applies in particular to holding or proceeding with a local inquiry or other hearing in respect of the plan under section 16; and at any such inquiry or hearing which is subsequently held or resumed a local planning authority need not give any person an opportunity of being heard in respect of any objection which has been heard at an examination, local inquiry or other hearing under section 20 or which the Secretary of State states that he has considered in making his decision. [In Section 18(3) after the words 'unitary development plan' will be inserted the words 'for an area in England' on a day appointed under the Local Government (Wales) Act 1994.]

19. Approval of unitary development plan by Secretary of State

(1) Subject to section 20, the Secretary of State may after considering a plan or part of a plan submitted to him under section 18(1) either approve it (in whole or in part and with or without modifications or reservations) or reject it.

(2) In considering a plan or part of a plan submitted to him under that section the Secretary of State may take into account any matters which he thinks relevant, whether or not they were taken into account in preparing the plan or that part of it.

(3) The Secretary of State shall give a local planning authority such statement as he considers appropriate of the reasons governing his decision on any plan or part of a plan submitted to him.

(4) Where the whole or part of Part I of a unitary development plan is approved by the Secretary of State with modifications, the local planning authority shall, before adopting the remainder of the plan, make such modifications in Part II as may be directed by the Secretary of State for bringing it into general conformity with Part I and, in the absence of any such direction, shall make such modifications for that purpose in Part II as appear to the authority to be required.

(5) Subject to section 287, a plan or part of a plan which is approved by the Secretary of State under this section shall become operative on such day as he may appoint.

20. Local inquiry, public examination and consultation by Secretary of State

(1) Before deciding whether or not to approve a plan or part of a plan submitted to him under section 18(1), the Secretary of State shall consider any objection to it so far as made in accordance with the regulations.

(2) Where the whole or part of Part II of a unitary development plan is submitted to the Secretary of State under section 18(1) (whether or not the whole or part of Part I is also submitted), then, if any objections have been made to the plan or the relevant part of it as mentioned in subsection (1), before deciding whether to approve it he shall cause a local inquiry or other hearing to be held for the purpose of considering those objections.

(3) The Secretary of State need not under subsection (1) consider any objections which have already been considered by the local planning authority and need not cause a local inquiry or other hearing to be held under subsection (2) if that authority have already held a local inquiry or other hearing into the objections under section 16 or the Secretary of State, on taking the plan or the relevant part of it into consideration, decides to reject it.

(4) Where the whole or part of Part I of a unitary development plan (but not the whole or any part of Part II) is submitted to the Secretary of State under section 18(1) he may cause a person or persons appointed by him for the purpose to hold an examination in public of such matters affecting the Secretary of State's consideration of the part of the plan submitted to him as he considers ought to be so examined.

(5) The Secretary of State may, after consultation with the Lord Chancellor, make regulations with respect to the procedure to be followed at any examination under subsection (4).

(6) The Secretary of State shall not be required to secure to any local planning authority or other person a right to be heard at an examination under subsection (4), and the bodies and persons who may take part shall be such only as he may, whether before or during the course of the examination, in his discretion invite to do so; but the person or persons holding the examination shall have power, exercisable either before or during the course of the examination, to invite additional bodies or persons to take part if it appears to him or them desirable to do so.

(7) An examination under subsection (4) shall constitute a statutory inquiry for the purposes of section 1(1)(c) of the Tribunals and Inquiries Act 1992 but shall not constitute such an inquiry for any other purpose of that Act.

(8) On considering a plan or part of a plan submitted to him under section 18(1) the Secretary of State may consult with or consider the views of any local planning authority or other person but he need not do so except as provided by this section.

Alteration of plans

21. Alteration or replacement of unitary development plan

(1) A local planning authority may at any time prepare proposals—
    (a) for alterations to the unitary development plan for their area; or
    (b) for its replacement.

(1A) If the Secretary of State directs them to do so, the authority shall prepare, within such time as he may direct, proposal for—
    (a) such alterations to the unitary development plan as he directs; or
    (b) its replacement.

(1B) An authority shall not, without the consent of the Secretary of State, prepare proposals in respect of a unitary development plan if the plan or any part of it has been approved by the Secretary of State.

(2) Subject to section 22, sections 12 to 20 (other than subsection (1) of section 12) shall apply in relation to the making of proposals under this section and to any alteration or replacement so proposed as they apply to the preparation of a unitary development plan under section 12 and to a plan prepared under that section.

(3) As soon as practicable after—
  (a) an order has been made under paragraph 5 of Schedule 32 to the Local Government, Planning and Land Act 1980 (designation of enterprise zone); or
  (b) a notification has been given under paragraph 11(1) of that Schedule (approval of modification of enterprise zone scheme),
the local planning authority for an area in which the zone is wholly or partly situated shall review any unitary development plan for that area in the light of the provisions of the scheme or modified scheme under that Schedule and prepare proposals under this section for any consequential alterations to the plan which they consider necessary.

22. [repealed by the Planning and Compensation Act 1991]

Joint plans

23. Joint unitary development plans

(1) A joint unitary development plan or joint proposals for the alteration or replacement of such a plan may be prepared by two or more local planning authorities in Greater London or by two or more local planning authorities in a metropolitan county; and the previous provisions of this Chapter shall, in relation to any such joint plan or proposals, have effect subject to the following provisions of this section.

(2) to (4) [repealed]

(5) Each of the local planning authorities by whom a joint unitary development plan is prepared shall have the duty imposed by subsection (2) of section 13 of making copies of the plan available for inspection.

(6) Objections to such a plan may be made to any of those authorities and the statement required by subsection (3) of section 13 to accompany copies of the plan shall state that objections may be so made.

(7) It shall be for each of the local planning authorities by whom a joint unitary development plan is prepared to adopt the plan under section 15(1) and they may do so as respects any part of their area to which the plan relates, but any modifications subject to which the plan is adopted must have the agreement of all those authorities.

(8) Where a unitary development plan has been prepared jointly, the power of preparing proposals in respect of the plan under section 21 may be exercised as respects their respective areas by any of the authorities by whom it was prepared and the Secretary of State may under that section direct any of them to prepare proposals as respects their respective areas.

(9) and (10) [repealed]

(11) The date of the coming into operation of a unitary development plan prepared jointly by two or more local planning authorities or for the alteration or replacement of such a plan in pursuance of proposals so prepared shall be a date jointly agreed by those authorities.

[23A. Joint unitary development plans: Wales

(1) A joint unitary development plan or joint proposals for the alteration or replacement of such a plan may be prepared by two or more local planning authorities in Wales for their areas if—
  (a) each of those areas adjoins each of the others; or
  (b) the Secretary of State has given his approval.

(2) Subsection (1) does not apply in relation to a joint plan for any area which consists of or includes a National Park.

(3) The previous provisions of this Chapter shall, in relation to any joint plan or proposals of a kind mentioned in subsection (1), have effect subject to the following provisions of this section.

(4) Each of the local planning authorities by whom a joint unitary development plan is prepared shall have the duty imposed under section 13(2) of making copies of the plan available for inspection.

(5) Objections to such a plan may be made to any of those authorities and the statement required by section 13(3) to accompany copies of the plan shall state that objections may be so made.

(6) It shall be for each of the local planning authorities by whom a joint unitary development plan is prepared to adopt the plan under section 15(1) and, subject to the provisions of this Chapter, they may do so as respects the part of their area to which the plan relates, but any modifications subject to which the plan is adopted must have the agreement of all those authorities.

(7) Where a unitary development plan has been prepared jointly, the power of preparing proposals in respect of the plan under section 21 may be exercised as respects their respective areas by any of the authorities by whom it was prepared and the Secretary of State may under that section direct any of them to prepare proposals as respects their respective areas.

(8) The date of the coming into operation of a unitary development plan prepared jointly by two or more local planning authorities or for the alteration or replacement of such a plan in pursuance of proposals so prepared shall be a date jointly agreed by those authorities.

23B. Unitary development plans for National Parks in Wales

(1) A unitary development plan shall be prepared for each National Park in Wales.

(2) A Welsh National Park development plan shall relate to an area prescribed in relation to the National Park in question by order made by the Secretary of State.

(3) The prescribed area in relation to a National Park which falls wholly within, but does not comprise the whole of, the area of a single local planning authority shall be—
    (a) where the local planning authority have so elected, the whole of the area of the local planning authority; and
    (b) in any other case—
        (i) the whole of the area of the National Park; or
        (ii) a composite area.

(4) The prescribed area in relation to any other Welsh National Park shall be—
    (a) the whole of the area of the National Park; or
    (b) a composite area.

(5) For the purposes of this section and section 23C, 'composite area', in relation to a National Park, means an area which consists of the whole of the Park together with any one or more other areas in Wales.

(6) The Secretary of State shall not under subsection (2) prescribe an area which is a composite area except with the consent of every local planning authority in whose area the prescribed area or any part of it would fall.

(7) Any order made by the Secretary of State under subsection (2) may make such saving or transitional provision as he considers appropriate.

(8) Where, by an order under subsection (2), the Secretary of State prescribes a composite area which comprises or includes part only of the area of a local planning authority, the provisions of this Chapter shall apply in relation to—
    (a) the Welsh National Park development plan in question, or
    (b) any proposals for its alteration or replacement,
subject to such modifications, if any, as may be prescribed by the order.

(9) Subsections (3) and (4) of section 10A do not apply for the purposes of—
(a) subsection (3) or (8) of this section, or
(b) section 23C(1), (2) or (4).
(10) For the purposes of this Act, 'Welsh National Park development plan' means a unitary development plan prepared for a National Park in Wales.

23C. Joint unitary development plans for National Parks in Wales
(1) A Welsh National Park development plan for a National Park which neither coincides with nor falls wholly within the area of a single local planning authority shall be a joint unitary development plan.
(2) A Welsh National Park development plan for any other National Park shall be a joint unitary development plan if it relates to a composite area unless the composite area coincides with or falls wholly within the area of a single local planning authority.
(3) Any Welsh National Park development plan which is required to be a joint plan shall be prepared by the authorities who will be the appropriate authorities in relation to the plan.
(4) For the purposes of this section, an authority are an appropriate authority in relation to a joint plan if—
(a) they are a local planning authority; and
(b) their area or any part of their area falls within the area to which the plan relates.
(5) Any proposals prepared under section 21 for the alteration or replacement of a joint plan of a kind mentioned in subsection (1) or (2) shall be joint proposals prepared by the appropriate authorities in relation to that plan, and any direction given by the Secretary of State under that section in relation to that plan shall be given jointly to those authorities.
(6) Subsections (3) to (6) and (8) of section 23A apply in relation to any joint plan or proposals of a kind mentioned in subsection (1), (2) or (5) as they apply in relation to any joint plan or proposals of a kind mentioned in section 23A(1).]
[Sections 23A to 23C were inserted by, and will come into effect on an appointed day order under, the Local Government (Wales) Act 1994.]

Supplementary

24. Disregard of certain representations
Notwithstanding anything in the previous provisions of this Chapter, neither the Secretary of State nor a local planning authority shall be required to consider representations or objections with respect to a unitary development plan or any proposals for the alteration or replacement of such a plan if it appears to the Secretary of State or, as the case may be, the authority that those representations or objections are in substance representations or objections with respect to things done or proposed to be done in pursuance of—
(a) an order or scheme under section 10, 14, 16, 18, 106(1) or (3) or 108(1) of the Highways Act 1980;
(b) an order or scheme under any provision replaced by the provisions mentioned in paragraph (a), namely, an order or scheme under section 7, 9, 11, 13 or 20 of the Highways Act 1959, section 3 of the Highways (Miscellaneous Provisions) Act 1961 or section 1 or 10 of the Highways Act 1971; or
(c) an order under section 1 of the New Towns Act 1981.

25. Default powers
(1) Where, by virtue of any of the previous provisions of this Chapter, any unitary development plan or proposals for the alteration or replacement of such a plan are required to be prepared, or steps are required to be taken for the adoption of any such plan or proposals, then—

(a) if at any time the Secretary of State is satisfied, after holding a local inquiry or other hearing, that the local planning authority are not taking the steps necessary to enable them to prepare or adopt such a plan or proposals within a reasonable period; or

(b) in a case where a period is specified for the preparation or adoption of any such plan or proposals, if no such plan or proposals have been prepared or adopted by the local planning authority within that period,

the Secretary of State may prepare and make the plan or any part of it or, as the case may be, alter or replace it, as he thinks fit.

(2) The previous provisions of this Chapter shall, so far as practicable, apply with any necessary modifications in relation to the doing of anything under this section by the Secretary of State and the thing so done.

(3) The authority mentioned in subsection (1) shall on demand repay to the Secretary of State so much of any expenses incurred by him in connection with the doing of anything which should have been done by them as he certifies to have been incurred in the performance of their functions.

26. Regulations and directions

(1) Without prejudice to the previous provisions of this Chapter, the Secretary of State may make regulations with respect to the form and content of unitary development plans and the procedure to be followed in connection with their preparation, withdrawal, adoption, submission, approval, making, alteration or replacement.

(2) Such regulations may in particular—

(a) provide for publicity to be given to the results of any review or survey carried out under section 11;

(b) provide for the notice to be given of or the publicity to be given to—

(i) matters included or proposed to be included in any unitary development plan,

(ii) the approval, adoption or making of any such plan or any alteration or replacement of it, or

(iii) any other prescribed procedural step,

and for publicity to be given to the procedure to be followed as mentioned in subsection (1);

(c) make provision with respect to the making and consideration of representations with respect to matters to be included in, or objections to, any such plan or proposals for its alteration or replacement;

(cc) make provision with respect to the circumstances in which representations with respect to the matters to be included in a plan or proposals are to be treated, for any of the purposes of this Chapter, as being objections made in accordance with the regulations;

(d) without prejudice to paragraph (b), provide for notice to be given to particular persons of the approval, adoption, alteration or replacement of any plan if they have objected to the plan and have notified the local planning authority of their wish to receive notice, subject (if the regulations so provide) to the payment of a reasonable charge;

(e) require or authorise a local planning authority to consult with, or consider the views of, other persons before taking any prescribed procedural step;

(f) require a local planning authority, in such cases as may be prescribed or in such particular cases as the Secretary of State may direct, to provide persons making a request in that behalf with copies of any plan or document which has been made public in compliance with the regulations or available for inspection under section 13(2), subject (if the regulations so provide) to the payment of a reasonable charge;

(ff) make provision for steps taken in compliance with the regulations in respect of a unitary development plan which has been withdrawn to be taken into account in prescribed circumstances for the purposes of complying with the regulations in respect of a subsequent unitary development plan;

(g) provide for the publication and inspection of any unitary development plan which has been adopted, approved or made or any document approved, adopted or made altering or replacing any such plan, and for copies of any such plan or document to be made available on sale.

(3) Regulations under this section may make different provision for different cases.

(4) Subject to the previous provisions of this Chapter and to any regulations under this section, the Secretary of State may give directions to any local planning authority or to local planning authorities generally—

(a) for formulating the procedure for the carrying out of their functions under this Chapter;

(b) for requiring them to give him such information as he may require for carrying out any of his functions under this Chapter.

27. Meaning of 'development plan' in Greater London and metropolitan counties

For the purposes of this Act and any other enactment relating to town and country planning, the Land Compensation Act 1961 and the Highways Act 1980, the development plan for any district in Greater London or a metropolitan county (whether the whole or part of the area of a local planning authority) shall be taken as consisting of—

(a) the provisions of the unitary development plan for the time being in force for that area or the relevant part of it, together with a copy of the local planning authority's resolution of adoption or the Secretary of State's notice of approval or, where part of the plan has been adopted and the remainder approved, copies of the resolution and the notice; and

(b) any alteration to that plan, together with a copy of the authority's resolution of adoption, or the Secretary of State's notice of approval, of the alteration or, where part of the alteration has been adopted and the remainder approved, copies of the resolution and the notice.

27A. Meaning of 'development plan' in relation to Wales

For the purposes of the enactments mentioned in section 27, the development plan for any area in Wales shall be taken as consisting of—

(a) the provisions of the unitary development plan for the time being in force for that area, together with a copy of the relevant local planning authority's resolution of adoption or of the Secretary of State's notice of approval or, where part of the plan has been adopted and the remainder approved, copies of the resolution and the notice; and

(b) any alteration to that plan, together with a copy of the relevant local planning authority's resolution of adoption, or the Secretary of State's notice of approval, of the alteration or, where parts of the alteration has been adopted and the remainder approved, copies of the resolution and the notice.

28. Commencement of Chapter I: transitional provisions

(1) Subject to subsection (2), the provisions of this Chapter shall come into force in the area of any local planning authority in Greater London or a metropolitan county (other than any area in that county which is part of a National Park) on such day as may be appointed in relation to that area by an order made by the Secretary of State.

(2) Subsection (1) does not apply in any area in relation to which an order has been made before the commencement of this Act under section 4(1) of the Local Government Act 1985 (commencement of Part I of Schedule 1 to that Act) and in any such area the provisions of this Chapter shall come into force at the commencement of this Act or, if later, on the day appointed by the order.

(3) Until a unitary development plan becomes operative under this Chapter for such an area as is mentioned in subsection (1) (or where parts of such a plan become operative on different dates until every part has become operative)—

(a) if it is the area of a local planning authority in a metropolitan county, Part I of Schedule 2 (which provides for existing plans to continue in force and applies some of the provisions of Chapter II) shall apply in relation to it;

(b) if it is the area of a local planning authority in Greater London, Part II of that Schedule (which makes similar provision) shall apply in relation to it; and

(c) Part III of that Schedule shall apply in relation to it for the purpose of making continuing provision for the transitional matters for which provision was made immediately before the commencement of this Act by Schedule 7 to the 1971 Act (old development plans etc.).

(4) The power to make orders under this section may be exercised so as to make different provision for different cases, including different provision for different areas.

[**28A. Application of Chapter I in relation to Wales: transitional provisions**

(1) Until a unitary development plan becomes fully operative for the area of any local planning authority in Wales—

(a) Part IA of Schedule 2, and

(b) Part III of Schedule 5 to the Local Government (Wales) Act 1994 (transitional provisions in relation to structure and local plans),

shall apply in relation to that area.

(2) For the purposes of this Chapter, a unitary development plan for the area of a local planning authority in Wales has become fully operative when—

(a) it has become operative under this Chapter, or

(b) where different parts have become operative at different times, when all parts of it have become so operative.

(3) Schedule 5 shall have effect—

(a) Part I making minor and consequential amendments to Part II of the planning Act,

(b) Part II inserting a new Part IA in Schedule 2 to the planning Act, and

(c) Part III making transitional provision, including provision with respect to the completion and adoption by new authorities of—

(i) local plans, and

(ii) proposals for alteration or replacement of structure plans and local plans, prepared or in course of preparation on 1st April 1996.

(4) Schedule 6 shall have effect—

(a) Part I making minor and consequential amendments to the 1972 Act in relation to National Parks and countryside functions, and

(b) Part II making minor and consequential amendments to enactments concerned with planning.]

[This section was introduced by, and will come into force on an appointed day order under, the Local Government (Wales) Act 1994.]

CHAPTER II
STRUCTURE AND LOCAL PLANS: NON-METROPOLITAN AREAS

Preliminary

29. Application of Chapter II to non-metropolitan areas in England

(1) This Chapter applies only to—

(a) the area of any local planniing authority in England outside Greater London and the metropolitan counties; and

(b) any part of a National Park in a metropolitan county in England.

(2) Subsection (1) is subject to the transitional provisions in—

(a) Schedule 2; and
(b) Part III of Schedule 5 to the Local Government (Wales) Act 1994.
[This section will be substituted by, and will come into force on an appointed day order under, the Local Government (Wales) Act 1994.]

Surveys, etc.

30. Survey of planning areas

(1) The local planning authority—
 (a) shall keep under review the matters which may be expected to affect the development of their area or the planning of its development; and
 (b) may, if they think fit, at any time institute a fresh survey of their area examining those matters.

(2) Without prejudice to the generality of subsection (1), the matters to be kept under review and examined under that subsection shall include—
 (a) the principal physical and economic characteristics of the area of the authority (including the principal purposes for which land is used) and, so far as they may be expected to affect that area, of any neighbouring areas;
 (b) the size, composition and distribution of the population of that area (whether resident or otherwise);
 (c) without prejudice to paragraph (a), the communications, transport system and traffic of that area and, so far as they may be expected to affect that area, of any neighbouring areas;
 (d) any considerations not mentioned in paragraph (a), (b) or (c) which may be expected to affect any matters so mentioned;
 (e) such other matters as may be prescribed or as the Secretary of State may in any particular case direct;
 (f) any changes already projected in any of the matters mentioned in any of the previous paragraphs and the effect which those changes are likely to have on the development of that area or the planning of such development.

(3) A survey under subsection (1)(b) may relate to only part of the area of an authority; and references in subsection (2) to the area of an authority or any neighbouring areas shall be construed accordingly.

(4) A local planning authority shall, for the purpose of discharging their functions under this section of examining and keeping under review any matters relating to the area of another such authority, consult with that other authority about those matters.

Structure plans

31. Structure plans: continuity, form and content

(1) Each structure plan approved by the Secretary of State under the 1971 Act with respect to the area of a local planning authority which is in operation immediately before the commencement of this Act shall continue in force after its commencement (subject to any alterations then in operation and to the following provisions of this Part).

(2) A structure plan shall contain a written statement formulating the authority's general policies in respect of the development and use of land in their area.

(3) The policies shall, subject to subsection (4), include policies in respect of—
 (a) the conservation of the natural beauty and amenity of the land;
 (b) the improvement of the physical environment; and
 (c) the management of traffic.

(4) Regulations under this section may prescribe the aspects of such development and use with which the general policies in a structure plan are to be concerned, in which case the policies shall be concerned with those aspects and no others.

(5) A structure plan shall also contain—

(a) such diagrams, illustrations or other descriptive or explanatory matter in respect of the general policies as may be prescribed; and
    (b) such other matters as the Secretary of State may, in any particular case, direct.
    (6) In formulating their general policies the authority shall have regard to—
    (a) any regional or strategic planning guidance given by the Secretary of State to assist them in the preparation of the plan;
    (b) current national policies;
    (c) the resources likely to be available; and
    (d) such other matters as the Secretary of State may prescribe or, in a particular case, direct.
    (7) Where there is in operation, by virtue of section 7(7) of the 1971 Act, a structure plan relating to part of the area of a local planning authority, the authority shall, within such period (if any) as the Secretary of State may direct, prepare proposals for replacing the structure plans for the time being in operation with a single structure plan relating to the whole of their area.
    (8) The following provisions of this Chapter apply to such replacement as they apply to replacement in exercise of the power in section 32(1)(b).
    (9) Regulations under this section may make different provision for different cases and shall be subject to any direction given, in a particular case, by the Secretary of State.
    (10) For the purposes of this section, except subsection (6)(b), 'policies' includes proposals.

32. Alteration and replacement of structure plans

    (1) A local planning authority may at any time prepare proposals—
    (a) for alterations to the structure plan for their area; or
    (b) for its replacement.
    (2) If the Secretary of State directs them to do so, the authority shall prepare, within such time as he may direct, proposals for—
    (a) such alterations to the structure plan as he directs; or
    (b) its replacement.
    (3) An authority shall not, without the consent of the Secretary of State, prepare proposals in respect of a structure plan if the plan or any part of it has been approved by the Secretary of State under section 35A.
    (4) Proposals for the alteration of a structure plan may relate to the whole or part of the area to which the plan relates.
    (5) Proposals prepared under this section shall be accompanied by an explanatory memorandum.
    (6) The explanatory memorandum shall state—
    (a) the reasons which in the opinion of the authority justify each of their proposals;
    (b) any information on which the proposals are based;
    (c) the relationship of the proposals to general policies for the development and use of land in neighbouring areas which may be expected to affect the area to which the proposals relate,
and may contain such illustrative material as the authority think appropriate.
    (7) Proposals for the alteration or replacement of a structure plan shall not become operative unless they are—
    (a) adopted by the authority (under section 35); or
    (b) approved by the Secretary of State (under section 35A).

33. Public participation

    (1) When preparing proposals for the alteration or replacement of a structure plan for their area and before finally determining their contents the local planning authority shall—

(a) comply with—
(i) any requirements imposed by regulations made under section 53; and
(ii) any particular direction given to them by the Secretary of State with respect to a matter falling within any of paragraphs (a) to (c) or (e) of subsection (2) of that section; and
(b) consider any representations made in accordance with those regulations.

(2) Where the authority have prepared proposals for the alteration or replacement of a structure plan they shall—
(a) make copies of the proposals and the explanatory memorandum available for inspection at such places as may be prescribed by those regulations;
(b) send a copy of the proposals and the explanatory memorandum to the Secretary of State; and
(c) comply with any requirements imposed by those regulations.

(3) Each copy made available for inspection or sent under subsection (2) shall be accompanied by a statement of the prescribed period within which objections may be made to the authority.

(4) In this section 'the prescribed period' means such period as may be prescribed by or determined in accordance with regulations made under section 53 and in this Chapter 'objections made in accordance with the regulations' means objections made—
(a) in accordance with regulations made under that section; and
(b) within the prescribed period.

(5) The persons who may make objections in accordance with the regulations include, in particular, the Secretary of State.

(6) The proposals shall not be adopted by the authority under section 35 until—
(a) after they have considered any objections made in accordance with the regulations; or
(b) if no such objections are made, after the expiry of the prescribed period.

34. Withdrawal of proposals for alteration and replacement of structure plans

(1) Proposals for the alteration or replacement of a structure plan may be withdrawn by the local planning authority at any time before they have adopted them or the Secretary of State has approved them.

(2) On the withdrawal of such proposals, the authority shall—
(a) withdraw the copies made available for inspection in accordance with section 33(2); and
(b) give notice that the proposals have been withdrawn to every person who has made an objection to them.

35. Adoption of proposals

(1) Subject to subsection (3) and sections 35A and 35B, the local planning authority may by resolution adopt proposals for the alteration or replacement of a structure plan, either as originally prepared or as modified so as to take account of—
(a) any objections to the proposals; or
(b) any other considerations which appear to them to be material.

(2) If it appears to the Secretary of State that the proposals are unsatisfactory he may, at any time before the local planning authority have adopted the proposals, direct the authority to modify the proposals in such respects as are indicated in the direction.

(3) An authority to whom such a direction is given shall not adopt the proposals unless—
(a) they satisfy the Secretary of State that they have made the modifications necessary to conform with the direction; or
(b) the direction is withdrawn.

(4) Subject to the following provisions of this Chapter and to section 287, proposals for the alteration or replacement of a structure plan shall become operative on the date on which they are adopted.

35A. Calling in of proposals for approval by Secretary of State

(1) The Secretary of State may, at any time before the local planning authority have adopted proposals for the alteration or replacement of a structure plan, direct that all or any part of the proposals shall be submitted to him for his approval.

(2) If he gives such a direction—

(a) the local planning authority shall not take any further steps for the adoption of any of the proposals until the Secretary of State has given his decision on the proposals or the relevant part of the proposals; and

(b) the proposals or the relevant part of the proposals shall not have effect unless approved by him and shall not require adoption by the authority under section 35.

(3) Subsection (2)(a) applies in particular to holding or proceeding with an examination in public under section 35B(1).

(4) The Secretary of State may, after considering proposals submitted to him in compliance with a direction under subsection (1)—

(a) approve them, in whole or in part and with or without modifications or reservations; or

(b) reject them.

(5) In considering proposals so submitted to him the Secretary of State—

(a) shall take into account any objections made in accordance with the regulations; and

(b) may take into account any matters which he thinks relevant, whether or not they were taken into account in preparing the proposals.

(6) For the purpose of taking into account any objection or matter, the Secretary of State may, but need not, consult with any local planning authority or other person.

(7) The Secretary of State shall give the authority such statement as he considers appropriate of the reasons governing his decision on any proposals submitted to him.

(8) Subject to section 287, proposals approved by the Secretary of State under this section shall become operative on such day as he may appoint.

35B. Examination in public

(1) Before adopting proposals for the alteration or replacement of a structure plan, the local planning authority shall, unless the Secretary of State otherwise directs, cause an examination in public to be held of such matters affecting the consideration of the proposals as—

(a) they consider ought to be so examined; or

(b) the Secretary of State directs.

(2) Where proposals are submitted to the Secretary of State in compliance with a direction under section 35A(1), he may cause an examination in public to be held of any matter specified by him.

(3) An examination in public shall be conducted by a person or persons appointed by the Secretary of State for the purpose.

(4) No person shall have a right to be heard at an examination in public.

(5) The following may take part in an examination in public—

(a) in the case of an examination held under subsection (1), the local planning authority; and

(b) in any case, any person invited to do so by the person or persons holding the examination or the person causing the examination to be held.

(6) The Secretary of State may, after consultation with the Lord Chancellor, make regulations with respect to the procedure to be followed at any examination in public.

(7) An examination in public shall constitute a statutory inquiry for the purposes of section 1(1)(c) of the Tribunals and Inquiries Act 1992 but shall not constitute such an inquiry for any other purpose of that Act.

35C. Duties to notify authorities responsible for local plans

(1) An authority responsible for a structure plan shall, where any proposals of theirs for the alteration or replacement of a structure plan are adopted or approved—

(a) notify any authority responsible for a local plan in their area that the proposals have been adopted or approved; and

(b) supply that authority with a statement that the local plan is or, as the case may be, is not in general conformity with the altered or new structure plan.

(2) A statement that a local plan is not in general conformity with a structure plan shall specify the respects in which it is not in such conformity.

(3) An authority responsible for a structure plan shall, where any proposals of theirs for the alteration or replacement of a structure plan are withdrawn, notify any authority responsible for a local plan in their area that the proposals have been withdrawn.

(4) Nothing in this section requires an authority to notify or supply a statement to themselves.

(5) For the purposes of this section an authority shall be regarded as responsible—

(a) for a structure plan, if they are entitled to prepare proposals for its alteration or replacement; and

(b) for a local plan, if they are under a duty to prepare a local plan or are entitled to prepare proposals for its alteration or replacement.

Local plans

36. Local plans

(1) The local planning authority shall, within such period (if any) as the Secretary of State may direct, prepare for their area a plan to be known as a local plan.

(2) A local plan shall contain a written statement formulating the authority's detailed policies for the development and use of land in their area.

(3) The policies shall include policies in respect of—

(a) the conservation of the natural beauty and amenity of the land;

(b) the improvement of the physical environment; and

(c) the management of traffic.

(4) A local plan shall be in general conformity with the structure plan.

(5) A local plan shall not contain—

(a) any policies in respect of the winning and working of minerals or the depositing of mineral waste, unless it is a plan for a National Park;

(b) any policies in respect of the depositing of refuse or waste materials other than mineral waste, unless it is a plan for a National Park or for an area where such depositing is not a county matter for the purposes of Schedule 1.

(6) A local plan shall also contain—

(a) a map illustrating each of the detailed policies; and

(b) such diagrams, illustrations or other descriptive or explanatory matter in respect of the policies as may be prescribed,

and may contain such descriptive or explanatory matter as the authority think appropriate.

(7) A local plan may designate any part of the authority's area as an action area, that is to say, an area which they have selected for the commencement during a prescribed period of comprehensive treatment by development, redevelopment or improvement (or partly by one and partly by another method).

(8) If an area is so designated the plan shall contain a description of the treatment proposed by the authority.

(9) In formulating their detailed policies, the authority shall have regard to—
  (a) such information and other considerations as the Secretary of State may prescribe or, in a particular case, direct; and
  (b) the provisions of any scheme under paragraph 3 of Schedule 32 to the Local Government, Planning and Land Act 1980 relating to land in their area which has been designated under that Schedule as an enterprise zone.
(10) Subject to the following provisions of this Chapter and section 287, a local plan shall become operative on the date on which it is adopted.
(11) For the purposes of this section 'policies' includes proposals.

37. Minerals local plans

(1) A mineral planning authority for an area other than a National Park shall, within such period (if any) as the Secretary of State may direct, prepare for their area a plan to be known as a minerals local plan.
(2) A minerals local plan shall contain a written statement formulating the authority's detailed policies for their area in respect of development consisting of the winning and working of minerals or involving the depositing of mineral waste.
(3) The local planning authority for a National Park shall, within such period (if any) as the Secretary of State may direct—
  (a) prepare for their area a plan to be known as a minerals local plan; or
  (b) include in their local plan their detailed policies in respect of development consisting of the winning and working of minerals or involving the depositing of mineral waste.
(4) In formulating the policies in a minerals local plan, the authority shall have regard to such information and other considerations as the Secretary of State may prescribe or, in a particular case, direct.
(5) Subsections (4), (6), (10) and (11) of section 36 apply with respect to minerals local plans as they apply with respect to local plans.
(6) The following provisions of this Chapter apply with respect to minerals local plans as they apply with respect to local plans, but as if references to a local planning authority were, in relation to an area other than a National Park, references to a mineral planning authority.

38. Waste policies

(1) In this section—
'waste policies' means detailed policies in respect of development which involves the depositing of refuse or waste materials other than mineral waste; and
'waste local plan' means a plan containing waste policies.
(2) A local planning authority other than an excluded authority shall, within such period (if any) as the Secretary of State may direct—
  (a) prepare a waste local plan for their area; or
  (b) include their waste policies in their minerals local plan.
(3) A local planning authority are an excluded authority for the purposes of subsection (2) if they are an authority—
  (a) for a National Park;
  (b) for an area where waste policies are not a county matter for the purposes of Schedule 1.
(4) A local planning authority for a National Park shall within such period (if any) as the Secretary of State may direct—
  (a) prepare a waste local plan for their area; or
  (b) include their waste policies in—
    (i) their minerals local plan; or
    (ii) their local plan.

Town and Country Planning Act 1990 35

(5) In formulating their waste policies, the authority shall have regard to such information and other considerations as the Secretary of State may prescribe or, in a particular case, direct.

(6) Subsections (4), (6), (10) and (11) of section 36 apply with respect to waste local plans as they apply with respect to local plans.

(7) The following provisions of this Chapter apply with respect to waste local plans as they apply with respect to local plans, but as if references to a local planning authority were references to the authority who are entitled to prepare a waste local plan.

39. Alteration and replacement of local plans

(1) A local planning authority may at any time prepare proposals—
   (a) for alterations to the local plan for their area; or
   (b) for its replacement.

(2) A local planning authority shall—
   (a) consider whether they need to prepare such proposals, if they have been supplied with a statement under section 35C that the local plan is not in general conformity with the structure plan; and
   (b) prepare such proposals, if they are directed to do so by the Secretary of State, within such period (if any) as he may direct.

(3) An authority shall not, without the consent of the Secretary of State, prepare such proposals if the plan or any part of it has been approved by the Secretary of State.

(4) Proposals for the alteration of a local plan may relate to the whole or part of the area to which the plan relates.

(5) Subject to the following provisions of this Chapter and section 287, proposals for the alteration or replacement of a local plan shall become operative on the date on which they are adopted.

40. Public participation

(1) When preparing a local plan for their area or proposals for its alteration or replacement and before finally determining the contents of the plan or the proposals the local planning authority shall—
   (a) comply with—
      (i) any requirements imposed by regulations made under section 53; and
      (ii) any particular direction given to them by the Secretary of State with respect to a matter falling within any of paragraphs (a) to (c) or (e) of subsection (2) of that section; and
   (b) consider any representations made in accordance with those regulations.

(2) Subject to section 46(1), where the authority have prepared a local plan or proposals for its alteration or replacement they shall—
   (a) make copies of the relevant documents available for inspection at such places as may be prescribed by those regulations;
   (b) send a copy of the relevant documents to the Secretary of State; and
   (c) comply with any requirements imposed by those regulations.

(3) In subsection (2) 'the relevant documents' means—
   (a) the plan or the proposals; and
   (b) any statement supplied under section 46(2).

(4) Each copy made available for inspection or sent under subsection (2) shall be accompanied by a statement of the prescribed period within which objections may be made to the authority.

(5) In this section 'the prescribed period' means such period as may be prescribed by or determined in accordance with regulations made under section 53 and in this Chapter 'objections made in accordance with the regulations' means objections made—

(a) in accordance with regulations made under that section; and

(b) within the prescribed period.

(6) The persons who may make objections in accordance with the regulations include, in particular, the Secretary of State.

(7) A local plan or proposals for its alteration or replacement shall not be adopted by the authority under section 43 until—

(a) after they have considered any objections made in accordance with the regulations; or

(b) if no such objections are made, after the expiry of the prescribed period.

41. [repealed by the Planning and Compensation Act 1991]

42. Objections: local inquiry or other hearing

(1) Where any objections have been made, in accordance with the regulations, to proposals for a local plan or for its alteration or replacement copies of which have been made available for inspection under section 40(2), the local planning authority shall cause a local inquiry or other hearing to be held for the purpose of considering the objections.

(2) The local planning authority may cause a local inquiry or other hearing to be held for the purpose of considering any other objections to the proposals.

(2A) No local inquiry or other hearing need be held under this section if all persons who have made objections have indicated in writing that they do not wish to appear.

(3) A local inquiry or other hearing shall be held by a person appointed by the Secretary of State or, in such cases as may be prescribed, by the authority themselves.

(4) Regulations may—

(a) make provision with respect to the appointment, and qualifications for appointment, of persons to hold a local inquiry or other hearing;

(b) include provision enabling the Secretary of State to direct a local planning authority to appoint a particular person, or one of a specified list or class of persons;

(c) make provision with respect to the remuneration and allowances of the person appointed.

(5) Subsections (2) and (3) of section 250 of the Local Government Act 1972 (power to summon and examine witnesses) apply to an inquiry held under this section.

(6) The Tribunals and Inquiries Act 1992 shall apply to a local inquiry or other hearing held under this section as it applies to a statutory inquiry held by the Secretary of State, but as if in section 10(1) of that Act (statement of reasons for decisions) the reference to any decision taken by the Secretary of State were a reference to a decision taken by a local authority.

43. Adoption of proposals

(1) Subject to the following provisions of this section and section 44, the local planning authority may by resolution adopt proposals for a local plan or for its alteration or replacement, either as originally prepared or as modified so as to take account of—

(a) any objections to the plan; or

(b) any other considerations which appear to them to be material.

(2) [repealed by the Planning and Compensation Act 1991]

(3) The authority shall not adopt any proposals which do not conform generally to the structure plan.

(4) After copies of the proposals have been sent to the Secretary of State and before they have been adopted by the local planning authority, the Secretary of State

Town and Country Planning Act 1990

may, if it appears to him that the proposals are unsatisfactory, direct the authority to modify the proposals in such respects as are indicated in the direction.

(5) An authority to whom a direction is given shall not adopt the proposals unless they satisfy the Secretary of State that they have made the modifications necessary to conform with the direction or the direction is withdrawn.

(6) Where an objection to the proposals has been made by the Minister of Agriculture, Fisheries and Food and the local planning authority do not propose to modify their proposals to take account of the objection—

(a) the authority shall send particulars of the objection to the Secretary of State, together with a statement of their reasons for not modifying their proposals to take account of it, and

(b) they shall not adopt the proposals unless the Secretary of State authorises them to do so.

44. Calling in of proposals for approval by Secretary of State

(1) After copies of proposals have been sent to the Secretary of State and before they have been adopted by the local planning authority, the Secretary of State may direct that the proposals or any part of them shall be submitted to him for his approval.

(2) If he gives such a direction—

(a) the authority shall not take any further steps for the adoption of any of the proposals until the Secretary of State has given his decision on the proposals or the relevant part of the proposals; and

(b) the proposals or the relevant part of the proposals shall not have effect unless approved by him and shall not require adoption by the authority under section 43.

(3) Where particulars of an objection made by the Minister of Agriculture, Fisheries and Food have been sent to the Secretary of State under section 43(6), then, unless the Secretary of State is satisfied that that Minister no longer objects to the proposals, he shall give a direction in respect of the proposals under this section.

45. Approval of proposals by Secretary of State

(1) The Secretary of State may after considering proposals submitted to him under section 44 either approve them (in whole or in part and with or without modifications or reservations) or reject them.

(2) In considering the proposals he may take into account any matters he thinks are relevant, whether or not they were taken into account in the proposals as submitted.

(3) Where on taking the proposals into consideration the Secretary of State does not determine then to reject them, he shall before determining whether or not to approve them—

(a) consider any objections to them made in accordance with the regulations,

(b) give any person who made such an objection which has not been withdrawn an opportunity of appearing before and being heard by a person appointed by him for the purpose, and

(c) if a local inquiry or other hearing is held, also give such an opportunity to the authority and such other persons as he thinks fit,

except so far as the objections have already been considered, or a local inquiry or other hearing into the objections has already been held, by the authority.

(4) In considering the proposals the Secretary of State may consult with or consider the views of any local planning authority or any other person; but he need not do so, or give an opportunity for the making of representations or objections, or cause a local inquiry or other hearing to be held, except as provided by subsection (3).

(5) Subject to section 287, proposals approved by the Secretary of State under this section shall become operative on such day as he may appoint.

Conformity between plans

46. Conformity between plans

(1) An authority responsible for a local plan shall not make copies available as mentioned in section 40(2) unless—

(a) they have served on the authority responsible for the structure plan in their area a copy of the plan or the proposals; and

(b) such period as may be prescribed has elapsed since they served the copy of the plan or proposals.

(2) Where a local planning authority have been served with a copy as mentioned in subsection (1) they shall, before the end of any period prescribed for the purposes of that subsection, supply the authority responsible for the local plan with—

(a) a statement that the plan or the proposals are in general conformity with the structure plan; or

(b) a statement that the plan or the proposals are not in such conformity.

(3) A statement that a plan or proposals are not in such conformity shall specify the respects in which the plan or proposals are not in such conformity.

(4) Any such statement shall be treated for the purposes of this Chapter as an objection made in accordance with the regulations.

(5) Nothing in this section requires an authority to serve a copy on or supply a statement to themselves.

(6) Where—

(a) a local planning authority propose to make, alter or replace a local plan;

(b) copies of proposals for the alteration or replacement of the structure plan for their area have been made available for inspection under section 33(2); and

(c) the authority mentioned in paragraph (a) include in any relevant copy of the plan or proposals a statement that they are making the permitted assumption,

the permitted assumption shall, subject to subsection (9), be made for all purposes (including in particular any question as to conformity between plans).

(7) In this section 'the permitted assumption' means the assumption that—

(a) the proposals mentioned in subsection (6)(b); or

(b) if any proposed modifications to those proposals are published in accordance with regulations made under section 53, the proposals as so modified,

have been adopted.

(8) For the purposes of subsection (6)(c) a copy is a relevant copy of a plan or proposals if it is—

(a) served under subsection (1)(a); or

(b) made available or sent under section 40(2).

(9) The permitted assumption shall not be made at any time after the authority mentioned in subsection (6)(a) know that the proposals mentioned in subsection (6)(b) have been withdrawn.

(10) The provisions of a local plan prevail for all purposes over any conflicting provisions in the relevant structure plan unless the local plan is one—

(a) stated under section 35C not to be in general conformity with the structure plan; and

(b) neither altered nor replaced after the statement was supplied.

(11) The Secretary of State may make regulations with respect to cases where—

(a) provisions in a structure plan or a local plan conflict with provisions in—

(i) a minerals local plan; or

(ii) a waste local plan;

(b) a structure plan and a local plan are made by the same authority and the provisions of the two plans conflict.

Town and Country Planning Act 1990

(12) Subsection (5) of section 35C applies for the purposes of this section as it applies for the purposes of that.

47. and 48. [repealed by the Planning and Compensation Act 1991]

Supplementary

49. Disregarding of representations with respect to development authorised by or under other enactments

Notwithstanding anything in the previous provisions of this Chapter, neither the Secretary of State nor a local planning authority need consider representations or objections with respect to a local plan or any proposal to alter or replace a structure plan or a local plan if under if it appears to the Secretary of State or, as the case may be, the authority that those representations or objections are in substance representations or objections with respect to things done or proposed to be done in pursuance of—

(a) an order or scheme under section 10, 14, 16, 18, 106(1) or (3) or 108(1) of the Highways Act 1980;

(b) an order or scheme under any provision replaced by the provisions of the Highways Act 1980 mentioned in paragraph (a) (namely, an order or scheme under section 7, 9, 11, 13 or 20 of the Highways Act 1959, section 3 of the Highways (Miscellaneous Provisions) Act 1961 or section 1 or 10 of the Highways Act 1971);

(c) an order under section 1 of the New Towns Act 1981.

50. Joint structure and local plans

(1) Where a structure plan has been prepared by two or more local planning authorities jointly, the power of making proposals under section 32 for the alteration or replacement of the plan may be exercised as respects their respective areas by any of the authorities by whom it was prepared, and the Secretary of State may under that section direct any of them to submit such proposals as respects their respective areas.

(2) [repealed by the Planning and Compensation Act 1991]

(4) Each of the authorities by whom proposals for the alteration or replacement of a joint structure plan have been prepared shall have the duty imposed by section 33(2) of making copies of the proposals and explanatory memorandum available for inspection.

(5) Where two or more local planning authorities jointly prepare proposals for the alteration replacement of a structure plan under this section, all or any of them may withdraw them under section 34(1) and on their doing so all the authorities shall comply with subsection (2) of that section.

(6) Where two or more local planning authorities jointly prepare proposals for the making, alteration, or replacement of a local plan—

(a) they each have the duty imposed by section 40(2) of making copies of the relevant documents available for inspection and objections to the proposals may be made to any of those authorities and the statement required by section 40(4) to accompany the relevant documents shall state that objections may be so made;

(b) it shall be for each of the local planning authorities to adopt the proposals under section 43(1), but any modifications subject to which the proposals are adopted must have the agreement of all those authorities.

(7) Where a structure plan has been jointly prepared by two or more local planning authorities, the duty—

(a) to notify and supply a statement under section 35C; and

(b) to supply a statement under section 46.

shall apply to each of those authorities.

(7A) Where a local plan, or proposals for its alteration or replacement have been jointly prepared by two or more local planning authorities—

(a) the requirement to serve a copy under subsection (1) of section 46; and

(b) the right to be supplied with a statement under subsection (2) of that section,

shall apply to each of those authorities.

(8) Where a local plan has been made jointly, the power of making proposals for its alteration, or replacement may be exercised as respects their respective areas by any of the authorities by whom it was made, and the Secretary of State may under section 39 direct any of them to make proposals as respects their respective areas.

(9) The date of the coming into operation—

(a) of proposals for the alteration or replacement of a structure plan prepared jointly by two or more local planning authorities; and

(b) of a local plan or proposals for its alteration or replacement so prepared,

shall be a date jointly agreed by those authorities.

51. Default powers

(1) Where, by virtue of any of the previous provisions of this Chapter, any survey is required to be carried out, or any local plan or proposals for the alteration or replacement of such a plan or of a structure plan are required to be prepared or submitted to the Secretary of State, or steps are required to be taken for the adoption of any local plan or any such proposals, then—

(a) if at any time the Secretary of State is satisfied, after holding a local inquiry or other hearing, that the relevant local planning authority are not carrying out the survey or are not taking the steps necessary to enable them to submit or adopt a local plan or such proposals within a reasonable period; or

(b) in a case where a period is specified for the submission or adoption of a local plan or any such proposals, if no such plan or proposals have been submitted or adopted within that period,

the Secretary of State may carry out the survey or prepare and make a local plan or, as the case may be, alter or replace such a plan or a structure plan, as he thinks fit.

(2) Where under subsection (1) the Secretary of State may do anything which should have been done by a local planning authority ('the defaulting authority') he may, if he thinks fit, authorise any other local planning authority who appear to him to have an interest in the proper planning of the area of the defaulting authority to do it.

(3) The previous provisions of this Chapter shall, so far as applicable, apply with any necessary modifications in relation to the doing of anything under this section by the Secretary of State or an authority other than the defaulting authority and the thing so done.

(4) The defaulting authority—

(a) shall on demand repay to the Secretary of State so much of any expenses incurred by him in connection with the doing of anything which should have been done by them as he certifies to have been incurred in the performance of their functions; and

(b) shall repay to any other authority who do under this section anything which should have been done by the defaulting authority any expenses certified by the Secretary of State to have been reasonably incurred by that other authority in connection with the doing of that thing.

51A. Urban development corporations

(1) The Secretary of State may direct—

(a) that a structure plan shall not operate; or

(b) that a local plan shall not be prepared or operate,

in relation to the area of an urban development corporation.

(2) The Secretary of State may direct that proposals for the alteration or replacement of a structure plan or a local plan shall not be prepared in relation to the area of an urban development corporation.

Town and Country Planning Act 1990

52. Reviews of plans in enterprise zones

(1) As soon as practicable after an order has been made under paragraph 5 of Schedule 32 to the Local Government, Planning and Land Act 1980 (adoption of enterprise zone scheme) or a notification has been given under paragraph 11 of that Schedule (modification of such a scheme) any local planning authority for an area in which the enterprise zone is wholly or partly situated shall consider whether they need, in the light of the provisions in the scheme or modified scheme, to prepare proposals for the alteration or replacement of any structure or local plan in relation to which they have power to prepare such proposals.

53. Supplementary provisions as to structure and local plans

(1) Without prejudice to the previous provisions of this Chapter, the Secretary of State may make regulations with respect to the form and content of structure and local plans and the procedure to be followed in connection with their preparation, withdrawal, adoption, submission, approval, making, alteration and replacement.

(2) In particular any such regulations may—

(a) provide for publicity to be given to the report of any survey carried out by a local planning authority under section 30;

(b) provide for the notice to be given of or the publicity to be given to—

(i) matters included or proposed to be included in any such plan,

(ii) the approval, adoption or making of any such plan or any alteration or replacement of it, or

(iii) any other prescribed procedural step,

and for publicity to be given to the procedure to be followed as mentioned in subsection (1);

(c) make provision with respect to the making and consideration of representations with respect to matters to be included in, or objections to, any such plan or proposals for its alteration, repeal or replacement;

(cc) make provision with respect to the circumstances in which representations with respect to the matters to be included in a plan or proposals are to be treated, for any of the purposes of this Chapter, as being objections made in accordance with the regulations;

(d) without prejudice to paragraph (b), provide for notice to be given to particular persons of the approval, adoption or alteration of any plan, if they have objected to the plan and have notified the relevant local planning authority of their wish to receive notice, subject (if the regulations so provide) to the payment of a reasonable charge for receiving it;

(e) require or authorise a local planning authority to consult with, or consider the views of, other persons before taking any prescribed procedural step;

(f) require a local planning authority, in such cases as may be prescribed or in such particular cases as the Secretary of State may direct, to provide persons making a request with copies of any plan or document which has been made public in compliance with the regulations or available for inspection under sections 33(2) or 40(2), subject (if the regulations so provide) to the payment of a reasonable charge;

(ff) make provision for steps taken in compliance with the regulations in respect of a plan or proposal which has been withdrawn to be taken into account in prescribed circumstances for the purposes of complying with the regulations in respect of a subsequent plan or proposal;

(g) provide for the publication and inspection of any structure plan or local plan which has been approved, adopted or made, or any document approved, adopted or made altering, repealing or replacing any such plan, and for copies of any such plan or document to be made available on sale.

(3) Regulations under this section may extend throughout England and Wales or to specified areas only and may make different provision for different cases.

(4) Subject to the previous provisions of this Chapter and to any regulations under this section, the Secretary of State may give directions to any local planning authority, or to local planning authorities generally—
  (a) for formulating the procedure for the carrying out of their functions under this Chapter;
  (b) for requiring them to give him such information as he may require for carrying out any of his functions under this Chapter.

54. Meaning of 'development plan' outside Greater London and the metropolitan counties

(1) Subject to subsection (4), for the purposes of this Act and any other enactment relating to town and country planning, the Land Compensation Act 1961 and the Highways Act 1980, the development plan for any district outside Greater London and the metropolitan counties (whether the whole or part of the area of a local planning authority) shall be taken as consisting of—
  (a) the provisions of the structure plan for the time being in operation in the area;
  (b) any alterations to that structure plan;
  (c) the provisions of the local plan and any minerals local plan or waste local plan for the time being in operation in the area;
  (d) any alterations to that local plan or minerals local plan or waste local plan, together with the resolutions of the authority who made or altered the plan or, as the case may be the Secretary of State's notice of approval.

(2) References in subsection (1) to the provisions of any plan, notices of approval, alterations and resolutions of adoption shall, in relation to a district forming part of the area to which they are applicable, be respectively construed as references to so much of those provisions, notices, alterations and resolutions as is applicable to the district.

(3) References in subsection (1) to notices of approval shall, in relation to any plan or alteration made by the Secretary of State under section 51, be construed as references to notices of the making of the plan or alteration.

(4) This section has effect subject to Part III of Schedule 2 (old development plans) and Part III of Schedule 4 to the Planning and Compensation Act 1991.

(5) Any reference in the Land Compensation Act 1961 to an area defined in the current development plan as an area of comprehensive development shall be construed as a reference to an action area for which a local plan is in force.

CHAPTER III
GENERAL

54A. Status of development plans

Where, in making any determination under the planning Acts, regard is to be had to the development plan, the determination shall be made in accordance with the plan unless material considerations indicate otherwise.

PART III
CONTROL OVER DEVELOPMENT

Meaning of development

55. Meaning of 'development'

(1) Subject to the following provisions of this section, in this Act, except where the context otherwise requires, 'development,' means the carrying out of building, engineering, mining or other operations in, on, over or under land, or the making of any material change in the use of any buildings or other land.

Town and Country Planning Act 1990 43

(1A) For the purposes of this Act 'building operations' includes—
 (a) demolition of buildings;
 (b) rebuilding;
 (c) structural alterations of or additions to buildings; and
 (d) other operations normally undertaken by a person carrying on business as a builder.

(2) The following operations or uses of land shall not be taken for the purposes of this Act to involve development of the land—
 (a) the carrying out for the maintenance, improvement or other alteration of any building of works which—
  (i) affect only the interior of the building, or
  (ii) do not materially affect the external appearance of the building,
and are not works for making good war damage or works begun after 5th December 1968 for the alteration of a building by providing additional space in it underground;
 (b) the carrying out on land within the boundaries of a road by a local highway authority of any works required for the maintenance or improvement of the road;
 (c) the carrying out by a local authority or statutory undertakers of any works for the purpose of inspecting, repairing or renewing any sewers, mains, pipes, cables or other apparatus; including the breaking open of any street or other land for that purpose;
 (d) the use of any buildings or other land within the curtilage of a dwellinghouse for any purpose incidental to the enjoyment of the dwellinghouse as such;
 (e) the use of any land for the purposes of agriculture or forestry (including afforestation) and the use for any of those purposes of any building occupied together with land so used;
 (f) in the case of buildings or other land which are used for a purpose of any class specified in an order made by the Secretary of State under this section, the use of the buildings or other land or, subject to the provisions of the order, of any part of the buildings or the other land, for any other purpose of the same class.
 (g) The demolition of any description of building specified in a direction given by the Secretary of State to local planning authorities generally or to a particular local planning authority.

(3) For the avoidance of doubt it is hereby declared that for the purposes of this section—
 (a) the use as two or more separate dwellinghouses of any building previously used as a single dwellinghouse involves a material change in the use of the building and of each part of it which is so used;
 (b) the deposit of refuse or waste materials on land involves a material change in its use, notwithstanding that the land is comprised in a site already used for that purpose, if—
  (i) the superficial area of the deposit is extended, or
  (ii) the height of the deposit is extended and exceeds the level of the land adjoining the site.

(4) For the purposes of this Act mining operations include—
 (a) the removal of material of any description—
  (i) from a mineral-working deposit;
  (ii) from a deposit of pulverised fuel ash or other furnace ash or clinker; or
  (iii) from a deposit of iron, steel or other metallic slags; and
 (b) the extraction of minerals from a disused railway embankment.

(4A) Where the placing or assembly of any tank in any part of any inland waters for the purpose of fish farming there would not, apart from this subsection, involve development of the land below, this Act shall have effect as if the tank resulted from carrying out engineering operations over that land; and in this subsection—

'fish farming' means the breeding, rearing or keeping of fish or shellfish (which includes any kind of crustacean and mollusc);
'inland waters' means waters which do not form part of the sea or of any creek, bay or estuary or of any river as far as the tide flows; and
'tank' includes any cage and any other structure for use in fish farming.

(5) Without prejudice to any regulations made under the provisions of this Act relating to the control of advertisements, the use for the display of advertisements of any external part of a building which is not normally used for that purpose shall be treated for the purposes of this section as involving a material change in the use of that part of the building.

56. Time when development begun

(1) Subject to the following provisions of this section, for the purposes of this Act development of land shall be taken to be initiated—

(a) if the development consists of the carrying out of operations, at the time when those operations are begun;

(b) if the development consists of a change in use, at the time when the new use is instituted;

(c) if the development consists both of the carrying out of operations and of a change in use, at the earlier of the times mentioned in paragraphs (a) and (b).

(2) For the purposes of the provisions of this Part mentioned in subsection (3) development shall be taken to be begun on the earliest date on which any material operation comprised in the development begins to be carried out.

(3) The provisions referred to in subsection (2) are sections 85(2), 86(6), 87(4), 89, 91, 92 and 94.

(4) In subsection (2) 'material operation' means—

(a) any work of construction in the course of the erection of a building;

(aa) any work of demolition of a building;

(b) the digging of a trench which is to contain the foundations, or part of the foundations, of a building;

(c) the laying of any underground main or pipe to the foundations, or part of the foundations, of a building or to any such trench as is mentioned in paragraph (b);

(d) any operation in the course of laying out or constructing a road or part of a road;

(e) any change in the use of any land which constitutes material development.

(5) In subsection (4)(e) 'material development' means any development other than—

(a) development for which planning permission is granted by a general development order for the time being in force and which is carried out so as to comply with any condition or limitation subject to which planning permission is so granted;

(b) development of a class specified in paragraph 1 or 2 of Schedule 3; and

(c) development of any class prescribed for the purposes of this subsection.

(6) In subsection (5) 'general development order' means a development order (within the meaning of section 59) made as a general order applicable (subject to such exceptions as may be specified in it) to all land in England and Wales.

Requirement for planning permission

57. Planning permission required for development

(1) Subject to the following provisions of this section, planning permission is required for the carrying out of any development of land.

(2) Where planning permission to develop land has been granted for a limited period, planning permission is not required for the resumption, at the end of that period, of its use for the purpose for which it was normally used before the permission was granted.

(3) Where by a development order planning permission to develop land has been granted subject to limitations, planning permission is not required for the use of that land which (apart from its use in accordance with that permission) is its normal use.

(4) Where an enforcement notice has been issued in respect of any development of land, planning permission is not required for its use for the purpose for which (in accordance with the provisions of this Part of this Act) it could lawfully have been used if that development had not been carried out.

(5) In determining for the purposes of subsections (2) and (3) what is or was the normal use of land, no account shall be taken of any use begun in contravention of this Part or of previous planning control.

(6) For the purposes of this section a use of land shall be taken to have been begun in contravention of previous planning control if it was begun in contravention of Part III of the 1947 Act, Part III of the 1962 Act or Part III of the 1971 Act.

(7) Subsection (1) has effect subject to Schedule 4 (which makes special provision about use of land on 1st July 1948).

58. Granting of planning permission: general
(1) Planning permission may be granted—
   (a) by a development order;
   (b) by the local planning authority (or, in the cases provided in this Part, by the Secretary of State) on application to the authority in accordance with a development order;
   (c) on the adoption or approval of a simplified planning zone scheme or alterations to such a scheme in accordance with section 82 or, as the case may be, section 86; or
   (d) on the designation of an enterprise zone or the approval of a modified scheme under Schedule 32 to the Local Government, Planning and Land Act 1980 in accordance with section 88 of this Act.

(2) Planning permission may also be deemed to be granted under section 90 (development with government authorisation).

(3) This section is without prejudice to any other provisions of this Act providing for the granting of permission.

Development orders

59. Development orders: general
(1) The Secretary of State shall by order (in this Act referred to as a 'development order') provide for the granting of planning permission.

(2) A development order may either—
   (a) itself grant planning permission for development specified in the order or for development of any class specified; or
   (b) in respect of development for which planning permission is not granted by the order itself, provide for the granting of planning permission by the local planning authority (or, in the cases provided in the following provisions, by the Secretary of State) on application to the authority in accordance with the provisions of the order.

(3) A development order may be made either—
   (a) as a general order applicable, except so far as the order otherwise provides, to all land, or
   (b) as a special order applicable only to such land or descriptions of land as may be specified in the order.

60. Permission granted by development order
(1) Planning permission granted by a development order may be granted either unconditionally or subject to such conditions or limitations as may be specified in the order.

(2) Without prejudice to the generality of subsection (1), where planning permission is granted by a development order for the erection, extension or alteration of any buildings, the order may require the approval of the local planning authority to be obtained with respect to the design or external appearance of the buildings.

(3) Without prejudice to the generality of subsection (1), where planning permission is granted by a development order for development of a specified class, the order may enable the Secretary of State or the local planning authority to direct that the permission shall not apply either—

(a) in relation to development in a particular area, or

(b) in relation to any particular development.

(4) Any provision of a development order by which permission is granted for the use of land for any purpose on a limited number of days in a period specified in that provision shall (without prejudice to the generality of references in this Act to limitations) be taken to be a provision granting permission for the use of land for any purpose subject to the limitation that the land shall not be used for any one purpose in pursuance of that provision on more than that number of days in that period.

61. Development orders: supplementary provisions

(1) A general development order may make different provision with respect to different descriptions of land.

(2) For the purpose of enabling development to be carried out in accordance with planning permission, or otherwise for the purpose of promoting proper development in accordance with the development plan, a development order may direct that any pre 1947 Act enactment, or any regulations, orders or byelaws made at any time under any such enactment—

(a) shall not apply to any development specified in the order, or

(b) shall apply to it subject to such modifications as may be so specified.

(3) In subsection (2) 'pre 1947 Act enactment' means—

(a) any enactment passed before 6th August 1947 (the date of the passing of the 1947 Act), and

(b) any enactment contained in the Highways Act 1980 which—

(i) is an enactment derived from the Highways Act 1959, and

(ii) re-enacts (with or without modifications) any such enactment as is mentioned in paragraph (a).

Applications for planning permission

62. Form and content of applications for planning permission

Any application to a local planning authority for planning permission—

(a) shall be made in such manner as may be prescribed by regulations under this Act; and

(b) shall include such particulars and be verified by such evidence as may be required by the regulations or by directions given by the local planning authority under them.

63. and 64. [repealed by the Planning and Compensation Act 1991]

Publicity for applications

65. Notice etc. of applications for planning permission

(1) A development order may make provision requiring—

(a) notice to be given of any application for planning permission, and

(b) any applicant for such permission to issue a certificate as to the interests in the land to which the application relates or the purpose for which it is used,

and provide for publicising such applications and for the form, content and service of such notices and certificates.

(2) Provision shall be made by a development order for the purpose of securing that, in the case of any application for planning permission, any person (other than the applicant) who on such date as may be prescribed by the order is an owner of the land to which the application relates, or a tenant of any agricultural holding any part of which is comprised in that land, is given notice of the application in such manner as may be required by the order.

(3) A development order may require an applicant for planning permission to certify, in such form as may be prescribed by the order, or to provide evidence, that any requirements of the order have been satisfied.

(4) A development order making any provision by virtue of this section may make different provision for different cases or different classes of development.

(5) A local planning authority shall not entertain an application for planning permission unless any requirements imposed by virtue of this section have been satisfied.

(6) If any person—
   (a) issues a certificate which purports to comply with any requirement imposed by virtue of this section and contains a statement which he knows to be false or misleading in a material particular; or
   (b) recklessly issues a certificate which purports to comply with any such requirement and contains a statement which is false or misleading in a material particular,
he shall be guilty of an offence.

(7) A person guilty of an offence under this section shall be liable on summary conviction to a fine not exceeding level 5 on the standard scale.

(8) In this section—
   'agricultural holding' has the same meaning as in the Agricultural Holdings Act 1986; and
   'owner' in relation to any land means any person who—
   (a) is the estate owner in respect of the fee simple;
   (b) is entitled to a tenancy granted or extended for a term of years certain of which not less than seven years remain unexpired; or
   (c) in the case of such applications as may be prescribed by a development order, is entitled to an interest in any mineral so prescribed,
and the reference to the interests in the land to which an application for planning permission relates includes any interest in any mineral in, on or under the land.

(9) Notwithstanding section 127 of the Magistrates' Courts Act 1980, a magistrates' court may try an information in respect of an offence under this section whenever laid.

66. to 68. [repealed by the Planning and Compensation Act 1991]

69. Registers of applications, etc.

(1) Every local planning authority shall keep, in such manner as may be prescribed by a development order, a register containing such information as may be so prescribed with respect to applications for planning permission

(2) The register shall contain—
   (a) information as to the manner in which such applications have been dealt with, and
   (b) such information as may be prescribed by a development order with respect to simplified planning zone schemes relating to zones in the authority's area.

(3) A development order may make provision for the register to be kept in two or more parts, each part containing such information relating to applications for planning permission as may be prescribed by the order.

(4) A development order may also make provision—

(a) for a specified part of the register to contain copies of applications and of any plans or drawings submitted with them; and

(b) for the entry relating to any application, and everything relating to it, to be removed from that part of the register when the application (including any appeal arising out of it) has been finally disposed of (without prejudice to the inclusion of any different entry relating to it in another part of the register).

(5) Every register kept under this section shall be available for inspection by the public at all reasonable hours.

Determination of applications

70. Determination of applications: general considerations

(1) Where an application is made to a local planning authority for planning permission—

(a) subject to sections 91 and 92, they may grant planning permission, either unconditionally or subject to such conditions as they think fit; or

(b) they may refuse planning permission.

(2) In dealing with such an application the authority shall have regard to the provisions of the development plan, so far as material to the application, and to any other material considerations.

(3) Subsection (1) has effect subject to section 65, and to the following provisions of this Act, to sections 66, 67, 72 and 73 of the Planning (Listed Buildings and Conservation Areas) Act 1990 and to section 15 of the Health Services Act 1976.

70A. Power of local planning authority to decline to determine applications

(1) A local planning authority may decline to determine an application for planning permission for the development of any land if—

(a) within the period of two years ending with the date on which the application is received, the Secretary of State has refused a similar application referred to him under section 77 or has dismissed an appeal against the refusal of a similar application; and

(b) in the opinion of the authority there has been no significant change since the refusal or, as the case may be, dismissal mentioned in paragraph (a) in the development plan, so far as material to the application, or in any other material considerations.

(2) For the purposes of this section an application for planning permission for the development of any land shall only be taken to be similar to a later application if the development and the land to which the applications relate are in the opinion of the local planning authority the same or substantially the same.

(3) The reference in subsection (1)(a) to an appeal against the refusal of an application includes an appeal under section 78(2) in respect of an application.

71. Consultations in connection with determinations under s. 70

(1) A development order may provide that a local planning authority shall not determine an application for planning permission before the end of such period as may be prescribed.

(2) A development order may require a local planning authority—

(a) to take into account in determining such an application such representations, made within such period, as may be prescribed; and

(b) to give to any person whose representations have been taken into account such notice as may be prescribed of their decision.

(2A) A development order making any provision by virtue of this section may make different provision for different cases or different classes of development.

(3) Before a local planning authority grant planning permission for the use of land as a caravan site, they shall, unless they are also the authority with power to issue a site licence for that land, consult the local authority with that power.

(4) In this section—
'prescribed' means prescribed by a development order;
'site licence' means a licence under Part 1 of the Caravan Sites and Control of Development Act 1960 authorising the use of land as a caravan site.

71A. Assessment of environmental effects

(1) The Secretary of State may by regulations make provision about the consideration to be given, before planning permission for development of any class specified in the regulations is granted, to the likely environmental effects of the proposed development.

(2) The regulations—

(a) may make the same provision as, or provision similar or corresponding to, any provision made, for the purposes of any Community obligation of the United Kingdom about the assessment of the likely effects of development on the environment, under section 2(2) of the European Communities Act 1972; and

(b) may make different provision for different classes of development.

(3) Where a draft of regulations made in exercise both of the power conferred by this section and the power conferred by section 2(2) of the European Communities Act 1972 is approved by resolution of each House of Parliament, section 333(3) shall not apply.

72. Conditional grant of planning permission

(1) Without prejudice to the generality of section 70(1), of planning may be imposed on the grant of planning permission under that section—

(a) for regulating the development or use of land in respect of which the application was made or requiring the carrying out of works on any such land, so far as appears to the local planning authority to be expedient for the purposes of or in connection with the development authorised by the permission;

(b) for requiring the removal of any buildings or works authorised by the permission, or the discontinuance of any use of land so authorised, at the end of a specified period, and the carrying out of any works required for the reinstatement of land at the end of that period.

(2) A planning permission granted subject to such a condition as is mentioned in subsection (1)(b) is in this Act referred to as 'planning permission granted for a limited period'.

(3) Where—

(a) planning permission is granted for development consisting of or including the carrying out of building or other operations subject to a condition that the operations shall be commenced not later than a time specified in the condition; and

(b) any building or other operations are commenced after the time so specified, the commencement and carrying out of those operations do not constitute development for which that permission was granted.

(4) Subsection (3)(a) does not apply to a condition attached to the planning permission by or under section 91 or 92.

(5) Part I of Schedule 5 shall have effect for the purpose of making special provision with respect to the conditions which may be imposed on the grant of planning permission for development consisting of the winning and working of minerals or involving the depositing of refuse or mineral waste, and subsection (2) has effect subject to paragraph 1(6)(a) of that Schedule.

73. Determination of applications to develop land without compliance with conditions previously attached

(1) This section applies, subject to subsection (4), to applications for planning permission for the development of land without complying with conditions subject to which a previous planning permission was granted.

(2) On such an application the local planning authority shall consider only the question of the conditions subject to which planning permission should be granted, and—

(a) if they decide that planning permission should be granted subject to conditions differing from those subject to which the previous permission was granted, or that it should be granted unconditionally, they shall grant planning permission accordingly, and

(b) if they decide that planning permission should be granted subject to the same conditions as those subject to which the previous permission was granted, they shall refuse the application.

(3) Special provision may be made with respect to such applications—

(a) by regulations under section 62 as regards the form and content of the application, and

(b) by a development order as regards the procedure to be followed in connection with the application.

(4) This section does not apply if the previous planning permission was granted subject to a condition as to the time within which the development to which it related was to be begun and that time has expired without the development having been begun.

73A. Planning permission for development already carried out

(1) On an application made to a local planning authority, the planning permission which may be granted includes planning permission for development carried out before the date of the application.

(2) Subsection (1) applies to development carried out—

(a) without planning permission;

(b) in accordance with planning permission granted for a limited period; or

(c) without complying with some condition subject to which planning permission was granted.

(3) Planning permission for such development may be granted so as to have effect from—

(a) the date on which the development was carried out; or

(b) if it was carried out in accordance with planning permission granted for a limited period, the end of that period.

74. Directions etc. as to method of dealing with applications

(1) Provision may be made by a development order for regulating the manner in which applications for planning permission to develop land are to be dealt with by local planning authorities, and in particular—

(a) for enabling the Secretary of State to give directions restricting the grant of planning permission by the local planning authority, either indefinitely or during such period as may be specified in the directions, in respect of any such development, or in respect of development of any such class, as may be so specified;

(b) for authorising the local planning authority, in such cases and subject to such conditions as may be prescribed by the order or by directions given by the Secretary of State under it, to grant planning permission for development which does not accord with the provisions of the development plan;

(c) for requiring that, before planning permission for any development is granted or refused, local planning authorities prescribed by the order or by directions given by the Secretary of State under it shall consult with such authorities or persons as may be so prescribed;

(d) for requiring the local planning authority to give to any applicant for planning permission, within such time as may be prescribed by the order, such notice as may be so prescribed as to the manner in which his application has been dealt with;

Town and Country Planning Act 1990

(e) for requiring the local planning authority to give any applicant for any consent, agreement or approval required by a condition imposed on a grant of planning permission notice of their decision on his application, within such time as may be so prescribed;

(f) for requiring the local planning authority to give to the Secretary of State, and to such other persons as may be prescribed by or under the order, such information as may be so prescribed with respect to applications for planning permission made to the authority, including information as to the manner in which any such application has been dealt with.

(1A) Provision may be made by a development order—

(a) for determining the persons to whom applications under this Act are to be sent; and

(b) for requiring persons to whom such applications are sent to send copies to other interested persons.

(2) Subsection (1) is subject to the provisions of sections 67(7) and 73(1) of the Planning (Listed Buildings and Conservation Areas) Act 1990.

75. Effect of planning permission

(1) Without prejudice to the provisions of this Part as to the duration, revocation or modification of planning permission, any grant of planning permission to develop land shall (except in so far as the permission otherwise provides) enure for the benefit of the land and of all persons for the time being interested in it.

(2) Where planning permission is granted for the erection of a building, the grant of permission may specify the purposes for which the building may be used.

(3) If no purpose is so specified, the permission shall be construed as including permission to use the building for the purpose for which it is designed.

76. Duty to draw attention to certain provisions for benefit of disabled

(1) This section applies when planning permission is granted for any development which will result in the provision—

(a) of a building or premises to which section 4 of the Chronically Sick and Disabled Persons Act 1970 applies (buildings or premises to which the public are to be admitted whether on payment or otherwise);

(b) of any of the following (being in each case, premises in which persons are employed to work—

(i) office premises, shop premises and railway premises to which the Offices, Shops and Railway Premises Act 1963 applies;

(ii) premises which are deemed to be such premises for the purposes of that Act; or

(iii) factories as defined by section 175 of the Factories Act 1961;

(c) of a building intended for the purposes of a university, university college or college, or of a school or hall of a university;

(d) of a building intended for the purposes of an institution within the PCFC funding sector; or

(e) of a building intended for the purposes of a school or an institution which provides higher education or further education (or both) and is maintained or assisted by a local education authority.

(2) The local planning authority granting the planning permission shall draw the attention of the person to whom the permission is granted—

(a) in the case of such a building or premises as are mentioned in subsection (1)(a)—

(i) to sections 4 and 7 of the Chronically Sick and Disabled Persons Act 1970; and

(ii) to the Code of Practice for Access of the Disabled to Buildings (British Standards Institution code of practice BS 5810: 1979) or any prescribed document replacing that code;

(b) in the case of such premises as are mentioned in subsection (1)(b), to sections 7 and 8A of that Act and to that code or any such prescribed document replacing it;

(c) in the case of such a building as is mentioned in subsection (1)(c), (d) or (e), to sections 7 and 8 of that Act and to Design Note 18 'Access for Disabled People to Educational Buildings' published in 1984 on behalf of the Secretary of State, or any prescribed document replacing that note.

(3) Expressions used in subsection (1)(d) and (e) and in the Education Act 1944 have the same meanings as in that Act.

Secretary of State's powers as respects planning applications and decisions

77. Reference of applications to Secretary of State

(1) The Secretary of State may give directions requiring applications for planning permission, or for the approval of any local planning authority required under a development order, to be referred to him instead of being dealt with by local planning authorities.

(2) A direction under this section—
 (a) may be given either to a particular local planning authority or to local planning authorities generally; and
 (b) may relate either to a particular application or to applications of a class specified in the direction.

(3) Any application in respect of which a direction under this section has effect shall be referred to the Secretary of State accordingly.

(4) Subject to subsection (5), where an application for planning permission is referred to the Secretary of State under this section, sections 70, 7(1) and (5), 73 and 73 shall apply, with any necessary modifications, as they apply to such an application which falls to be determined by the local planning authority and a development order may apply, with or without modifications, to an application so referred any requirements imposed by such an order by virtue of sections 65 to 71.

(5) Before determining an application referred to him under this section, the Secretary of State shall, if either the applicant or the local planning authority wish, give each of them an opportunity of appearing before, and being heard by, a person appointed by the Secretary of State for the purpose.

(6) Subsection (5) does not apply to an application for planning permission referred to a Planning Inquiry Commission under section 101.

(7) The decision of the Secretary of State on any application referred to him under this section shall be final.

78. Right to appeal against planning decisions and failure to take such decisions

(1) Where a local planning authority—
 (a) refuse an application for planning permission or grant it subject to conditions;
 (b) refuse an application for any consent, agreement or approval of that authority required by a condition imposed on a grant of planning permission or grant it subject to conditions; or
 (c) refuse an application for any approval of that authority required under a development order or grant it subject to conditions,
the applicant may by notice appeal to the Secretary of State.

(2) A person who has made such an application may also appeal to the Secretary of State if the local planning authority have done none of the following—
 (a) given notice to the applicant of their decision on the application;
 (aa) given notice to the applicant that they have exercised this power under section 70A to decline to determine the application

(b) given notice to him that the application has been referred to the Secretary of State in accordance with directions given under section 77,
within such period as may be prescribed by the development order or within such extended period as may at any time be agreed upon in writing between the applicant and the authority.

(3) Any appeal under this section shall be made by notice served within such time and in such manner as may be prescribed by a development order.

(4) The time prescribed for the service of such a notice must not be less than—
    (a) 28 days from the date of notification of the decision; or
    (b) in the case of an appeal under subsection (2), 28 days from the end of the period prescribed as mentioned in subsection (2) or, as the case may be, the extended period mentioned in that subsection.

(5) For the purposes of the application of sections 79(1), 253(2)(c), 266(1)(b) and 288(10)(b) in relation to an appeal under subsection (2), it shall be assumed that the authority decided to refuse the application in question.

79. Determination of appeals
(1) On an appeal under section 78 the Secretary of State may—
    (a) allow or dismiss the appeal, or
    (b) reverse or vary any part of the decision of the local planning authority (whether the appeal relates to that part of it or not),
and may deal with the application as if it had been made to him in the first instance.

(2) Before determining an appeal under section 78 the Secretary of State shall, if either the appellant or the local planning authority so wish, give each of them an opportunity of appearing before and being heard by a person appointed by the Secretary of State for the purpose.

(3) Subsection (2) does not apply to an appeal referred to a Planning Inquiry Commission under section 101.

(4) Subject to subsection (2), the provisions of section 70, 72(1) and (5), 73 and 73A and Part I of Schedule 5 shall apply, with any necessary modifications, in relation to an appeal to the Secretary of State under section 78 as they apply in relation to an application for planning permission which falls to be determined by the local planning authority and a development order may apply, with or without modifications, to such an appeal any requirements imposed by a development order by virtue of section 65 or 71.

(5) The decision of the Secretary of State on such an appeal shall be final.

(6) If, before or during the determination of such an appeal in respect of an application for planning permission to develop land, the Secretary of State forms the opinion that, having regard to the provisions of sections 70 and 72(1), the development order and any directions given under that order, planning permission for that development—
    (a) could not have been granted by the local planning authority; or
    (b) could not have been granted otherwise than subject to the conditions imposed,
he may decline to determine the appeal or to proceed with the determination.

(6A) If at any time before or during the determination of such an appeal it appears to the Secretary of State that the appellant is responsible for undue delay in the progress of the appeal, he may—
    (a) give the appellant notice that the appeal will be dismissed unless the appellant takes, within the period specified in the notice, such steps as are specified in the notice for the expedition of the appeal; and
    (b) if the appellant fails to take those steps within that period, dismiss the appeal accordingly.

(7) Schedule 6 applies to appeals under section 78, including appeals under that section as applied by or under any other provision of this Act.

80. and 81. [repealed by the Planning and Compensation Act 1991]

Simplified planning zones

82. Simplified planning zones

(1) A simplified planning zone is an area in respect of which a simplified planning zone scheme is in force.

(2) The adoption or approval of a simplified planning zone scheme has effect to grant in relation to the zone, or any part of it specified in the scheme, planning permission—

(a) for development specified in the scheme, or

(b) for development of any class so specified.

(3) Planning permission under a simplified planning zone scheme may be unconditional or subject to such conditions, limitations or exceptions as may be specified in the scheme.

83. Making of simplified planning zone schemes

(1) Every local planning authority shall consider, as soon as praticable after 2nd November 1987, the question for which part or parts of their area a simplified planning zone schemes is desirable, and then shall keep that question under review.

(2) If as a result of their original consideration or of any such review a local planning authority decide that it is desirable to prepare a scheme for any part of their area they shall do so; and a local planning authority may at any time decide—

(a) to make a simplified planning zone scheme, or

(b) to alter a scheme adopted by them, or

(c) with the consent of the Secretary of State, to alter a scheme approved by him.

(3) Schedule 7 has effect with respect to the making and alteration of simplified planning zone schemes and other related matters.

84. Simplified planning zone schemes; conditions and limitations on planning permission

(1) The conditions and limitations on planning permission which may be specified in a simplified planning zone scheme may include—

(a) conditions or limitations in respect of all development permitted by the scheme or in respect of particular descriptions of development so permitted, and

(b) conditions or limitations requiring the consent, agreement or approval of the local planning authority in relation to particular descriptions of permitted development.

(2) Different conditions or limitations may be specified in a simplified planning zone scheme for different cases or classes of case.

(3) Nothing in a simplified planning zone scheme shall affect the right of any person—

(a) to do anything not amounting to development, or

(b) to carry out development for which planning permission is not required or for which permission has been granted otherwise than by the scheme.

(4) No limitation or restriction subject to which permission has been granted otherwise than under the scheme shall affect the right of any person to carry out development for which permission has been granted under the scheme.

85. Duration of simplified planning zone scheme

(1) A simplified planning zone scheme shall take effect on the date of its adoption or approval and shall cease to have effect at the end of the period of 10 years beginning with that date.

(2) When the scheme ceases to have effect planning permission under it shall also cease to have effect except in a case where the development authorised by it has been begun.

86. Alteration of simplified planning zone scheme

(1) This section applies where alterations to a simplified planning zone scheme are adopted or approved.

(2) The adoption or approval of alterations providing for the inclusion of land in the simplified planning zone has effect to grant in relation to that land, or such part of it as is specified in the scheme, planning permission for development so specified or of any class so specified.

(3) The adoption or approval of alterations providing for the grant of planning permission has effect to grant such permission in relation to the simplified planning zone, or such part of it as is specified in the scheme, for development so specified or development of any class so specified.

(4) The adoption or approval of alterations providing for the withdrawal or relaxation of conditions, limitations or restrictions to which planning permission under the scheme is subject has effect to withdraw or relax the conditions, limitations or restrictions immediately.

(5) The adoption or approval of alterations providing for—
   (a) the exclusion of land from the simplified planning zone,
   (b) the withdrawal of planning permission, or
   (c) the imposition of new or more stringent conditions, limitations or restrictions to which planning permission under the scheme is subject,
has effect to withdraw permission, or to impose the conditions, limitations or restrictions, with effect from the end of the period of 12 months beginning with the date of the adoption or approval.

(6) The adoption or approval of alterations to a scheme does not affect planning permission under the scheme in any case where the development authorised by it has been begun.

87. Exclusion of certain descriptions of land or development

(1) The following descriptions of land may not be included in a simplified planning zone—
   (a) land in a National Park;
   (b) land in a conservation area;
   (c) land within the Broads;
   (d) land in an area designated under section 87 of the National Parks and Access to the Countryside Act 1949 as an area of outstanding natural beauty;
   (e) land identified in the development plan for the district as part of a green belt;
   (f) land in respect of which a notification or order is in force under section 28 or 29 of the Wildlife and Countryside Act 1981 (areas of special scientific interest).

(2) Where land included in a simplified planning zone becomes land of a description mentioned in subsection (1), that subsection does not operate to exclude it from the zone.

(3) The Secretary of State may by order provide that no simplified planning zone scheme shall have effect to grant planning permission—
   (a) in relation to an area of land specified in the order or to areas of land of a description so specified, or
   (b) for development of a description specified in the order.

(4) An order under subsection (3) has effect to withdraw such planning permission under a simplified planning zone scheme already in force with effect from the date on which the order comes into force, except in a case where the development authorised by the permission has been begun.

Enterprise zone schemes

88. Planning permission for development in enterprise zones

(1) An order designating an enterprise zone under Schedule 32 to local Government, Planning and Land Act 1980 shall (without more) have effect on the date on which the order designating the zone takes effect to grant planning permission for development specified in the scheme or for development of any class so specified.

(2) The approval of a modified scheme under paragraph 11 of that Schedule shall (without more) have effect on the date on which the modifications take effect to grant planning permission for development specified in the modified scheme or for development of any class so specified.

(3) Planning permission so granted shall be subject to such conditions or limitations as may be specified in the scheme or modified scheme or, if none is specified, shall be unconditional.

(4) Subject to subsection (5), where planning permission is so granted for any development or class of development the enterprise zone authority may direct that the permission shall not apply in relation—

(a) to a specified development; or
(b) to a specified class of development; or
(c) to a specified class of development in a specified area within the enterprise zone.

(5) An enterprise zone authority shall not give a direction under subsection (4) unless—

(a) they have submitted it to the Secretary of State, and
(b) he has notified them that he approves of their giving it.

(6) If the scheme or the modified scheme specifies, in relation to any development it permits, matters which will require approval by the enterprise zone authority, the permission shall have effect accordingly.

(7) The Secretary of State may by regulations make provision as to—

(a) the procedure for giving a direction under subsection (4); and
(b) the method and procedure relating to the approval of matters specified in a scheme or modified scheme as mentioned in subsection (6).

(8) Such regulations may modify any provision of the planning Acts or any instrument made under them or may apply any such provision or instrument (with or without modification) in making any such provision as is mentioned in subsection (7).

(9) Nothing in this section prevents planning permission being granted in relation to land in an enterprise zone otherwise than by virtue of this section (whether the permission is granted in pursuance of an application made under this Part or by a development order).

(10) Nothing in this section prejudices the right of any person to carry out development apart from this section.

89. Effect on planning permission of modification or termination of scheme

(1) Modifications to an enterprise zone scheme do not affect planning permission under the scheme in any case where the development authorised by it has been begun before the modifications take effect.

(2) When an area ceases to be an enterprise zone, planning permission under the scheme shall cease to have effect except in a case where the development authorised by it has been begun.

Deemed planning permission

90. Development with government authorisation

(1) Where the authorisation of a government department is required by virtue of an enactment in respect of development to be carried out by a local authority, or National Parks Authority or by statutory undertakers who are not a local authority, or

National Parks Authority that department may, on granting that authorisation, direct that planning permission for that development shall be deemed to be granted, subject to such conditions (if any) as may be specified in the direction.

(2) On granting a consent under section 36 or 37 of the Electricity Act 1989 in respect of any operation or change of use that constitutes development, the Secretary of State may direct that planning permission for that development and any ancillary development shall be deemed to be granted, subject to such conditions (if any) as may be specified in the direction.

(2A) On making an order under section 1 or 3 of the Transport and Works Act 1992 which includes provision for development, the Secretary of State may direct that planning permission for that development shall be deemed to be granted, subject to such conditions (if any) as may be specified in the direction.

(3) The provisions of this Act (except Part XII) shall apply in relation to any planning permission deemed to be granted by virtue of a direction under this section as if it had been granted by the Secretary of State on an application referred to him under section 77.

(4) For the purposes of this section development is authorised by a government department if—

(a) any consent, authority or approval to or for the development is granted by the department in pursuance of an enactment;

(b) a compulsory purchase order is confirmed by the department authorising the purchase of land for the purpose of the development;

(c) consent is granted by the department to the appropriation of land for the purpose of the development or the acquisition of land by agreement for that purpose;

(d) authority is given by the department—
 (i) for the borrowing of money for the purpose of the development, or
 (ii) for the application for that purpose of any money not otherwise so applicable; or

(e) any undertaking is given by the department to pay a grant in respect of the development in accordance with an enactment authorising the payment of such grants;

and references in this section to the authorisation of a government department shall be construed accordingly.

(5) In subsection (2) 'ancillary development', in relation to development consisting of the extension of a generating station, does not include any development which is not directly related to the generation of electricity by that station; and in this subsection 'extension' and 'generating station' have the same meanings as in Part I of the Electricity Act 1989.

[The references to National Park Authorities were introduced by the Environment Act 1995, see note to Section 4A supra.]

Duration of planning permission

91. General condition limiting duration of planning permission

(1) Subject to the provisions of this section, every planning permission granted or deemed to be granted shall be granted or, as the case may be, be deemed to be granted, subject to the condition that the development to which it relates must be begun not later than the expiration of—

(a) five years beginning with the date on which the permission is granted or, as the case may be, deemed to be granted; or

(b) such other period (whether longer or shorter) beginning with that date as the authority concerned with the terms of planning permission may direct.

(2) The period mentioned in subsection (1)(b) shall be a period which the authority consider appropriate having regard to the provisions of the development plan and to any other material considerations.

(3) If planning permission is granted without the condition required by subsection (1), it shall be deemed to have been granted subject to the condition that the development to which it relates must be begun not later than the expiration of five years beginning with the date of the grant.

(4) Nothing in this section applies—

(a) to any planning permission granted by development order;

(b) to any planning permission granted for development carried out before the grant of that permission

(c) to any planning permission granted for a limited period;

(d) to any planning permission for development consisting of the winning and working of minerals or involving the depositing of mineral waste which is granted (or deemed to be granted) subject to a condition that the development to which it relates must be begun before the expiration of a specified period after—

(i) the completion of other development consisting of the winning and working of minerals already being carried out by the applicant for the planning permission; or

(ii) the cessation of depositing of mineral waste already being carried out by the applicant for the planning permission;

(e) to any planning permission granted by an enterprise zone scheme;

(f) to any planning permission granted by a simplified planning zone scheme; or

(g) to any outline planning permission, as defined by section 92.

92. Outline planning permission

(1) In this section and section 91 'outline planning permission' means planning permission granted, in accordance with the provisions of a development order, with the reservation for subsequent approval by the local planning authority or the Secretary of State of matters not particularised in the application ('reserved matters').

(2) Subject to the following provisions of this section, where outline planning permission is granted for development consisting in or including the carrying out of building or other operations, it shall be granted subject to conditions to the effect—

(a) that, in the case of any reserved matter, application for approval must be made not later than the expiration of three years beginning with the date of the grant of outline planning permission; and

(b) that the development to which the permission relates must be begun not later than—

(i) the expiration of five years from the date of the grant of outline planning permission; or

(ii) if later, the expiration of two years from the final approval of the reserved matters or, in the case of approval on different dates, the final approval of the last such matter to be approved.

(3) If outline planning permission is granted without the conditions required by subsection (2), it shall be deemed to have been granted subject to those conditions.

(4) The authority concerned with the terms of an outline planning permission may, in applying subsection (2), substitute, or direct that there be substituted, for the periods of three years, five years or two years referred to in that subsection such other periods respectively (whether longer or shorter) as they consider appropriate.

(5) They may also specify, or direct that there be specified, separate periods under paragraph (a) of subsection (2) in relation to separate parts of the development to which the planning permission relates; and, if they do so, the condition required by paragraph (b) of that subsection shall then be framed correspondingly by reference to those parts, instead of by reference to the development as a whole.

(6) In considering whether to exercise their powers under subsections (4) and (5), the authority shall have regard to the provisions of the development plan and to any other material considerations.

93. Provisions supplementary to ss. 91 and 92

(1) The authority referred to in section 91(1)(b) or 92(4) is—

(a) the local planning authority or the Secretary of State, in the case of planning permission granted by them,

(b) in the case of planning permission deemed to be granted under section 90(1), the department on whose direction planning permission is deemed to be granted, and

(c) in the case of planning permission deemed to be granted under section 90(2), the Secretary of State.

(2) For the purposes of section 92, a reserved matter shall be treated as finally approved—

(a) when an application for approval is granted, or

(b) in a case where the application is made to the local planning authority and on an appeal to the Secretary of State against the authority's decision on the application the Secretary of State grants the approval, when the appeal is determined.

(3) Where a local planning authority grant planning permission, the fact that any of the conditions of the permission are required by the provisions of section 91 or 92 to be imposed, or are deemed by those provisions to be imposed, shall not prevent the conditions being the subject of an appeal under section 78 against the decision of the authority.

(4) In the case of planning permission (whether outline or other) which has conditions attached to it by or under section 91 or 92—

(a) development carried out after the date by which the conditions require it to be carried out shall be treated as not authorised by the permission; and

(b) an application for approval of a reserved matter, if it is made after the date by which the conditions require it to be made, shall be treated as not made in accordance with the terms of the permission.

94. Termination of planning permission by reference to time limit: completion notices

(1) This section applies where—

(a) by virtue of section 91 or 92, a planning permission is subject to a condition that the development to which the permission relates must be begun before the expiration of a particular period, that development has been begun within that period, but that period has elapsed without the development having been completed; or

(b) development has been begun in accordance with planning permission under a simplified planning zone scheme but has not been completed by the time the area ceases to be a simplified planning zone; or

(c) development has been begun in accordance with planning permission under an enterprise zone scheme but has not been completed by the time the area ceases to be an enterprise zone.

(2) If the local planning authority are of the opinion that the development will not be completed within a reasonable period, they may serve a notice ('a completion notice') stating that the planning permission will cease to have effect at the expiration of a further period specified in the notice.

(3) The period so specified must not be less than 12 months after the notice takes effect.

(4) A completion notice shall be served—

(a) on the owner of the land,

(b) on the occupier of the land, and

(c) on any other person who in the opinion of the local planning authority will be affected by the notice.

(5) The local planning authority may withdraw a completion notice at any time before the expiration of the period specified in it as the period at the expiration of which the planning permission is to cease to have effect.

(6) If they do so they shall immediately give notice of the withdrawal to every person who was served with the completion notice.

95. Effect of completion notice

(1) A completion notice shall not take effect unless and until it is confirmed by the Secretary of State.

(2) In confirming a completion notice the Secretary of State may substitute some longer period for that specified in the notice as the period at the expiration of which the planning permission is to cease to have effect.

(3) If, within such period as may be specified in a completion notice (which must not be less than 28 days from its service) any person on whom the notice is served so requires, the Secretary of State, before confirming the notice, shall give him and the local planning authority an opportunity of appearing before and being heard by a person appointed by the Secretary of State for the purpose.

(4) If a completion notice takes effect, the planning permission referred to in it shall become invalid at the expiration of the period specified in the notice (whether the original period specified under section 94(2) or a longer period substituted by the Secretary of State under subsection (2)).

(5) Subsection (4) shall not affect any permission so far as development carried out under it before the end of the period mentioned in that subsection is concerned.

96. Power of Secretary of State to serve completion notices

(1) If it appears to the Secretary of State to be expedient that a completion notice should be served in respect of any land, he may himself serve such a notice.

(2) A completion notice served by the Secretary of State shall have the same effect as if it had been served by the local planning authority.

(3) The Secretary of State shall not serve such a notice without consulting the local planning authority.

Revocation and modification of planning permission

97. Power to revoke or modify planning permission

(1) If it appears to the local planning authority that it is expedient to revoke or modify any permission to develop land granted on an application made under this Part, the authority may by order revoke or modify the permission to such extent as they consider expedient.

(2) In exercising their functions under subsection (1) the authority shall have regard to the development plan and to any other material considerations.

(3) The power conferred by this section may be exercised—

(a) where the permission relates to the carrying out of building or other operations, at any time before those operations have been completed;

(b) where the permission relates to a change of the use of any land, at any time before the change has taken place.

(4) The revocation or modification of permission for the carrying out of building or other operations shall not affect so much of those operations as has been previously carried out.

(5) References in this section to the local planning authority are to be construed in relation to development consisting of the winning and working of minerals as references to the mineral planning authority.

(6) Part II of Schedule 5 shall have effect for the purpose of making special provision with respect to the conditions that may be imposed by an order under this section which revokes or modifies permission for development—

(a) consisting of the winning and working of minerals; or

(b) involving the depositing of refuse or waste materials.

98. Procedure for s. 97 orders: opposed cases

(1) Except as provided in section 99, an order under section 97 shall not take effect unless it is confirmed by the Secretary of State.

(2) Where a local planning authority submit such an order to the Secretary of State for confirmation, they shall serve notice on—
- (a) the owner of the land affected,
- (b) the occupier of the land affected, and
- (c) any other person who in their opinion will be affected by the order.

(3) The notice shall specify the period within which any person on whom it is served may require the Secretary of State to give him an opportunity of appearing before, and being heard by, a person appointed by the Secretary of State for the purpose.

(4) If within that period such a person so requires, before the Secretary of State confirms the order he shall give such an opportunity both to him and to the local planning authority.

(5) The period referred to in subsection (3) must not be less than 28 days from the service of the notice.

(6) The Secretary of State may confirm an order submitted to him under this section either without modification or subject to such modifications as he considers expedient.

99. Procedure for s. 97 orders: unopposed cases

(1) This section applies where—
- (a) the local planning authority have made an order under section 97; and
- (b) the owner and the occupier of the land and all persons who in the authority's opinion will be affected by the order have notified the authority in writing that they do not object to it.

(2) Where this section applies, instead of submitting the order to the Secretary of State for confirmation the authority shall advertise in the prescribed manner the fact that the order has been made, and the advertisement must specify—
- (a) the period within which persons affected by the order may give notice to the Secretary of State that they wish for an opportunity of appearing before, and being heard by, a person appointed by the Secretary of State for the purpose; and
- (b) the period at the expiration of which, if no such notice is given to the Secretary of State, the order may take effect by virtue of this section without being confirmed by the Secretary of State.

(3) The authority shall also serve notice to the same effect on the persons mentioned in subsection (1)(b).

(4) The period referred to in subsection (2)(a) must not be less than 28 days from the date the advertisement first appears.

(5) The period referred to in subsection (2)(b) must not be less than 14 days from the expiration of the period referred to in subsection (2)(a).

(6) The authority shall send a copy of any advertisement published under subsection (2) to the Secretary of State not more than three days after the publication.

(7) If—
- (a) no person claiming to be affected by the order has given notice to the Secretary of State under subsection (2)(a) within the period referred to in that subsection, and
- (b) the Secretary of State has not directed within that period that the order be submitted to him for confirmation,

the order shall take effect at the expiry of the period referred to in subsection (2)(b), without being confirmed by the Secretary of State as required by section 98(1).

(8) This section does not apply—

(a) to an order revoking or modifying a planning permission granted or deemed to have been granted by the Secretary of State under this Part or Part VII, or

(b) to an order modifying any conditions to which a planning permission is subject by virtue of section 91 or 92.

100. Revocation and modification of planning permission by the Secretary of State

(1) If it appears to the Secretary of State that it is expedient that an order should be made under section 97, he may himself make such an order.

(2) Such an order which is made by the Secretary of State shall have the same effect as if it had been made by the local planning authority and confirmed by the Secretary of State.

(3) The Secretary of State shall not make such an order without consulting the local planning authority.

(4) Where the Secretary of State proposes to make such an order he shall serve notice on the local planning authority.

(5) The notice shall specify the period (which must not be less than 28 days from the date of its service) within which the authority may require an opportunity of appearing before and being heard by a person appointed by the Secretary of State for the purpose.

(6) If within that period the authority so require, before the Secretary of State makes the order he shall give the authority such an opportunity.

(7) The provisions of this Part and of any regulations made under this Act with respect to the procedure to be followed in connection with the submission by the local planning authority of any order under section 97 and its confirmation by the Secretary of State shall have effect, subject to any necessary modifications, in relation to any proposal by the Secretary of State to make such an order and its making by him.

(8) Subsections (5) and (6) of section 97 apply for the purposes of this section as they apply for the purposes of that.

References to Planning Inquiry Commission

101. Power to refer certain planning questions to Planning Inquiry Commission

(1) The Secretary of State may constitute a Planning Inquiry Commission to inquire into and report on any matter referred to them under subsection (2) in the circumstances mentioned in subsection (3).

(2) The matters that may be referred to a Planning Inquiry Commission are—

(a) an application for planning permission which the Secretary of State has under section 77 directed to be referred to him instead of being dealt with by a local planning authority;

(b) an appeal under section 78 (including that section as applied by or under any other provision of this Act);

(c) a proposal that a government department should give a direction under section 90(1) that planning permission shall be deemed to be granted for development by a local authority or National Park Authority or by statutory undertakers which is required by any enactment to be authorised by that department;

(d) a proposal that development should be carried out by or on behalf of a government department.

(3) Any of those matters may be referred to any such commission under this section if it appears expedient to the responsible Minister or Ministers that the question whether the proposed development should be permitted to be carried out should be the subject of a special inquiry on either or both of the following grounds—

Town and Country Planning Act 1990 63

(a) that there are considerations of national or regional importance which are relevant to the determination of that question and require evaluation, but a proper evaluation of them cannot be made unless there is a special inquiry for the purpose;

(b) that the technical or scientific aspects of the proposed development are of so unfamiliar a character as to jeopardise a proper determination of that question unless there is a special inquiry for the purpose.

(4) Part I of Schedule 8 shall have effect as respects the constitution of any such commission and its functions and procedure on references to it under this section, and the references in subsection (3) and in that Schedule to 'the responsible Minister or Ministers' shall be construed in accordance with Part II of that Schedule.

(5) In relation to any matter affecting both England and Wales, the functions of the Secretary of State under subsection (1) shall be exercised by the Secretaries of State for the time being having general responsibility in planning matters in relation to England and in relation to Wales acting jointly.

[The reference to a National Park Authority was introduced by the Environment Act 1995, see note to Section 4A supra.]

Other controls over development

102. Orders requiring discontinuance of use or alteration or removal of buildings or works

(1) If, having regard to the development plan and to any other material considerations, it appears to a local planning authority that it is expedient in the interests of the proper planning of their area (including the interests of amenity)—

(a) that any use of land should be discontinued or that any conditions should be imposed on the continuance of a use of land; or

(b) that any buildings or works should be altered or removed, they may by order—

(i) require the discontinuance of that use, or

(ii) impose such conditions as may be specified in the order on the continuance of it, or

(iii) require such steps as may be so specified to be taken for the alteration or removal of the buildings or works,

as the case may be.

(2) An order under this section may grant planning permission for any development of the land to which the order relates, subject to such conditions as may be specified in the order.

(3) Section 97 shall apply in relation to any planning permission granted by an order under this section as it applies in relation to planning permission granted by the local planning authority on an application made under this Part.

(4) The planning permission which may be granted by an order under this section includes planning permission, subject to such conditions as may be specified in the order, for development carried out before the date on which the order was submitted to the Secretary of State under section 103.

(5) Planning permission for such development may be granted so as to have effect from—

(a) the date on which the development was carried out; or

(b) if it was carried out in accordance with planning permission granted for a limited period, the end of that period.

(6) Where the requirements of an order under this section will involve the displacement of persons residing in any premises, it shall be the duty of the local planning authority, in so far as there is no other residential accommodation suitable to the reasonable requirements of those persons available on reasonable terms, to secure the provision of such accommodation in advance of the displacement.

(7) Subject to section 103(8), in the case of planning permission granted by an order under this section, the authority referred to in sections 91(1)(b) and 92(4) is the local planning authority making the order.

(8) The previous provisions of this section do not apply to the use of any land for development consisting of the winning and working of minerals or involving the depositing of refuse or waste materials except as provided in Schedule 9, and that Schedule shall have effect for the purpose of making provision as respects land which is or has been so used.

103. Confirmation by Secretary of State of s. 102 orders

(1) An order under section 102 shall not take effect unless it is confirmed by the Secretary of State, either without modification or subject to such modifications as he considers expedient.

(2) The power of the Secretary of State under this section to confirm an order subject to modifications includes power—

(a) to modify any provision of the order granting planning permission, as mentioned in subsections (2) to (5) of section 102;

(b) to include in the order any grant of planning permission which might have been included in the order as submitted to him.

(3) Where a local planning authority submit an order to the Secretary of State for his confirmation under this section, they shall serve notice—

(a) on the owner of the land affected,

(b) on the occupier of that land, and

(c) on any other person who in their opinion will be affected by the order.

(4) The notice shall specify the period within which any person on whom it is served may require the Secretary of State to give him an opportunity of appearing before, and being heard by, a person appointed by the Secretary of State for the purpose.

(5) If within that period such a person so requires, before the Secretary of State confirms the order, he shall give such an opportunity both to him and to the local planning authority.

(6) The period referred to in subsection (4) must not be less than 28 days from the service of the notice.

(7) Where an order under section 102 has been confirmed by the Secretary of State, the local planning authority shall serve a copy of the order on the owner and occupier of the land to which the order relates.

(8) Where the Secretary of State exercises his powers under subsection (2) in confirming an order granting planning permission, he is the authority referred to in sections 91(1)(b) and 92(4).

104. Power of the Secretary of State to make s. 102 orders

(1) If it appears to the Secretary of State that it is expedient that an order should be made under section 102, he may himself make such an order.

(2) Such an order made by the Secretary of State shall have the same effect as if it had been made by the local planning authority and confirmed by the Secretary of State.

(3) The Secretary of State shall not make such an order without consulting the local planning authority.

(4) Where the Secretary of State proposes to make such an order he shall serve notice on the local planning authority.

(5) The notice shall specify the period within which the authority may require an opportunity of appearing before and being heard by a person appointed by the Secretary of State for the purpose.

(6) If within that period the authority so require, before the Secretary of State makes the order he shall give the authority such an opportunity.

(7) The period referred to in subsection (5) must not be less than 28 days from the date of the service of the notice.

(8) The provisions of this Part and of any regulations made under this Act with respect to the procedure to be followed in connection with the submission by the local planning authority of any order under section 102, its confirmation by the Secretary of State and the service of copies of it as confirmed shall have effect, subject to any necessary modifications, in relation to any proposal by the Secretary of State to make such an order, its making by him and the service of copies of it.

105. Reviews by mineral planning authorities

(1) Every mineral planning authority shall undertake periodic reviews about the winning and working of minerals and the depositing of mineral waste in their area.

(2) Subject to regulations made by virtue of subsection (4) the duty under this section is, at such intervals as they think fit—

(a) to review every mining site in their area; and

(b) to consider whether they should make an order under section 97 or under paragraph 1,3,5 or 6 of Schedule 9, and if they do consider that they should make any such order, to make it.

(3) For the purposes of subsection (2) 'a mining site' means a site which—

(a) is being used the winning and working of minerals or the depositing of mineral waste;

(b) has been so used at any time during—

(i) the period of five years preceding the date of the beginning of the review; or

(ii) such other period preceding that date as may be prescribed; or

(c) is authorised to be so used.

(4) If regulations so require, the reviews shall be undertaken at prescribed intervals and shall cover such matters as may be prescribed.

[To be repealed as from a day to be appointed under the Environment Act 1995 Section 96(4).]

106. Planning obligations

(1) Any person interested in land in the area of a local planning authority may, by agreement or otherwise, enter into an obligation (referred to in this section and sections 106A and 106B as 'a planning obligation'), enforceable to the extent mentioned in subsection (3)—

(a) restricting the development or use of the land in any specified way;

(b) requiring specified operations or activities to be carried out in, on, under or over the land;

(c) requiring the land to, be used in any specified way; or

(d) requiring a sum or sums to be paid to the authority on a specified date or dates or periodically.

(2) A planning obligation may—

(a) be unconditional or subject to conditions;

(b) impose any restriction or requirement mentioned in subsection (1)(a) to (c) either indefinitely or for such period or periods as may be specified; and

(c) if it requires a sum or sums to be paid, require the payment of a specified amount or an amount determined in accordance with the instrument by which the obligation is entered into and, if it requires the payment of periodical sums, require them to be paid indefinitely or for a specified period.

(3) Subject to subsection (4) a planning obligation is enforceable by the authority identified in accordance with subsection (9)(d)—

(a) against the person entering into the obligation; and

(b) against any person deriving title from that person.

(4) The instrument by which a planning obligation is entered into may provide that a person shall not be bound by the obligation in respect of any period during which he no longer has an interest in the land.

(5) A restriction or requirement imposed under a planning obligation is enforceable by injunction.

(6) Without prejudice to subsection (5), if there is a breach of a requirement in a planning obligation to carry out any operations in, on, under or over the land to which the obligation relates, the authority by whom the obligation is enforceable may—

    (a) enter the land and carry out the operations; and

    (b) recover from the person or persons against whom the obligation is enforceable any expenses reasonably incurred by them in doing so.

(7) Before an authority exercise their power under subsection (6)(a) they shall give not less than twenty-one days' notice of their intention to do so to any person against whom the planning obligation is enforceable.

(8) Any person who wilfully obstructs a person acting in the exercise of a power under subsection (6)(a) shall be guilty of an offence and liable on summary conviction to a fine not exceeding level 3 on the standard scale.

(9) A planning obligation may not be entered into except by an instrument executed as a deed which—

    (a) states that the obligation is a planning obligation for the purposes of this section;

    (b) identifies the land in which the person entering into the obligation is interested;

    (c) identifies the person entering into the obligation and states what his interest in the land is; and

    (d) identifies the local planning authority by whom the obligation is enforceable.

(10) A copy of any such instrument shall be given to the authority so identified.

(11) A planning obligation shall be a local land charge and for the purposes of the Local Land Charges Act 1975 the authority by whom the obligation is enforceable shall be treated as the originating authority as respects such a charge.

(12) Regulations may provide for the charging on the land of—

    (a) any sum or sums required to be paid under a planning obligation; and

    (b) any expenses recoverable by a local planning authority under subsection (6)(b),

and this section and sections 106A and 106B shall have effect subject to any such regulations.

(13) In this section 'specified' means specified in the instrument by which the planning obligation is entered into and in this section and section 106A 'land' has the same meaning as in the Local Land Charges Act 1975.

106A. Modification and discharge of planning obligations

(1) A planning obligation may not be modified or discharged except—

    (a) by agreement between the authority by whom the obligation is enforceable and the person or persons against whom the obligation is enforceable; or

    (b) in accordance with this section and section 106B.

(2) An agreement falling within subsection (1)(a) shall not be entered into except by an instrument executed as a deed.

(3) A person against whom a planning obligation is enforceable may, at any time after the expiry of the relevant period, apply to the local planning authority by whom the obligation is enforceable for the obligation—

    (a) to have effect subject to such modifications as may be specified in the application; or

Town and Country Planning Act 1990

(b) to be discharged.

(4) In subsection (3) 'the relevant period' means—

(a) such period as may be prescribed; or

(b) if no period is prescribed, the period of five years beginning with the date on which the obligation is entered into.

(5) An application under subsection (3) for the modification of a planning obligation may not specify a modification imposing an obligation on any other person against whom the obligation is enforceable.

(6) Where an application is made to an authority under subsection (3), the authority may determine—

(a) that the planning obligation shall continue to have effect without modification;

(b) if the obligation no longer serves a useful purpose, that it shall be discharged; or

(c) if the obligation continues to serve a useful purpose, but would serve that purpose equally well if it had effect subject to the modifications specified in the application, that it shall have effect subject to those modifications.

(7) The authority shall give notice of their determination to the applicant within such period as may be prescribed.

(8) Where an authority determine that a planning obligation shall have effect subject to modifications, specified in the application, the obligation as modified shall be enforceable as if it had been entered into on the date on which notice of the determination was given to the applicant.

(9) Regulations may make provision with respect to—

(a) the form and content of applications under subsection (3);

(b) the publication of notices of such applications;

(c) the procedures for considering any representations made with respect to such applications; and

(d) the notices to be given to applicants of determinations under subsection (6).

(10) Section 84 of the Law of Property Act 1925 (power to discharge or modify restrictive covenants affecting land) does not apply to a planning obligation.

106B. Appeals

(1) Where a local planning authority—

(a) fail to give notice as mentioned in section 106A(7); or

(b) determine that a planning obligation shall continue to have effect without modification,

the applicant may appeal to the Secretary of State.

(2) For the purposes of an appeal under subsection (1)(a), it shall be assumed that the authority have determined that the planning obligation shall continue to have effect without modification.

(3) An appeal under this section shall be made by notice served within such period and in such manner as may be prescribed.

(4) Subsections (6) to (9) of section 106A apply in relation to appeals to the Secretary of State under this section as they apply in relation to applications to authorities under that section.

(5) Before determining the appeal the Secretary of State shall, if either the applicant or the authority so wish, give each of them an opportunity of appearing before and being heard by a person appointed by the Secretary of State for the purpose.

(6) The determination of an appeal by the Secretary of State under this section shall be final.

(7) Schedule 6 applies to appeals under this section.

PART IV
COMPENSATION FOR EFFECTS OF CERTAIN ORDERS, NOTICES, ETC.

Compensation for revocation of planning permission, etc.

107. Compensation where planning permission revoked or modified

(1) Subject to section 116, where planning permission is revoked or modified by an order under section 97, then if, on a claim made to the local planning authority within the prescribed time and in the prescribed manner, it is shown that a person interested in the land or in minerals in, on or under it—

(a) has incurred expenditure in carrying out work which is rendered abortive by the revocation or modification; or

(b) has otherwise sustained loss or damage which is directly attributable to the revocation or modification,

the local planning authority shall pay that person compensation in respect of that expenditure, loss or damage.

(2) For the purposes of this section, any expenditure incurred in the preparation of plans for the purposes of any work, or upon other similar matters preparatory to it, shall be taken to be included in the expenditure incurred in carrying out that work.

(3) Subject to subsection (2), no compensation shall be paid under this section in respect—

(a) of any work carried out before the grant of the permission which is revoked or modified, or

(b) of any other loss or damage arising out of anything done or omitted to be done before the grant of that permission (other than loss or damage consisting of depreciation of the value of an interest in land).

(4) In calculating for the purposes of this section the amount of any loss or damage consisting of depreciation of the value of an interest in land, it shall be assumed that planning permission would be granted

(a) subject to the condition set out in Schedule 10, for any development of the land of a class specified in paragraph 1 of Schedule 3;

(b) for any development of a class specified in paragraph 2 of Schedule 3.

(5) In this Part any reference to an order under section 97 includes a reference to an order under the provisions of that section as applied by section 102(3) (or, subject to section 116, by paragraph 1(3) of Schedule 9).

108. Compensation for refusal or conditional grant of planning permission formerly granted by development order

(1) Where—

(a) planning permission granted by a development order is withdrawn (whether by the revocation or amendment of the order or by the issue of directions under powers conferred by the order); and

(b) on an application made under Part III planning permission for development formerly permitted by that order is refused or is granted subject to conditions other than those imposed by that order,

section 107 shall apply as if the planning permission granted by the development order—

(i) had been granted by the local planning authority under Part III; and

(ii) had been revoked or modified by an order under section 97.

(2) Where planning permission granted by a development order is withdrawn by revocation or amendment of the order, this section applies only if the application referred to in subsection (1)(b) is made before the end of the period of 12 months beginning with the date on which the revocation or amendment came into operation.

(3) This section shall not apply in relation to planning permission for the development of operational land of statutory undertakers.

(4) Regulations made by virtue of this subsection may provide that subsection (1) shall not apply where planning permission granted by a development order for demolition of buildings or any description of buildings is withdrawn by the issue of directions under powers conferred by the order.

109. Apportionment of compensation for depreciation

(1) Where compensation becomes payable under section 107 which includes compensation for depreciation of an amount exceeding £20, the local planning authority—

(a) if it appears to them to be practicable to do so, shall apportion the amount of the compensation for depreciation between different parts of the land to which the claim for that compensation relates; and

(b) shall give particulars of any such apportionment to the claimant and to any other person entitled to an interest in land which appears to the authority to be substantially affected by the apportionment.

(2) In carrying out an apportionment under subsection (1)(a), the local planning authority shall divide the land into parts and shall distribute the compensation for depreciation between those parts, according to the way in which different parts of the land appear to the authority to be differently affected by the order or, in a case falling within section 108, the relevant planning decision, in consequence of which the compensation is payable.

(3) Regulations under this section shall make provision, subject to subsection (4)—

(a) for enabling the claimant and any other person to whom particulars of an apportionment have been given under subsection (1), or who establishes that he is entitled to an interest in land which is substantially affected by such an apportionment, if he wishes to dispute the apportionment, to require it to be referred to the Lands Tribunal;

(b) for enabling the claimant and every other person to whom particulars of any such apportionment have been so given to be heard by the Tribunal on any reference under this section of that apportionment; and

(c) for requiring the Tribunal, on any such reference, either to confirm or to vary the apportionment and to notify the parties of the decision of the Tribunal.

(4) Where on a reference to the Lands Tribunal under this section it is shown that an apportionment—

(a) relates wholly or partly to the same matters as a previous apportionment, and

(b) is consistent with that previous apportionment in so far as it relates to those matters,

the Tribunal shall not vary the apportionment in such a way as to be inconsistent with the previous apportionment in so far as it relates to those matters.

(5) On a reference to the Lands Tribunal by virtue of subsection (3), subsections (1) and (2), so far as they relate to the making of an apportionment, shall apply with the substitution, for references to the local planning authority, of references to the Lands Tribunal.

(6) In this section and section 110—

'compensation for depreciation' means so much of any compensation payable under section 107 as is payable in respect of loss or damage consisting of depreciation of the value of an interest in land,

'interest' (where the reference is to an interest in land) means the fee simple or a tenancy of the land and does not include any other interest in it, and

'relevant planning decision' means the planning decision by which planning permission is refused, or is granted subject to conditions other than those previously imposed by the development order.

110. Registration of compensation for depreciation

(1) Where compensation becomes payable under section 107 which includes compensation for depreciation of an amount exceeding £20, the local planning authority shall give notice to the Secretary of State that such compensation has become payable, specifying the amount of the compensation for depreciation and any apportionment of it under section 109.

(2) Where the Secretary of State is given such notice he shall cause notice of that fact to be deposited—

(a) with the council of the district [Welsh County, county borough] or London borough in which the land is situated, and

(b) if that council is not the local planning authority, with the local planning authority.

(3) Notices deposited under this section must specify—

(a) the order, or in a case falling within section 108 the relevant planning decision, and the land to which the claim for compensation relates; and

(b) the amount of compensation and any apportionment of it under section 109.

(4) Notices deposited under this section shall be local land charges, and for the purposes of the Local Land Charges Act 1975 the council with whom any such notice is deposited shall be treated as the originating authority as respects the charge constituted by it.

(5) In relation to compensation specified in a notice registered under this section, references in this Part to so much of the compensation as is attributable to a part of the land to which the notice relates shall be construed as follows—

(a) if the notice does not include an apportionment under section 109, the amount of the compensation shall be treated as distributed rateably according to area over the land to which the notice relates;

(b) if the notice includes such an apportionment—

(i) the compensation shall be treated as distributed in accordance with that apportionment as between the different parts of the land by reference to which the apportionment is made; and

(ii) so much of the compensation as, in accordance with the apportionment, is attributed to a part of the land shall be treated as distributed rateably according to area over that part.

[The words in [ ] in Section 110(2) were inserted by, and will come into force on an appointed day order under, the Local Government (Wales) Act 1994.]

111. Recovery of compensation under s. 107 on subsequent development

(1) No person shall carry out any development to which this section applies on land in respect of which a notice ('a compensation notice') is registered under section 110 until any amount which is recoverable under this section in accordance with section 112 in respect of the compensation specified in the notice has been paid or secured to the satisfaction of the Secretary of State.

(2) Subject to subsections (3) to (5), this section applies to any development—

(a) which is development of a residential, commercial or industrial character and consists wholly or mainly of the construction of houses, flats, shop or office premises, or industrial buildings (including warehouses), or any combination of them; or

(b) which consists in the winning and working of minerals; or

(c) to which, having regard to the probable value of the development, it is in the opinion of the Secretary of State reasonable that this section should apply.

(3) This section shall not apply to any development by virtue of subsection (2)(c) if, on an application made to him for the purpose, the Secretary of State has certified that, having regard to the probable value of the development, it is not in his opinion reasonable that this section should apply to it.

(4) Where the compensation under section 107 specified in the notice registered under section 110 became payable in respect of an order modifying planning permission or, in a case falling within section 108, of a relevant planning decision (within the meaning of section 109) granting conditional planning permission, this section shall not apply to development in accordance with that permission as modified by the order or, as the case may be, in accordance with those conditions.

(5) This section does not apply to any development—
    (a) of a class specified in paragraph 1 of Schedule 3 which is carried out in accordance with the condition set out in Schedule 10; or
    (b) of a class specified in paragraph 2 of Schedule 3.

112. Amount recoverable under s. 111 and provisions for payment or remission of it

(1) Subject to the following provisions of this section, the amount recoverable under section 111 in respect of the compensation specified in a notice registered under section 110—
    (a) if the land on which the development is to be carried out ('the development area') is identical with, or includes (with other land) the whole of, the land comprised in the notice, shall be the amount of compensation specified in the notice;
    (b) if the development area forms part of the land comprised in the notice, or includes part of that land together with other land not comprised in the notice, shall be so much of the amount of the compensation specified in the notice as is attributable to land comprised in the notice and falling within the development area.

(2) Where, in the case of any land in respect of which such a notice has been so registered, the Secretary of State is satisfied, having regard to the probable value of any proper development of that land, that no such development is likely to be carried out unless he exercises his powers under this subsection, he may, in the case of any particular development, remit the whole or part of any amount otherwise recoverable under section 111.

(3) Where part only of any such amount has been remitted in respect of any land, the Secretary of State shall cause the notice registered under section 110 to be amended by substituting in it, for the statement of the amount of the compensation, in so far as it is attributable to that land, a statement of the amount which has been remitted under subsection (2).

(4) Where, in connection with the development of any land, an amount becomes recoverable under section 111 in respect of the compensation specified in such a notice, then, except where, and to the extent that, payment of that amount has been remitted under subsection (2), no amount shall be recoverable under that section in respect of that compensation, in so far as it is attributable to that land, in connection with any subsequent development of it.

(5) No amount shall be recoverable under section 111 in respect of any compensation by reference to which a sum has become recoverable by the Secretary of State under section 308.

(6) An amount recoverable under section 111 in respect of any compensation shall be payable to the Secretary of State either—
    (a) as a single capital payment, or
    (b) as a series of instalments of capital and interest combined, or
    (c) as a series of other annual or periodical payments, of such amounts, and payable at such times, as the Secretary of State may direct.

(7) Before giving a direction under subsection (6)(c) the Secretary of State shall take into account any representations made by the person by whom the development is to be carried out.

(8) Except where the amount payable under subsection (6) is payable as a single

capital payment, it shall be secured by the person by whom the development is to be carried out in such manner (whether by mortgage, covenant or otherwise) as the Secretary of State may direct.

(9) If any person initiates any development to which section 111 applies in contravention of subsection (1) of that section, the Secretary of State may serve a notice on him—
  (a) specifying the amount appearing to the Secretary of State to be the amount recoverable under that section in respect of the compensation in question, and
  (b) requiring him to pay that amount to the Secretary of State within such period as may be specified in the notice.

(10) The period specified under subsection (9)(b) must not be less than three months after the service of the notice.

(11) Subject to subsection (12), any sum recovered by the Secretary of State under section 111 shall be paid to the local planning authority who paid the compensation to which that sum relates.

(12) Subject to subsection (13), in paying any such sum to the local planning authority, the Secretary of State shall deduct from it—
  (a) [repealed by the Planning and Compensation Act 1991]
  (b) the amount of any grant paid by him under Part XIV in respect of that compensation.

(13) If the sum recovered by the Secretary of State under section 111—
  (a) is an instalment of the total sum recoverable, or
  (b) is recovered by reference to development of part of the land in respect of which the compensation was payable,
any deduction to be made under subsection (12) shall be a deduction of such amount as the Secretary of State may determine to be the proper proportion of the amount referred to in that paragraph.

113. and 114. [repealed by the Planning and Compensation Act 1991]

115. Compensation in respect of orders under s. 102, etc.

(1) This section shall have effect where an order is made under section 102—
  (a) requiring a use of land to be discontinued,
  (b) imposing conditions on the continuance of it, or
  (c) requiring any buildings or works on land to be altered or removed.

(2) If, on a claim made to the local planning authority within the prescribed time and in the prescribed manner, it is shown that any person has suffered damage in consequence of the order—
  (a) by depreciation of the value of an interest to which he is entitled in the land or in minerals in, on or under it, or
  (b) by being disturbed in his enjoyment of the land or of such minerals,
that authority shall pay to that person compensation in respect of that damage.

(3) Without prejudice to subsection (2), any person who carries out any works in compliance with the order shall be entitled, on a claim made as mentioned in that subsection, to recover from the local planning authority compensation in respect of any expenses reasonably incurred by him in that behalf.

(4) Any compensation payable to a person under this section by virtue of such an order as is mentioned in subsection (1) shall be reduced by the value to him of any timber, apparatus or other materials removed for the purpose of complying with the order.

(5) Subject to section 116, this section applies where such an order as is mentioned in subsection (6) is made as it applies where an order is made under section 102.

(6) The orders referred to in subsection (5) are an order under paragraph 1 of Schedule 9—

(a) requiring a use of land to be discontinued, or
(b) imposing conditions on the continuance of it, or
(c) requiring any buildings or works or plant or machinery on land to be altered or removed,
or an order under paragraph 3, 5 or 6 of that Schedule.

116. Modification of compensation provisions in respect of mineral working etc.

(1) Regulations made by virtue of this section with the consent of the Treasury may provide that where an order is made under—

(a) section 97 modifying planning permission for development consisting of the winning and working of minerals or involving the depositing of mineral waste; or

(b) paragraph 1, 3, 5 or 6 of Schedule 9 with respect to such winning and working or depositing,

sections 107, 115, 117, 279 and 280 shall have effect subject, in such cases as may be prescribed, to such modifications as may be prescribed.

(2) Any such regulations may make provision—

(a) as to circumstances in which compensation is not to be payable;

(b) for the modification of the basis on which any amount to be paid by way of compensation is to be assessed;

(c) for the assessment of any such amount on a basis different from that on which it would otherwise have been assessed,

and may also make different provision for different cases and incidental or supplementary provision.

(3) No such regulations shall be made unless a draft of the instrument is laid before and approved by a resolution of each House of Parliament.

(4) Before making any such regulations the Secretary of State shall consult such persons as appear to him to be representative—

(a) of persons carrying out mining operations;
(b) of owners of interests in land containing minerals; and
(c) of mineral planning authorities.

General and supplemental provisions

117. General provisions as to compensation for depreciation under Part IV

(1) For the purpose of assessing any compensation to which this section applies, the rules set out in section 5 of the Land Compensation Act 1961 shall, so far as applicable and subject to any necessary modifications, have effect as they have effect for the purpose of assessing compensation for the compulsory acquisition of an interest in land.

(2) Subject to regulations by virtue of section 116, this section applies to any compensation which under the provisions of this Part is payable in respect of depreciation of the value of an interest in land.

(3) Where an interest in land is subject to a mortgage—

(a) any compensation to which this section applies, which is payable in respect of depreciation of the value of that interest, shall be assessed as if the interest were not subject to the mortgage;

(b) a claim for any such compensation may be made by any mortgagee of the interest, but without prejudice to the making of a claim by the person entitled to the interest;

(c) no compensation to which this section applies shall be payable in respect of the interest of the mortgagee (as distinct from the interest which is subject to the mortgage); and

(d) any compensation to which this section applies which is payable in respect of the interest which is subject to the mortgage shall be paid to the mortgagee, or, if there is more than one mortgagee, to the first mortgagee, and shall in either case be applied by him as if it were proceeds of sale.

118. Determination of claims for compensation

(1) Except in so far as may be otherwise provided by any regulations made under this Act, any question of disputed compensation under this Part shall be referred to and determined by the Lands Tribunal.

(2) In relation to the determination of any such question, the provisions of sections 2 and 4 of the Land Compensation Act 1961 shall apply subject to any necessary modifications and to the provisions of any regulations made under this Act.

PART V

119–136 [repealed by the Planning and Compensation Act 1991]

PART VI
RIGHTS OF OWNERS ETC. TO REQUIRE PURCHASE OF INTERESTS

CHAPTER 1
INTERESTS AFFECTED BY PLANNING DECISIONS OR ORDERS

Service of purchase notices

137. Circumstances in which purchase notices may be served

(1) This section applies where—

(a) on an application for planning permission to develop any land, permission is refused or is granted subject to conditions; or

(b) by an order under section 97 planning permission in respect of any land is revoked, or is modified by the imposition of conditions; or

(c) an order is made under section 102 or paragraph 1 of Schedule 9 in respect of any land.

(2) If—

(a) in the case mentioned in subsection (1)(a) or (b), any owner of the land claims that the conditions mentioned in subsection (3) are satisfied with respect to it, or

(b) in the case mentioned in subsection (1)(c), any person entitled to an interest in land in respect of which the order is made claims that the conditions mentioned in subsection (4) are satisfied with respect to it,

he may, within the prescribed time and in the prescribed manner, serve on the council of the district [Welsh county, county borough] or London borough in which the land is situated a notice (in this Act referred to as 'a purchase notice') requiring that council to purchase his interest in the land in accordance with this Chapter.

(3) The conditions mentioned in subsection (2)(a) are—

(a) that the land has become incapable of reasonably beneficial use in its existing state; and

(b) in a case where planning permission was granted subject to conditions or was modified by the imposition of conditions, that the land cannot be rendered capable of reasonably beneficial use by the carrying out of the permitted development in accordance with those conditions; and

(c) in any case, that the land cannot be rendered capable of reasonably beneficial use by the carrying out of any other development for which planning permission has been granted or for which the local planning authority or the Secretary of State has undertaken to grant planning permission.

(4) The conditions mentioned in subsection (2)(b) are—

(a) that by reason of the order the land is incapable of reasonably beneficial use in its existing state; and

(b) that it cannot be rendered capable of reasonably beneficial use by the carrying out of any development for which planning permission has been granted, whether by that order or otherwise.

(5) For the purposes of subsection (1)(a) and any claim arising in the circumstances mentioned in that subsection, the conditions referred to in sections 91 and 92 shall be disregarded.

(6) A person on whom a repairs notice has been served under section 48 of the Planning (Listed Buildings and Conservation Areas) Act 1990 shall not be entitled to serve a notice under this section in the circumstances mentioned in subsection (1)(a) in respect of the building in question—

(a) until the expiration of three months beginning with the date of the service of the repairs notice; and

(b) if during that period the compulsory acquisition of the building is begun in the exercise of powers under section 47 of that Act, unless and until the compulsory acquisition is discontinued.

(7) For the purposes of subsection (6) a compulsory acquisition—

(a) is started when the the notice required by section 12 of the Acquisition of Land Act 1981 or, as the case may be, paragraph 3 of Schedule 1 to that Act is served; and

(b) is discontinued—

(i) in the case of acquisition by the Secretary of State, when he decides not to make the compulsory purchase order; and

(ii) in any other case, when the order is withdrawn or the Secretary of State decides not to confirm it.

(8) No purchase notice shall be served in respect of an interest in land while the land is incapable of reasonably beneficial use by reason only of such an order as is mentioned in subsection (1)(c), except by virtue of a claim under subsection (2)(b). [The words in [ ] in Section 137(2) were inserted by, and will come into effect on an appointed day under, the Local Government (Wales) Act 1994.]

138. Circumstances in which land incapable of reasonably beneficial use

(1) Where, for the purpose of determining whether the conditions specified in section 137(3) or (4) are satisfied in relation to any land, any question arises as to what is or would in any particular circumstances be a reasonably beneficial use of that land, then, in determining that question for that purpose, no account shall be taken of any unauthorised prospective use of that land.

(2) A prospective use of land shall be regarded as unauthorised for the purposes of subsection (1)—

(a) if it would involve the carrying out of development other than any development specified in paragraph 1 or 2 of Schedule 3, or

(b) in the case of a purchase notice served in consequence of a refusal or conditional grant of planning permission, if it would contravene the condition set out in Schedule 10.

Duties of authorities on service of purchase notice

139. Action by council on whom purchase notice is served

(1) The council on whom a purchase notice is served shall serve on the owner by whom the purchase notice was served a notice (a 'response notice') stating either—

(a) that the council are willing to comply with the purchase notice; or

(b) that another local authority or statutory undertakers specified in the response notice have agreed to comply with it in their place; or

(c) that for reasons so specified the council are not willing to comply with the purchase notice and have not found any other local authority or statutory undertakers who will agree to comply with it in their place, and that they have sent the Secretary of State a copy of the purchase notice and of the response notice.

(2) A response notice must be served before the end of the period of three months beginning with the date of service of the purchase notice.

(3) Where the council on whom a purchase notice is served by an owner have served a response notice on him in accordance with subsection (1)(a) or (b), the council or, as the case may be, the other local authority or statutory undertakers specified in the response notice shall be deemed—

(a) to be authorised to acquire the interest of the owner compulsorily in accordance with the relevant provisions, and

(b) to have served a notice to treat in respect of it on the date of service of the response notice.

(4) Where the council propose to serve such a response notice as is mentioned in subsection (1)(c), they must first send the Secretary of State a copy—

(a) of the proposed response notice, and

(b) of the purchase notice.

(5) A notice to treat which is deemed to have been served by virtue of subsection (3)(b) may not be withdrawn under section 31 of the Land Compensation Act 1961.

140. Procedure on reference of purchase notice to Secretary of State

(1) Where a copy of a purchase notice is sent to the Secretary of State under section 139(4), he shall consider whether to confirm the notice or to take other action under section 141 in respect of it.

(2) Before confirming a purchase notice or taking such other action, the Secretary of State must give notice of his proposed action—

(a) to the person who served the purchase notice;

(b) to the council on whom it was served;

(c) [in England] outside Greater London—

(i) to the county planning authority and also, where that authority is a joint planning board, to the county council; and

(ii) if the district council on whom the purchase notice in question was served is a constituent member of a joint planning board, to that board;

[(cc) in Wales, to the local planning authority, where it is a joint planning board] and

(d) if the Secretary of State proposes to substitute any other local authority or statutory undertakers for the council on whom the notice was served, to them.

(3) A notice under subsection (2) shall specify the period (which must not be less than 28 days from its service) within which any of the persons on whom it is served may require the Secretary of State to give those persons an opportunity of appearing before, and being heard by, a person appointed by the Secretary of State for the purpose.

(4) If within that period any of those persons so require, before the Secretary of State confirms the purchase notice or takes any other action under section 141 in respect of it he must give those persons such an opportunity.

(5) If, after any of those persons have appeared before and been heard by the appointed person, it appears to the Secretary of State to be expedient to take action under section 141 otherwise than in accordance with the notice given by him, the Secretary of State may take that action accordingly.

[In Section 140(2) the words in [ ] were inserted by, and will come into effect on an appointed day under, the Local Government (Wales) Act 1994.]

141. Action by Secretary of State in relation to purchase notice

(1) Subject to the following provisions of this section and to section 142(3), if the Secretary of State is satisfied that the conditions specified in subsection (3) or, as the

Town and Country Planning Act 1990 77

case may be, subsection (4) of section 137 are satisfied in relation to a purchase notice, he shall confirm the notice.

(2) If it appears to the Secretary of State to be expedient to do so, he may, instead of confirming the purchase notice—

(a) in the case of a notice served on account of the refusal of planning permission, grant planning permission for the development in question;

(b) in the case of a notice served on account of planning permission for development being granted subject to conditions, revoke or amend those conditions so far as appears to him to be required in order to enable the land to be rendered capable of reasonably beneficial use by the carrying out of that development;

(c) in the case of a notice served on account of the revocation of planning permission by an order under section 97, cancel the order;

(d) in the case of a notice served on account of the modification of planning permission by such an order by the imposition of conditions, revoke or amend those conditions so far as appears to him to be required in order to enable the land to be rendered capable of reasonably beneficial use by the carrying out of the development in respect of which the permission was granted; or

(e) in the case of a notice served on account of the making of an order under section 102 or paragraph 1 of Schedule 9, revoke the order or, as the case may be, amend the order so far as appears to him to be required in order to prevent the land from being rendered incapable of reasonably beneficial use by the order.

(3) If it appears to the Secretary of State that the land, or any part of the land, could be rendered capable of reasonably beneficial use within a reasonable time by the carrying out of any other development for which planning permission ought to be granted, he may, instead of confirming the purchase notice, or, as the case may be, of confirming it so far as it relates to that part of the land, direct that, if an application for planning permission for that development is made, it must be granted.

(4) If it appears to the Secretary of State, having regard to the probable ultimate use of the land, that it is expedient to do so, he may, if he confirms the notice, modify it, either in relation to the whole or any part of the land, by substituting another local authority or statutory undertakers for the council on whom the notice was served.

(5) Any reference in section 140 to the taking of action by the Secretary of State under this section includes a reference to the taking by him of a decision not to confirm the purchase notice either on the grounds that any of the conditions referred to in subsection (1) are not satisfied or by virtue of section 142.

142. Power to refuse to confirm purchase notice where land has restricted use by virtue of previous planning permission

(1) This section applies where a purchase notice is served in respect of land which consists in whole or in part of land which has a restricted use by virtue of an existing planning permission.

(2) For the purposes of this section, land is to be treated as having a restricted use by virtue of an existing planning permission if it is part of a larger area in respect of which planning permission has previously been granted (and has not been revoked) and either—

(a) it remains a condition of the planning permission (however expressed) that that part shall remain undeveloped or be preserved or laid out in a particular way as amenity land in relation to the remainder; or

(b) the planning permission was granted on an application which contemplated (expressly or by necessary implication) that the part should not be comprised in the development for which planning permission was sought, or should be preserved or laid out as mentioned in paragraph (a).

(3) Where a copy of the purchase notice is sent to the Secretary of State under section 139(4), he need not confirm the notice under section 141(1) if it appears to

him that the land having a restricted use by virtue of an existing planning permission ought, in accordance with that permission, to remain undeveloped or, as the case may be, remain or be preserved or laid out as amenity land in relation to the remainder of the large area for which that planning permission was granted.

143. Effect of Secretary of State's action in relation to purchase notice

(1) Where the Secretary of State confirms a purchase notice—
   (a) the council on whom the purchase notice was served, or
   (b) if under section 141(4) the Secretary of State modified the purchase notice by substituting another local authority or statutory undertakers for that council, that other authority or those undertakers,
shall be deemed to be authorised to acquire the interest of the owner compulsorily in accordance with the relevant provisions, and to have served a notice to treat in respect of it on such date as the Secretary of State may direct.

(2) If, before the end of the relevant period, the Secretary of State has neither—
   (a) confirmed the purchase notice, nor
   (b) taken any such action in respect of it as is mentioned in section 141(2) or (3), nor
   (c) notified the owner by whom the notice was served that he does not propose to confirm the notice,
the notice shall be deemed to be confirmed at the end of that period, and the council on whom the notice was served shall be deemed to be authorised as mentioned in subsection (1) and to have served a notice to treat in respect of the owner's interest at the end of that period.

(3) Subject to subsection (4), for the purposes of subsection (2) the relevant period is—
   (a) the period of nine months beginning with the date of service of the purchase notice; or
   (b) if it ends earlier, the period of six months beginning with the date on which a copy of the purchase notice was sent to the Secretary of State.

(4) The relevant period does not run if the Secretary of State has before him at the same time both—
   (a) a copy of the purchase notice sent to him under section 139(4); and
   (b) a notice of appeal under section 78, 174 or 195 of this Act or under section 20 or 39 of the Planning (Listed Buildings and Conservation Areas) Act 1990 (appeals against refusal of listed building consent, etc. and appeals against listed building enforcement notices) or under section 21 of the Planning (Hazardous Substances) Act 1990 (appeals against decisions and failure to take decisions relating to hazardous substances) relating to any of the land to which the purchase notice relates.

(5) Where—
   (a) the Secretary of State has notified the owner by whom a purchase notice has been served of a decision on his part to confirm, or not to confirm, the notice; and
   (b) that decision is quashed under Part XII,
the purchase notice shall be treated as cancelled, but the owner may serve a further purchase notice in its place.

(6) The reference in subsection (5) to a decision to confirm, or not to confirm, the purchase notice includes—
   (a) any decision not to confirm the notice in respect of any part of the land to which it relates, and
   (b) any decision to grant any permission, or give any direction, instead of confirming the notice, either wholly or in part.

(7) For the purposes of determining whether a further purchase notice under subsection (5) was served within the period prescribed for the service of purchase

notices, the planning decision in consequence of which the notice was served shall be treated as having been made on the date on which the decision of the Secretary of State was quashed.

(8) A notice to treat which is deemed to have been served by virtue of subsection (1) or (2) may not be withdrawn under section 31 of the Land Compensation Act 1961.

Compensation

144. Special provisions as to compensation where purchase notice served

(1) Where compensation is payable by virtue of section 107 in respect of expenditure incurred in carrying out any works on land, any compensation payable in respect of the acquisition of an interest in the land in pursuance of a purchase notice shall be reduced by an amount equal to the value of those works.

(2) Where—
   (a) the Secretary of State directs under section 141(3) that, if an application for it is made, planning permission must be granted for the development of any land, and
   (b) on a claim made to the local planning authority within the prescribed time and in the prescribed manner, it is shown that the permitted development value of the interest in that land in respect of which the purchase notice was served is less than its Schedule 3 value,
that authority shall pay the person entitled to that interest compensation of an amount equal to the difference.

(3) If the planning permission mentioned in subsection (2)(a) would be granted subject to conditions for regulating the design or external appearance, or the size or height of buildings, or for regulating the number of buildings to be erected on the land, the Secretary of State may direct that in assessing any compensation payable under subsection (2) those conditions must be disregarded, either altogether or to such extent as may be specified in the direction.

(4) The Secretary of State may only give a direction under subsection (3) if it appears to him to be reasonable to do so having regard to the local circumstances.

(5) Sections 117 and 118 shall have effect in relation to compensation under subsection (2) as they have effect in relation to compensation to which those sections apply.

(6) In this section—
   'permitted development value', in relation to an interest in land in respect of which a direction is given under section 141(3), means the value of that interest calculated with regard to that direction, but on the assumption that no planning permission would be granted otherwise than in accordance with that direction, and
   'Schedule 3 value', in relation to such an interest, means the value of that interest calculated on the assumption that planning permission would be granted—
   (a) subject to the condition in Schedule 10, for any development of a class specified in paragraph 1 of Schedule 3; and
   (b) for any development of a class specified in paragraph 2 of Schedule 3.

(7) Where a purchase notice in respect of an interest in land is served in consequence of an order under section 102 or paragraph 1 of Schedule 9, then if—
   (a) that interest is acquired in accordance with this Chapter; or
   (b) compensation is payable in respect of that interest under subsection (2),
no compensation shall be payable in respect of that order under section 115.

Special provisions for requiring purchase of whole of partially affected agricultural unit

145. Counter-notice requiring purchase of remainder of agricultural unit

(1) This section applies where—

(a) an acquiring authority is deemed under this Chapter to have served notice to treat in respect of any agricultural land on a person ('the claimant') who has a greater interest in the land than as tenant for a year or from year to year (whether or not he is in occupation of the land), and

(b) the claimant has such an interest in other agricultural land ('the unaffected area') comprised in the same agricultural unit as that to which the notice relates.

(2) Where this section applies the claimant may serve on the acquiring authority a counter-notice—

(a) claiming that the unaffected area is not reasonably capable of being farmed, either by itself or in conjunction with other relevant land, as a separate agricultural unit; and

(b) requiring the acquiring authority to purchase his interest in the whole of the unaffected area.

(3) Subject to subsection (4), 'other relevant land' in subsection (2) means—

(a) land which is comprised in the same agricultural unit as the land to which the notice to treat relates and in which the claimant does not have such an interest as is mentioned in subsection (1); and

(b) land which is comprised in any other agricultural unit occupied by the claimant on the date on which the notice to treat is deemed to have been served and in respect of which he is then entitled to a greater interest than as tenant for a year or from year to year.

(4) Where a notice to treat has been served or is deemed under this Chapter or under Part III of the Compulsory Purchase (Vesting Declarations) Act 1981 to have been served in respect of any of the unaffected area or in respect of other relevant land as defined in subsection (3), then, unless and until the notice to treat is withdrawn, this section and section 146 shall have effect as if that land did not form part of the unaffected land or, as the case may be, did not constitute other relevant land.

(5) Where a counter-notice is served under subsection (2) the claimant shall also serve a copy of it on any other person who has an interest in the unaffected area (but failure to comply with this subsection shall not invalidate the counter-notice).

(6) A counter-notice under subsection (2) and any copy of that notice required to be served under subsection (5) must be served within the period of two months beginning with the date on which the notice to treat is deemed to have been served.

(7) This section is without prejudice to the rights conferred by sections 93 and 94 of the Lands Clauses (Consolidation) Act 1845 or section 8(2) and (3) of the Compulsory Purchase Act 1965 (provisions as to divided land).

146. Effect of counter-notice under s. 145

(1) If the acquiring authority do not within the period of two months beginning with the date of service of a counter-notice under section 145 agree in writing to accept the counter-notice as valid, the claimant or the authority may, within two months after the end of that period, refer it to the Lands Tribunal.

(2) On such a reference the Tribunal shall determine whether the claim in the counter-notice is justified and declare the counter-notice valid or invalid accordingly.

(3) Where a counter-notice is accepted as valid under subsection (1) or declared to be valid under subsection (2), the acquiring authority shall be deemed—

(a) to be authorised to acquire compulsorily the interest of the claimant in the land to which the requirement in the counter-notice relates under the same provision of this Chapter as they are authorised to acquire the other land in the agricultural unit in question; and

(b) to have served a notice to treat in respect of it on the date on which notice to treat is deemed to have been served under that provision.

(4) A claimant may withdraw a counter-notice at any time before the compensation payable in respect of a compulsory acquisition in pursuance of the counter-notice

has been determined by the Lands Tribunal or at any time before the end of six weeks beginning with the date on which it is determined.

(5) Where a counter-notice is withdrawn by virtue of subsection (4) any notice to treat deemed to have been served in consequence of it shall be deemed to have been withdrawn.

(6) Without prejudice to subsection (5), a notice to treat deemed to have been served by virtue of this section may not be withdrawn under section 31 of the Land Compensation Act 1961.

(7) The compensation payable in respect of the acquisition of an interest in land in pursuance of a notice to treat deemed to have been served by virtue of this section shall be assessed on the assumptions mentioned in section 5(2), (3) and (4) of the Land Compensation Act 1973.

(8) Where by virtue of this section the acquiring authority become or will become entitled to a lease of any land but not to the interest of the lessor—

(a) the authority shall offer to surrender the lease to the lessor on such terms as the authority consider reasonable;

(b) the question of what is reasonable may be referred to the Lands Tribunal by the authority or the lessor and, if at the expiration of the period of three months after the date of the offer mentioned in paragraph (a) the authority and the lessor have not agreed on that question and that question has not been referred to the Tribunal by the lessor, it shall be so referred by the authority;

(c) if that question is referred to the Tribunal, the lessor shall be deemed—

(i) to have accepted the surrender of the lease at the expiry of one month after the date of the determination of the Tribunal or on such other date as the Tribunal may direct, and

(ii) to have agreed with the authority on the terms of surrender which the Tribunal has held to be reasonable.

(9) For the purposes of subsection (8) any terms as to surrender contained in the lease shall be disregarded.

(10) Where the lessor—

(a) refuses to accept any sum payable to him by virtue of subsection (8), or

(b) refuses or fails to make out his title to the satisfaction of the acquiring authority,

they may pay into court any such sum payable to the lessor and section 9(2) and (5) of the Compulsory Purchase Act 1965 (deposit of compensation in cases of refusal to convey etc.) shall apply to that sum with the necessary modifications.

(11) Where an acquiring authority who become entitled to the lease of any land as mentioned in subsection (8) are a body incorporated by or under any enactment, the corporate powers of the authority shall, if they would not otherwise do so, include the power to farm that land.

147. Provisions supplemental to ss. 145 and 146

(1) Sections 145 and 146 apply in relation to the acquisition of interests in land by government departments which possess compulsory purchase powers as they apply in relation to the acquisition of interests in land by authorities who are not government departments.

(2) In sections 145, 146 and this section—

'agricultural' and 'agricultural land' have the meaning given in section 109 of the Agriculture Act 1947 and references to the farming of land include references to the carrying on in relation to the land of any agricultural activities;

'agricultural unit' has the meaning given in section 171(1);

'acquiring authority' has the same meaning as in the Land Compensation Act 1961; and 'government departments which possess compulsory purchase powers' means government departments being authorities possessing compulsory purchase powers within the meaning of that Act.

147A. This Chapter shall have effect as if—
(a) the bodies on whom a purchase notice may be served under section 137 included any National Park authority which is the local planning authority for the area in which the land is situated; and
(b) a National Park authority were a local authority for the purposes of this Act and the National Park for which it is the local planning authority were its area;
and the references in this Chapter and in section 288(10)(a) to a council and to a local authority shall be construed accordingly.
[Part III of the Environment Act 1995 which includes this new provision comes into force at the end of two months from the date of the Act's passing, i.e., July 1995.]

Supplemental

148. Interpretation of Chapter I
(1) In this Chapter—
'the relevant provisions' means—
(a) the provisions of Part IX, or
(b) in the case of statutory undertakers, any statutory provision (however expressed) under which they have power, or may be authorised, to purchase land compulsorily for the purposes of their undertaking; and
'statutory undertakers' includes public telecommunications operators.
(2) In the case of a purchase notice served by such a person as is mentioned in subsection (2)(b) of section 137, references in this Chapter to the owner of the land include references to that person unless the context otherwise requires.

CHAPTER II
INTERESTS AFFECTED BY PLANNING PROPOSALS: BLIGHT

Preliminary

149. Scope of Chapter II
(1) This Chapter shall have effect in relation to land falling within any paragraph of Schedule 13 (land affected by planning proposals of public authorities etc.); and in this Chapter such land is referred to as 'blighted land'.
(2) Subject to the provisions of sections 161 and 162, an interest qualifies for protection under this Chapter if—
(a) it is an interest in a hereditament or part of a hereditament and on the relevant date it satisfies one of the conditions mentioned in subsection (3); or
(b) it is an interest in an agricultural unit or part of an agricultural unit and on the relevant date it is the interest of an owner-occupier of the unit;
and in this Chapter such an interest is referred to as 'a qualifying interest'.
(3) The conditions mentioned in subsection (2)(a) are—
(a) that the annual value of the hereditament does not exceed such amount as may be prescribed for the purposes of this paragraph by an order made by the Secretary of State, and the interest is the interest of an owner-occupier of the hereditament; or
(b) that the interest is the interest of a resident owner-occupier of the hereditament.
(4) In this section 'the relevant date', in relation to an interest, means the date of service of a notice under section 150 in respect of it.
(5) In this Chapter 'blight notice' means a notice served under section 150, 161 or 162.

Blight notices

150. Notices requiring purchase of blighted land

(1) Where the whole or part of a hereditament or agricultural unit is comprised in blighted land a person claims that—

(a) he is entitled to a qualifying interest in that hereditament or unit;

(b) he has made reasonable endeavours to sell that interest or the land falls within paragraph 21 or paragraph 22 (disregarding the notes) of Schedule 13 and the powers of compulsory acquisition remain exercisable; and

(c) in consequence of the fact that the hereditament or unit or a part of it was, or was likely to be, comprised in blighted land, he has been unable to sell that interest except at a price substantially lower than that for which it might reasonably have been expected to sell if no part of the hereditament or unit were, or were likely to be, comprised in such land, he may serve on the appropriate authority a notice in the prescribed form requiring that authority to purchase that interest to the extent specified in, and otherwise in accordance with, this Chapter.

(2) Subject to subsection (3), subsection (1) shall apply in relation to an interest in part of a hereditament or unit as it applies in relation to an interest in the whole of a hereditament or unit.

(3) Subsection (2) shall not enable any person—

(a) if he is entitled to an interest in the whole of a hereditament or agricultural unit, to make any claim or serve any notice under this section in respect of his interest in part of a hereditament or unit; or

(b) if he is entitled to an interest only in part of a hereditament or agricultural unit, to make or serve any such claim or notice in respect of his interest in less than the whole of that part.

(4) In this Chapter—

(a) subject to section 161(1), 'the claimant', in relation to a blight notice, means the person who served that notice, and

(b) any reference to the interest of the claimant, in relation to a blight notice, is a reference to the interest which the notice requires the appropriate authority to purchase as mentioned in subsection (1).

151. Counter-notices objecting to blight notices

(1) Where a blight notice has been served in respect of a hereditament or an agricultural unit, the appropriate authority may serve on the claimant a counter-notice in the prescribed form objecting to the notice.

(2) A counter-notice under subsection (1) may be served at any time before the end of the period of two months beginning with the date of service of the blight notice.

(3) Such a counter-notice shall specify the grounds on which the appropriate authority object to the blight notice (being one or more of the grounds specified in subsection (4) or, as relevant, in section 159(1), 161(5) or 162(5)).

(4) Subject to the following provisions of this Act, the grounds on which objection may be made in a counter-notice to a notice served under section 150 are—

(a) that no part of the hereditament or agricultural unit to which the notice relates is comprised in blighted land;

(b) that the appropriate authority (unless compelled to do so by virtue of this Chapter) do not propose to acquire any part of the hereditament, or in the case of an agricultural unit any part of the affected area, in the exercise of any relevant powers;

(c) that the appropriate authority propose in the exercise of relevant powers to acquire a part of the hereditament or, in the case of an agricultural unit, a part of the affected area specified in the counter-notice, but (unless compelled to do so by virtue of this Chapter) do not propose to acquire any other part of that hereditament or area in the exercise of any such powers;

(d) in the case of land falling within paragraph 1, 3 or 13 but not 14, 15 or 16 of Schedule 13, that the appropriate authority (unless compelled to do so by virtue of this Chapter) do not propose to acquire in the exercise of any relevant powers any part of the hereditament or, in the case of an agricultural unit, any part of the affected area during the period of 15 years from the date of the counter-notice or such longer period from that date as many be specified in the counter-notice;

(e) that, on the date of service of the notice under section 150, the claimant was not entitled to an interest in any part of the hereditament or agricultural unit to which the notice relates;

(f) that (for reasons specified in the counter-notice) the interest of the claimant is not a qualifying interest;

(g) that the conditions specified in paragraphs (b) and (c) of section 150(1) are not fulfilled.

(5) Where the appropriate enactment confers power to acquire rights over land, subsection (4) shall have effect as if—

(a) in paragraph (b) after the word 'acquire' there were inserted the words 'or to acquire any rights over';

(b) in paragraph (c) for the words 'do not propose to acquire' there were substituted the words 'propose neither to acquire, nor to acquire any right over';

(c) in paragraph (d) after the words 'affected area' there were inserted 'or to acquire any right over any part of it'.

(6) An objection may not be made on the grounds mentioned in paragraph (d) of subsection (4) if it may be made on the grounds mentioned in paragraph (b) of that subsection.

(7) The grounds on which objection may be made in a counter-notice to a blight notice served by virtue of paragraph 19 of Schedule 13 shall not include those mentioned in subsection (4)(b) or (c).

(8) In this section 'relevant powers', in relation to blighted land falling within any paragraph of Schedule 13, means any powers under which the appropriate authority are or could be authorised—

(a) to acquire that land or to acquire any rights over it compulsorily as being land falling within that paragraph; or

(b) to acquire that land or any rights over it compulsorily for any of the relevant purposes;

and 'the relevant purposes', in relation to any such land, means the purposes for which, in accordance with the circumstances by virtue of which that land falls within the paragraph in question, it is liable to be acquired or is indicated as being proposed to be acquired.

152. Further counter-notices where certain proposals have come into force

(1) Where—

(a) an appropriate authority have served a counter-notice objecting to a blight notice in respect of any land falling within paragraph 1, 2, 3, 4 or 14 of Schedule 13 by virtue of Note (1) to that paragraph, and

(b) the relevant plan or alterations or, as the case may be, the relevant order or scheme comes into force (whether in its original form or with modifications),

the appropriate authority may serve on the claimant, in substitution for the counter-notice already served, a further counter-notice specifying different grounds of objection.

(2) Such a further counter-notice shall not be served—

(a) at any time after the end of the period of two months beginning with the date on which the relevant plan or alterations come into force; or

(b) if the objection in the counter-notice already served has been withdrawn or the Lands Tribunal has already determined whether or not to uphold that objection.

Town and Country Planning Act 1990 85

153. Reference of objection to Lands Tribunal: general

(1) Where a counter-notice has been served under section 151 objecting to a blight notice, the claimant may require the objection to be referred to the Lands Tribunal.

(2) Such a reference may be required under subsection (1) at any time before the end of the period of two months beginning with the date of service of the counter-notice.

(3) On any such reference, if the objection is not withdrawn, the Lands Tribunal shall consider—
   (a) the matters set out in the notice served by the claimant, and
   (b) the grounds of the objection specified in the counter-notice;
and, subject to subsection (4), unless it is shown to the satisfaction of the Tribunal that the objection is not well-founded, the Tribunal shall uphold the objection.

(4) An objection on the grounds mentioned in section 151(4)(b), (c) or (d) shall not be upheld by the Tribunal unless it is shown to the satisfaction of the Tribunal that the objection is well-founded.

(5) If the Tribunal determines not to uphold the objection, the Tribunal shall declare that the notice to which the counter-notice relates is a valid notice.

(6) If the Tribunal upholds the objection, but only on the grounds mentioned in section 151(4)(c), the Tribunal shall declare that the notice is a valid notice in relation to the part of the hereditament, or in the case of an agricultural unit the part of the affected area, specified in the counter-notice as being the part which the appropriate authority propose to acquire as mentioned in that notice, but not in relation to any other part of the hereditament or affected area.

(7) In a case falling within subsection (5) or (6), the Tribunal shall give directions specifying the date on which notice to treat (as mentioned in section 154) is to be deemed to have been served.

(8) This section shall have effect in relation to a further counter-notice served by virtue of section 152(1) as it has effect in relation to the counter-notice for which it is substituted.

154. Effect of valid blight notice

(1) Subsection (2) applies where a blight notice has been served and either—
   (a) no counter-notice objecting to that notice is served in accordance with this Chapter; or
   (b) where such a counter-notice has been served, the objection is withdrawn or, on a reference to the Lands Tribunal, is not upheld by the Tribunal.

(2) Where this subsection applies, the appropriate authority shall be deemed—
   (a) to be authorised to acquire compulsorily under the appropriate enactment the interest of the claimant in the hereditament, or in the case of an agricultural unit the interest of the claimant in so far as it subsists in the affected area, and
   (b) to have served a notice to treat in respect of it on the date mentioned in subsection (3).

(3) The date referred to in subsection (2)—
   (a) in a case where, on a reference to the Lands Tribunal, the Tribunal determines not to uphold the objection, is the date specified in directions given by the Tribunal in accordance with section 153(7);
   (b) in any other case, is the date on which the period of two months beginning with the date of service of the blight notice comes to an end.

(4) Subsection (5) applies where the appropriate authority have served a counter-notice objecting to a blight notice on the grounds mentioned in section 151(4)(c) and either—
   (a) the claimant, without referring that objection to the Lands Tribunal, and before the time for so referring it has expired—

(i) gives notice to the appropriate authority that he accepts the proposal of the authority to acquire the part of the hereditament or affected area specified in the counter-notice, and

(ii) withdraws his claim as to the remainder of that hereditament or area; or

(b) on a reference to the Lands Tribunal, the Tribunal makes a declaration in accordance with section 153(6) in respect of that part of the hereditament or affected area.

(5) Where this subsection applies, the appropriate authority shall be deemed—

(a) to be authorised to acquire compulsorily under the appropriate enactment the interest of the claimant in so far as it subsists in the part of the hereditament or affected area specified in the counter-notice (but not in so far as it subsists in any other part of that hereditament or area), and

(b) to have served a notice to treat in respect of it on the date mentioned in subsection (6).

(6) The date referred to in subsection (5)—

(a) in a case falling within paragraph (a) of subsection (4), is the date on which notice is given in accordance with that paragraph; and

(b) in a case falling within paragraph (b) of that subsection, is the date specified in directions given by the Lands Tribunal in accordance with section 153(7).

155. Effect on powers of compulsory acquisition of counter-notice disclaiming intention to acquire

(1) Subsection (2) shall have effect where the grounds of objection specified in a counter-notice served under section 151 consist of or include the grounds mentioned in paragraph (b) or (d) of subsection (4) of that section and either—

(a) the objection on the grounds mentioned in that paragraph is referred to and upheld by the Lands Tribunal; or

(b) the time for referring that objection to the Lands Tribunal expires without its having been so referred.

(2) If—

(a) a compulsory purchase order has been made under the appropriate enactment in respect of land which consists of or includes the whole or part of the hereditament or agricultural unit to which the counter-notice relates, or

(b) the land in question falls within paragraph 21 of Schedule 13;

any power conferred by that order or, as the case may be, by special enactment for the compulsory acquisition of the interest of the claimant in the hereditament or agricultural unit or any part of it shall cease to have effect.

(3) Subsection (4) shall have effect where the grounds of objection specified in a counter-notice under section 151 consist of or include the grounds mentioned in paragraph (c) of subsection (4) of that section and either—

(a) the objection on the grounds mentioned in that paragraph is referred to and upheld by the Lands Tribunal; or

(b) the time for referring that objection to the Lands Tribunal expires without its having been so referred;

and in subsection (4) any reference to 'the part of the hereditament or affected area not required' is a reference to the whole of that hereditament or area except the part specified in the counter-notice as being the part which the appropriate authority propose to acquire as mentioned in the counter-notice.

(4) If—

(a) a compulsory purchase order has been made under the appropriate enactment in respect of land which consists of or includes any of the part of the hereditament or affected area not required, or

(b) the land in question falls within paragraph 21 of Schedule 13,

Town and Country Planning Act 1990

any power conferred by that order or, as the case may be, by the special enactment for the compulsory acquisition of the interest of the claimant in any land comprised in the part of the hereditament or affected area not required shall cease to have effect.

156. Withdrawal of blight notice

(1) Subject to subsection (3), the person by whom a blight notice has been served may withdraw the notice at any time before the compensation payable in respect of a compulsory acquisition in pursuance of the notice has been determined by the Lands Tribunal or, if there has been such a determination, at any time before the end of the period of six weeks beginning with the date of the determination.

(2) Where a blight notice is withdrawn by virtue of subsection (1) any notice to treat deemed to have been served in consequence of it shall be deemed to have been withdrawn.

(3) A person shall not be entitled by virtue of subsection (1) to withdraw a notice after the appropriate authority have exercised a right of entering and taking possession of land in pursuance of a notice to treat deemed to have been served in consequence of that notice.

(4) No compensation shall be payable in respect of the withdrawal of a notice to treat which is deemed to have been withdrawn by virtue of subsection (2).

Compensation

157. Special provisions as to compensation for acquisitions in pursuance of blight notices

(1) Where—

   (a) an interest in land is acquired in pursuance of a blight notice, and

   (b) the interest is one in respect of which a compulsory purchase order is in force under section 1 of the Acquisition of Land Act 1981, as applied by section 47 of the Planning (Listed Buildings and Conservation Areas) Act 1990, containing a direction for minimum compensation under section 50 of that Act of 1990,

the compensation payable for the acquisition shall be assessed in accordance with that direction and as if the notice to treat deemed to have been served in respect of the interest under section 154 had been served in pursuance of the compulsory purchase order.

(2) Where—

   (a) an interest in land is acquired in pursuance of a blight notice, and

   (b) the interest is one in respect of which a compulsory purchase order is in force under section 290 of the Housing Act 1985 (acquisition of land for clearance);

the compensation payable for the acquisition shall be assessed in accordance with that Act and as if the notice to treat deemed to have been served in respect of the interest under section 154 had been served in pursuance of the compulsory purchase order.

(3) The compensation payable in respect of the acquisition by virtue of section 160 of an interest in land comprised in—

   (a) the unaffected area of an agricultural unit; or

   (b) if the appropriate authority have served a counter-notice objecting to the blight notice on the grounds mentioned in section 151(4)(c), so much of the affected area of the unit as is not specified in the counter-notice,

shall be assessed on the assumptions mentioned in section 5(2), (3) and (4) of the Land Compensation Act 1973.

(4) In subsection (3) the reference to 'the appropriate authority' shall be construed as if the unaffected area of an agricultural unit were part of the affected area.

Special provisions for requiring purchase of whole of partially affected agricultural unit

158. Inclusion in blight notices of requirement to purchase parts of agricultural units unaffected by blight

(1) This section applies where—

(a) a blight notice is served in respect of an interest in the whole or part of an agricultural unit, and

(b) on the date of service that unit or part contains land ('the unaffected area') which is not blighted land as well as land ('the affected area') which is such land.

(2) Where this section applies the claimant may include in the blight notice—

(a) a claim that the unaffected area is not reasonably capable of being farmed, either by itself or in conjunction with other relevant land, as a separate agricultural unit; and

(b) a requirement that the appropriate authority shall purchase his interest in the whole of the unit or, as the case may be, in the whole of the part of it to which the notice relates.

(3) Subject to section 159(4), 'other relevant land' in subsection (2) means—

(a) if the blight notice is served only in respect of part of land comprised in the agricultural unit, the remainder of it; and

(b) land which is comprised in any other agricultural unit occupied by the claimant on the date of service and in respect of which he is then entitled to an owner's interest as defined in section 168(4).

159. Objections to s. 158 notices

(1) The grounds on which objection may be made in a counter-notice to a blight notice served by virtue of section 158 shall include the ground that the claim made in the notice is not justified.

(2) Objection shall not be made to a blight notice served by virtue of section 158 on the grounds mentioned in section 151(4)(c) unless it is also made on the grounds mentioned in subsection (1).

(3) The Lands Tribunal shall not uphold an objection to a notice served by virtue of section 158 on the grounds mentioned in section 151(4)(c) unless it also upholds the objection on the grounds mentioned in subsection (1).

(4) Where objection is made to a blight notice served by virtue of section 158 on the ground mentioned in subsection (1) and also on those mentioned in section 151(4)(c), the Lands Tribunal, in determining whether or not to uphold the objection, shall treat that part of the affected area which is not specified in the counter-notice as included in 'other relevant land' as defined in section 158(3).

(5) If the Lands Tribunal upholds an objection but only on the ground mentioned in subsection (1), the Tribunal shall declare that the blight notice is a valid notice in relation to the affected area but not in relation to the unaffected area.

(6) If the Tribunal upholds an objection both on the ground mentioned in subsection (1) and on the grounds mentioned in section 151(4)(c) (but not on any other grounds) the Tribunal shall declare that the blight notice is a valid notice in relation to the part of the affected area specified in the counter-notice as being the part which the appropriate authority propose to acquire as mentioned in that notice but not in relation to any other part of the affected area or in relation to the unaffected area.

(7) In a case falling within subsection (5) or (6), the Tribunal shall give directions specifying a date on which notice to treat (as mentioned in sections 154 and section 160) is to be deemed to have been served.

(8) Section 153(6) shall not apply to any blight notice served by virtue of section 158.

160. Effect of notices served by virtue of s. 158

(1) In relation to a blight notice served by virtue of section 158—

(a) subsection (2) of section 154 shall have effect as if for the words 'or in the case of an agricultural unit the interest of the claimant in so far as it subsists in the affected area' there were substituted the words 'or agricultural unit'; and

Town and Country Planning Act 1990

(b) subsections (4) and (5) of that section shall not apply to any such blight notice.

(2) Where the appropriate authority have served a counter-notice objecting to a blight notice on the grounds mentioned in section 159(1), then if either—

(a) the claimant, without referring that objection to the Lands Tribunal and before the time for so referring it has expired, gives notice to the appropriate authority that he withdraws his claim as to the unaffected area; or

(b) on a reference to the Tribunal, the Tribunal makes a declaration in accordance with section 159(5),

the appropriate authority shall be deemed—

(i) to be authorised to acquire compulsorily under the appropriate enactment the interest of the claimant in so far as it subsists in the affected area (but not in so far as it subsists in the unaffected area), and

(ii) to have served a notice to treat in respect of it on the date mentioned in subsection (3).

(3) The date referred to in subsection (2)—

(a) in a case falling within paragraph (a) of subsection (2), is the date on which notice is given in accordance with that paragraph; and

(b) in a case falling within paragraph (b) of that subsection, is the date specified in directions given by the Tribunal in accordance with section 159(7).

(4) Where the appropriate authority have served a counter-notice objecting to a blight notice on the grounds mentioned in section 159(1) and also on the grounds mentioned in section 151(4)(c), then if either—

(a) the claimant, without referring that objection to the Lands Tribunal and before the time for so referring it has expired—

(i) gives notice to the appropriate authority that he accepts the proposal of the authority to acquire the part of the affected area specified in the counter-notice, and

(ii) withdraws his claim as to the remainder of that area and as to the unaffected area; or

(b) on a reference to the Tribunal, the Tribunal makes a declaration in accordance with section 159(6) in respect of that part of the affected area,

the appropriate authority shall be deemed to be authorised to acquire compulsorily under the appropriate enactment the interest of the claimant in so far as it subsists in the part of the affected area specified in the counter-notice (but not in so far as it subsists in any other part of that area or in the unaffected area) and to have served a notice to treat in respect of it on the date mentioned in subsection (5).

(5) The date referred to in subsection (4)—

(a) in a case falling within paragraph (a) of that subsection, is the date on which notice is given in accordance with that paragraph; and

(b) in a case falling within paragraph (b) of that subsection, is the date specified in directions given by the Tribunal in accordance with section 159(7).

(6) In relation to a blight notice served by virtue of section 158 references to 'the appropriate authority' and 'the appropriate enactment' shall be construed as if the unaffected area of an agricultural unit were part of the affected area.

Personal representatives, mortgagees and partnerships

161. Powers of personal representatives in respect of blight notice

(1) In relation to any time after the death of a person who has serve a blight notice, sections 151(1), 152(1), 153(1), 154(4) and (5), 156(1) and 160(2) and (4) shall apply as if any reference in them to the claimant were a reference to the claimant's personal representatives.

(2) Where the whole or part of a hereditament or agricultural unit is comprised in blighted land and a person claims that—

(a) he is the personal representative of a person ('the deceased') who at the date of his death was entitled to an interest in that hereditament or unit;
    (b) the interest was one which would have been a qualifying interest if a notice under section 150 had been served in respect of it on that date;
    (c) he has made reasonable endeavours to sell that interest or the land falls within paragraph 21 or paragraph 22 (disregarding the notes) of Schedule 13 and the powers of compulsory acquisition remain exercisable;
    (d) in consequence of the fact that the hereditament or unit or a part of it was, or was likely to be, comprised in blighted land, he has been unable to sell that interest except at a price substantially lower than that for which it might reasonably have been expected to sell if no part of the hereditament or unit were, or were likely to be, comprised in such land; and
    (e) one or more individuals are (to the exclusion of any body corporate) beneficially entitled to that interest,
he may serve on the appropriate authority a notice in the prescribed form requiring that authority to purchase that interest to the extent specified in, and otherwise in accordance with, this Chapter.
    (3) Subject to subsection (4), subsection (2) shall apply in relation to an interest in part of a hereditament or agricultural unit as it applies in relation to an interest in the whole of a hereditament or agricultural unit.
    (4) Subsection (3) shall not enable any person—
    (a) if the deceased was entitled to an interest in the whole of a hereditament or agricultural unit, to make any claim or serve any notice under this section in respect of the deceased's interest in part of the hereditament or unit; or
    (b) if the deceased was entitled to an interest only in part of the hereditament or agricultural unit, to make or serve any such claim or notice in respect of the deceased's interest in less than the whole of that part.
    (5) Subject to sections 151(7) and 159(2) and (3), the grounds on which objection may be made in a counter-notice under section 151 to a notice under this section are those specified in paragraphs (a) to (c) of subsection (4) of that section and, in a case to which it applies, the grounds specified in paragraph (d) of that subsection and also the following grounds—
    (a) that the claimant is not the personal representative of the deceased or that, on the date of the deceased's death, the deceased was not entitled to an interest in any part of the hereditament or agricultural unit to which the notice relates;
    (b) that (for reasons specified in the counter-notice) the interest of the deceased is not such as is specified in subsection (2)(b);
    (c) that the conditions specified in subsection (2)(c), (d) or (e) are not satisfied.

162. Power of mortgagees to serve blight notice

    (1) Where the whole or part of a hereditament or agricultural unit is comprised in blighted land and a person claims that—
    (a) he is entitled as mortgagee (by virtue of a power which has become exercisable) to sell an interest in the hereditament or unit, giving immediate vacant possession of the land;
    (b) he has made reasonable endeavours to sell that interest or the land falls within paragraph 21 or paragraph 22 (disregarding the notes) of Schedule 13 and the powers of compulsory acquisition remain exercisable; and
    (c) in consequence of the fact that the hereditament or unit or a part of it was, or was likely to be, comprised in blighted land, he has been unable to sell that interest except at a price substantially lower than that for which it might reasonably have been expected to sell if no part of the hereditament or unit were, or were likely to be, comprised in such land,

then, subject to the provisions of this section, he may serve on the appropriate authority a notice in the prescribed form requiring that authority to purchase that interest to the extent specified in, and otherwise in accordance with, this Chapter.

(2) Subject to subsection (3), subsection (1) shall apply in relation to an interest in part of a hereditament or unit as it applies in relation to an interest in the whole of a hereditament or unit.

(3) Subsection (2) shall not enable a person—
 (a) if his interest as mortgagee is in the whole of a hereditament or agricultural unit, to make any claim or serve any notice under this section in respect of any interest in part of the hereditament or unit; or
 (b) if his interest as mortgagee is only in part of a hereditament or agricultural unit, to make or serve any such notice or claim in respect of any interest in less than the whole of that part.

(4) Notice under this section shall not be served unless the interest which the mortgagee claims he has the power to sell—
 (a) could be the subject of a notice under section 150 served by the person entitled to it on the date of service of the notice under this section; or
 (b) could have been the subject of such a notice served by that person on a date not more than six months before the date of service of the notice under this section.

(5) Subject to sections 151(7) and 159(2) and (3), the grounds on which objection may be made in a counter-notice under section 151 to a notice under this section are those specified in paragraphs (a) to (c) of subsection (4) of that section and, in a case to which it applies, the grounds specified in paragraph (d) of that subsection and also the following grounds—
 (a) that, on the date of service of the notice under this section, the claimant had no interest as mortgagee in any part of the hereditament or agricultural unit to which the notice relates;
 (b) that (for reasons specified in the counter-notice) the claimant had not on that date the power referred to in subsection (1)(a);
 (c) that the conditions specified in subsection (1)(b) and (c) are not fulfilled;
 (d) that (for reasons specified in the counter-notice) neither of the conditions specified in subsection (4) was, on the date of service of the notice under this section, satisfied with regard to the interest referred to in that subsection.

163. Prohibition on service of simultaneous notices under ss. 150, 161 and 162

(1) No notice shall be served under section 150 or 161 in respect of a hereditament or agricultural unit, or any part of it, at a time when a notice already served under section 162 is outstanding with respect to it, and no notice shall be served under section 162 at a time when a notice already served under section 150 or 161 is outstanding with respect to the relevant hereditament, unit or part.

(2) For the purposes of subsection (1), a notice shall be treated as outstanding with respect to a hereditament, unit or part—
 (a) until it is withdrawn in relation to the hereditament, unit or part; or
 (b) in a case where an objection to the notice has been made by a counter-notice under section 151, until either—
  (i) the period of two months specified in section 153 elapses without the claimant having required the objection to be referred to the Lands Tribunal under that section; or
  (ii) the objection, having been so referred, is upheld by the Tribunal with respect to the hereditament, unit or part.

164. Special provisions as to partnerships

(1) This section shall have effect for the purposes of the application of this Chapter to a hereditament or agricultural unit occupied for the purposes of a partnership firm.

(2) Occupation for the purposes of the firm shall be treated as occupation by the firm, and not as occupation by any one or more of the partners individually, and the definitions of 'owner-occupier' in section 168(1) and (2) shall apply in relation to the firm accordingly.

(3) If, after the service by the firm of a blight notice, any change occurs (whether by death or otherwise) in the constitution of the firm, any proceedings, rights or obligations consequential upon that notice may be carried on or exercised by or against, or, as the case may be, shall be incumbent upon, the partners for the time being constituting the firm.

(4) Nothing in this Chapter shall be construed as indicating an intention to exclude the operation of the definition of 'person' in Schedule 1 to the Interpretation Act 1978 (by which, unless the contrary intention appears, 'person' includes any body of persons corporate or unincorporate) in relation to any provision of this Chapter.

(5) Subsection (2) shall not affect the definition of 'resident owner-occupier' in section 168(3).

Miscellaneous and supplementary provisions

165. Power of Secretary of State to acquire land affected by orders relating to new towns etc. where blight notice served

(1) Where a blight notice has been served in respect of land falling within paragraph 7, 8 or 9 of Schedule 13, then until such time as a development corporation is established for the new town or, as the case may be, an urban development corporation is established for the urban development area the Secretary of State shall have power to acquire compulsorily any interest in the land in pursuance of the blight notice served virtue of that paragraph.

(2) Where the Secretary of State acquires an interest under subsection (1), then—

(a) if the land is or becomes land within paragraph 8 or, as the case may be, paragraph 9(b) of Schedule 13, the interest shall be transferred by him to the development corporation established for the new town or, as the case may be, the urban development corporation established for the urban development area; and

(b) in any other case, the interest may be disposed of by him in such manner as he thinks fit.

(3) The Land Compensation Act 1961 shall have effect in relation to the compensation payable in respect of the acquisition of an interest by the Secretary of State under subsection (1) as if—

(a) the acquisition were by a development corporation under the New Towns Act 1981 or, as the case may be, by an urban development corporation under Part XVI of the Local Government, Planning and Land Act 1980;

(b) in the case of land within paragraph 7 of Schedule 13, the land formed part of an area designated as the site of a new town by an order which has come into operation under section 1 of the New Towns Act 1981; and

(c) in the case of land within paragraph 9(a) of Schedule 13, the land formed part of an area designated as an urban development area by an order under section 134 of the Local Government, Planning and Land Act 1980 which has come into operation.

166. Saving for claimant's right to sell whole hereditament, etc.

(1) The provisions of sections 151(4)(c), 153(6), 154(4) and (5) and 155(3) and (4) relating to hereditaments shall not affect—

(a) the right of a claimant under section 92 of the Lands Clauses Consolidation Act 1845 to sell the whole of the hereditament or, in the case of an agricultural unit, the whole of the affected area, which he has required the authority to purchase; or

(b) the right of a claimant under section 8 of the Compulsory Purchase Act 1965 to sell (unless the Lands Tribunal otherwise determines) the whole of the hereditament or, as the case may be, affected area which he has required that authority to purchase.

(2) In accordance with subsection (1)(b), in determining whether or not to uphold an objection relating to a hereditament on the grounds mentioned in section 151(4)(c), the Lands Tribunal shall consider (in addition to the other matters which they are required to consider) whether—

(a) in the case of a house, building or factory, the part proposed to be acquired can be taken without material detriment to the house, building or factory; or

(b) in the case of a park or garden belonging to a house, the part proposed to be acquired can be taken without seriously affecting the amenity or convenience of the house.

167. No withdrawal of constructive notice to treat

Without prejudice to the provisions of section 156(1) and (2), a notice to treat which is deemed to have been served by virtue of this Chapter may not be withdrawn under section 31 of the Land Compensation Act 1961.

168. Meaning of 'owner-occupier' and 'resident owner-occupier'

(1) Subject to the following provisions of this section, in this Chapter 'owner-occupier', in relation to a hereditament, means—

(a) a person who occupies the whole or a substantial part of the hereditament in right of an owner's interest in it, and has so occupied the hereditament or that part of it during the whole of the period of six months ending with the date of service; or

(b) if the whole or a substantial part of the hereditament was unoccupied for a period of not more than 12 months ending with that date, a person who so occupied the hereditament or, as the case may be, that part of it during the whole of a period of six months ending immediately before the period when it was not occupied.

(2) Subject to the following provisions of this section, in this Chapter 'owner-occupier', in relation to an agricultural unit, means a person who—

(a) occupies the whole of that unit and has occupied it during the whole of the period of six months ending with the date of service; or

(b) occupied the whole of that unit during the whole of a period of six months ending not more than 12 months before the date of service,

and, at all times material for the purposes of paragraph (a) or, as the case may be, paragraph (b) has been entitled to an owner's interest in the whole or part of that unit.

(3) In this Chapter 'resident owner-occupier', in relation to a hereditament, means—

(a) an individual who occupies the whole or a substantial part of the hereditament as a private dwelling in right of an owner's interest in it, and has so occupied the hereditament or, as the case may be, that part during the whole of the period of six months ending with the date of service; or

(b) if the whole or a substantial part of the hereditament was unoccupied for a period of not more than 12 months ending with that date, an individual who so occupied the hereditament or, as the case may be, that part during the whole of a period of six months ending immediately before the period when it was not occupied.

(4) In this section—

'owner's interest', in relation to a hereditament or agricultural unit, means a freehold interest in it or a tenancy of it granted or extended for a term of years certain not less than three years of which remain unexpired on the date of service; and

'date of service', in relation to a hereditament or agricultural unit, means the date of service of a notice in respect of it under section 150.

169. 'Appropriate authority' for purposes of Chapter II

(1) Subject to the following provisions of this section, in this Chapter 'the appropriate authority', in relation to any land, means the government department, local authority, National Park Authority or other body or person by whom, in accordance with the circumstances by virtue of which the land falls within any paragraph of Schedule 13, the land is liable to be acquired or is indicated as being proposed to be acquired or, as the case may be, any right over the land is proposed to be acquired.

(2) If any question arises—

(a) whether the appropriate authority in relation to any land for the purposes of this Chapter is the Secretary of State or a local highway authority; or

(b) which of two or more local highway authorities is the appropriate authority in relation to any land for those purposes; or

(c) which of two or more local authorities is the appropriate authority in relation to any land for those purposes,

that question shall be referred to the Secretary of State, whose decision shall be final.

(3) If any question arises which authority is the appropriate authority for the purposes of this Chapter—

(a) section 151(2) shall have effect as if the reference to the date of service of the blight notice were a reference to that date or, if it is later, the date on which that question is determined;

(b) section 162(4)(b) shall apply with the substitution for the period six months of a reference to that period extended by so long as it takes to obtain a determination of the question; and

(c) section 168(1)(b), (2)(b) and (3)(b) shall apply with the substitution for the reference to 12 months before the date of service of a reference to that period extended by so long as it takes to obtain a determination of the question.

(4) In relation to land falling within paragraph 7, 8 or 9 of Schedule 13, until such time as a development corporation is established for the new town or, as the case may be, an urban development corporation is established for the urban development area, this Chapter shall have effect as if 'the appropriate authority' were the Secretary of State.

(5) In relation to land falling within paragraph 19 of Schedule 13, 'the appropriate authority' shall be the highway authority for the highway in relation to which the order mentioned in that paragraph was made.

[The reference to a National Parks Authority was inserted by the Environment Act 1995, see note to Section 4A supra.]

170. 'Appropriate enactment' for purposes of Chapter II

(1) Subject to the following provisions of this section, in this Chapter 'the appropriate enactment', in relation to land falling within any paragraph of Schedule 13, means the enactment which provides for the compulsory acquisition of land as being land falling within that paragraph or, as respects paragraph 22(b), the enactment under which the compulsory purchase order referred to in that paragraph was made.

(2) In relation to land falling within paragraph 2, 3 or 4 of that Schedule, an enactment shall for the purposes of subsection (1) be taken to be an enactment which provides for the compulsory acquisition of land as being land falling within that paragraph if—

(a) the enactment provides for the compulsory acquisition of land for the purposes of the functions which are indicated in the development plan as being the functions for the purposes of which the land is allocated or is proposed to be developed; or

Town and Country Planning Act 1990   95

(b) where no particular functions are so indicated in the development plan, the enactment provides for the compulsory acquisition of land for the purposes of any of the functions of the government department, local authority, National Park Authority or other body for the purposes of whose functions the land is allocated or is defined as the site of proposed development.

(3) In relation to land falling within paragraph 2, 3 or 4 of that Schedule by virtue of Note (1) to that paragraph, 'the appropriate enactment' shall be determined in accordance with subsection (2) as if references in that subsection to the development plan were references to any such plan, proposal or modifications as are mentioned in paragraph (a), (b) or (c) of that Note.

(4) In relation to land falling within paragraph 5 or 6 of that Schedule, 'the appropriate enactment' shall be determined in accordance with subsection (2) as if references in that subsection to the development plan were references to the resolution or direction in question.

(5) In relation to land falling within paragraph 7, 8 or 9 of that Schedule, until such time as a development corporation is established for the new town or, as the case may be, an urban development corporation is established for the urban development area, this Chapter shall have effect as if 'the appropriate enactment' were section 165(1).

(6) In relation to land falling within paragraph 10 or 11 of that Schedule, 'the appropriate enactment' shall be section 290 of the Housing Act 1985.

(7) In relation to land falling within paragraph 19 of that Schedule, 'the appropriate enactment' shall be section 239(6) of the Highways Act 1980.

(8) In relation to land falling within paragraph 22 of that Schedule by virtue of Note (1) to that paragraph, 'the appropriate enactment' shall be the enactment which would provide for the compulsory acquisition of the land or of the rights over the land if the relevant compulsory purchase order were confirmed or made.

(9) Where, in accordance with the circumstances by virtue of which any land falls within any paragraph of that Schedule, it is indicated that the land is proposed to be acquired for highway purposes, any enactment under which a highway authority are or (subject to the fulfilment of the relevant conditions) could be authorised to acquire that land compulsorily for highway purposes shall, for the purposes of subsection (1), be taken to be an enactment providing for the compulsory acquisition of that land as being land falling within that paragraph.

(10) In subsection (9) the reference to the fulfilment of the relevant conditions is a reference to such one or more of the following as are applicable to the circumstances in question—

(a) the coming into operation of any requisite order or scheme made, or having effect as if made, under the provisions of Part II of the Highways Act 1980;

(b) the coming into operation of any requisite scheme made, or having effect as if made, under section 106(3) of that Act;

(c) the making or approval of any requisite plans.

(11) If, apart from this subsection, two or more enactments would be the appropriate enactment in relation to any land for the purposes of this Chapter, the appropriate enactment for those purposes shall be taken to be that one of those enactments under which, in the circumstances in question, it is most likely that (apart from this Chapter) the land would have been acquired by the appropriate authority.

(12) If any question arises as to which enactment is the appropriate enactment in relation to any land for the purposes of this Chapter, that question shall be referred—

(a) where the appropriate authority are a government department, to the Minister in charge of that department;

(b) where the appropriate authority are statutory undertakers, to the appropriate Minister; and

(c) in any other case, to the Secretary of State,
and the decision of the Minister or, as the case may be, the Secretary of State shall be final.
[The reference to a National Park Authority was inserted by the Environment Act 1995, see note to Section 4A supra.]

171. General interpretation of Chapter II

(1) Subject to the following provisions of this section, in this Chapter—
'the affected area', in relation to an agricultural unit, means so much of that unit as, on the date of service, consists of land falling within any paragraph of Schedule 13;
'agricultural' has the same meaning as in section 109 of the Agriculture Act 1947 and references to the farming of land include references to the carrying on in relation to the land of agricultural activities;
'agricultural unit' means land which is occupied as a unit for agricultural purposes, including any dwellinghouse or other building occupied by the same person for the purpose of farming the land;
'annual value' means—
   (a) in the case of a hereditament which is shown in a local non-domestic rating list and none of which consists of domestic property or property exempt from local non-domestic rating, the value shown in that list as the rateable value of that hereditament on the date of service;
   (b) in the case of a hereditament which is shown in a local non-domestic rating list and which includes domestic property or property exempt from local non-domestic rating, the sum of—
      (i) the value shown in that list as the rateable value of that hereditament on the date of service; and
      (ii) the value attributable to the non-rateable part of that hereditament in accordance with subsections (2) and (3);
   (c) in the case of any other hereditament, the value attributable to that hereditament in accordance with subsections (2) and (3);
'blight notice' has the meaning given in section 149(5);
'the claimant' has the meaning given in section 150(4);
'hereditament' means a relevant hereditament within the meaning of section 64(4)(a) to (c) of the Local Government Finance Act 1988;
'special enactment' means a local enactment, or a provision contained in an Act other than a local or private Act, which is a local enactment or provision authorising the compulsory acquisition of land specifically identified in it; and in this definition 'local enactment' means a local or private Act, or an order confirmed by Parliament or brought into operation in accordance with special parliamentary procedure.

(2) The value attributable to a hereditament, or the non-rateable part of it, in respect of domestic property shall be the value certified by the relevant valuation officer as being 5 per cent of the compensation which would be payable in respect of the value of that property if it were purchased compulsorily under statute with vacant possession and the compensation payable were calculated in accordance with Part II of the Land Compensation Act 1961 by reference to the relevant date.

(3) The value attributable to a hereditament, or the non-rateable part of it, in respect of property exempt from local non-domestic rating shall be the value certified by the relevant valuation officer as being the value which would have been shown as the rateable value of that property on the date of service if it were a relevant non-domestic hereditament consisting entirely of non-domestic property, none of which was exempt from local non-domestic rating.

Town and Country Planning Act 1990

(4) and which (apart from this subsection) would comprise separate hereditaments solely by reason of being divided by a boundary between rating areas shall be treated for the purposes of the definition of 'hereditament' in subsection (1) as if it were not so divided.

(5) In this section—
'date of service' has the same meaning as in section 168;
'relevant valuation officer' means the valuation officer who would have determined the rateable value in respect of the hereditament for the purposes of Part III of the Local Government Finance Act 1988 if the hereditament had fulfilled the conditions set out in section 42(1)(b) to (d) of that Act;
'relevant date' is the date by reference to which that determination would have been made;
and expressions used in the definition of 'annual value' in subsection (1) or in subsection (2) or (3) which are also used in Part III of that Act have the same meaning as in that Part.

PART VII
ENFORCEMENT

Introductory

171A. Expression used in connection with enforcement
(1) For the purposes of this Act—
　(a) carrying out development without the required planning permission; or
　(b) failing to comply with any condition or limitation subject to which planning permission has been granted,
constitutes a breach of planning control.
(2) For the purposes of this Act—
　(a) the issue of an enforcement notice (defined in section 172); or
　(b) the service of a breach of condition notice (defined in section 187A),
constitutes taking enforcement action.
(3) In this Part 'planning permission' includes permission under Part III of the 1947 Act, of the 1962 Act or of the 1971 Act.

171B. Time limits
(1) Where there has been a breach of planning control consisting in the carrying out without planning permission of building, engineering, mining or other operations in, on, over or under land, no enforcement action may be taken after the end of the period of four years beginning with the date on which the operations were substantially completed.
(2) Where there has been a breach of planning control consisting in the change of use of any building to use as a single dwellinghouse, no enforcement action may be taken after the end of the period of four years beginning with the date of the breach.
(3) In the case of any other breach of planning control, no enforcement action may be taken after the end of the period of ten years beginning with the date of the breach.
(4) The preceding subsections do not prevent—
　(a) the service of a breach of condition notice in respect of any breach of planning control if an enforcement notice in respect of the breach is in effect; or
　(b) taking further enforcement action in respect of any breach of planning control if, during the period of four years ending with that action being taken, the local planning authority have taken or purported to take enforcement action in respect of that breach.

Planning contravention notices

171C. Power to require information about activities on land

(1) Where it appears to the local planning authority that there may have been a breach of planning control in respect of any land, they may serve notice to that effect (referred to in this Act as a 'planning contravention notice') on any person who—

    (a) is the owner or occupier of the land or has any other interst in it; or

    (b) is carrying out operations on the land or is using it for any purpose.

(2) A planning contravention notice may require the person on whom it is served to give such information as to—

    (a) any operations being carried out on the land, any use of the land and any other activities being carried out on the land; and

    (b) any matter relating to the conditions or limitations subject to which any planning permission in respect of the land has been granted,

as may be specified in the notice.

(3) Without prejudice to the generality of subsection (2), the notice may require the person on whom it is served, so far as he is able—

    (a) to state whether or not the land is being used for any purpose specified in the notice or any operations or activities specified in the notice are being or have been carried out on the land;

    (b) to state when any use, operations or activities began;

    (c) to give the name and address of any person known to him to use or have used the land for any purpose or to be carrying out, or have carried out, any operations or activities on the land;

    (d) to give any information he holds as to any planning permission for any use or operations or any reason for planning permission not being required for any use or operations;

    (e) to state the nature of his interest (if any) in the land and the name and address of any other person known to him to have an interest in the land.

(4) A planning contravention notice may give notice of a time and place at which—

    (a) any offer which the person on whom the notice is served may wish to make to apply for planning permission, to refrain from carrying out any operations or activities or to undertake remedial works; and

    (b) any representations which he may wish to make about the notice,

will be considered by the authority, and the authority shall give him an opportunity to make in person any such offer or representations at that time and place.

(5) A planning contravention notice must inform the person on whom it is served—

    (a) of the likely consequences of his failing to respond to the notice and, in particular, that enforcement action may be taken; and

    (b) of the effect of section 186(5)(b).

(6) Any requirement of a planning contravention notice shall be complied with by giving information in writing to the local planning authority.

(7) The service of a planning contravention notice does not affect any other power exercisable in respect of any breach of planning control.

(8) In this section references to operations or activities on land include operations or activities in, under or over the land.

171D. Penalties for non-compliance with planning contravention notice

(1) If, at any time after the end of the period of twenty-one days beginning with the day on which a planning contravention notice has been served on any person, he has not complied with any requirement of the notice, he shall be guilty of an offence.

(2) An offence under subsection (1) may be charged by reference to any day or longer period of time and a person may be convicted of a second or subsequent

offence under that subsection by reference to any period of time following the preceding conviction for such an offence.

(3) It shall be a defence for a person charged with an offence under subsection (1) to prove that he had a reasonable excuse for failing to comply with the requirement.

(4) A person guilty of an offence under subsection (1) shall be liable on summary conviction to a fine not exceeding level 3 on the standard scale.

(5) If any person—
    (a) makes any statement purporting to comply with a requirement of a planning contravention notice which he knows to be false or misleading in a material particular; or
    (b) recklessly makes such a statement which is false or misleading in a material particular,
he shall be guilty of an offence.

(6) A person guilty of an offence under subsection (5) shall be liable on summary conviction to a fine not exceeding level 5 on the standard scale.

Enforcement notices

172. Issue of enforcement notice

(1) The local planning authority may issue a notice (in this Act referred to as an 'enforcement notice') where it appears to them—
    (a) that there has been a breach of planning control; and
    (b) that it is expedient to issue the notice, having regard to the provisions of the development plan and to any other material considerations.

(2) A copy of an enforcement notice shall be served—
    (a) on the owner and on the occupier of the land to which it relates; and
    (b) on any other person having an interest in the land, being an interest which, in the opinion of the authority, is materially affected by the notice.

(3) The service of the notice shall take place—
    (a) not more than twenty-eight days after its date of issue; and
    (b) not less than twenty-eight days before the date specified in it as the date on which it is to take effect.

173. Contents and effect of notice

(1) An enforcement notice shall state—
    (a) the matters which appear to the local planning authority to constitute the breach of planning control; and
    (b) the paragraph of section 171A(1) within which, in the opinion of the authority, the breach falls.

(2) A notice complies with subsection (1)(a) if it enables any person on whom a copy of it is served to know what those matters are.

(3) An enforcement notice shall specify the steps which the authority require to be taken, or the activities which the authority require to cease, in order to achieve, wholly or partly, any of the following purposes.

(4) Those purposes are—
    (a) remedying the breach by making any development comply with the terms (including conditions and limitations) of any planning permission which has been granted in respect of the land, by discontinuing any use of the land or by restoring the land to its condition before the breach took place; or
    (b) remedying any injury to amenity which has been caused by the breach.

(5) An enforcement notice may, for example, require—
    (a) the alteration or removal of any buildings or works;
    (b) the carrying out of any building or other operations;
    (c) any activity on the land not to be carried on except to the extent specified in the notice; or

(d) the contour of a deposit of refuse or waste materials on land to be modified by altering the gradient or gradients of its sides.

(6) Where an enforcement notice is issued in respect of a breach of planning control consisting of demolition of a building, the notice may require the construction of a building (in this section referred to as a 'replacement building') which, subject to subsection (7), is as similar as possible to the demolished building.

(7) A replacement building—

(a) must comply with any requirement imposed by any enactment applicable to the construction of buildings;

(b) may differ from the demolished building in any respect which, if the demolished building had been altered in that respect, would not have constituted a breach of planning control;

(c) must comply with any regulations made for the purposes of this subsection (including regulations modifying paragraphs (a) and (b)).

(8) An enforcement notice shall specify the date on which it is to take effect and, subject to sections 175(4) and 289(4A), shall take effect on that date.

(9) An enforcement notice shall specify the period at the end of which any steps are required to have been taken or any activities are required to have ceased and may specify different periods for different steps or activities; and, where different periods apply to different steps or activities, references in this Part to the period for compliance with an enforcement notice, in relation to any step or activity, are to the period at the end of which the step is required to have been taken or the activity is required to have ceased.

(10) An enforcement notice shall specify such additional matters as may be prescribed, and regulations may require every copy of an enforcement notice served under section 172 to be accompanied by an explanatory note giving prescribed information as to the right of appeal under section 174.

(11) Where—

(a) an enforcement notice in respect of any breach of planning control could have required any buildings or works to be removed or any activity to cease, but does not do so; and

(b) all the requirements of the notice have been complied with,

then, so far as the notice did not so require, planning permission shall be treated as having been granted by virtue of section 73A in respect of development consisting of the construction of the buildings or works or, as the case may be, the carrying out of the activities.

(12) Where—

(a) an enforcement notice requires the construction of a replacement building; and

(b) all the requirements of the notice with respect to that construction have been complied with,

planning permission shall be treated as having been granted by virtue of section 73A in respect of development consisting of that construction.

173A. Variation and withdrawal of enforcement notices

(1) The local planning authority may—

(a) withdraw an enforcement notice issued by them; or

(b) waive or relax any requirement of such a notice and, in particular, may extend any period specified in accordance with section 173(9).

(2) The powers conferred by subsection (1) may be exercised whether or not the notice has taken effect.

(3) The local planning authority shall, immediately after exercising the powers conferred by subsection (1), give notice of the exercise to every person who has been

served with a copy of the enforcement notice or would, if the notice were re-issued, be served with a copy of it.

(4) The withdrawal of an enforcement notice does not affect the power of the local planning authority to issue a further enforcement notice.

174. Appeal against enforcement notice

(1) A person having an interest in the land to which an enforcement notice relates or a relevant occupier may appeal to the Secretary of State against the notice, whether or not a copy of it has been served on him.

(2) An appeal may be brought on any of the following grounds—

(a) that, in respect of any breach of planning control which may be constituted by the matters stated in the notice, planning permission ought to be granted or, as the case may be, the condition or limitation concerned ought to be discharged;

(b) that those matters have not occurred;

(c) that those matters (if they occurred) do not constitute a breach of planning control;

(d) that, at the date when the notice was issued, no enforcement action could be taken in respect of any breach of planning control which may be constituted by those matters;

(e) that copies of the enforcement notice were not served as required by section 172;

(f) that the steps required by the notice to be taken, or that activities required by the notice to cease, exceed what was necessary to remedy any breach of planning control which may be constituted by those matters or, as the case may be to remedy any injury to amenity which has been caused any such breach;

(g) that any period specified in the notice in accordance with section 173(9) falls short of what should reasonably be allowed.

(3) An appeal under this section shall be made either—

(a) by giving written notice of the appeal to the Secretary of State before the date specified in the enforcement notice and the date on which it is to take effect; or

(b) by sending such notice to him in a properly addressed and pre-paid letter posted to him at such time that, in the ordinary course of post, it would be delivered to him before that date.

(4) A person who gives notice under subsection (3) shall submit to the Secretary of State, either when giving the notice or within the prescribed time, a statement in writing—

(a) specifying the grounds on which he is appealing against the enforcement notice; and

(b) giving such further information as may be prescribed.

(5) If, where more than one ground is specified in that statement, the appellant does not give information required under subsection (4)(b) in relation to each of those grounds within the prescribed time, the Secretary of State may determine the appeal without considering any ground as to which the appellant has failed to give such information within that time.

(6) In this section 'relevant occupier' means a person who—

(a) on the date on which the enforcement notice is issued occupies the land to which the notice relates by virtue of a licence; and

(b) continues so to occupy the land when the appeal is brought.

175. Appeals: supplementary provisions

(1) The Secretary of State may by regulations prescribe the procedure which is to be followed on appeals under section 174 and, in particular, but without prejudice to the generality of this subsection, may—

(a) require the local planning authority to submit, within such time as may be prescribed, a statement indicating the submissions which they propose to put forward on the appeal;

(b) specify the matters to be included in such a statement;
(c) require the authority or the appellant to give such notice of such an appeal as may be prescribed;
(d) require the authority to send to the Secretary of State, within such period from the date of the bringing of the appeal as may be prescribed, a copy of the enforcement notice and a list of the persons served with copies of it.

(2) The notice to be prescribed under subsection (1)(c) shall be such notice as in the opinion of the Secretary of State is likely to bring the appeal to the attention of persons in the locality in which the land to which the enforcement notice relates is situated.

(3) Subject to section 176(4), the Secretary of State shall, if either the appellant or the local planning authority so desire, give each of them an opportunity of appearing before and being heard by a person appointed by the Secretary of State for the purpose.

(4) Where an appeal is brought under section 174 the enforcement notice shall subject to any order under section 289(4A) be of no effect pending the final determination or the withdrawal of the appeal.

(5) Where any person has appealed to the Secretary of State against an enforcement notice, no person shall be entitled, in any other proceedings instituted after the making of the appeal, to claim that the notice was not duly served on the person who appealed.

(6) Schedule 6 applies to appeals under section 174, including appeals under that section as applied by regulations under any other provisions of this Act.

(7) Subsection (5) of section 250 of the Local Government Act 1972 (which authorises a Minister holding an inquiry under that section to make orders with respect to the costs of the parties) shall apply in relation to any proceedings before the Secretary of State on an appeal undersection 174 as if those proceedings were an inquiry held by the Secretary of State under section 250.

176. General provisions relating to determination of appeals

(1) On an appeal under section 174 the Secretary of State may—
    (a) correct any defect, error or misdescription in the enforcement notice; or
    (b) vary the terms of the enforcement notice,
if he is satisfied that the correction or variation will not cause injustice to the appellant or the local planning authority.

(2) Where the Secretary of State determines to allow the appeal, he may quash the notice.

(2A) The Secretary of State shall give any directions necessary to give effect to his determination on the appeal.

(3) The Secretary of State—
    (a) may dismiss an appeal if the appellant fails to comply with section 174(4) within the prescribed time; and
    (b) may allow an appeal and quash the enforcement notice if the local planning authority fail to comply with any requirement of regulations made by virtue of paragraph (a), (b), or (d) of section 175(1) within the prescribed period.

(4) If the Secretary of State proposes to dismiss an appeal under paragraph (a) of subsection (3) or to allow an appeal and quash the enforcement notice under paragraph (b) of that subsection, he need not comply with section 175(3).

(5) Where it would otherwise be a ground for determining an appeal under section 174 in favour of the appellant that a person required to be served with a copy of the enforcement notice was not served, the Secretary of State may disregard that fact if neither the appellant nor that person has been substantially prejudiced by the failure to serve him.

177. Grant or modification of planning permission on appeals against enforcement notices

(1) On the determination of an appeal under section 174, the Secretary of State may—

(a) grant planning permission in respect of the matters stated in the enforcement notice as constituting a breach of planning control, whether in relation to the whole or any part of those matters or in relation to the whole or any part of the land to which the notice relates.

(b) discharge any condition or limitation subject to which planning permission was granted;

(c) determine whether, on the date on which the appeal was made any existing use of the land was lawful, any operations which had been carried out in, on, over or under the land were lawful or any matter constituting a failure to comply with any condition or limitation subject to which planning permission was granted was lawful and, if so, issue a certificate under section 191.

(1A) The provisions of sections 191 to 194 mentioned in subsection (1B) shall apply for the purposes of subsection (1)(c) as they apply for the purposes of section 191, but as if—

(a) any reference to an application for a certificate were a reference to the appeal and any reference to the date of such an application were a reference to the date on which the appeal is made; and

(b) references to the local planning authority were references to the Secretary of State.

(1B) Those provisions are: sections 191(5) to (7), 193(4) (so far as it relates to the form of the certificate), (6) and (7) and 194.

(2) In considering whether to grant planning permission under subsection (1), the Secretary of State shall have regard to the provisions of the development plan, so far as material to the subject matter of the enforcement notice, and to any other material considerations.

(3) The planning permission that may be granted under subsection (1) is any planning permission that might be granted on an application under Part III.

(5) Where an appeal against an enforcement notice is brought under section 174, the appellant shall be deemed to have made an application for planning permission in respect of the matters stated in the enforcement notice as constituting a breach of planning control.

(5A) Where—

(a) the statement under subsection (4) of section 174 specifies the ground mentioned in subsection (2)(a) of that section:

(b) any fee is payable under regulations made by virtue of section 303 in respect of the application deemed to be made by virtue of the appeal; and

(c) the Secretary of State gives notice in writing to the appellant specifying the period within which the fee must be paid,

then, if that fee is not paid within that period, the appeal, so far as brought on that ground, and the application shall lapse at the end of that period.

(6) Any planning permission granted under subsection (1) on an appeal shall be treated as granted on the application deemed to have been made by the appellant.

(7) In relation to a grant of planning permission or a determination under subsection (1) the Secretary of State's decision shall be final.

(8) For the purposes of section 69 the Secretary of State's decision shall be treated as having been given by him in dealing with an application for planning permission made to the local planning authority.

178. Execution and costs of works required by enforcement notice

(1) Where any steps required by an enforcement notice to be taken are not taken within the period for compliance with the notice, the local planning authority may—

(a) enter the land and take the steps; and

(b) recover from the person who is then the owner of the land any expenses reasonably incurred by them in doing so.

(2) Where a copy of an enforcement notice has been served in respect of any breach of planning control—

(a) any expenses incurred by the owner or occupier of any land for the purpose of complying with the notice, and

(b) any sums paid by the owner of any land under subsection (1) in respect of expenses incurred by the local planning authority in taking steps required by such a notice to be taken,

shall be deemed to be incurred or paid for the use and at the request of the person by whom the breach of planning control was committed.

(3) Regulations made under this Act may provide that—

(a) section 276 of the Public Health Act 1936, (power of local authorities to sell materials removed in executing works under that Act subject to accounting for the proceeds of sale);

(b) section 289 of that Act (power to require the occupier of any premises to permit works to be executed by the owner of the premises); and

(c) section 294 of that Act (limit on liability of persons holding premises as agents or trustees in respect of the expenses recoverable under that Act),

shall apply, subject to such adaptations and modifications as may be specified in the regulations, in relation to any steps required to be taken by an enforcement notice.

(4) Regulations under subsection (3) applying section 289 of the Public Health Act 1936 may include adaptations and modifications for the purpose of giving the owner of land to which an enforcement notice relates the right, as against all other persons interested in the land, to comply with the requirements of the enforcement notice.

(5) Regulations under subsection (3) may also provide for the charging on the land of any expenses recoverable by a local planning authority under subsection (1).

(6) Any person who wilfully obstructs a person acting in the exercise of powers under subsection (1) shall be guilty of an offence and liable on summary conviction to a fine not exceeding level 3 on the standard scale.

(7) [repealed]

179. Offence where enforcement notice not complied with

(1) Where, at any time after the end of the period for complance with an enforcement notice, any step required by the notice to be taken has not been taken or any activity required by the notice to cease is being carried on, the person who is then the owner of the land is in breach of the notice.

(2) Where the owner of the land is in breach of an enforcement notice he shall be guilty of an offence.

(3) In proceedings against any person for an offence under subsection (2), it shall be a defence for him to show that he did everything he could be expected to do to secure compliance with the notice.

(4) A person who has control of or an interest in the land to which an enforcement notice relates (other than the owner) must not carry on any activity which is required by the notice to cease or cause or permit such an activity to be carried on.

(5) A person who, at any time after the end of the period for compliance with the notice, contravenes subsection (4) shall be guilty of an offence.

(6) An offence under subsection (2) or (5) may be charged by reference to any day or longer period of time and a person may be convicted of a second or subsequent offence under the subsection in question by reference to any period of time following the preceding conviction for such an offence.

(7) Where—
(a) a person charged with an offence under this section has not been served with a copy of the enforcement notice; and
(b) the notice is not contained in the appropriate register kept under section 188,
it shall be a defence for him to show that he was not aware of the existence of the notice.

(8) person guilty of an offence under this section shall be liable—
(a) on summary conviction, to a fine not exceeding £20,000; and
(b) on conviction on indictment, to a fine.

(9) In determining the amount of any fine to be imposed on a person convicted of an offence under this section, the court shall in particular have regard to any financial benefit which has accrued or appears likely to accrue to him in consequence of the offence.

180. Effect of planning permission, etc., on enforcement or breach of condition notice

(1) Where, after the service of—
(a) a copy of an enforcement notice; or
(b) a breach of condition notice,
planning permission is granted for any development carried out before the grant of that permission, the notice shall cease to have effect so far as inconsistent with that permission.

(2) Where after a breach of condition notice has been served any condition to which the notice relates is discharged, the notice shall cease to have effect so far as it requires any person to secure compliance with the condition in question.

(3) The fact that an enforcement notice or breach of condition notice has wholly or partly ceased to have effect by virtue of this section shall not affect the liability of any person for an offence in respect of a previous failure to comply, or secure compliance, with the notice.

181. Enforcement notice to have effect against subsequent development

(1) Compliance with an enforcement notice, whether in respect of—
(a) the completion, removal or alteration of any buildings or works;
(b) the discontinuance of any use of land; or
(c) any other requirements contained in the notice,
shall not discharge the notice.

(2) Without prejudice to subsection (1), any provision of an enforcement notice requiring a use of land to be discontinued shall operate as a requirement that it shall be discontinued permanently, to the extent that it is in contravention of Part III; and accordingly the resumption of that use at any time after it has been discontinued in compliance with the enforcement notice shall to that extent be in contravention of the enforcement notice.

(3) Without prejudice to subsection (1), if any development is carried out on land by way of reinstating or restoring buildings or works which have been removed or altered in compliance with an enforcement notice, the notice shall, notwithstanding that its terms are not apt for the purpose, be deemed to apply in relation to the buildings or works as reinstated or restored as it applied in relation to the buildings or works before they were demolished or altered; and, subject to subsection (4), the provisions of section 178(1) and (2) shall apply accordingly.

(4) Where, at any time after an enforcement notice takes effect—
(a) any development is carried out on land by way of reinstating or restoring buildings or works which have been removed or altered in compliance with the notice; and

(b) the local planning authority propose, under section 178(1), to take any steps required by the enforcement notice for the removal or alteration of the buildings or works in consequence of the reinstatement or restoration,
the local planning authority shall, not less than 28 days before taking any such steps, serve on the owner and occupier of the land a notice of their intention to do so.

(5) Where without planning permission a person carries out any development on land by way of reinstating or restoring buildings or works which have been removed or altered in compliance with an enforcement notice—

(a) he shall be guilty of an offence and shall be liable on summary conviction to a fine not exceeding level 5 on the standard scale, and

(b) no person shall be liable under section 179(2) for failure to take any steps required to be taken by an enforcement notice by way of removal or alteration of what has been so reinstated or restored.

182. Enforcement by the Secretary of State

(1) If it appears to the Secretary of State to be expedient that an enforcement notice should be issued in respect of any land, he may issue such a notice.

(2) The Secretary of State shall not issue such a notice without consulting the local planning authority.

(3) An enforcement notice issued by the Secretary of State shall have the same effect as a notice issued by the local planning authority.

(4) In relation to an enforcement notice issued by the Secretary of State, sections 178 and 181 shall apply as if for any reference in those sections to the local planning authority there were substituted a reference to the Secretary of State.

Stop notices

183. Stop notices

(1) Where the local planning authority consider it expedient that any relevant activity should cease before the expiry of the period for compliance with an enforcement notice, they may, when they serve the copy of the enforcement notice or afterwards, serve a notice (in this Act referred to as a 'stop notice') prohibiting the carrying out of that activity on the land to which the enforcement notice relates, or any part of that land specified in the stop notice.

(2) In this section and sections 184 and 186 'relevant activity' means any activity specified in the enforcement notice as an activity which the local planning authority require to cease and any activity carried out as part of that activity or associated with that activity.

(3) A stop notice may not be served where the enforcement notice has taken effect.

(4) A stop notice shall not prohibit the use of any building as a dwellinghouse.

(5) A stop notice shall not prohibit the carrying out of any activity if the activity has been carried out (whether continuously or not) for a period of more than four years ending with the service of the notice; and for the purposes of this subsection no account is to be taken of any period during which the activity was authorised by planning permission.

(5A) Subsection (5) does not prevent a stop notice prohibiting any activity consisting of, or incidental to, building, engineering, mining or other operations or the deposit of refuse or waste materials.

(6) A stop notice may be served by the local planning authority on any person who appears to them to have an interest in the land or to be engaged in any activity prohibited by the notice.

(7) The local planning authority may at any time withdraw a stop notice (without prejudice to their power to serve another) by serving notice to that effect on persons served with the stop notice.

184. Stop notices: supplementary provisions

(1) A stop notice must refer to the enforcement notice to which it relates and have a copy of that notice annexed to it.

(2) A stop notice must specify the date on which it will take effect (and it cannot be contravened until that date).

(3) That date—

(a) must not be earlier than three days after the date when the notice is served, unless the local planning authority consider that there are special reasons for specifying an earlier date and a statement of those reasons is served with the stop notice; and

(b) must not be later than twenty-eight days from the date when the notice is first served on any person.

(4) A stop notice shall cease to have effect when—

(a) the enforcement notice to which it relates is withdrawn or quashed; or

(b) the [period for compliance with the enforcement notice] expires; or

(c) notice of the withdrawal of the stop notice is first served under section 183(7).

(5) A stop notice shall also cease to have effect if or to the extent that the activities prohibited by it cease, on a variation of the enforcement notice, to be relevant activities.

(6) Where a stop notice has been served in respect of any land, the local planning authority may display there a notice (in this section and section 187 referred to as a 'site notice')—

(a) stating that a stop notice has been served and that any person contravening it may be prosecuted for an offence under section 187,

(b) giving the date when the stop notice takes effect, and

(c) indicating its requirements.

(7) If under section 183(7) the local planning authority withdraw a stop notice in respect of which a site notice was displayed, they must display a notice of the withdrawal in place of the site notice.

(8) A stop notice shall not be invalid by reason that a copy of the enforcement notice to which it relates was not served as required by section 172 if it is shown that the local planning authority took all such steps as were reasonably practicable to effect proper service.

185. Service of stop notices by Secretary of State

(1) If it appears to the Secretary of State to be expedient that a stop notice should be served in respect of any land, he may himself serve such a notice.

(2) A notice served by the Secretary of State under subsection (1) shall have the same effect as if it had been served by the local planning authority.

(3) The Secretary of State shall not serve such a notice without consulting the local planning authority.

186. Compensation for loss due to stop notice

(1) Where a stop notice is served under section 183 compensation may be payable under this section in respect of a prohibition contained in the notice only if—

(a) the enforcement notice is quashed on grounds other than those mentioned in paragraph (a) of section 174(2);

(b) the enforcement notice is varied (otherwise than on the grounds mentioned in that paragraph) so that any activity the carrying out of which is prohibited by the stop notice ceased to be a relevant activity;

(c) the enforcement notice is withdrawn by the local planning authority otherwise than in consequence of the grant by them of planning permission for the development to which the notice relates; or

(d) the stop notice is withdrawn.

(2) A person who, when the stop notice is first served, has an interest in or occupies the land to which the notice relates shall be entitled to be compensated by the local planning authority in respect of any loss or damage directly attributable to the prohibition contained in the notice or, in a case within subsection (1)(b), the prohibition of such of the activities prohibited by the stop notice as cease to be relevant activities.

(3) A claim for compensation under this section shall be made to the local planning authority within the prescribed time and in the prescribed manner.

(4) The loss or damage in respect of which compensation is payable under this section in respect of a prohibition shall include any sum payable in respect of a breach of contract caused by the taking of action necessary to comply with the prohibition.

(5) No compensation is payable under this section—

(a) in respect of the prohibition in a stop notice of any activity which, at any time when the notice is in force, constitutes or contributes to a breach of planning control; or

(b) in the case of a claimant who was required to provide information under section 171C or 330 or section 16 of the Local Government (Miscellaneous Provisions) Act 1976, in respect of any loss or damage suffered by him which could have been avoided if he had provided the information or had otherwise co-operated with the local planning authority when responding to the notice.

(6) Except in so far as may be otherwise provided by any regulations made under this Act, any question of disputed compensation under this Part shall be referred to and determined by the Lands Tribunal.

(7) In relation to the determination of any such question, the provisions of sections 2 and 4 of the Land Compensation Act 1961 shall apply subject to any necessary modifications and to the provisions of any regulations made under this Act.

187. Penalties for contravention of stop notice

(1) If any person contravenes a stop notice after a site notice has been displayed or the stop notice has been served on him he shall be guilty of an offence.

(1A) An offence under this section may be charged by reference to any day or longer period of time and a person may be convicted of a second or subsequent offence under this section by reference to any period of time following the preceding conviction for such an offence.

(1B) References in this section to contravening a stop notice include causing or permitting its contravention.

(2) A person guilty of an offence under this section shall be liable—

(a) on summary conviction, to a fine not exceeding £20,000; and

(b) on conviction on indictment, to a fine.

(2A) In determining the amount of any fine to be imposed on a person convicted of an offence under this section, the court shall in particular have regard to any financial benefit which has accrued or appears likely to accrue to him in consequence of the offence.

(3) In proceedings for an offence under this section it shall be a defence for the accused to prove—

(a) that the stop notice was not served on him, and

(b) that he did not know, and could not reasonably have been expected to know, of its existence.

Breach of condition

187A. Enforcement of conditions

(1) This section applies where planning permission for carrying out any development of land has been granted subject to conditions.

Town and Country Planning Act 1990

(2) The local planning authority may, if any of the conditions is not complied with, severe a notice (in this Act referred to as a 'breach of condition notice') on—
  (a) any person who is carrying out or has carried out the development; or
  (b) any person having control of the land,
requiring him to secure compliance with such of the conditions as are specified in the notice.

(3) References in this section to the person responsible are to the person on whom the breach of condition notice has been served.

(4) The conditions which may be specified in a notice served by virtue of subsection (2)(b) are any of the conditions regulating the use of the land.

(5) A breach of condition notice shall specify the steps which the authority consider ought to be taken, or the activities which the authority consider ought to cease, to secure compliance with the conditions specified in the notice.

(6) The authority may by notice served on the person responsible withdraw the breach of condition notice, but its withdrawal shall not affect the power to serve on him a further breach of condition notice in respect of the conditions specified in the earlier notice or any other conditions.

(7) The period allowed for compliance with the notice is—
  (a) such period of not less than twenty-eight days beginning with the date of service of the notice as may be specified in the notice; or
  (b) that period as extended by a further notice served by the local planning authority on the person responsible.

(8) If, at any time after the end of the period allowed for compliance with the notice—
  (a) any of the conditions specified in the notice is not complied with; and
  (b) the steps specified in the notice have not been taken or, as the case may be, the activities specified in the notice have not ceased,
the person responsible is in breach of the notice.

(9) If the person responsible is in breach of the notice he shall be guilty of an offence.

(10) An offence under subsection (9) may be charged by reference to any day or longer period of time and a person may be convicted of a second or subsequent offence under that subsection by reference to any period of time following the preceding conviction for such an offence.

(11) It shall be a defence for a person charged with an offence under subsection (9) to prove—
  (a) that he took all reasonable measures to secure compliance with the conditions specified in the notice; or
  (b) where the notice was served on him by virtue of subsection (2)(b), that he no longer had control of the land.

(12) A person who is guilty of an offence under subsection (9) shall be liable on summary conviction to a fine not exceeding level 3 on the standard scale.

(13) In this section—
  (a) 'conditions' includes limitations; and
  (b) references to carrying out any development include causing or permitting another to do so.

Injunctions

187B. Injunctions restraining breaches of planning control

(1) Where a local planning authority consider it necessary or expedient for any actual or apprehended breach of planning control to be restrained by injunction, they may apply to the court for an injunction, whether or not they have exercised or are proposing to exercise any of their other powers under this Part.

(2) On an application under subsection (1) the court may grant such an injunction as the court thinks appropriate for the purpose of restraining the breach.

(3) Rules of court may provide for such an injunction to be issued against a person whose identity is unknown.

(4) In this section 'the court' means the High Court or the county court.

Registers

188. Register of enforcement and stop notices

(1) Every district planning authority [every local planning authority for an area in Wales] and the council of every metropolitan district or London borough shall keep, in such manner as may be prescribed by a development order, a register containing such information as may be so prescribed with respect—

(a) to enforcement notices;

(b) to stop notices; and

(c) to breach of condition notices

which relate to land in their area.

(2) A development order may make provision—

(a) for the entry relating to any enforcement notice, stop notice, or breach of condition notice, and everything relating to any such notice, to be removed from the register in such circumstances as may be specified in the order; and

(b) for requiring a county planning authority to supply to a district planning authority such information as may be so specified with regard to enforcement notices issued and stop notices and breach of condition notices served by the county planning authority.

(3) Every register kept under this section shall be available for inspection by the public at all reasonable hours.

[In Section 188(1) the words in [ ] were inserted by, and will come into effect on an appointed day under, the Local Government (Wales) Act 1994.]

Enforcement of orders for discontinuance of use, etc.

189. Penalties for contravention of orders under s. 102 and Schedule 9

(1) Any person who without planning permission—

(a) uses land, or causes or permits land to be used—

(i) for any purpose for which an order under section 102 or paragraph 1 of Schedule 9 has required that its use shall be discontinued; or

(ii) in contravention of any condition imposed by such an order by virtue of subsection (1) of that section or, as the case may be, sub-paragraph (1) of that paragraph; or

(b) resumes, or causes or permits to be resumed, development consisting of the winning and working of minerals or involving the depositing of waste the resumption of which an order under paragraph 3 of that Schedule has prohibited; or

(c) contravenes, or causes or permits to be contravened, any such requirement as is specified in sub-paragraph (3) or (4) of that paragraph,

shall be guilty of an offence.

(2) Any person who contravenes any requirement of an order under paragraph 5 or 6 of that Schedule or who causes or permits any requirement of such an order to be contravened shall be guilty of an offence.

(3) Any person guilty of an offence under this section shall be liable—

(a) on summary conviction, to a fine not exceeding the statutory maximum; and

(b) on conviction on indictment, to a fine.

(4) It shall be a defence for a person charged with an offence under this section to prove that he took all reasonable measures and exercised all due diligence to avoid commission of the offence by himself or by any person under his control.

Town and Country Planning Act 1990

(5) If in any case the defence provided by subsection (4) involves an allegation that the commission of the offence was due to the act or default of another person or due to reliance on information supplied by another person, the person charged shall not, without the leave of the court, be entitled to rely on the defence unless, within a period ending seven clear days before the hearing, he has served on the prosecutor a notice in writing giving such information identifying or assisting in the identification of the other person as was then in his possession.

190. Enforcement of orders under s. 102 and Schedule 9
(1) This section applies where—
    (a) any step required by an order under section 102 or paragraph 1 of Schedule 9 to be taken for the alteration or removal of any buildings or works or any plant or machinery;
    (b) any step required by an order under paragraph 3 of that Schedule to be taken—
        (i) for the alteration or removal of plant or machinery; or
        (ii) for the removal or alleviation of any injury to amenity; or
    (c) any step for the protection of the environment required to be taken by an order under paragraph 5 or 6 of that Schedule,
has not been taken within the period specified in the order or within such extended period as the local planning authority or, as the case may be, the mineral planning authority may allow.
(2) Where this section applies the local planning authority or, as the case may be, the mineral planning authority may enter the land and take the required step.
(3) Where the local planning authority or, as the case may be, the mineral planning authority have exercised their power under subsection (2) they may recover from the person who is then the owner of the land any expenses reasonably incurred by them in doing so.
(4) [repealed by the Planning and Compensation Act 1991]
(5) Section 276 of the Public Health Act 1936 shall apply in relation to any works executed by an authority under subsection (2) as it applies in relation to works executed by a local authority under that Act.

Certificate of lawful use or development

191. Certificate of lawfulness of existing use or development
(1) If any person wishes to ascertain whether—
    (a) any existing use of buildings or other land is lawful;
    (b) any operations which have been carried out in, on, over or under land are lawful; or
    (c) any other matter constituting a failure to comply with any condition or limitation subject to which planning permission has been granted is lawful,
he may make an application for the purpose to the local planning authority specifying the land and describing the use, operations or other matter.
(2) For the purposes of this Act uses and operations are lawful at any time if—
    (a) no enforcement action may then be taken in respect of them (whether because they did not involve development or require planning permission or because the time for enforcement action has expired or for any other reason); and
    (b) they do not constitute a contravention of any of the requirements of any enforcement not then in force.
(3) For the purposes of this Act any matter constituting a failure to comply with any condition or, limitation subject to which planning permission has been granted is lawful at any time if—
    (a) the time for taking enforcement action in respect of the failure has then expired; and

(b) it does not constitute a contravention of any of the requirements of any enforcement notice or breach of condition notice then in force.

(4) If, on an application under this section, the local planning authority are provided with information satisfying them of the lawfulness at the time of the application of the use, operations or other matter described in the application, or that description as modified by the local planning authority or a description substituted by them, they shall issue a certificate to that effect; and in any other case they shall refuse the application.

(5) A certificate under this section shall—

(a) specify the land to which it relates;

(b) describe the use, operations or other matter in question (in the case of any use falling within one of the classes specified in an order under section 55(2)(f), identifying it by reference to that class);

(c) give the reasons for determining the use, operations or other matter to be lawful; and

(d) specify the date of the application for the certificate.

(6) The lawfulness of any use, operations or other matter for which a certificate is in force under this section shall be conclusively presumed.

(7) A certificate under this section in respect of any use shall also have effect, for the purposes of the following enactments, as if it were a grant of planning permission—

(a) section 3(3) of the Caravan Sites and Control of Development Act 1960;

(b) section 5(2) of the Control of Pollution Act 1974; and

(c) section 36(2)(a) of the Environmental Protection Act 1990.

192. Certificate of lawfulness of proposed use or development

(1) If any person wishes to ascertain whether—

(a) any proposed use of buildings or other land; or

(b) any operations proposed to be carried out in, on, over or under land,

would be lawful, he may make an application for the purpose to the local planning authority specifying the land and describing the use or operations in question.

(2) If, on an application under this section, the local planning authority are provided with information satisfying them that the use or operations described in the application would be lawful if instituted or begun at the time of the application, they shall issue a certificate to that effect; and in any other case they shall refuse the application.

(3) A certificate under this section shall—

(a) specify the land to which it relates;

(b) describe the use or operations in question (in the case of any use falling within one of the classes specified in an order under section 55(2)(f), identifying it by reference to that class);

(c) give the reasons for determining the use or operations to be lawful; and

(d) specify the date of the application for the certificate.

(4) The lawfulness of any use or operations for which a certificate is in force under this section shall be conclusively presumed unless there is a material change, before the use is instituted or the operations are begun, in any of the matters relevant to determining such lawfulness.

193. Certificates under sections 191 and 192: supplementary provisions

(1) An application for a certificate under section 191 or 192 shall be made in such manner as may be prescribed by a development order and shall include such particulars, and be verified by such evidence, as may be required by such an order or by any directions given under such an order or by the local planning authority.

(2) Provision may be made by a development order for regulating the manner in which applications for certificates under those sections are to be dealt with by local planning authorities.

(3) In particular, such an order may provide for requiring the authority—

(a) to give to any applicant within such time as may be prescribed by the order such notice as may be so prescribed as to the manner in which his application has been dealt with; and

(b) to give to the Secretary of State and to such other persons as may be prescribed by or under the order, such information as may be so prescribed with respect to such applications made to the authority, including information as to the manner in which any application has been dealt with.

(4) A certificate under either of those sections may be issued—

(a) for the whole or part of the land specified in the application; and

(b) where the application specifies two or more uses, operations or other matters, for all of them or some one or more of them;

and shall be in such form as may be prescribed by a development order.

(5) A certificate under section 191 or 192 shall not affect any matter constituting a failure to comply with any condition or limitation subject to which planning permission has been granted unless that matter is described in the certificate.

(6) In section 69 references to applications for planning permission shall include references to applications for certificates under section 191 or 192.

(7) A local planning authority may revoke a certificate under either of those sections if, on the application for the certificate—

(a) a statement was made or document used which was false in a material particular; or

(b) any material information was withheld.

(8) Provision may be made by a development order for regulating the manner in which certificates may be revoked and the notice to be given of such revocation.

194. Offences

(1) If any person, for the purpose of procuring a particular decision on an application (whether by himself or another) for the issue of a certificate under section 191 or 192—

(a) knowingly or recklessly makes a statement which is false or misleading in a material particular;

(b) with intent to deceive, uses any document which is false or misleading in a material particular; or

(c) with intent to deceive, withholds any material information,

he shall be guilty of an offence.

(2) A person guilty of an offence under subsection (1) shall be liable—

(a) on summary conviction, to a fine not exceeding the statutory maximum; or

(b) on conviction on indictment, to imprisonment for a term not exceeding two years, or a fine, or both.

(3) Notwithstanding section 127 of the Magistrates' Courts Act 1980, a magistrates' court may try an information in respect of an offence under subsection (1) whenever laid.

195. Appeals against refusal or failure to give decision on application

(1) Where an application is made to a local planning authority for a certificate under section 191 or 192 and—

(a) the application is refused or is refused in part, or

(b) the authority do not give notice to the applicant of their decision on the application within such period as may be prescribed by a development order or within such extended period as may at any time be agreed upon in writing between the applicant and the authority, the applicant may by notice appeal to the Secretary of State.

(2) On any such appeal, if and so far as the Secretary of State is satisfied—

(a) in the case of an appeal under subsection (1)(a), that the authority's refusal is not well-founded, or

(b) in the case of an appeal under subsection (1)(b), that if the authority had refused the application their refusal would not have been well-founded,

he shall grant the appellant a certificate under section 191 or, as the case may be, 192 accordingly or, in the case of a refusal in part, modify the certificate granted by the authority on the application.

(3) If and so far as the Secretary of State is satisfied that the authority's refusal is or, as the case may be, would have been well-founded, he shall dismiss the appeal.

(4) References in this section to a refusal of an application in part include a modification or substitution of the description in the application of the use, operations or other matter in question.

(5) For the purposes of the application of section 288(10)(b) in relation to an appeal in a case within subsection (1)(b) it shall be assumed that the authority decided to refuse the application in question.

(6) Schedule 6 applies to appeals under this section.

196. Further provisions as to references and appeals to the Secretary of State

(1) Before determining an appeal to him under section 195(1), the Secretary of State shall, if either the appellant or the local planning authority so wish, give each of them an opportunity of appearing before, and being heard by, a person appointed by the Secretary of State for the purpose.

(2) Where the Secretary of State grants a certificate under section 191 or 192 on such a reference or such an appeal, he shall give notice to the local planning authority of that fact.

(3) The decision of the Secretary of State on such an appeal shall be final.

(4) The information which may be prescribed as being required to be contained in a register kept under section 69 shall include information with respect to certificates under section 191 or 192 granted by the Secretary of State.

(5)—(7) [repealed by the Planning and Compensation Act 1991]

(8) Subsection (5) of section 250 of the Local Government Act 1972 (which authorises a Minister holding an inquiry under that section to make orders with respect to the costs of the parties) shall apply in relation to any proceedings before the Secretary of State on an appeal under section 195 as if those proceedings were an inquiry held by the Secretary of State under section 250.

Rights of entry for enforcement purposes

196A. Rights to enter without warrant

(1) Any person duly authorised in writing by a local planning authority may at any reasonable hour enter any land—

(a) to ascertain whether there is or has been any breach of planning control on the land or any other land;

(b) to determine whether any of the powers conferred on a local planning authority by this Part should be exercised in relation to the land or any other land;

(c) to determine how any such power should be exercised in relation to the land or any other land;

(d) to ascertain whether there has been compliance with any requirement imposed as a result of any such power having been exercised in relation to the land or any other land,

if there are reasonable grounds for entering for the purpose in question.

Town and Country Planning Act 1990

(2) Any person duly authorised in writing by the Secretary of State may at any reasonable hour enter any land to determine whether an enforcement notice should be issued in relation to the land or any other land, if there are reasonable grounds for entering for that purpose.

(3) The Secretary of State shall not so authorise any person without consulting the local planning authority.

(4) Admission to any building used as a dwellinghouse shall not be demanded as of right by virtue of subsection (1) or (2) unless twenty-four hours' notice of the intended entry has been given to the occupier of the building.

196B. Right to enter under warrant

(1) If it is shown to the satisfaction of a justice of the peace on sworn information in writing—

(a) that there are reasonable grounds for entering any land for any of the purposes mentioned in section 196A(1) or (2); and

(b) that—

(i) admission to the land has been refused, or a refusal is reasonably apprehended; or

(ii) the case is one of urgency,

the justice may issue a warrant authorising any person duly authorised in writing by a local planning authority or, as the case may be, the Secretary of State to enter the land.

(2) For the purposes of subsection (1)(b)(i) admission to land shall be regarded as having been refused if no reply is received to a request for admission within a reasonable period.

(3) A warrant authorises entry on one occasion only and that entry must be—

(a) within one month from the date of the issue of the warrant; and

(b) at a reasonable hour, unless the case is one of urgency.

196C. Rights of entry: supplementary provisions

(1) A person authorised to enter any land in pursuance of a right of entry conferred under or by virtue of section 196A or 196B (referred to in this section as 'a right of entry')—

(a) shall, if so required, produce evidence of his authority and state the purpose of his entry before so entering;

(b) may take with him such other persons as may be necessary; and

(c) on leaving the land shall, if the owner or occupier is not then present, leave it as effectively secured against trespassers as he found it.

(2) Any person who wilfully obstructs a person acting in the exercise of a right of entry shall be guilty of an offence and liable on summary conviction to a fine not exceeding level 3 on the standard scale.

(3) If any damage is caused to land or chattels in the exercise of a right of entry, compensation may be recovered by any person suffering the damage from the authority who gave the written authority for the entry or, as the case may be, the Secretary of State.

(4) The provisions of section 118 shall apply in relation to compensation under subsection (3) as they apply in relation to compensation under Part IV.

(5) If any person who enters any land, in exercise of a right of entry, discloses to any person any information obtained by him while on the land as to any manufacturing process or trade secret, he shall be guilty of an offence.

(6) Subsection (5) does not apply if the disclosure is made by a person in the course of performing his duty in connection with the purpose for which he was authorised to enter the land.

(7) A person who is guilty of an offence under subsection (5) shall be liable on summary conviction to a fine not exceeding the statutory maximum or on conviction on indictment to imprisonment for a term not exceeding two years or a fine or both.

(8) In sections 196A, and 196B and this section references to a local planning authority include, in relation to a building situated in Greater London, a reference to the Historic Buildings and Monuments Commission for England.

PART VIII
SPECIAL CONTROLS

CHAPTER I
TREES

General duty of planning authorities as respects trees

197. Planning permission to include appropriate provision for preservation and planting of trees

It shall be the duty of the local planning authority—

(a) to ensure, whenever it is appropriate, that in granting planning permission for any development adequate provision is made, by the imposition of conditions, for the preservation or planting of trees; and

(b) to make such orders under section 198 as appear to the authority to be necessary in connection with the grant of such permission, whether for giving effect to such conditions or otherwise.

Tree preservation orders

198. Power to make tree preservation orders

(1) If it appears to a local planning authority that it is expedient in the interests of amenity to make provision for the preservation of trees or woodlands in their area, they may for that purpose make an order with respect to such trees, groups of trees or woodlands as may be specified in the order.

(2) An order under subsection (1) is in this Act referred to as a 'tree preservation order'.

(3) A tree preservation order may, in particular, make provision—

(a) for prohibiting (subject to any exemptions for which provision may be made by the order) the cutting down, topping, lopping, uprooting, wilful damage or wilful destruction of trees except with the consent of the local planning authority, and for enabling that authority to give their consent subject to conditions;

(b) for securing the replanting, in such manner as may be prescribed by or under the order, of any part of a woodland area which is felled in the course of forestry operations permitted by or under the order;

(c) for applying, in relation to any consent under the order, and to applications for such consent, any of the provisions of this Act mentioned in subsection (4), subject to such adaptations and modifications as may be specified in the order.

(4) The provisions referred to in subsection (3)(c) are—

(a) the provisions of Part III relating to planning permission and to applications for planning permission, except sections 56, 62, 65, 69(3) and (4), 71, 91 to 96, 100 and 101 and Schedule 8; and

(b) sections 137 to 141, 143 and 144 (except so far as they relate to purchase notices served in consequence of such orders as are mentioned in section 137(1)(b) or (c));

(c) section 316.

(5) A tree preservation order may be made so as to apply, in relation to trees to be planted pursuant to any such conditions as are mentioned in section 197(a), as from the time when those trees are planted.

(6) Without prejudice to any other exemptions for which provision may be made by a tree preservation order, no such order shall apply—

(a) to the cutting down, uprooting, topping or lopping of trees which are dying or dead or have become dangerous, or

(b) to the cutting down, uprooting, topping or lopping of any trees in compliance with any obligations imposed by or under an Act of Parliament or so far as may be necessary for the prevention or abatement of a nuisance.

(7) This section shall have effect subject to—

(a) section 39(2) of the Housing and Planning Act 1986 (saving for effect of section 2(4) of the Opencast Coal Act 1958 on land affected by a tree preservation order despite its repeal); and

(b) section 15 of the Forestry Act 1967 (licences under that Act to fell trees comprised in a tree preservation order).

199. Form of and procedure applicable to orders

(1) A tree preservation order shall not take effect until it is confirmed by the local planning authority and the local planning authority may confirm any such order either without modification or subject to such modifications as they consider expedient.

(2) Provision may be made by regulations under this Act with respect—

(a) to the form of tree preservation orders, and

(b) to the procedure to be followed in connection with the making and confirmation of such orders.

(3) Without prejudice to the generality of subsection (2), the regulations may make provision—

(a) that, before a tree preservation order is confirmed by the local planning authority, notice of the making of the order shall be given to the owners and occupiers of land affected by the order and to such other persons, if any, as may be specified in the regulations;

(b) that objections and representations with respect to the order, if duly made in accordance with the regulations, shall be considered before the order is confirmed by the local planning authority; and

(c) that copies of the order, when confirmed by the authority, shall be served on such persons as may be specified in the regulations.

200. Orders affecting land where Forestry Commissioners interested

(1) In relation to land in which the Forestry Commissioners have an interest, a tree preservation order may be made only if—

(a) there is not in force in respect of the land a plan of operations or other working plan approved by the Commissioners under a forestry dedication covenant; and

(b) the Commissioners consent to the making of the order.

(2) For the purposes of subsection (1), the Forestry Commissioners are only to be regarded as having an interest in land if—

(a) they have made a grant or loan under section 1 of the Forestry Act 1979 in respect of it, or

(b) there is a forestry dedication covenant in force in respect of it.

(3) A tree preservation order in respect of such land shall not have effect so as to prohibit, or to require any consent for, the cutting down of a tree in accordance with a plan of operations or other working plan approved by the Forestry Commissioners, and for the time being in force, under a forestry dedication covenant or under the conditions of a grant or loan made under section 1 of the Forestry Act 1979.

(4) In this section—

(a) 'a forestry dedication covenant' means a covenant entered into with the Commissioners under section 5 of the Forestry Act 1967; and

(b) references to provisions of the Forestry Act 1967 and the Forestry Act 1979 include references to any corresponding provisions replaced by those provisions or by earlier corresponding provisions.

201. Provisional tree preservation orders

(1) If it appears to a local planning authority that a tree preservation order proposed to be made by that authority should take effect immediately without previous confirmation, they may include in the order as made by them a direction that this section shall apply to the order.

(2) Notwithstanding section 199(1), an order which contains such a direction—
    (a) shall take effect provisionally on such date as may be specified in it, and
    (b) shall continue in force by virtue of this section until—
        (i) the expiration of a period of six months beginning with the date on which the order was made; or
        (ii) the date on which the order is confirmed, whichever first occurs.

202. Power for Secretary of State to make tree preservation orders

(1) If it appears to the Secretary of State, after consultation with the local planning authority, to be expedient that a tree preservation order or an order amending or revoking such an order should be made, he may himself make such an order.

(2) Any order so made by the Secretary of State shall have the same effect as if it had been made by the local planning authority and confirmed by them under this Chapter.

(3) The provisions of this Chapter and of any regulations made under it with respect to the procedure to be followed in connection with the making and confirmation of any order to which subsection (1) applies and the service of copies of it as confirmed shall have effect, subject to any necessary modifications—
    (a) In relation to any proposal by the Secretary of State to make such an order,
    (b) in relation to the making of it by the Secretary of State, and
    (c) in relation to the service of copies of it as so made.

Compensation for loss or damage caused by orders, etc.

203. Compensation in respect of tree preservation orders

A tree preservation order may make provision for the payment by the local planning authority, subject to such exceptions and conditions as may be specified in the order, of compensation in respect of loss or damage caused or incurred in consequence—
    (a) of the refusal of any consent required under the order, or
    (b) of the grant of any such consent subject to conditions.

204. Compensation in respect of requirement as to replanting of trees

(1) This section applies where—
    (a) in pursuance of provision made by a tree preservation order, a direction is given by the local planning authority or the replanting of Secretary of State for securing the replanting of all or any part of a woodland area which is felled in the course of forestry operations permitted by or under the order; and
    (b) the Forestry Commissioners decide not to make any grant or loan under section 1 of the Forestry Act 1979 in respect of the replanting by reason that the direction frustrates the use of the woodland area for the growing of timber or other forest products for commercial purposes and in accordance with the rules or practice of good forestry.

(2) Where this section applies, the local planning authority exercising functions under the tree preservation order shall be liable, on the making of a claim in accordance with this section, to pay compensation in respect of such loss or damage, if any, as is caused or incurred in consequence of compliance with the direction.

(3) The Forestry Commissioners shall, at the request of the person under a duty to comply with such a direction as is mentioned in subsection (1)(a), give a certificate stating—
    (a) whether they have decided not to make such a grant or loan as is mentioned in subsection (1)(b), and

(b) if so, the grounds for their decision.

(4) A claim for compensation under this section must be served on the local planning authority—
  (a) within 12 months from the date on which the direction was given, or
  (b) where an appeal has been made to the Secretary of State against the decision of the local planning authority, within 12 months from the date of the decision of the Secretary of State on the appeal,
but subject in either case to such extension of that period as the local planning authority may allow.

205. Determination of compensation claims

(1) Except in so far as may be otherwise provided by any tree preservation order or any regulations made under this Act, any question of disputed compensation under section 203 or 204 shall be referred to and determined by the Lands Tribunal.

(2) In relation to the determination of any such question, the provisions of sections 2 and 4 of the Land Compensation Act 1961 shall apply subject to any necessary modifications and to the provisions of any regulations made under this Act.

Consequences of tree removal, etc.

206. Replacement of trees

(1) If any tree in respect of which a tree preservation order is for the time being in force—
  (a) is removed, uprooted or destroyed in contravention of the order, or
  (b) except in the case of a tree to which the order applies as part of a woodland,
is removed, uprooted or destroyed or dies at a time when its cutting down or uprooting is authorised only by virtue of section 198(6)(a),
it shall be the duty of the owner of the land to plant another tree of an appropriate size and species at the same place as soon as he reasonably can.

(2) The duty imposed by subsection (1) does not apply to an owner if on application by him the local planning authority dispense with it.

(3) In respect of trees in a woodland it shall be sufficient for the purposes of this section to replace the trees removed, uprooted or destroyed by planting the same number of trees—
  (a) on or near the land on which the trees removed, uprooted or destroyed stood, or
  (b) on such other land as may be agreed between the local planning authority and the owner of the land,
and in such places as may be designated by the local planning authority.

(4) In relation to any tree planted pursuant to this section, the relevant tree preservation order shall apply as it applied to the original tree.

(5) The duty imposed by subsection (1) on the owner of any land shall attach to the person who is from time to time the owner of the land.

207. Enforcement of duties as to replacement of trees

(1) If it appears to the local planning authority that—
  (a) the provisions of section 206, or
  (b) any conditions of a consent given under a tree preservation order which require the replacement of trees,
are not complied with in the case of any tree or trees, that authority may serve on the owner of the land a notice requiring him, within such period as may be specified in the notice, to plant a tree or trees of such size and species as may be so specified.

(2) A notice under subsection (1) may only be served within four years from the date of the alleged failure to comply with those provisions or conditions.

(3) A notice under subsection (1) shall specify a period at the end of which it is to take effect.

(4) The specified period shall be a period of not less than twenty-eight days beginning with the date of service of the notice.

(5) The duty imposed by section 206(1) may only be enforced as provided by this section and not otherwise.

208. Appeals against s. 207 notices

(1) A person on whom a notice under section 207(1) is served may appeal to the Secretary of State against the notice on any of the following grounds—

(a) that the provisions of section 206 or, as the case may be, the conditions mentioned in section 207(1)(b) are not applicable or have been complied with;

(aa) that in all the circumstances of the case the duty imposed by section 206(1) should be dispensed with in relation to any tree;

(b) that the requirements of the notice are unreasonable in respect of the period or the size or species of trees specified in it;

(c) that the planting of a tree or trees in accordance with the notice is not required in the interests of amenity or would be contrary to the practice of good forestry;

(d) that the place on which the tree is or trees are required to be planted is unsuitable for that purpose.

(2) An appeal under subsection (1) shall be made either—

(a) by giving written notice of the appeal to the Secretary of State before the end of the period specified in accordance with section 207(3); or

(b) by sending such notice to him in a properly addressed and pre-paid letter posted to him at such time that, in the ordinary course of post, it would be delivered to him before the end of that period.

(3) [repealed by the Planning and Compensation Act 1991]

(4) The notice shall indicate the grounds of the appeal and state the facts on which it is based.

(5) On any such appeal the Secretary of State shall, if either the appellant or the local planning authority so desire, give each of them an opportunity of appearing before and being heard by a person appointed by the Secretary of State for the purpose.

(6) Where such an appeal is brought, the notice under section 207(1) shall be of no effect pending the final determination or the withdrawal of the appeal.

(7) On such an appeal the Secretary of State may—

(a) correct any defect, error or misdescription in the notice; or

(b) vary any of its requirements,

if he is satisfied that the correction or variation will not cause injustice to the appellant or the local planning authority.

(8) Where the Secretary of State determines to allow the appeal, he may quash the notice.

(8A) The Secretary of State shall give any directions necessary to give effect to his determination on the appeal.

(9) Schedule 6 applies to appeals under this section.

(10) Where any person has appealed to the Secretary of State under this section against a notice, neither that person nor any other shall be entitled, in any other proceedings instituted after the making of the appeal, to claim that the notice was not duly served on the person who appealed.

(11) Subsection (5) of section 250 of the Local Government Act 1972 (which authorises a Minister holding an inquiry under that section to make orders with respect to the costs of the parties) shall apply in relation to any proceedings before the Secretary of State on an appeal under this section as if those proceedings were an inquiry held by the Secretary of State under section 250.

Town and Country Planning Act 1990

209. Execution and cost of works required by s. 207 notice
(1) If, within the period specified in a notice under section 207(1) for compliance with it, or within such extended period as the local planning authority may allow, any trees which are required to be planted by a notice under that section have not been planted, the local planning authority may—
    (a) enter the land and plant those trees, and
    (b) recover from the person who is then the owner of the land any expenses reasonably incurred by them in doing so.
(2) Where such a notice has been served—
    (a) any expenses incurred by the owner of any land for the purpose of complying with the notice, and
    (b) any sums paid by the owner of any land under subsection (1) in respect of expenses incurred by the local planning authority in planting trees required by such a notice to be planted,
shall be deemed to be incurred or paid for the use and at the request of any person, other than the owner, responsible for the cutting down, destruction or removal of the original tree or trees.
(3) Regulations made under this Act may provide that—
    (a) section 276 of the Public Health Act 1936 (power of local authorities to sell materials removed in executing works under that Act subject to accounting for the proceeds of sale),
    (b) section 289 of that Act (power to require the occupier of any premises to permit works to be executed by the owner of the premises); or
    (c) section 294 of that Act (limit on liability of persons holding premises as agents or trustees in respect of the expenses recoverable under that Act),
shall apply, subject to such adaptations and modifications as may be specified in the regulations, in relation to any steps required to be taken by a notice under section 207(1).
(4) Regulations under subsection (3) applying section 289 of the Public Health Act 1936 may include adaptations and modifications for the purpose of giving the owner of land to which such a notice relates the right, as against all other persons interested in the land, to comply with the requirements of the notice.
(5) Regulations under subsection (3) may also provide for the charging on the land of any expenses recoverable by a local authority or National Park Authority under subsection (1).
(6) Any person who wilfully obstructs a person acting in the exercise of the power under subsection (1)(a) shall be guilty of an offence and liable on summary conviction to a fine not exceeding level 3 on the standard scale.
[The reference to a National Park Authority was inserted by the Environment Act 1995; see note to Section 4A supra.]

210. Penalties for non-compliance with tree preservation order
(1) If any person, in contravention of a tree preservation order—
    (a) cuts down, uproots or wilfully destroys a tree, or
    (b) wilfully damages, tops or lops a tree in such a manner as to be likely to destroy it,
he shall be guilty of an offence.
(2) A person guilty of an offence under subsection (1) shall be liable—
    (a) on summary convicton to a fine not exceeding £20,000;
    (b) on conviction on indictment, to a fine.
(3) In determining the amount of any fine to be imposed on a person convicted of an offence under subsection (1), the court shall in particular have regard to any financial benefit which has accrued or appears likely to accrue to him in consequence of the offence.

(4) If any person contravenes the provisions of a tree preservation order otherwise than as mentioned in subsection (1), he shall be guilty of an offence and liable on summary conviction to a fine not exceeding level 4 on the standard scale.

(5) [repealed]

Trees in conservation areas

211. Preservation of trees in conservation areas

(1) Subject to the provisions of this section and section 212, any person who, in relation to a tree to which this section applies, does any act which might by virtue of section 198(3)(a) be prohibited by a tree preservation order shall be guilty of an offence.

(2) Subject to section 212, this section applies to any tree in a conservation area in respect of which no tree preservation order is for the time being in force.

(3) It shall be a defence for a person charged with an offence under subsection (1) to prove—

(a) that he served notice of his intention to do the act in question (with sufficient particulars to identify the tree) on the local planning authority in whose area the tree is or was situated; and

(b) that he did the act in question—

(i) with the consent of the local planning authority in whose area the tree is or was situated, or

(ii) after the expiry of the period of six weeks from the date of the notice but before the expiry of the period of two years from that date.

(4) Section 210 shall apply to an offence under this section as it applies to a contravention of a tree preservation order.

212. Power to disapply s. 211

(1) The Secretary of State may by regulations direct that section 211 shall not apply in such cases as may be specified in the regulations.

(2) Without prejudice to the generality of subsection (1), the regulations may be framed so as to exempt from the application of that section cases defined by reference to all or any of the following matters—

(a) acts of such descriptions or done in such circumstances or subject to such conditions as may be specified in the regulations;

(b) trees in such conservation areas as may be so specified;

(c) trees of a size or species so specified; or

(d) trees belonging to persons or bodies of a description so specified.

(3) The regulations may, in relation to any matter by reference to which an exemption is conferred by them, make different provision for different circumstances.

(4) Regulations under subsection (1) may in particular, but without prejudice to the generality of that subsection, exempt from the application of section 211 cases exempted from section 198 by subsection (6) of that section.

213. Enforcement of controls as respects trees in conservation areas

(1) If any tree to which section 211 applies—

(a) is removed, uprooted or destroyed in contravention of that section; or

(b) is removed, uprooted or destroyed or dies at a time when its cutting down or uprooting is authorised only by virtue of the provisions of such regulations under subsection (1) of section 212 as are mentioned in subsection (4) of that section,

it shall be the duty of the owner of the land to plant another tree of an appropriate size and species at the same place as soon as he reasonably can.

(2) The duty imposed by subsection (1) does not apply to an owner if on application by him the local planning authority dispense with it.

(3) The duty imposed by subsection (1) on the owner of any land attaches to the person who is from time to time the owner of the land and may be enforced as provided by section 207 and not otherwise.

214. Registers of s. 211 notices
It shall be the duty of a local planning authority to compile and keep available for public inspection free of charge at all reasonable hours and at a convenient place a register containing such particulars as the Secretary of State may determine of notices under section 211 affecting trees in their area.

Injunctions

214A. Injunctions
Where a local planning authority consider it necessary or expedient for an actual or apprehended offence under section 210 or 211 to be restrained by injunction, they may apply to the court for an injunction, whether or not they have exercised or are proposing to exercise any of their other powers under this Chapter.

(2) Subsections (2) to (4) of section 187B apply to an application under this section as they apply to an application under that section.

Rights of entry

214B. Rights to enter without warrant
(1) Any person duly authorised in writing by a local planning authority may enter any land for the purpose of—
  (a) surveying it in connection with making or confirming a tree preservation order with respect to the land;
  (b) ascertaining whether an offence under section 210 or 211 has been committed on the land; or
  (c) determining whether a notice under section 207 should be served on the owner of the land,
if there are reasonable grounds for entering for the purpose in question.

(2) Any person duly authorised in writing by the Secretary of State may enter any land for the purpose of surveying it in connection with making, amending or revoking a tree preservation order with respect to the land, if there are reasonable grounds for entering for that purpose.

(3) Any person who is duly authorised in writing by a local planning authority may enter any land in connection with the exercise of any functions conferred on the authority by or under this Chapter.

(4) Any person who is an officer of the Valuation Office may enter any land for the purpose of surveying it, or estimating its value, in connection with a claim for compensation in respect of any land which is payable by the local planning authority under this Chapter (other than section 204).

(5) Any person who is duly authorised in writing by the Secretary of State may enter any land in connection with the exercise of any functions conferred on the Secretary of State by or under this Chapter.

(6) The Secretary of State shall not authorise any person as mentioned in subsection (2) without consulting the local planning authority.

(7) Admission shall not be demanded as of right—
  (a) by virtue of subsection (1) or (2) to any building used as a dwellinghouse; or
  (b) by virtue of subsection (3), (4) or (5) to any land which is occupied,
unless twenty-four hours' notice of the intended entry has been given to the occupier.

(8) Any right to enter by virtue of this section shall be exercised at a reasonable hour.

214C. Right to enter under warrant

(1) If it is shown to the satisfaction of a justice of the peace on sworn information in writing—

(a) that there are reasonable grounds for entering any land for any of the purposes mentioned in section 214B(1) or (2); and

(b) that—

(i) admission to the land has been refused, or a refusal is reasonably apprehended; or

(ii) the case is one of urgency,

the justice may issue a warrant authorising any person duly authorised in writing by a local planning authority or, as the case may be, the Secretary of State to enter the land.

(2) For the purposes of subsection (1)(b)(i) admission to land shall be regarded as having been refused if no reply is received to a request for admission within a reasonable period.

(3) A warrant authorises entry on one occasion only and that entry must be—

(a) within one month from the date of the issue of the warrant; and

(b) at a reasonable hour, unless the case is one of urgency.

214D. Rights of entry: supplementary provisions

(1) Any power conferred under or by virtue of section 214B or 214C to enter land (referred to in this section as 'a right of entry') shall be construed as including power to take samples from any tree and samples of the soil.

(2) A person authorised to enter land in the exercise of a right of entry—

(a) shall, if so required, produce evidence of his authority and state the purpose of his entry before so entering;

(b) may take with him such other persons as may be necessary; and

(c) on leaving the land shall, if the owner or occupier is not then present, leave it as effectively secured against trespassers as he found it.

(3) Any person who wilfully obstructs a person acting in the exercise of a right of entry shall be guilty of an offence and liable on summary conviction to a fine not exceeding level 3 on the standard scale.

(4) If any damage is caused to land or chattels in the exercise of a right of entry, compensation may be recovered by any person suffering the damage from the authority who gave the written authority for the entry or, as the case may be, the Secretary of State.

(5) The provisions of section 118 shall apply in relation to compensation under subsection (4) as they apply in relation to compensation under Part IV.

CHAPTER II
LAND ADVERSELY AFFECTING AMENITY OF NEIGHBOURHOOD

215. Power to require proper maintenance of land

(1) If it appears to the local planning authority that the amenity of a part of their area, or of an adjoining area, is adversely affected by the condition of land in their area, they may serve on the owner and occupier of the land a notice under this section.

(2) The notice shall require such steps for remedying the condition of the land as may be specified in the notice to be taken within such period as may be so specified.

(3) Subject to the following provisions of this Chapter, the notice shall take effect at the end of such period as may be specified in the notice.

(4) That period shall not be less than 28 days after the service of the notice.

216. Penalty for non-compliance with s. 215 notice

(1) The provisions of this section shall have effect where a notice has been served under section 215.

(2) If any owner or occupier of the land on whom the notice was served fails to take steps required by the notice within the period specified in it for compliance with it, he shall be guilty of an offence and liable on summary conviction to a fine not exceeding level 3 on the standard scale.

(3) Where proceedings have been brought under subsection (2) against a person as the owner of the land and he has, at some time before the end of the compliance period, ceased to be the owner of the land, if he—

(a) duly lays information to that effect, and

(b) gives the prosecution not less than three clear days' notice of his intention,

he shall be entitled to have the person who then became the owner of the land brought before the court in the proceedings.

(4) Where proceedings have been brought under subsection (2) against a person as the occupier of the land and he has, at some time before the end of the compliance period, ceased to be the occupier of the land, if he—

(a) duly lays information to that effect, and

(b) gives the prosecution not less than three clear days' notice of his intention,

he shall be entitled to have brought before the court in the proceedings the person who then became the occupier of the land or, if nobody then became the occupier, the person who is the owner at the date of the notice.

(5) Where in such proceedings—

(a) it has been proved that any steps required by the notice under section 215 have not been taken within the compliance period, and

(b) the original defendant proves that the failure to take those steps was attributable, in whole or in part, to the default of a person specified in a notice under subsection (3) or (4),

then—

(i) that person may be convicted of the offence; and

(ii) if the original defendant also proves that he took all reasonable steps to ensure compliance with the notice, he shall be acquitted of the offence.

(6) If, after a person has been convicted under the previous provisions of this section, he does not as soon as practicable do everything in his power to secure compliance with the notice, he shall be guilty of a further offence and liable on summary conviction to a fine not exceeding [one-tenth of level 3 on the standard scale] for each day following his first conviction on which any of the requirements of the notice remain unfulfilled.

(7) Any reference in this section to the compliance period, in relation to a notice, is a reference to the period specified in the notice for compliance with it or such extended period as the local planning authority who served the notice may allow for compliance.

217. Appeal to magistrates' court against s. 215 notice

(1) A person on whom a notice under section 215 is served, or any other person having an interest in the land to which the notice relates, may, at any time within the period specified in the notice as the period at the end of which it is to take effect, appeal against the notice on any of the following grounds—

(a) that the condition of the land to which the notice relates does not adversely affect the amenity of any part of the area of the local planning authority who served the notice, or of any adjoining area;

(b) that the condition of the land to which the notice relates is attributable to, and such as results in the ordinary course of events from, the carrying on of operations or a use of land which is not in contravention of Part III;

(c) that the requirements of the notice exceed what is necessary for preventing the condition of the land from adversely affecting the amenity of any part of the area of the local planning authority who served the notice, or of any adjoining area;

(d) that the period specified in the notice as the period within which any steps required by the notice are to be taken falls short of what should reasonably be allowed.

(2) Any appeal under this section shall be made to a magistrates' court acting for the petty sessions area in which the land in question is situated.

(3) Where such an appeal is brought, the notice to which it relates shall be of no effect pending the final determination or withdrawal of the appeal.

(4) On such an appeal the magistrates' court may correct any informality, defect or error in the notice if satisfied that the informality, defect or error is not material.

(5) On the determination of such an appeal the magistrates' court shall give directions for giving effect to their determination, including, where appropriate, directions for quashing the notice or for varying the terms of the notice in favour of the appellant.

(6) Where any person has appealed to a magistrates' court under this section against a notice, neither that person nor any other shall be entitled, in any other proceedings instituted after the making of the appeal, to claim that the notice was not duly served on the person who appealed.

218. Further appeal to the Crown Court

Where an appeal has been brought under section 217, an appeal agains the decision of the magistrates' court on that appeal may be brought to the Crown Court by the appellant or by the local planning authority who served the notice in question under section 215.

219. Execution and cost of works required by s. 215 notice

(1) If, within the period specified in a notice under section 215 in accordance with subsection (2) of that section, or within such extended period as the local planning authority who served the notice may allow, any steps required by the notice to be taken have not been taken, the local planning authority who served the notice may—

(a) enter the land and take those steps, and

(b) recover from the person who is then the owner of the land any expenses reasonably incurred by them in doing so.

(2) Where a notice has been served under section 215—

(a) any expenses incurred by the owner or occupier of any land for the purpose of complying with the notice, and

(b) any sums paid by the owner of any land under subsection (1) in respect of expenses incurred by the local planning authority in taking steps required by such a notice,

shall be deemed to be incurred or paid for the use and at the request of the person who caused or permitted the land to come to be in the condition in which it was when the notice was served.

(3) Regulations made under this Act may provide that—

(a) section 276 of the Public Health Act 1936 (power of local authorities to sell materials removed in executing works under that Act subject to accounting for the proceeds of sale):

(b) section 289 of that Act (power to require the occupier of any premises to permit works to be executed by the owner of the premises); or

(c) section 294 of that Act (limit on liability of persons holding premises as agents or trustees in respect of the expenses recoverable under that Act),

shall apply, subject to such adaptations and modifications as may be specified in the regulations, in relation to any steps required to be taken by a notice under section 215.

(4) Regulations under subsection (3) applying section 289 of the Public Health Act 1936 may include adaptations and modifications for the purpose of giving the owner of land to which a notice under section 215 relates the right, as against all other persons interested in the land, to comply with the requirements of the enforcement notice.

(5) Regulations under subsection (3) may also provide for the charging on the land of any expenses recoverable by a local authority under subsection (1).

(6) [repealed]

CHAPTER III
ADVERTISEMENTS

Advertisement regulations

220. Regulations controlling display of advertisements

(1) Regulations under this Act shall make provision for restricting or regulating the display of advertisements so far as appears to the Secretary of State to be expedient in the interests of amenity or public safety.

(2) Without prejudice to the generality of subsection (1), any such regulations may provide—

(a) for regulating the dimensions, appearance and position of advertisements which may be displayed, the sites on which advertisements may be displayed and the manner in which they are to be affixed to the land;

(b) for requiring the consent of the local planning authority to be obtained for the display of advertisements, or of advertisements of any class specified in the regulations;

(c) for applying, in relation to any such consent and to applications for such consent, any of the provisions mentioned in subsection (3), subject to such adaptations and modifications as may be specified in the regulations;

(d) for the constitution, for the purposes of the regulations, of such advisory committees as may be prescribed by the regulations, and for determining the manner in which the expenses of any such committee are to be defrayed.

(3) The provisions referred to in subsection (2)(c) are—

(a) the provisions of Part III relating to planning permission and to applications for planning permission, except sections 56, 62, 65, 69(3) and (4), 71, 91 to 96, 100 and 101 and Schedule 8;

(b) sections 137 to 141, 143 and 144 (except so far as they relate to purchase notices served in consequence of such orders as are mentioned in section 137(l)(b) or (c));

(c) section 316.

(4) Without prejudice to the generality of the powers conferred by this section, regulations made for the purposes of this section may provide that any appeal from the decision of the local planning authority, on an application for their consent under the regulations, shall be to an independent tribunal constituted in accordance with the regulations, instead of being an appeal to the Secretary of State.

(5) If any tribunal is so constituted, the Secretary of State may pay to the chairman and members of the tribunal such remuneration, whether by way of salaries or by way of fees, and such reasonable allowances in respect of expenses properly incurred in the performance of their duties, as he may with the consent of the Treasury determine.

221. Power to make different advertisement regulations for different areas

(1) Regulations made for the purposes of section 220 may make different provision with respect to different areas, and in particular may make special provision—

(a) with respect to conservation areas;

(b) with respect to areas defined for the purposes of the regulations as experimental areas, and

(c) with respect to areas defined for the purposes of the regulations as areas of special control.

(2) An area may be defined as an experimental area for a prescribed period for the purpose of assessing the effect an amenity or public safety of advertisements of a prescribed description.

(3) An area may be defined as an area of special control if it is—

(a) a rural area, or

(b) an area which appears to the Secretary of State to require special protection on grounds of amenity.

(4) Without prejudice to the generality of subsection (1), the regulations may prohibit the display in an area of special control of all advertisements except advertisements of such classes (if any) as may be prescribed.

(5) Areas of special control for the purposes of regulations under this section may be defined by means of orders made or approved by the Secretary of State in accordance with the provisions of the regulations.

(6) Where the Secretary of State is authorised by the regulations to make or approve any such order as is mentioned in subsection (5), the regulations shall provide—

(a) for the publication of notice of the proposed order in such manner as may be prescribed,

(b) for the consideration of objections duly made to it, and

(c) for the holding of such inquiries or other hearings as may be prescribed,

before the order is made or approved.

(7) to (9) [repealed].

222. Planning permission not needed for advertisements complying with regulations

Where the display of advertisements in accordance with regulations made under section 220 involves development of land—

(a) planning permission for that development shall be deemed to be granted by virtue of this section, and

(b) no application shall be necessary for that development under Part III.

Repayment of expense of removing prohibited advertisements

223. Repayment of expense of removing prohibited advertisements

(1) Where, for the purpose of complying with any regulations made under section 220, works are carried out by any person—

(a) for removing an advertisement which was being displayed on 1st August 1948; or

(b) for discontinuing the use for the display of advertisements of a site used for that purpose on that date,

that person shall, on a claim made to the local planning authority within such time and in such manner as may be prescribed, be entitled to recover from that authority compensation in respect of any expenses reasonably incurred by him in carrying out those works.

(2) Except in so far as may be otherwise provided by any regulations made under this Act, any question of disputed compensation under this section shall be referred to and determined by the Lands Tribunal.

(3) In relation to the determination of any such question, the provisions of sections 2 and 4 of the Land Compensation Act 1961 shall apply subject to any necessary modifications and to the provisions of any regulations made under this Act.

Enforcement of control over advertisements

224. Enforcement of control as to advertisements

(1) Regulations under section 220 may make provision for enabling the local planning authority to require—

(a) the removal of any advertisement which is displayed in contravention of the regulations, or

(b) the discontinuance of the use for the display of advertisements of any site which is being so used in contravention of the regulations.

(2) For that purpose the regulations may apply any of the provisions of Part VII with respect to enforcement notices or the provisions of section 186, subject to such adaptations and modifications as may be specified in the regulations.

(3) Without prejudice to any provisions included in such regulations by virtue of subsection (1) or (2), if any person displays an advertisement in contravention of the regulations he shall be guilty of an offence and liable on summary conviction to a fine of such amount as may be prescribed, not exceeding level 3 on the standard scale and, in the case of a continuing offence, one tenth of level 3 on the standard scale for each day during which the offence continues after conviction.

(4) Without prejudice to the generality of subsection (3), a person shall be deemed to display an advertisement for the purposes of that subsection if—

(a) he is the owner or occupier of the land on which the advertisement is displayed; or

(b) the advertisement gives publicity to his goods, trade, business or other concerns.

(5) A person shall not be guilty of an offence under subsection (3) by reason only—

(a) of his being the owner or occupier of the land on which an advertisement is displayed, or

(b) of his goods, trade, business or other concerns being given publicity by the advertisement,

if he proves that it was displayed without his knowledge or consent.

225. Power to remove or obliterate placards and posters

(1) Subject to subsections (2) and (3), the local planning authority may remove or obliterate any placard or poster—

(a) which is displayed in their area; and

(b) which in their opinion is so displayed in contravention of regulations made under section 220.

(2) Subsection (1) does not authorise the removal or obliteration of a placard or poster displayed within a building to which there is no public right of access.

(3) Subject to subsection (4), where a placard or poster identifies the person who displayed it or caused it to be displayed, the local planning authority shall not exercise any power conferred by subsection (1) unless they have first given him notice in writing—

(a) that in their opinion it is displayed in contravention of regulations made under section 220; and

(b) that they intend to remove or obliterate it on the expiry of a period specified in the notice.

(4) Subsection (3) does not apply if—

(a) the placard or poster does not give his address, and

(b) the authority do not know it and are unable to ascertain it after reasonable inquiry.

(5) The period specified in a notice under subsection (3) must be not less than two days from the date of service of the notice.

PART IX
ACQUISITION AND APPROPRIATION OF LAND FOR PLANNING PURPOSES, ETC.

Aquisition for planning and public purposes

226. Compulsory acquisition of land for development and other planning purposes

(1) A local authority to whom this section applies shall, on being authorised to do so by the Secretary of State, have power to acquire compulsorily any land in their area which—

(a) is suitable for and required in order to secure the carrying out of development, redevelopment or improvement; or

(b) is required for a purpose which it is necessary to achieve in the interests of the proper planning of an area in which the land is situated.

(2) A local authority and the Secretary of State in considering for the purposes of subsection (1)(a) whether land is suitable for development, re-development or improvement shall have regard—

(a) to the provisions of the development plan, so far as material;

(b) to whether planning permission for any development on the land is in force; and

(c) to any other considerations which would be material for the purpose of determining an application for planning permission for development on the land.

(3) Where a local authority exercise their power under subsection (1) in relation to any land, they shall, on being authorised to do so by the Secretary of State, have power to acquire compulsorily—

(a) any land adjoining that land which is required for the purpose of executing works for facilitating its development or use; or

(b) where that land forms part of a common or open space or fuel or field garden allotment, any land which is required for the purpose of being given in exchange for the land which is being acquired.

(4) It is immaterial by whom the local authority propose that any activity or purpose mentioned in subsection (1) or (3)(a) should be undertaken or achieved (and in particular the local authority need not propose to undertake an activity or to achieve that purpose themselves).

(5) Where under subsection (1) the Secretary of State has power to authorise a local authority to whom this section applies to acquire any land compulsorily he may, after the requisite consultation, authorise the land to be so acquired by another authority, being a local authority within the meaning of this Act.

(6) Before giving an authorisation under subsection (5), the Secretary of State shall—

(a) if the land is in a non-metropolitan county [in England], consult with the councils of the county and the district;

(b) if the land is in a metropolitan district, consult with the council of the district;

[(bb) if the land is in Wales, consult with the council of the county or county borough]; and

(c) if the land is in a London borough, consult with the council of the borough.

(7) The Acquisition of Land Act 1981 shall apply to the compulsory acquisition of land under this section.

(8) The local authorities to whom this section applies are the councils of counties [county boroughs,], districts and London boroughs.

[In Section 226(6) and (8) the words in [ ] were inserted by, and will come into effect on an appointed day under, the Local Government (Wales) Act 1994.]

227. Acquisition of land by agreement

(1) The council of any county [county borough], district or London borough may acquire by agreement any land which they require for any purpose for which a local authority may be authorised to acquire land under section 226.

(2) The provisions of Part 1 of the Compulsory Purchase Act 1965 (so far as applicable), other than sections 4 to 8, section 10 and section 31, shall apply in relation to the acquisition of land under this section.

[In Section 227(1) the words in [ ] were inserted by and will come into effect on an appointed day under the Local Government (Wales) Act 1994.]

228. Compulsory acquisition of land by the Secretary of State for the Environment

(1) The Secretary of State for the Environment may acquire compulsorily—

(a) any land necessary for the public service; and

(b) any land which it is proposed to use not only for the public service but also—

(i) to meet the interests of proper planning of the area, or

(ii) to secure the best or most economic development or use of the land,

otherwise than for the public service.

(2) Where the Secretary of State has acquired or proposes to acquire any land under subsection (1) ('the primary land') and in his opinion other land ought to be acquired together with the primary land—

(a) in the interests of the proper planning of the area concerned; or

(b) for the purpose of ensuring that the primary land can be used, or developed and used, (together with that other land) in what appears to him to be the best or most economic way; or

(c) where the primary land or any land acquired, or which he proposes to acquire, by virtue of paragraph (a) or (b) of this subsection or of section 122(1)(a) or (b) of the Local Government, Planning and Land Act 1980, forms part of a common, open space or fuel or field garden allotment, for the purpose of being given in exchange for that land,

he may compulsorily acquire that other land.

(3) Subject to subsection (4), the power of acquiring land compulsorily under this section shall include power to acquire an easement or other right over land by the grant of a new right.

(4) Subsection (3) shall not apply to an easement or other right over any land which would for the purposes of the Acquisition of Land Act 1981 form part of a common, open space or fuel or field garden allotment.

(5) References in this section to the public service include the service in the United Kingdom—

(a) of any international organisation or institution whether or not the United Kingdom or Her Majesty's Government in the United Kingdom is or is to become a member;

(b) of any office or agency established by such an organisation or institution or for its purposes, or established in pursuance of a treaty (whether or not the United Kingdom is or is to become a party to the treaty);

(c) of a foreign sovereign Power or the Government of such a Power.

(6) For the purposes of subsection (5)(b) 'treaty' includes any international agreement and any, protocol or annex to a treaty or international agreement.

(7) The Acquisition of Land Act 1981 shall apply to any compulsory acquisition by the Secretary of State for the Environment under this section.

229. Appropriation of land forming part of common, etc.

(1) Any local authority may be authorised, by an order made by that authority and confirmed by the Secretary of State, to appropriate for any purpose for which that authority can be authorised to acquire land under any enactment any land to which this subsection applies which is for the time being held by them for other purposes.

(2) Subsection (1) applies to land which is or forms part of a common or fuel or field garden allotment (including any such land which is specially regulated by any enactment, whether public general or local or private), other than land which is Green Belt land within the meaning of the Green Belt (London and Home Counties) Act 1938.

(3) Section 19 of the Acquisition of Land Act 1981 (special provision with respect to compulsory purchase orders under that Act relating to land forming part of a

common, open space or fuel or field garden allotment) shall apply to an order under this section authorising the appropriation of land as it applies to a compulsory purchase order under that Act.

(4) Where land appropriated under this section was acquired under an enactment incorporating the Lands Clauses Acts, any works executed on the land after the appropriation has been effected shall, for the purposes of section 68 of the Lands Clauses Consolidation Act 1845 and section 10 of the Compulsory Purchase Act 1965, be deemed to have been authorised by the enactment under which the land was acquired.

(5) On an appropriation of land by a local authority under this section, where—

(a) the authority is not an authority to whom Part II of the 1959 Act applies;

(b) the land was immediately before the appropriation held by the authority for the purposes of a grant-aided function (within the meaning of that Act); or

(c) the land is appropriated by the authority for the purposes of such a function, such adjustments shall be made in the accounts of the local authority as the Secretary of State may direct.

(6) On an appropriation under this section which does not fall within subsection (5), such adjustment of accounts shall be made as is required by section 24(1) of the 1959 Act.

230. Acquisition of land for purposes of exchange

(1) Without prejudice to the generality of the powers conferred by sections 226 and 227, any power of a local authority to acquire land under those sections, whether compulsorily or by agreement, shall include power to acquire land required for giving in exchange—

(a) for land appropriated under section 229; or

(b) for Green Belt land appropriated in accordance with the Green Belt (London and Home Counties) Act 1938 for any purpose specified in a development plan.

(2) In subsection (1) 'Green Belt land' has the same meaning as in that Act.

231. Power of Secretary of State to require acquisition or development of land

(1) If the Secretary of State is satisfied after holding a local inquiry that the council of a county [County Borough], district or London borough have failed to take steps for the acquisition of any land which in his opinion ought to be acquired by them under section 226 he may by order require the council to take such steps as may be specified in the order for acquiring the land.

(2) If the Secretary of State is satisfied after holding a local inquiry that a local authority have failed to carry out, on land acquired by them under section 226 (or section 68 of the 1962 Act or section 112 of the 1971 Act) or appropriated by them under section 229 (or section 121 of the 1971 Act), any development which in his opinion ought to be carried out, he may by order require the authority to take such steps as may be specified in the order for carrying out the development.

(3) An order under this section shall be enforceable on the application of the Secretary of State by mandamus.

[In Section 231(1) the words in [ ] were inserted by, and will come into effect on an appointed day under, the Local Government (Wales) Act 1994.]

Appropriation, disposal and development of land held for planning purposes, etc.

232. Appropriation of land held for planning purposes

(1) Where any land has been acquired or appropriated by a local authority for planning purposes and is for the time being held by them for the purposes for which it was so acquired or appropriated, the authority may appropriate the land for any

purpose for which they are or may be authorised in any capacity to acquire land by virtue of or under any enactment not contained in this Part or in Chapter V of Part I of the Planning (Listed Buildings and Conservation Areas) Act 1990.

(2) Land which consists or forms part of a common, or formerly consisted or formed part of a common, and is held or managed by a local authority in accordance with a local Act shall not be appropriated under this section without the consent of the Secretary of State.

(3) Such consent may be given—

(a) either in respect of a particular appropriation or in respect of appropriations of any class, and

(b) either subject to or free from any conditions or limitations.

(4) Before appropriating under this section any land which consists of or forms part of an open space, a local authority—

(a) shall publish a notice of their intention to do so for at least two consecutive weeks in a newspaper circulating in their area; and

(b) shall consider any objections to the proposed appropriation which may be made to them.

(5) In relation to any appropriation under this section—

(a) subsection (4) of section 122 of the Local Government Act 1972 (which relates to the operation of section 68 of the Lands Clauses Consolidation Act 1845 and section 10 of the Compulsory Purchase Act 1965) shall have effect as it has effect in relation to appropriations under section 122 of that Act of 1972; and

(b) subsections (5) and (6) of section 229 of this Act shall have effect as they have effect in relation to appropriations under that section.

(6) In relation to any such land as is mentioned in subsection (1), this section shall have effect to the exclusion of the provisions of section 122(1) of the Local Government Act 1972.

233. Disposal by local authorities of land held for planning purposes

(1) Where any land has been acquired or appropriated by a local authority for planning purposes and is for the time being held by them for the purpose for which it was so acquired or appropriated, the authority may dispose of the land to such person, in such manner and subject to such conditions as appear to them to be expedient in order—

(a) to secure the best use of that or other land and any buildings or works which have been, or are to be, erected, constructed or carried out on it (whether by themselves or by any other person), or

(b) to secure the erection, construction or carrying out on it of any buildings or works appearing to them to be needed for the proper planning of the area of the authority.

(2) Land which consists of or forms part of a common, or formerly consisted or formed part of a common, and is held or managed by a local authority in accordance with a local Act shall not be disposed of under this section without the consent of the Secretary of State.

(3) The consent of the Secretary of State is also required where the disposal is to be for a consideration less than the best that can reasonably be obtained and is not—

(a) the grant of a term of seven years or less; or

(b) the assignment of a term of years of which seven years or less are unexpired at the date of the assignment.

(4) Before disposing under this section of any land which consists of or forms part of an open space, a local authority—

(a) shall publish a notice of their intention to do so for at least two consecutive weeks in a newspaper circulating in their area; and

(b) shall consider any objections to the proposed disposal which may be made to them.

(5) In relation to land acquired or appropriated for planning purposes for a reason mentioned in section 226(1)(a) or (3) the powers conferred by this section on a local authority, and on the Secretary of State in respect of the giving of consent to disposals under this section, shall be so exercised as to secure to relevant occupiers, so far as may be practicable, a suitable opportunity for accommodation.

(6) A person is a relevant occupier for the purposes of subsection (5) if—

(a) he was living or carrying on business or other activities on any such land as is mentioned in that subsection which the authority have acquired as mentioned in subsection (1),

(b) he desires to obtain accommodation on such land, and

(c) he is willing to comply with any requirements of the authority as to the development and use of such land;

and in this subsection 'development' includes redevelopment.

(7) In subsection (5) a suitable opportunity for accommodation means, in relation to any person, an opportunity to obtain accommodation on the land in question which is suitable to his reasonable requirements on terms settled with due regard to the price at which any such land has been acquired from him.

(8) In relation to any such land as is mentioned in subsection (1), this section shall have effect to the exclusion of section 123 of the Local Government Act 1972 (disposal of land by principal councils).

234. Disposal by Secretary of State of land acquired under s. 228

(1) The Secretary of State may dispose of land held by him and acquired by him or any other Minister under section 228 to such person, in such manner and subject to such conditions as appear to him expedient.

(2) In particular, the Secretary of State may under subsection (1) dispose of land held by him for any purpose in order to secure its use for that purpose.

235. Development of land held for planning purposes

(1) A local authority may—

(a) erect, construct or carry out on any land to which this section applies any building or work other than a building or work for the erection, construction or carrying out of which, whether by that local authority or by any other person, statutory power exists by virtue of, or could be conferred under, an alternative enactment; and

(b) repair, maintain and insure any buildings or works on such land and generally deal with such land in a proper course of management.

(2) This section applies to any land which—

(a) has been acquired or appropriated by a local authority for planning purposes, and

(b) is for the time being held by the authority for the purposes for which it was so acquired or appropriated.

(3) A local authority may exercise the powers conferred by subsection (1) notwithstanding any limitation imposed by law on their capacity by virtue of their constitution.

(4) A local authority may enter into arrangements with an authorised association for the carrying out by the association of any operation which, apart from the arrangements, the local authority would have power under this section to carry out, on such terms (including terms as to the making of payments or loans by the authority to the association) as may be specified in the arrangements.

(5) Nothing in this section shall be construed—

(a) as authorising any act or omission on the part of a local authority which is actionable at the suit of any person on any grounds other than such a limitation as is mentioned in subsection (3); or

(b) as authorising an authorised association to carry out any operation which they would not have power to carry out apart from subsection (4).

(6) In this section—

'alternative enactment' means any enactment which is not contained in this Part, in section 2, 5 or 6 of the Local Authorities (Land) Act 1963, in section 14(1) or (4) or 17(3) of the Industrial Development Act 1982 or in Chapter V of Part I of the Planning (Listed Buildings and Conservation Areas) Act 1990; and

'authorised association' means any society, company or body of persons—

(a) whose objects include the promotion, formation or management of garden cities, garden suburbs or garden villages and the erection, improvement or management of buildings for the working classes and others, and

(b) which does not trade for profit or whose constitution forbids the issue of any share or loan capital with interest or dividend exceeding the rate for the time being fixed by the Treasury.

Extinguishment of certain rights affecting acquired or appropriated land

236. Extinguishment of rights over land compulsorily acquired

(1) Subject to the provisions of this section, upon the completion of a compulsory acquisition of land under section 226, 228 or 230—

(a) all private rights of way and rights of laying down, erecting, continuing or maintaining any apparatus on, under or over the land shall be extinguished, and

(b) any such apparatus shall vest in the acquiring authority.

(2) Subsection (1) shall not apply—

(a) to any right vested in, or apparatus belonging to, statutory undertakers for the purpose of the carrying on of their undertaking, or

(b) to any right conferred by or in accordance with the telecommunications code on the operator of a telecommunications code system, or

(c) to any telecommunications apparatus kept installed for the purposes of any such system.

(3) In respect of any right or apparatus not falling within subsection (2), subsection (1) shall have effect subject—

(a) to any direction given by the acquiring authority before the completion of the acquisition that subsection (1) shall not apply to any right or apparatus specified in the direction; and

(b) to any agreement which may be made (whether before or after the completion of the acquisition) between the acquiring authority and the person in or to whom the right or apparatus in question is vested or belongs.

(4) Any person who suffers loss by the extinguishment of a right or the vesting of any apparatus under this section shall be entitled to compensation from the acquiring authority.

(5) Any compensation payable under this section shall be determined in accordance with the Land Compensation Act 1961.

237. Power to override easements and other rights

(1) Subject to subsection (3), the erection, construction or carrying out or maintenance of any building or work on land which has been acquired or appropriated by a local authority for planning purposes (whether done by the local authority or by a person deriving title under them) is authorised by virtue of this section if it is done in accordance with planning permission, notwithstanding that it involves—

(a) interference with an interest or right to which this section applies, or

(b) a breach of a restriction as to the user of land arising by virtue of a contract.

(2) Subject to subsection (3), the interests and rights to which this section applies are any easement, liberty, privilege, right or advantage annexed to land and adversely affecting other land, including any natural right to support.

(3) Nothing in this section shall authorise interference with any right of way or right of laying down, erecting, continuing or maintaining apparatus on, under or over land which is—

(a) a right vested in or belonging to statutory undertakers for the purpose of the carrying on of their undertaking, or

(b) a right conferred by or in accordance with the telecommunications code on the operator of a telecommunications code system.

(4) In respect of any interference or breach in pursuance of subsection (1), compensation—

(a) shall be payable under section 63 or 68 of the Lands Clauses Consolidation Act 1845 or under section 7 or 10 of the Compulsory Purchase Act 1965, and

(b) shall be assessed in the same manner and subject to the same rules as in the case of other compensation under those sections in respect of injurious affection where—

(i) the compensation is to be estimated in connection with a purchase under those Acts, or

(ii) the injury arises from the execution of works on land acquired under those Acts.

(5) Where a person deriving title under the local authority by whom the land in question was acquired or appropriated—

(a) is liable to pay compensation by virtue of subsection (4), and

(b) fails to discharge that liability,

the liability shall be enforceable against the local authority.

(6) Nothing in subsection (5) shall be construed as affecting any agreement between the local authority and any other person for indemnifying the local authority against any liability under that subsection.

(7) Nothing in this section shall be construed as authorising any act or omission on the part of any person which is actionable at the suit of any person on any grounds other than such an interference or breach as is mentioned in subsection (1).

238. Use and development of consecrated land

(1) Notwithstanding any obligation or restriction imposed under ecclesiastical law or otherwise in respect of consecrated land, any such land, which has been the subject of a relevant acquisition or appropriation, may subject to the following provisions of this section—

(a) if it has been acquired by a Minister, be used in any manner by him or on his behalf for any purpose for which he acquired the land; and

(b) in any other case, be used by any person in any manner in accordance with planning permission.

(2) Subsection (1) applies whether or not the land includes a building but it does not apply to land which consists of or forms part of a burial ground.

(3) Any use of consecrated land authorised by subsection (1) shall be subject—

(a) to compliance with the prescribed requirements with respect—

(i) to the removal and reinterment of any human remains, and

(ii) to the disposal of monuments and fixtures and furnishings; and

(b) to such provisions as may be prescribed for prohibiting or restricting the use of the land, either absolutely or until the prescribed consent has been obtained, so long as any church or other building used or formerly used for religious worship, or any part of it, remains on the land.

(4) Any use of land other than consecrated land which—

(a) has been the subject of a relevant acquisition or appropriation, and

(b) at the time of the acquisition or appropriation included a church or other building used or formerly used for religious worship or the site of such a church or building, shall be subject to compliance with such requirements as are mentioned in subsection (3)(a).

(5) Any regulations made for the purposes of subsection (3) or (4)—

(a) shall contain such provisions as appear to the Secretary of State to be requisite for securing that any use of land which is subject to compliance with the regulations shall, as nearly as may be, be subject to the same control as is imposed by law in the case of a similar use authorised by an enactment not contained in this Act or by a Measure, or as it would be proper to impose on a disposal of the land in question otherwise than in pursuance of an enactment or Measure;

(b) shall contain such requirements relating to the disposal of any such land as is mentioned in subsection (3) or (4) as appear to the Secretary of State requisite for securing that the provisions of those subsections are complied with in relation to the use of the land; and

(c) may contain such incidental and consequential provisions (including provision as to the closing of registers) as appear to the Secretary of State to be expedient for the purposes of the regulations.

(6) Nothing in this section shall be construed as authorising any act or omission on the part of any person which is actionable at the suit of any person on any grounds other than contravention of any such obligation, restriction or enactment as is mentioned in subsection (1).

239. Use and development of burial grounds

(1) Notwithstanding anything in any enactment relating to burial grounds or any obligation or restriction imposed under ecclesiastical law or otherwise in respect of them, any land consisting of a burial ground or part of a burial ground, which has been the subject of a relevant acquisition or appropriation, may—

(a) if it has been acquired by a Minister, be used in any manner by him or on his behalf for any purpose for which he acquired the land; and

(b) in any other case, be used by any person in any manner in accordance with planning permission.

(2) This section does not apply to land which has been used for the burial of the dead until the prescribed requirements with respect to the removal and reinterment of human remains, and the disposal of monuments, in or upon the land have been complied with.

(3) Nothing in this section shall be construed as authorising any act or omission on the part of any person which is actionable at the suit of any person on any grounds other than contravention of any such enactment, obligation or restriction as is mentioned in subsection (1).

240. Provisions supplemental to ss. 238 and 239

(1) Provision shall be made by any regulations made for the purposes of sections 238(3) and (4) and 239(2)—

(a) for requiring the persons in whom the land is vested to publish notice of their intention to carry out the removal and reinterment of any human remains or the disposal of any monuments;

(b) for enabling the personal representatives or relatives of any deceased person themselves to undertake—

(i) the removal and reinterment of the remains of the deceased, and

(ii) the disposal of any monument commemorating the deceased,

and for requiring the persons in whom the land is vested to defray the expenses of such removal, reinterment and disposal (not exceeding such amount as may be prescribed);

(c) for requiring compliance—

(i) with such reasonable conditions (if any) as may be imposed in the case of consecrated land, by the bishop of the diocese, with respect to the manner of removal and the place and manner of reinterment of any human remains and the disposal of any monuments, and

(ii) with any directions given in any case by the Secretary of State with respect to the removal and reinterment of any human remains.

(2) Subject to the provisions of any such regulations, no faculty is required—

(a) for the removal and reinterment in accordance with the regulations of any human remains, or

(b) for the removal or disposal of any monuments,

and section 25 of the Burial Act 1857 (prohibition of removal of human remains without the licence of the Secretary of State except in certain cases) does not apply to a removal carried out in accordance with the regulations.

(3) In sections 238 and 239 and this section—

'burial ground' includes any churchyard, cemetery or other ground, whether consecrated or not, which has at any time been set apart for the purposes of interment,

'monument' includes a tombstone or other memorial, and

'relevant acquisition or appropriation' means an acquisition made by a Minister, a local authority or statutory undertakers under this Part or Chapter V of Part I of the Planning (Listed Buildings and Conservation Areas) Act 1990 or compulsorily under any other enactment, or an appropriation by a local authority for planning purposes.

241. Use and development of open spaces

(1) Notwithstanding anything in any enactment relating to land which is or forms part of a common, open space or fuel or field garden allotment or in any enactment by which the land is specially regulated, such land which has been acquired by a Minister, a local authority or statutory undertakers under this Part or under Chapter V of Part I of the Planning (Listed Buildings and Conservation Areas) Act 1990 or compulsorily under any other enactment, or which has been appropriated by a local authority for planning purposes—

(a) if it has been acquired by a Minister, may be used in any manner by him or on his behalf for any purpose for which he acquired the land; and

(b) in any other case, may be used by any person in any manner in accordance with planning permission.

(2) Nothing in this section shall be construed as authorising any act or omission on the part of any person which is actionable at the suit of any person on any grounds other than contravention of any such enactment as is mentioned in subsection (1).

242. Overriding of rights of possession

If the Secretary of State certifies that possession of a house which—

(a) has been acquired or appropriated by a local authority for planning purposes, and

(b) is for the time being held by the authority for the purposes for which it was acquired or appropriated,

is immediately required for those purposes, nothing in the Rent Act 1977 or Part I of the Housing Act 1988 shall prevent the acquiring or appropriating authority from obtaining possession of the house.

Constitution of joint body to hold land for planning purposes

243. Constitution of joint body to hold land for planning purposes

(1) If it appears to the Secretary of State, after consultation with the local authorities concerned, to be expedient that any land acquired by a local authority for planning purposes should be held by a joint body, consisting of representatives of that authority and of any other local authority, he may by order provide for the establishment of such a joint body and for the transfer to that body of the land so acquired.

Town and Country Planning Act 1990 139

(2) Any order under this section providing for the establishment of a joint body may make such provision as the Secretary of State considers expedient with respect to the constitution and functions of that body.

(3) The provisions which may be included under subsection (2) include provisions—

(a) for incorporating the joint body;

(b) for conferring on them, in relation to land transferred to them as mentioned in subsection (1), any of the powers conferred on local authorities by this Part or Chapter V of Part I of the Planning (Listed Buildings and Conservation Areas) Act 1990 in relation to land acquired and held by such authorities for the purposes of this Part or that Chapter;

(c) for determining the manner in which their expenses are to be defrayed.

(4) Regulations under this Act may make such provision consequential upon or supplementary to the provisions of this section as appears to the Secretary of State to be necessary or expedient.

General and supplementary provisions

244. Powers of joint planning boards under Part IX

(1) A joint planning board or a board reconstituted under Schedule 17 to the Local Government Act 1972 shall, on being authorised to do so by the Secretary of State, have the same power to acquire land compulsorily as the local authorities to whom section 226 applies have under that section.

(2) Such a board shall have the same power to acquire land by agreement as the local authorities mentioned in subsection (1) of section 227 have under that subsection.

(3) Sections 226(1) and (7), 227, 229, 230, 232, 233 and 235 to 242 apply with the necessary modifications as if any such board were a local authority to which those sections applied.

(4) On being authorised to do so by the Secretary of State such a board shall have, for any purpose for which by virtue of this section they may acquire land compulsorily, the power which section 13 of the Local Government (Miscellaneous Provisions) Act 1976 confers on the local authorities to whom subsection (1) of that section applies to purchase compulsorily rights over land not in existence when their compulsory purchase is authorised, and subsections (2) to (5) of that section shall accordingly apply to the purchase of rights under this subsection as they apply to the purchase of rights under subsection (1) of that section.

[The words underlined in Section 244(1) will be repealed as from a day to be appointed under the Environment Act 1995.]

244A. Powers of National Park authorities under Part IX

(1) A National Park authority shall on being authorised to do so by the Secretary of State, have the same power to acquire land compulsorily as the local authorities to whom section 226 applies have under that section.

(2) A National Park authority shall have the same power to acquire land by agreement as the local authorities mentioned in subsection (1) of section 227 have under that subsection.

(3) Sections 226(1) and (7), 227, 229, 230, 232, 233 and 235 to 242 shall apply with the necessary modifications as if a National Park authority were a local authority to which those sections applied and as if the Park in relation to which it carries out functions were the authority's area.

[See above note to Section 4A for commencement.]

245. Modification of incorporated enactments for purposes of Part IX

(1) Where—

(a) it is proposed that land should be acquired compulsorily under section 226 or 228, and

(b) a compulsory purchase order relating to that land is submitted to the confirming authority in accordance with Part II of the Acquisition of Land Act 1981 or, as the case may be, is made in draft by the Secretary of State for the Environment in accordance with Schedule 1 to that Act,

the confirming authority or, as the case may be, that Secretary of State may disregard for the purposes of that Part or, as the case may be, that Schedule any objection to the order or draft which, in the opinion of that authority or Secretary of State, amounts in substance to an objection to the provisions of the development plan defining the proposed use of that or any other land.

(2) Where a compulsory purchase order authorising the acquisition of any land under section 226 is submitted to the Secretary of State in accordance with Part II of the Acquisition of Land Act 1981, then if the Secretary of State—

(a) is satisfied that the order ought to be confirmed so far as it relates to part of the land comprised in it; but

(b) has not for the time being determined whether it ought to be confirmed so far as it relates to any other such land,

he may confirm the order so far as it relates to the land mentioned in paragraph (a) and give directions postponing consideration of the order, so far as it relates to any other land specified in the directions, until such time as may be so specified.

(3) Where the Secretary of State gives directions under subsection (2), the notices required by section 15 of the Acquisition of Land Act 1981 to be published and served shall include a statement of the effect of the directions.

(4) In construing the Compulsory Purchase Act 1965 in relation to any of the provisions of this Part—

(a) references to the execution of the works shall be construed as including references to any erection, construction or carrying out of buildings or works authorised by section 237;

(b) in relation to the erection, construction or carrying out of any buildings or works so authorised, references in section 10 of that Act to the acquiring authority shall be construed as references to the person by whom the buildings or works in question are erected, constructed or carried out; and

(c) references to the execution of the works shall be construed as including also references to any erection, construction or carrying out of buildings or works on behalf of a Minister or statutory undertakers on land acquired by that Minister or those undertakers, where the buildings or works are erected, constructed or carried out for the purposes for which the land was acquired.

246. Interpretation of Part IX

(1) In this Part—

(a) any reference to the acquisition of land for planning purposes is a reference to the acquisition of it under section 226 or 227 of this Act or section 52 of the Planning (Listed Buildings and Conservation Areas) Act 1990 (or, as the case may be, under section 112 or 119 of the 1971 Act or section 68 or 71 of the 1962 Act); and

(b) any reference to the appropriation of land for planning purposes is a reference to the appropriation of it for purposes for which land can be (or, as the case may be, could have been) acquired under those sections.

(2) Nothing in sections 237 to 241 shall be construed as authorising any act or omission on the part of a local authority or body corporate in contravention of any limitation imposed by law on their capacity by virtue of their constitution.

(3) Any power conferred by section 238, 239 or 241 to use land in a manner mentioned in those sections shall be construed as a power so to use the land, whether

or not it involves the erection, construction or carrying out of any building or work or the maintenance of any building or work.

PART X
HIGHWAYS

Orders made by Secretary of State

247. Highways affected by development: orders by Secretary of State

(1) The Secretary of State may by order authorise the stopping up or diversion of any highway if he is satisfied that it is necessary to do so in order to enable development to be carried out—

(a) in accordance with planning permission granted under Part III, or

(b) by a government department.

(2) Such an order may make such provision as appears to the Secretary of State to be necessary or expedient for the provision or improvement of any other highway.

(3) Such an order may direct—

(a) that any highway provided or improved by virtue of it shall for the purposes of the Highways Act 1980 be a highway maintainable at the public expense;

(b) that the Secretary of State, or any county council, [county borough council] metropolitan district council or London borough council specified in the order or, if it is so specified, the Common Council of the City of London, shall be the highway authority for that highway;

(c) in the case of a highway for which the Secretary of State is to be the highway authority, that the highway shall, on such date as may be specified in the order, become a trunk road within the meaning of the Highways Act 1980.

(4) An order made under this section may contain such incidental and consequential provisions as appear to the Secretary of State to be necessary or expedient, including in particular—

(a) provision for authorising the Secretary of State, or requiring any other authority or person specified in the order—

(i) to pay, or to make contributions in respect of, the cost of doing any work provided for by the order or any increased expenditure to be incurred which is attributable to the doing of any such work; or

(ii) to repay, or to make contributions in respect of, any compensation paid by the highway authority in respect of restrictions imposed under section 1 or 2 of the Restriction of Ribbon Development Act 1935 in relation to any highway stopped up or diverted under the order;

(b) provision for the preservation of any rights of statutory undertakers in respect of any apparatus of theirs which immediately before the date of the order is under, in, on, over, along or across the highway to which the order relates.

(5) An order may be made under this section authorising the stopping up or diversion of any highway which is temporarily stopped up or diverted under any other enactment.

(6) The provisions of this section shall have effect without prejudice to—

(a) any power conferred on the Secretary of State by any other enactment to authorise the stopping up or diversion of a highway;

(b) the provisions of Part VI of the Acquisition of Land Act 1981; or

(c) the provisions of section 251(1).

[In Section 247(3)(b) the words in [ ] were inserted by, and will come into effect on an appointed day under, the Local Government (Wales) Act 1994.]

248. Highways crossing or entering route of proposed new highway, etc.

(1) This section applies where—

(a) planning permission is granted under Part III for constructing or improving, or the Secretary of State proposes to construct or improve, a highway ('the main highway'); and

(b) another highway crosses or enters the route of the main highway or is, or will be, otherwise affected by the construction or improvement of the main highway.

(2) Where this section applies, if it appears to the Secretary of State expedient to do so—

(a) in the interests of the safety of users of the main highway; or

(b) to facilitate the movement of traffic on the main highway,

he may by order authorise the stopping up or diversion of the other highway.

(3) Subsections (2) to (6) of section 247 shall apply to an order under this section as they apply to an order under that section, taking the reference in subsection (2) of that section to any other highway as a reference to any highway other than that which is stopped up or diverted under this section and the references in subsection (3) to a highway provided or improved by virtue of an order under that section as including a reference to the main highway.

249. Order extinguishing right to use vehicles on highway

(1) This section applies where—

(a) a local planning authority by resolution adopt a proposal for improving the amenity of part of their area, and

(b) the proposal involves the public ceasing to have any right of way with vehicles over a highway in that area, being a highway which is neither a trunk road nor a road classified as a principal road.

(2) The Secretary of State may, on an application by a local planning authority who have so resolved, by order provide for the extinguishment of any right which persons may have to use vehicles on that highway.

(3) An order under subsection (2) may include such provision as the Secretary of State (after consultation with every authority who are a local planning authority for the area in question and the highway authority) thinks fit for permitting the use on the highway of vehicles (whether mechanically propelled or not) in such cases as may be specified in the order, notwithstanding the extinguishment of any such right as is mentioned in that subsection.

(4) Such provision as is mentioned in subsection (3) may be framed by reference to—

(a) particular descriptions of vehicles, or

(b) particular persons by whom, or on whose authority, vehicles may be used, or

(c) the circumstances in which, or the times at which, vehicles may be used for particular purposes.

(5) No provision contained in, or having effect under, any enactment, being a provision prohibiting or restricting the use of footpaths, footways or bridleways shall affect any use of a vehicle on a highway in relation to which an order under subsection (2) has effect, where the use is permitted in accordance with provisions of the order included by virtue of subsection (3).

(6) If any authority who are a local planning authority for the area in which a highway to which an order under subsection (2) relates is situated apply to the Secretary of State in that behalf, he may by order revoke that order, and, if he does so, any right to use vehicles on the highway in relation to which the order was made which was extinguished by virtue of the order under that subsection shall be reinstated.

(7) Such an order as is mentioned in subsection (6) may make provision requiring the removal of any obstruction of a highway resulting from the exercise of powers under Part VIIA of the Highways Act 1980.

(8) Before making an application under subsection (2) or (6) the local planning authority shall consult with the highway authority (if different) and any other authority who are a local planning authority for the area in question.

(9) Subsections (2), (3), (4) and (6) of section 247 shall apply to an order under this section as they apply to an order under that section.

250. Compensation for orders under s. 249

(1) Any person who, at the time of an order under section 249(2) coming into force, has an interest in land having lawful access to a highway to which the order relates shall be entitled to be compensated by the local planning authority on whose application the order was made in respect of—

    (a) any depreciation in the value of his interest which is directly attributable to the order; and

    (b) any other loss or damage which is so attributable.

(2) [repealed by the Planning and Compensation Act 1991]

(3) A claim for compensation under this section shall be made to the local planning authority on whose application the order was made within the prescribed time and in the prescribed manner.

(4) For the purpose of assessing any such compensation the rules set out in section 5 of the Land Compensation Act 1961 shall, so far as applicable and subject to any necessary modifications, have effect as they have effect for the purpose of assessing compensation for the compulsory acquisition of an interest in land.

(5) Where an interest in land is subject to a mortgage—

    (a) any compensation to which this section applies which is payable in respect of depreciation of the value of that interest shall be assessed as if the interest were not subject to the mortgage;

    (b) a claim for any such compensation may be made by any mortgagee of the interest, but without prejudice to the making of a claim by the person entitled to the interest;

    (c) no compensation to which this section applies shall be payable in respect of the interest of the mortgagee (as distinct from the interest which is subject to the mortgage); and

    (d) any compensation to which this section applies which is payable in respect of the interest which is subject to the mortgage shall be paid to the mortgagee (or, if there is more than one mortgagee, to the first mortgagee) and shall in either case be applied by him as if it were proceeds of sale.

(6) Except in so far as may be otherwise provided by any regulations made under this Act, any question of disputed compensation under this section shall be referred to and determined by the Lands Tribunal.

(7) In relation to the determination of any such question, the provisions of sections 2 and 4 of the Land Compensation Act 1961 shall apply subject to any necessary modifications and to the provisions of any regulations made under this Act.

251. Extinguishment of public rights of way over land held for planning purposes

(1) Where any land has been acquired or appropriated for planning purposes and is for the time being held by a local authority for the purposes for which it was acquired or appropriated, the Secretary of State may by order extinguish any public right of way over the land if he is satisfied—

    (a) that an alternative right of way has been or will be provided; or

    (b) that the provision of an alternative right of way is not required.

(2) In this section any reference to the acquisition or appropriation of land for planning purposes shall be construed in accordance with section 246(1) as if this section were in Part IX.

(3) Subsection (1) shall also apply (with the substitution of a reference to the Broads Authority for the reference to the local authority) in relation to any land within the Broads which is held by the Broads Authority and which was acquired by, or

vested in, the Authority for any purpose connected with the discharge of any of its functions.

252. Procedure for making of orders

(1) Before making an order under section 247, 248, 249 or 251 the Secretary of State shall publish in at least one local newspaper circulating in the relevant area, and in the London Gazette, a notice—

    (a) stating the general effect of the order;

    (b) specifying a place in the relevant area where a copy of the draft order and of any relevant map or plan may be inspected by any person free of charge at all reasonable hours during a period of 28 days from the date of the publication of the notice ('the publication date'); and

    (c) stating that any person may within that period by notice to the Secretary of State object to the making of the order.

(2) Not later than the publication date, the Secretary of State shall serve a copy of the notice, together with a copy of the draft order and of any relevant map or plan—

    (a) on every local authority in whose area any highway or, as the case may be, any land to which the order relates is situated, and

    (aa) on any National Park authority which is the local planning authority for the area in which any highway or, as the case may be, any land to which the order relates is situated, and,

    (b) on any water, sewerage, hydraulic power or electricity undertakers or public gas supplier having any cables, mains, sewers, pipes or wires laid along, across, under or over any highway to be stopped up or diverted, or, as the case may be, any land over which a right of way is proposed to be extinguished, under the order.

(3) Not later than the publication date, the Secretary of State shall also cause a copy of the notice to be displayed in a prominent position at the ends of so much of any highway as is proposed to be stopped up or diverted or, as the case may be, of the right of way proposed to be extinguished under the order.

(4) If before the end of the period of 28 days mentioned in subsection (1)(b) an objection is received by the Secretary of State from any local authority, National Parks Authority or undertakers or public gas supplier on whom a notice is required to be served under subsection (2), or from any other person appearing to him to be affected by the order, and the objection is not withdrawn, then unless subsection (5) applies the Secretary of State shall cause a local inquiry to be held.

(5) If, in a case where the objection is made by a person other than such a local authority or undertakers or supplier, the Secretary of State is satisfied that in the special circumstances of the case the holding of such an inquiry is unnecessary he may dispense with the inquiry.

(6) Subsections (2) to (5) of section 250 of the Local Government Act 1972 (local inquiries: evidence and costs) shall apply in relation to an inquiry caused to be held by the Secretary of State under subsection (4).

(7) Where publication of the notice mentioned in subsection (1) takes place on more than one day, the references in this section to the publication date are references to the latest date on which it is published.

(8) After considering any objections to the order which are not withdrawn and, where a local inquiry is held, the report of the person who held the inquiry, the Secretary of State may, subject to subsection (9), make the order either without modification or subject to such modifications as he thinks fit.

(9) Where—

    (a) the order contains a provision requiring any such payment, repayment or contribution as is mentioned in section 247(4)(a); and

    (b) objection to that provision is duly made by an authority or person who would be required by it to make such a payment, repayment or contribution; and

Town and Country Planning Act 1990   145

(c) the objection is not withdrawn,
the order shall be subject to special parliamentary procedure.

(10) Immediately after the order has been made, the Secretary of State shall publish, in the manner specified in subsection (1), a notice stating that the order has been made and naming a place where a copy of the order may be seen at all reasonable hours.

(11) Subsections (2), (3) and (7) shall have effect in relation to a notice under subsection (10) as they have effect in relation to a notice under subsection (1).

(12) In this section—
'the relevant area', in relation to an order, means the area in which any highway or land to which the order relates is situated;
'local authority' means the council of a county, [county borough] district, parish [community] or London borough, a joint authority established by Part IV of the Local Government Act 1985, a housing action trust established under Part III of the Housing Act 1988 and the parish meeting of a rural parish not having a separate parish council;
and in subsection (2)—
    (i) the reference to water undertakers shall be construed as including a reference to the National Rivers Authority, and
    (ii) the reference to electricity undertakers shall be construed as a reference to holders of licences under section 6 of the Electricity Act 1989 who are entitled to exercise any power conferred by paragraph 1 of Schedule 4 to that Act.
[The references to a National Park Authority were introduced by the Environment Act 1995, see note to Section 4A supra, while the words in Section 252(12) in [ ] were inserted by, and will come into effect on an appointed day under, the Local Government (Wales) Act 1994.]

253. Procedure in anticipation of planning permission
(1) Where—
    (a) the Secretary of State would, if planning permission for any development had been granted under Part III, have power to make an order under section 247 or 248 authorising the stopping up or diversion of a highway in order to enable that development to be carried out, and
    (b) subsection (2), (3) or (4) applies,
then, notwithstanding that such permission has not been granted, the Secretary of State may publish notice of the draft of such an order in accordance with section 252.

(2) This subsection applies where the relevant development is the subject of an application for planning permission and either—
    (a) that application is made by a local authority, National Park Authority or statutory undertakers; or
    (b) that application stands referred to the Secretary of State in pursuance of a direction under section 77; or
    (c) the applicant has appealed to the Secretary of State under section 78 against a refusal of planning permission or of approval required under a development order or against a condition of any such permission or approval.

(3) This subsection applies where—
    (a) the relevant development is to be carried out by a local authority, National Park Authority or statutory undertakers and requires, by virtue of an enactment, the authorisation of a government department; and
    (b) the developers have made an application to the department for that authorisation and also requested a direction under section 90(1) that planning permission be deemed to be granted for that development.

(4) This subsection applies where the council of a county, [county borough] metropolitan district or London borough, National Park Authority or a joint planning

board certify that they have begun to take such steps, in accordance with regulations made by virtue of section 316, as are required to enable them to obtain planning permission for the relevant development.

(5) Section 252(8) shall not be construed as authorising the Secretary of State to make an order under section 247 or 248 of which notice has been published by virtue of subsection (1) until planning permission is granted for the development which occasions the making of the order.

[The references to National Parks Authorities were introduced by the Environment Act 1995, see note to Section 4A supra, while the words in section 253(4) in [ ] were inserted by, and will come into effect on an appointed day under, the Local Government (Wales) Act 1994.]

254. Compulsory acquisition of land in connection with highways

(1) The Secretary of State, or a local highway authority on being authorised by the Secretary of State to do so, may acquire land compulsorily—

(a) for the purpose of providing or improving any highway which is to be provided or improved in pursuance of an order under section 247, 248 or 249 or for any other purpose for which land is required in connection with the order; or

(b) for the purpose of providing any public right of way which is to be provided as an alternative to a right of way extinguished under an order under section 251.

(2) The Acquisition of Land Act 1981 shall apply to the acquisition of land under this section.

255. Concurrent proceedings in connection with highways

(1) In relation to orders under sections 247, 248 and 249, regulations made under this Act may make provision for securing that any proceedings required to be taken for the purposes of the acquisition of land under section 254 (as mentioned in subsection (1)(a) of that section) may be taken concurrently with any proceedings required to be taken for the purposes of the order.

(2) In relation to orders under section 251, regulations made under this Act may make provision for securing—

(a) that any proceedings required to be taken for the purposes of such an order may be taken concurrently with any proceedings required to be taken for the purposes of the acquisition of the land over which the right of way is to be extinguished; or

(b) that any proceedings required to be taken for the purposes of the acquisition of any other land under section 254 (as mentioned in subsection (1)(b) of that section) may be taken concurrently with either or both of the proceedings referred to in paragraph (a).

256. Telecommunication apparatus: orders by Secretary of State

(1) Where—

(a) in pursuance of an order under section 247, 248 or 249 a highway is stopped up or diverted or, as the case may be, any right to use vehicles on that highway is extinguished; and

(b) immediately before the date on which the order came into force there was under, in, on, over, along or across the highway any telecommunication apparatus kept installed for the purposes of a telecommunications code system,

the operator of that system shall have the same powers in respect of the apparatus as if the order had not come into force.

(2) Notwithstanding subsection (1), any person entitled to land over which the highway subsisted shall be entitled to require the alteration of the apparatus.

(3) Where—

(a) any such order provides for the improvement of a highway, for which the Secretary of State is not the highway authority, and

(b) immediately before the date on which the order came into force there was under, in, on, over, along or across the highway any telecommunication apparatus kept installed for the purposes of a telecommunications code system,
the local highway authority shall be entitled to require the alteration of the apparatus.

(4) Subsection (3) does not have effect so far as it relates to the alteration of any apparatus for the purpose of major highway works, major bridge works or major transport works within the meaning of Part III of the New Roads and Street Works Act 1991.

(5) Paragraph 1(2) of the telecommunications code (alteration of apparatus to include moving, removal or replacement of apparatus) shall apply for the purposes of this section as it applies for the purposes of that code.

(6) Paragraph 21 of the telecommunications code (restriction on removal of telecommunication apparatus) shall apply in relation to any entitlement conferred by this section to require the alteration, moving or replacement of any telecommunication apparatus as it applies in relation to an entitlement to require the removal of any such apparatus.

Orders by other authorities

257. Footpaths and bridleways affected by development: orders by other authorities

(1) Subject to section 259, a competent authority may by order authorise the stopping up or diversion of any, footpath or bridleway if they are satisfied that it is necessary to do so in order to enable development to be carried out—
    (a) in accordance with planning permission granted under Part III, or
    (b) by a government department.

(2) An order under this section may, if the competent authority are satisfied that it should do so, provide—
    (a) for the creation of an alternative highway for use as a replacement for the one authorised by the order to be stopped up or diverted, or for the improvement of an existing highway for such use;
    (b) for authorising or requiring works to be carried out in relation to any footpath or bridleway for whose stopping up or diversion, creation or improvement provision is made by the order;
    (c) or the preservation of any rights of statutory undertakers in respect of any apparatus of theirs which immediately before the date of the order is under, in, on, over, along or across any such footpath or bridleway;
    (d) for requiring any person named in the order to pay, or make contributions in respect of, the cost of carrying out any such works.

(3) An order may be made under this section authorising the stopping up or diversion of a footpath or bridleway which is temporarily stopped up or diverted under any other enactment.

(4) In this section 'competent authority' means—
    (a) in the case of development authorised by a planning permission, the local planning authority who granted the permission or, in the case of a permission granted by the Secretary of State, who would have had power to grant it; and
    (b) in the case of development carried out by a government department, the local planning authority who would have had power to grant planning permission on an application in respect of the development in question if such an application had fallen to be made.

258. Extinguishment of public rights of way over land held for planning purposes

(1) Where any land has been acquired or appropriated for planning purposes and is for the time being held by a local authority for the purposes for which it was

acquired or appropriated, then, subject to section 259, the local authority may by order extinguish any public right of way over the land, being a footpath or bridleway, if they are satisfied—

(a) that an alternative right of way has been or will be provided; or

(b) that the provision of an alternative right of way is not required.

(2) In this section any reference to the acquisition or appropriation of land for planning purposes shall be construed in accordance with section 246(1) as if this section were in Part IX.

(3) Subsection (1) shall also apply (with the substitution of a reference to the Broads Authority for the reference to the local authority) in relation to any land within the Broads which is held by the Broads Authority and which was acquired by, or vested in, the Authority for any purpose connected with the discharge of any of its functions.

259. Confirmation of orders made by other authorities

(1) An order made under section 257 or 258 shall not take effect unless confirmed by the Secretary of State or unless confirmed, as an unopposed order, by the authority who made it.

(2) The Secretary of State shall not confirm any such order unless satisfied as to every matter as to which the authority making the order are required under section 257 or, as the case may be, section 258 to be satisfied.

(3) The time specified—

(a) in an order under section 257 as the time from which a footpath or bridleway is to be stopped up or diverted; or

(b) in an order under section 258 as the time from which a right of way is to be extinguished,

shall not be earlier than confirmation of the order.

(4) Schedule 14 shall have effect with respect to the confirmation of orders under section 257 or 258 and the publicity for such orders after they are confirmed.

260. Telecommunication apparatus: orders by or on application of other authorities

(1) This section applies where—

(a) any order is made by a local authority under section 258(1), or on the application of a local authority under section 251(1), which extinguishes a public right of way; or

(b) any order is made by a competent authority under section 257 which authorises the stopping up or diversion of a footpath or bridleway,

and at the time of the publication of the notice required by section 252(1) or, as the case may be, paragraph 1 of Schedule 14 any telecommunication apparatus was kept installed for the purposes of a telecommunications code system under, in, on, over, along or across the land over which the right of way subsisted.

(2) In subsection (1) 'competent authority' has the same meaning as in section 257 and in the following provisions of this section references to the authority are to the authority who made the order or, as the case may be, to the authority on whose application it was made.

(3) The power of the operator of the telecommunications code system to remove the apparatus—

(a) shall, notwithstanding the making of the order, be exercisable at any time not later than the end of the period of three months from the date on which the right of way is extinguished or authorised to be stopped up or diverted; and

(b) if before the end of that period the operator of the system has given notice to the authority of his intention to remove the apparatus or a part of it, shall be exercisable in respect of the whole or, as the case may be, that part of the apparatus after the end of that period.

Town and Country Planning Act 1990 149

(4) The operator of the system may by notice given in that behalf to the authority not later than the end of that period abandon the telecommunication apparatus or any part of it.

(5) Subject to subsection (4), the operator of the system shall be deemed at the end of that period to have abandoned any part of the apparatus which the operator has then neither removed nor given notice of his intention to remove.

(6) The operator of the system shall be entitled to recover from the authority the expense of providing, in substitution for the apparatus and any other telecommunication apparatus connected with it which is rendered useless in consequence of the removal or abandonment of the first-mentioned apparatus, any telecommunication apparatus in such other place as the operator may require.

(7) Where under the previous provisions of this section the operator of the system has abandoned the whole or any part of any telecommunication apparatus, that apparatus or that part of it shall vest in the authority and shall be deemed, with its abandonment, to cease to be kept installed for the purposes of a telecommunications code system.

(8) As soon as reasonably practicable after the making of any such order as is mentioned in paragraph (a) or (b) of subsection (1) in circumstances in which that subsection applies in relation to the operator of any telecommunications code system, the person by whom the order was made shall give notice to the operator of the making of the order.

(9) Subsections (5) and (6) of section 256 apply for the purposes of this section as they apply for the purposes of that section.

Temporary highway orders: mineral workings

261. Temporary stopping up of highways for mineral workings

(1) Where the Secretary of State is satisfied—

(a) that an order made by him under section 247 for the stopping up or diversion of a highway is required for the purpose of enabling minerals to be worked by surface working; and

(b) that the highway can be restored, after the minerals have been worked, to a condition not substantially less convenient to the public,

the order may provide for the stopping up or diversion of the highway during such period as may be prescribed by or under the order and for its restoration at the expiration of that period.

(2) Where a competent authority within the meaning of section 257 are satisfied—

(a) that an order made by them under that section for the stopping up or diversion of a footpath or bridleway is required for the purpose of enabling minerals to be worked by surface working; and

(b) that the footpath or bridleway can be restored, after the minerals have been worked, to a condition not substantially less convenient to the public,

the order may provide for the stopping up or diversion of the footpath or bridleway during such period as may be prescribed by or under the order and for its restoration at the expiration of that period.

(3) Without prejudice to the provisions of section 247 or 257, any such order as is authorised by subsection (1) or (2) may contain such provisions as appear to the Secretary of State or, as the case may be, the competent authority to be expedient—

(a) for imposing upon persons who, apart from the order, would be subject to any liability with respect to the repair of the original highway during the period prescribed by or under the order a corresponding liability in respect of any highway provided in pursuance of the order;

(b) for the stopping up at the expiry of that period of any highway so provided and for the reconstruction and maintenance of the original highway;

and any provision included in the order in accordance with subsection (4) of section 247 or subsection (2) of section 257 requiring payment to be made in respect of any cost or expenditure under the order may provide for the payment of a capital sum in respect of the estimated amount of that cost or expenditure.

(4) In relation to any highway which is stopped up or diverted by virtue of an order under section 247 or 248, sections 271 and 272 shall have effect—

(a) as if for references to land which has been acquired as there mentioned and to the acquiring or appropriating authority there were substituted respectively references to land over which the highway subsisted and to the person entitled to possession of that land; and

(b) as if references in subsection (5) of each of those sections to a local authority or statutory undertakers included references to any person (other than a Minister) who is entitled to possession of that land,

and sections 275 to 278 shall have effect accordingly.

(5) Subsection (4) shall not apply to land constituting the site of a highway in respect of which opencast planning permission (within the meaning of section 51 of the Opencast Coal Act 1958) has been granted.

PART XI
STATUTORY UNDERTAKERS

Preliminary

262. Meaning of 'statutory undertakers'

(1) Subject to the following provisions of this section, in this Act 'statutory undertakers' means persons authorised by any enactment to carry on any railway, light railway, tramway, road transport, water transport, canal, inland navigation, dock, harbour, pier or lighthouse undertaking or any undertaking for the supply of hydraulic power and a relevant airport operator (within the meaning of Part V of the Airports Act 1986).

(2) Subject to the following provisions of this section, in this Act 'statutory undertaking' shall be construed in accordance with subsection (1) and, in relation to a relevant airport operator (within the meaning of that Part), means an airport to which that Part of that Act applies.

(3) Subject to subsection (5), for the purposes of the provisions mentioned in subsection (4) any public gas supplier, water or sewerage undertaker, the National Rivers Authority, the Post Office and the Civil Aviation Authority shall be deemed to be statutory undertakers and their undertakings statutory undertakings.

(4) The provisions referred to in subsection (3) are sections 55, 90, 101, 108(3), 139 to 141, 143, 148, 170(12)(b), 236(2)(a), 237 to 241, 245, 247(4)(b), 253, 257(2), 263(1) and (2), 264, 266 to 283, 288(10)(a), 306, 325(9), 336(2) and (3), paragraph 18 of Schedule 1 and Schedules 8, 13 and 14.

(5) Subsection (4) shall apply—

(a) as respects the Post Office, as if the reference to sections 55, 247(4)(b), 253 and 257(2) were omitted; and

(b) as respects the Post Office and the Civil Aviation Authority as if—

(i) the references to sections 245, 263(1) and (2) and 336(2) and (3) were omitted; and

(ii) after the words '266 to 283' there were inserted the words '(except section 271 as applied by section 13 of the Opencast Coal Act 1958)'.

(6) Any holder of a licence under section 6 of the Electricity Act 1989 shall be deemed to be a statutory undertaker and his undertaking a statutory undertaking—

(a) for the purposes of the provisions mentioned in subsection (7)(a), if he holds a licence under subsection (1) of that section;

(b) for the purposes of the provisions mentioned in subsection (7)(b), if he is entitled to exercise any power conferred by Schedule 3 to that Act; and

(c) for the purposes of the provisions mentioned in subsection (7)(c), if he is entitled to exercise any power conferred by paragraph 1 of Schedule 4 to that Act.

(7) The provisions referred to in subsection (6) are—

(a) sections 55, 108(3), 139 to 141, 143, 148, 236(2)(a), 237, 245, 253, 263(1) and (2), 264, 266 to 283, 288(10)(a), 306, 325(9) and 336(2) and (3), paragraph 18 of Schedule 1 and Schedule 13;

(b) sections 170(12)(b) and 238 to 241; and

(c) sections 247(4) and 257(2) and Schedule 14.

263. Meaning of 'operational land'

(1) Subject to the following provisions of this section and to section 264, in this Act 'operational land' means, in relation to statutory undertakers—

(a) land which is used for the purpose of carrying on their undertaking; and

(b) land in which an interest is held for that purpose.

(2) Paragraphs (a) and (b) of subsection (1) do not include land which, in respect of its nature and situation, is comparable rather with land in general than with land which is used, or in which interests are held, for the purpose of the carrying on of statutory undertakings.

(3) In sections 108(3), 266 to 283 and Part II of Schedule 8 'operational land', in relation to the Post Office and the Civil Aviation Authority, means land of the Post Office's or, as the case may be, of the Authority's of any such class as may be prescribed by regulations.

(4) Such regulations—

(a) shall be made—

(i) in the case of the Post Office, by the appropriate Minister and the Secretary of State acting jointly; and

(ii) in the case of the Civil Aviation Authority, by the appropriate Minister;

(b) may define a class of land by reference to any circumstances whatsoever, and

(c) in the case of the Civil Aviation Authority, may make provision for different circumstances, including prescribing different classes of land for the purposes of different provisions.

264. Cases in which land is to be treated as not being operational land

(1) This section applies where an interest in land is held by statutory undertakers for the purpose of carrying on their undertaking and—

(a) The interest was acquired by them on or after 6th December 1968; or

(b) it was held by them immediately before that date but the circumstances were then such that the land did not fall to be treated as operational land for the purposes of the 1962 Act.

(2) Where this section applies in respect of any land then, notwithstanding the provisions of section 263, the land shall not be treated as operational land for the purposes of this Act unless it falls within subsection (3) or (4).

(3) Land falls within this subsection if—

(a) there is, or at some time has been, in force with respect to it a specific planning permission for its development; and

(b) that development, if carried out, would involve or have involved its use for the purpose of the carrying on of the statutory undertakers' undertaking—

(4) Land falls within this subsection if—

(a) the undertakers' interest in the land was acquired by them as the result of a transfer under the provisions of the Transport Act 1968, the Transport (London) Act 1969, the Gas Act 1986, the Airports Act 1986, the Water Act 1989, or the Water Industry Act 1991 from other statutory undertakers; and

(b) immediately before transfer the land was operational land of those other undertakers.

(5) A specific planning permission for the purpose of subsection (3)(a) is a planning permission—

(a) granted on an application in that behalf made under Part III; or

(b) granted by provisions of a development order granting planning permission generally for development which has received specific parliamentary approval; or

(c) granted by a special development order in respect of development specifically described in the order; or

(d) deemed to be granted by virtue of a direction of a government department under section 90(1).

(6) In subsection (5)—

(a) the reference in paragraph (a) to Part III includes a reference to Part III of the 1971 Act and the enactments in force before the commencement of that Act, and replaced by Part III of it; and

(b) the reference in paragraph (b) to development which has received specific parliamentary approval is a reference to development authorised—

(i) by a local or private Act of Parliament,

(ii) by an order approved by both Houses of Parliament;

or

(iii) by an order which has been brought into operation in accordance with the provisions of the Statutory Orders (Special Procedure) Act 1945,

being an Act or order which designates specifically both the nature of the development authorised by it and the land upon which it may be carried out;

(c) the reference in paragraph (d) to section 90(1) includes a reference to section 40 of the 1971 Act, section 41 of the 1962 Act and section 35 of the 1947 Act.

(7) This section shall not apply to land in the case of which an interest of the Postmaster General's vested in the Post Office by virtue of section 16 of the Post Office Act 1969.

(8) Where an interest in land is held by the Civil Aviation Authority this section shall not apply for the purpose of determining whether the land is operational land in relation to the Authority for the purposes of this Act.

265. Meaning of 'the appropriate Minister'

(1) Subject to the following provisions of this section, in this Act 'the appropriate Minister' means—

(a) in relation to statutory undertakers carrying on any railway, light railway, tramway, road transport, dock, harbour, pier or lighthouse undertaking, the Civil Aviation Authority or a relevant airport operator (within the meaning of Part V of the Airports Act 1986), the Secretary of State for Transport;

(b) in relation to statutory undertakers carrying on an undertaking for the supply of hydraulic power, the Secretary of State for Trade and Industry;

(c) in relation to the Post Office, the Secretary of State for Trade and Industry; and

(d) in relation to any other statutory undertakers, the Secretary of State for the Environment.

(2) For the purposes of sections 170(12), 266 to 280, 325(9) and 336(2) and (3) and Part II of Schedule 8, 'the appropriate Minister', in relation to a public gas supplier or a holder of a licence under section 6 of the Electricity Act 1989, means the Secretary of State for Trade and Industry.

(3) For the purposes of sections 170(12), 266 to 280, 325(9) and 336(2) and (3) and Part II of Schedule 8 and Schedule 14 'the appropriate Minister'—

(a) in relation to the National Rivers Authority, means the Secretary of State or the Minister of Agriculture, Fisheries and Food; and

Town and Country Planning Act 1990 153

(b) in relation to a water or sewerage undertaker, means the Secretary of State.

(4) References in this Act to the Secretary of State and the appropriate Minister—

(a) if the appropriate Minister is not the one concerned as the Secretary of State, shall be construed as references to the Secretary of State and the appropriate Minister; and

(b) if the one concerned as the Secretary of State is also the appropriate Minister, shall be construed as references to him alone,

and similarly with references to a Minister and the appropriate Minister and with any provision requiring the Secretary of State to act jointly with the appropriate Minister.

Application of Part III to statutory undertakers

266. Applications for planning permission by statutory undertakers

(1) Where—

(a) an application for planning permission to develop land to which this subsection appliers is made by statutory undertakers and is referred to the Secretary of State under Part III; or

(b) an appeal is made to the Secretary of State under that Part from the decision on such an application; or

(c) such an application is deemed to be made under subsection (5) of section 177 on an appeal under section 174 by statutory undertakers,

the application or appeal shall be dealt with by the Secretary of State and the appropriate Minister.

(2) Subsection (1) applies

(a) to operational land; and

(b) to land in which the statutory undertakers hold or propose to acquire an interest with a view to its being used for the purpose of carrying on their undertaking, where the planning permission, if granted on the application or appeal, would be for development involving the use of the land for that purpose.

(3) [repealed by the Planning and Compensation Act 1991].

(4) Subject to the provisions of this Part as to compensation, the provisions of this Act shall apply to an application which is dealt with under this section by the Secretary of State and the appropriate Minister as if it had been dealt with by the Secretary of State.

(5) Subsection (2)(b) shall have effect in relation to the Civil Aviation Authority as if for the reference to development involving the use of land for the purpose of carrying on the Civil Aviation Authority's undertaking there were substituted a reference to development involving the use of land for such of the purposes of carrying on that undertaking as may be prescribed by the appropriate Minister.

267. Conditional grants of planning permission

Notwithstanding anything in Part III, planning permission to develop operational land of statutory undertakers shall not, except with their consent, be granted subject to conditions requiring—

(a) that any buildings or works authorised by the permission shall be removed, or

(b) that any use of the land so authorised shall be discontinued, at the end of a specified period.

268. Development requiring authorisation of government department

(1) The Secretary of State and the appropriate Minister shall not be required under section 266(1) to deal with an application for planning permission for the development of operational land if the authorisation of a government department is required in respect of that development.

(2) Subsection (1) does not apply where the relevant authorisation has been granted without any direction as to the grant of planning permission.

(3) For the purposes of this section development shall be taken to be authorised by a government department if—

(a) any consent, authority or approval to or for the development is granted by the department in pursuance of an enactment;

(b) a compulsory purchase order is confirmed by the department authorising the purchase of land for the purpose of the development;

(c) consent is granted by the department to the appropriation of land for the purpose of the development or the acquisition of land by agreement for that purpose;

(d) authority is given by the department for the borrowing of money for the purpose of the development, or for the application for that purpose of any money not otherwise so applicable; or

(e) any undertaking is given by the department to pay a grant in respect of the development in accordance with an enactment authorising the payment of such grants,

and references in this section to the authorisation of a government department shall be construed accordingly.

269. Revocation or modification of permission to develop operational land
In relation to any planning permission granted on the application of statutory undertakers for the development of operational land, the provisions of Part III with respect to the revocation and modification of planning permission shall have effect as if for any reference in them to the Secretary of State there were substituted a reference to the Secretary of State and the appropriate Minister.

270. Order requiring discontinuance of use etc. of operational land
The provisions of Part III with respect to the making of orders—

(a) requiring the discontinuance of any use of land;

(b) imposing conditions on the continuance of it; or

(c) requiring buildings or works on land to be altered or removed,

and the provisions of Schedule 9 with respect to the making of orders that Schedule shall have effect in relation to operational land of statutory undertakers as if for any reference in them to the Secretary of State there were substituted a reference to the Secretary of State and the appropriate Minister.

Extinguishment of rights of statutory undertakers, etc.

271. Extinguishment of rights of statutory undertakers: preliminary notices
(1) This section applies where any land has been acquired by a Minister, a local authority or statutory undertakers under Part IX of this Act or Chapter V of Part I of the Planning (Listed Buildings and Conservation Areas) Act 1990 or compulsorily under any other enactment or has been appropriated by a local authority for planning purposes, and—

(a) there subsists over that land a right vested in or belonging to statutory undertakers for the purpose of the carrying on of their undertaking, being a right of way or a right of laying down, erecting, continuing or maintaining apparatus on, under or over the land; or

(b) there is on, under or over the land apparatus vested in or belonging to statutory undertakers for the purpose of the carrying on of their undertaking.

(2) If the acquiring or appropriating authority is satisfied that the extinguishment of the right or, as the case may be, the removal of the apparatus, is necessary for the purpose of carrying out any development with a view to which the land was acquired or appropriated, they may serve on the statutory undertakers a notice—

(a) stating that at the end of the relevant period the right will be extinguished; or

(b) requiring that before the end of that period the apparatus shall be removed.

(3) The statutory undertakers on whom a notice is served under subsection (2) may, before the end of the period of 28 days from the date of service of the notice, serve a counter-notice on the acquiring or appropriating authority—
  (a) stating that they object to all or any of the provisions of the notice; and
  (b) specifying the grounds of their objection.
(4) If no counter-notice is served under subsection (3)—
  (a) any right to which the notice relates shall be extinguished at the end of the relevant period; and
  (b) if at the end of that period any requirement of the notice as to the removal of any apparatus has not been complied with, the acquiring or appropriating authority may remove the apparatus and dispose of it in any way the authority may think fit.
(5) If a counter-notice is served under subsection (3) on a local authority or on statutory undertakers, the authority or undertakers may either—
  (a) withdraw the notice (without prejudice to the service of a further notice); or
  (b) apply to the Secretary of State and the appropriate Minister for an order under this section embodying the provisions of the notice, with or without modification.
(6) If a counter-notice is served under subsection (3) on a Minister—
  (a) he may withdraw the notice (without prejudice to the service of a further notice); or
  (b) he and the appropriate Minister may make an order under this section embodying the provisions of the notice, with or without modification.
(7) In this section any reference to the appropriation of land for planning purposes shall be construed in accordance with section 246(1) as if this section were in Part IX.
(8) For the purposes of this section the relevant period, in relation to a notice served in respect of any right or apparatus, is the period of 28 days from the date of service of the notice or such longer period as may be specified in it in relation to that right or apparatus.

272. Extinguishment of rights of telecommunications code system operators: preliminary notices

(1) This section applies where any land has been acquired by a Minister, a local authority or statutory undertakers under Part IX of this Act or under Chapter V of Part I of the Planning (Listed Buildings and Conservation Areas) Act 1990 or compulsorily under any other enactment or has been appropriated by a local authority for planning purposes, and—
  (a) there subsists over that land a right conferred by or in accordance with the telecommunications code on the operator of a telecommunications code system, being a right of way or a right of laying down, erecting, continuing or maintaining apparatus on, under or over the land; or
  (b) there is on, under or over the land telecommunication apparatus kept installed for the purposes of any such system.
(2) If the acquiring or appropriating authority is satisfied, that the extinguishment of the right or, as the case may be, the removal of the apparatus is necessary for the purpose of carrying out any development with a view to which the land was acquired or appropriated, they may serve on the operator of the telecommunications code system a notice—
  (a) stating that at the end of the relevant period the right will be extinguished; or
  (b) requiring that before the end of that period the apparatus shall be removed.
(3) The operator of the telecommunications code system on whom a notice is served under subsection (2) may, before the end of the period of 28 days from the date of service of the notice, serve a counter-notice on the acquiring or appropriating authority—

(a) stating that he objects to all or any of the provisions of the notice; and
(b) specifying the grounds of his objection.

(4) If no counter-notice is served under subsection (3)—

(a) any right to which the notice relates shall be extinguished at the end of the relevant period; and

(b) if at the end of that period any requirement of the notice as to the removal of any apparatus has not been complied with, the acquiring or appropriating authority may remove the apparatus and dispose of it in any way the authority may think fit.

(5) If a counter-notice is served under subsection (3) on a local authority or on statutory undertakers, the authority or undertakers may either—

(a) withdraw the notice (without prejudice to the service of a further notice); or

(b) apply to the Secretary of State and the Secretary of State for Trade and Industry for an order under this section embodying the provisions of the notice, with or without modification.

(6) If a counter-notice is served under subsection (3) on a Minister—

(a) he may withdraw the notice (without prejudice to the service of a further notice); or

(b) he and the Secretary of State for Trade and Industry may make an order under this section embodying the provisions of the notice, with or withhout modification.

(7) In this section any reference to the appropriation of land for planning purposes shall be construed in accordance with section 246(1) as if this section were in Part IX.

(8) For the purposes of this section the relevant period, in relation to a notice served in respect of any right or apparatus, is the period of 28 days from the date of service of the notice or such longer period as may be specified in it in relation to that right or apparatus.

273. Notice for same purposes as ss. 271 and 272 but given by undertakers to developing authority

(1) Subject to the provisions of this section, where land has been acquired or appropriated as mentioned in section 271(1), and—

(a) there is on, under or over the land any apparatus vested in or belonging to statutory undertakers; and

(b) the undertakers claim that development to be carried out on the land is such as to require, on technical or other grounds connected with the carrying on of their undertaking, the removal or re-siting of the apparatus affected by the development,

the undertakers may serve on the acquiring or appropriating authority a notice claiming the right to enter on the land and carry out such works for the removal or re-siting of the apparatus or any part of it as may be specified in the notice.

(2) No notice under this section shall be served later than 21 days after the beginning of the development of land which has been acquired or appropriated as mentioned in section 271(1).

(3) Where a notice is served under this section, the authority on whom it is served may, before the end of the period of 28 days from the date of service, serve on the statutory undertakers a counter-notice—

(a) stating that they object to all or any of the provisions of the notice; and
(b) specifying the grounds of their objection.

(4) If no counter-notice is served under subsection (3), the statutory undertakers shall, after the end of that period, have the rights claimed in their notice.

(5) If a counter-notice is served under subsection (3), the statutory undertakers who served the notice under this section may either withdraw it or may apply to the Secretary of State and the appropriate Minister for an order under this section conferring on the undertakers the rights claimed in the notice or such modified rights

Town and Country Planning Act 1990

as the Secretary of State and the appropriate Minister think it expedient to confer on them.

(6) Where, by virtue of this section or of an order of Ministers under it, statutory undertakers have the right to execute works for the removal or re-siting of apparatus, they may arrange with the acquiring or appropriating authority for the works to be carried out by that authority, under the superintendence of the undertakers, instead of by the undertakers themselves.

(7) In subsection (1)(a), the reference to apparatus vested in or belonging to statutory undertakers shall include a reference to telecommunication apparatus kept installed for the purposes of a telecommunications code system.

(8) For the purposes of subsection (7), in this section—
  (a) references (except in subsection (1)(a)) to statutory undertakers shall have effect as references to the operator of any such system; and
  (b) references to the appropriate Minister shall have effect as references to the Secretary of State for Trade and Industry.

274. Orders under ss. 271 and 272

(1) Where a Minister and the appropriate Minister propose to make an order under section 271(6) or 272(6), they shall prepare a draft of the order.

(2) Before making an order under subsection (5) or (6) of section 271, or under subsection (5) or (6) of section 272, the Ministers proposing to make the order shall give the statutory undertakers or, as the case may be, the operator of the telecommunications code system on whom notice was served under subsection (2) of section 271 or, as the case may be, under subsection (2) of section 272 an opportunity of objecting to the application for, or proposal to make, the order.

(3) If any such objection is made, before making the order the Ministers shall consider the objection and give those statutory undertakers or, as the case may be, that operator (and, in a case falling within subsection (5) of either of those sections, the local authority or statutory undertakers on whom the counter-notice was served) an opportunity of appearing before, and being heard by, a person appointed for the purpose by the Secretary of State and the appropriate Minister.

(4) After complying with subsections (2) and (3) the Ministers may, if they think fit, make the order in accordance with the application or, as the case may be, in accordance with the draft order, either with or without modification.

(5) Where an order is made under section 271 or 272—
  (a) any right to which the order relates shall be extinguished at the end of the period specified in that behalf in the order; and
  (b) if, at the end of the period so specified in relation to any apparatus, any requirement of the order as to the removal of the apparatus has not been complied with, the acquiring or appropriating authority may remove the apparatus and dispose of it in any way the authority may think fit.

(6) In this section references to the appropriate Minister shall in the case of an order under section 272 be taken as references to the Secretary of State for Trade and Industry.

Extension or modification of statutory undertakers' functions

275. Extension or modification of functions of statutory undertakers

(1) The powers conferred by this section shall be exercisable where, on a representation made by statutory undertakers, it appears to the Secretary of State and the appropriate Minister to be expedient that the powers and duties of those undertakers should be extended or modified, in order—
  (a) to secure the provision of services which would not otherwise be provided, or satisfactorily provided, for any purpose in connection with which a local authority

or Minister may be authorised under Part IX of this Act or under Chapter V of Part I of the Planning (Listed Buildings and Conservation Areas) Act 1990 to acquire land or in connection with which any such person may compulsorily acquire land under any other enactment; or

(b) to facilitate an adjustment of the carrying on of the undertaking necessitated by any of the acts and events mentioned in subsection (2).

(2) The said acts and events are—

(a) the acquisition under Part IX of this Act or that Chapter or compulsorily under any other enactment of any land in which an interest was held, or which was used, for the purpose of the carrying on of the undertaking of the statutory undertakers in question;

(b) the extinguishment of a right or the imposition of any requirement by virtue of section 271 or 272;

(c) a decision on an application made by the statutory undertakers for planning permission to develop any such land as is mentioned in paragraph (a);

(d) the revocation or modification of planning permission granted on any such application;

(e) the making of an order under section 102 or paragraph 1 of Schedule 9 in relation to any such land.

(3) The powers conferred by this section shall also be exercisable where, on a representation made by a local authority or Minister, it appears to the Secretary of State and the appropriate Minister to be expedient that the powers and duties of statutory undertakers should be extended or modified in order to secure the provision of new services, or the extension of existing services, for any purpose in connection with which the local authority or Minister making the representation may be authorised under Part IX of this Act or under Chapter V of Part I of the Planning (Listed Buildings and Conservation Areas) Act 1990 to acquire land or in connection with which the local authority or Minister may compulsorily acquire land under any other enactment.

(4) Where the powers conferred by this section are exercisable, the Secretary of State and the appropriate Minister may, if they think fit, by order provide for such extension or modification of the powers and duties of the statutory undertakers as appears to them to be requisite in order—

(a) to secure the services in question, as mentioned in subsection (1)(a) or (3), or

(b) to secure the adjustment in question, as mentioned in subsection (1)(b), as the case may be.

(5) Without prejudice to the generality of subsection (4), an order under this section may make provision—

(a) for empowering the statutory undertakers—

(i) to acquire (whether compulsorily or by agreement) any land specified in the order, and

(ii) to erect or construct any buildings or works so specified;

(b) for applying in relation to the acquisition of any such land or the construction of any such works enactments relating to the acquisition of land and the construction of works;

(c) where it has been represented that the making of the order is expedient for the purposes mentioned in subsection (1)(a) or (3), for giving effect to such financial arrangements between the local authority or Minister and the statutory undertakers as they may agree, or as, in default of agreement, may be determined to be equitable in such manner and by such tribunal as may be specified in the order;

(d) for such incidental and supplemental matters as appear to the Secretary of State and the appropriate Minister to be expedient for the purposes of the order.

Town and Country Planning Act 1990 159

276. Procedure in relation to orders under s. 275

(1) As soon as possible after making such a representation as is mentioned in subsection (1) or subsection (3) of section 275 the statutory undertakers, the local authority or Minister making the representation shall—

(a) publish notice of the representation; and

(b) if the Secretary of State and the appropriate Minister so direct, serve a similar notice on such persons, or persons of such classes, as they may direct.

(2) A notice under subsection (1)—

(a) shall be published in such form and manner as the Secretary of State and the appropriate Minister may direct;

(b) shall give such particulars as they may direct of the matters to which the representation relates; and

(c) shall specify the time within which, and the manner in which, objections to the making of an order on the representation may be made.

(3) Orders under section 275 shall be subject to special parliamentary procedure.

277. Relief of statutory undertakers from obligations rendered impracticable

(1) Where, on a representation made by statutory undertakers, the appropriate Minister is satisfied that the fulfilment of any obligation incurred by those undertakers in connection with the carrying on of their undertaking has been rendered impracticable by an act or event to which this subsection applies, the appropriate Minister may, if he thinks fit, by order direct that the statutory undertakers shall be relieved of the fulfilment of that obligation, either absolutely or to such extent as may be specified in the order.

(2) Subsection (1) applies to the following acts and events—

(a) the compulsory acquisition under Part IX of this Act or under Chapter V of Part I of the Planning (Listed Buildings and Conservation Areas) Act 1990 or under any other enactment of any land in which an interest was held, or which was used, for the purpose of the carrying on of the undertaking of the statutory undertakers; and

(b) the acts and events specified in section 275(2)(b) to (e).

(3) The appropriate Minister may direct statutory undertakers who have made a representation to him under subsection (1) to publicise it in either or both of the following ways—

(a) by publishing in such form and manner as he may direct a notice, giving such particulars as he may direct of the matters to which the representation relates and specifying the time within which, and the manner in which, objections to the making of an order on the representation may be made;

(b) by serving such a notice on such persons, or persons of such classes, as he may direct.

(4) The statutory undertakers shall comply with any direction given to them under subsection (3) as soon as possible after the making of the representation under subsection (1).

(5) If any objection to the making of an order under this section is duly made and is not withdrawn before the order is made, the order shall be subject to special parliamentary procedure.

(6) Immediately after an order is made under this section by the appropriate Minister, he shall—

(a) publish a notice stating that the order has been made and naming a place where a copy of it may be seen at all reasonable hours; and

(b) serve a similar notice—

(i) on any person who duly made an objection to the order and has sent to the appropriate Minister a request in writing to serve him with the notice required by this subsection, specifying an address for service; and

(ii) on such other persons (if any) as the appropriate Minister thinks fit.

(7) Subject to subsection (8), and to the provisions of Part XII, an order under this section shall become operative on the date on which the notice required by subsection (6) is first published.

(8) Where in accordance with subsection (5) the order is subject to special parliamentary procedure, subsection (7) shall not apply.

278. Objections to orders under ss. 275 and 277

(1) For the purposes of sections 275 to 277, an objection to the making of an order shall not be treated as duly made unless—

(a) the objection is made within the time and in the manner specified in the notice required by section 276 or, as the case may be, section 277; and

(b) a statement in writing of the grounds of the objection is comprised in or submitted with the objection.

(2) Where an objection to the making of such an order is duly made in accordance with subsection (1) and is not withdrawn, the following provisions of this section shall have effect in relation to it.

(3) Unless the appropriate Minister decides without regard to the objection not to make the order, or decides to make a modification which is agreed to by the objector as meeting the objection, before he makes a final decision he—

(a) shall consider the grounds of the objection as set out in the statement; and

(b) may if he thinks fit, require the objector to submit within a specified period a further statement in writing as to any of the matters to which the objection relates.

(4) In so far as the appropriate Minister, after considering the grounds of the objection as set out in the original statement and in any such further statement, is satisfied that the objection relates to a matter which can be dealt with in the assessment of compensation, the appropriate Minister may treat the objection as irrelevant for the purpose of making a final decision.

(5) If—

(a) after considering the grounds of the objection as so set out, the appropriate Minister is satisfied that, for the purpose of making a final decision, he is sufficiently informed as to the matters to which the objection relates; or

(b) in a case where a further statement has been required, it is not submitted within the specified period,

the appropriate Minister may make a final decision without further investigation as to those matters.

(6) Subject to subsections (4) and (5), before making a final decision the appropriate Minister shall give the objector an opportunity of appearing before, and being heard by, a person appointed for the purpose by the appropriate Minister.

(7) If the objector takes that opportunity, the appropriate Minister shall give an opportunity of appearing and being heard on the same occasion to the statutory undertakers, local authority or Minister on whose representation the order is proposed to be made, and to any other persons to whom it appears to him to be expedient to give such an opportunity.

(8) Notwithstanding anything in the previous provisions of this section, if it appears to the appropriate Minister that the matters to which the objection relates are such as to require investigation by public local inquiry before he makes a final decision, he shall cause such an inquiry to be held.

(9) Where the appropriate Minister determines to cause such an inquiry to be held, any of the requirements of subsections (3) to (7) to which effect has not been given at the time of that determination shall be dispensed with.

(10) In this section any reference to making a final decision in relation to an order is a reference to deciding whether to make the order or what modification (if any) ought to be made.

Town and Country Planning Act 1990

(11) In the application of this section to an order under section 275, any reference to the appropriate Minister shall be construed as a reference to the Secretary of State and the appropriate Minister.

Compensation

279. Rights to compensation in respect of certain decisions and orders

(1) Statutory undertakers shall, subject to the following provisions of this Part, be entitled to compensation from the local planning authority—

(a) in respect of any decision made in accordance with section 266 by which planning permission to develop operational land of those undertakers is refused or is granted subject to conditions where—

(i) planning permission for that development would have been granted by a development order but for a direction given under such an order that planning permission so granted should not apply to the development; and

(ii) it is not development which has received specific parliamentary approval (within the meaning of section 264(6));

(b) in respect of any order under section 97, as modified by section 269, by which planning permission which was granted on the application of those undertakers for the development of any such land is revoked or modified.

(2) Where by virtue of section 271—

(a) any right vested in or belonging to statutory undertakers is extinguished; or

(b) any requirement is imposed on statutory undertakers,

those undertakers shall be entitled to compensation from the acquiring or appropriating authority at whose instance the right was extinguished or the requirement imposed.

(3) Where by virtue of section 272—

(a) any right vested in or belonging to an operator of a telecommunications code system is extinguished; or

(b) any requirement is imposed on such an operator,

the operator shall be entitled to compensation from the acquiring or appropriating authority at whose instance the right was extinguished or the requirement imposed.

(4) Where—

(a) works are carried out for the removal or re-siting of statutory undertakers' apparatus; and

(b) the undertakers have the right to carry out those works by virtue of section 273 or an order of Ministers under that section,

the undertakers shall be entitled to compensation from the acquiring or appropriating authority.

(5) Subsection (1) shall not apply in respect of a decision or order if—

(a) it relates to land acquired by the statutory undertakers after 7th January 1947; and

(b) the Secretary of State and the appropriate Minister include in the decision or order a direction that subsection (1) shall not apply to it.

(6) The Secretary of State and the appropriate Minister may only give a direction under subsection (5) if they are satisfied, having regard to the nature, situation and existing development of the land and of any neighbouring land, and to any other material considerations, that it is unreasonable that compensation should be recovered in respect of the decision or order in question.

(7) For the purposes of this section the conditions referred to in sections 91 and 92 shall be disregarded.

280. Measure of compensation to statutory undertakers, etc.

(1) Where statutory undertakers are entitled to compensation

(a) as mentioned in subsection (1), (2) or (4) of section 279;

(b) under the provisions of section 115 in respect of an order made under section 102 or paragraph 1, 3, 5 or 6 of Schedule 9, as modified by section 270; or

(c) in respect of a compulsory acquisition of land which has been acquired by those undertakers for the purposes of their undertaking, where the first-mentioned acquisition is effected under a compulsory purchase order confirmed or made without the appropriate Minister's certificate,

or the operator of a telecommunications code system is entitled to compensation as mentioned in section 279(3), the amount of the compensation shall (subject to section 281) be an amount calculated in accordance with this section.

(2) Subject to subsections (4) to (6), that amount shall be the aggregate of—

(a) the amount of any expenditure reasonably incurred in acquiring land, providing apparatus, erecting buildings or doing work for the purpose of any adjustment of the carrying on of the undertaking or, as the case may be, the running of the telecommunications code system rendered necessary by the proceeding giving rise to compensation (a 'business adjustment');

(b) the appropriate amount for loss of profits; and

(c) where the compensation is under section 279(2) or (3), and is in respect of the imposition of a requirement to remove apparatus, the amount of any expenditure reasonably incurred by the statutory undertakers or, as the case may be, the operator in complying with the requirement, reduced by the value after removal of the apparatus removed.

(3) In subsection (2) 'the appropriate amount for loss of profits' means—

(a) where a business adjustment is made, the aggregate of—

(i) the estimated amount of any decrease in net receipts from the carrying on of the undertaking or, as the case may be, the running of the telecommunications code system pending the adjustment, in so far as the decrease is directly attributable to the proceeding giving rise to compensation; and

(ii) such amount as appears reasonable compensation for any estimated decrease in net receipts from the carrying on of the undertaking or, as the case may be, the running of the telecommunications code system in the period after the adjustment has been completed, in so far as the decrease is directly attributable to the adjustment;

(b) where no business adjustment is made, such amount as appears reasonable compensation for any estimated decrease in net receipts from the carrying on of the undertaking or, as the case may be, the running of the telecommunications code system which is directly attributable to the proceeding giving rise to compensation.

(4) Where a business adjustment is made, the aggregate amount mentioned in subsection (2) shall be reduced by such amount (if any) as appears to the Lands Tribunal to be appropriate to offset—

(a) the estimated value of any property (whether moveable or immoveable) belonging to the statutory undertakers or the operator and used for the carrying on of their undertaking or, as the case may be, the running of the telecommunications code system which in consequence of the adjustment ceases to be so used, in so far as the value of the property has not been. taken into account under paragraph (c) of that subsection; and

(b) the estimated amount of any increase in net receipts from the carrying on of the undertaking or the running of the telecommunications code system in the period after the adjustment has been completed, in so far as that amount has not been taken into account in determining the amount mentioned in paragraph (b) of that subsection and is directly attributable to the adjustment.

(5) Where a business adjustment is made the aggregate amount mentioned in subsection (2) shall be further reduced by any amount which appears to the Lands

Tribunal to be appropriate, having regard to any increase in the capital value of immoveable property belonging to the statutory undertakers or the operator which is directly attributable to the adjustment, allowance being made for any reduction made under subsection (4)(b).

(6) Where—
   (a) the compensation is under section 279(4); and
   (b) the acquiring or appropriating authority carry out the works,
then, in addition to any reduction falling to be made under subsection (4) or (5), the aggregate amount mentioned in subsection (2) shall be reduced by the actual cost to the authority of carrying out the works.

(7) References in this section to a decrease in net receipts shall be construed as references—
   (a) to the amount by which a balance of receipts over expenditure is decreased;
   (b) to the amount by which a balance of expenditure over receipts is increased;
or
   (c) where a balance of receipts over expenditure is converted into a balance of expenditure over receipts, to the aggregate of the two balances;
and references to an increase in net receipts shall be construed, accordingly.

(8) In this section—
'proceeding giving rise to compensation' means—
   (a) except in relation to compensation under section 279(4), the particular action (that is to say, the decision, order, extinguishment of a right, imposition of a requirement or acquisition) in respect of which compensation falls to be assessed, as distinct from any development or project in connection with which that action may have been taken;
   (b) in relation to compensation under section 279(4), the circumstances making it necessary for the apparatus in question to be removed or re-sited;
'the appropriate Minister's certificate' means such a certificate as is mentioned in section 16 of or paragraph 3 of Schedule 3 to the Acquisition of Land Act 1981.

281. Exclusion of s. 280 at option of statutory undertakers

(1) Where statutory undertakers are entitled to compensation in respect of such a compulsory acquisition as is mentioned in section 280(1)(c), the statutory undertakers may by notice in writing under this section elect that the compensation shall be ascertained in accordance with the enactments (other than rule (5) of the rules set out in section 5 of the Land Compensation Act 1961) which would be applicable apart from section 280.

(2) If the statutory undertakers so elect the compensation shall be ascertained accordingly.

(3) An election under this section may be made either in respect of the whole of the land comprised in the compulsory acquisition in question or in respect of part of that land.

(4) Any notice under this section shall be given to the acquiring authority before the end of the period of two months from the date of service of notice to treat in respect of the interest of the statutory undertakers.

282. Procedure for assessing compensation

(1) Where the amount of any such compensation as is mentioned in subsection (1) of section 280 falls to be ascertained in accordance with the provisions of that section, the compensation shall, in default of agreement, be assessed by the Lands Tribunal, if apart from this section it would not fall to be so assessed.

(2) For the purposes of any proceedings arising before the Lands Tribunal in respect of compensation falling to be ascertained as mentioned in subsection (1), the provisions of sections 2 and 4 of the Land Compensation Act 1961 shall apply as they

apply to proceedings on a question referred to the Tribunal under section 1 of that Act, but with the substitution in section 4 of that Act, for references to the acquiring authority, of references to the person from whom the compensation is claimed.

Advertisements

283. Display of advertisements on operational land
Sections 266 to 270 and 279(1), (5) and (6) do not apply in relation to the display of advertisements on operational land of statutory undertakers.

PART XII
VALIDITY

284. Validity of development plans and certain orders, decisions and directions

(1) Except in so far as may be provided by this Part, the validity of—

(a) a structure plan, local plan, minerals local plan, waste local plan or unitary development plan or any alteration, or replacement of any such plan, whether before or after the plan, alteration, or replacement has been approved or adopted; or

(b) a simplified planning zone scheme or an alteration of such a scheme, whether before or after the adoption or approval of the scheme or alteration; or

(c) an order under any provision of Part X except section 251(1), whether before or after the order has been made; or

(d) an order under section 277, whether before or after the order has been made; or

(e) any such order as is mentioned in subsection (2), whether before or after it has been confirmed; or

(f) any such action on the part of the Secretary of State as is mentioned in subsection (3),

shall not be questioned in any legal proceedings whatsoever.

(2) The orders referred to in subsection (1)(e) are—

(a) any order under section 97 or under the provisions of that section as applied by or under any other provision of this Act;

(b) any order under section 102;

(c) any tree preservation order;

(d) any order made in pursuance of section 221(5);

(e) any order under paragraph 1, 3, 5 or 6 of Schedule 9.

(3) The action referred to in subsection (1)(f) is action on the part of the Secretary of State of any of the following descriptions—

(a) any decision on an application for planning permission referred to him under section 77;

(b) any decision on an appeal under section 78;

(c) [repealed by the Planning and Compensation Act 1991]

(d) any decision to confirm a completion notice under section 95;

(e) any decision to grant planning permission under paragraph (a) of section 177(1) or to discharge a condition or limitation under paragraph (b) of that section;

(f) any decision to confirm or not to confirm a purchase notice including—

(i) any decision not to confirm such a notice in respect of part of the land to which it relates, or

(ii) any decision to grant any permission, or give any direction, instead of confirming such a notice, either wholly or in part;

(g) any decision on an appeal under section 195(1);

(h) any decision relating—

(i) to an application for consent under a tree preservation order,

(ii) to an application for consent under any regulations made in accordance with section 220 or 221, or

Town and Country Planning Act 1990

(iii) to any certificate or direction under any such order or regulations, whether it is a decision on appeal or a decision on an application referred to the Secretary of State for determination in the first instance.

(4) Nothing in this section shall affect the exercise of any jurisdiction of any court in respect of any refusal or failure on the part of the Secretary of State to take any such action as is mentioned in subsection (3).

285. Validity of enforcement notices and similar notices

(1) The validity of an enforcement notice shall not, except by way of an appeal under Part VII, be questioned in any proceedings whatsoever on any of the grounds on which such an appeal may be brought.

(2) Subsection (1) shall not apply to proceedings brought under section 179 against a person who—
   (a) has held an interest in the land since before the enforcement notice was issued under that Part;
   (b) did not have a copy of the enforcement notice served on him under that Part; and
   (c) satisfies the court—
      (i) that he did not know and could not reasonably have been expected to know that the enforcement notice had been issued; and
      (ii) that his interests have been substantially prejudiced by the failure to serve him with a copy of it.

(3) Subject to subsection (4), the validity of a notice which has been served under section 215 on the owner and occupier of the land shall not, except by way of an appeal under Chapter II of Part VIII, be questioned in any proceedings whatsoever on either of the grounds specified in section 217(1)(a) or (b).

(4) Subsection (3) shall not prevent the validity of such a notice being questioned on either of those grounds in proceedings brought under section 216 against a person on whom the notice was not served, but who has held an interest in the land since before the notice was served on the owner and occupier of the land, if he did not appeal against the notice under that Chapter.

(5) and (6) [repealed]

286. Challenges to validity on ground of authority's powers

(1) The validity of any permission, determination or certificate granted, made or issued or purporting to have been granted, made or issued by a local planning authority in respect of—
   (a) an application for planning permission;
   (b) [repealed by the Planning and Compensation Act 1991]
   (c) an application for a certificate under section 191 or 192;
   (d) an application for consent to the display of advertisements under section 220; or
   (e) a determination under section 302 or Schedule 15,
shall not be called in question in any legal proceedings, or in any proceedings under this Act which are not legal proceedings, on the ground that the permission, determination or certificate should have been granted, made or given by some other local planning authority.

(2) The validity of any order under section 97 revoking or modifying planning permission, any order under section 102 or paragraph 1 of Schedule 9 requiring discontinuance of use, or imposing conditions on continuance of use, or requiring the alteration or removal of buildings or works, or any enforcement notice under section 172 or stop notice under section 183 or a breach of condition notice order section 187A, being an order or notice purporting to have been made, issued or served by a local planning authority, shall not be called in question in any such proceedings on the ground—

(a) in the case of an order or notice purporting to have been made, issued or served by a district planning authority, that they failed to comply with paragraph 11(2) of Schedule 1;

(b) in the case of an order or notice purporting to have been made, issued or served by a county planning authority, that they had no power to make, issue or serve it because it did not relate to a county matter within the meaning of that Schedule.

287. Proceedings for questioning validity of development plans and certain schemes and orders

(1) If any person aggrieved by a unitary development plan or a local plan, minerals local plan or waste local plan or by any alteration or replacement of any such plan or structure plan, desires to question the validity of the plan or, as the case may be, the alteration or replacement on the ground—

(a) that it is not within the powers conferred by Part II, or

(b) that any requirement of that Part or of any regulations made under it has not been complied with in relation to the approval or adoption of the plan or, as the case may be, it's alteration or replacement,

he may make an application to the High Court under this section.

(2) On any application under this section the High Court—

(a) may by interim order wholly or in part suspend the operation of the plan, or, as the case may be, the alteration, or replacement, either generally or in so far as it affects any property of the applicant, until the final determination of the proceedings;

(b) if satisfied that the plan or, as the case may be, the alteration, repeal or replacement is wholly or to any extent outside the powers conferred by Part II, or that the interests of the applicant have been substantially prejudiced by the failure to comply with any requirement of that Part or of any regulations made under it, may wholly or in part quash the plan or, as the case may be,

the alteration or replacement either generally or in so far as it affects any property of the applicant.

(3) Subsections (1) and (2) shall apply, subject to any necessary modifications, to a simplified planning zone scheme or an alteration of such a scheme or to an order under section 247, 248, 249, 251, 257, 258 or 277 as they apply to any plan or any alteration or replacement there mentioned.

(4) An application under this section must be made within six weeks from the relevant date.

(5) For the purposes of subsection (4) the relevant date is—

(a) in the case of an application in respect of such a plan as is mentioned in subsection (1), the date of the publication of the first notice of the approval or adoption of the plan, alteration or replacement required by regulations under section 26 or, as the case may be, section 53,

(b) in the case of an application by virtue of subsection (3) in respect of a simplified planning zone scheme or an alteration of such a scheme, the date of the publication of the first notice of the approval or adoption of the scheme or alteration required by regulations under paragraph 13 of Schedule 7,

(c) in the case of an application by virtue of subsection (3) in respect of an order under section 247, 248, 249, or 251, the date on which the notice required by section 252(10) is first published,

(d) in the case of an application by virtue of subsection (3) in respect of an order under section 257 or 258, the date on which the notice required by paragraph 7 of Schedule 14 is first published in accordance with that paragraph,

(e) in the case of an application by virtue of subsection (3) in respect of an order under section 277, the date on which the notice required by subsection (6) of that section is first published;

Town and Country Planning Act 1990

but subject, in the case of those orders mentioned in paragraphs (c) and (e) to which section 292 applies, to that section.

(6) In their application to simplified planning zone schemes and their alteration, subsections (1) and (2) shall have effect as if they referred to Part III instead of Part II.

288. Proceedings for questioning the validity of other orders, decisions and directions

(1) If any person—
    (a) is aggrieved by any order to which this section applies and wishes to question the validity of that order on the grounds—
        (i) that the order is not within the powers of this Act, or
        (ii) that any of the relevant requirements have not been complied with in relation to that order; or
    (b) is aggrieved by any action on the part of the Secretary of State to which this section applies and wishes to question the validity of that action on the grounds—
        (i) that the action is not within the powers of this Act, or
        (ii) that any of the relevant requirements have not been complied with in relation to that action,
he may make an application to the High Court under this section.

(2) Without prejudice to subsection (1), if the authority directly concerned with any order to which this section applies, or with any action on the part of the Secretary of State to which this section applies, wish to question the validity of that order or action on any of the grounds mentioned in subsection (1), the authority may make an application to the High Court under this section.

(3) An application under this section must be made within six weeks from the date on which the order is confirmed (or, in the case of an order under section 97 which takes effect under section 99 without confirmation, the date on which it takes effect) or, as the case may be, the date on which the action is taken.

(4) This section applies to any such order as is mentioned in subsection (2) of section 284 and to any such action on the part of the Secretary of State as is mentioned in subsection (3) of that section.

(5) On any application under this section the High Court—
    (a) may, subject to subsection (6), by interim order suspend the operation of the order or action, the validity of which is questioned by the application, until the final determination of the proceedings;
    (b) if satisfied that the order or action in question is not within the powers of this Act, or that the interests of the applicant have been substantially prejudiced by a failure to comply with any of the relevant requirements in relation to it, may quash that order or action.

(6) Paragraph (a) of subsection (5) shall not apply to applications questioning the validity of tree preservation orders.

(7) In relation to a tree preservation order, or to an order made in pursuance of section 221(5), the powers conferred on the High Court by subsection (5) shall be exercisable by way of quashing or (where applicable) suspending the operation of the order either in whole or in part, as the court may determine.

(8) References in this section to the confirmation of an order include the confirmation of an order subject to modifications as well as the confirmation of an order in the form in which it was made.

(9) In this section 'the relevant requirements', in relation to any order or action to which this section applies, means any requirements of this Act or of the Tribunals and Inquiries Act 1992 or of any order, regulations or rules made under this Act or under that Act which are applicable to that order or action.

(10) Any reference in this section to the authority directly concerned with any order or action to which this section applies—

(a) in relation to any such decision as is mentioned in section 284(3)(f), is a reference to the council on whom the notice in question was served and, in a case where the Secretary of State has modified such a notice, wholly or in part, by substituting another local authority or statutory undertakers for that council, includes a reference to that local authority or those statutory undertakers;

(b) in any other case, is a reference to the. authority who made the order in question or made the decision or served the notice to which the proceedings in question relate, or who referred the matter to the Secretary of State, or, where the order or notice in question was made or served by him, the authority named in the order or notice.

289. Appeals to High Court relating to enforcement notices and notices under s. 207

(1) Where the Secretary of State gives a decision in proceedings on an appeal under Part VII against an enforcement notice the appellant or the local planning authority or any other person having an interest in the land to which the notice relates may, according as rules of court may provide, either appeal to the High Court against the decision on a point of law or require the Secretary of State to state and sign a case for the opinion of the High Court.

(2) Where the Secretary of State gives a decision in proceedings on an appeal under Part VIII against a notice under section 207, the appellant or the local planning authority or any person (other than the appellant) on whom the notice was served may, according as rules of court may provide, either appeal to the High Court against the decision on a point of law or require the Secretary of State to state and sign a case for the opinion of the High Court.

(3) At any stage of the proceedings on any such appeal as is mentioned in subsection (1), the Secretary of State may state any question of law arising in the course of the proceedings in the form of a special case for the decision of the High Court.

(4) A decision of the High Court on a case stated by virtue of subsection (3) shall be deemed to be a judgment of the court within the meaning of section 16 of the Supreme Court Act 1981 (jurisdiction of the Court of Appeal to hear and determine appeals from any judgment of the High Court).

(4A) In proceedings brought by virtue of this section in respect of an enforcement notice, the High Court or, as the case may be, the Court of Appeal may, on such terms if any as the Court thinks fit (which may include terms requiring the local planning authority to give an undertaking as to damages or any other matter), order that the notice shall have effect, or have effect to such extent as may be specified in the order, pending the final determination of those proceedings and any re-hearing and determination by the Secretary of State.

(4B) Where proceedings are brought by virtue of this section in respect of any notice under section 207, the notice shall be of no effect pending the final determination of those proceedings and any re-hearing and determination by the Secretary of State.

(5) In relation to any proceedings in the High Court or the Court of Appeal brought by virtue of this section the power to make rules of court shall include power to make rules—

(a) prescribing the powers of the High Court or the Court of Appeal with respect to the remitting of the matter with the opinion or direction of the court for re-hearing and determination by the Secretary of State; and

(b) providing for the Secretary of State, either generally or in such circumstances as may be prescribed by the rules, to be treated as a party to any such proceedings and to be entitled to appear and to be heard accordingly.

(5A) Rules of court may also provide for the High Court or, as the case may be, the Court of Appeal to give directions as to the exercise, until such proceedings in respect of an enforcement notice are finally concluded and any re-hearing and determination by the Secretary of State has taken place, of any other powers in respect of the matters to which such a notice relates.

(6) No proceedings in the High Court shall be brought by virtue of this section except with the leave of that Court and no appeal to the Court of Appeal shall be so brought except with the leave of the Court of Appeal or of the High Court.

(7) In this section 'decision' includes a direction or order, and references to the giving of a decision shall be construed accordingly.

290. [repealed by the Planning and Compensation Act 1991]

291. Special provisions as to decisions relating to statutory undertakers
In relation to any action which—

(a) apart from the provisions of Part XI would fall to be taken by the Secretary of State and, if so taken, would be action falling within section 284(3); but

(b) by virtue of that Part, is required to be taken by the Secretary State and the appropriate Minister,

the provisions of sections 284 and 288 shall have effect (subject to section 292) as if any reference in those provisions to the Secretary of State were a reference to the Secretary of State and the appropriate Minister.

292. Special provisions as to orders subject to special parliamentary procedure

(1) Where an order under section 247, 248, 249 or 277 is subject to special parliamentary procedure, then—

(a) if the order is confirmed by Act of Parliament under section 6 of the Statutory Orders (Special Procedure) Act 1945, sections 284 and 287 shall not apply to the order;

(b) in any other case, section 287 shall have effect in relation to the order as if, in subsection (4) of that section, for the reference to the date there mentioned there were substituted a reference to the date on which the order becomes operative under section 6 of that Act ('the operative date').

(2) Where by virtue of Part XI any such action as is mentioned in section 291 is required to be embodied in an order, and that order is subject to special parliamentary procedure, then—

(a) if the order in which the action is embodied is confirmed by Act of Parliament under section 6 of that Act, sections 284 and 288 shall not apply;

(b) in any other case, section 288 shall apply with the substitution for any reference to the date on which the action is taken of a reference to the operative date.

PART XIII
APPLICATION OF ACT TO CROWN LAND

Preliminary

293. Preliminary definitions

(1) In this Part—

'Crown land' means land in which there is a Crown interest or a Duchy interest;
'Crown interest' means an interest belonging to Her Majesty in right of the Crown or belonging to a government department or held in trust for Her Majesty for the purposes of a government department;
'Duchy interest' means an interest belonging to Her Majesty in right of the Duchy of Lancaster or belonging to the Duchy of Cornwall;
'private interest' means an interest which is neither a Crown interest nor a Duchy interest.

(2) For the purposes of this Part 'the appropriate authority', in relation to any land—

(a) in the case of land belonging to Her Majesty in right of the Crown and forming part of the Crown Estate, means the Crown Estate Commissioners;

(b) in relation to any other land belonging to Her Majesty in right of the Crown, means the government department having the management of that land;

(c) in relation to land belonging to Her Majesty in right of the Duchy of Lancaster, means the Chancellor of the Duchy;

(d) in relation to land belonging to the Duchy of Cornwall, means such person as the Duke of Cornwall, or the possessor for the time being of the Duchy of Cornwall, appoints;

(e) in the case of land belonging to a government department or held in trust for Her Majesty for the purposes of a government department, means that department.

(3) If any question arises as to what authority is the appropriate authority in relation to any land, that question shall be referred to the Treasury, whose decision shall be final.

(4) A person who is entitled to occupy Crown land by virtue of a licence in writing shall be treated for the purposes of section 296(1)(c), so far as applicable to Parts III, VII and VIII, and sections 294(2) to (7), 295, 299 and 300 as having an interest in land and references in section 299 to the disposal of an interest in Crown land, and in that section and sections 294(2) and 300 to a private interest in such land, shall be construed accordingly.

Application of Act as respects Crown land

294. Control of development on Crown land: special enforcement notices

(1) No enforcement notice shall be issued under section 172 in respect of development carried out by or on behalf of the Crown after 1st July 1948 on land which was Crown land at the time when the development was carried out.

(2) The following provisions of this section apply to development of Crown land carried out otherwise than by or on behalf of the Crown at a time when no person is entitled to occupy it by virtue of a private interest.

(3) Where—

(a) it appears to a local planning authority that development to which this subsection applies has taken place in their area, and

(b) they consider it expedient to do so having regard to the provisions of the development plan and to any other material considerations,

they may issue a notice under this section (a 'special enforcement notice').

(4) No special enforcement notice shall be issued except with the consent of the appropriate authority.

(5) A special enforcement notice shall specify—

(a) the matters alleged to constitute development to which this section applies; and

(b) the steps which the authority issuing the notice require to be taken for restoring the land to its condition before the development took place or for discontinuing any use of the land which has been instituted by the development.

(6) A special enforcement notice shall also specify—

(a) the date on which it is to take effect ('the specified date'), and

(b) the period within which any such steps as are mentioned in subsection (5)(b) are to be taken.

(7) A special enforcement notice may specify different periods for the taking of different steps.

Town and Country Planning Act 1990 171

295. Supplementary provisions as to special enforcement notices

(1) Not later than 28 days after the date of the issue of a special enforcement notice and not later than 28 days before the specified date, the local planning authority who issued it shall serve a copy of it—

   (a) on the person who carried out the development alleged in the notice;
   (b) on any person who is occupying the land when the notice is issued; and
   (c) on the appropriate authority.

(2) The local planning authority need not serve a copy of the notice on the person mentioned in subsection (1)(a) if they are unable after reasonable enquiry to identify or trace him.

(3) Any such person as mentioned in subsection (1)(a) or (b) may appeal against the notice to the Secretary of State on the ground that the matters alleged in the notice—

   (a) have not taken place, or
   (b) do not constitute development to which section 294 applies.

(4) A person may appeal against a special enforcement notice under subsection (3) whether or not he was served with a copy of it.

(5) The provisions contained in or having effect under sections 174(3) to (5), 175(1) to (4) and 176(1) to (4) shall apply to special enforcement notices issued by local planning authorities and to appeals against them under subsection (3) as they apply to enforcement notices and to appeals under section 174.

(6) The Secretary of State may by regulations apply to special enforcement notices and to appeals under subsection (3) such other provisions of this Act (with such modifications as he thinks fit) as he thinks necessary or expedient.

296. Exercise of powers in relation to Crown land

(1) Notwithstanding any interest of the Crown in Crown land, but subject to the following provisions of this section—

   (a) a plan approved, adopted or made under Part II of this Act or Part II of the 1971 Act may include proposals relating to the use of Crown land;
   (b) any power to acquire land compulsorily under Part IX may be exercised in relation to any interest in Crown land which is for the time being held otherwise than by or on behalf of the Crown;
   (c) any restrictions or powers imposed or conferred by Part III, VII except sections 196A and 196B or VIII, by the provisions of Part VI relating to purchase notices, or by any of the provisions of sections 266 to 270, shall apply and be exercisable in relation to Crown land, to the extent of any interest in it for the time being held otherwise than by or on behalf of the Crown.

(2) Except with the consent of the appropriate authority—

   (a) no order or notice shall be made, issued or served under any of the provisions of section 102, 103, 171C, 172, 173A, 183, 187A, 187B, 198, 199 or 215 or Schedule 9 or under any of those provisions as applied by any order or regulations made under Part VIII, in relation to land which for the time being is Crown land;
   (aa) in relation to land which for the time being is Crown land—
      (i) a planning obligation shall not be enforced by injunction; and
      (ii) the power to enter land conferred by section 106(6) shall not be exercised;
   (b) no interest in land which for the time being is Crown land shall be acquired compulsorily under Part IX.

(3) No purchase notice shall be served in relation to any interest in Crown land unless—

   (a) an offer has been previously made by the owner of that interest to dispose of it to the appropriate authority on equivalent terms, and
   (b) that offer has been refused by the appropriate authority.

(4) In subsection (3) 'equivalent terms' means that the price payable for the interest shall be equal to (and shall, in default of agreement, be determined in the same manner as) the compensation which would be payable in respect of it if it were acquired in pursuance of a purchase notice.

(5) The rights conferred by the provisions of Chapter II of Part VI shall be exercisable by a person who (within the meaning of those provisions) is an owner-occupier of a hereditament or agricultural unit which is Crown land, or is a resident owner-occupier of a hereditament which is Crown land, in the same way as they are exercisable in respect of a hereditament or agricultural unit which is not Crown land, and those provisions shall apply accordingly.

297. Agreements relating to Crown land

(1) The appropriate authority and the local planning authority for the area in which any Crown land is situated may make agreements for securing the use of the land, so far as may be prescribed by any such agreement, in conformity with the provisions of the development plan applicable to it.

(2) Any such agreement may contain such consequential provisions, including provisions of a financial character, as may appear to be necessary or expedient having regard to the purposes of the agreement.

(3) An agreement made under this section by a government department shall not have effect unless it is approved by the Treasury.

(4) In considering whether to make or approve an agreement under this section relating—
    (a) to land belonging to a government department, or
    (b) to land held in trust for Her Majesty for the purposes of a government department,
the department and the Treasury shall have regard to the purposes for which the land is held by or for the department.

298. Supplementary provisions as to Crown and Duchy interests

(1) Where there is a Crown interest in any land, sections 109 to 112 shall have effect in relation to any private interest or Duchy interest as if the Crown interest were a private interest.

(2) Where there is a Duchy interest in any land, those sections shall have effect in relation to that interest or any private interest as if the Duchy interest were a private interest.

(3) Where, in accordance with an agreement under section 297, the approval of a local planning authority is required in respect of any development of land in which there is a Duchy interest, sections 109 to 112 shall have effect in relation to the withholding of that approval, or the giving of it subject to conditions, as if it were a refusal of planning permission or, as the case may be, a grant of planning permission subject to conditions.

Provisions relating to anticipated disposal of Crown land

299. Application for planning permission etc. in anticipation of disposal of Crown land

(1) This section has effect for the purpose of enabling Crown land, or an interest in Crown land, to be disposed of with the benefit of planning permission or a certificate under section 192.

(2) Notwithstanding the interest of the Crown in the land in question, an application for any such permission or certificate may be made by—
    (a) the appropriate authority; or
    (b) any person authorised by that authority in writing;

Town and Country Planning Act 1990 173

and, subject to subsections (3) to (5), all the statutory provisions relating to the making and determination of any such application shall accordingly apply as if the land were not Crown land.

(3) Any planning permission granted by virtue of this section shall apply only—

(a) to development carried out after the land in question has ceased to be Crown land; and

(b) so long as that land continues to be Crown land, to development carried out by virtue of a private interest in the land.

(4) Any application made by virtue of this section for a certificate under section 192 shall be determined as if the land were not Crown land.

(5) The Secretary of State may by regulations—

(a) modify or exclude any of the statutory provisions referred to in subsection (2) in their application by virtue of that subsection and any other statutory provisions in their application to permissions or certificates granted or made by virtue of this section;

(b) make provision for requiring a local planning authority to be notified of any disposal of, or of an interest in, any Crown land in respect of which an application has been made by virtue of this section; and

(c) make such other provision in relation to the making and determination of applications by virtue of this section as he thinks necessary or expedient.

(6) This section shall not be construed as affecting any right to apply for any such permission or certificate as is mentioned in subsection (1) in respect of Crown land in a case in which such an application can be made by virtue of a private interest in the land.

(7) In this section 'statutory provisions' means provisions contained in or having effect under any enactment.

299A. Crown planning obligations

(1) The appropriate authority in relation to any Crown interest or Duchy interest in land in the area of a local planning authority may enter into an obligation falling within any of paragraphs (a) to (d) of section 106(1) (in this section referred to as a 'planning obligation') enforceable to the extent mentioned in subsection (3).

(2) A planning obligation may not be entered into except by an instrument executed as a deed which—

(a) states that the obligation is a planning obligation for the purposes of this section;

(b) identifies the land in relation to which the obligation is entered into;

(c) identifies the appropriate authority who are entering into the obligation and states what the Crown or Duchy interest in the land is; and

(d) identifies the local planning authority by whom the obligation is enforceable.

(3) A planning obligation entered into under this section is enforceable—

(a) against any person with a private interest deriving from the Crown or Duchy interest stated in accordance with subsection (2)(c);

(b) by the authority identified in accordance with subsection (2)(d).

(4) Subject to subsection (5), subsections (2), (4) to (8) and (10) to (13) of section 106 and sections 106A and 106B apply to a planning obligation entered into under this section as they apply to a planning obligation entered into under that section.

(5) The consent of the appropriate authority must be obtained to—

(a) the enforcement by injunction of a planning obligation against a person in respect of land which is Crown land; and

(b) the exercise, in relation to Crown land, of the power to enter land conferred by section 106(6) (as applied by subsection (4)).

300. Tree preservation orders in anticipation of disposal of Crown land

(1) A local planning authority may make a tree preservation order in respect of Crown land in which no interest is for the time, being held otherwise than by or on behalf of the Crown, if they consider it expedient to do so for the purpose of preserving trees or woodlands on the land in the event of its ceasing to be Crown land or becoming-subject to a private interest.

(2) No tree preservation order shall be made by virtue of this section except with the consent of the appropriate authority.

(3) A tree preservation order made by virtue of this section shall not take effect until the first occurrence of a relevant event.

(4) For the purposes of subsection (3), a relevant event occurs in relation to any land if it ceases to be Crown land or becomes subject to a private interest.

(5) A tree preservation order made by virtue of this section—
 (a) shall not require confirmation under section 199 until after the occurrence of the event by virtue of which it takes effect; and
 (b) shall by virtue of this subsection continue in force until—
  (i) the expiration of the period of six months beginning with the occurrence of that event; or
  (ii) the date on which the order is confirmed,
whichever first occurs.

(6) Where a tree preservation order takes effect in accordance with subsection (3), the appropriate authority shall as soon as practicable give to the authority who made the order a notice in writing of the name and address of the person who has become entitled to the land in question or to a private interest in it.

(7) The procedure prescribed under section 199 in connection with the confirmation of a tree preservation order shall apply in relation to an order made by virtue of this section as if the order were made on the date on which the notice under subsection (6) is received by the authority who made it.

301. Requirement of planning permission for continuance of use instituted by the Crown

(1) A local planning authority in whose area any Crown land is situated may agree with the appropriate authority that subsection (2) shall apply to such use of land by the Crown as is specified in the agreement, being a use resulting from a material change made or proposed to be made by the Crown in the use of the land.

(2) Where an agreement is made under subsection (1) in respect of any Crown land, then, if at any time the land ceases to be used by the Crown for the purposes specified in the agreement, this Act shall have effect in relation to any subsequent private use of the land as if—
 (a) the specified use by the Crown had required planning permission, and
 (b) that use had been authorised by planning permission granted subject to a condition requiring its discontinuance at that time.

(3) The condition referred to in subsection (2) shall not be enforceable against any person who had a private interest in the land at the time when the agreement was made unless the local planning authority by whom the agreement was made have notified him of the making of the agreement and of the effect of that subsection.

(4) An agreement made under subsection (1) by a local planning authority shall be a local land charge, and for the purposes of the Local Land Charges Act 1975 the local planning authority by whom such an agreement is made shall be treated as the originating authority as respects the charge constituted by the agreement.

(5) In this section 'private use' means use otherwise than by or on behalf of the Crown, and references to the use of land by the Crown include references to its use on behalf of the Crown.

Enforcement in respect of war-time breaches of planning control by the Crown

302. Enforcement in respect of war-time breaches of planning control by the Crown

(1) This section applies where during the war period—
 (a) works not complying with planning control were carried out on land, or
 (b) a use of land not complying with planning control was begun by or on behalf of the Crown.

(2) Subject to subsection (4), if at any time after the end of the war period there subsists in the land a permanent or long-term interest which is neither held by or on behalf of the Crown nor subject to any interest or right to possession so held, the planning control shall, so long as such an interest subsists in the land, be enforceable in respect of those works or that use notwithstanding—
 (a) that the works were carried out or the land used by or on behalf of the Crown, or
 (b) the subsistence in the land of any interest held by or on behalf of the Crown in reversion (whether immediate or not) expectant on the termination of that permanent or long-term interest.

(3) A person entitled to make an application under this subsection with respect to any land may apply at any time before the relevant date to an authority responsible for enforcing any planning control for a determination—
 (a) whether works on the land carried out, or a use of the land begun, during the war period fail to comply with any planning control which the authority are responsible for enforcing, and
 (b) if so, whether the works or use should be deemed to comply with that control.

(4) Where any works on land carried out, or use of land begun, during the war period remain or continues after the relevant date and no such determination has been given, the works or use shall by virtue of this subsection be treated for all purposes as complying with that control unless steps for enforcing the control have been begun before that date.

(5) Schedule 15 shall have effect for the purpose of making supplementary provision concerning the enforcement of breaches of planning control to which this section applies and the making and determination of applications under subsection (3).

(6) In this section and that Schedule—
 'authority responsible for enforcing planning control' means, in relation to any works on land or use of land, the authority empowered by virtue of section 75 of the 1947 Act or of paragraph 34 of Schedule 24 to the 1971 Act (including that paragraph as it continues in effect by virtue of Schedule 3 to the Planning (Consequential Provisions) Act 1990) to serve an enforcement notice in respect of it or the authority who would be so empowered if the works had been carried out, or the use begun, otherwise than in compliance with planning control;
 'the relevant date', in relation to any land, means the date with which the period of five years from the end of the war period ends, but for the purposes of this definition any time during which, notwithstanding subsection (2), planning control is unenforceable by reason of the subsistence in or over the land of any interest or right to possession held by or on behalf of the Crown shall be disregarded;
 'owner' has the same meaning as in the Housing Act 1985 and 'owned' shall be construed accordingly;
 'permanent or long-term interest', in relation to any land, means the fee simple in the land, a tenancy of the land granted for a term of more than ten years and

not subject to a subsisting right of the landlord to determine the tenancy at or before the expiration of ten years from the beginning of the term, or a tenancy granted for a term of ten years or less with a right of renewal which would enable the tenant to prolong the term of the tenancy beyond ten years;

'tenancy' includes a tenancy under an underlease and a tenancy under an agreement for a lease or underlease, but does not include an option to take a tenancy and does not include a mortgage;

'war period' means the period extending from 3rd September 1939 to 26th March 1946;

'works' includes any building, structure, excavation or other work on land.

(7) References in this section and that Schedule to non-compliance with planning control mean—

(a) in relation to works on land carried out, or a use of land begun, at a time when the land was subject to a resolution to prepare a scheme under the Town and Country Planning Act 1932, that the works were carried out or the use begun otherwise than in accordance with the terms of an interim development order or of permission granted under such an order;

(b) in relation to works on land carried out, or a use of land begun, at a time when the land was subject to such a scheme, that the works were carried out or the use begun otherwise than in conformity with the provisions of the scheme;

and references in this Act to compliance with planning control shall be construed accordingly.

(8) References in this section and that Schedule to the enforcement of planning control shall be construed as references to the exercise of the powers conferred by section 75 of the 1947 Act or by paragraph 34 of Schedule 24 to the 1971 Act (including that paragraph as it continues in effect by virtue of Schedule 3 to the Planning (Consequential Provisions) Act 1990).

PART XIV
FINANCIAL PROVISIONS

303. Fees for planning applications, etc.

(1) The Secretary of State may by regulations make such provision as he thinks fit for the payment of a fee of the prescribed amount to a local planning authority in respect of an application made to them under the planning Acts or any order or regulations made under them for any permission, consent, approval, determination or certificate.

(2) Regulations under subsection (1) may provide for the transfer of prescribed fees received in respect of any description of application by an authority to whom applications fall to be made to any other authority by whom applications of that description fall to be dealt with.

(3) The Secretary of State may by regulations make such provision as he thinks fit for the payment—

(a) of fees of prescribed amounts to him and to the local planning authority in respect of any application for planning permission deemed to be made under section 177(5); and

(b) of a fee of the prescribed amount to him in respect of any other application for planning permission which is deemed to be made to him under this Act or any order or regulations made under it.

(4) Regulations under subsection (1) or (3) may provide for the remission or refunding of a prescribed fee (in whole or in part) in prescribed circumstances.

(5) No such regulations shall be made unless a draft of the regulations has been laid before and approved by a resolution of each House of Parliament.

(6) The reference to the planning Acts in subsection (1) does not include a reference to section 302 of this Act.

304. Grants for research and education

The Secretary of State may, with the consent of the Treasury, make grants for assisting establishments engaged in promoting or assisting research relating to, and education with respect to, the planning and design of the physical environment.

305. Contributions by Ministers towards compensation paid by local authorities

(1) Where—

(a) compensation is payable by a local authority, National Park Authority under this Act in consequence of any decision or order to which this section applies, and

(b) that decision or order was given or made wholly or partly in the interest of a service which is provided by a government department and the cost of which is defrayed out of money provided by Parliament,

the Minister responsible for the administration of that service may pay to that authority a contribution of such amount as he may with the consent of the Treasury determine.

(2) This section applies to any decision or order given or made under Part III, the provisions of Part VI relating to purchase notices, Part VII, Part VIII or Schedule 5, 6 or 9.

[The reference to a National Parks Authority was inserted by the Environment Act 1995, see note to Section 4A supra.]

306. Contributions by local authorities and statutory undertakers

(1) Without prejudice to section 274 of the Highways Act 1980 (contributions by local authorities to expenses of highway authorities), any local authority may contribute towards any expenses incurred by a local highway authority—

(a) in the acquisition of land under Part IX of this Act or Chapter V of Part I of the Planning (Listed Buildings and Conservation Areas) Act 1990,

(b) in the construction or improvement of roads on land so acquired, or

(c) in connection with any development required in the interests of the proper planning of the area of the local authority.

(2) Any local authority and any statutory undertakers may contribute towards—

(a) any expenses incurred by a local planning authority in or in connection with the carrying out of a survey or the preparation of a unitary development plan or a local plan, minerals local plan or waste local plan or the alteration or replacement of such a plan or a structure plan under Part II;

(b) any expenses incurred by a local planning authority or a mineral planning authority in or in connection with the performance of any of their functions under Part III, the provisions of Part VI relating to purchase notices, Part VII (except sections 196A and 196B), Part VIII (except section 207), Part IX or Schedule 5 or 9.

(3) Where any expenses are incurred by a local authority in the payment of compensation payable in consequence of anything done under Part III, the provisions of Part VI relating to purchase notices, Part VII (except section 196A and 196B), Part VIII, or Schedule 5 or 9, the Secretary of State may, if it appears to him to be expedient to do so, require any other local authority to contribute towards those expenses such sum as appears to him to be reasonable, having regard to any benefit accruing to that authority by reason of the proceeding giving rise to the compensation.

(4) Subsection (3) shall apply in relation to payments made by a local authority to any statutory undertakers in accordance with financial arrangements to which effect is given under section 275(5)(c), as it applies in relation to compensation payable by such an authority in consequence of anything done under Part III, Part VIII or Schedule 5 or 9, and the reference in that subsection to the proceeding giving rise to the compensation shall be construed accordingly.

(5) For the purposes of this section, contributions made by a local planning authority towards the expenditure of a joint advisory committee shall be deemed to

be expenses incurred by that authority for the purposes for which that expenditure is incurred by the committee.

(6) This section shall have effect as if the references to a local authority included references to a National Park authority.

[Inserted by the Environment Act 1995, see note to Section 4A supra.]

307. Assistance for acquisition of property where objection made to blight notice in certain cases

(1) The council of a county, [county borough] district or London borough may advance money to any person for the purposes of enabling him to acquire a hereditament or agricultural unit in respect of which a counter-notice has been served under section 151 specifying the grounds mentioned in subsection (4)(d) of that section as, or as one of, the grounds of objection.

(2) No advance may be made under subsection (1) in the case of a hereditament if its annual value exceeds such amount as may be prescribed for the purposes of section 149(3)(a).

(3) An advance under subsection (1) may be made subject to such conditions as the council may think fit.

[The words in Section 307(1) in [ ] were inserted by, and will come into effect on an appointed day order under, the Local Government (Wales) Act 1994.]

308. Recovery from acquiring authorities of sums paid by way of compensation

(1) This section applies where—

(a) an interest in land is compulsorily acquired or is sold to an authority possessing compulsory purchase powers, and

(b) a notice is registered under section 110(2) in respect of any of the land acquired or sold (whether before or after the completion of the acquisition or sale) in consequence of a planning decision or order made before the service of the notice to treat, or the making of the contract, in pursuance of which the acquisition or sale is effected.

(2) Where this section applies the Secretary of State shall, subject to the following provisions of this section, be entitled to recover from the acquiring authority a sum equal to so much of the amount of the compensation specified in the notice as (in accordance with section 110(5) is to be treated as attributable to that land.

(3) If immediately after the completion of the acquisition or sale, there is outstanding some interest in the land acquired or sold to which a person other than the acquiring authority is entitled, the sum referred to in subsection (2) shall not accrue due until that interest either ceases to exist or becomes vested in the acquiring authority.

(4) No sum shall be recoverable under this section in the case of a compulsory acquisition or sale where the Secretary of State is satisfied that the interest in question is being acquired for the purposes of the use of the land as a public open space.

(5) Where the Secretary of State recovers a sum under this section in respect of any land by reason that it is land in respect of which a notice is registered under the provisions of section 110, section 112(11) to (13) shall have effect in relation to that sum as if it were a sum recovered as mentioned in section 112(11).

(6) In this section 'interest' (where the reference is to an interest in land) mean the fee simple or a tenancy of the land and does not include any other interest in it.

309. [repealed by the Planning and Compensation Act 1991]

310. Sums recoverable from acquiring authorities reckonable for purposes of grant

Where—

(a) a sum is recoverable from any authority under section 308 by reference to an acquisition or purchase of an interest in land, and

(b) grant became or becomes payable to that or some other authority under an enactment in respect of that acquisition or purchase or of a subsequent appropriation of the land,

the power conferred by that enactment to pay the grant shall include, and shall be deemed always to have included, power to pay a grant in respect of that sum as if it had been expenditure incurred by the acquiring authority in connection with the acquisition or purchase.

311. Expenses of government departments

(1) The following expenses of the Secretary of State shall be paid out of money provided by Parliament—

(a) any expenses incurred by the Secretary of State under subsection (5) of section 220 or in the payment of expenses of any committee established under that section;

(b) any sums necessary to enable the Secretary of State to make any payments becoming payable by him under Part IV;

(c) any expenses incurred by the Secretary of State under Part X;

(d) any expenses incurred by the Secretary of State in the making of grants under section 304;

(e) any administrative expenses incurred by the Secretary of State for the purposes of this Act.

(2) There shall be paid out of money provided by Parliament any expenses incurred by any government department (including the Secretary of State)—

(a) in the acquisition of land under Part IX;

(b) in the payment of compensation under section 236(4), 279(2) or 325;

(c) under section 240(1)(b); or

(d) under section 305.

312. [repealed by the Planning and Compensation Act 1991]

313. General provision as to receipts of Secretary of State

Subject to the provisions of section 112, any sums received by the Secretary of State under any provision of this Act shall be paid into the Consolidated Fund.

314. Expenses of county councils

The council of a county may direct that any expenses incurred by them under the provisions specified in Parts I and II of Schedule 16 shall be treated as special expenses of a county council chargeable upon such part of the county as may be specified in the directions.

PART XV
MISCELLANEOUS AND GENERAL PROVISIONS

Application of Act in special cases

315. Power to modify Act in relation to minerals

(1) In relation to development consisting of the winning and working of minerals or involving the depositing of mineral waste, the provisions specified in Parts I and II of Schedule 16 shall have effect subject to such adaptations and modifications as may be prescribed.

(2) In relation to interests in land consisting of or comprising minerals (being either the fee simple or tenancies of such land), the provisions specified in Part III of Schedule 16 shall have effect subject to such adaptations and modifications as may be prescribed.

(3) Regulations made for the purposes of this section may only be made with the consent of the Treasury and shall be of no effect unless they are approved by resolution of each House of Parliament.

(4) Any regulations made by virtue of subsection (1) shall not apply—

(a) to the winning and working, on land held or occupied with land used for the purposes of agriculture, of any minerals reasonably required for the purposes of that use, including the fertilisation of the land so used and the maintenance, improvement or alteration of buildings or works on it which are occupied or used for those purposes; or

(b) to development consisting of the winning and working of any minerals vested in the British Coal Corporation, being development to which any of the provisions of the planning Acts relating to operational land of statutory undertakers apply by virtue of regulations made under section 317.

(5) Nothing in subsection (1) or (4) shall be construed as affecting the prerogative right of Her Majesty (whether in right of the Crown or of the Duchy of Lancaster) or of the Duke of Cornwall to any gold or silver mine.

316. Land of interested planning authorities and development by them

(1) The provisions of Parts III, VII and VIII of this Act shall apply in relation to—
   (a) land of interested planning authorities; and
   (b) the development of any land by interested planning authorities or by such authorities jointly with any other persons,
subject to regulations made by virtue of this section.

(2) The regulations may, in relation to such land or such development—
   (a) provide for any of those provisions to apply subject to prescribed exceptions or modifications or not to apply;
   (b) make new provision as to any matter dealt with in any of those provisions;
   (c) make different provision in relation to different classes of land or development.

(3) Without prejudice to subsection (2), the regulations may provide—
   (a) subject to subsection (5), for applications for planning permission to develop such land, or for such development, to be determined by the authority concerned, by another interested planning authority or by the Secretary of State; and
   (b) for the procedure to be followed on such applications,
and, in the case of applications falling to be determined by an interested planning authority, they may regulate the authority's arrangements for the discharge of their functions, notwithstanding anything in section 101 of the Local Government Act 1972.

(4) The regulations shall—
   (a) provide for section 71(3), and any provision made by virtue of section 65 or 71 by a development order, to apply to applications for planning permission to develop such land, or for such development, subject to prescribed exceptions or modifications, or
   (b) make corresponding provision.

(5) In the case of any application for planning permission to develop land of an interested planning authority where—
   (a) the authority do not intend to develop the land themselves or jointly with any other person; and
   (b) if it were not such land, the application would fall to be determined by another body,
the regulations shall provide for the application to be determined by that other body, unless the application is referred to the Secretary of State under section 77.

(6) In this section 'interested planning authority', in relation to any land, means any body which exercises any of the functions of a local planning authority in relation

to that land; and for the purposes of this section land is land of an authority if the authority have any interest in it.

(7) This section applies to any consent required in respect of any land as it applies to planning permission to develop land.

(8) Subsection (1) does not apply to sections 76, 90(2) and (5) and 223.

316A. Local planning authorities as statutory undertakers

In relation to statutory undertakers who are local planning authorities, section 283 and the provisions specified in that section shall have effect subject to such exceptions and modifications as may be prescribed.

317. [repealed by the Coal Industry Act 1994]

318. Ecclesiastical property

(1) Without prejudice to the provisions of the Acquisition of Land Act 1981 with respect to notices served under that Act, where under any of the provisions of this Act a notice or copy of a notice is required to be served on an owner of land, and the land is ecclesiastical property, a similar notice or copy of a notice shall be served on the Church Commissioners.

(2) Where the fee simple of any ecclesiastical property is in abeyance—

(a) if the property is situated elsewhere than in Wales, then for the purposes of the provisions specified in Part VI of Schedule 16 the fee simple shall be treated as being vested in the Church Commissioners;

(b) in any case, the fee simple shall, for the purposes of a compulsory acquisition of the property under Part IX, be treated as being vested in the Church Commissioners, and any notice to treat shall be served, or be deemed to have been served, accordingly.

(3) Any compensation payable under Part IV, section 186, Part VIII (except section 204) or section 250 in respect of land which is ecclesiastical property—

(a) shall in the case of glebe land, be paid to the Church Commissioners; and

(b) shall, in the case of diocesan glebe land, be paid to the Diocesan Board of Finance in which the land is vested, and (in either case) be applied by them for the purposes for which the proceeds of a sale by agreement of the land would be applicable under any enactment or Measure authorising or disposing of the proceeds of such a sale.

(4) Any sum which under any of the provisions specified in Part III of Schedule 16 is payable in relation to land which is, or on 1st July 1948 was, ecclesiastical property, and apart from this subsection would be payable to an incumbent—

(a) shall be paid to the Church Commissioners, and

(b) shall be applied by them for the purposes mentioned in subsection (3).

(5) Where any sum is recoverable under section 111, 112, 133 or 327 in respect of any such land, the Church Commissioners may apply any money or securities held by them in the payment of that sum.

(6) In this section 'ecclesiastical property' means land belonging to an ecclesiastical benefice, or being or forming part of a church subject to the jurisdiction of a bishop of any diocese or the site of such a church, or being or forming part of a burial ground subject to such jurisdiction or being diocesan glebe land; and 'Diocesan Board of Finance' and 'diocesan glebe land' have the same meaning as in the Endowments and Glebe Measure Act 1976.

319. The Isles of Scilly

(1) This Act applies to the Isles of Scilly subject to such exceptions, adaptations and modifications as the Secretary of State may by order direct.

(2) An order under this section may in particular provide for the exercise by the Council of the Isles of Scilly of any functions exercisable by a local planning authority or mineral planning authority.

(3) Before making an order under this section the Secretary of State shall consult with that Council.

Local inquiries and other hearings

320. Local inquiries
(1) The Secretary of State may cause a local inquiry to be held for the purposes of the exercise of any of his functions under any of the provisions of this Act.

(2) Subsections (2) to (5) of section 250 of the Local Government Act 1972 (local inquiries: evidence and costs) apply to an inquiry held by virtue of this section.

321. Planning inquiries to be held in public subject to certain exceptions
(1) This section applies to any inquiry held under section 320(1), paragraph 6 of Schedule 6 or paragraph 5 of Schedule 8.

(2) Subject to subsection (3), at any such inquiry oral evidence shall be heard in public and documentary evidence shall be open to public inspection.

(3) If the Secretary of State is satisfied in the case of any such inquiry—

(a) that giving evidence of a particular description or, as the case may be, making it available for inspection would be likely to result in the disclosure of information as to any of the matters mentioned in subsection (4); and

(b) that the public disclosure of that information would be contrary to the national interest,

he may direct that evidence of the description indicated in the direction shall only be heard or, as the case may be, open to inspection at that inquiry by such persons or persons of such descriptions as he may specify in the direction.

(4) The matters referred to in subsection (3)(a) are

(a) national security; and

(b) the measures taken or to be taken to ensure the security of any premises or property.

322. Orders as to costs of parties where no local inquiry held
(1) This section applies to proceedings under this Act where the Secretary of State is required, before reaching a decision, to give any person an opportunity of appearing before and being heard by a person appointed by him.

(2) The Secretary of State has the same power to make orders under section 250(5) of the Local Government Act 1972 (orders with respect to the costs of the parties) in relation to proceedings to which this section applies which do not give rise to a local inquiry as he has in relation to a local inquiry.

322A. Orders as to costs: supplementary
(1) This section applies where—

(a) for the purposes of any proceedings under this Act—

(i) the Secretary of State is required, before a decision is reached, to give any person an opportunity, or ask any person whether he wishes, to appear before and be heard by a person appointed by him; and

(ii) arrangements are made for a local inquiry or hearing to be held;

(b) the inquiry or hearing does not take place; and

(c) if it had taken place, the Secretary of State or a person appointed by him would have had power to make an order under section 250(5) of the Local Government Act 1972 requiring any party to pay any costs of any other party.

(2) Where this section applies the power to make such an order may be exercised, in relation to costs incurred for the purposes of the inquiry or hearing, as if it had taken place.

323. Procedure on certain appeals and applications
(1) The Secretary of State may by regulations prescribe the procedure to be followed in connection with proceedings under this Act where he is required, before

reaching a decision, to give any person an opportunity of appearing before and being heard by a person appointed by him and which are to be disposed of without an inquiry or hearing to which rules under section 11 of the Tribunals and Inquiries Act 1992 apply.

(2) The regulations may in particular make provision as to the procedure to be followed—

(a) where steps have been taken with a view to the holding of such an inquiry or hearing which does not take place, or

(b) where steps have been taken with a view to the determination of any matter by a person appointed by the Secretary of State and the proceedings are the subject of a direction that the matter shall instead be determined by the Secretary of State, or

(c) where steps have been taken in pursuance of such a direction and a further direction is made revoking that direction,

and may provide that such steps shall be treated as compliance, in whole or in part, with the requirements of the regulations.

(3) The regulations may also—

(a) provide for a time limit within which any party to the proceedings must submit representations in writing and any supporting documents;

(b) prescribe the time limit (which may be different for different classes of proceedings) or enable the Secretary of State to give directions setting the time limit in a particular case or class of case;

(c) empower the Secretary of State to proceed to a decision taking into account only such written representations and supporting documents as were submitted within the time limit; and

(d) empower the Secretary of State, after giving the parties written notice of his intention to do so, to proceed to a decision notwithstanding that no written representations were made within the time limit, if it appears to him that he has sufficient material before him to enable him to reach a decision on the merits of the case.

Rights of entry

324. Rights of entry

(1) Any person authorised in writing by the Secretary of State or by a local planning authority may at any reasonable time enter any land for the purpose of surveying it in connection with—

(a) the preparation, approval, adoption or making of a unitary development plan or a local plan, minerals local plan or waste local plan relating to the land under Part II or the alteration of such a plan or a structure plan relating to the land under that Part, including the carrying out of any survey under that Part;

(b) any application under Part III or sections 220 or 221 or under any order or regulations made under any of those provisions, for any permission, consent or determination to be given or made in connection with that land or any other land under that Part or any of those sections or under any such order or regulations;

(c) any proposal by the local planning authority or by the Secretary of State to make, issue or serve any order or notice under Part other than sections 94 and 96), or Chapter 2 or 3 of Part VIII or under any order or regulations made under any of those provisions.

(2) [repealed by the Planning and Compensation Act 1991]

(3) Any person duly authorised in writing by the local planning authority may at any reasonable time enter any land for the purpose of exercising a power conferred on the authority by section 225 if—

(a) the land is unoccupied; and

(b) it would be impossible to exercise the power without entering the land.

(4) [repealed by the Planning and Compensation Act 1991]

(5) Any person who is an officer of the Valuation Office or is duly authorised in writing by a local planning authority may at any reasonable time enter any land for the purpose of surveying it, or estimating its value, in connection with a claim for compensation in respect of that land or any other land which is payable by the local planning authority under Part IV, section 186, Chapters 2 or 3 of Part VIII section 250(1) or Part XI (other than section 279(2) or (3) or 280(1)(c)).

(6) Any person who is an officer of the Valuation Office or is duly authorised in writing by a local authority or Minister authorised to acquire land under section 226 or 228 or by a local authority who have power to acquire land under Part IX may at any reasonable time enter any land for the purpose of surveying it, or estimating its value, in connection with any proposal to acquire that land or any other land or in connection with any claim for compensation in respect of any such acquisition.

(7) Any person duly authorised in writing by the Secretary of State or by a local planning authority may at any reasonable time enter any land in respect of which an order or notice has been made or served as mentioned in subsection (1)(c) for the purpose of ascertaining whether the order or notice has been complied with.

(8) Subject to section 325, any power conferred by this section to survey land shall be construed as including power to search and bore for the purpose of ascertaining the nature of the subsoil or the presence of minerals in it.

(9) In subsections (1)(c) and (7) references to a local planning authority include, in relation to a building situated in Greater London, a reference to the Historic Buildings and Monuments Commission for England.

325. Supplementary provisions as to rights of entry

(1) A person authorised under section 324 to enter any land—

(a) shall, if so required, produce evidence of his authority and state the purpose of his entry before so entering, and

(b) shall not demand admission as of right to any land which is occupied unless 24 hours' notice of the intended entry has been given to the occupier.

(2) Any person who wilfully obstructs a person acting in the exercise of his powers under section 324 shall be guilty of an offence and liable on summary conviction to a fine not exceeding level 3 on the standard scale.

(3) If any person who, in compliance with the provisions of section 324, is admitted into a factory, workshop or workplace discloses to any person any information obtained by him in it as to any manufacturing process or trade secret, he shall be guilty of an offence.

(4) Subsection (3) does not apply if the disclosure is made by a person in the course of performing his duty in connection with the purpose for which he was authorised to enter the land.

(5) A person who is guilty of an offence under subsection (3) shall be liable on summary conviction to a fine not exceeding the statutory maximum or on conviction on indictment to imprisonment for a term not exceeding two years or a fine or both.

(6) Where any damage is caused to land or chattels—

(a) in the exercise of a right of entry conferred under section 324, or

(b) in the making of any survey for the purpose of which any such right of entry has been so conferred;

compensation may be recovered by any person suffering the damage from the Secretary of State or authority on whose behalf the entry was effected.

(7) The provisions of section 118 shall apply in relation to compensation under subsection (6) as they apply in relation to compensation under Part IV.

(8) No person shall carry out under section 324 any works authorised by virtue of subsection (8) of that section unless notice of his intention to do so was included in the notice required by subsection (1).

(9) The authority of the appropriate Minister shall be required for the carrying out under that section of works so authorised if the land in question is held by statutory undertakers, and they object to the proposed works on the ground that the execution of the works would be seriously detrimental to the carrying on of their undertaking.

Miscellaneous and general provisions

326. and 327. [repealed by the Planning and Compensation Act 1991]

328. Settled land and land of universities and colleges

(1) The purposes authorised for the application of capital money—
 (a) by section 73 of the Settled Land Act 1925 and by that section as applied by section 28 of the Law of Property Act 1925 in relation to trusts for sale; and
 (b) by section 26 of the Universities and College Estates Act 1925,
shall include the payment of any sum recoverable under section 111 or 112.

(2) The purposes authorised as purposes for which money may be raised by mortgage—
 (a) by section 71 of the Settled Land Act 1925 and by that section as so applied; and
 (b) by section 30 of the Universities and College Estates Act 1925,
shall include the payment of any sum so recoverable.

329. Service of notices

(1) Any notice or other document required or authorised to be served or given under this Act may be served or given either—
 (a) by delivering it to the person on whom it is to be served or to whom it is to be given; or
 (b) by leaving it at the usual or last known place of abode of that person or, in a case where an address for service has been given by that person, at that address; or
 (c) by sending it in a prepaid registered letter, or by the recorded delivery service, addressed to that person at his usual or last known place of abode or, in a case where an address for service has been given by that person, at that address; or
 (d) in the case of an incorporated company or body, by delivering it to the secretary or clerk of the company or body at their registered or principal office or sending it in a prepaid registered letter, or by the recorded delivery service, addressed to the secretary or clerk of the company or body at that office.

(2) Where the notice or document is required or authorised to be served on any person as having an interest in premises, and the name of that person cannot be ascertained after reasonable inquiry, or where the notice or document is required or authorised to be served on any person as an occupier of premises, the notice or document shall be taken to be duly served if—
 (a) it is addressed to him either by name or by the description of 'the owner' or, as the case may be, 'the occupier' of the premises (describing them) and is delivered or sent in the manner specified in subsection (1)(a), (b) or (c); or
 (b) it is so addressed and is marked in such a manner as may be prescribed for securing that it is plainly identifiable as a communication of importance and—
  (i) it is sent to the premises in a prepaid registered letter or by the recorded delivery service and is not returned to the authority sending it, or
  (ii) it is delivered to some person on those premises, or is affixed conspicuously to some object on those premises.

(3) Where
 (a) the notice or other document is required to be served on or given to all persons who have interests in or are occupiers of premises comprised in any land, and
 (b) it appears to the authority required or authorised to serve or give the notice or other document that any part of that land is unoccupied,

the notice or document shall be taken to be duly served on all persons having interests in, and on any occupiers of, premises comprised in that part of the land (other than a person who has given to that authority an address for the service of the notice or document on him) if it is addressed to 'the owners and any occupiers' of that part of the land (describing it) and is affixed conspicuously to some object on the land.

(4) This section is without prejudice to section 233 of the Local Government Act 1972 (general provisions as to service of notices by local authorities).

330. Power to require information as to interests in land

(1) For the purpose of enabling the Secretary of State or a local authority to make an order or issue or serve any notice or other document which, by any of the provisions of this Act, he or they are authorised or required to make, issue or serve, the Secretary of State or the local authority may by notice in writing require the occupier of any premises and any person who, either directly or indirectly, receives rent in respect of any premises to give in writing such information as to the matters mentioned in subsection (2) as may be so specified.

(2) Those matters are—

(a) the nature of the interest in the premises of the person on whom the notice is served;

(b) the name and address of any other person known to him as having an interest in the premises;

(c) the purpose for which the premises are being used,

(d) the time when that use began;

(e) the name and address of any person known to the person on whom the notice is served as having used the premises for that purpose;

(f) the time when any activities being carried out on the premises began.

(3) A notice under subsection (1) may require information to be given within 21 days after the date on which it is served, or such longer time as may be specified in it, or as the Secretary of State or, as the case may be, the local authority may allow.

(4) Any person who, without reasonable excuse, fails to comply with a notice served on him under subsection (1) shall be guilty of an offence and liable on summary conviction to a fine not exceeding level 3 on the standard scale.

(5) Any person who, having been required by a notice under subsection (1) to give any information, knowingly makes any misstatement in respect of it shall be guilty of an offence and liable on summary conviction to a fine not exceeding the statutory maximum or on conviction on indictment to imprisonment for a term not exceeding two years or to a fine, or both.

(6) This section shall have effect as if the references to a local authority included references to a National Park authority.

[Introduced by the Environment Act 1995, see note to section 4A supra.]

331. Offences by corporations

(1) Where an offence under this Act which has been committed by a body corporate is proved to have been committed with the consent or connivance of, or to be attributable to any neglect on the part of—

(a) a director, manager, secretary or other similar officer of the body corporate, or

(b) any person who was purporting to act in any such capacity,

he as well as the body corporate shall be guilty of that offence and be liable to be proceeded against accordingly.

(2) In subsection (1) 'director', in relation to any body corporate—

(a) which was established by or under an enactment for the purpose of carrying on under national ownership an industry or part of an industry or undertaking, and

(b) whose affairs are managed by its members,

means a member of that body corporate.

332. Combined applications

(1) Regulations made under this Act may provide for the combination in a single document, made in such form and transmitted to such authority as may be prescribed, of—

(a) an application for planning permission in respect of any development; and

(b) an application required, under any enactment specified in the regulations, to be made to a local authority in respect of that development.

(2) Before making any regulations under this section, the Secretary of State shall consult with such local authorities or associations of local authorities as appear to him to be concerned.

(3) Different provision may be made by any such regulations in relation to areas in which different enactments are in force.

(4) If an application required to be made to a local authority under an enactment specified in any such regulations is made in accordance with the provisions of the regulations, it shall be valid notwithstanding anything in that enactment prescribing, or enabling any authority to prescribe, the form in which, or the manner in which, such an application is to be made.

(5) Subsection (4) shall have effect without prejudice to—

(a) the validity of any application made in accordance with the enactment in question; or

(b) any provision of that enactment enabling a local authority to require further particulars of the matters to which the application relates.

(6) In this section 'application' includes a submission.

333. Regulations and orders

(1) The Secretary of State may make regulations under this Act—

(a) for prescribing the form of any notice, order or other document authorised or required by this Act to be served, made or issued by any local authority or National Park Authority;

(b) for any purpose for which regulations are authorised or required to be made under this Act (other than a purpose for which regulations are authorised or required to be made by another Minister).

(2) Any power conferred by this Act to make regulations shall be exercisable by statutory instrument.

(3) Any statutory instrument containing regulations made under this Act (except regulations under section 88 and regulations which by virtue of this Act are of no effect unless approved by a resolution of each House of Parliament) shall be subject to annulment in pursuance of a resolution of either House of Parliament.

(4) The power to make development orders and orders under sections 2, 28, 55(2)(f), 87, 149(3)(a) and 319 shall be exercisable by statutory instrument.

(5) Any statutory instrument—

(a) which contains an order under section 2 which has been made after a local inquiry has been held in accordance with subsection (2) of that section; or

(b) which contains a development order or an order under section 28, 87 or 149(3)(a),

shall be subject to annulment in pursuance of a resolution of either House of Parliament.

(6) Without prejudice to subsection (5), where a development order makes provision for excluding or modifying any enactment contained in a public general Act (other than any of the enactments specified in Schedule 17) the order shall not have effect until that provision is approved by a resolution of each House of Parliament.

(7) Without prejudice to section 14 of the Interpretation Act 1978, any power conferred by any of the provisions of this Act to make an order, shall include power to vary or revoke any such order by a subsequent order.

[The reference to a National Park Authority was introduced by the Environment Act 1995, see note to Section 4A supra.]

334. Licensing planning areas

(1) Where the united district for which, by an order under section 2, a joint planning board is constituted comprises a licensing planning area, or the whole or part of such a united district is included in a licensing planning area, the Secretary of State may by order revoke or vary any order in force under Part VII of the Licensing Act 1964 so far as may be necessary or expedient in consequence of the order under section 2.

(2) Subject to subsection (1), nothing in any order made under section 2 shall affect the validity of any order in force under Part VII of the Licensing Act 1964 if made before the date of the order under section 2.

335. Act not excluded by special enactments

For the avoidance of doubt it is hereby declared that the provisions of this Act, and any restrictions or powers imposed or conferred by it in relation to land, apply and may be exercised in relation to any land notwithstanding that provision is made by any enactment in force at the passing of the 1947 Act, or by any local Act passed at any time during the Session of Parliament held during the regnal years 10 & 11 Geo. 6, for authorising or regulating any development of the land.

336. Interpretation

(1) In this Act, except in so far as the context otherwise requires and subject to the following provisions of this section and to any transitional provision made by the Planning (Consequential Provisions) Act 1990—

'the 1944 Act' means the Town and Country Planning Act 1944;
'the 1947 Act' means the Town and Country Planning Act 1947;
'the 1954 Act' means the Town and Country Planning Act 1954;
'the 1959 Act' means the Town and Country Planning Act 1959;
'the 1962 Act' means the Town and Country Planning Act 1962;
'the 1968 Act' means the Town and Country Planning Act 1968;
'the 1971 Act' means the Town and Country Planning Act 1971;
'acquiring authority', in relation to the acquisition of an interest in land (whether compulsorily or by agreement) or to a proposal so to acquire such an interest, means the government department, local authority or other body by whom the interest is, or is proposed to be, acquired;
'advertisement' means any word, letter, model, sign, placard, board, notice, awning, blind, device or representation, whether illuminated or not, in the nature of, and employed wholly or partly for the purposes of, advertisement, announcement or direction, and (without prejudice to the previous provisions of this definition) includes any hoarding or similar structure used or designed, or adapted for use, and anything else principally used, or designed or adapted principally for use, for the display of advertisements, and references to the display of advertisements shall be construed accordingly;
'aftercare condition' has the meaning given in paragraph 2(2) of Schedule 5;
'aftercare scheme' has the meaning given in paragraph 2(3) of Schedule 5;
'agriculture' includes horticulture, fruit growing, seed growing, dairy farming, the breeding and keeping of livestock (including any creature kept for the production of food, wool, skins or fur, or for the purpose of its use in the farming of land), the use of land as grazing land, meadow land, osier land, market gardens and nursery grounds, and the use of land for woodlands where that use is ancillary to the farming of land for other agricultural purposes, and 'agricultural' shall be construed accordingly;

'the appropriate Minister' has the meaning given in section 265;
'authority possessing compulsory purchase powers', in relation to the compulsory acquisition of an interest in land, means the person or body of persons effecting the acquisition and, in relation to any other transaction relating to an interest in land, means any person or body of persons who could be or have been authorised to acquire that interest compulsorily for the purposes for which the transaction is or was effected or a body (being a parish council, community council or parish meeting) on whose behalf a district council or county council [or county borough council] could be or have been so authorised;
'authority to whom Part II of the 1959 Act applies' means a body of any of the descriptions specified in Part I of Schedule 4 to the 1959 Act;
'breach of condition notice' has the meaning given in section 187A;
'breach of planning control' has the meaning given in section 171A;
'bridleway' has the same meaning as in the Highways Act 1980;
'the Broads' has the same meaning as in the Norfolk and Suffolk Broads Act 1988;
'building' includes any structure or erection, and any part of a building, as so defined, but does not include plant or machinery comprised in a building;
'buildings or works' includes waste materials, refuse and other matters deposited on land, and references to the erection or construction of buildings or works shall be construed accordingly and references to the removal of buildings or works include demolition of buildings and filling in of trenches;
'building operations' has the meanining given by section 55;
'caravan site' has the meaning given in section 1(4) of the Caravan Sites and Control of Development Act 1960;
'clearing', in relation to land, means the removal of buildings or materials from the land, the levelling of the surface of the land, and the carrying out of such other operations in relation to it as may be prescribed;
'common' includes any land subject to be enclosed under the Inclosure Acts 1845 to 1882, and any town or village green;
'compulsory acquisition' does not include the vesting in a person by an Act of Parliament of property previously vested in some other person;
'conservation area' means an area designated under section 69 of the Planning (Listed Buildings and Conservation Areas) Act 1990;
'depositing of mineral waste' means any process whereby a mineral-working deposit is created or enlarged and 'depositing of refuse or waste material' includes the depositing of mineral waste;
'development' has the meaning given in section 55, and 'develop' shall be construed accordingly;
'development order' has the meaning given in section 59;
'development plan' shall be construed in accordance with sections 27 [27A] and 54 (but subject to the transitional provisions in Schedule 2 and Part III of Schedule 4 to the Planning and Compensation Act 1991);
'disposal' means disposal by way of sale, exchange or lease, or by way of the creation of any easement, right or privilege, or in any other manner, except by way of appropriation, gift or mortgage, and 'dispose of' shall be construed accordingly;
'enactment' includes an enactment in any local or private Act of Parliament and an order, rule, regulation, byelaw or scheme made under an Act of Parliament;
'enforcement notice' means a notice under section 172;
'engineering operations' includes the formation or laying out of means of access to highways;
'enterprise zone scheme' means a scheme or modified scheme having effect to grant planning permission in accordance with section 88;

'erection', in relation to buildings as defined in this subsection, includes extension, alteration and re-erection;
'footpath' has the same meaning as in the Highways Act 1980;
'fuel or field garden allotment' means any allotment set out as a fuel allotment, or a field garden allotment, under an Inclosure Act;
'functions' includes powers and duties;
'government department' includes any Minister of the Crown;
'the Greater London Development Plan' means the development plan submitted to the Minister of Housing and Local Government under section 25 of the London Government Act 1963 and approved by the Secretary of State under section 5 of the 1962 Act or the corresponding-provision of the 1971 Act;
'highway' has the same meaning as in the Highways Act 1980 ;
'improvement', in relation to a highway, has the same meaning as in the Highways Act 1980;
'joint planning board' has the meaning given in section 2;
'land' means any corporeal hereditament, including a building, and, in relation to the acquisition of land under Part IX, includes any interest in or right over land;
'lease' includes an underlease and an agreement for a lease or underlease, but does not include an option to take a lease or a mortgage, and 'leasehold interest' means the interest of the tenant under a lease as so defined;
'local authority' (except in section 252 and subject to subsection (10) below and section 71(7) of the Environment Act 1995) means—

    (a) charging authority, a precepting authority (except the Receiver for the Metropolitan Police District), <u>a combined police authority</u> or a combined fire authority, as those expressions are defined in section 144 of the Local Government Finance Act 1988;

    (b) levying body within the meaning of section 74 of that Act; and

    (c) a body as regards which section 75 of that Act applies;

and includes any joint board or joint committee if all the constituent authorities are local authorities within paragraph (a), (b) or (c);
'local highway authority' means a highway authority other than the Secretary of State;
'local planning authority' shall be construed in accordance with Part I;
'London borough' includes the City of London, references to the council of a London borough or the clerk to such a council being construed, in relation to the City, as references to the Common Council of the City and the town clerk of the City respectively;
'means of access' includes any means of access, whether private or public, for vehicles or for foot passengers, and includes a street;
'mineral planning authority' has the meaning given in section 1(4);
'mineral-working deposit' means any deposit of material remaining after minerals have been extracted from land or otherwise deriving from the carrying out of operations for the winning and working of minerals in, on or under land;
'minerals' includes all substances of a kind ordinarily worked for removal by underground or surface working, except that it does not include peat cut for purposes other than sale;
'Minister' means any Minister of the Crown or other government department;
'mortgage' includes any charge or lien on any property for securing money or money's worth;
'open space' means any land laid out as a public garden, or used for the purposes of public recreation, or land which is a disused burial ground;
'operational land' has the meaning given in section 263;

'owner', in relation to any land, means a person, other than a mortgagee not in possession, who, whether in his own right or as trustee for any other person, is entitled to receive the rack rent of the land or, where the land is not let at a rack rent, would be so entitled if it were so let;
'the planning Acts' means this Act, the Planning (Listed Buildings and Conservation Areas) Act 1990, the Planning (Hazardous Substances) Act 1990 and the Planning (Consequential Provisions) Act 1990;
'planning contravention notice' has the meaning given in section 171C;
'planning decision' means a decision made on an application under Part III;
'planning permission' means permission under Part III;
'planning permission granted for a limited period' has the meaning given in section 72(2);
'prescribed' (except in relation to matters expressly required or authorised by this Act to be prescribed in some other way) means prescribed by regulations under this Act;
'public gas supplier' has the same meaning as in Part I of the Gas Act 1986;
'purchase notice' has the meaning given in section 137;
'replacement of open space', in relation to any area, means the rendering of land available for use as an open space, or otherwise in an undeveloped state, in substitution for land in that area which is so used;
'restoration condition' has the meaning given in paragraph 2(2) of Schedule 5;
'simplified planning zone' and 'simplified planning zone scheme' shall be construed in accordance with sections 82 and 83;
'statutory undertakers' and 'statutory undertaking' have the meanings given in section 262;
'steps for the protection of the environment' has the meaning given paragraph 5(4) of Schedule 9;
'stop notice' has the meaning given in section 183;
'suspension order' has the meaning given in paragraph 5 of Schedule 9; and
'supplementary suspension order' has the meaning given in paragraph 6 of Schedule 9;
'tenancy' has the same meaning as in the Landlord and Tenant Act 1954;
'tree preservation order' has the meaning given in section 198;
'urban development area' and 'urban development corporation' have the same meanings as in Part XVI of the Local Government, Planning and Land Act 1980;
'use', in relation to land, does not include the use of land for the carrying out of any building or other operations on it;
'Valuation Office' means the Valuation Office of the Inland Revenue Department;
'war damage' has the meaning given in the War Damage Act 1943.
'the winning and working of minerals' includes the extraction of minerals from a mineral working deposit.

[(1A) In this Act—
  (a) any reference to a county (other than one to a county planning authority) shall be construed, in relation to Wales, as including a reference to a county borough;
  (b) any reference to a county council shall be construed, in relation to Wales, as including a reference to a county borough council; and
  (c) section 17(4) and (5) of the Local Government (Wales) Act 1994 (references to counties and districts to be construed generally in relation to Wales as references to counties and county boroughs) shall not apply.]

(2) If, in relation to anything required or authorised to be done under this Act, any question arises as to which Minister is or was the appropriate Minister in relation to any statutory undertakers, that question shall be determined by the Treasury.

(3) If any question so arises whether land of statutory undertakers is operational land, that question shall be determined by the Minister who is the appropriate Minister in relation to those undertakers.

(4) Words in this Act importing a reference to service of a notice to treat shall be construed as including a reference to the constructive service of such a notice which, by virtue of any enactment, is to be deemed to be served.

(5) With respect to references in this Act to planning decisions—

(a) in relation to a decision altered on appeal by the reversal or variation of the whole or part of it, such references shall be construed as references to the decision as so altered;

(b) in relation to a decision upheld on appeal, such references shall be construed as references to the decision of the local planning authority and not to the decision of the Secretary of State on the appeal;

(c) in relation to a decision given on an appeal in the circumstances mentioned in section 78(2), such references shall be construed as references to the decision so given;

(d) the time of a planning decision, in a case where there is or was an appeal, shall be taken to be or have been the time of the decision as made by the local planning authority (whether or not that decision is or was altered on that appeal) or, in the case of a decision given on an appeal in the circumstances mentioned in section 78(2), the end of the period there mentioned.

(6) Section 56 shall apply for determining for the purposes of this Act when development of land shall be taken to be initiated.

(7) In relation to the sale or acquisition of an interest in land—

(a) in a case where the interest is or was conveyed or assigned without a preliminary contract, references in this Act to a contract are references to the conveyance or assignment; and

(b) references to the making of a contract are references to the execution of it.

(8) In this Act—

(a) references to a person from whom title is derived by another person include references to any predecessor in title of that other person;

(b) references to a person deriving title from another person include references to any successor in title of that other person;

(c) references to deriving title are references to deriving title either directly or indirectly.

(9) References in the planning Acts to any of the provisions of Parts III, VII and VIII include, except where the context otherwise requires, references to those provisions as modified under section 316(1) to (3).

(10) In section 90, Chapter I of Part VI, and sections 324(2) and 330 'local authority', in relation to land in the Broads, includes the Broads Authority.

[In Section 336(1) the words in [ ] and Section 336(1A) were inserted by, and will come into effect on an appointed day order under, the Local Government (Wales) Act 1994, while the reference in Section 336(1)(a) to a 'combined police authority' is to be repealed as from an appointed day by the Police and Magistrates' Courts Act 1994.]

337. Short title, commencement and extent

(1) This Act may be cited as the Town and Country Planning Act 1990.

(2) Except as provided in Part II and in Schedule 4 to the Planning (Consequential Provisions) Act 1990, this Act shall come into force at the end of the period of three months beginning with the day on which it is passed.

(3) This Act extends to England and Wales only.

Section 1.   SCHEDULE 1
LOCAL PLANNING AUTHORITIES: DISTRIBUTION OF FUNCTIONS

Preliminary

1.—(1) In this Schedule 'county matter' means in relation to any application, order or notice—

(a) the winning and working of minerals in, on or under land (whether by surface or underground working) or the erection of any building, plant, or machinery—

    (i) which it is proposed to use in connection with the winning and working of minerals or with their treatment or disposal in or on land adjoining the site of the working; or

    (ii) which a person engaged in mining operations proposes to use in connection with the grading, washing, grinding or crushing of minerals;

(b) the use of land, or the erection of any building, plant or machinery on land, for the carrying out of any process for the preparation or adaptation for sale of any mineral or the manufacture of any article from a mineral where—

    (i) the land forms part of or adjoins a site used or proposed to be used for the winning and working of minerals; or

    (ii) the mineral is, or is proposed to be, brought to the land from a site used, or proposed to be used, for the winning and working of minerals by means of a pipeline, conveyor belt, aerial ropeway, or similar plant or machinery, or by private road, private waterway or private railway;

(c) the carrying out of searches and tests of mineral deposits or the erection of any building, plant or machinery which it is proposed to use in connection with them;

(d) the depositing of mineral waste;

(e) the use of land for any purpose required in connection with the transport by rail or water of aggregates (that is to say, any of the following, namely—

    (i) sand and gravel;

    (ii) crushed rock;

    (iii) artificial materials of appearance similar to sand, gravel or crushed rock and manufactured or otherwise derived from iron or steel slags, pulverised fuel ash, clay or mineral waste),

or the erection of any building, plant or machinery which it is proposed to use in connection with them;

(f) the erection of any building, plant or machinery which it is proposed to use for the coating of roadstone or the production of concrete or of concrete products or artificial aggregates, where the building, plant or, machinery is to be erected in or on land which forms part of or adjoins a site used or proposed to be used—

    (i) for the winning and working of minerals; or

    (ii) for any of the purposes mentioned in paragraph (e) above;

(g) the erection of any building, plant or machinery which it is proposed to use for the manufacture of cement;

(h) the carrying out of operations in, on, over or under land, or a use of land, where the land is or forms part of a site used or formerly used for the winning and working of minerals and where the operations or use would conflict with or prejudice compliance with a restoration condition or an aftercare condition;

(i) the carrying out of operations in, on, over or under land, or any use of land, which is situated partly in and partly outside a National Park;

(j) the carrying out of any operation which is, as respects the area in question, a prescribed operation or an operation of a prescribed class or any use which is, as respects that area, a prescribed use or use of a prescribed class.

Development plans

2. The functions of a local planning authority—
  (a) under sections 30 to 35B, 38(2) and 50(1), (4), (5) and (7) shall be exercisable by the county planning authority and not by the district planning authority;
  (b) under section 36, 39, 40, 42 to 44 and 50(6), (7A) and (8) shall be exercisable by the district planning authority and not by the county planning authority;
and references to a local planning authority in those sections shall be construed accordingly.

Planning and special control

3.—(1) The functions of a local planning authority of determining—
  (a) applications for planning permission;
  (b) applications for a certificate under section 191 or 192;
  (c) applications for an established use certificate under section 192;
shall, subject to sub-paragraph (2), be exercised by the district planning authority.

(2) The functions of a local planning authority of determining any such application as is mentioned in sub-paragraph (1) which relates to a county matter shall be exercised by the county planning authority.

(3) to (6) [repealed by the Planning and Compensation Act 1991]

(7) The previous provisions of this paragraph shall not apply to applications relating to land in a National Park, but paragraph 4 shall apply to such applications instead.

4.—(1) Each of the following applications, namely—
  (d) applications for consent to the display of advertisements under section 220,
shall, if relating to land in a National Park, be made to the district planning authority who shall, unless it falls to be determined by them, send it on to the county planning authority and, in the case of an application for planning permission, shall send a copy to the local highway authority, except where the local highway authority are a local planning authority and except in any case or class of case with respect to which the local highway authority otherwise direct.

(2) Where any application for planning permission, for a certificate under section 191 or 192 or for consent to the display of advertisements under section 220, relating in each case to land in a National Park or an application so relating for approval of a matter reserved under an outline planning permission within the meaning of section 92 falls to be determined by a National Park Authority or <u>county planning authority</u>, that authority shall before determining it consult with any authority which (but for Section 4A) would be <u>or, as the case may be, which is</u> the district planning authority for the area in which the land to which the application relates is situated.
[The references to National Park Authorities were introduced by the Environment Act 1995, see note to Section 4A supra, while the words underlined will be repealed as from a day to be appointed under that Act.]

5.—(1) The Secretary, of State may include in a development order such provisions as he thinks fit enabling a local highway authority to impose restrictions on the grant by the local planning authority of planning permission for the following descriptions of development relating to land in the area of the local highway authority—
  (a) the formation, laying out or alteration of any means of access to a road classified under section 12(3) of the Highways Act 1980 or section 27 of the Local Government Act 1966 or to a proposed road the route of which has been adopted by

Town and Country Planning Act 1990 195

resolution of the local highway authority and notified as such to the local planning authority;

(b) any other operations or use of land which appear to the local highway authority to be likely to result in a material increase in the volume of traffic entering or leaving such a classified or proposed road, to prejudice the improvement or construction of such a road or to result in a material change in the character of traffic entering, leaving or using such a road.

(2) The reference to a local planning authority in sub-paragraph (1) shall not be construed as including a reference to an urban development corporation who are the local planning authority by virtue of an order under section 149 of the Local Government, Planning and Land Act 1980, and no provision of a development order which is included in it by virtue of that paragraph is to be construed as applying to such a corporation.

(3) The Secretary of State may include in a development order provision enabling a local highway authority to impose restrictions on the grant by an urban development corporation who are the local planning authority of planning permission for such descriptions of development as may be specified in the order.

6.—(1) A development order may also include provision requiring a county planning authority who are determining any application mentioned in paragraph 3 and relating to a county matter, or an application for approval of a matter reserved under an outline planning permission within the meaning of section 92 and so relating, to give the district planning authority for the area in which the land to which the application relates is situated an opportunity to make recommendations to the county planning authority as to the manner in which the application is determined, and to take into account any such recommendations.

(2) It may also include provision requiring a county or district planning authority who have received any application so mentioned or any application for such approval (including any such application relating to land in a National Park) to notify the district or, as the case may be, county planning authority of the terms of their decision, or, where the application is referred to the Secretary of State, the date when it was so referred and, when notified to them, the terms of his decision.
[The words underlined will be repealed as from a date to be appointed under the Environment Act 1995.]

7.—(1) It shall be the duty of a local planning authority in a non-metropolitan county when exercising their functions under section 70 to seek the achievement of the general objectives of the structure plan for the time being in force in their area.

(2) Subject to sub-paragraph (4), the district planning authority shall consult the county planning authority for their area before determining any application to which this sub-paragraph applies.

(3) Sub-paragraph (2) applies to any application for planning permission for the carrying out—
  (a) of any development of land which would materially conflict with or prejudice the implementation—
    (i) of any policy contained in a structure plan which has been adopted or approved;
    (ii) of any policy contained in proposals made available for inspection under section 33(2);
    (iii) [repealed by the Planning and Compensation Act 1991]
    (iv) of a fundamental provision of a development plan to which paragraph 2 of Part III of Schedule 2 applies, so far as the development plan is in force in the district planning authority's area;
    (v) of any policy contained in a minerals local plan or a waste local plan which has been adopted or approved;

(vi) of any policy contained in proposals for the making, alteration or replacement of a minerals local plan or a waste local plan which have been made available for inspection under section 40(2);

(vii) of any proposal contained in a local plan which was prepared by the county planning authority and continued in operation by virtue of paragraph 44 of Schedule 4 to the Planning and Compensation Act 1991;

(viii) of any proposal contained in proposals in respect of a local plan which have been prepared by the county planning authority and are adopted or approved by virtue of paragraph 43 of that Schedule or made available for inspection in pursuance of that paragraph;.

(b) of any development of land which would, by reason of its scale or nature or the location of the land, be of major importance for the implementation of a structure plan;

(c) of any development of land in an area which the county planning authority have notified to the district planning authority, in writing, as an area in which development is likely to affect or be affected by the winning and working of minerals, other than coal;

(d) of any development of land which the county planning authority have notified the district planning authority, in writing, that they themselves propose to develop;

(e) of any development of land which would prejudice the carrying out of development proposed by the county planning authority and notified to the district planning authority under paragraph (d);

(f) of any development of land in England in respect of which the county planning authority have notified the district planning authority, in writing, that it is proposed that it shall be used for waste disposal;

(g) of any development of land which would prejudice a proposed use of land for waste disposal notified to the district planning authority under paragraph (f).

(4) The district planning authority may determine any application to which sub-paragraph (2) applies without the consultation required by that sub-paragraph if the county planning authority have given them directions authorising them to do so.

(5) A direction under sub-paragraph (4) may relate to a class of applications or to a particular application.

(6) Subject to sub-paragraph (7), where the district planning authority are required to consult the county planning authority before determining an application for planning permission—

(a) they shall give the county planning authority notice that they propose to consider the application and send them a copy of it; and

(b) they shall not determine it until the expiration of such period from the date of the notice as a development order may provide.

(7) A district planning authority may determine an application for planning permission before the expiration of such a period as is mentioned in sub-paragraph (6)(b)—

(a) if they have received representations concerning the application from the county planning authority before the expiration of that period; or

(b) if the county planning authority have notified them that they do not wish to make representations.

(8) Where a district planning authority are required to consult the county planning authority before determining an application for planning permission, they shall in determining it take into account any representations relating to it which they have received from the county planning authority before the expiration of the period mentioned in sub-paragraph (6)(b).

Town and Country Planning Act 1990

8.—(1) A local planning authority who have the function of determining applications for planning permission shall, if requested to do so by the council of any parish [or community] situated in their area, notify the council of—
    (a) any relevant planning application; and
    (b) any alteration to that application accepted by the authority.
(2) In sub-paragraph (1) 'a relevant planning application' means an application which—
    (a) relates to land in the parish [or community]; and
    (b) is an application for—
        (i) planning permission; or
        (ii) approval of a matter reserved under an outline planning permission within the meaning of section 92.
(3) Any request made for the purposes of sub-paragraph (1) shall be in writing and state that the council wishes to be notified of all relevant applications or all applications of a description specified in the request.
(4) An authority shall comply with the duty to notify a council of an application by—
    (a) sending the council a copy of the application; or
    (b) indicating to the council the nature of the development which is the subject of the application and identifying the land to which it relates,
and any notification falling within paragraph (b) shall be in writing.
(5) An authority shall comply with their duty to notify a council of an alteration by—
    (a) sending a copy of the alteration to the council; or
    (b) informing the council in writing of its general effect,
but they need not notify a council of an alteration which in their opinion is trivial.
(6) A development order may require a local planning authority which is dealing with an application of which a council is entitled to be notified—
    (a) to give the council an opportunity to make representations to them as to the manner in which the application should be determined;
    (b) to take into account any such representations;
    (c) to notify the council of the terms of their decision or, where the application is referred to the Secretary of State, the date when it was so referred and, when notified to them, the terms of his decision.
[The words in [ ] are to be omitted by, and as from an appointed day under, the Local Government (Wales) Act 1994.]

9.—(1) The functions of local planning authorities under the provisions of this Act relating to simplified planning zone schemes shall be exercised in non-metropolitan counties by the district planning authorities.
(2) and (3) [repealed]

10. Elsewhere than in a National Park, the functions of a local planning authority under section 94 shall be exercisable by the district planning authority, except that where the relevant planning permission was granted by the county planning authority, those functions, so far as relating to that permission, shall be exercisable by the county planning authority and also by the district planning authority after consulting the county planning authority.

11.—(1) The functions of a local planning authority of—
    (a) making orders under section 97 revoking or modifying planning permission, or under section 102 requiring discontinuance of use, imposing conditions on continuance of use or requiring the alteration or removal of buildings or works, or
    (b) issuing enforcement notices under section 172 or serving planning contravention notices under section 171 or stop notices under section 183 or breach of condition notices under section 187A,

shall, subject to sub-paragraphs (2) to (4), be exercisable by the district planning authority.

(2) In a case where it appears to the district planning authority of a district in a non-metropolitan county that the functions mentioned in sub-paragraph (1) relate to county matters, they shall not exercise those functions without first consulting the county planning authority.

(3) Subject to sub-paragraph (4), in a non-metropolitan county those functions shall also be exercisable by a county planning authority in a case where it appears to that authority that they relate to a matter which should properly be considered a county matter.

(4) In relation to a matter which is a county matter by virtue of any of the provisions of paragraph 1(1)(a) to (h) the functions of a local planning authority specified in sub-paragraph (1)(b) shall only be exercisable by the county planning authority in their capacity as mineral planning authority.

12. In sections 178(1), 181(4)(b) and 190(2) to (5) any reference to the local planning authority shall be construed as a reference to the authority who issued the notice or made the order in question or, in the case of an notice issued or an order made by the Secretary of State, the authority named in the notice or order.

12A. The functions of a local planning authorit under section 187B are exercisable by any body having the function of taking enforcement action in respect of the breach in question.

13.—(1) A county planning authority may only make a tree preservation order—
  (a) if they make it in pursuance of section 197(b);
  (b) if it relates to land which does not lie wholly within the area of a single district planning authority;
  (c) if it relates to land in which the county planning authority hold an interest; or
  (d) if it relates to land in a National Park.

(2) Where a local planning authority have made a tree preservation order under section 198 or the Secretary of State has made such an order by virtue of section 202, the powers of varying or revoking the order and the powers of dispensing with section 206 or serving, or appearing on an appeal relating to, a notice under section 207 shall be exercisable only by the authority who made the order or, in the case of an order made by the Secretary of State, the authority named in the order.
[In paragraph 13(1), for 'A county planning authority' there shall be substituted 'In the case of any area for which there is both a district planning authority and a county planning authority, the county planning authority'. The words underlined will be repealed and the substitution will be made as from a day to be appointed under the Environment Act 1995.]

14. The functions of local planning authorities under sections 69, 211, 214, 220, 221, 224 and 225, and in non-metropolitan counties the functions under section 215, are exercisable by district planning authorities.

15.—(1) The copy of the notice required to be served by paragraph 4(5) of Schedule 8 on a local planning authority shall, in the case of a proposal that a government department should give a direction under section 90(1) or that development should be carried out by or on behalf of a government department, be served on the local planning authority who, in the opinion of the Secretary of State, would have been responsible for dealing with an application for planning permission for the development in question if such an application had fallen to be made.

(2) References in paragraphs 3(2) and 5(1) of that Schedule to the local planning authority shall be construed as references to the local planning authority on whom that copy is required to be served.

Compensation

16.—(1) Claims for payment of compensation under section 107 (including that section as applied by section 108) and sections 115(1) to (4), 186 and 223 shall, subject to sub-paragraph (3), be made to and paid by the local planning authority who took the action by virtue of which the claim arose or, where that action was taken by the Secretary of State, the local planning authority from whom the appeal was made to him or who referred the matter to him or, in the case of an order made or notice served by him by virtue of section 100, 104 or 185, the appropriate authority, and references in those sections to a local planning authority shall be construed accordingly.

(2) In this paragraph 'appropriate authority' means—

    (a) in the case of a claim for compensation under section 107 or 108, the local planning authority who granted, or are to be treated for the purposes of section 107 as having granted, the planning permission the revocation or modification of which gave rise to the claim;

    (b) in the case of a claim for compensation under section 115(1) to (4) or 186, the local planning authority named in the relevant order or stop notice of the Secretary of State;

    (c) in the case of a claim for compensation under section 223, the district planning authority.

(3) The Secretary of State may after consultation with all the authorities concerned direct that where a local planning authority is liable to pay compensation under any of the provisions mentioned in sub-paragraph (1) in any particular case or class of case they shall be entitled to be reimbursed the whole of the compensation or such proportion of it as he may direct from one or more authorities specified in the direction.

(4) The local planning authority by whom compensation is to he paid and to whom claims for compensation are to be made under section 144(2) shall be the district planning authority.

17. Claims for payment of compensation under a tree preservation order by virtue of section 203, and claims for payment of compensation under section 204 by virtue of directions given in pursuance of such an order, shall be made to and paid by the local planning authority who made the order or, in the case of an order made by the Secretary of State, the authority named in the order; and the reference in section 204(2) to the authority exercising functions under the tree preservation order shall have effect subject to the provisions of this paragraph.

18. The local planning authority by whom compensation is to be paid under section 279(1)(a) to statutory undertakers shall be the authority who referred the application for planning permission to the Secretary of State and the appropriate Minister, or from whose decision the appeal was made to them or who served the enforcement notice appealed against, as the case may be.

The Crown

19.—(1) Elsewhere than in a metropolitan county or a National Park the functions conferred by section 302 and Schedule 15 on the authority responsible for enforcing planning control shall, subject to sub-paragraph (3)—

    (a) in the case of works on or a use of land which in the opinion of the district planning authority relates to a county matter, be exercised by the county planning authority;

    (b) in any other case be exercised by the district planning authority.

(2) As respects an area in a National Park [to which Section 4 applies] outside a metropolitan county those functions shall be exercised by the county planning authority.

[(2A) As respects the area of any National Park for which a National Park authority is the local planning authority those functions shall be exercised by that authority.]

(3) Every application made under subsection (3) of that section to an authority responsible for enforcing planning control shall be made to the district planning authority who, in the case of an application falling to be determined by the county planning authority, shall send it on to the latter.

(4) A county planning authority determining any such application shall give the district planning authority for the area in which the land to which the application relates is situated an opportunity to make recommendations to the county planning authority as to the manner in which the application should be determined and shall take any such recommendations into account.

(5) A county or district planning authority who have dealt with any such application shall notify the district or, as the case may be, the county planning authority of the terms of their determination or, in a case where the application has been referred to the Secretary of State, the date when it was so referred.

[The references to National Park authorities were introduced by the Environment Act 1995, see note to Section 4A supra, while the words underlined will be repealed as from a day to be appointed under the 1995 Act.]

Miscellaneous

20.—(1) The local planning authority whom the Secretary of State is required to consult under section 100(3), 104(3), 196A(3), 201(1) or 214B(6) or serve with a notice of his proposals under section 100(4) or 104(4) shall be the county planning authority or the district planning authority, as he thinks appropriate, and references in sections 100(2), (3) and (4) and 104(2), (3) and (4) and 202 to the local planning authority shall be construed accordingly.

(2) In sections 96, 182 and 185 any reference to the local planning authority shall be construed as a reference to the county planning authority or the district planning authority, as the Secretary of State thinks appropriate.

(3) In relation to land in the area of a joint planning board, a person entering into a planning obligation under section 106 or 299A may identify the council of the county in which the land is situated as the authority by whom the obligation is enforceable.

(4) In paragraph 16 of Schedule 13 the reference to the local planning authority shall be construed—

 (a) in relation to land in a National Park outside a metropolitan county, as a reference to the county planning authority; and

 (b) in relation to land elsewhere, as a reference to the district planning authority.

  [(i) in paragraph (a), for 'outside a metropolitan county' there shall be substituted 'which is land in an area the local planning authority for which comprises both a county planning authority and a district planning authority'; and

  (ii) in paragraph (b), for 'elsewhere' there shall be substituted 'other land in an area the local planning authority for which comprises both a county planning authority and a district planning authority'.

The words underlined will be repealed and the substitution made as from a day to be appointed under the Environment Act 1995.]

21.—(1) Subject to sub-paragraph (2), the provisions of this Schedule do not apply in Greater London.

(2) Paragraph 5(3) of this Schedule applies in Greater London and paragraph 2(3) of Part I and of Part II of Schedule 2 shall apply as respects the temporary application

of paragraph 7(1) of this Schedule in the metropolitan counties and in Greater London respectively.

SCHEDULE 1A
DISTRIBUTION OF LOCAL PLANNING AUTHORITY FUNCTIONS: WALES

1.—(1) Where a local planning authority are not the local highway authority, the Secretary of State may include in a development order such provisions as he thinks fit enabling the local highway authority to impose restrictions on the grant by the local planning authority of planning permission for the following descriptions of development relating to land in the area of the local highway authority—

    (a) the formation, laying out or alteration of any means of access to—

        (i) a road classified under section 12(3) of the Highways Act 1980 or section 27 of the Local Government Act 1966: or

        (ii) a proposed road the route of which has been adopted by resolution of the local highway authority and notified as such to the local planning authority;

    (b) any other operations or use of land which appear to the local highway authority to be likely to—

        (i) result in a material increase in the volume of traffic entering or leaving such a classified or proposed road;

        (ii) prejudice the improvement or construction of such a road; or

        (iii) result in a material change in the character of traffic entering, leaving or using such a road.

(2) The reference to a local planning authority in sub-paragraph (1) shall not be construed as including a reference to an urban development corporation who are the local planning authority by virtue of an order under section 149 of the Local Government, Planning and Land Act 1980, and no provision of a development order which is included in it by virtue of that sub-paragraph is to be construed as applying to such a corporation.

(3) The Secretary of State may include in a development order provision enabling a local highway authority to impose restrictions on the grant by an urban development corporation who are the local planning authority of planning permission for such descriptions of development as may be specified in the order.

2.—(1) A local planning authority who have the function of determining applications for planning permission shall, if requested to do so by the council for any community or group of communities situated in their area, notify that council of—

    (a) any relevant planning application; and

    (b) any alteration to that application accepted by the authority.

(2) In sub-paragraph (1) 'relevant planning application' means an application which—

    (a) relates to land in the community or (as the case may be) one of the communities concerned; and

    (b) is an application for—

        (i) planning permission; or

        (ii) approval of a matter reserved under an outline planning permission within the meaning of section 92.

(3) Any request made for the purposes of sub-paragraph (1) shall be in writing and shall state that the community council wishes to be notified of all relevant applications or all applications of a description specified in the request.

(4) An authority shall comply with the duty to notify a community council of an application by—

    (a) sending the council a copy of the application; or

    (b) indicating to the council the nature of the development which is the subject of the application and identifying the land to which it relates,

and any notification falling within paragraph (b) shall be in writing.

(5) An authority shall comply with their duty to notify a community council of an alteration by—
  (a) sending a copy of the alteration to the council; or
  (b) informing the council in writing of its general effect.
but they need not notify a community council of an alteration which in their opinion is trivial.

(6) A development order may require a local planning authority who are dealing with an application of which a community council is entitled to be notified—
  (a) to give to the council an opportunity to make representations to them as to the manner in which the application should be determined;
  (b) to take into account any such representations;
  (c) to notify the council of the terms of their decision or, where the application is referred to the Secretary of State, the date when it was so referred and, when notified to them, the terms of his decision.

3. Paragraphs 4 to 10 apply only in relation to any area for which, by virtue of any provision of or made under section 6, 7 or 8, there is more than one local planning authority.

4. In sections 178(1), 181(4)(b) and 190(2), (3) and (5) any reference to the local planning authority shall be construed as a reference to the authority who issued the notice or made the order in question or, in the case of a notice issued or an order made by the Secretary of State, the authority named in the notice or order.

5. The functions of a local planning authority under section 187B are exercisable by any body having the function of taking enforcement action in respect of the breach in question.

6. Where a local planning authority have made a tree preservation order under section 198 or the Secretary of State has made such an order by virtue of section 202, the powers of varying or revoking the order and the powers of dispensing with section 206 or serving, or appearing on an appeal relating to, a notice under section 207 shall he exercisable only by the authority who made the order or, in the case of an order made by the Secretary of State, the authority named in the order.

7.—(1) The copy of the notice required to be served by paragraph 4(5) of Schedule 8 on a local planning authority shall, in the case of a proposal that a government department should give a direction under section 90(1) or that development should be carried out by or on behalf of a government department, be served on the local planning authority who, in the opinion of the Secretary of State, would have been responsible for dealing with an application for planning permission for the development in question if such an application had fallen to be made.

[This Schedule was added by, and will come into force on an appointed day order under, the Local Government (Wales) Act 1994.]

Sections 28 and 54.   SCHEDULE 2
DEVELOPMENT PLANS: TRANSITIONAL PROVISIONS

PART I
THE METROPOLITAN COUNTIES

Continuation of structure plans, local plans and old development plans

1.—(1) Subject to paragraphs 2 and 3—
  (a) the structure plan,
  (b) any local plan; and
  (c) any old development plan,
which immediately before the commencement of this Act was in force in the area of a local planning authority in a metropolitan county (or in that and other areas) shall continue in force in respect of the area of that authority until a unitary development plan for that area becomes operative under Chapter I of Part II of this Act or, where

parts of a unitary development plan become operative on different dates, until every part of it has become operative.

(2) A plan which continues in force by virtue of this paragraph shall, while it continues in force, be treated for the purposes of this Act, any other enactment relating to town and country planning, the Land Compensation Act 1961 and the Highways Act 1980 as being, or being comprised in, the development plan in respect of the area in question.

(3) In this paragraph 'old development plan' means any plan which was in force in the area in question immediately before the commencement of this Act by virtue of Schedule 7 to the 1971 Act and paragraph 18 of Schedule 1 to the Local Government Act 1985.

Revocation of structure plan

2.—(1) Where under Chapter I of Part II of this Act the Secretary of State approves all or any of Part I of a unitary development plan he may by order—

(a) wholly or partly revoke a structure plan continued in force by paragraph 1, either in its application to the whole of the area of a local planning authority or in its application to part of that area; and

(b) make such consequential amendments to that plan as appear to him to be necessary or expedient.

(2) Before making an order under this paragraph the Secretary of State shall consult the local planning authority for the area to which the unitary development plan relates.

(3) Until the structure plan for an area in a metropolitan county ceases to be operative under paragraph 1 or this paragraph, paragraph 7(1) of Schedule 1 shall apply in that area with the omission of the words 'in a non-metropolitan county'.

3. [repealed by the Planning and Compensation Act 1991]

Incorporation of current local plan in unitary development plan

4.—(1) Sub-paragraph (2) applies where—

(a) a local plan is in force in the area of a local planning authority;

(b) a unitary development plan is being prepared;

(c) the local planning authority who are preparing that plan have published in the prescribed manner a statement in the prescribed form identifying a policy included in the plan as an existing policy; and

(d) a local inquiry or other hearing is held for the purpose of considering any objection to the plan.

(2) Where this sub-paragraph applies, the person holding the inquiry or other hearing need not allow an objector to appear if he is satisfied that—

(a) the objection is to a policy identified in the statement published under sub-paragraph (1)(c);

(b) the policy so identified is an existing policy; and

(c) there has been no significant change in circumstances affecting the existing policy since it first formed part of the plan mentioned in sub-paragraph (1)(a).

(3) In this paragraph 'existing policy' means a policy or proposal the substance of which (however expressed) was contained in a local plan in force as mentioned in sub-paragraph (1)(a).

PART IA
WALES

Continuation of structure, local and old development plans

1.—(1) Every existing plan which relates to any part of Wales shall continue in force on and after 1st April 1996.

(2) When a unitary development plan has become fully operative for the area of a local planning authority in Wales—
   (a) any existing plan which is for the time being in force; and
   (b) any interim plan,
shall cease to have effect in respect of its plan area to the extent that it is comprised in the area of that local planning authority.

(3) Any existing plan or interim plan shall, while it continues in force in respect of the area, or part of the area, of any local planning authority in Wales, be treated for the purposes of—
   (a) this Act,
   (b) any other enactment relating to town and country planning,
   (c) the Land Compensation Act 1961, and
   (d) the Highways Act 1980,
as being, or as being comprised in, the development plan in respect of that area or, as the case may be, that part of that area.

(4) Sub-paragraphs (1) to (3) have effect subject to the provisions of this Part of this Schedule and the 1994 Act transitional provisions.

(5) In this paragraph—
'the 1994 Act transitional provisions' means the provisions of Part III of Schedule 5 to the Local Government (Wales) Act 1994;
'existing plan' means a—
   (a) structure plan;
   (b) local plan; or
   (c) old development plan,
to the extent that it was in force in respect of any area in Wales immediately before 1st April 1996 (and includes any alteration made to, or replacement of, the plan after that date under the 1994 Act transitional provisions);
'interim plan' means any modified plan (within the meaning of the 1994 Act transitional provisions) which comes into force in respect of any area in Wales on or after 1st April 1996 under those provisions;
'old development plan' means any plan which was in force immediately before 1st April 1996 by virtue of Schedule 7 to the Town and Country Planning Act 1971 and Part III of this Schedule; and
'plan area', in relation to an existing plan or interim plan, means the area in respect of which it was in force immediately before 1st April 1996 or, as the case may be, comes into force on or after that date.

Revocation of structure plan

2.—(1) Where under chapter I of Part II of this Act the Secretary of State approves all or any of Part I of a unitary development plan for the whole or part of the area of a local planning authority in Wales ('the relevant whole or part area'), he may by order—
   (a) wholly or partly revoke an existing plan which is a structure plan in respect of the plan area, to the extent that it is comprised in the relevant whole or part area or any part of it; and
   (b) make such consequential amendments to that existing plan as appear to him to be necessary or expedient.

(2) Before making an order under this paragraph, the Secretary of State shall consult the local planning authority for the area to which the unitary development plan relates.

Incorporation of current policy in unitary development plan

3.—(1) This paragraph applies where—

(a) a unitary development plan is being prepared for the area of a local planning authority in Wales;

(b) the local planning authority preparing that plan have published in the prescribed manner a statement in the prescribed form identifying a policy included in the plan as an existing policy;

(c) one or more local plans is or, as the case may be, are together in force throughout the policy area; and

(d) a local inquiry or other hearing is held for the purpose of considering any objection to the plan.

(2) The person holding the inquiry or other hearing need not allow an objector to appear if he is satisfied that—

(a) the objection is to a policy identified in the statement published under sub-paragraph (1)(b);

(b) the policy so identified is an existing policy; and

(c) there has been no significant change in circumstances affecting the existing policy since it first formed part of any plan mentioned in sub-paragraph (1)(c).

(3) In this paragraph—

'existing policy' means a policy the substance of which (however expressed) was contained in the local plan or local plans mentioned in sub-paragraph (1)(c);

'policy' includes a proposal; and

'policy area' means so much of the area of the local planning authority to which the policy concerned relates.

Meaning of 'local plan'

4. In this Part of this Schedule, 'local plan' includes—
    (a) a minerals local plan;
    (b) a waste local plan;
    (c) a local plan adopted or approved before the commencement of Part I of Schedule 4 to the Planning and Compensation Act 1991 or under Part II of that Schedule.

[This schedule was added by, and will come into force on an appointed day order under, the Local Government (Wales) Act 1994.]

PART II
GREATER LONDON

Continuation of Greater London Development Plan, local plans and old development plans

1.—(1) Subject to paragraphs 2 and 3—
    (a) the Greater London Development Plan,
    (b) any local plan; and
    (c) any old development plan,

which immediately before the commencement of this Act was in force in the area, of a local planning authority in Greater London (or in that and other areas) shall continue in force in respect of the area of that authority until a unitary development plan for that area becomes operative under Chapter I of Part II of this Act or, where parts of a unitary development plan become operative on different dates, until every part of it has become operative.

(2) A plan which continues in force by virtue of this paragraph shall, while it continues in force, be treated for the purposes of this Act, any other enactment relating to town and country planning, the Land Compensation Act 1961 and the Highways Act 1980 as being, or being comprised in, the development plan in respect of the area in question.

(3) In this paragraph 'old development plan' has the same meaning as in paragraph 1 of Part I of this Schedule.

Revocation of Greater London Development Plan

2.—(1) Where under Chapter I of Part II of this Act the Secretary of State approves all or any of Part I of a unitary development plan he may by order—

(a) wholly or partly revoke the Greater London Development Plan, either in its application to the whole of the area of a local planning authority or in its application to part of that area; and

(b) make such consequential amendments to that plan as appear to him to be necessary or expedient.

(2) Before making an order under this paragraph the Secretary of State shall consult the local planning authority for the area to which the unitary development plan relates.

(3) Until the Greater London Development Plan ceases to be operative in an area under paragraph 1 or this paragraph, paragraph 7(1) of Schedule 1 shall apply in that area—

(a) with the omission of the words 'in a non-metropolitan county'; and

(b) with the substitution for the reference to the structure plan of a reference to that Plan.

3. to 16. [repealed by the Planning and Compensation Act 1991]

Incorporation of current local plan in unitary development plan

17.—(1) Sub-paragraph (2) applies where—

(a) a local plan is in force in the area of a local planning authority;

(b) a unitary development plan is being prepared;

(c) the local planning authority who are preparing that plan have published in the prescribed manner a statement in the prescribed form identifying a policy included in the plan as an existing policy; and

(d) a local inquiry or other hearing is held for the purpose of considering any objection to the plan.

(2) Where this sub-paragraph applies, the person holding the inquiry or other hearing need not allow an objector to appear if he is satisfied that—

(a) the objection is to a policy identified in the statement published under sub-paragraph (1)(c);

(b) the policy so identified is an existing policy; and

(c) there has been no significant change in circumstances affecting the existing policy since it first formed part of the plan mentioned in sub-paragraph (1)(a).

(3) In this paragraph 'existing policy' means a policy or proposal the substance of which (however expressed) was contained in a local plan in force as mentioned in sub-paragraph (1)(a).

18. [repealed]

PART III
OLD DEVELOPMENT PLAN

Preliminary

1. In this Part of this Schedule 'old development plan' means a development plan to which paragraph 2 of Schedule 7 to the 1971 Act (continuation in force of development plans prepared before structure plans became operative) applied immediately before the commencement of this Act.

Continuation in force of old development plans

2. Any old development plan which immediately before the commencement of this Act was in force as respects any district shall, subject to the provisions of this Part

of this Schedule, continue in force as respects that district and be treated for the purposes of this Act, any other enactment relating to town and country planning, the Land Compensation Act 1961 and the Highways Act 1980 as being comprised in the development plan for that district.

Other plans to prevail over old development plans

3. Subject to the following provisions of this Part of this Schedule, where by virtue of paragraph 2 the old development plan for any district is treated as being comprised in a development plan for that district—

(a) if there is a conflict between any of its provisions and those of the structure plan for that district, or, in the case of Greater London, the Greater London Development Plan the provisions of the structure plan or, as the case may be, that Plan shall be taken to prevail for the purposes of Parts III, V, VI, VII, VIII and IX of this Act and of the Planning (Listed Buildings and Conservation Areas) Act 1990 and the Planning (Hazardous Substances) Act 1990; and

(b) if there is a conflict between any of its provisions and those of a local plan, the provisions of the local plan shall be taken to prevail for those purposes.

Street authorisation maps

4. Where immediately before the commencement of this Act a street authorisation map prepared in pursuance of the Town and Country Planning (Development Plans) Regulations 1965 or the Town and Country Planning (Development Plans for Greater London) Regulations 1966 was treated for the purposes of the 1971 Act as having been adopted as a local plan for a district by a local planning authority, it shall continue to be so treated.

Development plans for compensation purposes

5. Where there is no local plan in force in a district, then, for any of the purposes of the Land Compensation Act 1961—

(a) the development plan or current development plan shall as respects that district be taken as being whichever of the following plans gives rise to those assumptions as to the grant of planning permission which are more favourable to the owner of the land acquired, for that purpose, namely the structure plan or, as the case may be, the Greater London Development Plan, so far as applicable to the district, and any alterations to it, together with the Secretary of State's notice of approval of the plan and alterations, and the old development plan;

(b) land situated in an area defined in the current development plan as an area of comprehensive development shall be taken to be situated in whichever of the following areas leads to such assumptions as are mentioned in paragraph (a), namely any area wholly or partly within that district selected by the structure plan or, as the case may be, the Greater London Development Plan as an action area and the area so defined in the old development plan.

Discontinuance of old development plan on adoption of local plan

6. Subject to paragraph 8, on the adoption or approval of a local plan under section 43 or 45 or paragraph 10 of Part II of this Schedule so much of any old development plan as relates to the area to which the local plan relates shall cease to have effect.

7. The Secretary of State may by order direct that any of the provisions of the old development plan shall continue in force in relation to the area to which the local plan relates.

8. If the Secretary of State makes an order under paragraph 7, the provisions of the old development plan specified in the order shall continue in force to the extent so specified.

9. Subject to paragraph 10, the Secretary of State may by order wholly or partly revoke a development plan continued in force under this Schedule whether in its application. to the whole of the area of a local planning authority or in its application to part of that area and make such consequential amendments to the plan as appear to him to be necessary or expedient.

10. Before making an order with respect to a development plan under paragraph 7 or 9, the Secretary of State shall consult with the local planning authority for the area to which the plan relates.

Sections 55, 107 and 114. SCHEDULE 3
DEVELOPMENT NOT CONSTITUTING NEW DEVELOPMENT

PART I
DEVELOPMENT NOT RANKING FOR COMPENSATION UNDER s. 114

1. The carrying out of—
  (a) the rebuilding, as often as occasion may require, of any building which was in existence on 1st July 1948, or of any building which was in existence before that date but was destroyed or demolished after 7th January 1937, including the making good of war damage sustained by any such building,
  (b) the rebuilding, as often as occasion may require, of any building erected after 1st July 1948 which was in existence at a material date;
  (c) the carrying out for the maintenance, improvement or other alteration of any building, of works which—
    (i) affect only the interior of the building, or do not materially affect the external appearance of the building, and
    (ii) are works for making good war damage,
so long as the cubic content of the original building is not substantially exceeded.

2. The use as two or more separate dwellinghouses of any building which at a material date was used as a single dwellinghouse.

PART II

[3 to 8 repealed by the Planning and Compensation Act 1991]

PART III

SUPPLEMENTARY PROVISIONS

9. Where after 1st July 1948—
  (a) any buildings or works have been erected or constructed, or any use of land has been instituted, and
  (b) any condition imposed under Part III of this Act, limiting the period for which those buildings or works may be retained, or that use may be continued, has effect in relation to those buildings or works or that use,
this Schedule shall not operate except as respects the period specified in that condition.

10.—(1) Any reference in this Schedule to the cubic content of a building shall be construed as a reference to that content as ascertained by external measurement.

(2) For the purposes of paragraph 1 the cubic content of a building is substantially increased or exceeded—
  (a) in the case of a dwellinghouse, if it is increased or exceeded by more than one-tenth or 1,750 cubic feet, whichever is the greater; and

(b) in any other case, if it is increased or exceeded by more than one-tenth.

11. [repealed by the Planning and Compensation Act 1991]

12.—(1) In this Schedule 'at a material date' means at either
   (a) 1st July 1948; or
   (b) the date by reference to which this Schedule falls to be applied in the particular case in question.

(2) Sub-paragraph (1)(b) shall not apply in relation to any buildings, works or use of land in respect of which, whether before or after the date mentioned in that sub-paragraph, an enforcement notice served before that date has become or becomes effective.

13.—(1) In relation to a building erected after 1st July 1948 which results from the carrying out of any such works as are described in paragraph 1, any reference in this Schedule to the original building is a reference to the building in relation to which those works were carried out and not to the building resulting from the carrying out of those works.

(2) This paragraph does not apply for the purposes of sections 111 and 138.

14. [repealed]

Section 57(7). SCHEDULE 4
SPECIAL PROVISIONS AS TO LAND USE IN 1948

1. Where on 1st July 1948 land was being temporarily used for a purpose other than the purpose for which it was normally used, planning permission is not required for the resumption of the use of the land for the latter purpose before 6th December 1968.

2. Where on 1st July 1948 land was normally used for one purpose and was also used on occasions, whether at regular intervals or not, for another purpose, planning permission is not required in respect of the use of the land for that other purpose on similar occasions on or after 6th December 1968 if the land has been used for that other purpose on at least one similar occasion since 1st July 1948 and before the beginning of 1968.

3. Where land was unoccupied on 1st July 1948, but had before that date been occupied at some time on or after 7th January 1937, planning permission is not required in respect of any use of the land begun before 6th December 1968 for the purpose for which the land was last used before 1st July 1948.

4. Notwithstanding anything in paragraphs 1 to 3, the use of land as a caravan site shall not, by virtue of any of those paragraphs, be treated as a use for which planning permission is not required, unless the land was so used on one occasion at least during the period of two years ending with 9th March 1960.

Sections 72(5), 79(4), 97(5) and Schedule 9.
SCHEDULE 5
CONDITIONS RELATING TO MINERAL WORKING
PART I
CONDITIONS IMPOSED ON GRANT OF PERMISSION

Duration of development

1.—(1) Every planning permission for development—
   (a) consisting of the winning and working of minerals; or
   (b) involving the depositing of mineral waste,

shall be subject to a condition as to the duration of the development.

(2) Except where a condition is specified under sub-paragraph (3), the condition in the case of planning permission granted or deemed to be granted after 22nd February 1982 is that the winning and working of minerals or the depositing of mineral waste must cease not later than the expiration of the period of 60 years beginning with the date of the permission.

(3) An authority granting planning permission after that date or directing after that date that planning permission shall be deemed to be granted may specify a longe or shorter period than 60 years, and if they do so, the condition is that the winning and working of minerals or the depositing of mineral waste must cease not later than the expiration of a period of the specified length beginning with the date of the permission.

(4) A longer or shorter period than 60 years may be prescribed for the purposes of sub-paragraphs (2) and (3).

(5) The condition in the case of planning permission granted or deemed to have been granted before 22nd February 1982 is that the winning and working of minerals or the depositing of mineral waste must cease not later than the expiration of the period of 60 years beginning with that date.

(6) A condition to which planning permission for development is subject by virtue of this paragraph—

(a) is not to be regarded for the purposes of the planning Acts as a condition such as is mentioned in section 72(1)(b); but

(b) is to be regarded for the purposes of sections 78 and 79 as a condition imposed by a decision of the local planning authority, and may accordingly be the subject of an appeal under section 78.

Power to impose aftercare conditions

2.—(1) Where—

(a) planning permission for development consisting of the winning and working of minerals or involving the depositing of refuse or waste materials is granted, and

(b) the permission is subject to a condition requiring that after the winning and working is completed or the depositing has ceased, the site shall be restored by the use of any or all of the following, namely, subsoil, topsoil and soil-making material,

it may be granted subject also to any such condition as the mineral planning authority think fit requiring that such steps shall be taken as may be necessary to bring land to the required standard for whichever of the following uses is specified in the condition, namely—

(i) use for agriculture;
(ii) use for forestry; or
(iii) use for amenity.

(2) In this Act—

(a) a condition such as is mentioned in paragraph (b) of sub-paragraph (1) is referred to as 'a restoration condition'; and

(b) a condition requiring such steps to be taken as are mentioned in that sub-paragraph is referred to as 'an aftercare condition'.

(3) An aftercare condition may either—

(a) specify the steps to be taken; or

(b) require that the steps be taken in accordance with a scheme (in this Act referred to as an 'aftercare scheme') approved by the mineral planning authority.

(4) A mineral planning authority may approve an aftercare scheme in the form in which it is submitted to them or may modify it and approve it as modified.

(5) The steps that may be specified in an aftercare condition or an aftercare scheme may consist of planting, cultivating, fertilising, watering, draining or otherwise treating the land.

(6) Where a step is specified in a condition or a scheme, the period during which it is to be taken may also be specified, but no step may be required to be taken after the expiry of the aftercare period.

(7) In sub-paragraph (6) 'the aftercare period' means a period of five years from compliance with the restoration condition or such other maximum period after compliance with that condition as may be prescribed; and in respect of any part of a site, the aftercare period shall commence on compliance with the restoration condition in respect of that part.

(8) The power to prescribe maximum periods conferred by sub-paragraph (7) includes power to prescribe maximum periods differing according to the use specified.

(9) In this paragraph 'forestry' means the growing of a utilisable crop of timber.

Meaning of 'required standard'

3.—(1) In a case where—
  (a) the use specified in an aftercare condition is a use for agriculture; and
  (b) the land was in use for agriculture at the time of the grant of the planning permission or had previously been used for that purpose and had not at the time of the grant been used for any authorised purpose since its use for agriculture ceased; and
  (c) the Minister has notified the mineral planning authority of the physical characteristics of the land when it was last used for agriculture,
the land is brought to the required standard when its physical characteristics are restored, so far as it is practicable to do so, to what they were when it was last used for agriculture.

(2) In any other case where the use specified in an aftercare condition is a use for agriculture, the land is brought to the required standard when it is reasonably fit for that use.

(3) Where the use specified in an aftercare condition is a use for forestry, the land is brought to the required standard when it is reasonably fit for that use.

(4) Where the use specified in an aftercare condition is a use for amenity, the land is brought to the required standard when it is suitable for sustaining trees, shrubs or other plants.

(5) In this paragraph
  'authorised' means authorised by planning permission;
  'forestry' has the same meaning as in paragraph 2; and
  'the Minister' means—
    (a) in relation to England, the Minister of Agriculture, Fisheries and Food; and
    (b) in relation to Wales, the Secretary of State.

Consultations

4.—(1) Before imposing an aftercare condition, the mineral planning authority shall consult—
  (a) the Minister, where they propose that the use specified in the condition shall be a use for agriculture; and
  (b) the Forestry Commission, where they propose that the use so specified shall be a use for forestry,
as to whether it is appropriate to specify that use.

(2) Where after consultations required by sub-paragraph (1) the mineral planning authority are satisfied that the use that they ought to specify is a use for agriculture or for forestry, they shall consult—
  (a) where it is for agriculture, the Minister; and
  (b) where it is for forestry, the Forestry Commission,
with regard to whether the steps to be taken should be specified in the aftercare condition or in an aftercare scheme.

(3) The mineral planning authority shall also consult the Minister or, as the case may be, the Forestry Commission—
   (a) as to the steps to be specified in an aftercare condition which specifies a use for agriculture or for forestry; and
   (b) before approving an aftercare scheme submitted in accordance with an aftercare condition which specifies such a use.

(4) The mineral planning authority shall also, from time to time as they consider expedient, consult the Minister or the Commission, as the case may be, as to whether the steps specified in an aftercare condition or an aftercare scheme are being taken.

[(4A) Without prejudice to the application of this paragraph in relation to consultation with the Forestry Commission, where the Minister is consulted pursuant to any provision of this paragraph—
   (a) he is not required to inspect any land or to express a view on any matter or question; and
   (b) he is not precluded from responding in general terms or otherwise in terms which are not specific to the land in question.]

(5) In this paragraph 'forestry' and 'the Minister' have the same meanings as in paragraph 3.

[Paragraph 4(4A) was inserted by, and will be brought into force as from a day appointed under, the Environment Act 1995.]

Certificate of compliance

5. If, on the application of any person with an interest in land in respect of which an aftercare condition has been imposed, the mineral planning authority are satisfied that the condition has been complied with they shall issue a certificate to that effect.

Recovery of expenses of compliance

6. A person who has complied with an aftercare condition but who has not himself won and worked minerals or deposited refuse or waste materials shall be entitled, subject to any condition to the contrary contained in a contract which is enforceable against him by the person who last carried out such operations, to recover from that person any expenses reasonably incurred in complying with the aftercare condition.

PART II
CONDITIONS IMPOSED ON REVOCATION OR MODIFICATION OF PERMISSION

7. An order under section 97 may in relation to planning permission for development consisting of the winning and working of minerals or involving the depositing of refuse or waste materials include such aftercare condition as the mineral planning authority think fit if—
   (a) it also includes a restoration condition; or
   (b) a restoration condition has previously been imposed in relation to the land by virtue of any provision of this Act.

8. Paragraphs 2(3) to (9) and 3 to 6 shall apply in relation to an aftercare condition so imposed as they apply in relation to such a condition imposed under paragraph 2.

9. In this Schedule any reference to a mineral planning authority shall be construed, in relation to the exercise of functions with respect to the depositing of refuse or waste materials (other, than mineral waste), as; a reference to the authority entitled to discharge such functions.

Sections 79, 175, 195, 208. SCHEDULE 6
DETERMINATION OF CERTAIN APPEALS BY PERSON APPOINTED
BY SECRETARY OF STATE

Determination of appeals by appointed person

1.—(1) The Secretary of State may by regulations prescribe classes of appeals under sections 78, 106B, 174, 195 and 208 [and paragraphs 6(11) and (12) and 11(1) of Schedule 13 and paragraph 9(1) of Schedule 14 to the Environment Act 1995.], which are to be determined by a person appointed by the Secretary of State for the purpose instead of by the Secretary of State.

(2) Those classes of appeals shall be so determined except in such classes of case—
   (a) as may for the time being be prescribed, or
   (b) as may be specified in directions given by the Secretary of State.

(3) Regulations made for the purpose of this paragraph may provide for the giving of publicity to any directions given by the Secretary of State under this paragraph.

(4) This paragraph shall not affect any provision in this Act or any instrument made under it that an appeal shall lie to, or a notice of appeal shall be served on, the Secretary of State.

(5) A person appointed under this paragraph is referred to in this Schedule as 'an appointed person'.

Powers and duties of appointed person

2.—(1) An appointed person shall have the same powers and duties—
   (a) in relation to an appeal under section 78, as the Secretary of State has under subsections (1) (4) and (6) of section 79;
   (aa) in relation to an appeal under section 106B, as he was under that section;
   (b) in relation to an appeal under section 174, as he has under sections 176(1), (2) and (5) and 177(1) to (4);
   (c) in relation to an appeal under section 195, as he has under subsections (2) and 3) of that section and subsection (5) of section 196;
   (d) in relation to an appeal under section 208, as he has under subsections (7) to (8A) of that section.

(2) Sections 79(2), 106B(4) 175(3), 196(1) and 208(5) shall not apply to an appeal which falls to be determined by an appointed person, but before, it is determined the Secretary of State shall ask the appellant and the local planning authority whether they wish to appear before and be heard by the appointed person.

(3) If both the parties express a wish not to appear and be heard the appeal may be determined without their being heard.

(4) If either of the parties expresses a wish to appear and be heard, the appointed person shall give them both an opportunity of doing so.

(5) Sub-paragraph (2) does not apply in the case of an appeal under section 78 if the appeal is referred to a Planning Inquiry Commission under section 101.

(6) Where an appeal has been determined by an appointed person, his decision shall be treated as that of the Secretary of State.

(7) Except as provided by Part XII, the validity of that decision shall not be questioned in any proceedings whatsoever.

(8) It shall not be a ground of application to the High Court under section 288, or of appeal to the High Court under section 289 that an appeal ought to have been determined by the Secretary of State and not by an appointed person, unless the appellant or the local planning authority challenge the appointed person's power to determine the appeal before his decision on the appeal is given.

(9) Where in any enactment (including this Act) there is a reference to the Secretary of State in a context relating or capable of relating to an appeal to which

this Schedule applies or to anything done or authorised or required to be done by, to or before the Secretary of State on or in connection with any such appeal, then so far as the context permits it shall be construed, in relation to an appeal determined or falling to be determined by an appointed person, as a reference to him.

Determination of appeals by Secretary of State

3.—(1) The Secretary of State may, if he thinks fit, direct that an appeal which would otherwise fall to be determined by an appointed person shall instead be determined by the Secretary of State.

(2) Such a direction shall state the reasons for which it is given and shall be served on the person, if any, so appointed, the appellant, the local planning authority and any person who has made representations relating to the subject matter of the appeal which the authority are required to take into account under any provision of a development order made by virtue of section 71(2)(a).

(3) Where in consequence of such a direction an appeal falls to be determined by the Secretary of State, the provisions of this Act which are relevant to the appeal shall, subject to the following provisions of this paragraph, apply to the appeal as if this Schedule had never applied to it.

(4) The Secretary of State shall give the appellant, the local planning authority and any person who has made any such representations as mentioned in sub-paragraph (2) an opportunity of appearing before and being heard by a person appointed by the Secretary of State for that purpose if—

(a) the reasons for the direction raise matters with respect to which any of those persons have not made representations; or

(b) in the case of the appellant or the local planning authority, either of them was not asked in pursuance of paragraph 2(2) whether they wished to appear before and be heard by the appointed person, or expressed no wish in answer to that question, or expressed a wish to appear and be heard, but was not given an opportunity of doing so.

(5) Sub-paragraph (4) does not apply in the case of an appeal under section 78 if the appeal is referred to a Planning Inquiry Commission under section 101.

(6) Except as provided by sub-paragraph (4), the Secretary of State need not give any person an opportunity of appearing before and being heard by a person appointed for the purpose, or of making fresh representations or making or withdrawing any representations already made.

(7) In determining the appeal the Secretary of State may take into account any report made to him by any person previously appointed to determine it.

4.—(1) The Secretary of State may by a further direction revoke a direction under paragraph 3 at any time before the determination of the appeal.

(2) Such a further direction shall state the reasons for which it is given and shall be served on the person, if any, previously appointed to determine the appeal, the appellant, the local planning authority and any person who has made representations relating to the subject matter of the appeal which the authority are required to take into account under any provision of a development order made by virtue of section 71(2)(a).

(3) Where such a further direction has been given, the provisions of this Schedule relevant to the appeal shall apply, subject to sub-paragraph (4), as if no direction under paragraph 3 had been given.

(4) Anything done by or on behalf of the Secretary of State in connection with the appeal which might have been done by the appointed person (including any arrangements made for the holding of a hearing or local inquiry) shall, unless that person directs otherwise, be treated as having been done by him.

Appointment of another person to determine appeal

5.—(1) At any time before the appointed person has determined the appeal the Secretary of State may—
 (a) revoke his appointment; and
 (b) appoint another person under paragraph 1 to determine the appeal instead.
 (2) Where such a new appointment is made the consideration of the appeal or any inquiry or other hearing in connection with it shall be begun afresh.
 (3) Nothing in sub-paragraph (2) shall require—
 (a) the question referred to in paragraph 2(2) to be asked again with reference to the new appointed person if before his appointment it was asked with reference to the previous appointed person (any answers being treated as given with reference to the new appointed person); or
 (b) any person to be given an opportunity of making fresh representations or modifying or withdrawing any representations already made.

Local inquiries and hearings

6.—(1) Whether or not the parties to an appeal have asked for an opportunity to appear and be heard, an appointed person—
 (a) may hold a local inquiry in connection with the appeal; and
 (b) shall do so if the Secretary of State so directs.
 (2) Where an appointed person—
 (a) holds a hearing by virtue of paragraph 2(4); or
 (b) holds an inquiry by virtue of this paragraph,
an assessor may be appointed by the Secretary of State to sit with the appointed person at the hearing or inquiry to advise him on any matters arising, notwithstanding that the appointed person is to determine the appeal.
 (3) Subject to sub-paragraph (4), the costs of any such hearing or inquiry shall be defrayed by the Secretary of State.
 (4) Subsections (2) to (5) of section 250 of the Local Government Act 1972 (local inquiries: evidence and costs) apply to an inquiry held under this paragraph with the following adaptations—
 (a) with the substitution in subsection (4) (recovery of costs of holding the inquiry) for the references to the Minister causing the inquiry to be held of references to the Secretary of State; and
 (b) with the substitution in subsection (5) (orders as to the costs of the parties) for the reference to the Minister causing the inquiry to be held of a reference to the appointed person or the Secretary of State.
 (5) The appointed person or the Secretary of State has the same power to make orders under section 250(5) of that Act (orders with respect to costs of the parties) in relation to proceedings under this Schedule which do not give rise to an inquiry as he has in relation to such an inquiry.

Supplementary provisions

7. If before or during the determination of an appeal under section 78 which is to be or is being determined in accordance with paragraph 1, the Secretary of State forms the opinion mentioned in section 79(6), he may direct that the determination shall not be begun or proceeded with.

8.—(1) The Tribunals and Inquiries Act 1992 shall apply to a local inquiry or other hearing held in pursuance of this Schedule as it applies to a statutory inquiry held by the Secretary of State, but as if in section 12(1) of that Act (statement of reasons for decisions) the reference to any decision taken by the Secretary of State were a reference to a decision taken by an appointed person.

(2) Where an appointed person is an officer of the Department of the Environment or the Welsh Office the functions of determining an appeal and doing anything in connection with it conferred on him by this Schedule shall be treated for the purposes of the Parliamentary Commissioner Act 1967—

(a) if he was appointed by the Secretary of State for the time being having general responsibility in planning matters in relation to England, as functions of that Department; and

(b) if he was appointed by the Secretary of State for the time being having general responsibility in planning matters in relation to Wales, as functions of the Welsh Office.

Section 83. SCHEDULE 7
SIMPLIFIED PLANNING ZONES

General

1.—(1) A simplified planning zone scheme shall consist of a map and a written statement, and such diagrams, illustrations and descriptive matter as the local planning authority think appropriate for explaining or illustrating the provisions of the scheme.

(2) A simplified planning zone scheme shall specify—
 (a) the development or classes of development permitted by the scheme,
 (b) the land in relation to which permission is granted, and
 (c) any conditions, limitations or exceptions subject to which it is granted;
and shall contain such other matters as may be prescribed.

Notification of proposals to make or alter scheme

2. An authority who decide under section 83(2) to make or alter a simplified planning zone scheme shall—
 (a) notify the Secretary of State of their decision as soon as practicable, and
 (b) determine the date on which they will begin to prepare the scheme or the alterations.

Power of Secretary of State to direct making or alteration of scheme

3.—(1) If a person requests a local planning authority to make or alter a simplified planning zone scheme but the authority—
 (a) refuse to do so, or
 (b) do not within the period of three months from the date of the request decide to do so,
he may, subject to sub-paragraph (2), require them to refer the matter to the Secretary of State.

(2) A person may not require the reference of the matter to the Secretary of State if—
 (a) In the case of a request to make a scheme, a simplified planning zone scheme relating to the whole or part of the land specified in the request has been adopted or approved within the 12 months preceding his request;
 (b) in the case of a request to alter the scheme, the scheme to which the request relates was adopted or approved, or any alteration to it has been adopted or approved, within that period.

(3) The Secretary of State shall, as soon as practicable after a matter is referred to him—
 (a) send the authority a copy of any representations made to him by the applicant which have not been made to the authority, and
 (b) notify the authority that if they wish to make any representations in the matter they should do so, in writing, within 28 days.

(4) After the Secretary of State has—
(a) considered the matter and any written representations made by the applicant or the authority, and
(b) carried out such consultations with such persons as he thinks fit,
he may give the authority a simplified planning zone direction.

(5) The Secretary of State shall notify the applicant and the authority of his decision and of his reasons for it.

4.—(1) A simplified planning zone direction is—
(a) if the request was for the making of a scheme, a direction to make a scheme which the Secretary of State considers appropriate; and
(b) if the request was for the alteration of a scheme, a direction to alter it in such manner as he considers appropriate,
and, in either cases required the local planning authority to take all the steps required by this Schedule for the adoption of proposals for the making or, as the case may be, alteration of a scheme.

(2) A direction under sub-paragraph (1)(a) or (b) may extend—
(a) to the land specified in the request to the authority,
(b) to any part of the land so specified, or
(c) to land which includes the whole or part of the land so specified;
and accordingly may direct that land shall be added to or excluded from an existing simplified planning zone.

Steps to be taken before depositing proposals

5.—(1) A local planning authority proposing to make or alter a simplified planning zone scheme shall, before determining the content of their proposals, comply with this paragraph.

(2) They shall—
(a) consult the Secretary of State having responsibility for highways as to the effect any proposals they may make might have on existing or future highways,
(b) If they are the district planning authority, consult the county council—
(i) as county planning authority, and
(ii) as to the effect which any matters the district planning authority are considering including in the proposals might have on existing or future highways, and
(c) consult or notify such persons as regulations may require them to consult or, as the case may be, notify.

(3) They shall take such steps as may be prescribed or as the Secretary of State may, in a particular case, direct to publicise—
(a) the fact that they propose to make or alter a simplified planning zone scheme, and
(b) the matters which they are considering including in the proposals.

(4) They shall consider any representations that are made in accordance with regulations.

Procedure after deposit of proposals

6. Where a local planning authority have prepared a proposed simplified planning zone scheme, or proposed alterations to a simplified planning zone scheme, they shall—
(a) make copies of the proposed scheme or alterations available for inspection at such places as may be prescribed,
(b) take such steps as may be prescribed for the purpose of advertising the fact that the proposed scheme or alterations are so available and the places at which, and times during which, they may be inspected,

(c) take such steps as may be prescribed for inviting objections to be made within such period as may be prescribed, and

(d) send a copy of the proposed scheme or alterations to the Secretary of State and to the Secretary of State having responsibility for highways and, if they are the district planning authority, to the county council.

7. [repealed by the Planning and Compensation Act 1991]

Procedure for dealing with objections

8.—(1) Where objections to the proposed scheme or alterations are made, the local planning authority may—

(a) for the purpose of considering the objections, cause a local inquiry or other hearing to be held by a person appointed by the Secretary of State or, in such cases as may be prescribed, appointed by the authority, or

(b) require the objections to be considered by a person appointed by the Secretary of State.

(2) A local planning authority shall exercise the power under sub-paragraph (1), or paragraph (a) or (b) of that sub-paragraph, if directed to do so by the Secretary of State.

(3) [repealed by the Planning and Compensation Act 1991]

(4) Regulations may—

(a) make provision with respect to the appointment, and qualifications for appointment, of persons for the purposes of this paragraph;

(b) include provision enabling the Secretary of State to direct a local planning authority to appoint a particular person, or one of a specified list or class of persons;

(c) make provision with respect to the remuneration and allowances of the person appointed.

(5) Subsections (2) and (3) of section 250 of the Local Government Act 1972 (power to summon and examine witnesses) apply to an inquiry held under this paragraph.

(6) The Tribunals and Inquiries Act 1992 applies to a local inquiry or other hearing held under this paragraph as it applies to a statutory inquiry held by the Secretary of State, with the substitution in section 12(1) (statement of reasons for decision) for the references to a decision taken by the Secretary of State of references to a decision taken by a local authority.

Adoption of proposals by local planning authority

9.—(1) After the expiry of the period for making objections or, if objections have been made in accordance with the regulations, after considering those objections and the views of any person holding an inquiry or hearing or considering the objections under paragraph 8, the local planning authority may by resolution adopt the proposals (subject to the following provisions of this paragraph and paragraph 10).

(2) The authority may adopt the proposals as originally prepared or as modified so as to take account of—

(a) any such objections as are mentioned in sub-paragraph (1) or any other objections to the proposals, or

(b) any other considerations which appear to the authority to be material.

(3) If, before the proposals have been adopted by the local planning authority, it appears to the Secretary of State that they are unsatisfactory, he may direct the authority to modify the proposals in such respects as are indicated in the direction.

(4) An authority to whom such a direction is given shall not adopt the proposals unless—

(a) they satisfy the Secretary of State that they have made the modifications necessary to conform with the direction, or

(b) the direction is withdrawn.

Calling in of proposals for approval by Secretary of State

10.—(1) Before the proposals have been adopted by the local planning authority the Secretary of State may direct that they shall be submitted to him for his approval.

(2) If the Secretary of State gives such a direction—

(a) the authority shall not take any further steps for the adoption of the proposals, and in particular shall not hold or proceed with a local inquiry or other hearing or any consideration of objections in respect of the proposals under paragraph 8; and

(b) the proposals shall not have effect unless approved by the Secretary of State and shall not require adoption by the authority.

Approval of proposals by Secretary of State

11.—(1) The Secretary of State may after considering proposals submitted to him under paragraph 10 either approve them, in whole or in part and with or without modifications, or reject them.

(2) In considering the proposals the Secretary of State may take into account any matters he thinks are relevant, whether or not they were taken into account in the proposals as submitted to him.

(3) Where on taking the proposals into consideration the Secretary of State does not determine then to reject them he shall, before determining whether or not to approve them, consider any objections made in accordance with regulations (and not withdrawn) except objections which—

(a) have already been considered by the local planning authority or by a person appointed by the Secretary of State, or

(b) have already been considered at a local inquiry or other hearing.

(4) The Secretary of State may—

(a) for the purpose of considering any objections and the views of the local planning authority and of such other persons as he thinks fit, cause a local inquiry or other hearing to be held by a person appointed by him, or

(b) require such objections and views to be considered by a person appointed by him.

(5) In considering the proposals the Secretary of State may consult with, or consider the views of, any local planning authority or any other person; but he need not do so, or give an opportunity for the making or consideration of representations or objections, except so far as he is required to do so by sub-paragraph (3).

Default powers

12.—(1) Where—

(a) a local planning authority are directed under paragraph 3 to make a simplified planning zone scheme which the Secretary of State considers appropriate or to alter such a scheme in such manner as he considers appropriate, and

(b) the Secretary of State is satisfied, after holding a local inquiry or other hearing, that the authority are not taking within a reasonable period the steps required by this Schedule for the adoption of proposals for the making or, as the case may be, alteration of a scheme,

he may himself make a scheme or, as the case may be, the alterations.

(2) Where under this paragraph anything which ought to have been done by a local planning authority is done by the Secretary of State, the previous provisions of

this Schedule apply, so far as practicable, with any necessary modifications, in relation to the doing of that thing by the Secretary of State and the thing so done.

(3) Where the Secretary of State incurs expenses under this paragraph in connection with the doing of anything which should have been done by a local planning authority, so much of those expenses as may be certified by the Secretary of State to have been incurred in the performance of functions of that authority shall on demand be repaid by the authority to the Secretary of State.

Regulations and directions

13.—(1) Without prejudice to the previous provisions of this Schedule, the Secretary of State may make regulations with respect—
   (a) to the form and content of simplified planning zone schemes, and
   (b) to the procedure to be followed in connection with their preparation, withdrawal, adoption, submission, approval, making or alteration.

(2) Any such regulations may in particular—
   (a) provide for the notice to be given of, or the publicity to be given to—
      (i) matters included or proposed to be included in a simplified planning zone scheme, and
      (ii) the adoption or approval of such a scheme, or of any alteration of it, or any other prescribed procedural step,
and for publicity to be given to the procedure to be followed in these respects;
   (b) make provision with respect to the making and consideration of representations as to matters to be included in, or objections to, any such scheme or proposals for its alteration;
   (bb) make provision with respect to the circumstances in which representations with respect to the matters to be included in such a scheme or proposals for its alteration are to be treated, for the purposes of this Schedule, as being objections made in accordance with regulations;
   (c) without prejudice to paragraph (a), provide for notice to be given to particular persons of the adoption or approval of a simplified planning zone scheme, or an alteration to such a scheme, if they have objected to the proposals and have notified the local planning authority of their wish to receive notice, subject (if the regulations so provide) to the payment of a reasonable charge;
   (d) require or authorise a local planning authority to consult with, or consider the views of, other persons before taking any prescribed procedural step;
   (e) require a local planning authority, in such cases as may be prescribed or in such particular cases as the Secretary of State may direct, to provide persons making a request with copies of any document which has been made, subject (if the regulations so provide) to the payment of a reasonable charge;
   (f) provide for the publication and inspection of a simplified planning zone scheme which has been adopted or approved, or any document adopted or approved altering such a scheme, and for copies of any such scheme or document to be made available on sale.

(3) Regulations under this paragraph may extend throughout England and Wales or to specified areas only and may make different provision for different cases.

(4) Subject to the previous provisions of this Schedule and to any regulations under this paragraph, the Secretary of State may give directions to any local planning authority or to local planning authorities generally—
   (a) for formulating the procedure for the carrying out of their functions under this Schedule;
   (b) for requiring them to give him such information as he may require for carrying out any of his functions under this Schedule.

Section 101(4).

SCHEDULE 8
PLANNING INQUIRY COMMISSIONS

PART I
CONSTITUTION AND PROCEDURE ON REFERENCES

Constitution of Commissions

1.—(1) A Planning Inquiry Commission shall consist of a chairman and not less than two nor more than four other members appointed by the Secretary of State.

(2) The Secretary of State may—

(a) pay to the members of any such commission such remuneration and allowances as he may with the consent of the Treasury determine, and

(b) provide for each such commission such officers or servants, and such accommodation, as appears to him expedient to provide for the purpose of assisting the commission in the discharge of their functions.

(3) The validity of any proceedings of any such commission shall not be affected by any vacancy among the members of the commission or by any defect in the appointment of any member.

(4) In relation to any matter affecting both England and Wales—

(a) the functions of the Secretary of State under sub-paragraph (1) shall be exercised by the Secretaries of State for the time being having general responsibility in planning matters in relation to England and in relation to Wales acting jointly, and

(b) his functions under sub-paragraph (2) shall be exercised by one of those Secretaries of State authorised by the other to act on behalf of both of them for the purposes of that sub-paragraph.

Reference to a Planning Inquiry Commission

2.—(1) Two or more of the matters mentioned in section 101(2) may be referred to the same commission if it appears to the responsible Minister or Ministers that they relate to proposals to carry out development for similar purposes on different sites.

(2) Where a matter referred to a commission under section 101 relates to a proposal to carry out development for any purpose at a particular site, the responsible Minister or Ministers may also refer to the commission the question whether development for that purpose should instead be carried out at an alternative site.

(3) On referring a matter to a commission, the responsible Minister or Ministers—

(a) shall state in the reference the reasons for the reference, and

(b) may draw the attention of the commission to any points which seem to him or them to be relevant to their inquiry.

Functions of Planning Inquiry Commission on reference

3.—(1) A commission inquiring into a matter referred to them under section 101 shall—

(a) identify and investigate the considerations relevant to, or the technical or scientific aspects of, that matter which in their opinion are relevant to the question whether the proposed development should be permitted to be carried out, and

(b) assess the importance to be attached to those considerations or aspects.

(2) If—

(a) in the case of a matter mentioned in section 101(2)(a), (b) or (c), the applicant, or

(b) in any case, the local planning authority,

so wish, the commission shall give to each of them, and, in the case of an application or appeal mentioned in section 101(2)(a) or (b), also to any person who has made representations relating to the subject matter of the application or appeal which the authority are required to take into account under any provision of a development order made by virtue of section 71(2)(a), an opportunity of appearing before and being heard by one or more members of the commission.

(3) The commission shall then report to the responsible Minister or Ministers on the matter referred to them.

(4) A commission may, with the approval of the Secretary of State and at his expense, arrange for the carrying out (whether by the commission themselves or by others) of research of any kind appearing to them to be relevant to a matter referred to them for inquiry and report.

(5) In sub-paragraph (4) 'the Secretary of State,' in relation to any matter affecting both England and Wales, means—

(a) the Secretary of State for the time being having general responsibility in planning matters in relation to England, or

(b) the Secretary of State for the time being having responsibility in relation to Wales,

acting, by arrangements between the two of them, on behalf of both.

Procedure on reference to a Planning Inquiry Commission

4.—(1) A reference to a Planning Inquiry Commission of a proposal that development should be carried out by or on behalf of a government department may be made at any time.

(2) A reference of any other matter mentioned in section 101 may be made at any time before, but not after, the determination of the relevant application referred under section 77 or the relevant appeal under section 78 or, as the case may be, the giving of the relevant direction under section 90(1).

(3) The fact that an inquiry or other hearing has been held into a proposal by a person appointed by any Minister for the purpose shall not prevent a reference of the proposal to a Planning Inquiry Commission.

(4) Notice of the making of a reference to any such commission shall be published in the prescribed manner.

(5) A copy of the notice must be served on the local planning authority for the area in which it is proposed that the relevant development will be carried out, and—

(a) in the case of an application for planning permission referred under section 77 or an appeal under section 78, on the applicant and any person who has made representations relating to the subject matter of the application or appeal which the authority are required to take into account under any provision of a development order made by virtue of section 71(2)(a);

(b) On the case of a proposal that a direction should be given under section 90(1) with respect to any development, on the local authority, National Park Authority or statutory undertakers applying for authorisation to carry out that development.

(6) Subject to the provisions of this paragraph and paragraph 5 and to any directions given to them by the responsible Minister or Ministers, a Planning Inquiry Commission shall have power to regulate their own procedure.

[The reference to a National Park Authority was inserted by the Environment Act 1995, see note to Section 4A supra.]

Local inquiries held by Planning Inquiry Commission

5.—(1) A Planning Inquiry Commission shall, for the purpose of complying with paragraph 3(2), hold a local inquiry; and they may hold such an inquiry, if they think it necessary for the proper discharge of their functions, notwithstanding that neither the applicant nor the local planning authority want an opportunity to appear and be heard.

(2) Where a Planning Inquiry Commission are to hold a local inquiry under sub-paragraph (1) in connection with a matter referred to them, and it appears to the responsible Minister or Ministers, in the case of some other matter falling to be determined by a Minister of the Crown and required or authorised by an enactment other than this paragraph to be the subject of a local inquiry, that the two matters are so far cognate that they should be considered together, he or, as the case may be, they may direct that the two inquiries be held concurrently or combined as one inquiry.

(3) An inquiry held by a commission under this paragraph shall be treated for the purposes of the Tribunals and Inquiries Act 1992 as one held by a Minister in pursuance of a duty imposed by a statutory provision.

(4) Subsections (2) to (5) of section 250 of the Local Government Act 1972 (local inquiries: evidence and costs) shall apply in relation to an inquiry held under sub-paragraph (1) as they apply in relation to an inquiry caused to be held by a Minister under subsection (1) of that section, with the substitution for references to the Minister causing the inquiry to be held (other than the first reference in subsection (4)) of references to the responsible Minister or Ministers.

PART II
MEANING OF 'THE RESPONSIBLE MINISTER OR MINISTERS'

6. In relation to the matters specified in the first column of the Table below (which are matters mentioned in subsection (2)(a), (b), (c) or (d) of section 101 as matters which may be referred to a Planning Inquiry Commission under that section) 'the responsible Minister or Ministers' for the purposes of that section and this Schedule—

(a) in the case of a matter affecting England only, are those specified opposite in the second column of the Table;

(b) in the case of a matter affecting Wales only, are those specified opposite in the third column of the Table; and

(c) in the case of a matter affecting both England and Wales, are those specified opposite in the fourth column of the Table.

7. Where an entry in the second, third or fourth columns of the Table specifies two or more Ministers, that entry shall be construed as referring to those Ministers acting jointly.

TABLE

Referred matter	Affecting England only	Affecting Wales only	Affecting both England and Wales
1. Application for planning permission or appeal under section 78 relating to land to which section 266(1) applies.	The Secretary of State for the time being having general responsibility in planning matters in relation to England and the appropriate Minister (if different).	The Secretary of State for the time being having general responsibility in planning matters in relation to Wales and the appropriate Minister (if different).	The Secretaries of State for the time being having general responsibility in planning matters in relation to England and in relation to Wales the and appropriate Minister (if different).
2. Application for planning permission or appeal under section 78 relating to land to which section 266(1) does not apply.	The Secretary of State for the time being having general responsibility in planning matters in relation to England.	The Secretary of State for the time being having general responsibility in planning matters in relation to Wales.	The Secretaries of State for the time being having general responsibility in planning matters in relation to England and in relation to Wales.
3. Proposal that a government department should give a direction under section 90(1) or that development should be carried out by or on behalf of a government department.	The Secretary of State for the time being having general responsibility in planning matters in relation to England and the Minister (if different) in charge of the government department concerned.	The Secretary of State for the time being having general responsibility in planning matters in relation to Wales and the Minister (if different) in charge of the government department concerned.	The Secretaries of State for the time being having general responsibility in planning matters in relation to England and in relation to Wales and the Minister (if different) in charge of the government department concerned.

Section 102(8).

SCHEDULE 9
REQUIREMENTS RELATING TO DISCONTINUANCE OF MINERAL WORKING

Orders requiring discontinuance of mineral working

1.—(1) If, having regard to the development plan and to any other material considerations, it appears to a mineral planning authority that it is expedient in the interests of the proper planning of their area (including the interests of amenity)—
    (a) that any use of land for—
        (i) development consisting of the winning and working of minerals; or
        (ii) the depositing of refuse or waste materials,
should be discontinued or that any conditions should be imposed on the continuance of the winning and working or the depositing;
    (b) that any buildings or works on land so used should be altered or removed; or

(c) that any plant or machinery used for the winning and working or the depositing should be altered or removed,

the mineral planning authority may by order require the discontinuance of that use, or impose such conditions as may be specified in the order on the continuance of it or, as the case may be, require such steps as may be so specified to be taken for the alteration or removal of the buildings or works or plant or machinery.

(2) An order under this paragraph may grant planning permission for any development of the land to which the order relates, subject to such conditions as may be—
- (a) required by paragraph 1 of Schedule 5; or
- (b) specified in the order.

(3) Subsections (3) to (5) and (7) of section 102 and section 103 apply to orders under this paragraph as they apply to orders under section 102, but as if—
- (a) references to the local planning authority were references to the mineral planning authority; and
- (b) the reference in section 103(2)(a) to subsection (2) of section 102 were a reference to sub-paragraph (2).

2.—(1) Any order under paragraph 1 may impose a restoration condition.

(2) If such an order—
- (a) includes a restoration condition, or
- (b) a restoration condition has previously been imposed in relation to the land by virtue of any provision of this Act,

the order may also include any such aftercare condition as the mineral planning authority think fit.

(3) Paragraphs 2(3) to (9) and 3 to 6 of Schedule 5 shall apply in relation to an aftercare condition imposed under this paragraph as they apply in relation to such a condition imposed under paragraph 2 of that Schedule, but with the substitution for sub-paragraphs (1) and (2) of paragraph 3 of that Schedule of sub-paragraphs (4) and (5) below.

(4) In a case where—
- (a) the use specified in the aftercare condition is a use for agriculture;
- (b) the land was in use for agriculture immediately before the development began, or had previously been used for agriculture and had not been used for any authorised purpose since its use for agriculture ceased; and
- (c) the Minister has notified the mineral planning authority of the physical characteristics of the land when it was last used for agriculture,

the land is brought to the required standard when its physical characteristics are restored, so far as it is practicable to do so, to what they were when it was last used for agriculture.

(5) In any other case where the use specified in the aftercare condition is a use for agriculture, the land is brought to the required standard when it is reasonably fit for that use.

Prohibition of resumption of mineral working

3.—(1) Where it appears to the mineral planning authority—
- (a) that development of land—
  - (i) consisting of the winning and working of minerals; or
  - (ii) involving the depositing of mineral waste,

has occurred; but
- (b) the winning and working or depositing has permanently ceased,

the mineral planning authority may by order—
  - (i) prohibit the resumption of the winning and working or the depositing; and

(ii) impose, in relation to the site, any such requirement as is specified in sub-paragraph (3).

(2) The mineral planning authority may assume that the winning and working or the depositing has permanently ceased only when—

(a) no winning and working or depositing has occurred, to any substantial extent, at the site for a period of at least two years; and

(b) it appears to the mineral planning authority, on the evidence available to them at the time when they make the order, that resumption of the winning and working or the depositing to any substantial extent at the site is unlikely.

(3) The requirements mentioned in sub-paragraph (1) are—

(a) a requirement to alter or remove plant or machinery which was used for the purpose of the winning and working or the depositing or for any purpose ancillary to that purpose;

(b) a requirement to take such steps as may be specified in the order, within such period as may be so specified, for the purpose of removing or alleviating any injury to amenity which has been caused by the winning and working or depositing, other than injury due to subsidence caused by underground mining operations;

(c) a requirement that any condition subject to which planning permission for the development was granted or which has been imposed by virtue of any provision of this Act shall be complied with; and

(d) a restoration condition.

(4) If—

(a) an order under this paragraph includes a restoration condition; or

(b) a restoration condition has previously been imposed in relation to the site by virtue of any provision of this Act,

the order under this paragraph may include any such aftercare condition as the mineral planning authority think fit.

(5) Paragraphs 2(3) to (9) and 3 to 6 of Schedule 5 apply in relation to an aftercare condition imposed under this paragraph as they apply to such a condition imposed under paragraph 2 of this Schedule.

4.—(1) An order under paragraph 3 shall not take effect unless it is confirmed by the Secretary of State, either without modification or subject to such modifications as he considers expedient.

(2) Where a mineral planning authority submit such an order to the Secretary of State for his confirmation under this paragraph, the authority shall serve notice of the order—

(a) on any person who is an owner or occupier of any of the land to which the order relates, and

(b) on any other person who in their opinion will be affected by it.

(3) The notice shall specify the period within which any person on whom the notice is served may require the Secretary of State to give him an opportunity of appearing before, and being heard by, a person appointed by the Secretary of State for that purpose.

(4) If within that period such a person so requires, before the Secretary of State confirms the order he shall give such an opportunity both to him and to the mineral planning authority.

(5) The period referred to in sub-paragraph (3) must not be less than 28 days from the service of the notice.

(6) Where an order under paragraph 3 has been confirmed by the Secretary of State, the mineral planning authority shall serve a copy of the order on every person who was entitled to be served with notice under sub-paragraph (2).

(7) When an order under paragraph 3 takes effect any planning permission for the development to which the order relates shall cease to have effect.

(8) Sub-paragraph (7) is without prejudice to the power of the mineral planning authority, on revoking the order, to make a further grant of planning permission for development consisting of the winning and working of minerals or involving the depositing of mineral waste.

Orders after suspension of winning and working of minerals

5.—(1) Where it appears to the mineral planning authority—
  (a) that development of land—
    (i) consisting of the winning and working of minerals; or
    (ii) involving the depositing of mineral waste,
has occurred; but
  (b) the winning and working or depositing has been temporarily suspended,
the mineral planning authority may by order require that steps be taken for the protection of the environment.

(2) An order under sub-paragraph (1) is in this Act referred to as a 'suspension order'.

(3) The mineral planning authority may assume that the winning and working or the depositing has been temporarily suspended only when—
  (a) no such winning and working or depositing has occurred, to any substantial extent, at the site for a period of at least twelve months; but
  (b) it appears to the mineral planning authority, on the evidence available to them at the time when they make the order, that a resumption of such winning and working or depositing to a substantial extent is likely.

(4) In this Act 'steps for the protection of the environment' means steps for the purpose—
  (a) of preserving the amenities of the area in which the land in, on or under which the development was carried out is situated during the period while the winning and working or the depositing is suspended;
  (b) of protecting that area from damage during that period; or
  (c) of preventing any deterioration in the condition of the land during that period.

(5) A suspension order shall specify a period, commencing with the date on which it is to take effect, within which any required step for the protection of the environment is to be taken and may specify different periods for the taking of different steps.

Supplementary suspension orders

6.—(1) At any time when a suspension order is in operation the mineral planning authority may by order direct—
  (a) that steps for the protection of the environment shall be taken in addition to or in substitution for any of the steps which the suspension order or a previous order under this sub-paragraph specified as required to be taken; or
  (b) that the suspension order or any order under this sub-paragraph shall cease to have effect.

(2) An order under sub-paragraph (1) is in this Act referred to as a 'supplementary suspension order'.

Confirmation and coming into operation of suspension orders

7.—(1) Subject to sub-paragraph (2), a suspension order or a supplementary suspension order shall not take effect unless it is confirmed by the Secretary of State, either without modification or subject to such modifications as he considers expedient.

(2) A supplementary suspension order revoking a suspension order or a previous supplementary suspension order and not requiring that any fresh step shall be taken for the protection of the environment shall take effect without confirmation.

(3) Sub-paragraphs (2) to (5) of paragraph 4 shall have effect in relation to a suspension order or supplementary suspension order submitted to the Secretary of State for his confirmation as they have effect in relation to an order submitted to him for his confirmation under that paragraph.

(4) Where a suspension order or supplementary suspension order has been confirmed by the Secretary of State, the mineral planning authority shall serve a copy of the order on every person who was entitled to be served with notice of the order by virtue of sub-paragraph (3).

Registration of suspension orders as local land charges

8. A suspension order or a supplementary suspension order shall be a local land charge.

Review of suspension orders

9.—(1) It shall be the duty of a mineral planning authority—

(a) to undertake in accordance with the, following provisions of this paragraph reviews of suspension orders and supplementary suspension orders which are in operation in their area; and

(b) to determine whether they should make in relation to any land to which a suspension order or supplementary suspension order applies—
  (i) an order under paragraph 3; or
  (ii) supplementary suspension order.

(2) The first review of a suspension order shall be undertaken not more than five years from the date on which the order takes effect.

(3) Each subsequent review shall be undertaken not more than five years after the previous review.

(4) If a supplementary suspension order is in operation for any part of the area for which a suspension order is in operation, they shall be reviewed together.

(5) If a mineral planning authority have made a supplementary suspension order which requires the taking of steps for the protection of the environment in substitution for all the steps required to be taken by a previous suspension order or supplementary suspension order, the authority shall undertake reviews of the supplementary suspension order in accordance with sub-paragraphs (6) and (7).

(6) The first review shall be undertaken not more than five years from the date on which the order takes effect.

(7) Each subsequent review shall be undertaken not more than five years after the previous review.

(8) The duties to undertake reviews imposed by this paragraph are in addition to and not in substitution for the duties imposed by section 105.

Resumption of mineral working after suspension order

10.—(1) Subject to sub-paragraph (2), nothing in a suspension order or a supplementary suspension order shall prevent the recommencement of development consisting of the winning and working of minerals or involving the depositing of mineral waste at the site in relation to which the order has effect.

(2) No person shall recommence such development without first giving the mineral planning authority notice of his intention to do so.

(3) A notice under sub-paragraph (2) shall specify the date on which the person giving the notice intends to recommence the development.

(4) The mineral planning authority shall revoke the order if the winning and working of minerals or the depositing of mineral waste has recommenced to a substantial extent at the site in relation to which the order has effect.

(5) If the authority do not revoke the order before the end of the period of two months from the date specified in the notice under sub-paragraph (2), the person who gave that notice may apply to the Secretary of State for the revocation of the order.

(6) Notice of an application under sub-paragraph (5) shall be given by the applicant to the mineral planning authority.

(7) If he is required to do so by the person who gave the notice or by the mineral planning authority, the Secretary of State shall, before deciding whether to revoke the order, give him and the mineral planning authority an opportunity of appearing before, and being heard by, a person appointed by the Secretary of State for the purpose.

(8) If the Secretary of State is satisfied that the winning and working of minerals or the depositing of mineral waste has recommenced to a substantial extent at the site in relation to which the order has effect, he shall revoke the order.

(9) If the Secretary of State revokes an order by virtue of sub-paragraph (8), he shall give notice of its revocation—

(a) to the person who applied to him for the revocation, and
(b) to the mineral planning authority.

Default powers of Secretary of State

11.—(1) If it appears to the Secretary of State to be expedient that any order under paragraph 1, 3, 5 or 6 should be made, he may himself make such an order.

(2) Such an order which is made by the Secretary of State shall have the same effect as if it had been made by the mineral planning authority and confirmed by the Secretary of State.

(3) The Secretary of State shall not make such an order without consulting the mineral planning authority.

(4) Where the Secretary of State proposes to make an order under paragraph 1 he shall serve a notice of the proposal on the mineral planning authority.

(5) The notice shall specify the period (which must not be less than 28 days from the date of its service) within which the authority may require an opportunity of appearing before and being heard by a person appointed by the Secretary of State for the purpose.

(6) If within that period the authority so require, before the Secretary of State makes the order he shall give the authority such an opportunity.

(7) The provisions of this Schedule and of any regulations made under this Act with respect to the procedure to be followed in connection with the submission by the mineral planning authority of any order to which sub-paragraph (1) applies, its confirmation by the Secretary of State and the service of copies of it as confirmed shall have effect, subject to any necessary modifications, in relation to any proposal by the Secretary of State to make such an order, its making by him and the service of copies of it.

Interpretation

12. In this Schedule any reference to a mineral planning authority shall be construed, in relation to the exercise of functions with respect to the depositing of refuse or waste materials (other than mineral waste), as a reference to the authority entitled to discharge such functions.

Sections 111 and 114. SCHEDULE 10
CONDITION TREATED AS APPLICABLE TO REBUILDING AND ALTERATIONS

1. Where the building to be rebuilt or altered is the original building, the amount of gross floor space in the building as rebuilt or altered which may be used for any

purpose shall not exceed by more than ten per cent. the amount of gross floor space which was last used for that purpose in the original building.

2. Where the building to be rebuilt or altered is not the original building, the amount of gross floor space in the building as rebuilt or altered which may be used for any purpose shall not exceed the amount of gross floor space which was last used for that purpose in the building before the rebuilding or alteration.

3. In determining under this Schedule the purpose for which floor space was last used in any building, no account shall be taken of any use in respect of which an effective enforcement notice has been or could be served or, in the case of a use which has been discontinued, could have been served immediately before the discontinuance.

4.—(1) For the purposes of this Schedule gross floor space shall be ascertained by external measurement.

(2) Where different parts of a building are used for different purposes, floor space common to those purposes shall be apportioned rateably.

5. In relation to a building erected after 1st July 1948 which is a building resulting from the carrying out of any such works as are described in paragraph 1 of Schedule 3, any reference in this Schedule to the original building is a reference to the building in relation to which those works were carried out and not to the building resulting from the carrying out of those works.

SCHEDULE 11

[Schedule 11 repealed by the Planning and Compensation Act 1991.]

SCHEDULE 12

[Schedule 12 repealed by the Planning and Compensation Act 1991.]

Section 149. SCHEDULE 13
BLIGHTED LAND

Land allocated for public authority functions in development plans etc.

1. Land indicated in a structure plan in force for the district in which it is situated either—
   (a) as land which may be required for the purposes—
      (i) of the functions of a government department, local authority, National Park Authority or statutory undertakers, or
      (ii) of the establishment or running by a public telecomunications operator of a telecommunication system, or
   (b) as land which may be included in an action area.

Notes

(1) In this paragraph the reference to a structure plan in force includes a reference to—
   (a) proposals for the alteration or replacement of a structure plan which have been made available for inspection under section 33(2); or
   (b) any proposed modifications to those proposals which have been published in accordance with regulations under section 53.

(2) Note (1) shall cease to apply when the copies of the proposals made available for inspection have been withdrawn under section 34.

(3) Note (1) shall also cease to apply when—
   (a) the relevant proposals become operative (whether in their original form or with modifications), or

(b) the Secretary of State decides to reject the proposals and notice of the decision has been given by advertisement.

(4) In Note (1) references to anything done under any provision include reference to anything done under that provision as it applies by virtue of section 51.

(5) This paragraph does not apply to land situated in a district for which a local plan is in operation, where that plan—
   (a) allocates any land in the district for the purposes of such functions as are mentioned in this paragraph; or
   (b) defines any land in the district as the site of proposed development for the purposes of any such functions.

(5A) In Note (5) the reference to a local plan in operation includes a reference to a minerals local plan, a waste local plan, which in either case is in operation, and to a local plan continued in operation by virtue of paragraph 44 of Schedule 4 to the Planning and Compensation Act 1991.

(6) This paragraph does not apply to land within paragraph 5 or 6.

(7) In the application of this paragraph to Greater London the reference to a structure plan shall be construed as a reference to the Greater London Development Plan and Notes (1) to (4) shall be omitted.

[The reference to a National Park Authority was introduced by the Environment Act 1995, see note to Section 4A supra.]

2. Land which—
   (a) is allocated for the purposes of any such functions as are mentioned in paragraph 1(a)(i) or (ii) by a local plan in operation for the district, or
   (b) is land defined in such a plan as the site of proposed development for the purposes of any such functions.

Notes

(1) In this paragraph the reference to a local plan in operation includes a reference to a minerals local plan, a waste local plan, which in either case paragraph 44 of Schedule 4 to the Planning and Compensation Act 1991, is in operation, and to a local plan continued in operation by virtue of and also includes—
   (a) proposals for the making or alteration and replacement of any such plan where copies of the proposals have been made available for inspection under section 40(2) or by virtue of paragraph 43 of Schedule 4 to the Planning and Compensation Act 1991; and
   (b) any proposed modifications to those proposals which have been published in accordance with regulations under section 53.

(2) [repealed by the Planning and Compensation Act 1991]

(3) Note (1) shall also cease to apply when—
   (a) the relevant plan or proposals become operative (whether in their original form or with modifications), or
   (b) the Secretary of State decides to reject, or the local planning authority decide to abandon, the plan or proposals and notice of the decision has been given by advertisement.

(4) In Note (1) references to anything done under any provision include references to anything done under that provision as it applies by virtue of section 51.

3. Land indicated in a unitary development plan in force [for the district in which] it is situated—
   (a) as land which may be required for the purpose of any such functions as are mentioned in paragraph 1(a)(i) or (ii), or
   (b) as land which may be included in an action area.

Notes

(1) In this paragraph the reference to a unitary development plan includes references to—

(a) a unitary development plan of which copies have been made available for inspection under section 13(2);

(b) proposals for the alteration or replacement of a unitary development plan of which copies have been made available for inspection under that provision as applied by section. 21(2);

(c) modifications proposed to be made by the local planning authority or the Secretary of State to any such plan or proposals as are mentioned in paragraph (a) or (b), being modifications of which notice has been given in accordance with regulations under Chapter I of Part II.

(2) Note (1) shall cease to apply when the copies of the plan or proposals made available for inspection have been withdrawn under section 14(2) (but section 14(4) shall not invalidate any blight notice served by virtue of Note (1) before the withdrawal of copies of the plan or proposals).

(3) Note (1) shall also cease to apply when—

(a) the relevant plan or proposals become operative (whether in their original form or with modifications), or

(b) the Secretary of State decides to reject, or the local planning authority decide to withdraw, the plan or proposals and notice of the decision has been given by advertisement.

(4) In Note (1) references to anything done under any provision include references to anything done under that provision as it applies by virtue of section 25(2). [For the words in [ ] will be substituted on a day to be appointed under the Local Government (Wales) Act 1994.]

4. Land which by a unitary development plan is allocated for the purposes, or defined as the site, of proposed development for any such functions as are mentioned in paragraph 1(a)(i) or (ii).

Notes

(1) In this paragraph the reference to a unitary development plan includes references to—

(a) a unitary development plan of which copies have been made available for inspection under section 13(2):

(b) proposals for the alteration or replacement of a unitary development plan of which copies have been made available for inspection under that provision as applied by section 21(2);

(c) modifications proposed to be made by the local planning authority or the Secretary of State to any such plan or proposals as are mentioned in paragraph (a) or (b), being modifications of which notice has been given in accordance with regulations under Chapter I of Part II.

(2) Note (1) shall cease to apply when the copies of the plan or proposals made available for inspection have been withdrawn under section 14(2) (but section 14(4) shall not invalidate any blight notice served by virtue of Note (1) before the withdrawal of copies of the plan or proposals),

(3) Note (1) shall also cease to apply when—

(a) the relevant plan or proposals become operative (whether in their original form or with modifications), or

(b) the Secretary of State decides to reject, or the local planning authority decide to withdraw, the plan or proposals and notice of the decision has been given by advertisement.

(4) In Note (1) references to anything done under any provision include references to anything done under that provision as it applies by virtue of section 25(2).

5. Land indicated in a plan (other than a development plan) approved by a resolution passed by a local planning authority for the purpose of the exercise of their powers under Part III as land which may be required for the purposes of any such functions as are mentioned in paragraph 1(a)(i) or (ii).

6. Land in respect of which a local planning authority—
    (a) have resolved to take action to safeguard it for development for the purposes of any such functions as are mentioned in paragraph 5, or
    (b) have been directed by the Secretary of State to restrict the grant of planning permission in order to safeguard it for such development.

New towns and urban development areas

7. Land within an area described as the site of a proposed new town in the draft of an order in respect of which a notice has been published under paragraph 2 of Schedule 1 to the New Towns Act 1981.

Note

Land shall cease to be within this paragraph when—
    (a) the order comes into operation (whether in the form of the draft or with modifications), or
    (b) the Secretary of State decides not to make the order.

8. Land within an area designated as the site of a proposed new town by an order which has come into operation under section 1 of the New Towns Act 1981.

9. Land which is—
    (a) within an area intended to be designated as an urban development area by an order which has been made under section 134 of the Local Government, Planning and Land Act 1980 but has not come into effect; or
    (b) within an area which has been so designated by an order under that section which has come into effect.

Clearance and renewal areas

10. Land within an area declared to be a clearance area by a resolution under section 289 of the Housing Act 1985.

11. Land which—
    (a) is surrounded by or adjoining an area declared to be a clearance area by resolution under section 289 of the Housing Act 1985, and
    (b) is land which a local authority have determined to purchase under section 290 of that Act.

12. Land indicated by information published in pursuance of section 92 of the Local Government and Housing Act 1989 as land which a local authority propose to acquire in exercise of their powers under Part VII of that Act (renewal areas).

Highways

13. Land indicated in a development plan (otherwise than by being dealt with in a manner mentioned in paragraphs 1, 2, 3 and 4) as—
    (a) land on which a highway is proposed to be constructed, or
    (b) land to be included in a highway as proposed to be improved or altered.

14. Land on or adjacent to the line of a highway proposed to be constructed, improved or altered, as indicated in an order or scheme which has come into operation under Part II of the Highways Act 1980 (or under the corresponding provisions of Part II of the Highways Act 1959 or section 1 of the Highways Act 1971), being land in relation to which a power of compulsory acquisition conferred by any of the provisions of Part XII of that Act of 1980 (including a power compulsorily to acquire any right by virtue of section 250) may become exercisable, as being land required for purposes of construction, improvement or alteration as indicated in the order or scheme.

Notes

(1) In this paragraph the reference to an order or scheme which has come into operation includes a reference to an order or scheme which has been submitted for confirmation to, or been prepared in draft by, the Minister of Transport or the Secretary of State under Part II of that Act of 1980 and in respect of which a notice has been published under paragraph 1, 2 or 10 of Schedule 1 to that Act.

(2) Note (1) shall cease to apply when—
   (a) the relevant order or scheme comes into operation (whether in its original form or with modifications), or
   (b) the Secretary of State decides not to confirm or make the order or scheme.

(3) In this paragraph the reference to land required for purposes of construction, improvement or alteration as indicated in an order or scheme includes a reference to land required for the purposes of section 246(1) of the Highways Act 1980.

15. Land shown on plans approved by a resolution of a local highway authority as land comprised in the site of a highway as proposed to be constructed, improved or altered by that authority.

16. Land comprised in the site of a highway as proposed to be constructed, improved or altered by the Secretary of State if he has given written notice of the proposal, together with maps or plans sufficient to identify the land in question, to the local planning authority.

17. Land shown on plans approved by a resolution of a local highway authority as land proposed to be acquired by them for the purposes of section 246(1) of the Highways Act 1980.

18. Land shown in a written notice given by the Secretary of State to the local planning authority as land proposed to be acquired by him for the purposes of section 246(1) of the Highways Act 1980 in connection with a highway which he proposes to provide.

New streets

19. Land which
   (a) either—
     (i) is within the outer lines prescribed by an order under section 188 of the Highways Act 1980 (orders prescribing minimum width of new streets) or section 159 of the Highways Act 1959 (which is the predecessor of that section); or
     (ii) has a frontage to a highway declared to be a new street by an order under section 30 of the Public Health Act 1925 and lies within the minimum width of the street prescribed by any byelaws or local Act applicable by virtue of the order; and
   (b) is, or is part of—
     (i) a dwelling erected before, or under construction on, the date on which the order is made; or
     (ii) the curtilage of any such dwelling.

Note

This paragraph does not include any land in which the appropriate authority have previously acquired an interest either in pursuance of a blight notice served by virtue of this paragraph or by agreement in circumstances such that they could have been required to acquire it in pursuance of such a notice.

General improvement areas

20. Land indicated by information published in pursuance of section 257 of the Housing Act 1985 as land which a local authority propose to acquire in the exercise of their powers under the provisions of Part VIII of that Act relating to general improvement areas.

Compulsory purchase

21. Land authorised by a special enactment to be compulsorily acquired, or land falling within the limits of deviation within which powers of compulsory acquisition conferred by a special enactment are exercisable.

22. Land in respect of which—
(a) a compulsory purchase order is in force; or
(b) there is in force a compulsory purchase order providing for the acquisition of a right or rights over that land;
and the appropriate authority have power to serve, but have not served, notice to treat in respect of the land or, as the case may be, the right or rights.

Notes

(1) This paragraph applies also to land in respect of which—
(a) a compulsory purchase order has been submitted for confirmation to, or been prepared in draft by, a Minister, and
(b) a notice has been published under paragraph 3(1)(a) of Schedule 1 to the Acquisition of Land Act 1981 or under any corresponding enactment applicable to it.
(2) Note (1) shall cease to apply when—
(a) the relevant compulsory purchase order comes into force (whether in its original form or with modifications); or
(b) the Minister concerned decides not to confirm or make the order.

23. Land—
(a) the compulsory acquisition of which is authorised by an order under section 1 or 3 of the Transport and Works Act 1992, or
(b) which falls within the limits of deviation within which powers of compulsory acquisition conferred by such an order are exercisable, or
(c) which is the subject of a proposal, contained in an application made in accordance with rules under section 6 of that Act or in a draft order prepared under section 7(3) of that Act, that it should be such land.

[N.B. Under Schedule 5 paragraphs 21 and 22 of the Local Government (Wales) Act 1994, the foregoing Schedule will be modified as from an appointed day as follows:

21.—(1) Paragraph 1 of Schedule 13 to the Planning Act (blighted land) shall apply with the omission of Notes (2), (5A) and (7) and as modified by sub-paragraphs (2) to (6).

(2) References to a structure plan in force for the district in which land is situated are to be read as if they were references to a structure plan in force where that land is situated by virtue of Part IA of Schedule 2 to the planning Act.

(3) Note (1) to that paragraph shall apply as if—
(a) in paragraph (a), after 'inspection' there were inserted 'before 1st April 1996' and at the end there were added 'and not withdrawn before that date'
(b) after that paragraph there were inserted—

(aa) modified structure plan proposals made available for inspection under that section as it is applied by virtue of Part III of Schedule 5 to the Local Government (Wales) Act 1994;';

(c) in paragraph (b), after 'published' there were inserted 'either before 1st April 1996' and at the end there were added 'or after that date in accordance with regulations or a direction made by virtue of that Part of that Schedule'.

(4) Note (3) to that paragraph shall apply as if, after paragraph (b), there were inserted—

'or

(c) copies of the unitary development plan for the area in which the land is situated have been made available under section 13(2).'

(5) Note (4) to that paragraph shall apply as if at the end there were added 'or paragraph 13 of Schedule 5 to the Local Government (Wales) Act 1994'.

(6) In note (5) to that paragraph—

(a) the reference to a local plan is to be read as if it were a reference to—

(i) a local plan within the meaning of paragraph 4 of Part IA of Schedule 2 to the planning Act; or

(ii) a modified plan in force where that land is situated; and

(b) any reference to a district for which a local plan is in operation is to be read as if it were a reference to the area in which the plan mentioned in paragraph (a)(i) or (ii) is in force by virtue of Part IA of Schedule 2 to the planning Act.

Planning blight: local plans and modified plans

22.—(1) Paragraph 2 of Schedule 13 to the planning Act (blighted land) shall apply as modified by sub-paragraphs (2) to (5).

(2) Paragraph (a) shall apply as if for 'for the district' there were substituted 'where the land is situated'.

(3) Note (1) to that paragraph shall apply as if—

(a) for the words from 'includes a reference' to 'also' there were substituted 'is a reference to a local plan within the meaning of paragraph 4 of Part IA of Schedule 2 or a modified plan within the meaning of Part III of Schedule 5 to the Local Government (Wales) Act 1994, and, until copies of the unitary development plan for the area in which the land is situated have been made available under section 13(2).';

(b) in paragraph (a), after 'proposals have' there were inserted 'before 1st April 1996', and after '1991' there were inserted 'and not withdrawn before that date'; and

(c) in paragraph (b)—

(i) after 'published' there were inserted 'either before 1st April 1996', and

(ii) at the end of that paragraph there were added 'or after that date in accordance with regulations or a direction made by virtue of Part III of Schedule 5 to the Local Government (Wales) Act 1994'.

(4) Note (3) to that paragraph shall apply as if, in paragraph (b), the words 'the local planning authority decide to abandon' were omitted.

(5) Note (4) to that paragraph shall apply as if, at the end, there were added 'or paragraph 13 of Schedule 5 to the Local Government (Wales) Act 1994'.]

Section 259.

SCHEDULE 14
PROCEDURE FOR FOOTPATHS AND BRIDLEWAYS ORDERS

PART I
CONFIRMATION OF ORDERS

1. Before an order under section 257 or 258 is submitted to the Secretary of State for confirmation or confirmed as an unopposed order, the authority by whom the order was made shall give notice in the prescribed form—

(a) stating the general effect of the order and that it has been made and is about to be submitted for confirmation or to be confirmed as an unopposed order;
(b) naming a place in the area in which the land to which the order relates is situated where a copy of the order may be inspected free of charge and copies of it may be obtained at a reasonable charge at all reasonable hours; and
(c) specifying the time (which must not be less than 28 days from the date of the first publication of the notice) within which, and the manner in which, representations or objections with respect to the order may be made.
(2) Subject to sub-paragraphs (6) and (7), the notice to be given under sub-paragraph (1) shall be given—
(a) by publication in at least one local newspaper circulating in the area in which the land to which the order relates is situated; and
(b) by serving a similar notice on—
(i) every owner, occupier and lessee (except tenants for a month or a period less than a month and statutory tenants within the meaning of the Rent Act 1977) of any of that land; and
(ii) every council, the council of every rural parish [or community] and the parish meeting of every rural parish not having a separate council, being a council or parish whose area includes any of that land; and
[(iia) any National Park authority for a National Park which includes any of that land; and]
(iii) any statutory undertakers to whom there belongs, or by whom there is used, for the purposes of their undertaking, any apparatus under, in, on, over, along or across that land; and
(iv) every person on whom notice is required to be served in pursuance of sub-paragraph (4); and
(v) such other persons as may be prescribed in relation to the area in which that land is situated or as the authority may consider appropriate; and
(c) by causing a copy of the notice to be displayed in a prominent position—
(i) at the ends of so much of any footpath or bridleway as is to be stopped up, diverted or extinguished by the order;
(ii) at council offices in the locality of the land to which the order relates; and
(iii) at such other places as the authority may consider appropriate.
(3) In sub-paragraph (2)—
'council' means a county council, [a county borough council] a district council, a London borough council or a joint authority established by Part IV of the Local Government Act 1985;
'council offices' means offices or buildings acquired or provided by a council or by the council of a parish or community or the parish meeting of a parish not having a separate parish council.
(4) Any person may, on payment of such reasonable charge as the authority may consider appropriate, require an authority to give him notice of all such orders under section 257 or 258 as are made by the authority during a specified period, are of a specified description and relate to land comprised in a specified area.
(5) In sub-paragraph (4) 'specified' means specified in the requirement.
(6) Except where an owner, occupier or lessee is a local authority, National Park Authority or statutory undertaker, the Secretary of State may in any particular case direct that it shall not be necessary to comply with sub-paragraph (2)(b)(i).
(7) If the Secretary of State gives a direction under sub-paragraph (6) in the case of any land, then—
(a) in addition to publication the notice shall be addressed to 'the owners and any occupiers' of the land (describing it); and

(b) copy or copies of the notice shall be affixed to some conspicuous object or objects on the land.

(8) sub-paragraph (2)(b) and (c) and, where applicable, sub-paragraph (7) shall be complied with not less than 28 days before the expiry of the time specified in the notice.

(9) notice required to be served by sub-paragraph (2)(b)(i), (ii), (iii) or (v) shall be accompanied by a copy of the order.

(10) A notice required to be displayed by sub-paragraph (2)(c)(i) at the ends of so much of any way as is affected by the order shall be accompanied by a plan showing the general effect of the order so far as it relates to that way.

[The references to a National Park Authority were introduced by the Environment Act 1995, see note to Section 4A supra, while the words in [ ] in sub-paragraph (2)(b)(ii) and (3) were inserted by, and will come into effect on an appointed day order under, the Local Government (Wales) Act 1994.]

2. If no representations or objections are duly made, or if any so. made are withdrawn, the authority by whom the order was made may, instead of submitting the order to the Secretary of State, themselves confirm the order (but without any modification).

3.—(1) This paragraph applies where any representation or objection which has been duly made is not withdrawn.

(2) If the objection is made by a local authority or a National Park Authority the Secretary of State shall, before confirming the order, cause a local inquiry to be held.

(3) If the representation or objection is made by a person other than a local authority the Secretary of State shall, before confirming the order, either—

(a) cause a local inquiry to be held; or

(b) give any person by whom any representation or objection has been duly made and not withdrawn an opportunity of being heard by a person appointed by the Secretary of State for the purpose.

(4) After considering the report of the person appointed under sub-paragraph (2) or (3) to hold the inquiry or hear representations or objections, the Secretary of State may confirm the order, with or without modifications.

(5) In the case of an order under section 257, if objection is made by statutory undertakers on the ground that the order provides for the creation of a public right of way over land covered by works used for the purpose of their undertaking, or over the curtilage of such land, and the objection is not withdrawn, the order shall be subject to special parliamentary procedure.

(6) Notwithstanding anything in the previous provisions of this paragraph, the Secretary of State shall not confirm an order so as to affect land not affected by the order as submitted to him, except after—

(a) giving such notice as appears to him requisite of his proposal so to modify the order, specifying the time (which must not be less than 28 days from the date of the first publication of the notice) within which, and the manner in which, representations or objections with respect to the proposal may be made;

(b) holding a local inquiry or giving any person by whom any representation or objection has been duly made and not withdrawn an opportunity of being heard by a person appointed by the Secretary of State for the purpose; and

(c) considering the report of the person appointed to hold the inquiry or, as the case may be, to hear representations or objections.

(7) In the case of an order under section 257, if objection is made by statutory undertakers on the ground that the order as modified would provide for the creation of a public right of way over land covered by works used for the purposes of their undertaking or over the curtilage of such land, and the objection is not withdrawn, the order shall be subject to special parliamentary procedure.

[The reference to a National Park Authority was inserted by the Environment Act 1995, see note to Section 4A supra.]

4.—(1) A decision of the Secretary of State under paragraph 3 shall, except in such classes of case as may for the time being be prescribed or as may be specified in directions given by the Secretary of State, be made by a person appointed by the Secretary of State for the purpose instead of by the Secretary of State.

(2) A decision made by a person so appointed shall be treated as a decision of the Secretary of State.

(3) The Secretary of State may, if he thinks fit, direct that a decision which, by virtue of sub-paragraph (1) and apart from this sub-paragraph, falls to be made by a person appointed by the Secretary of State shall instead be made by the Secretary of State.

(4) A direction under sub-paragraph (3) shall
    (a) state the reasons for which it is given; and
    (b) be served on the person, if any, so appointed, the authority and any person by whom a representation or objection has been duly made and not withdrawn.

(5) Where the Secretary of State has appointed a person to make a decision under paragraph 3 the Secretary of State may, at any time before the making of the decision. appoint another person to make it instead of the person first appointed to make it.

(6) Where by virtue of sub-paragraph (3) or (5) a particular decision falls to be made by the Secretary of State or any other person instead of the person first appointed to make it, anything done by or in relation to the latter shall be treated as having been done by or in relation to the former.

(7) Regulations under this Act may provide for the giving of publicity to any directions given by the Secretary of State under this paragraph.

5.—(1) The Secretary of State shall not confirm an order under section 257 which extinguishes a right of way over land under, in, on, over, along or across which there is any apparatus belonging to or used by statutory undertakers for the purposes of their undertaking, unless the undertakers have consented to the confirmation of the order.

(2) Any such consent may be given subject to the condition that there are included in the order such provisions for the protection of the undertakers as they may reasonably require.

(3) The consent of statutory undertakers to any such order shall not be unreasonably withheld.

(4) Any question arising under this paragraph whether the withholding of consent is unreasonable, or whether any requirement is reasonable, shall be determined by whichever Minister is the appropriate Minister in relation to the statutory undertakers concerned.

6. Regulations under this Act may, subject to this Part of this Schedule, make such provision as the Secretary of State thinks expedient as to the procedure on the making, submission and confirmation of orders under sections 257 and 258.

PART II
PUBLICITY FOR ORDERS CONFIRMATION

7.—(1) As soon as possible after an order under section 257 or 258 has been confirmed by the Secretary of State or confirmed as an unopposed order, the authority by whom the order was made—
    (a) shall publish, in the manner required by paragraph 1(2)(a), a notice in the prescribed form—

(i) describing the general effect of the order,
(ii) stating that it has been confirmed, and
(iii) naming a place in the area in which the land to which the order relates is situated where a copy of the order as confirmed may be inspected free of charge and copies of it may be obtained at a reasonable charge at all reasonable hours;

(b) shall serve a similar notice on any persons on whom notices were required to be served under paragraph 1(2)(b) or (7); and

(c) shall cause similar notices to be displayed in a similar manner as the notices required to be displayed under paragraph 1(2)(c).

(2) No such notice or copy need be served on a person unless he has sent to the authority a request in that behalf, specifying an address for service.

(3) A notice required to be served by sub-paragraph (1)(b) on—

(a) a person on whom notice was required to be served by paragraph 1(2)(b)(i), (ii) or (iii); or

(b) in the case of an order which has been confirmed with modifications, a person on whom notice was required to be served by paragraph 1(2)(b)(v),

shall be accompanied by a copy of the order as confirmed.

(4) As soon as possible after a decision not to confirm an order under section 257 or 258, the authority by whom the order was made shall give notice of the decision by serving a copy of it on any persons on whom notices were required to be served under paragraph 1(2)(b) or (7).

8. Where an order under section 257 or 258 has come into force otherwise than—

(a) on the date on which it was confirmed by the Secretary of State or confirmed as an unopposed order; or

(b) at the expiration of a specified period beginning with that date,

then as soon as possible after it has come into force the authority by whom it was made shall give notice of its coming into force by publication in at least one local newspaper circulating in the area in which the land to which the order relates is situated.

Section 302(5).   **SCHEDULE 15**
ENFORCEMENT AS RESPECTS WAR-TIME BREACHES BY THE CROWN OF PLANNING CONTROL

Preliminary

1. In this Schedule an application under section 302(3) and a determination given on such an application are referred to respectively as 'a compliance determination application' and 'a compliance determination'.

Making of compliance determination applications

2.—(1) A compliance determination application may be made with respect to any land—

(a) by the owner or occupier of the land, or

(b) by any person who proves that he has or intends to acquire an interest in the land which will be affected by a compliance determination or that he has borne any of the cost of carrying out works on the land during the war period.

(2) In the case of land owned or occupied by or on behalf of the Crown, or leased to, or to a person acting on behalf of, the Crown, or land with respect to which it is proved that there is held, or intended to be acquired, by or on behalf of the Crown an interest in the land which will be affected as mentioned in sub-paragraph (1) or that any of the cost there mentioned has been borne by the Crown, a compliance determination application may be made by any person acting on behalf of the Crown.

3. A compliance determination application shall be accompanied by such plans and other information as are necessary to enable the application to be determined.

4.—(1) The authority to whom a compliance determination application is made shall within 14 days from the receipt of the application publish notice of it in one or more local newspapers circulating in the area in which the land is situated and serve notice of it on any person appearing to the authority to be specially affected by the application.

(2) The authority shall take into consideration any representations made to them in connection with the application within 14 days from the publication of the notice.

Determination of applications

5.—(1) Where a compliance determination application is made to an authority the authority shall determine whether the works or use in question fail to comply with any planning control which the authority are responsible for enforcing and, if so, shall specify the control in question.

(2) Where the authority determine that works or a use fail so to comply they shall further determine whether having regard to all relevant circumstances the works or use shall, notwithstanding the failure, be deemed so to comply, either unconditionally or subject to such conditions as to the time for which the works or use may be continued, the carrying out of alterations, or other matters, as the authority think expedient.

Appeals against compliance determinations or failure to make such determinations

6.—(1) Where the applicant is aggrieved by a compliance determination, or where a person by whom representations have been made as mentioned in paragraph 4 is aggrieved by such a determination, he may appeal to the Secretary of State.

(2) The applicant may also appeal if he is aggrieved by the failure of the authority to determine the application within two months from the last day on which representations under paragraph 4 may be made and has served notice on the authority that he appeals to the Secretary of State.

(3) An appeal under this paragraph must be made within the period of 28 days after the applicant has notice of the determination or, in the case of an appeal under sub-paragraph (2), after the applicant has served notice on the authority of the appeal, or within such extended period as the Secretary of State may allow.

7.—(1) On such an appeal the Secretary of State may give, in substitution for the determination, if any, given by the authority, such determination as appears to him to be proper having regard to all relevant circumstances, or, if he is satisfied that the applicant was not a person entitled to make the application, may decide that the application is not to be entertained.

(2) At any stage of the proceedings on such an appeal to him the Secretary of State may, and shall if so directed by the High Court, state in the form of a special case for the opinion of the High Court any question of law arising in connection with the appeal.

8. Subject to paragraph 9 and to any determination or decision of the Secretary of State on an appeal under paragraph 7, any compliance determination shall be final and any such failure to give a determination as mentioned in paragraph 6(2) shall be taken on the service of the notice there mentioned as a final refusal by the authority to entertain the application, and any determination or decision of the Secretary of State on an appeal under paragraph 7 shall be final.

Fresh applications where alteration in circumstances

9. Where a compliance determination has been given that works on land or a use of land shall not be deemed to comply with planning control or shall be deemed to comply with it subject to conditions, then if a person entitled to make a compliance determination application with respect to the land satisfies the authority or on appeal the Secretary of State that there has been a material change of circumstances since the previous application was determined, he may make a subsequent application and on such an application the authority or on appeal the Secretary of State may substitute for the compliance determination such determination as appears proper having regard to all relevant circumstances.

References of application to Secretary of State

10.—(1) If it appears to the Secretary of State that it is expedient, having regard to considerations affecting the public interest (whether generally or in the locality concerned), that any compliance determination application to an authority or any class or description of such applications, should instead of being determined by the authority be referred to him for decision, he may give directions to the authority requiring that application, or applications of that class or description, to be so referred.

(2) This Schedule shall apply to any such reference as if it were an appeal under paragraph 6(2) following failure of the authority to entertain the application.

Information

11. The Secretary of State may give directions to any authority responsible for enforcing planning control requiring them to furnish him with such information with respect to compliance determination applications received by them as he considers necessary or expedient in connection with the exercise of his functions under this Schedule.

Opportunity for hearing

12. On any compliance determination application or any appeal under this Schedule the applicant or, in the case of an application referred to the Secretary of State for decision or an appeal to the Secretary of State, the applicant or the authority responsible for enforcing the planning control in question, may require the authority by whom the application is to be determined or, as the case may be, the Secretary of State to give him or them an opportunity before the application or appeal is determined of appearing before and being heard by a person appointed by the authority or, as the case may be, the Secretary of State for the purpose.

Notice of proposed enforcement

13.—(1) This paragraph applies where before the relevant date any person proposes to take steps for enforcing a planning control in the case of such works or such a use as mentioned in subsection (1) of section 302.

(2) Subject to sub-paragraph (4), unless a compliance determination application has been made in relation to the land which has not been finally determined, that person shall serve on every owner and occupier of the land not less than 28 days' notice of the proposal, and if within that period any person makes such an application in relation to the land and within seven days of making it serves on the person proposing to take steps as aforesaid notice that the application has been made, no steps for enforcing the control shall be taken until the final determination of the application.

(3) If such an application has been made which has not been finally determined, no such steps shall be taken until the final determination of it.

(4) No notice shall be required under sub-paragraph (2) if steps for enforcing a planning control in the case of any works on land are begun within 28 days of the final determination of a compliance determination application in relation to the land.

(5) For the purpose of this paragraph a compliance determination application shall be treated as having been finally determined notwithstanding that a subsequent application may be made under paragraph 9.

Power of entry

14.—(1) At any time before the relevant date any officer of an authority responsible for enforcing planning control shall, on producing, if so required, some duly authenticated document showing his authority to act for the purposes of this paragraph, have a right, subject to the provisions of this paragraph, to enter any premises at all reasonable hours—

(a) for the purpose of ascertaining whether there are on the premises any works carried out during the war period which do not comply with planning control, or whether a use of the premises continues which was begun during that period and does not comply with it;

(b) where a compliance determination application has been made to the authority, for the purpose of obtaining any information required by the authority for the exercise of their functions under section 302 and this Schedule in relation to the application.

(2) Admission to any premises which are occupied shall not be demanded as of right unless 24 hours' notice of the intended entry has been served on the occupier.

(3) Any person who wilfully obstructs any officer of an authority acting in the exercise of his powers under this section shall be liable on summary conviction to a fine not exceeding level 1 on the standard scale.

(4) If any person who in compliance with this paragraph is admitted into a factory, workshop or workplace, discloses to any person any information obtained by him in, it with regard to any manufacturing process or trade secret, he shall, unless such disclosure was made in the performance of his duty, be liable on summary conviction to a fine not exceeding level 3 on the standard scale or to imprisonment for a term not exceeding three months.

Service of notices

15.—(1) Any notice or other document required or authorised to be served under this Schedule may be served on any person either by delivering it to him, or by leaving it at his proper address or by post.

(2) Any such document required or authorised to be served upon an incorporated company or body shall be duly served if it is served upon the secretary or clerk of the company or body.

(3) For the purposes of this paragraph and of section 7 of the Interpretation Act 1978, the proper address of any person upon whom any such document is to be served is—

(a) in the case of the secretary or clerk of any incorporated company or body, that of the registered or principal office of the company or body, and

(b) in any other case, the last known address of the person to be served.

(4) If it is not practicable after reasonable enquiry to ascertain the name or address of an owner or occupier of land on whom any such document is to be served, the document may be served by addressing it to him by the description of 'owner' or 'occupier' of the premises (describing them) to which it relates, and by delivering it to some person on the premises or, if there is no person on the premises to whom it can be delivered, by affixing it, or a copy of it, to some conspicuous part of the premises.

Supplementary provisions

16. Parts XIV and XV do not apply to section 302 and this Schedule.

SCHEDULE 16
PROVISIONS OF THE PLANNING ACT REFERRED TO IN SECTIONS 314 TO 319
PART I

Section 1(1), (2), (3) and (5). [Section 1(1) to (3), (5) and (6)]
Section 2.
Section 9.
Section 55.
Section 57.
Section 59.
Section 60 except subsection (4).
Sections 61 and 62.
Section 69(1), (2) and (5).
Section 70.
Section 70A.
Section 72(1) to (4).
Section 73A.
Section 74.
Section 75.
Section 77 with the omission in subsection (4) of the reference to sections 65.
Sections 78 and 79(1) to (5).
Section 90(1), (3) and (4).
Sections 96 to 98 except subsection (5) of section 97.
Section 100.
Sections 102 to 104 except subsection (8) of section 102.
Section 106 to 106B.
Section 107.
Section 108.
Section 115.
Sections 117 and 118.
Section 137 except subsections (6) and (7).
Section 138.
Section 139(1) to (4).
Sections 140 and 141.
Sections 143 and 144.
Section 148.
Section 175(5).
Sections 178 to 182.
Section 185.
Section 186(6) and (7).
Section 188.
Section 189.
Section 190 (in so far as it applies to orders under section 102).
Section 192.
Sections 196A to 196C.
Sections 198 to 200.
Sections 202 and 203.
Section 205.
Section 208(10).

Section 209(6).
Section 210.
Section 211(4).
Sections 214A to 214D.
Sections 215 to 224.
Section 227.
Sections 229 to 233.
Sections 235 to 247.
Sections 251 and 252.
Sections 254 to 256.
Section 260.
Section 263.
Section 265(1) and (4).
Sections 266 to 272.
Sections 274 to 278.
Section 279 except subsection (4).
Section 280 except subsections (6) and (8)(b).
Sections 281 to 283.
Section 284(1) except paragraphs (e) and (f).
Section 285.
Section 287.
Section 289.
Section 292 with the omission in subsection (2) of the references to section 288.
Section 293(1) to (3).
Section 294(1).
Section 296(1) (the reference in paragraph (c) to Part III not being construed as referring to section 65), and (2) to (4).
Section 297.
Sections 305 and 306.
Section 314.
Section 315.
Section 316.
Section 318 except subsections (2)(a), (4) and (5).
Section 324(1), (3) and (5) to (9).
Section 325.
Section 330.
Section 334.
Paragraphs 13 and 20(3) of Schedule 1.
Schedule 3.
Paragraphs 1 to 3 of Schedule 4.
Schedule 17.
Any other provisions of the planning Acts in so far as they apply, or have effect for the purposes of, any of the provisions specified above.
[The substitute reference at the head of the table in [ ] will come into effect on an appointed day order under the Local Government (Wales) Act 1994.]

PART II

Sections 30 to 49.
Section 50(5).
Section 51.
Sections 53 and 54.
Section 56(2) to (6) with the omission in subsection (3) of the references to sections 85, 86(6) and 87(4).

Section 65.
Section 69(3) and (4).
Section 79(6) to (7).
Sections 91 to 93.
Section 94(1)(a) and (2) to (6).
Section 95.
Section 99.
Section 101.
Section 137(6) and (7).
Section 142.
Section 157(1) and (2).
Sections 162 and 163.
Section 166.
Sections 171A to 171D.
Sections 172 to 174.
Section 175(1) to (4) and (6).
Sections 176 and 177.
Sections 183 and 184.
Section 186(1) to (5).
Sections 187 to 187B.
Sections 191 to 196.
Section 208(9).
Section 226.
Section 228(1), (3), (4) and (7).
Sections 248, 249 and 250.
Section 253.
Section 257.
Section 258(1).
Section 259.
Section 261.
Section 264(1) to (6).
Section 273.
Section 279(4).
Section 280(6) and (8)(b).
Section 304.
Section 307.
Section 331.
Paragraphs 3 to 12 of Part II of Schedule 2, Part III of Schedule 2, Schedules 6 and 14.

PART III

Sections 109 to 112.
Section 298.
Sections 308 to 310.
Section 318(4) and (5).
Section 328.
Any other provisions of the planning Acts in so far as they apply, or have effect for the purposes of, any of the provisions specified above.

PART IV

[repealed by the Planning and Compensation Act 1991]

PART V

[repealed by the Planning and Compensation Act 1991]

PART VI

Section 60(4).
Section 65.
Section 71(1) and (2) and (2A).
Sections 149 to 151.
Section 153(1) to (7).
Sections 154 to 156.
Section 161(1) in so far as it relates to provisions mentioned in this Part of this Schedule.
Section 164.
Sections 168 to 171.
Section 284 except subsection (1)(a) to (d).
Section 285(5) and (6).
Section 288.
Section 291.
Section 292(2).
Section 296(1) (construed as if the reference to Part III were a reference only to section 65) and (5).
Section 318(2) except paragraph (b).
In Schedule 13, paragraphs 1 to 4, 12 to 16 and 20 to 22.
Any other provisions of this Act in so far as they apply, or have effect for the purpose of, any of the provisions specified above.

SCHEDULE 17

ENACTMENTS EXEMPTED FROM SECTION 333(6)

1. [repealed by the Environmental Protection Act 1990]

2. The following provisions of the Highways Act 1980—
section 73(1) to (3), (6) and (9) to (11)
section 74 (except subsection (6))
section 241
section 261(5) and, so far as it relates to it, section 261(6)
section 307(5) and (7)
Schedule 9.

3. The following further provisions of the Highways Act 1980—
    (a) [repealed by the Planning and Compensation Act 1991]
    (b) section 247(6) so far as applicable for the purposes of section 241 of that Act;
    (c) in section 307—
        (i) subsections (1) to (3) so far as applicable for the purposes of section 73 of that Act;
        (ii) subsections (1), (3) and (6) so far as applicable for the purposes of section 74 of that Act;
    (d) section 311 so far as applicable for the purposes of section 74 of that Act.

4. Section 279 of the Highways Act 1980 so far as the purposes in question are the purposes of the exercise by a county council [county borough council] or metropolitan district council in relation to roads maintained by that council of their powers under section 73(1) to (3), (6) and (9) to (11) or section 241 of that Act.

5. Any enactment making such provision as might by virtue of any Act of Parliament have been made in relation to the area to which the order applies by means of a byelaw, order or regulation not requiring confirmation by Parliament.

6. Any enactment which has been previously excluded or modified by a development order, and any enactment having substantially the same effect as any such enactment.

[The words in [ ] in paragraph 4 were inserted by, and will come into effect on an appointed day order under, the Local Government (Wales) Act 1994.]

PLANNING (LISTED BUILDINGS AND CONSERVATION AREAS) ACT 1990
(1990, c. 9)
(as amended)

PART I
LISTED BUILDINGS
CHAPTER I
LISTING OF SPECIAL BUILDINGS

Section
1. Listing of buildings of special architectural or historic interest.
2. Publication of lists.
3. Temporary listing: building preservation notices.
4. Temporary listing in urgent cases.
5. Provisions applicable on lapse of building preservation notice.
6. Issue of certificate that building not intended to be listed.

CHAPTER II
AUTHORISATION OF WORKS AFFECTING LISTED BUILDINGS

Control of works in respect of listed buildings
7. Restriction on works affecting listed buildings.
8. Authorisation of works: listed building consent.
9. Offences.

Applications for listed building consent
10. Making of applications for listed building consent.
11. Certificates as to applicant's status etc.
12. Reference of certain applications to Secretary of State.
13. Duty to notify Secretary of State of applications.
14. Duty of London borough councils to notify Commission.
15. Directions concerning notification of applications etc.
16. Decision on application.

Grant of consent subject to conditions
17. Power to impose conditions on grant of listed building consent.
18. Limit of duration of listed building consent.
19. Application for variation or discharge of conditions.

Appeals
20. Right to appeal against decision or failure to take decision.
21. Appeals: supplementary provisions.
22. Determination of appeals.

Revocation and modification of consent
23. Revocation and modification of listed building consent by local planning authority.
24. Procedure for s. 23 orders: opposed cases.
25. Procedure for s. 23 orders: unopposed cases.
26. Revocation and modification of listed building consent by the Secretary of State.

CHAPTER III
RIGHTS OF OWNERS ETC.

Compensation

27. [Repealed by the Planning and Compensation Act 1991.]
28. Compensation where listed building consent revoked or modified.
29. Compensation for loss or damage caused by service of building preservation notice.
30. Local planning authorities for compensation purposes.
31. General provisions as to compensation for depreciation under this Part.

Listed building purchase notices

32. Purchase notice on refusal or conditional grant of listed building consent.
33. Action by council on whom listed building purchase notice served.
34. Procedure on reference of listed building purchase notice to Secretary of State.
35. Action by Secretary of State in relation to listed building purchase notice.
36. Effect of Secretary of State's action in relation to listed building purchase notice.
37. Reduction of compensation on acquisition where s. 28 compensation payable.

CHAPTER IV
ENFORCEMENT

38. Power to issue listed building enforcement notice.
39. Appeal against listed building enforcement notice.
40. Appeals: supplementary provisions.
41. Determination of appeals under s. 39.
42. Execution of works required by listed building enforcement notice.
43. Penalties for non-compliance with listed building enforcement notice.
44. Effect of listed building consent on listed building enforcement notice.
44A. Injunctions.
45. Commission to have concurrent enforcement functions in London.
46. Enforcement by the Secretary of State.

CHAPTER V
PREVENTION OF DETERIORATION AND DAMAGE

Compulsory acquisition of listed building in need of repair

47. Compulsory acquisition of listed building in need of repair.
48. Repairs notice as preliminary to acquisition under s. 47.
49. Compensation on compulsory acquisition of listed building.
50. Minimum compensation in case of listed building deliberately left derelict.
51. Ending of rights over land compulsorily acquired.

Acquisition by agreement

52. Acquisition of land by agreement.

Management of acquired buildings

53. Management of listed buildings acquired under this Act.

Urgent preservation

54. Urgent works to preserve unoccupied listed buildings.
55. Recovery of expenses of works under s. 54.
56. Dangerous structure orders in respect of listed buildings.

Grants for repair and maintenance

57. Power of local authority to contribute to preservation of listed buildings etc.
58. Recovery of grants under s. 57.

Damages to listed buildings

59. Acts causing or likely to result in damage to listed buildings.

CHAPTER VI
MISCELLANEOUS AND SUPPLEMENTAL

Exceptions for church buildings and ancient monuments

60. Exceptions for ecclesiastical buildings and redundant churches.
61. Exceptions for ancient monuments etc.

Validity of instruments, decisions and proceedings
62. Validity of certain orders and decisions.
63. Proceedings for questioning validity of other orders, decisions and directions.
64. Validity of listed building enforcement notices.
65. Appeals to High Court relating to listed building enforcement notices.

Special considerations affecting planning functions
66. General duty as respects listed buildings in exercise of planning functions.
67. Publicity for applications affecting setting of listed buildings.
68. Reference to Commission of planning applications involving listed buildings in Greater London.

PART II
CONSERVATION AREAS

Designation
69. Designation of conservation areas.
70. Designation of conservation areas: supplementary provisions.

General duties of planning authorities
71. Formulation and publication of proposals for preservation and enhancement of conservation areas.
72. General duty as respects conservation areas in exercise of planning functions.
73. Publicity for applications affecting conservation areas.

Control of demolition
74. Control of demolition in conservation areas.
75. Cases in which s. 74 does not apply.
76. Urgent works to preserve unoccupied buildings in conservation areas.

Grants
77. Grants and loans for preservation or enhancement of conservation areas.
78. Recovery of grants under s. 77.

Town schemes
79. Town scheme agreements.
80. Grants for repairing of buildings in town schemes.

PART III
GENERAL

Authorities exercising functions under Act
81. Authorities exercising functions under Act.

Special cases
82. Application of Act to land and works of local planning authorities.
83. Exercise of powers in relation to Crown land.
84. Application for listed building or conservation area consent in anticipation of disposal of Crown land.
85. [Repealed by the Coal Industry Act 1994.]
86. Ecclesiastical property.
87. Settled land.

Miscellaneous provisions
88. Rights of entry.
88A. Warrants to enter land.
88B. Rights of entry: supplementary provisions.
89. Application of certain general provisions of principal Act.
90. Financial provisions.

PART IV
SUPPLEMENTAL

91. Interpretation.
92. Application of Act to Isles of Scilly.

93. Regulations and orders.
94. Short title, commencement and extent.

SCHEDULES
Schedule 1 Buildings formerly subject to building preservation orders.
Schedule 2 Lapse of building preservation notices.
Schedule 3 Determination of certain appeals by person appointed by Secretary of State.
Schedule 4 Further provisions as to exercise of functions by different authorities.

An Act to consolidate certain enactments relating to special controls in respect of buildings and areas of special architectural or historic interest with amendments to give effect to recommendations of the Law Commission. [24th May 1990]

PART I
LISTED BUILDINGS
CHAPTER I
LISTING OF SPECIAL BUILDINGS

1. Listing of buildings of architectural or historic interest

(1) For the purposes of this Act and with a view to the guidance of local planning authorities in the performance of their functions under this Act and the principal Act in relation to buildings of special architectural or historic interest, the Secretary of State shall compile lists of such buildings, or approve, with or without modifications, such lists compiled by the Historic Buildings and Monuments Commission for England (in this Act referred to as 'the Commission') or by other persons or bodies of persons, and may amend any list so compiled or approved.

(2) The Secretary of State shall not approve any list compiled by the Commission if the list contains any building situated outside England.

(3) In considering whether to include a building in a list compiled or approved under this section, the Secretary of State may take into account not only the building itself but also—

(a) any respect in which its exterior contributes to the architectural or historic interest of any group of buildings of which it forms part; and

(b) the desirability of preserving, on the ground of its architectural or historic interest, any feature of the building consisting of a man-made object or structure fixed to the building or forming part of the land and comprised within the curtilage of the building.

(4) Before compiling, approving (with or without modifications) or amending any list under this section the Secretary of State shall consult—

(a) in relation to buildings which are situated in England, with the Commission; and

(b) with such other persons or bodies of persons as appear to him appropriate as having special knowledge of, or interest in, buildings of architectural or historic interest.

(5) In this Act 'listed building' means a building which is for the time being included in a list compiled or approved by the Secretary of State under this section; and for the purposes of this Act—

(a) any object or structure fixed to the building;

(b) any object or structure within the curtilage of the building which, although not fixed to the building, forms part of the land and has done so since before 1st July 1948,

shall be treated as part of the building.

(6) Schedule 1 shall have effect for the purpose of making provision as to the treatment as listed buildings of certain buildings formerly subject to building preservation orders.

2. Publication of lists

(1) As soon as possible after any list has been compiled or approved under section 1 or any amendments of such a list have been made, a copy of so much of the list as relates to any district, [Welsh county, county borough] or London borough or, as the case may be, of so much of the amendments as so relates, certified by or on behalf of the Secretary of State to be a true copy, shall be deposited—

    (a) in the case of a London borough, with the council of the borough and with the chief officer of the Commission; [. . .]

    (b) in the case of a district—

        (i) with the district council;

        (ii) with the county planning authority whose area or any part of whose area includes the district, or any part of it; and

        (iii) where the district council are not the district planning authority, with that authority; [and

    (c) in the case of a Welsh county or county borough—

        (i) with the county council or (as the case may be) the county borough council; and

        (ii) with the local planning authority, if different from that council.]

(2) Any copy deposited under subsection (1) shall be a local land charge, and the council with whom a copy is deposited shall be treated for the purposes of the Local Land Charges Act 1975 as the originating authority as respects the charge constituted by the deposit.

(3) As soon as possible after the inclusion of any building in a list under section 1 (whether it is included when the list is compiled, approved or amended) or as soon as possible after any such list has been amended by the exclusion of any building from it—

    (a) the Secretary of State shall inform the council of the district, [Welsh county, county borough] or London borough in whose area the building is situated of the inclusion or exclusion; and

    (b) the council shall serve a notice in the prescribed form on every owner and occupier of the building, stating that the building has been included in or excluded from the list.

(4) The Secretary of State shall keep available for public inspection free of charge at reasonable hours and at a convenient place, copies of all lists and amendments of lists, compiled, approved or made by him under section 1.

(5) Every authority with whom copies of any list or amendments are deposited under this section shall similarly keep available copies of so much of any such list or amendment as relates to buildings within their area.

(6) For the purposes of subsection (5) the Commission shall be taken to be an authority whose area is Greater London.

[The words in Section 2 in [ ] were inserted by, and will take effect on an appointed day order under, the Local Government (Wales) Act 1994.]

3. Temporary listing: building preservation notices

(1) If it appears to a local planning authority [in Wales, or to a local planning authority in England who are not] a county planning authority, that a building in their area which is not a listed building—

    (a) is of special architectural or historic interest; and

    (b) is in danger of demolition or of alteration in such a way as to affect its character as a building of such interest,

they may serve on the owner and occupier of the building a notice (in this Act referred to as a 'building preservation notice').

(2) A building preservation notice served by a local planning authority shall—

(a) state that the building appears to them to be of special architectural or historic interest and that they have requested the Secretary of State to consider including it in a list compiled or approved under section 1; and

(b) explain the effect of subsections (3) to (5) and Schedule 2.

(3) A building preservation notice—

(a) shall come into force as soon as it has been served on both the owner and occupier of the building to which it relates; and

(b) subject to subsection (4), shall remain in force for six months from the date when it is served or, as the case may be, last served.

(4) A building preservation notice shall cease to be in force if the Secretary of State—

(a) includes the building in a list compiled or approved under section 1, or

(b) notifies the local planning authority in writing that he does not intend to do so.

(5) While a building preservation notice is in force with respect to a building, the provisions of this Act (other than section 59) and the principal Act shall have effect in relation to the building as if it were a listed building.

(6) If, following the service of a building preservation notice, the Secretary of State notifies the local planning authority that he does not propose to include the building in a list compiled or approved under section 1, the authority shall immediately give notice of that decision to the owner and occupier of the building.

(7) Following such a notification by the Secretary of State no further building preservation notice in respect of the building shall be served by the local planning authority within the period of 12 months beginning with the date of the notification.

(8) The Commission shall, as respects any London borough, have concurrently with the council of that borough the functions of a local planning authority under this section; and references to the local planning authority shall be construed accordingly. [The words in [ ] in Section 3 were inserted by, and will come into effect on an appointed day order under, the Local Government (Wales) Act 1994.]

4. Temporary listing in urgent cases

(1) If it appears to the local planning authority to be urgent that a building preservation notice should come into force, they may, instead of serving the notice on the owner and occupier of the building, affix the notice conspicuously to some object on the building.

(2) The affixing of a notice under subsection (1) shall be treated for all the purposes of section 3, this section, sections 5 and 10 to 26 and Schedule 2 as service of the notice.

(3) A notice which is so affixed must explain that by virtue of being so affixed it is treated as being served for those purposes.

(4) The Commission shall, as respects any London borough, have concurrently with the council of that borough the functions of a local planning authority under this section; and references to the local planning authority shall be construed accordingly.

5. Provisions applicable on lapse of building preservation notice

Schedule 2 to this Act shall have effect as respects the lapse of building preservation notices.

6. Issue of certificate that building not intended to be listed

(1) Where—

(a) application has been made for planning permission for any development involving the alteration, extension or demolition of a building; or

(b) any such planning permission has been granted;

the Secretary of State may, on the application of any person, issue a certificate stating that he does not intend to list the building.

(2) The issue of such a certificate in respect of a building shall—
    (a) preclude the Secretary of State for a period of 5 years from the date of issue from exercising in relation to that building any of the powers conferred on him by section 1; and
    (b) preclude the local planning authority for that period from serving a building preservation notice in relation to it.
(3) Notice of an application under subsection (1) shall be given to the local planning authority within whose area the building is situated at the same time as the application is submitted to the Secretary of State.
(4) In this section 'local planning authority', in relation to a building in Greater London, includes the Commission.

CHAPTER II
AUTHORISATION OF WORKS AFFECTING LISTED BUILDINGS

Control of works in respect of listed buildings

7. Restriction on works affecting listed buildings
Subject to the following provisions of this Act, no person shall execute or cause to be executed any works for the demolition of a listed building or for its alteration or extension in any manner which would affect its character as a building of special architectural or historic interest, unless the works are authorised.

8. Authorisation of works: listed building consent
(1) Works for the alteration or extension of a listed building are authorised if—
    (a) written consent for their execution has been granted by the local planning authority or the Secretary of State; and
    (b) they are executed in accordance with the terms of the consent and of any conditions attached to it.
(2) Works for the demolition of a listed building are authorised if—
    (a) such consent has been granted for their execution;
    (b) notice of the proposal to execute the works has been given to the Royal Commission;
    (c) after such notice has been given either—
        (i) for a period of at least one month following the grant of such consent, and before the commencement of the works, reasonable access to the building has been made available to members or officers of the Royal Commission for the purpose of recording it; or
        (ii) the Secretary of the Royal Commission, or another officer of theirs with authority to act on their behalf for the purposes of this section, has stated in writing that they have completed their recording of the building or that they do not wish to record it; and
    (d) the works are executed in accordance with the terms of the consent and of any conditions attached to it.
(3) Where—
    (a) works for the demolition of a listed building or for its alteration or extension are executed without such consent; and
    (b) written consent is granted by the local planning authority or the Secretary of State for the retention of the works,
the works are authorised from the grant of that consent.
(4) In this section 'the Royal Commission' means—
    (a) in relation to England, the Royal Commission on the Historical Monuments of England; and
    (b) in relation to Wales, the Royal Commission on Ancient and Historical Monuments in Wales.

(5) The Secretary of State may by order provide that subsection (2) shall have effect with the substitution for the references to the Royal Commission of references to such other body as may be so specified.

(6) Such an order—

(a) shall apply in the case of works executed or to be executed on or after such date as may be specified in the order; and

(b) may apply in relation to either England or Wales, or both.

(7) Consent under subsection (1), (2) or (3) is referred to in this Act as 'listed building consent'.

9. Offences

(1) If a person contravenes section 7 he shall be guilty of an offence.

(2) Without prejudice to subsection (1), if a person executing or causing to be executed any works in relation to a listed building under a listed building consent fails to comply with any condition attached to the consent, he shall be guilty of an offence.

(3) In proceedings for an offence under this section it shall be a defence to prove the following matters—

(a) that works to the building were urgently necessary in the interests of safety or health or for the preservation of the building;

(b) that it was not practicable to secure safety or health or, as the case may be, the preservation of the building by works of repair or works for affording temporary support or shelter;

(c) that the works carried out were limited to the minimum measures immediately necessary; and

(d) that notice in writing justifying in detail the carrying out of the works was given to the local planning authority as soon as reasonably practicable.

(4) A person who is guilty of an offence under this section shall be liable—

(a) on summary conviction, to imprisonment for a term not exceeding six months or a fine not exceeding £20,000, or both; or

(b) on conviction on indictment, to imprisonment for a term not exceeding two years or a fine, or both.

(5) In determining the amount of any fine to be imposed on a person convicted of an offence under this section, the court shall in particular have regard to any financial benefit which has accrued or appears likely to accrue to him in consequence of the offence.

Applications for listed building consent

10. Making of applications for listed building consent

(1) Except as provided in sections 12 to 15, an application for listed building consent shall be made to and dealt with by the local planning authority.

(2) Such an application shall be made in such form as the authority may require and shall contain—

(a) sufficient particulars to identify the building to which it relates, including a plan;

(b) such other plans and drawings as are necessary to describe the works which are the subject of the application; and

(c) such other particulars as may be required by the authority.

(3) Provision may be made by regulations under this Act with respect to—

(a) the manner in which such applications are to be made;

(b) the manner in which they are to be advertised; and

(c) the time within which they are to be dealt with by local planning authorities or, as the case may be, by the Secretary of State.

11. Certificates as to applicant's status etc

(1) Regulations under this Act may provide that an application for listed building consent shall not be entertained unless it is accompanied by one of the following certificates in the prescribed form and signed by or on behalf of the applicant—

(a) a certificate stating that, at the beginning of the period of 21 days ending with the date of the application, no person (other than the applicant) was the owner of any of the building to which the application relates;

(b) a certificate stating that the applicant has given the requisite notice of the application to all the persons (other than himself) who at the beginning of that period were owners of any of the building to which the application relates;

(c) a certificate stating—

(i) that the applicant is unable to issue a certificate in accordance with paragraph (a) or (b);

(ii) that he has given the requisite notice of the application to such one or more of the persons mentioned in paragraph (b) as are specified in the certificate; and

(iii) that he has taken such steps as are reasonably open to him (specifying them) to ascertain the names and addresses of the remainder of those persons but has been unable to do so;

(d) a certificate stating—

(i) that the applicant is unable to issue a certificate in accordance with paragraph (a); and

(ii) that he has taken such steps as are reasonably open to him (specifying them) to ascertain the names and addresses of the persons mentioned in paragraph (b) but has been unable to do so.

(2) Where such provision is made any such certificate as is mentioned in subsection (1)(b) or (c) must set out—

(a) the names of the persons to whom the applicant has given the requisite notice of the application;

(b) the addresses at which notice was given to them; and

(c) the date of service of each such notice.

(3) Such regulations may require that any such certificate as is mentioned in subsection (1)(c) or (d) shall also contain a statement that the requisite notice of the application, as set out in the certificate, has on a date specified in the certificate (which must not be earlier than the beginning of the period mentioned in subsection (1)(a)) been published in a local newspaper circulating in the locality in which the building is situated.

(4) Such regulations may also require that where an application is accompanied by such a certificate as is mentioned in subsection (1)(b),(c) or (d), the local planning authority—

(a) shall not determine the application before the end of the period of 21 days beginning with the date appearing from the certificate to be the latest of the dates of service of notices as mentioned in the certificate, or, if later, the date of publication of a notice as so mentioned;

(b) shall in determining the application take into account any representations relating to it which are made to them before the end of that period by any person who satisfies them that he is an owner of any of the building to which the application relates; and

(c) shall give notice of their decision to every person who has made representations which they were required to take into account in accordance with paragraph (b).

(5) Such regulations may also make provision as to who, in the case of any building, is to be treated as the owner for the purposes of any provision made by virtue of this section.

(6) If any person—

(a) issues a certificate which purports to comply with the requirements of regulations made by virtue of this section and contains a statement which he knows to be false or misleading in a material particular; or

(b) recklessly issues a certificate which purports to comply with those requirements and contains a statement which is false or misleading in a material particular,

he shall be guilty of an offence and liable on summary conviction to a fine not exceeding level 3 on the standard scale.

(7) Subject to subsection (5), in this section 'owner' means a person who is for the time being the estate owner in respect of the fee simple or is entitled to a tenancy granted or extended for a term of years certain of which not less than seven years remain unexpired.

12. Reference of certain applications to Secretary of State

(1) The Secretary of State may give directions requiring applications for listed building consent to be referred to him instead of being dealt with by the local planning authority.

(2) A direction under this section may relate either to a particular application, or to applications in respect of such buildings as may be specified in the direction.

(3) An application in respect of which a direction under this section has effect shall be referred to the Secretary of State accordingly.

(3A) An application for listed building consent shall, without any direction by the Secretary of State, be referred to the Secretary of State instead of being dealt with by the local planning authority in any case where the consent is required in consequence of proposals included in an application for an order under section 1 or 3 of the Transport and Works Act 1992.

(4) Before determining an application referred to him under this section, the Secretary of State shall, if either the applicant or the authority so wish, give each of them an opportunity of appearing before, and being heard by, a person appointed by the Secretary of State.

(5) The decision of the Secretary of State on any application referred to him under this section shall be final.

13. Duty to notify Secretary of State of application

(1) If a local planning authority (other than a London borough council) to whom application is made for listed building consent, or a London borough council to whom such an application is made by the Commission, intend to grant listed building consent they shall first notify the Secretary of State of the application, giving particulars of the works for which the consent is required.

(2) The Secretary of State may within the period of 28 days beginning with the date of such a notification—

(a) direct the reference of the application to him under section 12; or

(b) give notice to the authority that he requires further time in which to consider whether to require such a reference.

(3) The local planning authority shall not grant listed building consent until—

(a) the period mentioned in subsection (2) has expired without the Secretary of State directing the reference of the application to him or giving them notice under paragraph (b) of that subsection; or

(b) the Secretary of State has notified them that he does not intend to require the reference of the application.

14. Duty of London borough councils to notify Commission

(1) Where an application for listed building consent is made to a planning authority which is a London borough council—

(a) unless the authority have determined to refuse it, they shall notify the Commission of the application, giving particulars of the works for which the consent is required; and

(b) the authority shall not grant the consent unless they are authorised or directed to do so under subsection (2)(a).

(2) On receipt of such a notification the Commission may—

(a) subject to subsection (6), give the local planning authority directions as to the granting of the application or authorise them to determine the application as they think fit; or

(b) direct them to refuse the application.

(3) If the Commission intend to exercise either of their powers under subsection (2)(a), they shall notify the Secretary of State of the application giving particulars of the works for which the consent is required.

(4) Where the Commission direct the local planning authority under subsection (2)(b) to refuse listed building consent, the authority may, within 28 days from the date of the direction, notify the Secretary of State of the application giving particulars of the works for which the consent is required.

(5) The Secretary of State may within the period of 28 days beginning with the date of a notification under subsection (3) or (4)—

(a) direct the reference of the application to him; or

(b) give notice to the authority who notified him or, as the case may be, the Commission that he requires further time in which to consider whether to require such a reference.

(6) The Commission shall not direct the local planning authority under subsection (2)(a) to grant the application or authorise them to determine it as they think fit unless—

(a) the period mentioned in subsection (5) has expired without the Secretary of State directing the reference of the application to him or giving them notice under paragraph (b) of that subsection; or

(b) he has notified them that he does not intend to require the reference of the application.

(7) Where the local planning authority notify the Secretary of State as mentioned in subsection (4), they shall not refuse the application unless—

(a) a period of 28 days beginning with the date of the notification has expired without the Secretary of State directing the reference of the application to him or giving them notice under subsection (5)(b); or

(b) he has notified the authority that he does not intend to require the reference of the application.

(8) Where, after receiving notification under subsection (4), the Secretary of State directs the reference of the application to him, before determining the application he shall, if either the applicant or the authority or, as the case may be, the Commission so desire, give each of them an opportunity of appearing before, and being heard by, a person appointed by the Secretary of State.

(9) Subsection (1) shall not apply where the application for listed building consent is made by the Commission.

15. Directions concerning notification of applications etc

(1) The Secretary of State may direct that, in the case of such descriptions of applications for listed building consent as he may specify, sections 13 and 14 shall not apply.

(2) Where a direction is in force under subsection (1) in respect of any description of application, local planning authorities may determine applications of that description in any manner they think fit, without notifying the Secretary of State or, as the case may be, the Commission.

Planning (Listed Buildings and Conservation Areas) Act 1990 259

(3) Before giving a direction under subsection (1) in respect of any description of application for consent to the demolition of a building in England, the Secretary of State shall consult the Commission.

(4) Where a direction is in force under subsection (1), the Secretary of State may direct a local planning authority that section 13 or, as the case may be, section 14 shall nevertheless apply—
    (a) to a particular application for listed building consent; or
    (b) to such descriptions of application for listed building consent as are specified in the direction;
and such a direction has effect in relation to any such application which has not been disposed of by the authority by their granting or refusing consent.

(5) Without prejudice to sections 10 to 14, the Secretary of State may give directions to local planning authorities requiring them, in such cases or classes of case as may be specified in the directions, to notify him and such other persons as may be so specified—
    (a) of any applications made to the authorities for listed building consent; and
    (b) of the decisions taken by the authorities on those applications.

(6) Directions under subsection (1) or (5) may be given to authorities generally or to particular authorities or descriptions of authority.

16. Decision on application

(1) Subject to the previous provisions of this Part, the local planning authority or, as the case may be, the Secretary of State may grant or refuse an application for listed building consent and, if they grant consent, may grant it subject to conditions.

(2) In considering whether to grant listed building consent for any works the local planning authority or the Secretary of State shall have special regard to the desirability of preserving the building or its setting or any features of special architectural or historic interest which it possesses.

(3) Any listed building consent shall (except in so far as it otherwise provides) enure for the benefit of the building and of all persons for the time being interested in it.

Grant of consent subject to conditions

17. Power to impose conditions on grant of listed building consent

(1) Without prejudice to the generality of section 16(1), the conditions subject to which listed building consent may be granted may include conditions with respect to—
    (a) the preservation of particular features of the building, either as part of it or after severance from it;
    (b) the making good, after the works are completed, of any damage caused to the building by the works;
    (c) the reconstruction of the building or any part of it following the execution of any works, with the use of original materials so far as practicable and with such alterations of the interior of the building as may be specified in the conditions.

(2) A condition may also be imposed requiring specified details of the works (whether or not set out in the application) to be approved subsequently by the local planning authority or, in the case of consent granted by the Secretary of State, specifying whether such details are to be approved by the local planning authority or by him.

(3) Listed building consent for the demolition of a listed building may be granted subject to a condition that the building shall not be demolished before—
    (a) a contract for the carrying out of works of redevelopment of the site has been made; and

(b) planning permission has been granted for the redevelopment for which the contract provides.

18. Limit of duration of listed building consent

(1) Subject to the provisions of this section, every listed building consent shall be granted subject to the condition that the works to which it relates must be begun not later than the expiration of—

(a) five years beginning with the date on which the consent is granted; or

(b) such other period (whether longer or shorter) beginning with that date as the authority granting the consent may direct, being a period which the authority considers appropriate having regard to any material considerations.

(2) If listed building consent is granted without the condition required by subsection (1), it shall be deemed to have been granted subject to the condition that the works to which it relates must be begun not later than the expiration of five years beginning with the date of the grant.

(3) Nothing in this section applies to any consent to the retention of works granted under section 8(3).

19. Application for variation or discharge of conditions

(1) Any person interested in a listed building with respect to which listed building consent has been granted subject to conditions may apply to the local planning authority for the variation or discharge of the conditions.

(2) The application shall indicate what variation or discharge of conditions is applied for.

(3) Sections 10 to 15 apply to such an application as they apply to an application for listed building consent.

(4) On such an application the local planning authority or, as the case may be, the Secretary of State may vary or discharge the conditions attached to the consent, and may add new conditions consequential upon the variation or discharge, as they or he thinks fit.

Appeals

20. Right to appeal against decision or failure to take decision

(1) Where a local planning authority—

(a) refuse an application for listed building consent or grant it subject to conditions;

(b) refuse an application for the variation or discharge of conditions subject to which such consent has been granted or grant it and add new conditions; or

(c) refuse an application for approval required by a condition imposed on the granting of listed building consent with respect to details of works or grant it subject to conditions,

the applicant, if aggrieved by the decision, may appeal to the Secretary of State.

(2) A person who has made such an application may also appeal to the Secretary of State if the local planning authority have neither—

(a) given notice to the applicant of their decision on the application; nor

(b) in the case of such an application as is mentioned in paragraph (a) or (b) of subsection (1), given notice to the applicant that the application has been referred to the Secretary of State in accordance with directions given under section 12,

within the relevant period from the date of the receipt of the application, or within such extended period as may at any time be agreed upon in writing between the applicant and the authority.

(3) In this section 'the relevant period' means—

(a) in the case of such an application as is mentioned in paragraph (a) or (b) of subsection (1), such period as may be prescribed; and

(b) in the case of such an application for approval as is mentioned in paragraph (c) of subsection (1), the period of eight weeks from the date of the receipt of the application.

(4) For the purposes of the application of sections 22(1) and 63(7)(b) in relation to an appeal under subsection (2) it shall be assumed that the authority decided to refuse the application in question.

21. Appeals: supplementary provisions

(1) An appeal under section 20 must be made by notice served in the prescribed manner within such period as may be prescribed.

(2) The period which may be prescribed under subsection (1) must not be less than—

(a) in the case of an appeal under subsection (1) of section 20, 28 days from the receipt by the applicant of notification of the decision; or

(b) in the case of an appeal under subsection (2) of that section, 28 days from the end of the relevant period (within the meaning of that section) or, as the case may be, the extended period there mentioned.

(3) The notice of appeal may include as the ground or one of the grounds of the appeal a claim that the building is not of special architectural or historic interest and ought to be removed from any list compiled or approved by the Secretary of State under section 1.

(4) In the case of a building with respect to which a listed building preservation notice is in force, the notice may include a claim that the building should not be included in such a list.

(5) Regulations under this Act may provide that an appeal in respect of an application for listed building consent or for the variation or discharge of conditions subject to which such consent has been granted shall not be entertained unless it is accompanied by a certificate in the prescribed form and corresponding to one of those described in subsection (1) of section 11.

(6) Any such regulations may also include provisions corresponding to those which may be included in the regulations which may be made by virtue of section 11.

(7) If any person—

(a) issues a certificate which purports to comply with the requirements of regulations made by virtue of subsection (5) or (6) and contains a statement which he knows to be false or misleading in a material particular; or

(b) recklessly issues a certificate which purports to comply with those requirements and contains a statement which is false or misleading in a material particular,

he shall be guilty of an offence and liable on summary conviction to a fine not exceeding level 3 on the standard scale.

22. Determination of appeals

(1) The Secretary of State may allow or dismiss an appeal under section 20 or may reverse or vary any part of the authority's decision (whether or not the appeal relates to that part), and—

(a) may deal with the application as if it had been made to him in the first instance; and

(b) may exercise his power under section 1 to amend any list compiled or approved under that section by removing from it the building to which the appeal relates.

(2) Before determining the appeal, the Secretary of State shall, if either the applicant or the local planning authority so wish, give each of them an opportunity of appearing before, and being heard by, a person appointed by the Secretary of State for the purpose.

(3) The decision of the Secretary of State on the appeal shall be final.

(4) Schedule 3 applies to appeals under section 20.

Revocation and modification of consent

23. Revocation and modification of listed building consent by local planning authority

(1) If it appears to the local planning authority that it is expedient to revoke or modify any listed building consent granted on an application under this Act, the authority may by order revoke or modify the consent to such extent as they consider expedient.

(2) In performing their functions under subsection (1) the local planning authority shall have regard to the development plan and to any other material considerations.

(3) The power conferred by this section to revoke or modify listed building consent in respect of any works may be exercised at any time before those works have been completed, but the revocation or modification shall not affect so much of those works as has been previously carried out.

24. Procedure for s. 23 orders: opposed cases

(1) Except as provided in section 25, an order made by a local planning authority under section 23 shall not take effect unless it is confirmed by the Secretary of State.

(2) Where a local planning authority submit such an order to the Secretary of State for confirmation they shall serve notice on—

   (a) the owner of the building affected;
   (b) the occupier of that building; and
   (c) any other person who in their opinion will be affected by the order.

(3) The notice shall specify the period (which must not be less than 28 days after its service) within which any person on whom it is served may require an opportunity of appearing before and being heard by a person appointed by the Secretary of State for the purpose.

(4) If within that period a person on whom the notice is served so requires, the Secretary of State shall give such an opportunity both to that person and to the local planning authority before he confirms the order.

(5) The Secretary of State may confirm an order submitted to him under this section either without modification or subject to such modifications as he considers expedient.

25. Procedure for s. 23 orders: unopposed cases

(1) This section shall have effect where—

   (a) the local planning authority have made an order under section 23 revoking or modifying a listed building consent granted by them; and
   (b) the owner and occupier of the land and all persons who in the authority's opinion will be affected by the order have notified the authority in writing that they do not object to the order.

(2) Where this section applies, instead of submitting the order to the Secretary of State for confirmation the authority shall—

   (a) advertise in the prescribed manner the fact that the order has been made, specifying in the advertisement—
      (i) the period within which persons affected by the order may give notice to the Secretary of State that they wish for an opportunity of appearing before and being heard by a person appointed by him for the purpose; and
      (ii) the period at the end of which, if no such notice is given to the Secretary of State, the order may take effect by virtue of this section without being confirmed by him;
   (b) serve notice to the same effect on the persons mentioned in subsection (1)(b);
   (c) send a copy of any such advertisement to the Secretary of State not more than three days after its publication.

(3) If—
(a) no person claiming to be affected by the order has given notice to the Secretary of State as mentioned in subsection (2)(a)(i) within the period referred to in that subsection; and
(b) the Secretary of State has not directed within that period that the order be submitted to him for confirmation,
the order shall take effect at the end of the period referred to in subsection (2)(a)(ii) without being confirmed by the Secretary of State as required by section 24(1).

(4) The period referred to in subsection (2)(a)(i) must not be less than 28 days from the date on which the advertisement first appears.

(5) The period referred to in subsection (2)(a)(ii) must not be less than 14 days from the end of the period referred to in subsection (2)(a)(i).

26. Revocation and modification of listed building consent by the Secretary of State

(1) If it appears to the Secretary of State that it is expedient that an order should be made under section 23 revoking or modifying any listed building consent granted on an application under this Act, he may himself make such an order revoking or modifying the consent to such extent as he considers expedient.

(2) In performing his functions under subsection (1) the Secretary of State shall have regard to the development plan and to any other material considerations.

(3) The Secretary of State shall not make an order under that subsection without consulting the local planning authority.

(4) Where the Secretary of State proposes to make such an order he shall serve notice on—
(a) the owner of the building affected;
(b) the occupier of that building; and
(c) any other person who in his opinion will be affected by the order.

(5) The notice shall specify the period (which must not be less than 28 days after its service) within which any person on whom it is served may require an opportunity of appearing before and being heard by a person appointed by the Secretary of State for the purpose.

(6) If within that period a person on whom it is served so requires, before the Secretary of State makes the order he shall give such an opportunity both to him and to the local planning authority.

(7) The power conferred by this section to revoke or modify listed building consent in respect of any works may be exercised at any time before those works have been completed, but the revocation or modification shall not affect so much of those works as has been previously carried out.

(8) An order under this section shall have the same effect as if it had been made by the local planning authority under section 23 and confirmed by the Secretary of State under section 24.

CHAPTER III
RIGHTS OF OWNERS ETC.

Compensation

27. [repealed by the Planning and Compensation Act 1991]

28. Compensation where listed building consent revoked or modified

(1) This section shall have effect where listed building consent is revoked or modified by an order under section 23 (other than an order which takes effect by virtue of section 25).

(2) If on a claim made to the local planning authority within the prescribed time and in the prescribed manner, it is shown that a person interested in the building—

(a) has incurred expenditure in carrying out works which are rendered abortive by the revocation or modification; or

(b) has otherwise sustained loss or damage which is directly attributable to the revocation or modification,

the authority shall pay that person compensation in respect of that expenditure, loss or damage.

(3) Subject to subsection (4), no compensation shall be paid under this section in respect of—

(a) any works carried out before the grant of the listed building consent which is revoked or modified; or

(b) any other loss or damage (not being loss or damage consisting of depreciation of the value of an interest in land) arising out of anything done or omitted to be done before the grant of that consent.

(4) For the purposes of this section, expenditure incurred in the preparation of plans for the purposes of any works, or upon other similar matters preparatory to any works, shall be taken to be included in the expenditure incurred in carrying out those works.

29. Compensation for loss or damage caused by service of building preservation notice

(1) This section applies where a building preservation notice ceases to have effect without the building having been included in a list compiled or approved by the Secretary of State under section 1.

(2) Any person who at the time when the notice was served had an interest in the building shall, on making a claim to the authority within the prescribed time and in the prescribed manner, be entitled to be paid compensation by the local planning authority in respect of any loss or damage directly attributable to the effect of the notice.

(3) The loss or damage in respect of which compensation is payable under subsection (2) shall include a sum payable in respect of any breach of contract caused by the necessity of discontinuing or countermanding any works to the building on account of the building preservation notice being in force with respect to it.

30. Local planning authorities for compensation purposes

(1) Subject to subsection (2)—

(a) [repealed by the Planning and Compensation Act 1991]

(b) Claims under section 28 shall be made to and paid by the local planning authority who made the order in question or, where it was made by the Secretary of State under section 26, the local planning authority who are treated as having made it under that section;

(c) claims under section 29 shall be made to and paid by the local planning authority who served the building preservation notice,

and references in those sections to a local planning authority shall be construed accordingly.

(2) The Secretary of State may after consultation with all the authorities concerned direct that where a local planning authority is liable to pay compensation under section 28 or 29 in any particular case or class of case they shall be entitled to be reimbursed the whole of the compensation or such proportion of it as he may direct from one or more authorities specified in the direction.

(3) This section does not apply in Greater London.

31. General provisions as to compensation for depreciation under this Part

(1) For the purpose of assessing any compensation to which this section applies, the rules set out in section 5 of the Land Compensation Act 1961 shall, so far as

applicable and subject to any necessary modifications, have effect as they have effect for the purpose of assessing compensation for the compulsory acquisition of an interest in land.

(2) This section applies to any compensation which is payable under sections 28 and 29 in respect of depreciation of the value of an interest in land.

(3) Where an interest in land is subject to a mortgage—

(a) any compensation to which this section applies, which is payable in respect of depreciation of the value of that interest, shall be assessed as if the interest were not subject to the mortgage;

(b) a claim for any such compensation may be made by any mortgagee of the interest, but without prejudice to the making of a claim by the person entitled to the interest;

(c) no compensation to which this section applies shall be payable in respect of the interest of the mortgagee (as distinct from the interest which is subject to the mortgage); and

(d) any compensation to which this section applies which is payable in respect of the interest which is subject to the mortgage shall be paid to the mortgagee, or, if there is more than one mortgagee, to the first mortgagee, and shall in either case be applied by him as if it were proceeds of sale.

(4) Except in so far as may be otherwise provided by any regulations made under this Act, any question of disputed compensation under sections 28 and 29 shall be referred to and determined by the Lands Tribunal.

(5) In relation to the determination of any such question, the provisions of sections 2 and 4 of the Land Compensation Act 1961 shall apply subject to any necessary modifications and to the provisions of any regulations made under this Act.

Listed building purchase notices

32. Purchase notice on refusal or conditional grant of listed building consent

(1) Where—

(a) listed building consent in respect of a building is refused, or granted subject to conditions, or is revoked or modified by an order under section 23 or 26; and

(b) any owner of the building claims—

(i) that the conditions mentioned in subsection (2) are satisfied with respect to it and any land comprising the building, or contiguous or adjacent to it, and owned with it; and

(ii) that the conditions mentioned in subsection (3) are satisfied with respect to that land,

he may, within the prescribed time and in the prescribed manner, serve on the council of the district, [Welsh county, county borough] or London borough in which the building and land are situated a notice (in this Act referred to as a 'listed building purchase notice') requiring that council to purchase his interest in the building and land in accordance with sections 33 to 37.

(2) The conditions mentioned in subsection (1)(b)(i) are—

(a) that the building and land in respect of which the notice is served have become incapable of reasonably beneficial use in their existing state;

(b) in a case where listed building consent has been granted subject to conditions with respect to the execution of the works or has been modified by the imposition of such conditions, that the land cannot be rendered capable of such use by the carrying out of the works in accordance with those conditions; and

(c) in any case, that the land cannot be rendered capable of such use by the carrying out of any other works for which listed building consent has been granted or for which the local planning authority or the Secretary of State has undertaken to grant such consent.

(3) The conditions mentioned in subsection (1)(b)(ii) are that the use of the land is substantially inseparable from that of the building and that it ought to be treated, together with the building, as a single holding.

(4) In determining for the purpose of subsection (2) what is or would in any particular circumstances be a reasonably beneficial use of land, no account shall be taken of any prospective use which would involve the carrying out of development (other than any development specified in paragraph 1 or 2 of Schedule 3 to the principal Act) or any works requiring listed building consent which might be executed to the building, other than works for which the local planning authority or the Secretary of State have undertaken to grant such consent.

[(4A) This section and sections 33 to 37 shall have effect as if—
    (a) the bodies on whom a listed building purchase notice may be served under this section included any National Park authority which is the local planning authority for the area in which the building and land in question are situated; and
    (b) a National Park authority were a local authority for the purposes of this Act and the Park for which it is the local planning authority were its area;
and the references in those sections and in section 63(7)(a) to a council and to a local authority shall be construed accordingly.]

(5) References in sections 33 to 37 to the land are to the building and the land in respect of which the notice under subsection (1) is served.

[Subsection (4A) was inserted by, and will have effect from a day appointed under, the Environment Act 1995, while the words in [ ] in Section 32(1) were inserted by, and will have effect under, the Local Government (Wales) Act 1994.]

33. Action by council on whom listed building purchase notice served

(1) The council on whom a listed building purchase notice is served by an owner shall serve on him a notice stating either—
    (a) that the council are willing to comply with the purchase notice; or
    (b) that another local authority or statutory undertakers specified in the notice under this subsection have agreed to comply with it in their place; or
    (c) that for reasons so specified the council are not willing to comply with the purchase notice and have not found any other local authority or statutory undertakers who will agree to comply with it in their place and that they have transmitted to the Secretary of State a copy of the purchase notice and of the notice under this subsection.

(2) A notice under subsection (1) must be served before the end of the period of three months beginning with the date of service of the listed building purchase notice.

(3) Where such a notice as is mentioned in paragraph (a) or (b) of subsection (1) has been duly served, the council or, as the case may be, the other local authority or statutory undertakers specified in the notice shall be deemed—
    (a) to be authorised to acquire the interest of the owner compulsorily in accordance with the provisions of section 47; and
    (b) to have served a notice to treat in respect of it on the date of service of the notice under that subsection.

(4) Where the council propose to serve such a notice as is mentioned in subsection (1)(c), they shall first send to the Secretary of State a copy of—
    (a) the proposed notice; and
    (b) the listed building purchase notice which was served on them.

34. Procedure on reference of listed building purchase notice to Secretary of State

(1) Where a copy of a listed building purchase notice is sent to the Secretary of State under section 33(4), he shall consider whether to confirm the notice or to take other action under section 35 in respect of it.

(2) Before confirming such a notice or taking such other action, the Secretary of State shall give notice of his proposed action—
(a) to the person who served the notice;
(b) to the council on whom it was served;
(c) outside Greater London—
(i) [in England] to the county planning authority and also, where that authority is a joint planning board, to the county council; and
(ii) if the district council on whom the purchase notice in question was served is a constituent member of a joint planning board, to that board; and
[(cc) in Wales, to the local planning authority, where it is a joint planning board;]
(d) if the Secretary of State proposes to substitute any other local authority or statutory undertakers for the council on whom the notice was served, to them.

(3) A notice under subsection (2) shall specify the period (which must not be less than 28 days from its service) within which any of the persons on whom it is served may require the Secretary of State to give him an opportunity of appearing before and being heard by a person appointed by him for the purpose.

(4) If any of those persons so require, before the Secretary of State confirms the listed building purchase notice or takes any other action under section 35 in respect of it, he shall give such an opportunity to each of them.

(5) If after any of those persons have appeared before and been heard by the appointed person, it appears to the Secretary of State to be expedient to take action under section 35 otherwise than in accordance with the notice given by him, the Secretary of State may take that action accordingly.
[The words in [ ] were inserted by, and will have effect on an appointed day order under, the Local Government (Wales) Act 1994.]

35. Action by Secretary of State in relation to listed building purchase notice

(1) Subject to the following provisions of this section, if the Secretary of State is satisfied that the conditions specified in section 32(2)(a) to (c) are satisfied in the case of any listed building purchase notice, he shall confirm the notice.

(2) If the Secretary of State is satisfied that those conditions are fulfilled only in respect of part of the land, he shall confirm the notice only in respect of that part and the notice shall have effect accordingly.

(3) The Secretary of State shall not confirm the notice unless he is satisfied that the land comprises such land contiguous or adjacent to the building as is in his opinion required—
(a) for preserving the building or its amenities, or
(b) for affording access to it, or
(c) for its proper control or management.

(4) If it appears to the Secretary of State to be expedient to do so he may, instead of confirming the notice—
(a) in the case of a notice served on account of the refusal of listed building consent for any works, grant such consent for those works;
(b) in the case of a notice served on account of such consent being granted subject to conditions, revoke or amend those conditions so far as it appears to him to be required in order to enable the land to be rendered capable of reasonably beneficial use by the carrying out of those works;
(c) in the case of a notice served on account of such consent being revoked by an order under section 23 or 26, cancel the order revoking the consent; or
(d) in the case of a notice served on account of such consent being modified by such an order by the imposition of conditions, revoke or amend those conditions so far as appears to him to be required in order to enable the land to be rendered capable

of reasonably beneficial use by the carrying out of the works in respect of which the consent was granted.

(5) If it appears to the Secretary of State that the land (or any part of it) could be rendered capable of reasonably beneficial use within a reasonable time by the carrying out—

(a) of any other works for which listed building consent ought to be granted, or

(b) of any development for which planning permission ought to be granted,

he may, instead of confirming the listed building purchase notice (or confirming it so far as it relates to that part), direct that if an application is made for such consent for those works or, as the case may be, for planning permission for that development, it shall be granted.

(6) If it appears to the Secretary of State, having regard to the probable ultimate use of the building or its site, that it is expedient to do so, he may, if he confirms the notice, modify it either in relation to the whole or any part of the land, by substituting another local authority or statutory undertakers for the council on whom the notice was served.

(7) Any reference in section 34 to the taking of action by the Secretary of State under this section includes a reference to the taking by him of a decision not to confirm the notice on the grounds that any of the conditions referred to in subsection (1) are not satisfied.

36. Effect of Secretary of State's action in relation to listed building purchase notice

(1) Where the Secretary of State confirms a listed building purchase notice, the council on whom the notice was served shall be deemed—

(a) to be authorised to acquire the owner's interest in the land compulsorily in accordance with the provisions of section 47; and

(b) to have served a notice to treat in respect of it on such date as the Secretary of State may direct.

(2) If before the end of the relevant period the Secretary of State has neither—

(a) confirmed the listed building purchase notice; nor

(b) notified the owner by whom it was served that he does not propose to confirm it; nor

(c) taken any such action in respect of it as is mentioned in subsection (4) or (5) of section 35,

the notice shall be deemed to be confirmed at the end of that period and the council on whom it was served shall be deemed to have been authorised as mentioned in subsection (1)(a) and to have served a notice to treat in respect of the owner's interest at the end of that period.

(3) Where a listed building purchase notice is confirmed in respect of only part of the land, references in this section to the owner's interest in the land are references to the owner's interest in that part.

(4) Where a listed building purchase notice is modified under section 35(6) by the substitution of another local authority or statutory undertakers for the council on whom the notice was served, the reference in subsection (1) to that council is to that other local authority or those statutory undertakers.

(5) In this section 'the relevant period' means, subject to subsection (6) below—

(a) the period of nine months beginning with the date of the service of the listed building purchase notice; or

(b) if it ends earlier, the period of six months beginning with the date on which a copy of the notice was sent to the Secretary of State.

(6) The relevant period does not run if the Secretary of State has before him at the same time both—

(a) a copy of the listed building purchase notice sent to him under section 33(4); and

(b) a notice of appeal under section 20 or section 39 relating to any of the land to which the listed building purchase notice relates.

(7) Where any decision by the Secretary of State to confirm or not to confirm a listed building purchase notice (including any decision to confirm the notice only in respect of part of the land, or to give any direction as to the granting of listed building consent or planning permission) is quashed under section 63, the notice shall be treated as cancelled but the owner may serve a further notice in its place.

(8) For the purposes of determining whether such a further notice has been served within the period prescribed for the service of listed building purchase notices, the decision concerning listed building consent on account of which the notice has been served shall be treated as having been made on the date on which the Secretary of State's decision was quashed.

37. Reduction of compensation on acquisition where s. 28 compensation payable

Where compensation is payable under section 28 in respect of expenditure incurred in carrying out any works to a building, any compensation which then becomes payable in respect of the acquisition of an interest in the land in pursuance of a listed building purchase notice shall be reduced by an amount equal to the value of those works.

CHAPTER IV
ENFORCEMENT

38. Power to issue listed building enforcement notice

(1) Where it appears to the local planning authority—

(a) that any works have been or are being executed to a listed building in their area; and

(b) that the works are such as to involve a contravention of section 9(1) or (2),

they may, if they consider it expedient to do so having regard to the effect of the works on the character of the building as one of special architectural or historic interest, issue a notice under this section (in this Act referred to as a 'listed building enforcement notice').

(2) A listed building enforcement notice shall specify the alleged contravention and require such steps as may be specified in the notice to be taken—

(a) for restoring the building to its former state; or

(b) if the authority consider that such restoration would not be reasonably practicable or would be undesirable, for executing such further works specified in the notice as they consider necessary to alleviate the effect of the works which were carried out without listed building consent; or

(c) for bringing the building to the state in which it would have been if the terms and conditions of any listed building consent which has been granted for the works had been complied with.

(3) A listed building enforcement notice—

(a) shall specify the date on which it is to take effect and, subject to sections 39(3) and 65(3A), shall take effect on that date, and

(b) shall specify the period within which any steps are required to be taken and may specify different periods for different steps,

and, where different periods apply to different steps, references in this Part to the period for compliance with a listed building enforcement notice, in relation to any step, are to the period within which the step is required to be taken.

(4) A copy of a listed building enforcement notice shall be served, not later than 28 days after the date of its issue and not later than 28 days before the date specified in it as the date on which it is to take effect—
    (a) on the owner and on the occupier of the building to which it relates; and
    (b) on any other person having an interest in that building which in the opinion of the authority is materially affected by the notice.
(5) The local planning authority may—
    (a) withdraw a listed building enforcement notice (without prejudice to their power to issue another); or
    (b) waive or relax any requirement of such a notice and, in particular, may extend the period specified in accordance with section 38(3),
and the powers conferred by this subsection may be exercised whether or not the notice has taken effect.
(6) The local planning authority shall, immediately after exercising the powers conferred by subsection (5), give notice of the exercise to every person who has been served with a copy of the listed building enforcement notice or would, if the notice were re-issued, be served with a copy of it.
(7) Where a listed building enforcement notice imposes any such requirement as is mentioned in subsection (2)(b), listed building consent shall be deemed to be granted for any works of demolition, alteration or extension of the building executed as a result of compliance with the notice.

39. Appeal against listed building enforcement notice

(1) A person having an interest in the building to which a listed building enforcement notice relates or a relevant occupier may appeal to the Secretary of State against the notice on any of the following grounds—
    (a) that the building is not of special architectural or historic interest;
    (b) that the matters alleged to constitute a contravention of section 9(1) or (2) have not occurred;
    (c) that those matters (if they occurred) do not constitute such a contravention.
    (d) that works to the building were urgently necessary in the interests of safety or health or for the preservation of the building, that it was not practicable to secure safety or health or, as the case may be, the preservation of the building by works of repair or works for affording temporary support or shelter, and that the works carried out were limited to the minimum measures immediately necessary;
    (e) that listed building consent ought to be granted for the works, or that any relevant condition of such consent which has been granted ought to be discharged, or different conditions substituted;
    (f) that copies of the notice were not served as required by section 38(4);
    (g) except in relation to such a requirement as is mentioned in section 38(2)(b) or (c), that the requirements of the notice exceed what is necessary for restoring the building to its condition before the works were carried out;
    (h) that the period specified in the notice as the period within which any step required by the notice is to be taken falls short of what should reasonably be allowed;
    (i) that the steps required by the notice for the purpose of restoring the character of the building to its former state would not serve that purpose;
    (j) that steps required to be taken by virtue of section 38(2)(b) exceed what is necessary to alleviate the effect of the works executed to the building;
    (k) that steps required to be taken by virtue of section 38(2)(c) exceed what is necessary to bring the building to the state in which it would have been if the terms and conditions of the listed building consent had been complied with.
(2) An appeal under this section shall be made either—

Planning (Listed Buildings and Conservation Areas) Act 1990 271

(a) by giving written notice of the appeal to the Secretary of State before the date specified in the listed building enforcement notice as the date on which it is to take effect; or

(b) by sending such notice to him in a properly addressed and pre-paid letter posted to him at such time that, in the ordinary course of post, it would be delivered to him before that date.

(3) Where such an appeal is brought the listed building enforcement notice shall subject to any order under section 65(3A) be of no effect pending the final determination or the withdrawal of the appeal.

(4) A person who gives notice of appeal under this section shall submit to the Secretary of State, either when giving the notice or within such time as may be prescribed, a statement in writing—

(a) specifying the grounds on which he is appealing against the listed building enforcement notice; and

(b) giving such further information as may be prescribed.

(5) If, where more than one ground is specified in the statement, the appellant does not give information required under subsection (4)(b) in relation to each of those grounds within the prescribed time, the Secretary of State may determine the appeal without considering any ground as to which the appellant has failed to give such information within that time.

(6) Where any person has appealed to the Secretary of State under this section against a notice, no person shall be entitled, in any other proceedings instituted after the making of the appeal, to claim that the notice was not duly served on the person who appealed.

(7) In this section 'relevant occupier' means a person who—

(a) on the date on which the listed building enforcement notice is issued occupies the building to which the notice relates by virtue of a licence . . . and

(b) continues so to occupy the building when the appeal is brought.

40. Appeals: supplementary provisions

(1) The Secretary of State may by regulations prescribe the procedure which is to be followed on appeals under section 39, and in particular, but without prejudice to the generality of this subsection may—

(a) require the local planning authority to submit, within such time as may be prescribed, a statement indicating the submissions which they propose to put forward on the appeal;

(b) specify the matters to be included in such a statement;

(c) require the authority or the appellant to give such notice of such an appeal as may be prescribed, being notice which in the opinion of the Secretary of State is likely to bring the appeal to the attention of persons in the locality in which the building in question is situated;

(d) require the authority to send to the Secretary of State, within such period from the date of the bringing of the appeal as may be prescribed, a copy of the enforcement notice and a list of the persons served with copies of it.

(2) Subject to section 41(4), the Secretary of State shall, if either the appellant or the local planning authority so wish, give each of them an opportunity of appearing before and being heard by a person appointed by the Secretary of State for the purpose.

(3) Schedule 3 applies to appeals under section 39.

41. Determination of appeals under s. 39

(1) On an appeal under section 39 the Secretary of State may—

(a) correct any defect, error or misdescription in the listed building enforcement notice; or

(b) vary the terms of the listed building enforcement notice,
if he is satisfied that the correction or variation will not cause injustice to the appellant or the local planning authority.

(2) Where the Secretary of State determines to allow the appeal, he may quash the notice.

(2A) The Secretary of State shall give any directions necessary to give effect to his determination on the appeal.

(3) The Secretary of State—

(a) may dismiss such an appeal if the appellant fails to comply with section 39(4) within the prescribed time; and

(b) may allow such an appeal and quash the listed building enforcement notice if the local planning authority fail to comply within the prescribed period with any requirement imposed by regulations made by virtue of section 40(1)(a),(b) or (d).

(4) If the Secretary of State proposes to dismiss an appeal under paragraph (a) of subsection (3) or to allow an appeal and quash the listed building enforcement notice under paragraph (b) of that subsection he need not comply with section 40(2).

(5) Where it would otherwise be a ground for determining an appeal in favour of the appellant that a person required to be served with a copy of the listed building enforcement notice was not served, the Secretary of State may disregard that fact if neither the appellant nor that person has been substantially prejudiced by the failure to serve him.

(6) On the determination of an appeal the Secretary of State may—

(a) grant listed building consent for the works to which the listed building enforcement notice relates or for part only of those works;

(b) discharge any condition or limitation subject to which listed building consent was granted and substitute any other condition, whether more or less onerous;

(c) if he thinks fit, exercise his power under section 1 to amend any list compiled or approved under that section by removing from it the building to which the appeal relates.

(7) Any listed building consent granted by the Secretary of State under subsection (6) shall be treated as granted on an application for the same consent under section 10 and the Secretary of State's decision in relation to the grant shall be final.

(8) Subsection (5) of section 250 of the Local Government Act 1972 (which authorises a Minister holding an inquiry under that section to make orders with respect to the costs of the parties) shall apply in relation to any proceedings before the Secretary of State on an appeal under section 39 as if those proceedings were an inquiry held by the Secretary of State under section 50.

42. Execution of works required by listed building enforcement notice

(1) If any of the steps specified in the listed building enforcement notice have not been taken within the period for compliance with the notice, the authority may—

(a) enter the land and take those steps, and

(b) recover from the person who is then the owner of the land any expenses reasonably incurred by them in doing so.

(2) Where a listed building enforcement notice has been served in respect of a building—

(a) any expenses incurred by the owner or occupier of the building for the purpose of complying with it, and

(b) any sums paid by the owner of the building under subsection (1) in respect of expenses incurred by the local planning authority in taking steps required by it,

shall be deemed to be incurred or paid for the use and at the request of the person who carried out the works to which the notice relates.

(3) Regulations under this Act may provide that all or any of the following sections of the Public Health Act 1936, namely—

(a) section 276 (power of local authorities to sell materials removed in executing works under that Act subject to accounting for the proceeds of sale);
(b) section 289 (power to require the occupier of any premises to permit works to be executed by the owner of the premises);
(c) section 294 (limit on liability of persons holding premises as agents or trustees in respect of the expenses recoverable under that Act),
shall apply, subject to such adaptations and modifications as may be specified in the regulations, in relation to any steps required to be taken by a listed building enforcement notice.

(4) Regulations under subsection (3) applying all or any of section 289 of that Act may include adaptations and modifications for the purpose of giving the owner of land to which such a notice relates the right, as against all other persons interested in the land, to comply with the requirements of the notice.

(5) Regulations under subsection (3) may also provide for the charging on the land on which the building stands of any expenses recoverable by a local planning authority under subsection (1).

(6) Any person who wilfully obstructs a person acting in the exercise of powers under subsection (1) shall be guilty of an offence and liable on summary conviction to a fine not exceeding level 3 on the standard scale.

43. Offence where listed building enforcement notice not complied with

(1) Where, at any time after the end of the period for compliance with the notice, any step required by a listed building enforcement notice to be taken has not been taken, the person who is then owner of the land is in breach of the notice.

(2) If at any time the owner of the land is in breach of a listed building enforcement notice he shall be guilty of an offence.

(3) An offence under this section may be charged by reference to any day or longer period of time and a person may be convicted of a second or subsequent offence under this section by reference to any period of time following the preceding conviction for such an offence.

(4) In proceedings against any person for an offence under this section, it shall be a defence for him to show—
(a) that he did everything he could be expected to do to secure that all the steps required by the notice were taken; or
(b) that he was not served with a copy of the listed building enforcement notice and was not aware of its existence.

(5) A person guilty of an offence under this section shall be liable—
(a) on summary conviction, to a fine not exceeding £20,000; and
(b) on conviction on indictment, to a fine.

(6) In determining the amount of any fine to be imposed on a person convicted of an offence under this section, the court shall in particular have regard to any financial benefit which has accrued or appears likely to accrue to him in consequence of the offence.

44. Effect of listed building consent on listed building enforcement notice

(1) If, after the issue of a listed building enforcement notice, consent is granted under section 8(3)—
(a) for the retention of any work to which the notice relates; or
(b) permitting the retention of works without compliance with some condition subject to which a previous listed building consent was granted,
the notice shall cease to have effect in so far as it requires steps to be taken involving the works not being retained or, as the case may be, for complying with that condition.

(2) The fact that such a notice has wholly or partly ceased to have effect under subsection (1) shall not affect the liability of any person for an offence in respect of a previous failure to comply with that notice.

44A. Injunctions

(1) Where a local planning authority consider it necessary or expedient for any actual or apprehended contravention of section 9(1) or (2) to be restrained by injunction, they may apply to the court for an injunction, whether or not they have exercised or are proposing to exercise any of their other powers under this Part.

(2) On an application under subsection (1) the court may grant such an injunction as the court thinks appropriate for the purpose of restraining the contravention.

(3) Rules of court may, in particular, provide for such an injunction to be issued against a person whose identity is unknown.

(4) The references in subsection (1) to a local planning authority include, as respects England, the Commission.

(5) In this section 'the court' means the High Court or the county court.

45. Commission to have concurrent enforcement functions in London

The Commission shall, as respects any London borough, have concurrently with the council of that borough the functions of a local planning authority under sections 38 to 43; and references to the local planning authority in those provisions shall be construed accordingly.

46. Enforcement by the Secretary of State

(1) If it appears to the Secretary of State to be expedient that a listed building enforcement notice should be issued in respect of any land, he may issue such a notice.

(2) Before the Secretary of State serves a notice under subsection (1) he shall consult—

(a) the local planning authority; and
(b) if the land is situated in England, the Commission.

(3) A listed building enforcement notice issued by the Secretary of State shall have the same effect as a notice issued by the local planning authority.

(4) In relation to a listed building enforcement notice issued by the Secretary of State, section 42 shall apply as if for any reference in that section to the local planning authority there were substituted a reference to the Secretary of State.

(5) References in this section to the local planning authority shall in the case of an authority for an area [in England] outside Greater London be construed as references to the district planning authority.

[The words in [ ] were inserted by, and will come into effect on an appointed day order under, the Local Government (Wales) Act 1994.]

CHAPTER V
PREVENTION OF DETERIORATION AND DAMAGE

Compulsory acquisition of listed building in need of repair

47. Compulsory acquisition of listed building in need of repair

(1) If it appears to the Secretary of State that reasonable steps are not being taken for properly preserving a listed building he—

(a) may authorise the appropriate authority to acquire compulsorily under this section the building and any relevant land; or
(b) may himself compulsorily acquire them under this section.

(2) The Acquisition of Land Act 1981 shall apply to compulsory acquisition under this section.

(3) The Secretary of State shall not make or confirm a compulsory purchase order for the acquisition of any building by virtue of this section unless—

(a) In the case of the acquisition of a building situated in England otherwise than by the Commission, he has consulted with the Commission; and

(b) in any case, he is satisfied that it is expedient to make provision for the preservation of the building and to authorise its compulsory acquisition for that purpose.

(4) Any person having an interest in a building which it is proposed to acquire compulsorily under this section may, within 28 days after the service of the notice required by section 12 of that Act of 1981 or, as the case may be, paragraph 3(1) of Schedule 1 to that Act, apply to a magistrates' court acting for the petty sessions area within which the building is situated for an order staying further proceedings on the compulsory purchase order.

(5) If on an application under subsection (4) the court is satisfied that reasonable steps have been taken for properly preserving the building, the court shall make an order accordingly.

(6) Any person aggrieved by the decision of a magistrates' court on an application under subsection (4) may appeal against the decision to the Crown Court.

(7) In this section—
'the appropriate authority' means—
(a) the council of the county, [county borough] or district in which the building is situated, or
(b) in the case of a building situated in Greater London, the Commission or the council of the London borough in which the building is situated, or
(c) in the case of a building situated outside Greater London, the joint planning board for the area in which the building is situated; or
(d) in the case of a building situated within the Broads, the Broads Authority;
'relevant land', in relation to any building, means the land comprising or contiguous or adjacent to it which appears to the Secretary of State to be required for preserving the building or its amenities, or for affording access to it, or for its proper control or management.
[The words in [ ] were inserted by, and will come into effect on an appointed day order under, the Local Government (Wales) Act 1994.]

48. Repairs notice as preliminary to acquisition under s. 47

(1) The compulsory purchase of a building under section 47 shall not be started by the appropriate authority or by the Secretary of State unless at least two months previously the authority or, as the case may be, the Secretary of State has served on the owner of the building a notice under this section (in this section referred to as a 'repairs notice')—
(a) specifying the works which the appropriate authority or, as the case may be, the Secretary of State considers reasonably necessary for the proper preservation of the building; and
(b) explaining the effect of sections 47 to 50,
and the repairs notice has not been withdrawn.

(2) Where—
(a) a building is demolished after a repairs notice has been served in respect of it by an appropriate authority or the Secretary of State, but
(b) the Secretary of State is satisfied that he would have confirmed or, as the case may be, would have made a compulsory purchase order in respect of the building had it not been demolished,
the demolition of the building shall not prevent the authority or the Secretary of State from being authorised under section 47 to acquire compulsorily the site of the building.

(3) An appropriate authority or the Secretary of State may at any time withdraw a repairs notice served by them on any person; and if they do so, they shall immediately give him notice of the withdrawal.

(4) The Secretary of State shall consult with the Commission before he serves or withdraws a repairs notice in relation to a building situated in England.

(5) Where a repairs notice has been served on a person in respect of a building, he shall not be entitled to serve a listed building purchase notice in respect of it—
  (a) until the expiration of three months beginning with the date of the service of the repairs notice; or
  (b) if during that period the compulsory acquisition of the building is begun under section 47, unless and until the compulsory acquisition is discontinued.

(6) For the purposes of this section a compulsory acquisition—
  (a) is started when the notice required by section 12 of the Acquisition of Land Act 1981 or, as the case may be, paragraph 3(1) of Schedule 1 to that Act is served; and
  (b) is discontinued—
    (i) in the case of acquisition by the Secretary of State, when he decides not to make the compulsory purchase order; and
    (ii) in any other case, when the order is withdrawn or the Secretary of State decides not to confirm it.

(7) In this section 'appropriate authority' has the same meaning as in section 47.

49. Compensation on compulsory acquisition of listed building
Subject to section 50, for the purpose of assessing compensation in respect of any compulsory acquisition of land including a building which immediately before the date of the compulsory purchase order was listed, it shall be assumed that listed building consent would be granted for any works—
  (a) for the alteration or extension of the building; or
  (b) for the demolition of the building for the purpose of development of any class specified in Schedule 3 to the principal Act (development not constituting new development).

50. Minimum compensation in case of listed building deliberately left derelict
(1) Where the appropriate authority within the meaning of section 47—
  (a) propose to acquire a building compulsorily under that section; and
  (b) are satisfied that the building has been deliberately allowed to fall into disrepair for the purpose of justifying its demolition and the development or re-development of the site or any adjoining site,
they may include in the compulsory purchase order as submitted to the Secretary of State for confirmation a direction for minimum compensation.

(2) Subject to the provisions of this section, where the Secretary of State acquires a building compulsorily under section 47, he may, if he is satisfied as mentioned in subsection (1)(b), include a direction for minimum compensation in the compulsory purchase order.

(3) Without prejudice to so much of section 12 of the Acquisition of Land Act 1981 or, as the case may be, paragraph 3(1) of Schedule 1 to that Act (notices stating effect of compulsory purchase order or, as the case may be, draft order) as requires the notice to state the effect of the order, the notice required to be served in accordance with that provision shall—
  (a) include a statement that a direction for minimum compensation has been included in the order or, as the case may be, in the draft order prepared by the Secretary of State in accordance with Schedule 1 to that Act; and
  (b) explain the meaning of the expression 'direction for minimum compensation'.

(4) A direction for minimum compensation, in relation to a building compulsorily acquired, is a direction that for the purpose of assessing compensation it is to be assumed, notwithstanding anything to the contrary in the Land Compensation Act 1961, the principal Act, or this Act—

(a) that planning permission would not be granted for any development or re-development of the site of the building; and

(b) that listed building consent would not be granted for any works for the demolition, alteration or extension of the building other than development or works necessary for restoring it to and maintaining it in a proper state of repair.

(5) If a compulsory purchase order is confirmed or made with the inclusion of a direction for minimum compensation, the compensation in respect of the compulsory acquisition shall be assessed in accordance with the direction.

(6) Where such a direction is included in a compulsory purchase order or, as the case may be, in a draft order prepared by the Secretary of State, any person having an interest in the building may, within 28 days after the service of the notice mentioned in subsection (3), apply to a magistrates' court acting for the petty sessions area in which the building is situated for an order that no such direction be included in the compulsory purchase order as confirmed or made by the Secretary of State.

(7) If the court to which an application is made under subsection (6) is satisfied that the building in respect of which the application is made has not been deliberately allowed to fall into disrepair for the purpose mentioned in subsection (1)(b) the court shall make the order applied for.

(8) A person aggrieved by the decision of a magistrates' court on an application under subsection (6) may appeal against the decision to the Crown Court.

(9) The rights conferred by subsections (6) and (8) shall not prejudice those conferred by section 47(4) and (6).

51. Ending of rights over land compulsorily acquired

(1) Subject to the provisions of this section, upon the completion of a compulsory acquisition of land under section 47—

(a) all private rights of way and rights of laying down, erecting, continuing or maintaining any apparatus on, under or over the land shall be extinguished, and

(b) any such apparatus shall vest in the acquiring authority.

(2) Subsection (1) shall not apply—

(a) to any right vested in, or apparatus belonging to, statutory undertakers for the purpose of the carrying on of their undertaking, or

(b) to any right conferred by or in accordance with the telecommunications code on the operator of a telecommunications code system, or

(c) to any telecommunication apparatus kept installed for the purposes of any such system.

(3) In respect of any right or apparatus not falling within subsection (2), subsection (1) shall have effect subject—

(a) to any direction given by the acquiring authority before the completion of the acquisition that subsection (1) shall not apply to any right or apparatus specified in the direction; and

(b) to any agreement which may be made (whether before or after the completion of the acquisition) between the acquiring authority and the person in or to whom the right or apparatus in question is vested or belongs.

(4) Any person who suffers loss by the extinguishment of a right or the vesting of any apparatus under this section shall be entitled to compensation from the acquiring authority.

(5) Any compensation payable under this section shall be determined in accordance with the Land Compensation Act 1961.

Acquisition by agreement

52. Acquisition of land by agreement

(1) The council of any county, [county borough], district or London borough or a joint planning board for an area outside Greater London may acquire by agreement—

(a) any building appearing to them to be of special architectural or historic interest; and

(b) any land comprising or contiguous or adjacent to such a building which appears to the Secretary of State to be required—
  (i) for preserving the building or its amenities, or
  (ii) for affording access to it, or
  (iii) for its proper control or management.

(2) The provisions of Part I of the Compulsory Purchase Act 1965 (so far as applicable), other than sections 4 to 8, 10 and 31, shall apply in relation to the acquisition of land under subsection (1), but references in that Part to the execution of the works shall be construed as including references to—

(a) any erection, construction or carrying out of buildings or works authorised by section 237 of the principal Act; and

(b) any erection, construction or carrying out of buildings or works on behalf of a Minister or statutory undertakers on land acquired by that Minister or those undertakers, where the buildings or works are erected, constructed or carried out for the purposes for which the land was acquired.

[The words in [ ] were inserted by, and will come into effect on an appointed day order under, the Local Government (Wales) Act 1994.]

Management of acquired buildings

53. Management of listed buildings acquired under this Act

(1) Where—
  (a) a local authority or joint planning board acquire any building or other land under section 47(1) or 52(1)(a) or (b); or
  (b) the Commission acquire any building or other land under section 47(1),
they may make such arrangements as to its management, use or disposal as they consider appropriate for the purpose of its preservation.

(2) Where the Secretary of State acquires any building or other land under section 47(1), he may—
  (a) make such arrangements as he thinks fit as to the management, custody or use of the building or land; and
  (b) dispose of or otherwise deal with any such building or land as he may from time to time determine.

(3) The Commission may be a party to such arrangements as are mentioned in subsection (2) if they relate to property situated in England.

Urgent preservation

54. Urgent works to preserve unoccupied listed buildings

(1) A local authority may execute any works which appear to them to be urgently necessary for the preservation of a listed building in their area.

(2) If it appears to the Secretary of State that any works are urgently necessary for the preservation of a listed building—
  (a) if the building is in England, he shall authorise the Commission to execute any works specified in the authorisation which appear to him to be urgently necessary for its preservation; or
  (b) if the building is in Wales, he may himself execute any works which appear to him to be urgently necessary for its preservation.

(3) The works which may be executed under this section may consist of or include works for affording temporary support or shelter for the building.

(4) If the building is occupied works may be carried out only to those parts which are not in use.

(5) The owner of the building must be given not less than seven days' notice in writing of the intention to carry out the works and, in the case of works authorised under subsection (2)(a), the Commission shall give that notice.

(6) A notice under subsection (5) shall describe the works proposed to be carried out.

(7) As respects buildings in Greater London, the functions of a local authority under this section are exercisable concurrently by the Commission and the relevant London borough council.

55. Recovery of expenses of works under s. 54

(1) This section has effect for enabling the expenses of works executed under section 54 to be recovered by the authority who carried out the works, that is to say the local authority, the Commission or the Secretary of State or, in the case of works carried out by the Commission on behalf of the Secretary of State, the Secretary of State.

(2) That authority may give notice to the owner of the building requiring him to pay the expenses of the works.

(3) Where the works consist of or include works for affording temporary support or shelter for the building—

(a) the expenses which may be recovered include any continuing expenses involved in making available the apparatus or materials used; and

(b) notices under subsection (2) in respect of any such continuing expenses may be given from time to time.

(4) The owner may within 28 days of the service of the notice represent to the Secretary of State—

(a) that some or all of the works were unnecessary for the preservation of the building; or

(b) in the case of works for affording temporary support or shelter, that the temporary arrangements have continued for an unreasonable length of time; or

(c) that the amount specified in the notice is unreasonable; or

(d) that the recovery of that amount would cause him hardship,

and the Secretary of State shall determine to what extent the representations are justified.

(5) The Secretary of State shall give notice of his determination, the reasons for it and the amount recoverable—

(a) to the owner of the building; and

(b) if the authority who gave notice under subsection (2) is a local authority or the Commission, to them.

56. Dangerous structure orders in respect of listed buildings

Before taking any steps with a view to—

(a) the making of an order in respect of a listed building under section 77(1)(a) of the Building Act 1984 or section 65 or 69(1) of the London Building Acts (Amendment) Act 1939; or

(b) the service of a notice under section 79(1) of that Act of 1984 or section 62(2) of that Act of 1939,

a local planning authority shall consider whether they should instead exercise their powers under sections 47 and 48 or section 54.

Grants for repair and maintenance

57. Power of local authority to contribute to preservation of listed buildings etc

(1) A local authority may contribute towards the expenses incurred or to be incurred in the repair or maintenance—

(a) of a listed building which is situate in or in the vicinity of their area; or

(b) of a building in their area which is not listed but appears to them to be of architectural or historic interest.

(2) At the time of making such a contribution the local authority may also contribute towards the expenses incurred, or to be incurred, in the upkeep of any garden occupied with the building and contiguous or adjacent to it.

(3) A contribution under this section may be made by grant or loan.

(4) A contribution by way of loan may be made upon such terms and conditions as the local authority may determine including (but without prejudice to the foregoing) a term that the loan shall be free of interest.

(5) A local authority—

(a) may renounce their right to repayment of such a loan or any interest for the time being outstanding, and

(b) by agreement with the borrower may otherwise vary any of the terms and conditions on which such a loan is made.

(6) A local authority may require as a condition of the making by them of a contribution under this section by way of grant towards the expenses of the repair or maintenance or upkeep of any property that the person to whom the grant is made shall enter into an agreement with them for the purpose of enabling the public to have access to the property or part of it during such period and at such times as the agreement may provide.

(7) In this section and in section 58 'local authority' means—

(a) the council of a county, [county borough,] borough or district,

(b) a joint planning board constituted under section 2 of the principal Act, and

(c) in relation to a building or land in the Broads, the Broads Authority.

[The words in [ ] were inserted by, and will come into effect on an appointed day under, the Local Government (Wales) Act 1994.]

58. Recovery of grants under s.57

(1) If, during the period of three years beginning with the day on which a grant is made under section 57 towards the repair or maintenance or upkeep of any property ('the grant property'), the grantee disposes of the interest held by him in the property on that day or any part of that interest, by way of sale or exchange or lease for a term of not less than 21 years, the local authority may recover the amount of the grant, or such part of it as they think fit, from the grantee in any court of competent jurisdiction.

(2) If the grantee gives the whole of that interest to any person (whether directly or indirectly, but otherwise than by will) subsection (1) shall have effect as if the donee were the grantee.

(3) If the grantee gives part of that interest to any person (whether directly or indirectly, but otherwise than by will) subsection (1) shall have effect as if any disposal or part disposal of that interest by the donee were a disposal by the grantee.

(4) If any condition imposed on the making of a grant to which this section applies is contravened or not complied with, the grantor may recover the amount of the grant, or such part of it as he thinks fit, from the grantee.

(5) Nothing in this section entitles a grantor to recover amounts in the aggregate exceeding the amount of the grant (for example by virtue of a breach of more than one condition or disposals of several parts of an interest in the grant property).

Damage to listed buildings

59. Acts causing or likely to result in damage to listed buildings

(1) If, with the intention of causing damage to a listed building, any relevant person does or permits the doing of any act which causes or is likely to result in

damage to the building, he shall be guilty of an offence and liable on summary conviction to a fine not exceeding level 3 on the standard scale.

(2) A person is a relevant person for the purpose of subsection (1) if apart from that subsection he would be entitled to do or permit the act in question.

(3) Subsection (1) does not apply to an act for the execution—

(a) of works authorised by planning permission granted or deemed to be granted in pursuance of an application under the principal Act; or

(b) of works for which listed building consent has been given under this Act.

(4) If a person convicted of an offence under this section fails to take such reasonable steps as may be necessary to prevent any damage or further damage resulting from the offence, he shall be guilty of a further offence and liable on summary conviction to a fine not exceeding one tenth of level three on the standard scale for each day on which the failure continues.

CHAPTER VI
MISCELLANEOUS AND SUPPLEMENTAL

Exceptions for church buildings and ancient monuments

60. Exceptions for ecclesiastical buildings and redundant churches

(1) The provisions mentioned in subsection (2) shall not apply to any ecclesiastical building which is for the time being used for ecclesiastical purposes.

(2) Those provisions are sections 3, 4, 7 to 9, 47, 54 and 59.

(3) For the purposes of subsection (1), a building used or available for use by a minister of religion wholly or mainly as a residence from which to perform the duties of his office shall be treated as not being an ecclesiastical building.

(4) For the purposes of sections 7 to 9 a building shall be taken to be used for the time being for ecclesiastical purposes if it would be so used but for the works in question.

(5) The Secretary of State may by order provide for restricting or excluding the operation of subsections (1) to (3) in such cases as may be specified in the order.

(6) An order under this section may—

(a) make provision for buildings generally, for descriptions of building or for particular buildings;

(b) make different provision for buildings in different areas, for buildings of different religious faiths or denominations or according to the use made of the building;

(c) make such provision in relation to a part of a building (including, in particular, an object or structure falling to be treated as part of the building by virtue of section 1(5)) as may be made in relation to a building and make different provision for different parts of the same building;

(d) make different provision with respect to works of different descriptions or according to the extent of the works;

(e) make such consequential adaptations or modifications of the operation of any other provision of this Act or the principal Act, or of any instrument made under either of those Acts, as appear to the Secretary of State to be appropriate.

(7) Sections 7 to 9 shall not apply to the execution of works for the demolition, in pursuance of a pastoral or redundancy scheme (within the meaning of the Pastoral Measure 1983), of a redundant building (within the meaning of that Measure) or a part of such a building.

61. Exceptions for ancient monuments etc

(1) The provisions mentioned in subsection (2) shall not apply to any building for the time being included in the schedule of monuments compiled and maintained under section 1 of the Ancient Monuments and Archaeological Areas Act 1979.

(2) Those provisions are sections 3, 4, 7 to 9, 47, 54 and 59.

Validity of instruments, decisions and proceedings

62. Validity of certain orders and decisions

(1) Except as provided by section 63, the validity of—

(a) any order under section 23 or 26 (whether before or after it has been confirmed); or

(b) any such decision by the Secretary of State as is mentioned in subsection (2),

shall not be questioned in any legal proceedings whatsoever.

(2) Those decisions are—

(a) any decision on an application referred to the Secretary of State under section 12 or on an appeal under section 20;

(b) any decision to confirm or not to confirm a listed building purchase notice including—

(i) any decision not to confirm such a notice in respect of part of the land to which it relates, and

(ii) any decision to grant any consent, or give any direction, in lieu of confirming such a notice, either wholly or in part;

(c) any decision to grant listed building consent under paragraph (a) of section 41(6) or to discharge a condition or limitation under paragraph (b) of that section.

(3) Nothing in this section shall affect the exercise of any jurisdiction of any court in respect of any refusal or failure on the part of the Secretary of State to take any such decision as is mentioned in subsection (2).

63. Proceedings for questioning validity of other orders, decisions and directions

(1) If any person is aggrieved by any such order or decision as is mentioned in section 62(1) and wishes to question its validity on the grounds—

(a) that it is not within the powers of this Act, or

(b) that any of the relevant requirements have not been complied with in relation to it,

he may make an application to the High Court under this section.

(2) Without prejudice to subsection (1), if the authority directly concerned with any such order or decision wish to question its validity on any of those grounds, the authority may make an application to the High Court under this section.

(3) An application under this section must be made within six weeks from the date on which the order is confirmed (or, in the case of an order under section 23 which takes effect under section 25 without confirmation, the date on which it takes effect) or, as the case may be, the date on which the action is taken.

(4) On any application under this section the High Court—

(a) may by interim order suspend the operation of the order or decision, the validity of which is questioned by the application, until the final determination of the proceedings; and

(b) if satisfied—

(i) that the order or decision is not within the powers of this Act, or

(ii) that the interests of the applicant have been substantially prejudiced by a failure to comply with any of the relevant requirements in relation to it,

may quash that order or decision.

(5) References in this section to the confirmation of an order include the confirmation of an order subject to modifications.

(6) In this section 'the relevant requirements', in relation to any order or decision, means any requirements of this Act or of the Tribunals and Inquiries Act 1992 or of any order, regulations or rules made under either of those Acts which are applicable to that order or decision.

(7) For the purposes of subsection (2) the authority directly concerned with an order or decision is—
  (a) in relation to any such decision as is mentioned in section 62(2)(b)—
    (i) the council on whom the listed building purchase notice was served, and
    (ii) in a case where the Secretary of State has modified the notice wholly or in part by substituting another local authority or statutory undertakers for that council, also that authority or those statutory undertakers; and
  (b) otherwise, the authority who—
    (i) made the order or decision to which the proceedings in question relate, or
    (ii) referred the matter to the Secretary of State, or
    (iii) if the order was made by him, are the authority named in it.

64. Validity of listed building enforcement notices

The validity of a listed building enforcement notice shall not, except by way of an appeal under section 39, be questioned in any proceedings whatsoever on any of the grounds on which such an appeal may be brought.

65. Appeals to High Court relating to listed building enforcement notices

(1) Where the Secretary of State gives a decision in proceedings on an appeal under section 39 against a listed building enforcement notice, the appellant or the local planning authority or any other person having an interest in the land to which the notice relates may, according as rules of court may provide, either appeal to the High Court against the decision on a point of law or require the Secretary of State to state and sign a case for the opinion of the High Court.

(2) At any stage of the proceedings on any such appeal, the Secretary of State may state any question of law arising in the course of the proceedings in the form of a special case for the decision of the High Court.

(3) A decision of the High Court on a case stated by virtue of subsection (2) shall be deemed to be a judgment of the court within the meaning of section 16 of the Supreme Court Act 1981 (jurisdiction of the Court of Appeal to hear and determine appeals from any judgment of the High Court).

(3A) In proceedings brought by virtue of this section, the High Court or, as the case may be, the Court of Appeal may, on such terms, if any, as the Court thinks fit (which may include terms requiring the local planning authority to give an undertaking as to damages or any other matter), order that the listed building enforcement notice shall have effect, or have effect to such extent as may be specified in the order, pending the final determination of those proceedings and any re-hearing and determination by the Secretary of State.

(4) In relation to any proceedings in the High Court or the Court of Appeal brought by virtue of this section the power to make rules of court shall include power to make rules—
  (a) prescribing the powers of the High Court or the Court of Appeal with respect to the remitting of the matter with the opinion or direction of the court for re-hearing and determination by the Secretary of State; and
  (b) providing for the Secretary of State, either generally or in such circumstances as may be prescribed by the rules, to be treated as a party to any such proceedings and to be entitled to appear and to be heard accordingly.

(5) No proceedings in the High Court shall be brought by virtue of this section except with the leave of that Court and no appeal to the Court of Appeal shall be so brought except with the leave of the Court of Appeal or of the High Court.

(6) In this section 'decision' includes a direction or order, and references to the giving of a decision shall be construed accordingly.

(7) In the case of a listed building enforcement notice issued by the Commission subsection (1) shall apply as if the reference to the local planning authority were a reference to the Commission.

Special considerations affecting planning functions

66. General duty as respects listed buildings in exercise of planning functions

(1) In considering whether to grant planning permission for development which affects a listed building or its setting, the local planning authority or, as the case may be, the Secretary of State shall have special regard to the desirability of preserving the building or its setting or any features of special architectural or historic interest which it possesses.

(2) Without prejudice to section 72, in the exercise of the powers of appropriation, disposal and development (including redevelopment) conferred by the provisions of sections 232, 233 and 235(1) of the principal Act, a local authority shall have regard to the desirability of preserving features of special architectural or historic interest, and in particular, listed buildings.

(3) The reference in subsection (2) to a local authority includes a reference to a joint planning board and a board reconstituted in pursuance of Schedule 17 to the Local Government Act 1972.
[The words underlined are to be repealed under the Environment Act 1995 by an appointed day order.]

67. Publicity for applications affecting setting of listed buildings

(1) This section applies where an application for planning permission for any development of land is made to a local planning authority and the development would, in the opinion of the authority, affect the setting of a listed building.

(2) The local planning authority shall—
 (a) publish in a local newspaper circulating in the locality in which the land is situated; and
 (b) for not less than seven days display on or near the land,
a notice indicating the nature of the development in question and naming a place within the locality where a copy of the application, and of all plans and other documents submitted with it, will be open to inspection by the public at all reasonable hours during the period of 21 days beginning with the date of publication of the notice under paragraph (a).

(3) In a case where the land is situated in England, the local planning authority shall send a copy of the notice to the Commission.

(4) Where the Secretary of State, after consulting with the Commission, notifies a local planning authority in writing that subsection (3) shall not affect the authority as regards any notice relating to any kind of application specified in the notification, then that subsection shall not affect the authority as regards any such notice.

(5) The Secretary of State shall send the Commission a copy of any notification made under subsection (4).

(6) The application shall not be determined by the local planning authority before—
 (a) the expiry of the period of 21 days referred to in subsection (2); or
 (b) if later, the expiry of the period of 21 days beginning with the date on which the notice required by that subsection to be displayed was first displayed.

(7) In determining any application for planning permission to which this section applies, the local planning authority shall take into account any representations relating to the application which are received by them before the periods mentioned in subsection (6) have elapsed.

(8) In this section references to planning permission do not include references to planning permissions falling within section 73A of the principal Act.

68. Reference to Commission of planning applications involving listed buildings in Greater London

(1) Without prejudice to his powers by virtue of section 74(1) of the principal Act, the Secretary of State may by regulations provide for any application for planning permission to which this section applies to be referred to the Commission before it is dealt with by the local planning authority.

(2) This section applies to an application for planning permission for any development in Greater London which would, in the opinion of the local planning authority to which the application is made, involve the demolition, in whole or in part, or a material alteration, of a listed building.

(3) Regulations under this section may—

(a) provide for the Commission to give the referring authority directions as to the manner in which an application is to be dealt with; and

(b) provide that an application which satisfies such conditions as may be specified in the regulations need not be referred to the Commission.

PART II
CONSERVATION AREAS

Designation

69. Designation of conservation areas

(1) Every local planning authority—

(a) shall from time to time determine which parts of their area are areas of special architectural or historic interest the character or appearance of which it is desirable to preserve or enhance, and

(b) shall designate those areas as conservation areas.

(2) It shall be the duty of a local planning authority from time to time to review the past exercise of functions under this section and to determine whether any parts or any further parts of their area should be designated as conservation areas; and, if they so determine, they shall designate those parts accordingly.

(3) The Secretary of State may from time to time determine that any part of a local planning authority's area which is not for the time being designated as a conservation area is an area of special architectural or historic interest the character or appearance of which it is desirable to preserve or enhance; and, if he so determines, he may designate that part as a conservation area.

(4) The designation of any area as a conservation area shall be a local land charge.

70. Designation of conservation areas: supplementary provisions

(1) The functions of a local planning authority under section 69 and this section shall also be exercisable in Greater London by the Commission.

(2) Before making a determination under section 69 the Commission shall consult the council of each London borough of which any part is included in the area to which the proposed determination relates.

(3) Before making a determination under section 69(3) the Secretary of State shall consult the local planning authority.

(4) Before designating any area in Greater London as a conservation area the Commission shall obtain the consent of the Secretary of State.

(5) A local planning authority shall give notice of the designation of any part of their area as a conservation area under section 69(1) or (2) and of any variation or cancellation of any such designation—

(a) to the Secretary of State; and

(b) if it affects an area in England and the designation or, as the case may be, the variation or cancellation was not made by the Commission, to the Commission.

(6) The Secretary of State shall give notice of the designation of any part of the area of a local planning authority as a conservation area under section 69(3) and of any variation or cancellation of any such designation—
   (a) to the authority; and
   (b) if it affects an area in England, to the Commission.

(7) A notice under subsection (5) or (6) shall contain sufficient particulars to identify the area affected.

(8) Notice of any such designation, variation or cancellation as is mentioned in subsection (5) or (6), with particulars of its effect, shall be published in the London Gazette and in at least one newspaper circulating in the area of the local planning authority, by that authority or, as the case may be, the Secretary of State.

General duties of planning authorities

71. Formulation and publication of proposals for preservation and enhancement of conservation areas

(1) It shall be the duty of a local planning authority from time to time to formulate and publish proposals for the preservation and enhancement of any parts of their area which are conservation areas.

(2) Proposals under this section shall be submitted for consideration to a public meeting in the area to which they relate.

(3) The local planning authority shall have regard to any views concerning the proposals expressed by persons attending the meeting.

72. General duty as respects conservation areas in exercise of planning functions

(1) In the exercise, with respect to any buildings or other land in a conservation area, of any functions under or by virtue of powers under any of the provisions mentioned in subsection (2), special attention shall be paid to the desirability of preserving or enhancing the character or appearance of that area.

(2) The provisions referred to in subsection (1) are the planning Acts and Part I of the Historic Buildings and Ancient Monuments Act 1953 and sections 70 and 73 of the Leasehold Reform, Housing and Urban Development Act 1993.

73. Publicity for applications affecting conservation areas

(1) Where an application for planning permission for any development of land is made to a local planning authority and the development would, in the opinion of the authority, affect the character or appearance of a conservation area, subsections (2) to (7) of section 67 shall apply as they apply in the circumstances mentioned in subsection (1) of that section.

(2) In this section references to planning permission do not include references to planning permissions falling within section 73A of the principal Act.

Control of demolition

74. Control of demolition in conservation areas

(1) A building in a conservation area shall not be demolished without the consent of the appropriate authority (in this Act referred to as 'conservation area consent').

(2) The appropriate authority for the purposes of this section is—
   (a) in relation to applications for consent made by local planning authorities, the Secretary of State; and
   (b) in relation to other applications for consent, the local planning authority or the Secretary of State.

(3) Sections 7 to 26, 28, 32 to 46, 56, 62 to 65, 66(1), 82(2) to (4), 83(1)(b),(3) and (4) and 90(2) to (4) have effect in relation to buildings in conservation areas as they have effect in relation to listed buildings subject to such exceptions and modifications as may be prescribed by regulations.

(4) Any such regulations may make different provision—
    (a) in relation to applications made by local planning authorities, and
    (b) in relation to other applications.

75. Cases in which s. 74 does not apply

(1) Section 74 does not apply to—
    (a) listed buildings;
    (b) ecclesiastical buildings which are for the time being used for ecclesiastical purposes;
    (c) buildings for the time being included in the schedule of monuments compiled and maintained under section 1 of the Ancient Monuments and Archaeological Areas Act 1979; or
    (d) buildings in relation to which a direction under subsection (2) is for the time being in force.

(2) The Secretary of State may direct that section 74 shall not apply to any description of buildings specified in the direction.

(3) A direction under subsection (2) may be given either to an individual local planning authority exercising functions under that section or to local planning authorities generally.

(4) The Secretary of State may vary or revoke a direction under subsection (b) by a further direction under that subsection.

(5) For the purposes of subsection (1)(b), a building used or available for use by a minister of religion wholly or mainly as a residence from which to perform the duties of his office shall be treated as not being as ecclesiastical building.

(6) For the purposes of sections 7 to 9 as they apply by virtue of section 74(3) a building shall be taken to be used for the time being for ecclesiastical purposes if it would be so used but for the works in question.

(7) The Secretary of State may by order provide for restricting or excluding the operation of subsection (1)(b) in such cases as may be specified in the order.

(8) An order under subsection (7) may—
    (a) make provision for buildings generally, for descriptions of building or for particular buildings;
    (b) make different provision for buildings in different areas, for buildings of different religious faiths or denominations or according to the use made of the building;
    (c) make such provision in relation to a part of a building (including, in particular, an object or structure falling to be treated as part of the building by virtue of section 1(5)) as may be made in relation to a building and make different provision for different parts of the same building;
    (d) make different provision with respect to works of different descriptions or according to the extent of the works;
    (e) make such consequential adaptations or modifications of the operation of any other provision of this Act or the principal Act, or of any instrument made under either of those Acts, as appear to the Secretary of State to be appropriate.

(9) Regulations under this Act may provide that subsections (5) to (8) shall have effect subject to such exceptions and modifications as may be prescribed, and any such regulations may make different provision—
    (a) in relation to applications made by local planning authorities, and
    (b) in relation to other applications.

(10) Any proceedings on or arising out of an application for conservation area consent made while section 74 applies to a building shall lapse if it ceases to apply to it, and any such consent granted with respect to the building shall also lapse.

(11) The fact that that section has ceased to apply to a building shall not affect the liability of any person to be prosecuted and punished for an offence under section 9 or 43 committed with respect to the building while that section did apply to it.

76. Urgent works to preserve unoccupied buildings in conservation areas

(1) If it appears to the Secretary of State that the preservation of a building in a conservation area is important for maintaining the character or appearance of that area, he may direct that section 54 shall apply to it as it applies to listed buildings.

(2) The Secretary of State shall consult the Commission before giving a direction under subsection (1) in respect of a building in England.

Grants

77. Grants and loans for preservation or enhancement of conservation areas

(1) If in the opinion of the Commission any relevant expenditure has made or will make a significant contribution towards the preservation or enhancement of the character or appearance of any conservation area situated in England or any part of such an area, they may make grants or loans for the purposes of defraying the whole or part of that expenditure.

(2) If in the opinion of the Secretary of State any relevant expenditure has made or will make a significant contribution towards the preservation or enhancement of the character or appearance of any conservation area situated in Wales or any part of such an area, he may make grants or loans for the purposes of defraying the whole or part of that expenditure.

(3) Expenditure is relevant for the purposes of subsection (1) or (2) if it has been or is to be incurred in or in connection with, or with a view to the promotion of, such preservation or enhancement as is mentioned in that subsection.

(4) A grant or loan under this section may be made subject to such conditions as the Commission or, as the case may be, the Secretary of State may think fit to impose.

(5) Any loan under subsection (1) shall be made on such terms as to repayment, payment of interest and otherwise as the Commission may determine.

(6) Any loan under subsection (2) shall be made on such terms as to repayment, payment of interest and otherwise as the Secretary of State may with the approval of the Treasury determine.

(7) Unless the making of a grant or loan under this section appears to the Secretary of State to be a matter of immediate urgency, before making the grant or loan, the Secretary of State shall consult the Historic Buildings Council for Wales as to its making and the conditions subject to which it should be made.

(8) The Secretary of State may pay such remuneration and allowances as he may with the approval of the Treasury determine to any member of the Historic Buildings Council for Wales by whom services are rendered in connection with any question as to the exercise of his powers under this section.

(9) If any such member is also a member of the House of Commons, those payments shall extend only to allowances in respect of travelling and subsistence expenses, and any other expenses necessarily incurred by him in connection with those services.

78. Recovery of grants under s. 77

(1) This section applies to any grant under section 77 made on terms that it shall be recoverable under this section.

(2) A grant shall only be regarded as made on those terms if before or on making the grant the grantor gives the grantee notice in writing—

(a) summarising the effect of this section; and

(b) if the grant is made for the purpose of defraying the whole or part of expenditure in relation to any particular property ('the grant property'), specifying the recovery period.

(3) In this section 'the recovery period' means the period, beginning with the day on which the grant is made and ending not more than ten years after that day, during which the grant is to be recoverable in accordance with subsection (4).

(4) If during the recovery period the grantee disposes of the interest which was held by him in the grant property on the day on which the grant was made or any part of that interest by way of sale or exchange or lease for a term of not less than 21 years, the grantor may recover the amount of the grant, or such part of it as the grantor thinks fit, from the grantee.

(5) If the grantee gives the whole of that interest to any person (whether directly or indirectly, but otherwise than by will) subsection (4) shall have effect as if the donee were the grantee.

(6) If the grantee gives part of that interest to any person (whether directly or indirectly, but otherwise than by will) subsection (4) shall have effect as if any disposal or part disposal of that interest by the donee were a disposal by the grantee.

(7) If any condition imposed on the making of a grant to which this section applies is contravened or not complied with, the grantor may recover the amount of the grant, or such part of it as he thinks fit, from the grantee.

(8) Nothing in this section entitles a grantor to recover amounts in the aggregate exceeding the amount of the grant (for example by virtue of a breach of more than one condition or disposals of several parts of an interest in the grant property).

Town schemes

79. Town scheme agreements

(1) The Commission and one or more local authorities in England, or the Secretary of State and one or more local authorities in Wales, may enter an agreement (in this Act referred to as a 'town scheme agreement') that a specified sum of money shall be set aside for a specified period of years for the purpose of making grants for the repair of buildings which are—

(a) included in a list compiled for the purposes of such an agreement by the parties to the agreement, or by them and other such authorities, or

(b) shown on a map prepared for those purposes by the parties, or by them and such other authorities.

(2) Before such a list is compiled or such a map is prepared by the Secretary of State and any local authorities as respects any buildings in Wales they shall consult the Historic Buildings Council for Wales.

(3) In this section 'local authority' means—

(a) a county council;

[(aa) a county borough council;]

(b) a district council;

(c) in relation to any building situated within the Broads, the Broads Authority;

[(ca) in relation to any building in a National Park for which a National Park authority is the local planning authority, that authority;]

(d) a London borough council or the Common Council of the City of London;

(e) the Council of the Isles of Scilly.

[The reference to a National Park authority was introduced by the Environment Act 1995, see the note to section 4A of the Town and Country Planning Act 1990, supra, while the reference to a county borough council was inserted by, and will come into effect on an appointed day under, the Local Government (Wales) Act 1994.]

80. Grants for repairing of buildings in town schemes

(1) The Commission may make grants for the purpose of defraying the whole or part of any expenditure incurred or to be incurred in the repair of any building which—

(a) is the subject of a town scheme agreement;

(b) is situated in a conservation area in England; and

(c) appears to the Commission to be of architectural or historic interest.

(2) The Secretary of State may make grants for the purpose of defraying the whole or part of any expenditure incurred or to be incurred in the repair of any building which—

(a) is the subject of a town scheme agreement;
(b) is situated in a conservation area in Wales; and
(c) appears to him to be of architectural or historic interest.

(3) A grant under this section may be made subject to conditions imposed by the Commission or, as the case may be, the Secretary of State for such purposes as the Commission or, as the case may be, the Secretary of State thinks fit.

(4) Unless the making of a grant under this section appears to the Secretary of State to be a matter of immediate urgency, before he makes such a grant he may consult with the Historic Buildings Council for Wales as to the making of the grant and as to the conditions subject to which it should be made.

(5) The Commission or the Secretary of State may—

(a) pay any grant under this section to any authority which is a party to a town scheme agreement; and
(b) make arrangements with any such authority for the way in which the agreement is to be carried out.

(6) Those arrangements may include such arrangements for the offer and payment of grants under this section as the parties may agree.

(7) Section 78(4) to (8) shall apply to a grant under this section as it applies to a grant under that section, but taking the recovery period to be three years beginning with the day on which the grant is made.

PART III
GENERAL

Authorities exercising functions under Act

81. Authorities exercising functions under Act

In this Act 'local planning authority' shall be construed in accordance with Part I of the principal Act and Schedule 4 to this Act (which makes further provision as to the exercise of functions under this Act).

Special cases

82. Application of Act to land and works of local planning authorities

(1) In relation to land of a local planning authority, section 1(1), (2) and (4) and sections 2, and 39(6) shall have effect subject to such exceptions and modifications as may be prescribed.

(2) The provisions mentioned in subsection (3) shall have effect for the purpose of applications by local planning authorities relating to the execution of works for the demolition, alteration or extension of listed buildings, subject to such exceptions and modifications as may be prescribed.

(3) Those provisions are sections 1(3), (5) and (6), 3 to 5, 7 to 29, 32 to 50 (except section 39(6)), 60(1) to (4) (as it applies as respects the provisions mentioned in this subsection), 62 to 65, 67(2)(b), (6) and (7), 73(1), Schedules 1 and 2, paragraph 2 of Schedule 4 (as it applies to Schedule 1) and paragraph 4(1) of Schedule 4 (as it applies as respects the provisions mentioned in this subsection).

(4) Regulations under this section may in particular provide—

(a) for the making of applications for listed building consent to the Secretary of State; and
(b) for the issue or service by him of notices under section 2(3) and the provisions mentioned in subsection (3).

Planning (Listed Buildings and Conservation Areas) Act 1990   291

83. Exercise of powers in relation to Crown land

(1) Notwithstanding any interest of the Crown in Crown land, but subject to the following provisions of this section—

(a) a building which for the time being is Crown land may be included in a list compiled or approved by the Secretary of State under section 1;

(b) any restrictions imposed or powers conferred by sections 1 to 26, 32 to 46, 54 to 56, 59 to 61, 66(1), 67, 68, 73 or 76 or Schedule 1, 2 or 3 shall apply and be exercisable in relation to Crown land to the extent of any interest in it for the time being held otherwise than by or on behalf of the Crown;

(c) any power to acquire land compulsorily under section 47 may be exercised in relation to any interest in the land which is for the time being held otherwise than by or on behalf of the Crown.

(2) Except with the consent of the appropriate authority—

(a) no notice shall be issued or served under section 38 in relation to land which for the time being is Crown land;

(b) no interest in land which for the time being is Crown land shall be acquired compulsorily under section 47.

(3) No listed building enforcement notice shall be issued in respect of works executed by or on behalf of the Crown in respect of a building which was Crown land at the time when the works were executed.

(4) No listed building purchase notice shall be served in relation to any interest in Crown land unless—

(a) an offer has been previously made by the owner of that interest to dispose of it to the appropriate authority on terms that the price payable for it—

(i) shall be equal to the compensation which would be payable in respect of it if it were acquired in pursuance of such a notice, or

(ii) in default of agreement, shall be determined in a similar manner to that in which that compensation would be determined; and

(b) that offer has been refused by the appropriate authority.

(5) In this section—

'Crown land' means land in which there is a Crown interest or a Duchy interest;

'Crown interest' means an interest belonging to Her Majesty in right of the Crown, or belonging to a government department, or held in trust for Her Majesty for the purposes of a government department;

'Duchy interest' means an interest belonging to Her Majesty in right of the Duchy of Lancaster or belonging to the Duchy of Cornwall.

(6) A person who is entitled to occupy Crown land by virtue of a licence in writing shall be treated as having an interest in land for the purposes of subsection (1)(b) so far as applicable to sections 1 to 26, 38 to 46, 54 to 56, 59 to 61, 66(1), 67, 68, 73 and 76 and Schedule 1, 2 or 3.

(7) For the purposes of this section 'the appropriate authority', in relation to any land—

(a) in relation to land belonging to Her Majesty in right of the Crown and forming part of the Crown Estate, means the Crown Estate Commissioners;

(b) in relation to any other land belonging to Her Majesty in right of the Crown, means the government department having the management of that land;

(c) in relation to land belonging to Her Majesty in right of the Duchy of Lancaster, means the Chancellor of the Duchy;

(d) in relation to land belonging to the Duchy of Cornwall, means such person as the Duke of Cornwall or the possessor for the time being of the Duchy of Cornwall appoints;

(e) in the case of land belonging to a government department or held in trust for Her Majesty for the purposes of a government department, means that department.

(8) If any question arises as to what authority is the appropriate authority in relation to any land, that question shall be referred to the Treasury, whose decision shall be final.

84. Application for listed building or conservation area consent in anticipation of disposal of Crown land

(1) This section has effect for the purpose of enabling Crown land, or an interest in Crown land, to be disposed of with the benefit of listed building consent or conservation area consent.

(2) Notwithstanding the interest of the Crown in the land in question, an application for any such consent may be made—
   (a) by the appropriate authority; or
   (b) by any person authorised by that authority in writing;
and, subject to subsections (3) and (4), all the statutory provisions relating to the making and determination of any such application shall accordingly apply as if the land were not Crown land.

(3) Any listed building consent or conservation area consent granted by virtue of this section shall apply only—
   (a) to works carried out after the land in question has ceased to be Crown land; and
   (b) so long as that land continues to be Crown land, to works carried out by virtue of a private interest in the land.

(4) The Secretary of State may by regulations—
   (a) modify or exclude any of the statutory provisions referred to in subsection (2) in their application by virtue of that subsection and any other statutory provisions in their application to consents granted or made by virtue of this section;
   (b) make provision for requiring a local planning authority to be notified of any disposal of, or of an interest in, any Crown land in respect of which an application has been made by virtue of this section; and
   (c) make such other provision in relation to the making and determination of applications by virtue of this section as he thinks necessary or expedient.

(5) This section shall not be construed as affecting any right to apply for any listed building consent or conservation area consent in respect of Crown land in a case in which such an application can be made by virtue of a private interest in the land.

(6) In this section—
   'statutory provisions' means provisions contained in or having effect under any enactment;
   'private interest' means an interest which is neither a Crown interest nor a Duchy interest;
and references to the disposal of an interest in Crown land include references to the grant of an interest in such land.

(7) Subsections (5), (7) and (8) of section 83 apply for the purposes of this section as they apply for the purposes of that section.

(8) A person who is entitled to occupy Crown land by virtue of a licence in writing shall be treated for the purposes of this section as having an interest in land and references to the disposal or grant of an interest in Crown land and to a private interest in such land shall be construed accordingly.

85. [repealed by the Coal Industry Act 1994]

86. Ecclesiastical property

(1) Without prejudice to the provisions of the Acquisition of Land Act 1981 with respect to notices served under that Act, where under any of the provisions of this Act a notice or copy of a notice is required to be served on an owner of land, and the land

is ecclesiastical property, a similar notice or copy of a notice shall be served on the Church Commissioners.

(2) Where the fee simple of any ecclesiastical property is in abeyance—

(a) if the property is situated in England, then for the purposes of section 11, this subsection (other than paragraph (b)) and sections 62, 63 and 83(1) and any other provisions of this Act so far as they apply or have effect for the purposes of any of those provisions, the fee simple shall be treated as being vested in the Church Commissioners;

(b) in any case, the fee simple shall, for the purposes of a compulsory acquisition of the property under section 47, be treated as being vested in the Church Commissioners, and any notice to treat shall be served, or be deemed to have been served, accordingly.

(3) Any compensation payable under section 29 in respect of land which is ecclesiastical property—

(a) shall in the case of land which is not diocesan glebe land, be paid to the Church Commissioners; and

(b) shall in the case of diocesan glebe land, be paid to the Diocesan Board of Finance in which the land is vested, and shall, (in either case) be applied by them for the purposes for which the proceeds of a sale by agreement of the land would be applicable under any enactment or Measure authorising or disposing of the proceeds of such a sale.

(4) In this section 'ecclesiastical property' means land belonging to an ecclesiastical benefice, or being or forming part of a church subject to the jurisdiction of a bishop of any diocese or the site of such a church, or being or forming part of a burial ground subject to such jurisdiction or being diocesan glebe land; and 'Diocesan Board of Finance' and 'diocesan glebe land' have the same meaning as in the Endowment and Glebe Measure 1976.

87. Settled land.

The classes of works specified in Part II of Schedule 3 to the Settled Land Act 1925 (which specifies improvements which may be paid for out of capital money, subject to provisions under which repayment out of income may be required to be made) shall include works specified by the Secretary of State as being required for properly maintaining a listed building which is settled land within the meaning of that Act.

Miscellaneous provisions

88. Rights of entry

(1) Any person duly authorised in writing by the Secretary of State may at any reasonable time enter any land for the purpose of surveying any building on it or any other land in connection with a proposal to include the building in, or exclude it from, a list compiled or approved under section 1.

(2) Any person duly authorised in writing by the Secretary of State, a local planning authority or, where the authorisation relates to a building situated in Greater London, the Commission may at any reasonable time enter any land for any of the following purposes—

(a) surveying it or any other land in connection with any proposal by the authority or the Secretary of State to make, issue or serve any order or notice under any of the provisions of sections 1 to 26, 38, 40, 46, 54, 55, 60, 68, 75 or 76 or under any order or regulations made under any of them, or any notice under section 48;

(b) ascertaining whether any such order or notice has been complied with in relation to the land or any other land;

(c) ascertaining whether an offence has been, or is being, committed with respect to any building on the land, or any other land, under section 9, 11 or 43;

(d) ascertaining whether any building on the land or any other land is being maintained in a proper state of repair.

(3) Any person duly authorised in writing by the Secretary of State, a local authority or, where the authorisation relates to a building situated in Greater London, the Commission may at any reasonable time enter any land for any of the following purposes—

(a) ascertaining whether an offence has been or is being committed under section 59 in relation to the land or any other land;

(b) ascertaining whether any of the functions conferred by section 54 should or may be exercised in connection with the land or any other land; or

(c) exercising any of those functions in connection with the land or any other land.

(4) Any person who is an officer of the Valuation Office or is duly authorised in writing by a local planning authority may at any reasonable time enter any land for the purpose of surveying it, or estimating its value, in connection with a claim for compensation payable by the authority under section 28 or 29 in respect of any land.

(5) Any person who is an officer of the Valuation Office or is duly authorised in writing by a local authority having power to acquire land under sections 47 to 52 may at any reasonable time enter any land for the purpose of surveying it, or estimating its value, in connection with any proposal to acquire that land or any other land or in connection with any claim for compensation in respect of any such acquisition.

(6) Subject to section 88B(8) any power conferred by this section to survey land shall be construed as including power to search and bore for the purpose of ascertaining the nature of the subsoil.

88A. Warrants to enter land

(1) If it is shown to the satisfaction of a justice of the peace on sworn information in writing—

(a) that there are reasonable grounds for entering any land for any of the purposes mentioned in section 88; and

(b) that—

(i) admission to the land has been refused, or a refusal is reasonably apprehended; or

(ii) the case is one of urgency,

the justice may issue a warrant authorising any person duly authorised in writing by the appropriate authority to enter the land.

(2) In subsection (1) 'the appropriate authority' means the person who may authorise entry on the land under section 88 for the purpose in question.

(3) For the purposes of subsection (1)(b)(i) admission to land shall be regarded as having been refused if no reply is received to a request for admission within a reasonable period.

(4) A warrant authorises entry on one occasion only and that entry must be—

(a) within one month from the date of the issue of the warrant; and

(b) at a reasonable hour, unless the case is one of urgency.

88B. Rights of entry; supplementary provisions

(1) A person authorised under section 88 to enter any land shall not demand admission as of right to any land which is occupied unless twenty-four hours notice of the intended entry has been given to the occupier.

(2) A person authorised to enter land in pursuance of a right of entry conferred under or by virtue of section 88 or 88A (referred to in this section as 'a right of entry')—

(a) shall, if so required, produce evidence of his authority and state the purpose of his entry before so entering;

(b) may take with him such other persons as may be necessary; and

(c) on leaving the land shall, if the owner or occupier is not then present, leave it as effectively secured against trespassers as he found it.

(3) Any person who wilfully obstructs a person acting in the exercise of a right of entry shall be guilty of an offence and liable on summary conviction to a fine not exceeding level 3 on the standard scale.

(4) If any person who enters any land, in exercise of a right of entry, discloses to any person any information obtained by him while on the land as to any manufacturing process or trade secret, he shall be guilty of an offence.

(5) Subsection (4) does not apply if the disclosure is made by a person in the course of performing his duty in connection with the purpose for which he was authorised to enter the land.

(6) A person who is guilty of an offence under subsection (4) shall be liable—

(a) on summary conviction to a fine not exceeding the statutory maximum, or

(b) on conviction on indictment to imprisonment for a term not exceeding two years or a fine or both.

(7) If any damage is caused to land or chattels in the exercise of—

(a) a right of entry; or

(b) a power conferred by virtue of section 88(6) in connection with such a right, compensation may be recovered by any person suffering the damage from the authority who gave the written authority for the entry or, as the case may be, the Secretary of State; and section 118 of the principal Act shall apply in relation to compensation under this subsection as it applies in relation to compensation under Part IV of that Act.

(8) No person shall carry out any works in exercise of a power conferred under section 88 unless notice of his intention to do so was included in the notice required by subsection (1).

(9) The authority of the appropriate Minister shall be required for the carrying out of works in exercise of a power conferred under section 88 if—

(a) the land in question is held by statutory undertakers; and

(b) they object to the proposed works on the ground that the execution of the works would be seriously detrimental to the carrying on of their undertaking.

(10) Section 265(1) and (3) of the principal Act (meaning of 'appropriate Minister') applies for the purposes of subsection (9) as it applies for the purposes of section 325(9) of the principal Act.

89. Application of certain general provisions of principal Act

(1) Subject to subsection (2), the following provisions of the principal Act shall apply for the purposes of this Act as they apply for the purposes of that Act, namely—

section 320 (local inquiries),
section 322 (orders as to costs of parties where no inquiry held),
section 322A (orders as to costs: supplementary),
section 323 (procedure on certain appeals and applications),
section 329 (service of notices),
section 330 (power to require information as to interests in land),
section 331 (offences by corporations).

(2) Section 331 of that Act shall not apply to offences under section 59 of this Act.

(3) In the application of Section 330 by this section references to a local authority include the Commission.

90. Financial provisions

(1) Where—

(a) compensation is payable by a local authority under this Act in consequence of any decision or order given or made under Chapters I, II or IV of Part I or sections 32 to 37, 60 or Schedule 3; and

(b) the decision or order in consequence of which it is payable was given or made wholly or partly in the interest of a service which is provided by a government department and the cost of which is defrayed out of money provided by Parliament, the Minister responsible for the administration of that service may pay that authority a contribution of such amount as he may with the consent of the Treasury determine.

(2) Any local authority and any statutory undertakers may contribute towards any expenses incurred by a local planning authority in or in connection with the performance of any of their functions under the provisions of Chapters I to V of Part I (other than sections 27 to 31, 53, 54, 55, 57, 58) and sections 66 and 68 and Schedule 1.

(3) Where any expenses are incurred by a local authority in the payment of compensation payable in consequence of anything done under Chapters I, II or IV of Part I or sections 32 to 37, 56, 59, 60, 66(1), 67, 68 or 73, the Secretary of State may, if it appears to him to be expedient to do so, require any other local authority to contribute towards those expenses such sum as appears to him to be reasonable, having regard to any benefit accruing to that authority by reason of the proceeding giving rise to the compensation.

(4) For the purposes of subsections (2) and (3), contributions made by a local planning authority towards the expenditure of a joint advisory committee shall be deemed to be expenses incurred by that authority for the purposes for which that expenditure is incurred by the committee.

(5) The council of a county may direct that any expenses incurred by them under the provisions specified in subsection (6) shall be treated as special expenses of a county council chargeable upon such part of the county as may be specified in the directions.

(6) Those provisions are—
(a) sections 1(1) to (5), 2(1) to (3), 51, 52, 64, 65, 66(2), 82(1) and (4)(b), 83, 86 (except subsection (2)(a)), 87, 88 (except subsection (3)) and subsections (1) to (4) of this section and any other provisions of the planning Acts in so far as they apply, or have effect for the purposes of, any of those provisions; and
(b) sections 1(6), 3, 4, 5, 7 to 29, 32 to 50 (except 39(6)), 60(1) to (4), 61, 66(1), 67(2)(b), (6) and (7), 73(1) (so far as it applies to section 67(2)(b), (6) and (7)), 82(2), (3) and (4)(a) and Schedules 1, 2 and 3.

(7) There shall be paid out of money provided by Parliament—
(a) any sums necessary to enable the Secretary of State to make any payments becoming payable by him under sections 27 to 29;
(b) any expenses incurred by any government department (including the Secretary of State) in the acquisition of land under sections 47 to 52 or in the payment of compensation under section 51(4) or 88(7) or under subsection (1);
(c) any administrative expenses incurred by the Secretary of State for the purposes of this Act.

(8) Any sums received by the Secretary of State under this Act shall be paid into the Consolidated Fund.

PART IV
SUPPLEMENTAL

91. Interpretation

(1) In this Act, except in so far as the context otherwise requires—
'building preservation notice' has the meaning given in section 3(1);
'the Commission' means the Historic Buildings and Monuments Commission for England;
'conservation area' means an area for the time being designated under section 69;
'conservation area consent' has the meaning given in section 74(1);

'listed building' has the meaning given in section 1(5);
'listed building consent' has the meaning given in section 8(7);
'listed building enforcement notice' has the meaning given in section 38(1);
'listed building purchase notice' has the meaning given in section 32(1);
'local planning authority' shall be construed in accordance with section 81;
'prescribed', except in relation to matters expressly required or authorised by this Act to be prescribed in some other way, means prescribed by regulations under this Act;
'the principal Act' means the Town and Country Planning Act 1990;
'town scheme agreement' has the meaning given in section 79.

(2) Subject to subsections (6) and (7) and except in so far as the context otherwise requires, the following expressions have the same meaning as in the principal Act—
'the 1962 Act'
'acquiring authority'
'the Broads'
'building'
'compulsory acquisition'
'development'
'development order'
'development plan'
'disposal'
'enactment'
'functions'
'government department'
'joint planning board'
'land'
'lease'
'local authority'
'London borough'
'minerals'
'Minister'
'owner'
'the planning Acts'
'planning permission'
'public gas supplier'
'use'
'Valuation Office',
but this subsection does not affect the meaning of 'owner' in section 11.

(3) In this Act 'statutory undertakers' has the same meaning as in the principal Act except that—

(a) in sections 33 to 36 it shall be deemed to include references to a public telecommunications operator;

(b) in sections 33 to 36, 51(2)(a) and 90(2) it shall be deemed to include the Post Office, the Civil Aviation Authority, a public gas supplier, a holder of a licence under section 6 of the Electricity Act 1989, the National Rivers Authority and every water or sewerage undertaker.

(4) References in the planning Acts to any of the provisions mentioned in section 82 include, except where the context otherwise requires, references to those provisions as modified under that section.

(5) Words in this Act importing a reference to service of a notice to treat shall be construed as including a reference to the constructive service of such a notice which, by virtue of any enactment, is to be deemed to be served.

(6) In sections 33 to 36, 53(1) 54, 55 and 88(3) 'local authority', in relation to a building or land in the Broads, includes the Broads Authority.

(7) For the purposes of subsection (1)(b) of section 57 and subsection (2) of that section as it applies for the purposes of that subsection the definition of 'building' in the principal Act shall apply with the omission of the words 'but does not include any plant or machinery comprised in a building'.

92. Application of Act to Isles of Scilly

(1) The Secretary of State shall, after consultation with the Council of the Isles of Scilly, by order provide for the application to those Isles of the provisions of this Act specified in subsection (2) as if those Isles were a separate county.

(2) The provisions referred to in subsection (1) are—

(a) sections 1(1) to (5), 2(1) to (3), 51, 52, 64, 65, 66(2), 82(1) and (4)(b), 83, 84, 86 (except subsection (2)(a)), 87, 88 (except subsection (3)), 90(1) to (4) and any other provisions of the planning Acts in so far as they apply, or have effect for the purposes of, any of those provisions; and

(b) sections 1(6), 3, 4, 5, 7 to 29, 32 to 50 (except 39(6)), 60(1) to (4), 61, 66(1), 67(2)(b), (6) and (7), 73(1) (so far as it applies to section 67(2)(b), (6) and (7)), 75(1), (5) and (6), 82(2), (3) and (4)(a) and Schedules 1, 2 and 3.

(3) The Secretary of State, may, after consultation with the Council of the Isles of Scilly, by order provide for the application to those Isles of sections 2(4) and (5), 53 to 55, 59, 67(1) to (6), 69 to 72, 73(1), 74 to 76 and 88(3) and paragraph 4 of Schedule 4 as if those Isles were a separate county or district.

(4) Any order under this section may provide for the application of provisions to the Isles subject to such modifications as may be specified in the order.

93. Regulations and orders

(1) The Secretary of State may make regulations under this Act—

(a) for prescribing the form of any notice, order or other document authorised or required by any of the provisions of this Act to be served, made or issued by any local authority, or National Park Authority;

(b) for any purpose for which regulations are authorised or required to be made under this Act.

(2) Any power conferred by this Act to make regulations shall be exercisable by statutory instrument.

(3) Any statutory instrument containing regulations made under this Act shall be subject to annulment in pursuance of a resolution of either House of Parliament.

(4) The power to make orders under sections 8(5), 60, 75(7) and 92 shall be exercisable by statutory instrument.

(5) Any statutory instrument which contains an order under section 60 or 75(7) shall be subject to annulment in pursuance of a resolution of either House of Parliament.

(6) Any order under section 60 or 75(7) may contain such supplementary and incidental provisions as may appear to the Secretary of State appropriate.

(7) Without prejudice to section 14 of the Interpretation Act 1978, any power conferred by this Act to make an order shall include power to vary or revoke any such order by a subsequent order.

[The reference to a National Park Authority was inserted by the Environment Act 1995, see the note to Section 4A of the Town and Country Planning Act 1990 supra.]

94. Short title, commencement and extent

(1) This Act may be cited as the Planning (Listed Buildings and Conservation Areas) Act 1990.

(2) Except as provided in Schedule 4 to the Planning (Consequential Provisions) Act 1990, this Act shall come into force at the end of the period of three months beginning with the day on which it is passed.

(3) This Act extends to England and Wales only.

SCHEDULE 1
BUILDINGS FORMERLY SUBJECT TO BUILDING PRESERVATION ORDERS

1. Subject to paragraph 2, every building which immediately before 1st January 1969 was subject to a building preservation order under Part III of the 1962 Act, but was not then included in a list compiled or approved under section 32 of that Act, shall be deemed to be a listed building.

2.—(1) The Secretary of State may at any time direct, in the case of any building, that paragraph 1 shall no longer apply to it.

(2) The local planning authority in whose area a building in respect of which such a direction is given is situated shall, on being notified of the direction, give notice of it to the owner and occupier of the building.

(3) Before giving such a direction in relation to a building situated in England, the Secretary of State shall consult with the Commission who shall in turn consult with the local planning authority and the owner and occupier of the building.

(4) Before giving such a direction in relation to a building not situated in England, the Secretary of State shall consult with the local planning authority and the owner and occupier of the building.

3. In the case of a building to which paragraph 1 applies—

(a) a notice of appeal under section 20 may include a claim that the Secretary of State should give a direction under paragraph 2 with respect to the building and on such an appeal the Secretary of State may give such a direction; and

(b) such a direction may also be given on an appeal under section 39.

SCHEDULE 2
LAPSE OF BUILDING PRESERVATION NOTICES

1. This Schedule applies where a building preservation notice ceases to be in force by virtue of—

(a) the expiry of the six month period mentioned in subsection (3)(b) of section 3; or

(b) the service of a notification by the Secretary of State under subsection (4)(b) of that section.

2. The fact that the notice has ceased to be in force shall not affect the liability of any person to be prosecuted and punished for an offence under section 9 or 43 committed with respect to the building while it was in force.

3. Any proceedings on or arising out of an application for listed building consent with respect to the building made while the notice was in force and any such consent granted while it was in force shall lapse.

4.—(1) Any listed building enforcement notice served by the local planning authority while the building preservation notice was in force shall cease to have effect.

(2) Any proceedings on it under sections 38 to 40 shall lapse.

(3) Notwithstanding sub-paragraph (1), section 42(1) and (2) shall continue to have effect as respects any expenses incurred by the local authority, owner or occupier as mentioned in that section and with respect to any sums paid on account of such expenses.

[(4) The reference to a local authority in sub-paragraph (3) above includes a reference to any National Park authority which is the local planning authority for any area.]

[This provision was inserted by the Environment Act 1995, see the note to section 4A of the Town and Country Planning Act 1990 supra.]

SCHEDULE 3
DETERMINATION OF CERTAIN APPEALS BY PERSON APPOINTED BY SECRETARY OF STATE

Determination of appeals by appointed person

1.—(1) The Secretary of State may by regulations prescribe the classes of appeals under sections 20 and 39 which are to be determined by a person appointed by the Secretary of State for the purpose instead of by the Secretary of State.

(2) Appeals of a prescribed class shall be so determined except in such classes of case as may for the time being be prescribed or as may be specified in directions given by the Secretary of State.

(3) Regulations made for the purpose of this paragraph may provide for the giving of publicity to any directions given by the Secretary of State under this paragraph.

(4) This paragraph shall not affect any provision in this Act or any instrument made under it that an appeal shall lie to, or a notice of appeal shall be served on, the Secretary of State.

(5) A person appointed under this paragraph is referred to in this Schedule as 'an appointed person'.

Powers and duties of appointed person

2.—(1) An appointed person shall have the same powers and duties—

(a) in relation to an appeal under section 20, as the Secretary of State has under subsection (1) of section 22 and paragraph 2 of Schedule 1; and

(b) in relation to an appeal under section 39, as he has under section 41(1), (2),(2A), (5) or (6) and paragraph 2 of Schedule 1.

(2) Sections 22(2) and 40(2) shall not apply to an appeal which falls to be determined by an appointed person, but before it is determined the Secretary of State shall ask the appellant and the local planning authority whether they wish to appear before and be heard by the appointed person.

(3) If both the parties express a wish not to appear and be heard the appeal may be determined without their being heard.

(4) If either of the parties expresses a wish to appear and be heard, the appointed person shall give them both an opportunity of doing so.

(5) Where an appeal has been determined by an appointed person, his decision shall be treated as that of the Secretary of State.

(6) Except as provided by sections 62 to 65, the validity of that decision shall not be questioned in any proceedings whatsoever.

(7) It shall not be a ground of application to the High Court under section 63, or of appeal to the High Court under section 65, that an appeal ought to have been determined by the Secretary of State and not by an appointed person, unless the appellant or the local planning authority challenge the appointed person's power to determine the appeal before his decision on the appeal is given.

(8) Where in any enactment (including this Act) there is a reference to the Secretary of State in a context relating or capable of relating—

(a) to an appeal under section 20 or 39, or

(b) to anything done or authorised or required to be done by, to or before the Secretary of State on or in connection with any such appeal,

then so far as the context permits it shall be construed, in relation to an appeal determined or falling to be determined by an appointed person, as a reference to him.

Determination of appeals by Secretary of State

3.—(1) The Secretary of State may, if he thinks fit, direct that an appeal which would otherwise fall to be determined by an appointed person shall instead be determined by the Secretary of State.

(2) Such a direction shall state the reasons for which it is given and shall be served on the appellant, the local planning authority, any person who made representations relating to the subject matter of the appeal which the authority were required to take into account by regulations made under section 11(4) and, if any person has been appointed under paragraph 1, on him.

(3) Where in consequence of such a direction an appeal under section 20 or 39 falls to be determined by the Secretary of State himself, the provisions of this Act which are relevant to the appeal shall, subject to the following provisions of this paragraph, apply to the appeal as if this Schedule had never applied to it.

(4) The Secretary of State shall give the appellant, the local planning authority and any person who has made such representations as are referred to in sub-paragraph (2) an opportunity of appearing before and being heard by a person appointed by the Secretary of State for that purpose if—

    (a) the reasons for the direction raise matters with respect to which any of those persons have not made representations; or

    (b) in the case of the appellant and the local planning authority, either of them was not asked in pursuance of paragraph 2(2) whether they wished to appear before and be heard by the appointed person, or expressed no wish in answer to that question, or expressed a wish to appear and be heard but was not given an opportunity of doing so.

(5) Except as provided by sub-paragraph (4), the Secretary of State need not give any person an opportunity of appearing before and being heard by a person appointed for the purpose, or of making fresh representations or making or withdrawing any representations already made.

(6) In determining the appeal the Secretary of State may take into account any report made to him by any person previously appointed to determine it.

4.—(1) The Secretary of State may by a further direction revoke a direction under paragraph 3 at any time before the determination of the appeal.

(2) Such a further direction shall state the reasons for which it is given and shall be served on the person, if any, previously appointed to determine the appeal, the appellant, the local planning authority and any person who made representations relating to the subject matter of the appeal which the authority were required to take into account by regulations made under section 11(4).

(3) Where such a further direction has been given the provisions of this Schedule relevant to the appeal shall apply, subject to sub-paragraph (4), as if no direction under paragraph 3 had been given.

(4) Anything done by or on behalf of the Secretary of State in connection with the appeal which might have been done by the appointed person (including any arrangements made for the holding of a hearing or local inquiry) shall unless that person directs otherwise, be treated as having been done by him.

Appointment of another person to determine appeal

5.—(1) At any time before the appointed person has determined the appeal the Secretary of State may—

    (a) revoke his appointment; and

    (b) appoint another person under paragraph 1 to determine the appeal instead.

(2) Where such a new appointment is made the consideration of the appeal or any inquiry or other hearing in connection with it shall be begun afresh.

(3) Nothing in sub-paragraph (2) shall require—

    (a) the question referred to in paragraph 2(2) to be asked again with reference to the new appointed person if before his appointment it was asked with reference to the previous appointed person (any answers being treated as given with reference to the new appointed person); or

(b) any person to be given an opportunity of making fresh representations or modifying or withdrawing any representations already made.

Local inquiries and hearings

6.—(1) Whether or not the parties to an appeal have asked for an opportunity to appear and be heard, an appointed person—
  (a) may hold a local inquiry in connection with the appeal; and
  (b) shall do so if the Secretary of State so directs.

(2) Where an appointed person—
  (a) holds a hearing by virtue of paragraph 2(4); or
  (b) holds an inquiry by virtue of this paragraph,
an assessor may be appointed by the Secretary of State to sit with the appointed person at the hearing or inquiry to advise him on any matters arising, notwithstanding that the appointed person is to determine the appeal.

(3) Subject to sub-paragraph (4), the costs of any such hearing or inquiry shall be paid by the Secretary of State.

(4) Section 250(2) to (5) of the Local Government Act 1972 (local inquiries: evidence and costs) applies to an inquiry held by virtue of this paragraph with the following adaptations—
  (a) for the references in subsection (4) (recovery of costs of holding the inquiry) to the Minister causing the inquiry to be held, there shall be substituted references to the Secretary of State; and
  (b) for the reference in subsection (5) (orders as to the costs of the parties) to the Minister causing the inquiry to be held, there shall be substituted a reference to the appointed person or the Secretary of State.

(5) Subject to sub-paragraph (6), at any such inquiry oral evidence shall be heard in public and documentary evidence shall be open to public inspection.

(6) If the Secretary of State is satisfied in the case of any such inquiry—
  (a) that giving evidence of a particular description or, as the case may be, making it available for inspection would be likely to result in the disclosure of information as to any of the matters mentioned in subparagraph (7); and
  (b) that the public disclosure of that information would be contrary to the national interest,
he may direct that evidence of the description indicated in the direction shall only be heard or, as the case may be, open to inspection at that inquiry by such persons or persons of such descriptions as he may specify in that direction.

(7) The matters referred to in sub-paragraph (6)(a) are—
  (a) national security; and
  (b) the measures taken or to be taken to ensure the security of any premises or property.

(8) The appointed person or the Secretary of State has the same power to make orders under section 250(5) of the Local Government Act 1972 (orders with respect to costs of the parties) in relation to proceedings under this Schedule which do not give rise to an inquiry as he has in relation to such an inquiry.

Supplementary provisions

7.—(1) The Tribunals and Inquiries Act 1992 shall apply to a local inquiry or other hearing held in pursuance of this Schedule as it applies to a statutory inquiry held by the Secretary of State, but as if in section 12(1) of that Act (statement of reasons for decisions) the reference to any decision taken by the Secretary of State were a reference to a decision taken by an appointed person.

(2) Where an appointed person is an officer of the Department of the Environment or the Welsh Office the functions of determining an appeal and doing anything

in connection with it conferred on him by this Schedule shall be treated for the purposes of the Parliamentary Commissioner Act 1967—
  (a) if he was appointed by the Secretary of State for the time being having general responsibility in planning matters in relation to England, as functions of that Department; and
  (b) if he was appointed by the Secretary of State for the time being having general responsibility in planning matters in relation to Wales, as functions of the Welsh Office.

SCHEDULE 4
FURTHER PROVISIONS AS TO EXERCISE OF FUNCTIONS BY DIFFERENT AUTHORITIES

1.—(1) Subsection (3) of section 1 of the principal Act (which provides that outside London, the metropolitan counties and the Isles of Scilly planning functions are exercisable by both county and district planning authorities) shall have effect subject to paragraphs 2, 4 and 5, and that section and section 2 of the principal Act (joint planning boards) shall have effect subject to paragraph 3.
  [(2) This Schedule shall apply in relation to Wales as if—
  (a) paragraphs 2 to 5 were omitted;
  (b) in paragraph 7, each reference to a district planning authority (or which is to be construed as such a reference) were a reference to the local planning authority.]
[Inserted by and to take effect under the Local Government (Wales) Act 1994.]
  2. Subject to sections 4, 4A, 6, 7, 8 and 8A of the principal Act (which make provision as to the exercise of planning functions in National Parks, enterprise zones, urban development areas and housing action areas) and to the following provisions, outside Greater London the functions of a local planning authority under sections 7 to 26, 38, 42, paragraph 2(2) of Schedule 1 and Schedule 2 shall be exercised by the district planning authority.
['4' is to be repealed under the Environment Act 1995.]
  3. Where an application for listed building consent under section 10 relating to land in a National Park falls to be determined by a National Park Authority or <u>county planning authority</u>, that authority—
  (a) shall send a copy of the application, as soon as practicable and in any event not later than seven days after they have received it, to any authority only which (but for section 4A) would be <u>or, as the case may be, which is the district planning authority for the area in which the land to which the application relates is situated; and</u>
  (b) shall before determining the application consult the <u>district planning</u> authority. [The words underlined are to be repealed and replaced by the words 'any such' and all other modifications brought about under the Environment Act 1995, see note to Section 4A of the Town and Country Planning Act 1990 supra.]
  4.—(1) Subject to sections <u>4(3) and (4)</u>, 6, 7, 8 and 8A of the principal Act, the functions of a local planning authority under sections 67(2) and (3), 69, 70 and 74 and paragraph 2(3) and (4) of Schedule 1 shall be exercisable—
  (a) in Greater London or a metropolitan county [or in any National Park for which a National Park Authority is the local planning authority], by the local planning authority;
  (b) in any part of a National Park <u>outside a metropolitan county</u>, by the county planning authority; and
  (c) elsewhere, by the district planning authority;
but outside a National Park a county planning authority shall also have power to make determinations and designations under section 69.
[The words underlined are to be repealed and replaced by 'to which paragraph (a) above does not apply' under the Environment Act 1995, see note to Section 4A of the Town and Country Planning Act 1990 supra.]

(2) Before making a determination under section 69 a county planning authority or National Park Authority shall consult the council of each district of which any part is included in the area to which the proposed determination relates. [The reference to a National Park Authority was inserted by the Environment Act 1995.]

(3) Where it is the duty of the district planning authority to take the steps required by section 67(2) in relation to an application which falls to be determined by the county planning authority, the district planning authority shall as soon as possible after taking those steps notify the county planning authority of the steps which they have taken and the date on which they took them.

5. For the purposes of sections 3 and 4, 7 to 26, 38, 42, 56, 66(1), 67, 69 to 75, 82, 84 and 88(2)(c) and (d) and the provisions of this Schedule so far as they relate to those provisions, the Broads Authority shall be the sole district planning authority in respect of the Broads, and in relation to a building or land within the Broads—

(a) the references to the district planning authority in section 2(1)(b)(iii) and in paragraph 4(1)(c) of this Schedule, so far as that paragraph relates to paragraph 2(3) and (4) of Schedule 1, include that Authority; and

(b) for the purposes of sections 6, 44A, 88(2)(a) and (b) and 88A 'local planning authority' includes that Authority.

6. The validity of any consent or determination granted or made or purported to be granted or made by a local planning authority in respect of an application for listed building consent or conservation area consent shall not be called in question in any legal proceedings, or in any proceedings under this Act which are not legal proceedings, on the ground that the consent or determination should have been granted or made by some other local planning authority.

7.—(1) The Secretary of State may from time to time direct a district planning authority to submit to him for his approval within a period specified in the direction the arrangements which the authority propose to make to obtain specialist advice in connection with their functions under sections 3, 4, 8, 10 to 26, 38, 42, 66(1), 69 to 72, 74 and 75.

(2) If the Secretary of State is not satisfied about any such arrangements he may direct the district planning authority and another local planning authority specified in the direction—

(a) to enter into an agreement under section 113 of the Local Government Act 1972 for the placing at the disposal of the district planning authority, for the purpose of giving them any such specialist advice, of the services of officers employed by that other authority who are qualified to give such advice; or

(b) to enter into arrangements, containing terms specified in the direction or terms on lines laid down by him, for the discharge by that other authority of any of those functions.

(3) Before giving a direction under sub-paragraph (2) the Secretary of State shall consult with the district planning authority and the other authority concerned.

ENVIRONMENT ACT 1995
(1995, c. 25)

SCHEDULES

Section
96 Mineral Planning Permissions
Schedule 9 —Para 13 Listed and historic buildings
Schedule 13—Review of old mineral planning permissions
Schedule 14—Periodic review of mineral planning permissions

[The 1995 Act is generally to be brought into effect by appointed day orders made under Section 125. However, Part III, which relates to National Parks, including

Environment Act 1995

planning functions in National Parks, came into force at the end of two months beginning with the date of the Act's passage. In this edition references to Scotland and to Scottish legislation are omitted.]

[19th July 1995]

Mineral planning permissions

96.—(1)   Schedules 13 and 14 to this Act shall have effect.

(2)   This section, those Schedules as they apply to England and Wales, and the 1990 Act shall have effect as if this section and those Schedules (as so applying) were included in Part III of that Act.

(3)   . . . [omitted in this edition]

(4)   Section 105 of the 1990 Act . . . shall cease to have effect.

(5)   Without prejudice to the generality of sections 59 to 61 of the 1990 Act . . . a development order may make, in relation to any planning permission which is granted by a development order for minerals development, provision similar to any provision made by Schedule 13 or 14 to this Act.

(6)   In this section and those Schedules—

. . . [omitted in this edition]

'the 1990 Act' means the Town and Country Planning Act 1990;

[portions omitted or rendered as . . . in the extracts from the 1995 Act relate to Scotland]

SCHEDULE 9

Listed and historic buildings

13.—(1)   In the case of a building situated in a National Park for which a National Park authority is the local planning authority, that authority and no other authority shall be the appropriate authority for the purposes of sections 47 to 51 of the Planning (Listed Buildings and Conservation Areas) Act 1990 (purchase of listed buildings etc in need of repair); and the reference to a local authority in section 88(5) of that Act (rights of entry) and in section 6 of the Historic Buildings and Ancient Monuments Act 1953 (under which grants for the acquisition of buildings in Wales may be made) shall have effect accordingly,

(2)   In relation to any building or land in any such National Park, the powers conferred on a county council or county borough council by section 52 of that Act of 1990 (power to acquire building and land by agreement) shall be exercisable by the National Park authority, and not (without prejudice to their powers apart from that section) by any other authority; and subsection (2) of that section shall have effect accordingly.

(3)   Section 53(1) of that Act (management of listed buildings etc. acquired under the Act) shall apply in relation to the powers conferred by virtue of this paragraph on a National Park authority as it applies in relation to the powers conferred by sections 47 and 52 of that Act on a local authority.

(4)   That Act shall have effect as if a National Park authority were a local authority for the purposes of—

(a)   sections 54 and 55 of that Act (urgent works to preserve listed buildings etc.), and

(b)   sections 57 and 58 of that Act (power of local authorities to contribute towards preservation of listed buildings etc.),

and, in relation to those provisions, as if the relevant Park were the authority's area.

(5)   In relation to the powers conferred on a National Park authority by virtue of this paragraph, section 88 of that Act (powers of entry) shall have effect as if references in that section to a local authority included references to a National Park authority.

(6) References to a local authority in section 90(1) to (4) of that Act (financial provisions) shall be deemed to include references to a National Park authority.

SCHEDULE 13
REVIEW OF OLD MINERAL PLANNING PERMISSIONS

Interpretation

1.—(1) In this Schedule—
'dormant site' means a Phase I or Phase II site in, on or under which no minerals development has been carried out to any substantial extent at any time in the period beginning on 22nd February 1982 and ending with 6th June 1995 otherwise than by virtue of a planning permission which is not a relevant planning permission relating to the site;
'first list', in relation to a mineral planning authority, means the list prepared by them pursuant to paragraph 3 below;
'mineral planning authofity'—
    (a) as respects England and Wales, means a mineral planning authority within the meaning of the 1990 Act, and
    (b) . . .
'mineral site' has the meaning given by sub-paragraph (2) below;
'National Park' means an area designated as such under section 5(3) of the National Parks and Access to the Countryside Act 1949;
'old mining permission' has the meaning given—
    (a) as respects England and Wales, by section 22(1) of the 1991 Act, and
    (b) . . .
'owner' in relation to any land—
    (a) as respects England and Wales, means any person who—
        (i) is the estate owner in respect of the fee simple, or
        (ii) is entitled to a tenancy granted or extended for a term of years certain of which not less than seven years remains unexpired; and
    (b) . . .
'Phase I site' and 'Phase II site' have the meaning given by paragraph 2 below;
'relevant planning permission' means any planning permission, other than an old mining permission or a planning permission granted by a development order, granted after 30th June 1948 for minerals development; and
'second list', in relation to a mineral planning authority, means the list prepared by them pursuant to paragraph 4 below.

(2) For the purposes of this Schedule, but subject to sub-paragraph (3) below, 'mineral site' means—
    (a) in a case where it appears to the mineral planning authority to be expedient to treat as a single site the aggregate of the land to which any two or more relevant planning permissions relate, the aggregate of the land to which those permissions relate; and
    (b) in any other case, the land to which a relevant planning permission relates,

(3) In determining whether it appears to them to be expedient to treat as a single site the aggregate of the land to which two or more relevant planning permissions relate a mineral planning authority shall have regard to any guidance issued for the purpose by the Secretary of State.

(4) Any reference (however expressed) in this Schedule to an old mining permission or a relevant planning permission relating to a mineral site is a reference to the mineral site, or some part of it, being the land to which the permission relates; and where any such permission authorises the carrying out of development consisting

of the winning and working of minerals but only in respect of any particular mineral or minerals, that permission shall not be taken, for the purposes of this Schedule, as relating to any other mineral in, on or under the land to which the permission relates.

(5) For the purposes of this Schedule, a mineral site which is a Phase I site or a Phase II site is active if it is not a dormant site.

(6) For the purposes of this Schedule, working rights are restricted in respect of a mineral site if any of—

(a) the size of the area which may be used for the winning and working of minerals or the depositing of mineral waste;

(b) the depth to which operations for the winning and working of minerals may extend;

(c) the height of any deposit of mineral waste;

(d) the rate at which any particular mineral may be extracted;

(e) the rate at which any particular mineral waste may be deposited;

(f) the period at the expiry of which any winning or working of minerals or depositing of mineral waste is to cease; or

(g) the total quantity of minerals which may be extracted from, or of mineral waste which may be deposited on, the site,

is restricted or reduced in respect of the mineral site in question.

(7) For the purposes of this Schedule, where an application is made under paragraph 9 below for the determination of the conditions to which the relevant planning permissions relating to the mineral site to which the application relates are to be subject, those conditions are finally determined when—

(a) the proceedings on the application, including any proceedings on or in consequence of an application under section 288 of the 1990 Act . . . have been determined, and

(b) any time for appealing under paragraph 11(1) below, or applying or further applying under paragraph 9 below, (where there is a right to do so) has expired.

Phase I and II sites

2.—(1) This paragraph has effect for the purposes of determining which mineral sites are Phase I sites, which are Phase II sites, and which are neither Phase I nor Phase II sites.

(2) A mineral site is neither a Phase I site nor a Phase II site where—

(a) all the relevant planning permissions which relate to the site have been granted after 21st February 1982; or

(b) some only of the relevant planning permissions which relate to the site have been granted after 21st February 1982, and the parts of the site to which those permissions relate constitute the greater part of that site.

(3) With the exception of those mineral sites which, by virtue of sub-paragraph (2) above, are neither Phase I nor Phase II sites, every mineral site is either a Phase I site or a Phase II site.

(4) Subject to sub-paragraph (2) above, where any part of a mineral site is situated within—

(a) a National Park;

(b) a site in respect of which a notification under section 28 of the Wildlife and Countryside Act 1981 (sites of special scientific interest) is in force;

(c) an area designated under section 87 of the National Parks and Access to the Countryside Act 1949 as an area of outstanding natural beauty;

(d) . . .

(e) . . .

that site is a Phase I site.

(5) Subject to sub-paragraphs (2) and (4) above, where—

(a) all the relevant planning permissions which relate to a mineral site, and which were not granted after 21st February 1982, were granted after the relevant day in 1969; or

(b) the parts of a mineral site to which relate such of the relevant planning permissions relating to the site as were granted after the relevant day in 1969 but before 22nd February 1982 constitute a greater part of the site than is constituted by those parts of the site to which no such relevant planning permission relates but to which a relevant planning permission granted on or before the relevant day in 1969 does relate,

the mineral site is a Phase II site.

(6) In sub-paragraph (5) above, 'the relevant day in 1969' means—
   (a) as respects England and Wales, 31st March 1969; and
   (b) . . .

(7) Every other mineral site, that is to say any mineral site other than one—
   (a) which is, by virtue of sub-paragraph (2) above, neither a Phase I nor a Phase II site; or
   (b) which is a Phase I site by virtue of sub-paragraph (4) above; or
   (c) which is a Phase II site by virtue of sub-paragraph (5) above,
is a Phase I site.

(8) In ascertaining, for the purposes of sub-paragraph (2) or (5) above, whether any parts of a mineral site constitute the greater part of that site, or whether a part of a mineral site is greater than any other part, that mineral site shall be treated as not including any part of the site—
   (a) to which an old mining permission relates; or
   (b) which is a part where minerals development has been (but is no longer being) carried out and which has, in the opinion of the mineral planning authority, been satisfactorily restored;
but no part of a site shall be treated, by virtue of paragraph (b) above, as being not included in the site unless the mineral planning authority are satisfied that any aftercare conditions which relate to that part have, so far as relating to that part, been complied with.

The 'first list'

3.—(1) A mineral planning authority shall, in accordance with the following provisions of this paragraph, prepare a list of mineral sites in their area ('the first list').

(2) A site shall, but shall only, be included in the first list if it is a mineral site in the area of the mineral planning authority and is either—
   (a) an active Phase I site;
   (b) an active Phase II site; or
   (c) a dormant site.

(3) In respect of each site included in the first list, the list shall indicate whether the site is an active Phase I site, an active Phase II site or a dormant site.

(4) In respect of each active Phase I site included in the first list, that list shall specify the date by which an application is to be made to the mineral planning authority under paragraph 9 below.

(5) Any date specified pursuant to sub-paragraph (4) above shall be a date—
   (a) not earlier than the date upon which expires the period of 12 months from the date on which the first list is first advertised in accordance with paragraph 5 below, and
   (b) not later than the date upon which expires the period of three years from the date upon which the provisions of this Schedule come into force.

(6) The preparation of the first list shall be completed before the day upon which it is first advertised in accordance with paragraph 5 below.

The 'second list'

4.—(1) A mineral planning authority shall, in accordance with the following provisions of this paragraph, prepare a list of the active Phase II sites in their area ('the second list').

(2) The second list shall include each mineral site in the mineral planning authority's area which is an active Phase II site.

(3) In respect of each site included in the second list, that list shall indicate the date by which an application is to be made to the mineral planning authority under paragraph 9 below.

(4) Subject to paragraph (5) below, any date specified pursuant to sub-paragraph (3) above shall be a date—

(a) not earlier than the date upon which expires the period of 12 months from the date on which the second list is first advertised in accordance with paragraph 5 below, and

(b) not later than the date upon which expires the period of six years from the date upon which the provisions of this Schedule come into force.

(5) The Secretary of State may by order provide that sub-paragraph (4)(b) above shall have effect as if for the period of six years referred to in that paragraph there were substituted such longer period specified in the order.

(6) The power of the Secretary of State to make an order under sub-paragraph (5) above shall be exercisable by statutory instrument; and any statutory instrument containing such an order shall be subject to annulment in pursuance of a resolution of either House of Parliament.

(7) The preparation of the second list shall be completed before the day upon which it is first advertised in accordance with paragraph 5 below.

Advertisement of the first and second lists

5.—(1) This paragraph makes provision for the advertisement of the first and second lists prepared by a mineral planning authority.

(2) The mineral planning authority shall advertise each of the first and second lists by causing to be published, in each of two successive weeks, in one or more newspapers circulating in its area, notice of the list having been prepared.

(3) In respect of each of those lists, such notice shall—

(a) state that the list has been prepared by the authority; and

(b) specify one or more places within the area of the authority at which the list may be inspected, and in respect of each such place specify the times (which shall be reasonable times) during which facilities for inspection of the list will be afforded.

(4) In respect of the first list, such notice shall—

(a) be first published no later than the day upon which expires the period of three months from the date upon which the provisions of this Schedule come into force;

(b) explain the general effect of a mineral site being classified as a dormant site or, as the case may be, as an active Phase I site or an active Phase II site;

(c) explain the consequences which will occur if no application is made under paragraph 9 below in respect of an active Phase I site included in the list by the date specified in the list for that site;

(d) explain the effects for any dormant or active Phase I or II site not included in the list of its not being included in the list and—

(i) set out the right to make an application to the authority for that site to be included in the list;

(ii) set out the date by which such an application must be made; and

(iii) state that the owner of such a site has a right of appeal against any decision of the authority upon such an application; and

(e) explain that the owner of an active Phase I site has a right to apply for postponement of the date specified in the list for the making of an application under paragraph 9 below, and set out the date by which an application for such postponement must be made.

(5) In respect of the second list, such notice shall—

(a) be first published no later than the day upon which expires the period of three years, or such longer period as the Secretary of State may by order specify, from the date upon which the provisions of this Schedule come into force; and

(b) explain the consequences which will occur if no application is made under paragraph 9 below in respect of an active Phase II site included in the list by the date specified in the list for that site.

(6) The power of the Secretary of State to make an order under sub-paragraph (5) above shall be exercisable by statutory instrument; and any statutory instrument containing such an order shall be subject to annulment in pursuance of a resolution of either House of Parliament.

Applications for inclusion in the first list of sites not included in that list as originally prepared and appeals from decisions upon such applications

6.—(1) Any person who is the owner of any land, or is entitled to an interest in a mineral, may, if that land or interest is not a mineral site included in the first list and does not form part of any mineral site included in that list, apply to the mineral planning authority for that land or interest to be included in that list.

(2) An application under sub-paragraph (1) above shall be made no later than the day upon which expires the period of three months from the day when the first list was first advertised in accordance with paragraph 5 above.

(3) Where the mineral planning authority consider that—

(a) the land or interest is, or forms part of, any dormant or active Phase I or II site, they shall accede to the application; or

(b) part only of the land or interest is, or forms part of, anv dormant or active Phase I or II site, they shall accede to the application so far as it relates to that part of the land or interest,

but shall otherwise refuse the application.

(4) On acceding, whether in whole or in part, to an application made under sub-paragraph (1) above, the mineral planning authority shall amend the first list as follows—

(a) where they consider that the land or interest, or any part of the land or interest, is a dormant site or an active Phase I or II site, they shall add the mineral site consisting of the land or interest or, as the case may be, that part, to the first list and shall cause the list to indicate whether the site is an active Phase I site, an active Phase II site or a dormant site;

(b) where they consider that the land or interest, or any part of the land or interest, forms part of any mineral site included in the first list, they shall amend the entry in the first list for that site accordingly.

(5) Where the mineral planning authority amend the first list in accordance with sub-paragraph (4) above, they shall also—

(a) in a case where an active Phase I site is added to the first list pursuant to paragraph (a) of that sub-paragraph, cause that list to specify, in respect of that site, the date by which an application is to be made to the mineral planning authority under paragraph 9 below;

(b) in a case where—

(i) the entry for an active Phase I site included in the first list is amended pursuant to paragraph (b) of that sub-paragraph; and

(ii) the date specified in that list in respect of that site as the date by which an application is to be made to the mineral planning authority under paragraph 9

Environment Act 1995   311

below is a date falling less than 12 months after the date upon which the authority make their decision upon the application in question,
cause that date to be amended so as to specify instead the date upon which expires the period of 12 months from the date on which the applicant is notified under sub-paragraph (10) below of the authority's decision upon his application.

(6) Any date specified pursuant to sub-paragraph (5)(a) above shall be a date—
    (a) not earlier than the date upon which expires the period of 12 months from the date on which the applicant is notified under sub-paragraph (10) below of the mineral planning authority's decision upon his application, and
    (b) not later than the later of—
        (i) the date upon which expires the period of three years from the date upon which the provisions of this Schedule come into force; and
        (ii) the date mentioned in paragraph (a) above.

(7) On acceding, whether in whole or in part, to an application made under sub-paragraph (1) above, the mineral planning authority shall, if the second list has been first advertised in accordance with paragraph 5 above prior to the time at which they make their decision on the application, amend the second list as follows—
    (a) where they consider that the land or interest, or any part of the land or interest, is an active Phase II site, they shall add the mineral site consisting of the land or interest or, as the case may be, that part, to the second list;
    (b) where they consider that the land or interest, or any part of the land or interest, forms part of any active Phase II site included in the second list, they shall amend the entry in that list for that site accordingly.

(8) Where the mineral planning authority amend the second list in accordance with sub-paragraph (7) above, they shall also—
    (a) in a case where an active Phase II site is added to the second list pursuant to paragraph (a) of that sub-paragraph, cause that list to specify, in respect of that site, the date by which an application is to be made to the authority under paragraph 9 below;
    (b) in a case where—
        (i) the entry for an active Phase II site included in the second list is amended pursuant to paragraph (b) of that sub-paragraph; and
        (ii) the date specified in that list in respect of that site as the date by which an application is to be made to the authority under paragraph 9 below is a date falling less than 12 months after the date upon which the authority make their decision upon the application in question,
cause that date to be amended so as to specify instead the date upon which expires the period of 12 months from the date on which the applicant is notified under sub-paragraph (10) below of the authority's decision upon his application.

(9) Any date specified pursuant to sub-paragraph (8)(a) above shall be a date—
    (a) not earlier than the date upon which expires the period of 12 months from the date on which the applicant is notified under sub-paragraph (10) below of the mineral planning authority's decision upon his application, and
    (b) not later than the later of—
        (i) the date upon which expires the period of six years from the date upon which the provisions of this Schedule come into force; and
        (ii) the date mentioned in paragraph (a) above.

(10) When a mineral planning authority determine an application made under sub-paragraph (1) above, they shall notify the applicant in writing of their decision and, in a case where they have acceded to the application, whether in whole or in part, shall supply the applicant with details of any amendment to be made to the first or second list in accordance with sub-paragraph (4) or (8) above.

(11) Where a mineral planning authority—

(a) refuse an application made under sub-paragraph (1) above; or

(b) accede to such an application only so far as it relates to part of the land or interest in respect of which it was made,

the applicant may by notice appeal to the Secretary of State.

(12) A person who has made such an application may also appeal to the Secretary of State if the mineral planning authority have not given notice to the applicant of their decision on the application within eight weeks of their having received the application or within such extended period as may at any time be agreed upon in writing between the applicant and the authority.

(13) An appeal under sub-paragraph (11) or (12) above must be made by giving notice of appeal to the Secretary of State before the end of the period of six months beginning with—

(a) In the case of an appeal under sub-paragraph (11) above, the determination; or

(b) in the case of an appeal under sub-paragraph (12) above, the end of the period of eight weeks mentioned in that sub-paragraph or, as the case may be, the end of the extended period mentioned in that sub-paragraph.

Postponement of the date specified in the first or second list for review of the permissions relating to a Phase I or II site in cases where the existing conditions are satisfactory

7.—(1) Any person who is the owner of any land, or of any interest in any mineral, comprised in—

(a) an active Phase I site included in the first list; or

(b) an active Phase II site included in the second list,

may apply to the mineral planning authority for the postponement of the date specified in that list in respect of that site as the date by which an application is to be made to the authority under paragraph 9 below (in this paragraph referred to as 'the specified date').

(2) Subject to sub-paragraph (3) below, an application under sub-paragraph (1) above shall be made no later than the day upon which expires the period of three months from the day when—

(a) in the case of an active Phase I site, the first list; or

(b) in the case of an active Phase II site, the second list,

was first advertised in accordance with paragraph 5 above.

(3) In the case of—

(a) an active Phase I site—

(i) added to the first list in accordance with paragraph 6(4)(a) above; or

(ii) in respect of which the entry in the first list was amended in accordance with paragraph 6(4)(b; above;

or

(b) an active Phase II site—

(i) added to the second list in accordance with paragraph 6(7)(a) above; or

(ii) in respect of which the entry in the second list was amended in accordance with paragraph 6(7)(b) above,

an application under sub-paragraph (1) above shall be made no later than the day upon which expires the period of three months from the day on which notice was given under paragraph 6(10) above of the mineral planning authority's decision to add the site to or, as the case may be, so to amend the list in question.

(4) An application under sub-paragraph (1) above shall be in writing and shall—

(a) set out the conditions to which each relevant planning permission relating to the site is subject,

(b) set out the applicant's reasons for considering those conditions to be satisfactory;

Environment Act 1995

(c) set out the date which the applicant wishes to be substituted for the specified date; and

(d) be accompanied by the appropriate certificate (within the meaning of sub-paragraph (5) or (6) below).

(5) For the purposes of sub-paragraph (4) above, as respects England and Wales the appropriate certificate is such a certificate—

(a) as would be required, under section 65 of the 1990 Act (notice etc. of applications for planning permission) and any provision of a development order made by virtue of that section, to accompany the application if it were an application for planning permission for minerals development, but

(b) with such modifications as are required for the purposes of this paragraph, and section 65(6) of that Act (offences) shall also have effect in relation to any certificate purporting to be the appropriate certificate,

(6) . . .

(7) Where the mineral planning authority receive an application made under sub-paragraph (1) above—

(a) if they consider the conditions referred to in sub-paragraph (4)(a) above to be satisfactory they shall agree to the specified date being postponed in which event they shall determine the date to be substituted for that date;

(b) in any other case they shall refuse the application.

(8) Where the mineral planning authority agree to the specified date being postponed they shall cause the first or, as the case may be, the second list to be amended accordingly.

(9) When a mineral planning authority determine an application made under sub-paragraph (1) above, they shall notify the applicant in writing of their decision and, in a case where they have agreed to the postponement of the specified date, shall notify the applicant of the date which they have determined should be substituted for the specified date.

(10) Where, within three months of the mineral planning authority having received an application under sub-paragraph (1) above, or within such extended period as may at any time be agreed upon in writing between the applicant and the authority, the authority have not given notice, under sub-paragraph (9) above, to the applicant of their decision upon the application, the authority shall be treated as—

(a) having agreed to the specified date being postponed; and

(b) having determined that the date referred to in sub-paragraph (4)(c) above be substituted for the specified date,

and sub-paragraph (8) above shall apply accordingly.

Service on owners etc. of notice of preparation of the first and second lists

8.—(1) The mineral planning authority shall, no later than the date upon which the first list is first advertised in accordance with paragraph 5 above, serve notice in writing of the first list having been prepared on each person appearing to them to be the owner of any land, or entitled to an interest in any mineral, included within a mineral site included in the first list, but this sub-paragraph is subject to sub-paragraph (7) below.

(2) A notice required to be served by sub-paragraph (1) above shall—

(a) indicate whether the mineral site in question is a dormant site or an active Phase I or II site; and

(b) Where that site is an active Phase I site—

(i) indicate the date specified in the first list in relation to that site as the date by which an application is to be made to the mineral planning authority under paragraph 9 below;

(ii) explain the consequences which will occur if such an application is not made by the date so specified; and

(iii) explain the right to apply to have that date postponed, and indicate the date by which such an application must be made.

(3) Where, in relation to any land or mineral included in an active Phase I site, the mineral planning authority—

(a) has served notice on any person under sub-paragraph (1) above; and

(b) has received no application under paragraph 9 below from that person by the date falling eight weeks before the date specified in the first list as the date by which such applications should be made in respect of the site in question,

the authority shall serve a written reminder on that person, and such a reminder shall—

(i) indicate that the land or mineral in question is included in an active Phase I site;

(ii) comply with the requirements of sub-paragraph (2)(b)(i) and (ii) above; and

(iii) be served on that person on or before the date falling four weeks before the date specified in the first list in respect of that site as the date by which an application is to be made to the authority under paragraph 9 below.

(4) The mineral planning authority shall, no later than the date upon which the second list is first advertised in accordance with paragraph 5 above, serve notice in writing of the second list having been prepared on each person appearing to them to be the owner of any land, or entitled to an interest in any mineral, included within an active Phase II site included in the second list, but this sub-paragraph is subject to sub-paragraph (7) below.

(5) A notice required to be served by sub-paragraph (4) above shall—

(a) indicate that the mineral site in question is an active Phase II site; and

(b) indicate the date specified in the second list in relation to that site as the date by which an application is to be made to the mineral planning authority under paragraph 9 below;

(c) explain the consequences which will occur if such an application is not made by the date so specified; and

(d) explain the right to apply to have that date postponed, and indicate the date by which such an application must be made.

(6) Where, in relation to any land or mineral included in an active Phase II site, the mineral planning authority—

(a) has served notice on any person under sub-paragraph (4) above; and

(b) has received no application under paragraph 9 below from that person by the date falling eight weeks before the date specified in the second list as the date by which such applications should be made in respect of the site in question,

the authority shall serve a written reminder on that person, and such a reminder shall—

(i) comply with the requirements of sub-paragraph (5)(a) to (c) above; and

(ii) be served on that person on or before the date falling four weeks before the date specified in the second list in respect of that site as the date by which an application is to be made to the authority under paragraph 9 below.

(7) Sub-paragraph (1) or (4) above shall not require the mineral planning authority to serve notice under that sub-paragraph upon any person whose identity or address for service is not known to and cannot practicably, after reasonable inquiry, be ascertained by them, but in any such case the authority shall cause to be firmly affixed, to each of one or more conspicuous objects on the land or, as the case may be, on the surface of the land above the interest in question, a copy of the notice which they would (apart from the provisions of this sub-paragraph) have had to serve under that sub-paragraph on the owner of that land or interest.

(8) If, in a case where sub-paragraph (7) above applies, no person makes an application to the authority under paragraph 9 below in respect of the active Phase I

or II site which includes the land or interest in question by the date falling eight weeks before the date specified in the first or, as the case may be, the second list as the date by which such applications should be made in respect of that site, the authority shall cause to be firmly affixed, to each of one or more conspicuous objects on the land or, as the case may be, on the surface of the land above the interest in question, a copy of the written reminder that would, in a case not falling within sub-paragraph (7) above, have been served under sub-paragraph (3) or (6) above.

(9) Where by sub-paragraph (7) or (8) above a copy of any notice is required to be affixed to an object on any land that copy shall—
    (a) be displayed in such a way as to be easily visible and legible;
    (b) be first displayed—
        (i) in a case where the requirement arises under sub-paragraph (7) above, no later than the date upon which the first or, as the case may be, the second list is first advertised in accordance with paragraph 5 above; or
        (ii) in a case where the requirement arises under sub-paragraph (8) above, no later than the date falling four weeks before the date specified in the first or, as the case may be, the second list in respect of the site in question as the date by which an application is to be made to the authority under paragraph 9 below; and
    (c) be left in position for at least the period of 21 days from the date when it is first displayed, but where the notice is, without fault or intention of the authority, removed, obscured or defaced before that period has elapsed, that requirement shall be treated as having been complied with if the authority has taken reasonable steps for protection of the notice and, if need be, its replacement.

(10) In sub-paragraphs (7) and (8) above, any reference to a conspicuous object on any land includes, in a case where the person serving a notice considers that there are no or insufficient such objects on the land, a reference to a post driven into or erected upon the land by the person serving the notice for the purpose of having affixed to it the notice in question.

(11) Where the mineral planning authority, being required—
    (a) by sub-paragraph (3) or (6) above to serve a written reminder on any person; or
    (b) by sub-paragraph (8) above to cause a copy of such a reminder to be displayed in the manner set out in that sub-paragraph,
fail to comply with that requirement by the date specified for the purpose, they may at any later time serve or, as the case may be, cause to be displayed, such a written reminder and, in any such case, the date by which an application in relation to the mineral site in question is to be made under paragraph 9 below is the date upon which expires the period of three months from the date when the reminder was served or posted in accordance with the provisions of this sub-paragraph.

Applications for approval of conditions and appeals in cases where the conditions approved are not those proposed

9.—(1) Any person who is the owner of any land, or who is entitled to an interest in a mineral, may, if that land or mineral is or forms part of a dormant site or an active Phase I or II site, apply to the mineral planning authority to determine the conditions to which the relevant planning permissions relating to that site are to be subject.

(2) An application under this paragraph shall be in writing and shall—
    (a) identify the mineral site to which the application relates;
    (b) specify the land or minerals comprised in the site of which the applicant is the owner or, as the case may be, in which the applicant is entitled to an interest;
    (c) identify any relevant planning permissions relating to the site;
    (d) identify, and give an address for, each other person that the applicant knows or, after reasonable inquiry, has cause to believe to be an owner of any land, or entitled to any interest in any mineral, comprised in the site;

(e) set out the conditions to which the applicant proposes the permissions referred to in paragraph (c) above should be subject; and

(f) be accompanied by the appropriate certificate (within the meaning of sub-paragraph (3) or (4) below).

(3) For the purposes of sub-paragraph (2) above, as respects England and Wales the appropriate certificate is such a certificate—

(a) as would be required, under section 65 of the 1990 Act (notice etc. of applications for planning permission) and any provision of a development order made by virtue of that section, to accompany the application if it were an application for planning permission for minerals development, but

(b) with such modifications as are required for the purposes of this paragraph, and section 65(6) of that Act (offences) shall also have effect in relation to any certificate purporting to be the appropriate certificate.

(4) [omitted]

(5) Section 65 of the 1990 Act . . . (by virtue of which a development order may provide for publicising applications for planning permission) shall have effect, with any necessary modifications, as if subsection (1) of that section also authorised a development order to provide for publicising applications under this paragraph.

(6) Where the mineral planning authority receive an application under this paragraph in relation to a dormant site or an active Phase I or II site they shall determine the conditions to which each relevant planning permission relating to the site is to be subject; and any such permission shall, from the date when the conditions to which it is to be subject are finally determined, have effect subject to the conditions which are determined under this Schedule as being the conditions to which it is to be subject.

(7) The conditions imposed by virtue of a determination under sub-paragraph (6) above—

(a) may include any conditions which may be imposed on a grant of planning permission for minerals development;

(b) may be in addition to, or in substitution for, any existing conditions to which the permission in question is subject.

(8) In determining that a relevant planning permission is to be subject to any condition relating to development for which planning permission is granted by a development order, the mineral planning authority shall have regard to any guidance issued for the purpose by the Secretary of State.

(9) Subject to sub-paragraph (10) below, where, within the period of three months from the mineral planning authority having received an application under this paragraph, or within such extended period as may at any time be agreed upon in writing between the applicant and the authority, the authority have not given notice to the applicant of their decision upon the application, the authority shall be treated as having at the end of that period or, as the case may be, that extended period, determined that the conditions to which any relevant planning permission to which the application relates is to be subject are those specified in the application as being proposed in relation to that permission; and any such permission shall, from that time, have effect subject to those conditions.

(10) Where a mineral planning authority, having received an application under this paragraph, are of the opinion that they are unable to determine the application unless further details are supplied to them, they shall within the period of one month from having received the application give notice to the applicant—

(a) stating that they are of such opinion; and

(b) specifying the further details which they require,

and where the authority so serve such a notice the period of three months referred to in sub-paragraph (9) above shall run not from the authority having received the

Environment Act 1995

application but from the time when the authority have received all the further details specified in the notice.

(11) Without prejudice to the generality of sub-paragraph (10) above, the further details which may be specified in a notice under that sub-paragraph include any—

(a) information, plans or drawings; or

(b) evidence verifying any particulars of details supplied to the authority in respect of the application in question,

which it is reasonable for the authority to request for the purpose of enabling them to determine the application.

Notice of determination of conditions to be accompanied by additional information in certain cases

10.—(1) This paragraph applies in a case where—

(a) on an application made to the mineral planning authority under paragraph 9 above in respect of an active Phase I or II site the authority determine under that paragraph the conditions to which the relevant planning permissions relating to the site are to be subject;

(b) those conditions differ in any respect from the proposed conditions set out in the application; and

(c) the effect of the conditions, other than any restoration or aftercare conditions, so determined by the authority, as compared with the effect of the conditions, other than any restoration or aftercare conditions, to which the relevant planning permissions in question were subject immediately prior to the authority making the determination, is to restrict working rights in respect of the site.

(2) In a case where this paragraph applies, the mineral planning authority shall, upon giving to the applicant notice of the conditions determined by the authority under paragraph 9 above, also give to the applicant notice—

(a) stating that the conditions determined by the authority differ in some respect from the proposed conditions set out in the application;

(b) stating that the effect of the conditions, other than any restoration or aftercare conditions, determined bv the authority, as compared with the effect of the conditions, other than any restoration or aftercare conditions, to which the relevant planning permissions relating to the site in question were subject immediately prior to the making of the authority's determination, is to restrict working rights in respect of the site;

(c) identifying the working rights so restricted; and

(d) stating whether, in the opinion of the authority, the effect of that restriction of working rights would be such as to prejudice adversely to an unreasonable degree—

(i) the economic viability of operating the site; or

(ii) the asset value of the site.

(3) In determining whether, in their opinion, the effect of that restriction of working rights would be such as is mentioned in sub-paragraph (2)(d) above, a mineral planning authority shall have regard to any guidance issued for the purpose by the Secretary of State.

(4) In this paragraph, 'the applicant' means the person who made the application in question under paragraph 9 above.

Right to appeal against mineral planning authority's determination of conditions etc.

11.—(1) Where the mineral planning authority—

(a) on an application under paragraph 9 above determine under that paragraph conditions that differ in any respect from the proposed conditions set out in the application; or

(b) give notice, under paragraph (d) of paragraph 10(2) above, stating that, in their opinion, the restriction of working rights in question would not be such as to

prejudice adversely to an unreasonable degree either of the matters referred to in sub-paragraphs (i) and (ii) of the said paragraph (d),
the person who made the application may appeal to the Secretary of State.

(2) An appeal under sub-paragraph (1) above must be made by giving notice of appeal to the Secretary of State before the end of the period of six months beginning with the date on which the authority give notice to the applicant of their determination or, as the case may be, stating their opinion.

Permissions ceasing to have effect

12.—(1) Subject to paragraph 8(11) above, where no application under paragraph 9 above in respect of an active Phase I or II site has been served on the mineral planning authority by the date specified in the first or, as the case may be, the second list as the date by which applications under that paragraph in respect of that site are to be made, or by such later date as may at any time be agreed upon in writing between the applicant and the authority, each relevant planning permission relating to the site shall cease to have effect, except insofar as it imposes any restoration or aftercare condition, on the day following the last date on which such an application may be made.

(2) The reference in sub-paragraph (1) above to the date specified in the first or, as the case may be, the second list as the date by which applications under paragraph 9 above are to be made in respect of any Phase I or II site is a reference to the date specified for that purpose in respect of that site in that list as prepared by the mineral planning authority or, where that date has been varied by virtue of any provision of this Schedule, to that date as so varied.

(3) Subject to sub-paragraph (4) below, no relevant planning permission which relates to a dormant site shall have effect to authorise the carrying out of minerals development unless—

(a) an application has been made under paragraph 9 above in respect of that site; and

(b) that permission has effect in accordance with sub-paragraph (6) of that paragraph.

(4) A relevant planning permission which relates to a Phase I or II site not included in the first list shall cease to have effect, except insofar as it imposes any restoration or aftercare condition, on the day following the last date on which an application under sub-paragraph (1) of paragraph 6 above may be made in respect of that site unless an application has been made under that sub-paragraph by that date in which event, unless the site is added to that list, such a permission shall cease to have effect when the following conditions are met—

(a) the proceedings on that application, including any proceedings on or in consequence of the application under section 288 of the 1990 Act . . . have been determined, and

(b) any time for appealing under paragraph 6(11) or (12) above, or applying or further applying under paragraph 6(1) above, (where there is a right to do so) has expired.

Reference of applications to the Secretary of State

13—(1) The Secretary of State may give directions requiring applications under paragraph 9 above to any mineral planning authority to be referred to him for determination instead of being dealt with by the authority.

(2) Any such direction may relate either to a particular application or to applications of a class specified in the direction.

(3) Where an application is referred to the Secretary of State in accordance with such a direction—

(a) subject to paragraph (b) below, the following provisions of this Schedule—
   (i) paragraph 9(6) and (7),
   (ii) paragraph 10, and
   (iii) paragraph 14 so far as relating to applications under paragraph 9 above,
shall apply, with any necessary modifications, as they apply to applications which fall to be determined by the mineral planning authority;
   (b) before determining the application the Secretary of State must, if either the applicant or the mineral planning authority so wish, give each of them an opportunity of appearing before and being heard by a person appointed by the Secretary of State for the purpose; and
   (c) the decision of the Secretary of State on the application shall be final.

Two or more applicants

14.—(1) Where a mineral planning authority has received from any person a duly made application under paragraph 7(1) or 9 above—
   (a) that person may not make any further application under the paragraph in question in respect of the same site; and
   (b) if the application has been determined, whether or not in the case of an application under paragraph 9 above it has been finally determined, no other person may make an application under the paragraph in question in respect of the same site
   (2) Where—
   (a) a mineral planning authority has received from any person in respect of a mineral site a duly made application under paragraph 7(1) or 9 above; and
   (b) the authority receives from another person a duly made application under the paragraph in question in respect of the same site,
then for the purpose of the determination of the applications and any appeal against such a determination, this Schedule shall have effect as if the applications were a single application received by the authority on the date on which the later application was received by the authority and references to the applicant shall be read as references to either or any of the applicants.

Compensation

15.—(1) This paragraph applies in a case where—
   (a) an application made under paragraph 9 above in respect of an active Phase I or II site is finally determined; and
   (b) the requirements of either sub-paragraph (2) or (3) below are satisfied.
   (2) The requirements, referred to in sub-paragraph (1)(b) above, of this sub-paragraph are—
   (a) that the conditions to which the relevant planning permissions relating to the site are to be subject were determined by the mineral planning authority;
   (b) no appeal was made under paragraph 11(1)(a) above in respect of that determination or any such appeal was withdrawn or dismissed; and
   (c) the authority gave notice under paragraph (d) of paragraph 10(2) above and either—
      (i) that notice stated that, in the authority's opinion, the restriction of working rights in question would be such as to prejudice adversely to an unreasonable degree either of the matters referred to in sub-paragraphs (i) and (ii) of the said paragraph (d); or
      (ii) that notice stated that, in the authority's opinion, the restriction in question would not be such as would so prejudice either of those matters but an appeal under paragraph 11(1) above in respect of the giving of the notice has been allowed.
   (3) The requirements, referred to in sub-paragraph (1)(b) above, of this sub-paragraph are that the conditions to which the relevant planning permissions are to

be subject were determined by the Secretary of State (whether upon an appeal under paragraph 11(1)(a) above or upon a reference under paragraph 13 above) and—
> (a) in a case where those conditions were determined upon an appeal under paragraph 11(1)(a) above either—
>> (i) the mineral planning authority gave notice under paragraph (d) of paragraph 10(2) above stating that, in their opinion, the restriction of working rights in question would be such as to prejudice adversely to an unreasonable degree either of the matters referred to in sub-paragraphs (i) and (ii) of the said paragraph (d), or
>> (ii) the authority gave a notice under the said paragraph (d) stating that, in their opinion, the restriction in question would not be such as would so prejudice either of those matters but an appeal under paragraph 11(1)(b) above in respect of the giving of that notice has been allowed;

or
> (b) in a case where those conditions were determined upon a reference under paragraph 13 above, the Secretary of State gave notice under paragraph (d) of paragraph 10(2) above stating that, in his opinion, the restriction of working rights in question would be such as to prejudice adversely to an unreasonable degree either of the matters referred to in sub-paragraphs (i) and (ii) of the said paragraph (d).

(4) In a case to which this paragraph applies—
> (a) as respects England and Wales, Parts IV and XI of the 1990 Act, or
> (b) . . .

shall have effect as if an order made under section 97 of the 1990 Act . . . had been confirmed by the Secretary of State under section 98 of the 1990 Act . . . at the time when the application in question was finally determined and, as so confirmed, had effect to modify those permissions to the extent specified in sub-paragraph (5) below.

(5) For the purposes of sub-paragraph (4) above, the order which is treated by virtue of that sub-paragraph as having been made under section 97 of the 1990 Act . . . is one whose only effect adverse to the interests of any person having an interest in the land or minerals comprised in the mineral site is to restrict working rights in respect of the site to the same extent as the relevant restriction.

(6) For the purposes of section 116 of the 1990 Act . . . and of any regulations made under those sections, the permissions treated as being modified by the order mentioned in sub-paragraph (4) above shall be treated as if they were planning permissions for development which neither consists of nor includes any minerals development.

Appeals: general procedural provisions

16.—(1) This paragraph applies to appeals under any of the following provisions of this Schedule—
> (a) paragraph 6(11) or (12) above; or
> (b) paragraph 11(1) above.

(2) Notice of appeal in respect of an appeal to which this paragraph applies shall be given on a form supplied by or on behalf of the Secretary of State for use for that purpose, and giving, so far as reasonably practicable, the information required by that form.

(3) Paragraph 6 of Schedule 2 to the 1991 Act (determination of appeals) shall, as respects England and Wales, apply to an appeal to which this paragraph applies as it applies to an appeal under paragraph 5 of that Schedule.

(4) As respects England and Wales, sections 284 to 288 of the 1990 Act (validity of certain decisions and proceedings for questioning their validity) shall have effect as if the action mentioned in section 284(3) of that Act included any decision of the Secretary of State—
> (a) on an appeal to which this paragraph applies; or

(b) on an application under paragraph 9 above referred to him under paragraph 13 above.
(5) [omitted]
(6) [omitted]
(7) [omitted]

SCHEDULE 14
PERIODIC REVIEW OF MINERAL PLANNING PERMISSIONS

Duty to carry out periodic reviews

1. The mineral planning authority shall, in accordance with the provisions of this Schedule, cause periodic reviews to be carried out of the mineral permissions relating to a mining site.

Interpretation

2.—(1) For the purposes of this Schedule—
'first review date' in relation to a mining site, shall, subject to paragraph 5 below, be ascertained in accordance with paragraph 3 below;
'mineral permission' means any planning permission, other than a planning permission granted by a development order, for minerals development;
'mineral planning authority'—
    (a) as respects England and Wales, means a mineral planning authority within the meaning of the 1990 Act, and
    (b) [omitted]
'mining site' means—
    (a) in a case where it appears to the mineral planning authority to be expedient to treat as a single site the aggregate of the land to which any two or more mineral permissions relate, the aggregate of the land to which those permissions relate; and
    (b) in any other case, the land to which a mineral permission relates;
'old mining permission' has the meaning given—
    (a) as respects England and Wales, by section 22(1) of the 1991 Act, and
    (b) [omitted]
'owner' in relation to any land—
    (a) as respects England and Wales, means any person who—
        (i) is the estate owner in respect of the fee simple, or
        (ii) is entitled to a tenancy granted or extended for a term of years certain of which not less than seven years remains unexpired; and
    (b) [omitted]

(2) In determining whether it appears to them to be expedient to treat as a single site the aggregate of the land to which two or more mineral permissions relate a mineral planning authority shall have regard to any guidance issued for the purpose by the Secretary of State.

(3) Any reference (however expressed) in this Schedule to a mining site being a site to which relates—
    (a) an old mining permission; or
    (b) a mineral permission,
is a reference to the mining site, or some part of it, being the land to which the permission relates.

(4) For the purposes of this Schedule, an application made under paragraph 6 below is finally determined when—
    (a) the proceedings on the application, including any proceedings on or in consequence of an application under section 288 of the 1990 Act . . . have been determined, and

(b) any time for appealing under paragraph 9(1) below, or applying or further applying under paragraph 6 below, (where there is a right to do so) has expired.

The first review date

3.—(1) Subject to sub-paragraph (7) below, in a case where the mineral permissions relating to a mining site include an old mining permission, the first review date means—

(a) the date falling fifteen years after the date upon which, pursuant to an application made under paragraph 2 of Schedule 2 to the 1991 Act . . . the conditions to which that old mining permission is to be subject are finally determined under that Schedule; or

(b) where there are two or more old mining permissions relating to that site, and the date upon which those conditions are finally determined is not the same date for each of those permissions, the date falling fifteen years after the date upon which was made the last such final determination to be so made in respect of any of those permissions,

and paragraph 10(2) of Schedule 2 to the 1991 Act . . . (meaning of 'finally determined') shall apply for the purposes of this sub-paragraph as it applies for the purposes of section 22 of and Schedule 2 to the 1991 Act . . . .

(2) Subject to sub-paragraph (7) below, in the case of a mining site which is a Phase I or II site within the meaning of Schedule 13 to this Act, the first review date means the date falling fifteen years after the date upon which, pursuant to an application made under paragraph 9 of that Schedule, there is determined under that paragraph the conditions to which the relevant planning permissions (within the meaning of that Schedule) relating to the site are to be subject.

(3) Subject to sub-paragraphs (4) and (7) below, in the case of a mining site—

(a) which is not a Phase I or II site within the meaning of Schedule 13 to this Act; and

(b) to which no old mining permission relates,

the first review date is the date falling fifteen years after the date upon which was granted the most recent mineral permission which relates to the site.

(4) Where, in the case of a mining site falling within sub-paragraph (3) above, the most recent mineral permission relating to that site relates, or the most recent such permissions (whether or not granted on the same date) between them relate, to part only of the site, and in the opinion of the mineral planning authority it is expedient, for the purpose of ascertaining, under that sub-paragraph, the first review date in respect of that site, to treat that permission or those permissions as having been granted at the same time as the last of the other mineral permissions relating to the site, the first review date for that site shall be ascertained under that sub-paragraph accordingly.

(5) A mineral planning authority shall, in deciding whether they are of such an opinion as is mentioned in sub-paragraph (4) above, have regard to any guidance issued by the Secretary of State for the purpose.

(6) Subject to sub-paragraph (7) below, in the case of a mining site—

(a) to which relates a mineral permission in respect of which an order has been made under section 97 of the 1990 Act . . ., or

(b) in respect of which, or any part of which, an order has been made under paragraph 1 of Schedule 9 to the 1990 Act . . .,

the first review date shall be the date falling fifteen years after the date upon which the order took effect or, in a case where there is more than one such order, upon which the last of those orders to take effect took effect.

(7) In the case of a mining site for which the preceding provisions of this paragraph have effect to specify two or more different dates as the first review date, the first review date shall be the latest of those dates.

Service of notice of first periodic review

4.—(1) The mineral planning authority shall, in connection with the first periodic review of the mineral permissions relating to a mining site, no later than 12 months before the first review date, serve notice upon each person appearing to them to be the owner of any land, or entitled to an interest in any mineral, included in that site.

(2) A notice required to be served under sub-paragraph (1) above shall—
 (a) specify the mining site to which it relates;
 (b) identify the mineral permissions relating to that site;
 (c) state the first review date;
 (d) state that the first review date is the date by which an application must be made for approval of the conditions to which the mineral permissions relating to the site are to be subject and explain the consequences which will occur if no such application is made by that date; and
 (e) explain the right to apply for postponement of the first review date and give the date by which such an application has to be made.

(3) Where, in relation to any land or mineral included in a mining site, the mineral planning authority—
 (a) has served notice on any person under sub-paragraph (1) above; and
 (b) has received no application under paragraph 6 below from that person by the date falling eight weeks before the first review date,
the authority shall serve a written reminder on that person.

(4) A reminder required to be served under sub-paragraph (3) above shall—
 (a) indicate that the land or mineral in question is included in a mining site;
 (b) comply with the requirements of sub-paragraph (2)(a) to (d) above; and
 (c) be served on the person in question on or before the date falling four weeks before the first review date.

(5) Sub-paragraph (1) above shall not require the mineral planning authority to serve notice under that sub-paragraph upon any person whose identity or address for service is not known to and cannot practicably, after reasonable inquiry, be ascertained by them, but in any such case the authority shall cause to be firmly affixed, to each of one or more conspicuous objects on the land or, as the case may be, on the surface of the land above the interest in question, a copy of the notice which they would (apart from the provisions of this sub-paragraph) have had to serve under that sub-paragraph on the owner of that land or interest.

(6) If, in a case where sub-paragraph (5) above applies, no person makes an application to the authority under paragraph 6 below in respect of the mining site which includes the land or interest in question by the date falling eight weeks before the first review date, the authority shall cause to be firmly affixed, to each of one or more conspicuous objects on the land or, as the case may be, on the surface of the land above the interest in question, a copy of the written reminder that would, in a case not falling within sub-paragraph (5) above, have been served under sub-paragraph (3) above.

(7) Where by sub-paragraph (5) or (6) above a copy of any notice is required to be affixed to an object on any land that copy shall—
 (a) be displayed in such a way as to be easily visible and legible;
 (b) be first displayed—
  (i) in a case where the requirement arises under sub-paragraph (5) above, no later than 12 months before the first review date; or
  (ii) in a case where the requirement arises under sub-paragraph (6) above, no later than the date falling four weeks before the first review date;
and
 (c) be left in position for at least the period of 21 days from the date when it is first displayed, but where the notice is, without fault or intention of the authority,

removed, obscured or defaced before that period has elapsed, that requirement shall be treated as having been complied with if the authority has taken reasonable steps for protection of the notice and, if need be, its replacement.

(8) In sub-paragraphs (5) and (6) above, any reference to a conspicuous object on any land includes, in a case where the person serving a notice considers that there are no or insufficient such objects on the land, a reference to a post driven into or erected upon the land by the person serving the notice for the purpose of having affixed to it a copy of the notice in question.

Application for postponement of the first review date

5.—(1) Any person who is the owner of any land, or of any interest in any mineral, comprised in a mining site may, no later than the day upon which expires the period of three months from the day upon which notice was served upon him under paragraph 4 above, apply under this paragraph to the mineral planning authority for the postponement of the first review date.

(2) An application under this paragraph shall be in writing and shall set out—
  (a) the conditions to which each mineral permission relating to the site is subject;
  (b) the applicant's reasons for considering those conditions to be satisfactory; and
  (c) the date which the applicant wishes to have substituted for the first review date.

(3) Where the mineral planning authority receive an application made under this paragraph—
  (a) if they consider the conditions referred to in sub-paragraph (2)(a) above to be satisfactory they shall agree to the first review date being postponed in which event they shall determine the date to be substituted for that date;
  (b) in any other case they shall refuse the application.

(4) When a mineral planning authority determine an application made under this paragraph, they shall notify the applicant in writing of their decision and, in a case where they have agreed to the postponement of the first review date, shall notify the applicant of the date which they have determined should be substituted for the first review date.

(5) Where, within the period of three months of the mineral planning authority having received an application under this paragraph, or within such extended period as may at any time be agreed upon in writing between the applicant and the authority, the authority have not given notice, under sub-paragraph (4) above, to the applicant of their decision upon the application, the authority shall be treated as having, at the end of that period or, as the case may be, that extended period—
  (a) agreed to the first review date being postponed; and
  (b) determined that the date referred to in sub-paragraph (2)(c) above be substituted for the first review date.

Application to determine the conditions to which the mineral permissions relating to a mining site are to be subject

6.—(1) Any person who is the owner of any land, or who is entitled to an interest in a mineral, may, if that land or mineral is or forms part of a mining site, apply to the mineral planning authority to determine the conditions to which the mineral permissions relating to that site are to be subject.

(2) An application under this paragraph shall be in writing and shall—
  (a) identify the mining site in respect of which the application is made and state that the application is made in connection with the first periodic review of the mineral permissions relating to that site;

(b) specify the land or minerals comprised in the site of which the applicant is the owner or, as the case may be, in which the applicant is entitled to an interest;

(c) identify the mineral permissions relating to the site;

(d) identify, and give an address for, each other person that the applicant knows or, after reasonable inquiry, has cause to believe to be an owner of any land, or entitled to any interest in any mineral, comprised in the site;

(e) set out the conditions to which the applicant proposes the permissions referred to in paragraph (c) above should be subject; and

(f) be accompanied by the appropriate certificate (within the meaning of sub-paragraph (3) or (4) below).

(3) For the purposes of sub-paragraph (2) above, as respects England and Wales the appropriate certificate is such a certificate—

(a) as would be required, under section 65 of the 1990 Act and any provision of a development order made by virtue of that section, to accompany the application if it were an application for planning permission for minerals development, but

(b) with such modifications as are required for the purposes of this paragraph, and section 65(6) of the 1990 Act shall also have effect in relation to any certificate purporting to be the appropriate certificate.

(4) . . .

(5) Where the mineral planning authority receive an application under this paragraph in relation to a mining site they shall determine the conditions to which each mineral permission relating to the site is to be subject.

(6) The conditions imposed by virtue of a determination under sub-paragraph (5) above—

(a) may include any conditions which may be imposed on a grant of planning permission for minerals development;

(b) may be in addition to, or in substitution for, any existing conditions to which the permission in question is subject.

(7) In determining that a mineral permission is to be subject to any condition relating to development for which planning permission is granted by a development order, the mineral planning authority shall have regard to any guidance issued for the purpose by the Secretary of State.

(8) Subject to sub-paragraph (9) below, where, within the period of three months of the mineral planning authority having received an application under this paragraph, or within such extended period as may at any time be agreed upon in writing between the applicant and the authority, the authority have not given notice to the applicant of their decision upon the application, the authority shall be treated as having at the end of that period or, as the case may be, that extended period, determined that the conditions to which any mineral permission to which the application relates is to be subject are those specified in the application as being proposed in relation to that permission; and any such permission shall, from that time, have effect subject to those conditions.

(9) Where a mineral planning authority, having received an application under this paragraph, are of the opinion that they are unable to determine the application unless further details are supplied to them, they shall within the period of one month from having received the application give notice to the applicant—

(a) stating that they are of such opinion; and

(b) specifying the further details which they require,

and where the authority so serve such a notice the period of three months referred to in sub-paragraph (8) above shall run not from the authority having received the application but from the time when the authority have received all the further details specified in the notice.

(10) Without prejudice to the generality of sub-paragraph (9) above, the further details which may be specified in a notice under that sub-paragraph include any—

(a) information, plans or drawings; or
(b) evidence verifying any particulars of details supplied to the authority in respect of the application in question,
which it is reasonable for the authority to request for the purpose of enabling them to determine the application.

Permissions ceasing to have effect

7. Where no application under paragraph 6 above in respect of a mining site has been served on the mineral planning authority by the first review date, or by such later date as may at any time be agreed upon in writing between the applicant and the authority, each mineral permission—
   (a) relating to the site; and
   (b) identified in the notice served in relation to the site under paragraph 4 above,
shall cease to have effect, except insofar as it imposes any restoration or aftercare condition, on the day following the first review date or, as the case may be, such later agreed date.

Reference of applications to the Secretary of State

8.—(1) The Secretary of State may give directions requiring applications made under paragraph 6 above to any mineral planning authority to be referred to him for determination instead of being dealt with by the authority.

(2) A direction under sub-paragraph (1) above may relate either to a particular application or to applications of a class specified in the direction.

(3) Where an application is referred to the Secretary of State in accordance with a direction under sub-paragraph (1) above—
   (a) subject to paragraph (b) below, paragraph 6(5) and (6) above, and paragraph 11 below so far as relating to applications under paragraph 6 above, shall apply, with any necessary modifications, to his determination of the application as they apply to the determination of applications by the mineral planning authority;
   (b) before determining the application the Secretary of State must, if either the applicant or the mineral planning authority so wish, give each of them an opportunity of appearing before and being heard by a person appointed by the Secretary of State for the purpose; and
   (c) the decision of the Secretary of State on the application shall be final.

Appeals

9.—(1) Where on an application under paragraph 6 above the mineral planning authority determine conditions that differ in any respect from the proposed conditions set out in the application, the applicant may appeal to the Secretary of State.

(2) An appeal under sub-paragraph (1) above must be made by giving notice of appeal to the Secretary of State, before the end of the period of six months beginning with the determination, on a form supplied by or on behalf of the Secretary of State for use for that purpose, and giving, so far as reasonably practicable, the information required by that form.

(3) Paragraph 6 of Schedule 2 to the 1991 Act (determination of appeals) shall, as respects England and Wales, apply to appeals under sub-paragraph (1) above as it applies to appeals under paragraph 5 of that Schedule.

(4) As respects England and Wales, sections 284 to 288 of the 1990 Act shall have effect as if the action mentioned in section 284(3) of that Act included any decision of the Secretary of State—
   (a) on an appeal under sub-paragraph (1) above; or
   (b) on an application under paragraph 6 above referred to him under paragraph 8 above.

(5) [omitted]
(6) [omitted]
(7) [omitted]

Time from which conditions determined under this Schedule are to take effect

10.—(1) Where an application has been made under paragraph 6 above in respect of a mining site, each of the mineral permissions relating to the site shall, from the time when the application is finally determined, have effect subject to the conditions to which it is determined under this Schedule that that permission is to be subject.

(2) Sub-paragraph (1) above is without prejudice to paragraph 6(8) above.

Two or more applicants

11.—(1) Where a mineral planning authority have received from any person a duly made application under paragraph 5 or 6 above—
    (a) that person may not make any further application under the paragraph in question in respect of the same site; and
    (b) if the application has been determined, whether or not in the case of an aplication under paragraph 6 above it has been finally determined, no other person may make an application under the paragraph in question in respect of the same site.

(2) Where—
    (a) a mineral planning authority have received from any person in respect of a mineral site a duly made application under paragraph 5 or 6 above; and
    (b) the authority receives from another person a duly made application under the paragraph in question in respect of the same site,
then for the purpose of the determination of the applications and any appeal against such a determination, this Schedule shall have effect as if the applications were a single application received by the authority on the date on which the later application was received by the authority and references to the applicant shall be read as references to either or any of the applicants.

Second and subsequent periodic reviews

12.—(1) In this paragraph, in relation to a mining site, but subject to paragraph 5 above as applied by sub-paragraph (2) below, 'review date' means—
    (a) in the case of the second periodic review, the date falling fifteen years after the date upon which was finally determined an application made under paragraph 6 above in respect of the site; and
    (b) in the case of subsequent periodic reviews, the date falling fifteen years after the date upon which there was last finally determined under this Schedule an application made in respect of that site under paragraph 6 above as applied by sub-paragraph (2) below.

(2) Paragraphs 4 to 11 above shall apply in respect of the second or any subsequent periodic review of the mineral permissions relating to a mining site as they apply to the first such periodic review, but as if—
    (a) any reference in those paragraphs to the 'first review date' were a reference to the review date; and
    (b) the references in paragraphs 4(1) and 6(2)(a) above to the first periodic review were references to the periodic review in question.

Compensation

13.—(1) This paragraph applies where—
    (a) an application made under paragraph 6 above in respect of a mining site is finally determined; and

(b) the conditions to which the mineral permissions relating to the site are to be subject, as determined under this Schedule, differ in any respect from the proposed conditions set out in the application; and

(c) the effect of the new conditions, except insofar as they are restoration or aftercare conditions, as compared with the effect of the existing conditions, except insofar as they were restoration or aftercare conditions, is to restrict working rights in respect of the site.

(2) For the purposes of this paragraph—

'the new conditions' in relation to a mining site, means the conditions, determined under this Schedule, to which the mineral permissions relating to the site are to be subject; and

'the existing conditions', in relation to a mining site, means the conditions to which the mineral permissions relating to the site were subject immediately prior to the final determination of the application made under paragraph 6 above in respect of that site.

(3) For the purposes of this paragraph, working rights are restricted in respect of a mining site if any of—

(a) the size of the area which may be used for the winning and working of minerals or the depositing of mineral waste;

(b) the depth to which operations for the winning and working of minerals may extend;

(c) the height of any deposit of mineral waste;

(d) the rate at which any particular mineral may be extracted;

(e) the rate at which any particular mineral waste may be deposited;

(f) the period at the expiry of which any winning or working of minerals or depositing of mineral waste is to cease; or

(g) the total quantity of minerals which may be extracted from, or of mineral waste which may be deposited on, the site,

is restricted or reduced in respect of the mining site in question.

(4) In a case to which this paragraph applies, but subject to sub-paragraph (6) below, as respects England and Wales, Parts IV and XI of the 1990 Act . . . shall have effect as if an order made under section 97 of the 1990 Act . . .—

(a) had been confirmed by the Secretary of State under section 98 of the 1990 Act . . . at the time when the application in question was finally determined; and

(b) as so confirmed, had effect to modify those permissions to the extent specified in sub-paragraph (6) below.

(5) For the purposes of this paragraph, the order referred to in sub-paragraph (4) above is one whose only effect adverse to the interests of any person having an interest in the land or minerals comprised in the mineral site is to restrict working rights in respect of the site to the same extent as the relevant restriction.

(6) For the purposes of section 116 of the 1990 Act . . . and of any regulations made under those sections, the permissions treated as being modified by the order mentioned in sub-paragraph (4) above shall be treated as if they were planning permissions for development which neither consists of nor includes any minerals development.

TOWN AND COUNTRY PLANNING (ENVIRONMENTAL ASSESSMENT AND PERMITTED DEVELOPMENT) REGULATIONS 1995
(SI 1995, No. 417)

1. Citation and commencement

These Regulations may be cited as the Town and Country Planning (Environmental Assessment and Permitted Development) Regulations 1995 and shall come into force on 3rd June 1995.

2. Interpretation

In these Regulations, unless the context otherwise requires—

'prospective developer' means a person, other than a relevant planning authority or a person who intends to undertake development with such an authority (whether or not with any other person), who is minded to undertake development which appears to him to be relevant development;

'relevant development' means development of any description specified in Schedule 2 to the Town and Country Planning (General Permitted Development) Order 1995 other than development of any description specified in article 3(12) of that Order;

'relevant planning authority' means the body by whom, assuming no direction were given under section 77 of the Town and Country Planning Act 1990, an application for planning permission in respect of the development concerned would be determined;

'Schedule 1' means Schedule 1 to the Town and Country Planning (Assessment of Environmental Effects) Regulations 1988; and

'Schedule 2' means Schedule 2 to those Regulations.

3. Opinion as to need for environmental statement

(1) A prosective developer may apply to the relevant planning authority for their opinion as to whether the relevant development specified in the application is within a description mentioned in Schedule 1 or Schedule 2, and, if so, within which descrption, and if within a description mentioned in Schedule 2, whether it would be likely to have significant effects on the environment by virtue of factors such as its nature, size or location.

(2) An application under paragraph (1) shall be accompanied by—
   (a) a plan sufficient to identify the land;
   (b) a brief description of the nature and purpose of the development and of its possible effects on the environment;
   (c) such other information or representations as the prospective developer may wish to provide or make.

(3) An authority which receives an application under paragraph (1) shall, if they consider that they have not been provided with sufficient information to give an opinion on the questions raised, notify the prospective developer of the particular points on which they require further information; and the information so requested shall be provided within such reasonable period as may be specified in the notice or such longer period as may be agreed in writing between the authority and the prospective developer.

(4) The authority shall give to the prospective developer written notice of their opinion within the period of 3 weeks beginning with the date of receipt of the application or such longer period as may be agreed in writing with the prospective developer; and if it is their opinion that the relevant development is—
   (a) within a description mentioned in Schedule 1, or
   (b) within a description mentioned in Schedule 2 and likely to have significant effects on the environment,
they shall provide with the opinion a written statement of their reasons for being of that opinion.

4. Discretions by the Secretary of State

(1) Where an authority—
   (a) give an opinion inv the terms mentioned in regulations 3(4)(a) or (b); or
   (b) fail to give an opinion within the period specified or agreed (as the case may be) for the purposes of regulation 3(4),

the prospective developer may apply to the Secretary of State, in accordance with the following provisions of this regulation, for his direction on the matter.

(2) An application under this regulation shall be accompanied by—

(a) a copy of the application under regulation 3(1) and of the documents which accompanied it;

(b) a copy of the notice (if any) given by the authority under regulation 3(3) and of the information (if any) supplied in response to that notice;

(c) a copy of the authority's opinion (if any) and of the statement of reasons which accompanied it; and

(d) such additional information or representations as the prospective developer may wish to provide or make.

(3) The prospective developer shall send to the relevant planning authority, at such time as he applies to the Secretary of State, a copy of the application under this regulation and of any additional information or representations made in accordance with paragraph (2)(d).

(4) If the Secretary of State considers that the information provided in accordance with paragraph (2) is insufficient to enable him to give a direction, he shall notify the prospective developer and the relevant planning authority of the matters in respect of which he requires further information; and the information so requested shall be provided by the prospective developer within such reasonable period as may be specified in the notice or such longer period as may be agreed in writing between the prospective developer and the Secretary of State.

(5) The Secretary of State shall issue a direction within the period of three weeks beginning with the date of receipt of the application or such longer period as he may reasonably require.

(6) The Secretary of State shall send a copy of his direction to the prospective developer and to the relevant planning authority; and where he concludes that the develoment is—

(a) within a description mentioned in Schedule 1; or

(b) within a description mentioned in Schedule 2 and likely to have significant environmental effects,

he shall send with the copy of the direction a written statement of the reasons for his conclusion.

5. Proposed development in which a relevant planning authority has an interest

(1) For the purposes of this regulation, 'developer' means—

(a) a relevant planning authority who are minded to undertake development (whether alone or with another or others) which appears to them to be relevant development; or

(b) a person who is minded to undertake development with a relevant planning authority (whether or not with any other person) which appears to him to be relevant development.

(2) A developer may apply in writing to the Secretary of State for an opinion as to whether the development is within a description mentioned in Schedule 1 or Schedule 2, and, if so, within which description, and if within a description mentioned in Schedule 2, whether it would be likely to have significant effects on the environment by virtue of factors such as its nature, size or location.

(3) An application under paragraph (2) shall be accompanied by—

(a) a plan sufficient to identify the land;

(b) a brief description of the nature and purpose of the relevant development and of its possible effects on the environment;

(c) such other information or representations as the developer may wish to provide or make.

(4) If the Secretary of State considers that the information provided in accordance with paragraph (3) is insufficient to enable him to give an opinion, he shall notify the developer and, where that person is not the relevant planning authority, that authority, of the matters in respect of which he requires further information; and the information so requested shall be provided by the developer within such reasonable period as may be specified in the notice or such longer period as may be agreed in writing between the developer and the Secretary of State.

(5) The Secretary of State shall give to the developer written notice of his opinion within the period of 3 weeks beginning with the date of receipt of the application or such longer period as he may reasonably require; and if it is his opinion that the relevant development is—

    (a) within a description mentioned in Schedule 1, or

    (b) within a description mentioned in Schedule 2 and likely to have significant effects on the environment,

he shall provide with the opinion a written statement of his reasons for being of that opinion.

(6) Where the developer is not the relevant planning authority, the Secretary of State shall send to that authority a copy of the opinion and of the statement of reasons (if any) given in accordance with paragraph (5).

6. Public inspection of opinions and directions

(1) The relevant planning authority shall make available for public inspection at all reasonable hours at the place where the appropriate register (or relevant section of that register) is kept a copy of—

    (a) every opinion given by the authority under regulation 3;

    (b) the accompanying statement of reasons (if any);

    (c) the application to which the opinion relates;

    (d) the documents which accompanied the application;

    (e) every direction or opinion received by the authority under regulation 4 or 5; and

    (f) the statement of reasons (if any) accompanying each such direction or opinion,

and those copies shall remain so available for a period of two years or until particulars of the opinion or direction are entered in Part I of the register in accordance with paragraph (2), whichever is the sooner.

(2) Where particulars of an application for planning permission are entered in Part I of the appropriate register, the local planning authority shall take steps to secure that that Part also contains such particulars of—

    (a) any opinion given under regulation 3; and

    (b) any direction or opinion given under regulation 4 or 5,

as are relevant to the development which is the subject of the application.

(3) In this regulation, 'appropriate register' means the register kept pursuant to section 69 of the Town and Country Planning Act 1990 on which particulars of an application for planning permission for the development concerned are required to be entered.

THE TOWN AND COUNTRY PLANNING (GENERAL PERMITTED DEVELOPMENT) ORDER 1995
(SI 1995, No. 418)
Brought into force: 3rd June 1995

ARTICLE

1. Citation, commencement and interpretation.
2. Application.
3. Permitted development.
4. Directions restricting permitted development.
5. Approval of Secretary of State for article 4(1) directions.
6. Notice and confirmation of article 4(2) directions.
7. Directions restricting permitted development under Class B of Part 22 or Class B of Part 23.
8. Directions.
9. Revocations.

SCHEDULE 1

PART
1. Article 1(4) land.
2. Article 1(5) land.
3. Article 1(6) land.

SCHEDULE 2
PERMITTED DEVELOPMENT

PART
1. Development within the curtilage of a dwellinghouse.
2. Minor operations.
3. Changes of use.
4. Temporary buildings and uses.
5. Caravan sites.
6. Agricultural buildings and operations.
7. Forestry buildings and operations.
8. Industrial and warehouse development.
9. Repairs to unadopted streets and private ways.
10. Repairs to services.
11. Development under local or private Acts or orders.
12. Development by local authorities.
13. Development by local highway authorities.
14. Development by drainage bodies.
15. Development by the National Rivers Authority.
16. Development by or on behalf of sewerage undertakers.
17. Development by statutory undertakers.
18. Aviation development.
19. Development ancillary to mining operations.
20. Coal mining development by the Coal Authority and licensed operators.
21. Waste tipping at a mine.
22. Mineral exploration.
23. Removal of material from mineral-working deposits.
24. Development by telecommunications code system operators.
25. Other telecommunications development.
26. Development by the Historic Buildings and Monuments Commission for England.
27. Use by members of certain recreational organisations.
28. Development at amusement parks.
29. Driver information systems.
30. Toll road facilities.
31. Demolition of buildings.
32. Schools, colleges, universities and hospitals.
33. Closed circuit television cameras.

[omitted]

SCHEDULE 3

The Secretary of State for the Environment, as respects England, and the Secretary of State for Wales, as respects Wales, in exercise of the powers conferred on them by sections 59, 60, 61, 74 and 333(7) of the Town and Country Planning Act 1990, Section 54 of the Coal Industry Act 1994) and of all other powers enabling them in that behalf, hereby make the following Order—

1. Citation, commencement and interpretation

(1) This Order may be cited as the Town and Country Planning (General Permitted Development) Order 1995 and shall come into force on 3rd June 1995.

(2) In this Order, unless the context otherwise requires—
'the Act' means the Town and Country Planning Act 1990;
'the 1960 Act' means the Caravan Sites and Control of Development Act 1960;
'aerodrome' means an aerodrome as defined in article 106 of the Air Navigation Order 1989 (interpretation) which is—
    (a) licensed under that Order,
    (b) a Government aerodrome,
    (c) one at which the manufacture, repair or maintenance of aircraft is carried out by a person carrying on business as a manufacturer or repairer of aircraft,
    (d) one used by aircraft engaged in the public transport of passengers or cargo or in aerial work, or
    (e) one identified to the Civil Aviation Authority before 1st March 1986 for inclusion in the UK Aerodrome Index,
and, for the purposes of this definition, the terms 'aerial work', 'Government aerodrome' and 'public transport' have the meanings given in article 106;
'aqueduct' does not include an underground conduit;
'area of outstanding natural beauty' means an area designated as such by an order made by the Countryside Commission, as respects England, or the Countryside Council for Wales, as respects Wales, under section 87 of the National Parks and Access to the Countryside Act 1949 (designation of areas of outstanding natural beauty) as confirmed by the Secretary of State;
'building'—
    (a) includes any structure or erection and, except in Parts 24, 25 and 33, and Class A of Part 31, of Schedule 2, includes any part of a building, as defined in this article; and
    (b) does not include plant or machinery and, in Schedule 2, except in Class B of Part 31 and Part 33, does not include any gate, fence, wall or other means of enclosure;
'caravan' has the same meaning as for the purposes of Part I of the 1960 Act (caravan sites);
'caravan site' means land on which a caravan is stationed for the purpose of human habitation and land which is used in conjunction with land on which a caravan is so stationed;
'classified road' means a highway or proposed highway which—
    (a) is a classified road or a principal road by virtue of section 12(1) of the Highways Act 1980 (general provision as to principal and classified roads); or
    (b) is classified by the Secretary of State for the purposes of any enactment by virtue of section 12(3) of that Act;
'cubic content' means the cubic content of a structure or building measured externally;
'dwellinghouse' does not include a building containing one or more flats, or a flat contained within such a building;

'erection', in relation to buildings as defined in this article, includes extension, alteration, or re-erection;

'existing', in relation to any building or any plant or machinery or any use, means (except in the definition of 'original') existing immediately before the carrying out, in relation to that building, plant, machinery or use, of development described in this Order;

'flat' means a separate and self-contained set of premises constructed or adapted for use for the purpose of a dwelling and forming part of a building from some other part of which it is divided horizontally;

'floor space' means the total floor space in a building or buildings;

'industrial process' means a process for or incidental to any of the following purposes—

(a) the making of any article or part of any article (including a ship or vessel, or a film, video or sound recording);

(b) the altering, repairing, maintaining, ornamenting, finishing, cleaning, washing, packing, canning, adapting for sale, breaking up or demolition of any article; or

(c) the getting, dressing or treatment of minerals in the course of any trade or business other than agriculture, and other than a process carried out on land used as a mine or adjacent to and occupied together with a mine;

'land drainage' has the same meaning as in section 116 of the Land Drainage Act 1976 (interpretation);

'listed building' has the same meaning as in section 1 of the Planning (Listed Buildings and Conservation Areas) Act 1990 (listing of buildings of special architectural or historic interest);

'by local advertisement' means by publication of the notice in at least one newspaper circulating in the locality in which the area or, as the case may be, the whole or relevant part of the conservation area to which the direction relates is situated;

'machinery' includes any structure or erection in the nature of machinery;

'microwave' means that part of the radio spectrum above 1,000 MHz;

'microwave antenna' means a satellite antenna or a terrestrial microwave antenna;

'mine' means any site on which mining operations are carried out;

'mining operations' means the winning and working of minerals in, on or under land, whether by surface or underground working;

'notifiable pipe-line' means a pipe-line, as defined in section 65 of the Pipe-lines Act 1962 (meaning of pipe-line), which contains or is intended to contain a hazardous substance, as defined in regulation 2(1) of the Notification Regulations (interpretation), except—

(a) a pipe-line the construction of which has been authorised under section 1 of the Pipe-lines Act 1962 (cross-country pipe-lines not to be constructed without the Minister's authority); or

(b) a pipe-line which contains or is intended to contain no hazardous substance other than—

(i) a flammable gas (as specified in item 1 of Part II of Schedule 1 to the Notification Regulations (classes of hazardous substances not specifically named in Part I)) at a pressure of less than 8 bars absolute; or

(ii) a liquid or mixture of liquids, as specified in item 4 of Part II of that Schedule;

'Notification Regulations' means the Notification of Installations Handling Hazardous Substances Regulations 1982;

'original' means, in relation to a building existing on 1st July 1948, as existing on that date and, in relation to a building built on or after 1st July 1948, as so built;

'plant' includes any structure or erection in the nature of plant;
'private way' means a highway not maintainable at the public expense and any other way other than a highway;
'proposed highway' has the same meaning as in section 329 of the Highways Act 1980 (further provision as to interpretation);
'public service vehicle' means a public service vehicle within the meaning of section 1 of the Public Passenger Vehicles Act 1981 (definition of public service vehicles) or a tramcar or trolley vehicle within the meaning of section 192(1) of the Road Traffic Act 1988 (general interpretation);
'satellite antenna' means apparatus designed for transmitting microwave radio energy to satellites or receiving it from them, and includes any mountings or brackets attached to such apparatus;
'scheduled monument' has the same meaning as in section 1(11) of the Ancient Monuments and Archaeological Areas Act 1979 (schedule of monuments);
'by site display' means by the posting of the notice by firm affixture to some object, sited and displayed in such a way as to be easily visible and legible by members of the public;
'site of archaeological interest' means land which is included in the schedule of monuments compiled by the Secretary of State under section 1 of the Ancient Monuments and Archaeological Areas Act 1979 (schedule of monuments), or is within an area of land which is designated as an area of archaeological importance under section 33 of that Act (designation of areas of archaeological importance), or which is within a site registered in any record adopted by resolution by a county council and known as the County Sites and Monuments Record;
'site of special scientific interest' means land to which section 28(1) of the Wildlife and Countryside Act 1981 (areas of special scientific interest) applies;
'statutory undertaker' includes, in addition to any person mentioned in section 262(1) of the Act (meaning of statutory undertakers), the Post Office, the Civil Aviation Authority, the National Rivers Authority, any water undertaker, any public gas supplier, and any licence holder within the meaning of section 64(1) of the Electricity Act 1989 (interpretation etc. of Part 1);
'terrestrial microwave antenna' means apparatus designed for transmitting or receiving terrestrial microwave radio energy between two fixed points;
'trunk road' means a highway or proposed highway which is a trunk road by virtue of section 10(1) or 19 of the Highways Act 1980 (general provisions as to trunk roads, and certain special roads and other highways to become trunk roads) or any other enactment or any instrument made under any enactment;
'the Use Classes Order' means the Town and Country Planning (Use Classes) Order 1987.

(3) Unless the context otherwise requires, any reference in this Order to the height of a building or of plant or machinery shall be construed as a reference to its height when measured from ground level; and for the purposes of this paragraph 'ground level' means the level of the surface of the ground immediately adjacent to the building or plant or machinery in question or, where the level of the surface of the ground on which it is situated or is to be situated is not uniform, the level of the highest part of the surface of the ground adjacent to it.

(4) The land referred to elsewhere in this Order as article 1(4) land is the land described in Part 1 of Schedule 1 to this Order (land in listed counties).

(5) The land referred to elsewhere in this Order as article 1(5) land is the land described in Part 2 of Schedule 1 to this Order (National Parks, areas of outstanding natural beauty and conservation areas etc.).

(6) The land referred to elsewhere in this Order as article 1(6) land is the land described in Part 3 of Schedule 1 to this Order (National Parks and adjoining land and the Broads).

2. Application

(1) This Order applies to all land in England and Wales, but where land is the subject of a special development order, whether made before or after the commencement of this Order, this Order shall apply to that land only to such extent and subject to such modifications as may be specified in the special development order.

(2) Nothing in this Order shall apply to any permission which is deemed to be granted under section 222 of the Act (planning permission not needed for advertisements complying with regulations).

3. Permitted development

(1) Subject to the provisions of this Order and regulations 60 to 63 of the Conservation (Natural Habitats, &c.) Regulations 1994 (general development orders), planning permission is hereby granted for the classes of development described as permitted development in Schedule 2.

(2) Any permission granted by paragraph (1) is subject to any relevant exception, limitation or condition specified in Schedule 2.

(3) References in the following provisions of this Order to permission granted by Schedule 2 or by any Part, Class or paragraph of that Schedule are references to the permission granted by this article in relation to development described in that Schedule or that provision of that Schedule.

(4) Nothing in this Order permits development contrary to any condition imposed by any planning permission granted or deemed to be granted under Part III of the Act otherwise than by this Order.

(5) The permission granted by Schedule 2 shall not apply if—

(a) in the case of permission granted in connection with an existing building, the building operations involved in the construction of that building are unlawful;

(b) in the case of permission granted in connection with an existing use, that use is unlawful.

(6) The permission granted by Schedule 2 shall not, except in relation to development permitted by Parts 9, 11, 13 or 30, authorise any development which requires or involves the formation, laying out or material widening of a means of access to an existing highway which is a trunk road or classified road, or creates an obstruction to the view of persons using any highway used by vehicular traffic, so as to be likely to cause danger to such persons.

(7) Any development falling within Part 11 of Schedule 2 authorised by an Act or order subject to the grant of any consent or approval shall not be treated for the purposes of this Order as authorised unless and until that consent or approval is obtained, except where the Act was passed or the order made after 1st July 1948 and it contains provision to the contrary.

(8) Schedule 2 does not grant permission for the laying or construction of a notifiable pipe-line, except in the case of the laying or construction of a notifiable pipe-line by a public gas supplier in accordance with Class F of Part 17 of that Schedule.

(9) Except as provided in Part 31, Schedule 2 does not permit any development which requires or involves the demolition of a building, but in this paragraph 'building' does not include part of a building.

(10) Subject to paragraph (I 2), development is not permitted by this Order if an application for planning permission for that development would be a Schedule 1 application or a Schedule 2 application within the meaning of the Town and Country Planning (Assessment of Environmental Effects) Regulations 1988 ('the Environmental Assessment Regulations') (descriptions of development).

(11) Where—

(a) the local planning authority have given an opinion under regulation 3 of the Town and Country Planning (Environmental Assessment and Permitted Development) Regulations 1995 ('the Permitted Development Regulations') (opinion as to need for environmental statement) that an application for particular development would be a Schedule 1 application or a Schedule 2 application within the meaning of the Environmental Assessment Regulations and the Secretary of State has issued no direction to the contrary under regulation 4 of the Permitted Development Regulations (directions by the Secretary of State); or

(b) the Secretary of State has given an opinion under regulation 5 of the Permitted Development Regulations (proposed development in which a relevant planning authority has an interest) that an application for particular development would be a Schedule 1 application or a Schedule 2 application within the meaning of the Environmental Assessment Regulations,

the development to which that opinion relates shall be treated, for the purposes of paragraph (10), as development which is not permitted by this Order.

(12) Paragraph (10) does not apply to—

(a) development which comprises or forms part of a project serving national defence purposes;

(b) development which consists of the carrying out by a drainage body within the meaning of the Land Drainage Act 1991 of improvement works within the meaning of the Land Drainage Improvement Works (Assessment of Environmental Effects) Regulations 1988;

(c) development which consists of the installation of an electric line (within the meaning of Part I of the Electricity Act 1989 (electricity supply)) which replaces an existing line (as defined in regulation 2 of the Overhead Lines (Exemption) Regulations 1990 (interpretation)) and in respect of which consent under section 37 of that Act (consent required for overhead lines) is not required by virtue of regulation 3(1)(e) of those Regulations (exemptions from section 37(1) of the Electricity Act 1989): provided that, in the circumstances mentioned in paragraph (1)(a) or (b) of regulation 5 of those Regulations (further restrictions on the exemptions contained in regulation 3), the determination for the purposes of that regulation that there is not likely to be a significant adverse effect on the environment shall have been made otherwise than as mentioned in paragraph (2) of that regulation;

(d) development for which permission is granted by Part 7, Class D of Part 8, Part 11, Class B of Part 12, Class F(a) of Part 17, Class A or Class B of Part 20 or Class B of Part 21 of Schedule 2;

(e) development for which permission is granted by Class C or Class D of Part 20, Class A of Part 21 or Class B of Part 22 of Schedule 2 where the land in, on or under which the development is to be carried out is—

(i) in the case of Class C or Class D of Part 20, on the same authorised site,

(ii) in the case of Class A of Part 21, on the same premises or, as the case may be, the same ancillary mining land,

(iii) in the case of Class B of Part 22, on the same land or, as the case may be, on land adjoining that land,

as that in, on or under which development of any description permitted by the same Class has been carried out before 3rd June 1995;

(f) the completion of any development begun before 3rd June 1995.

4. Directions restricting permitted development

(1) If the Secretary of State or the appropriate local planning authority is satisfied that it is expedient that development described in any Part, Class or paragraph in Schedule 2, other than Class B of Part 22 or Class B of Part 23, should not be carried out unless permission is granted for it on an application, he or they may give a direction under this paragraph that the permission granted by article 3 shall not apply to—

(a) all or any development of the Part, Class or paragraph in question in an area specified in the direction; or

(b) any particular development, failing within that Part, Class or paragraph, which is specified in the direction,

and the direction shall specify that it is made under this paragraph.

(2) If the appropriate local planning authority is satisfied that it is expedient that any particular development described in paragraph (5) below should not be carried out within the whole or any part of a conservation area unless permission is granted for it on an application, they may give a direction under this paragraph that the permission granted by article 3 shall not apply to all or any particular development of the Class in question within the whole or any part of the conservation area, and the direction shall specify the development and conservation area or part of that area to which it relates and that it is made under this paragraph.

(3) A direction under paragraph (1) or (2) shall not affect the carrying out of—

(a) development permitted by Part II authorised by an Act passed after 1st July 1948 or by an order requiring the approval of both Houses of Parliament approved after that date;

(b) any development in an emergency; or

(c) any development mentioned in Part 24, unless the direction specifically so provides.

(4) A direction given or having effect as if given under this article shall not, unless the direction so provides, affect the carrying out by a statutory undertaker of the following descriptions of development—

(a) the maintenance of bridges, buildings and railway stations;

(b) the alteration and maintenance of railway track, and the provision and maintenance of track equipment, including signal boxes, signalling apparatus and other appliances and works required in connection with the movement of traffic by rail;

(c) the maintenance of docks, harbours, quays, wharves, canals and towing paths;

(d) the provision and maintenance of mechanical apparatus or appliances (including signalling equipment) required for the purposes of shipping or in connection with the embarking, disembarking, loading, discharging or transport of passengers, livestock or goods at a dock, quay, harbour, bank, wharf or basin;

(e) any development required in connection with the improvement, maintenance or repair of watercourses or drainage works;

(f) the maintenance of buildings, runways, taxiways or aprons at an aerodrome;

(g) the provision, alteration and maintenance of equipment, apparatus and works at an aerodrome, required in connection with the movement of traffic by air (other than buildings, the construction, erection, reconstruction or alteration of which is permitted by Class A of Part 18 of Schedule 2).

(5) The development referred to in paragraph (2) is development described in—

(a) Class A of Part 1 of Schedule 2, consisting of the enlargement, improvement or other alteration of a dwellinghouse, where any part of the enlargement, improvement or alteration would front a relevant location;

(b) Class C of Part 1 of that Schedule, where the alteration would be to a roof slope which fronts a relevant location;

(c) Class D of Part 1 of that Schedule, where the external door in question fronts a relevant location;

(d) Class E of Part 1 of that Schedule, where the building or enclosure, swimming or other pool to be provided would front a relevant location, or where the part of the building or enclosure maintained, improved or altered would front a relevant location;

(e) Class F of Part 1 of that Schedule, where the hard surface would front a relevant location;

(f) Class H of Part 1 of that Schedule, where the part of the building or other structure on which the satellite antenna is to be installed, altered or replaced fronts a relevant location;

(g) Part 1 of that Schedule, consisting of the erection, alteration or removal of a chimney on a dwellinghouse or on a building within the curtilage of a dwellinghouse;

(h) Class A of Part 2 of that Schedule, where the gate, fence, wall or other means of enclosure would be within the curtilage of a dwellinghouse and would front a relevant location;

(i) Class C of Part 2 of that Schedule, consisting of the painting of the exterior of any part, which fronts a relevant location, of—
  (i) a dwellinghouse; or
  (ii) any building or enclosure within the curtilage of a dwellinghouse;

(j) Class B of Part 31 of that Schedule, where the gate, fence, wall or other means of enclosure is within the curtilage of a dwellinghouse and fronts a relevant location.

(6) In this article and in articles 5 and 6—
'appropriate local planning authority' means—
  (a) in relation to a conservation area in a non-metropolitan county, the county planning authority or the district planning authority; and
  (b) in relation to any other area, the local planning authority whose function it would be to determine an application for planning permission for the development to which the direction relates or is proposed to relate;
'relevant location' means a highway, waterway or open space.

5. Approval of Secretary of State for article 4(1) directions

(1) Except in the cases specified in paragraphs (3) and (4), a direction by a local planning authority under article 4(1) requires the approval of the Secretary of State, who may approve the direction with or without modifications.

(2) On making a direction under article 4(1) or submitting such a direction to the Secretary of State for approval—
  (a) a county planning authority shall give notice of it to any district planning authority in whose district the area to which the direction relates is situated; and
  (b) except in metropolitan districts, a district planning authority shall give notice of it to the county planning authority, if any.

(3) Unless it affects the carrying out of development by a statutory undertaker as provided by article 4(4), the approval of the Secretary of State is not required for a direction which relates to—
  (a) a listed building;
  (b) a building which is notified to the authority by the Secretary of State as a building of architectural or historic interest; or
  (c) development within the curtilage of a listed building,
and does not relate to land of any other description.

(4) Subject to paragraph (6), the approval of the Secretary of State is not required for a direction made under article 4(1) relating only to development permitted by any of Parts 1 to 4 or Part 31 of Schedule 2, if the relevant authority consider the development would be prejudicial to the proper planning of their area or constitute a threat to the amenities of their area.

(5) A direction not requiring the Secretary of State's approval by virtue of paragraph (4) shall, unless disallowed or approved by the Secretary of State, expire at the end of six months from the date on which it was made.

(6) Paragraph (4) does not apply to a second or subsequent direction relating to the same development or to development of the same Class or any of the same

Classes, in the same area or any part of that area as that to which the first direction relates or related.

(7) The local planning authority shall send a copy of any direction made by them to which paragraph (4) applies to the Secretary of State not later than the date on which notice of that direction is given in accordance with paragraph (10) or (12).

(8) The Secretary of State may give notice to the local planning authority that he has disallowed any such direction and the direction shall then cease to have effect.

(9) The local planning authority shall as soon as reasonably practicable give notice that a direction has been disallowed in the same manner as notice of the direction was given.

(10) Subject to paragraph (12), notice of any direction made under article 4(1) shall be served by the appropriate local planning authority on the owner and occupier of every part of the land within the area to which the direction relates as soon as practicable after the direction has been made or, where the direction is required to be approved by the Secretary of State, as soon as practicable after it has been so approved; and a direction shall come into force in respect of any part of the land within the area to which the direction relates on the date on which notice is so served on the occupier of that part, or, if there is no occupier, on the owner.

(11) If a direction to which paragraph (4) applies is approved by the Secretary of State within the period of six months referred to in paragraph (5), then (unless paragraph (12) applies) the authority who made the direction shall, as soon as practicable, serve notice of that approval on the owner and occupier of every part of the land within the area to which the direction relates; and where the Secretary of State has approved the direction with modifications the notice shall indicate the effect of the modifications.

(12) Where in the case of a direction under article 4(1)(a) an authority consider that individual service in accordance with paragraph (10) or (11) is impracticable for the reasons set out in paragraph (14) they shall publish a notice of the direction, or of the approval, by local advertisement.

(13) A notice published pursuant to paragraph (12) shall contain a statement of the effect of the direction and of any modification made to it by the Secretary of State, and shall name a place or places where a copy of the direction, and of a map defining the area to which it relates, may be seen at all reasonable hours.

(14) The reasons referred to in paragraph (12) are that the number of owners and occupiers within the area to which the direction relates makes individual service impracticable, or that it is difficult to identify or locate one or more of them.

(15) Where notice of a direction has been published in accordance with paragraph (12), the direction shall come into force on the date on which the notice is first published.

(16) A local planning authority may, by making a subsequent direction and without the approval of the Secretary of State, cancel any direction made by them under article 4(1), and the Secretary of State may make a direction cancelling any direction under article 4(1) made by the local planning authority.

(17) Paragraphs (10) and (12) to (15) shall apply to any direction made under paragraph (16).

6. Notice and confirmation of article 4(2) directions

(1) Notice of any direction made under article 4(2) shall, as soon as practicable after the direction has been made, be given by the appropriate local planning authority—

    (a) by local advertisement; and

    (b) subject to paragraphs (4) and (5), by serving the notice on the owner and occupier of every dwellinghouse within the whole or the relevant part of the conservation area to which the direction relates.

(2) The notice referred to in paragraph (1) shall—
  (a) include a description of the development and the conservation area or part of that area to which the direction relates, and a statement of the effect of the direction;
  (b) specify that the direction is made under article 4(2) of this Order;
  (c) name a place where a copy of the direction, and a copy of the map defining the conservation area or part of that area to which it relates, may be seen at all reasonable hours; and
  (d) specify a period of at least 21 days, stating the date on which that period begins, within which any representations concerning the direction may be made to the local planning authority.

(3) The direction shall come into force in respect of any part of the land within the conservation area or part of that area to which it relates—
  (a) on the date on which the notice is served on the occupier of that part of the land or, if there is no occupier, on the owner; or
  (b) if paragraph (4) or (5) applies, on the date on which the notice is first published in accordance with paragraph (1)(a).

(4) The local planning authority need not serve notice on an owner or occupier in accordance with paragraph (1)(b) where they consider that individual service on that owner or occupier is impracticable because it is difficult to identify or locate him.

(5) The local planning authority need not serve any notice in accordance with paragraph (1)(b) where they consider that the number of owners or occupiers within the conservation area or part of that area to which the direction relates makes individual service impracticable.

(6) On making a direction under article 4(2)
  (a) a county planning authority shall give notice of it to any district planning authority in whose district the conservation area or part of that area to which the direction relates is situated; and
  (b) except in metropolitan districts, a district planning authority shall give notice of it to the county planning authority, if any.

(7) A direction under article 4(2) shall expire at the end of six months from the date on which it was made unless confirmed by the appropriate local planning authority in accordance with paragraphs (8) and (9) before the end of that six month period.

(8) In deciding whether to confirm a direction made under article 4(2), the local planning authority shall take into account any representations received during the period specified in the notice referred to in paragraph (2)(d).

(9) The local planning authority shall not confirm the direction until a period of at least 28 days has elapsed following the latest date on which any notice relating to the direction was served or published.

(10) The appropriate local planning authority shall as soon as practicable give notice that a direction has been confirmed in the same manner as in paragraphs (1)(a) and (b) above.

7. Directions restricting permitted development under Class B of Part 22 or Class B of Part 23

(1) If, on receipt of a notification from any person that he proposes to carry out development within Class B of Part 22 or Class B of Part 23 of Schedule 2, a mineral planning authority are satisfied as mentioned in paragraph (2) below, they may, within a period of 21 days beginning with the receipt of the notification, direct that the permission granted by article 3 of this Order shall not apply to the development, or to such part of the development as is specified in the direction.

(2) The mineral planning authority may make a direction under this article if they are satisfied that it is expedient that the development, or any part of it, should not be carried out unless permission for it is granted on an application because—

(a) the land on which the development is to be carried out is within—
 (i) a National Park,
 (ii) an area of outstanding natural beauty,
 (iii) a site of archaeological interest, and the operation to be carried out is not one described in the Schedule to the Areas of Archaeological Importance (Notification of Operations) (Exemption) Order 1984 (exempt operations),
 (iv) a site of special scientific interest, or
 (v) the Broads;
(b) the development, either taken by itself or taken in conjunction with other development which is already being carried out in the area or in respect of which notification has been given in pursuance of the provisions of Class B of Part 22 or Class B of Part 23, would cause serious detriment to the amenity of the area in which it is to be carried out or would adversely affect the setting of a building shown as Grade I in the list of buildings of special architectural or historic interest compiled by the Secretary of State under section 1 of the Planning (Listed Buildings and Conservation Areas) Act 1990 (listing of buildings of special architectural or historic interest);
(c) the development would constitute a serious nuisance to the inhabitants of a nearby residential building, hospital or school; or
(d) the development would endanger aircraft using a nearby aerodrome.

(3) A direction made under this article shall contain a statement as to the day on which (if it is not disallowed under paragraph (5) below) it will come into force, which shall be 29 days from the date on which notice of it is sent to the Secretary of State in accordance with paragraph (4) below.

(4) As soon as is reasonably practicable a copy of a direction under this article shall be sent by the mineral planning authority to the Secretary of State and to the person who gave notice of the proposal to carry out development.

(5) The Secretary of State may, at any time within a period of 28 days beginning with the date on which the direction is made, disallow the direction; and immediately upon receipt of notice in writing from the Secretary of State that he has disallowed the direction, the mineral planning authority shall give notice in writing to the person who gave notice of the proposal that he is authorised to proceed with the development.

8. Directions

Any power conferred by this Order to give a direction includes power to cancel or vary the direction by a subsequent direction.

9. Revocations

The statutory instruments specified in column 1 of Schedule 3 are hereby revoked to the extent specified in column 3.

SCHEDULE 1

PART 1
ARTICLE 1(4) LAND

Land within the following counties—
 Cleveland, Cornwall, Cumbria, Devon, Durham, Dyfed, Greater Manchester, Gwynedd, Humberside, Lancashire, Merseyside, Northumberland, North Yorkshire, South Yorkshire, Tyne and Wear, West Glamorgan, West Yorkshire.

PART 2
ARTICLE 1(5) LAND

Land within—
 (a) a National Park;

(b) an area of outstanding natural beauty;
(c) an area designated as a conservation area under section 69 of the Planning (Listed Buildings and Conservation Areas) Act 1990 (designation of conservation areas);
(d) an area specified by the Secretary of State and the Minister of Agriculture, Fisheries and Food for the purposes of section 41(3) of the Wildlife and Countryside Act 1981 (enhancement and protection of the natural beauty and amenity of the countryside);
(e) the Broads.

PART 3
ARTICLE 1(6) LAND

Land within a National Park or within the following areas—
(a) In England, the Broads or land outside the boundaries of a National Park, which is within the parishes listed below—
in the district of Allerdale—
Blindcrake, Bothel and Threapland, Bridekirk, Brigham, Broughton, Broughton Moor, Camerton, Crosscanonby, Dean, Dearham, Gilcrux, Great Clifton, Greysouthen, Little Clifton, Loweswater, Oughterside and Allerby, Papcastle, Plumbland, Seaton, Winscales;
in the borough of Copeland—
Arlecdon and Frizington, Cleator Moor, Distington, Drigg and Carleton, Egremont, Gosforth, Haile, Irton with Santon, Lamplugh, Lowca, Lowside Quarter, Millom, Millom Without, Moresby, Parton, Ponsonby, St Bees, St Bridget's Beckermet, St John's Beckermet, Seascale, Weddicar;
in the district of Eden—
Ainstable, Asby, Bandleyside, Bolton, Brough, Brough Sowerby, Brougham, Castle
Sowerby, Catterlen, Clifton, Cliburn, Crackenthorpe, Crosby Garrett, Crosby Ravensworth, Culgaith, Dacre, Dufton, Glassonby, Great Salkeld, Great Strickland,
Greystoke, Hartley, Hesket, Hillbeck, Hunsonby, Hutton, Kaber, Kings Meaburn, Kirkby Stephen, Kirby Thore, Kirkoswald, Langwathby, Lazonby, Little Strickland, Long Marton, Lowther, Mallerstang, Milburn, Morland, Mungrisdale, Murton, Musgrave, Nateby, Newbiggin, Newby, Orton, Ousby, Ravenstonedale, Shap, Skelton, Sleagill, Sockbridge and Tirril, Soulby, Stainmore, Tebay, Temple Sowerby, Thrimby, Waitby, Warcop, Wharton, Winton, Yanwath and Eamont Bridge;
in the borough of High Peak—
Chapel-en-le-Frith, Charlesworth, Chinley Buxworth and Brownside, Chisworth, Green Fairfield, Hartington Upper Quarter, Hayfield, King Sterndale, Tintwistle, Wormhill;
in the district of South Lakeland—
Aldingham, Angerton, Arnside, Barbon, Beetham, Blawith and Subberthwaite, Broughton West, Burton, Casterton, Docker, Egton-with-Newland, Fawcett Forest, Firbank, Grayrigg, Helsington, Heversham, Hincaster, Holme, Hutton Roof, Killington, Kirkby Ireleth, Kirkby Lonsdale, Lambrigg, Levens, Lower Allithwaite, Lower Holker, Lowick, Lupton, Mansergh, Mansriggs, Middleton, Milnthorpe, Natland, New Hutton, Old Hutton and Holmescales, Osmotherley, Pennington, Preston Patrick, Preston Richard, Scalthwaiterigg, Sedgwick, Skelsmergh, Stainton, Strickland Ketel, Strickland Roger, Urswick, Whinfell, Whitwell and Selside;

in the district of West Derbyshire—
Aldwark, Birchover, Stanton; and
(b) In Wales, land outside the boundaries of a National Park which is—
(i) within the communities listed below —
in the borough of Aberconwy —
Caerhun, Dolgaffog;
in the borough of Arfon—
Betws Garmon, Bontnewydd, Llanberis, Llanddeiniolen, Llandwrog, Llanllyfni, Llanwnda, Waunfawr;
in the district of Meirionnydd—
Arthog, Corris, Llanfrothen, Penrhyndeudraeth; or
(ii) within the specified parts of the communities listed below—
in the borough of Aberconwy, those parts of the following communities which were on 31st March 1974 within the former rural district of Nant Conway—
Conwy, Henryd, Llanddoged and Maenan, Llanrwst, Llansanffraid Glan Conwy;
in the borough of Arfon, those parts of the following communities which were on 31st March 1974 within the former rural district of Gwyrfai—
Caernarfon, Llandygai, Llanrug, Pentir, Y Felinheli;
in the district of Dwyfor, that part of the community of Porthmadog which was on 31st March 1974 within the former rural district of Deudraeth and those parts of the following communities which were on that date within the former rural district of Gwyrfai —
Clynnog, Dolbenmaen, Llanaelhaearn;
in the district of Glyndwr, those parts of the following communities which were on 31st March 1974 within the former rural district of Penllyn—
Llandrillo, Llangwm;
in the district of Meirionnydd, those parts of the following communities which were on 31st March 1974 within the former rural district of Deudraeth—
Ffestiniog, Talsarnau;
and those parts of the following communities which were on that date within the former rural district of Dolgellau—
Barmouth, Mawddwy;
and that part of the community of Llandderfel which was on that date within the former rural district of Penllyn.

Article 3   SCHEDULE 2

PART 1
DEVELOPMENT WITHIN THE CURTILAGE OF A DWELLINGHOUSE

Class A
Permitted **A. The enlargement, improvement or other alteration of a**
development **dwellinghouse.**
Development   A.1   Development is not permitted by Class A if—
not permitted   (a) the cubic content of the resulting building would exceed the cubic content of the original dwellinghouse—
(i) in the case of a terrace house or in the case of a dwellinghouse on article 1(5) land, by more than 50 cubic metres or 10%, whichever is the greater,
(ii) in any other case, by more than 70 cubic metres or 15%, whichever is the greater,
(iii) in any case, by more than 115 cubic metres;

(b) the part of the building enlarged, improved or altered would exceed in height the highest part of the roof of the original dwellinghouse;

(c) the part of the building enlarged, improved or altered would be nearer to any highway which bounds the curtilage of the dwellinghouse than—

    (i) the part of the original dwellinghouse nearest to that highway, or

    (ii) any point 20 metres from that highway,

whichever is nearer to the highway;

(d) in the case of development other than the insertion, enlargement, improvement or other alteration of a window in an existing wall of a dwellinghouse, the part of the building enlarged, improved or altered would be within 2 metres of the boundary of the curtilage of the dwellinghouse and would exceed 4 metres in height;

(e) the total area of ground covered by buildings within the curtilage (other than the original dwellinghouse) would exceed 50% of the total area of the curtilage (excluding the ground area of the original dwellinghouse);

(f) it would consist of or include the installation, alteration or replacement of a satellite antenna;

(g) it would consist of or include the erection of a building within the curtilage of a listed building; or

(h) it would consist of or include an alteration to any part of the roof

A.2 In the case of a dwellinghouse on any article 1(5) land, development is not permitted by Class A if it would consist of or include the cladding of any part of the exterior with stone, artificial stone, timber, plastic or tiles.

Interpretation of Class A

A.3 For the purposes of Class A—

(a) the erection within the curtilage of a dwellinghouse of any building with a cubic content greater than 10 cubic metres shall be treated as the enlargement of the dwellinghouse for all purposes (including calculating cubic content) where—

    (i) the dwellinghouse is on article 1(5) land, or

    (ii) in any other case, any part of that building would be within 5 metres of any part of the dwellinghouse;

(b) where any part of the dwellinghouse would be within 5 metres of an existing building within the same curtilage, that building shall be treated as forming part of the resulting building for the purpose of calculating the cubic content.

Class B
Permitted development

B. The enlargement of a dwellinghouse consisting of an addition or alteration to its roof.

Development not permitted

B.1 Development is not permitted by Class B if—

(a) any part of the dwellinghouse would, as a result of the works, exceed the height of the highest part of the existing roof;

(b) any part of the dwellinghouse would, as a result of the works, extend beyond the plane of any existing roof slope which fronts any highway;

(c) it would increase the cubic content of the dwellinghouse by more than 40 cubic metres, in the case of a terrace house, or 50 cubic metres in any other case;

(d) the cubic content of the resulting building would exceed the cubic content of the original dwellinghouse—
    (i) in the case of a terrace house by more than 50 cubic metres or 10%, whichever is the greater,
    (ii) in any other case, by more than 70 cubic metres or 15%, whichever is the greater, or
    (iii) in any case, by more than 115 cubic metres; or
(e) the dwellinghouse is on article 1(5) land.

Class C
Permitted development

C. Any other alteration to the roof of a dwellinghouse.

Development not permitted

C.1 Development is not permitted by Class C if it would result in a material alteration to the shape of the dwellinghouse.

Class D
Permitted development

D. The erection or construction of a porch outside any external door of a dwellinghouse.

Development not permitted

D.1 Development is not permitted by Class D if—
    (a) the ground area (measured externally) of the structure would exceed 3 square metres;
    (b) any part of the structure would be more than 3 metres above ground level; or
    (c) any part of the structure would be within 2 metres of any boundary of the curtilage of the dwellinghouse with a highway.

Class E
Permitted development

E. The provision within the curtilage of a dwellinghouse of any building or enclosure, swimming or other pool required for a purpose incidental to the enjoyment of the dwellinghouse as such, or the maintenance, improvement or other alteration of such a building or enclosure.

Development not permitted

E.1 Development is not permitted by Class E if—
    (a) it relates to a dwelling or a satellite antenna;
    (b) any part of the building or enclosure to be constructed or provided would be nearer to any highway which bounds the curtilage than—
        (i) the part of the original dwellinghouse nearest to that highway, or
        (ii) any point 20 metres from that highway,
whichever is nearer to the highway;
    (c) where the building to be constructed or provided would have a cubic content greater than 10 cubic metres, any part of it would be within 5 metres of any part of the dwellinghouse;
    (d) the height of that building or enclosure would exceed—
        (i) 4 metres, in the case of a building with a ridged roof, or
        (ii) 3 metres, in any other case;
    (e) the total area of ground covered by buildings or enclosures within the curtilage (other than the original dwellinghouse) would exceed 50% of the total area of the curtilage (excluding the ground area of the original dwellinghouse); or
    (f) in the case of any article 1(5) land or land within the curtilage of a listed building, it would consist of the provision,

The Town and Country Planning (General Permitted Development) Order 1995 347

alteration or improvement of a building with a cubic content greater than 10 cubic metres.

Interpretation of Class E
E.2 For the purposes of Class E—
'purpose incidental to the enjoyment of the dwellinghouse as such' includes the keeping of poultry, bees, pet animals, birds or other livestock for the domestic needs or personal enjoyment of the occupants of the dwellinghouse.

Class F Permitted development

F. The provision within the curtilage of a dwellinghouse of a hard surface for any purpose incidental to the enjoyment of the dwellinghouse as such.

Class G Permitted development

G. The erection or provision within the curtilage of a dwellinghouse of a container for the storage of oil for domestic heating.

Development not permitted
G.1 Development is not permitted by Class G if—
   (a) the capacity of the container would exceed 3,500 litres;
   (b) any part of the container would be more than 3 metres above ground level; or
   (c) any part of the container would be nearer to any highway which bounds the curtilage than—
      (i) the part of the original building nearest to that highway, or
      (ii) any point 20 metres from that highway,
whichever is nearer to the highway.

Class H Permitted development

H. The installation, alteration or replacement of a satellite antenna on a dwellinghouse or within the curtilage of a dwellinghouse.

Development not permitted
H.1 Development is not permitted by Class H if—
   (a) the size of the antenna (excluding any projecting feed element, reinforcing rim, mountings and brackets) when measured in any dimension would exceed—
      (i) 45 centimetres in the case of an antenna to be installed on a chimney;
      (ii) 90 centimetres in the case of an antenna to be installed on or within the curtilage of a dwellinghouse on article 1(4) land other than on a chimney;
      (iii) 70 centimetres in any other case;
   (b) the highest part of an antenna to be installed on a roof or a chimney would, when installed, exceed in height—
      (i) in the case of an antenna to be installed on a roof, the highest part of the roof;
      (ii) in the case of an antenna to be installed on a chimney, the highest part of the chimney;
   (c) there is any other satellite antenna on the dwellinghouse or within its curtilage;
   (d) in the case of article 1(5) land, it would consist of the installation of an antenna—
      (i) on a chimney;
      (ii) on a building which exceeds 15 metres in height;

Conditions (iii) on a wall or roof slope which fronts a waterway in the Broads or a highway elsewhere.

H.2 Development is permitted by Class H subject to the following conditions—

(a) an antenna installed on a building shall, so far as practicable, be sited so as to minimise its effect on the external appearance of the building;

(b) an antenna no longer needed for the reception or transmission of microwave radio energy shall be removed as soon as reasonably practicable.

Interpretation of Part 1

1. For the purposes of Part 1—

'resulting building' means the dwellinghouse as enlarged, improved or altered, taking into account any enlargement, improvement or alteration to the original dwellinghouse, whether permitted by this Part or not; and

'terrace house' means a dwellinghouse situated in a row of three or more dwellinghouses used or designed for use as single dwellings, where—

(a) it shares a party wall with, or has a main wall adjoining the main wall of, the dwellinghouse on either side; or

(b) if it is at the end of a row, it shares a party wall with or has a main wall adjoining the main wall of a dwellinghouse which fulfils the requirements of sub-paragraph (a) above.

PART 2
MINOR OPERATIONS

Class A
Permitted development

A. The erection, construction, maintenance, improvement or alteration of a gate, fence, wall or other means of enclosure.

Development not permitted

A.1 Development is not permitted by Class A if—

(a) the height of any gate, fence, wall or means of enclosure erected or constructed adjacent to a highway used by vehicular traffic would, after the carrying out of the development, exceed one metre above ground level;

(b) the height of any other gate, fence, wall or means of enclosure erected or constructed would exceed two metres above ground level;

(c) the height of any gate, fence, wall or other means of enclosure maintained, improved or altered would, as a result of the development, exceed its former height or the height referred to in sub-paragraph (a) or (b) as the height appropriate to it if erected or constructed, whichever is the greater; or

(d) it would involve development within the curtilage of, or to a gate, fence, wall or other means of enclosure surrounding, a listed building.

Class B
Permitted development

B. The formation, laying out and construction of a means of access to a highway which is not a trunk road or a classified road, where that access is required in connection with development permitted by any Class in this Schedule (other than by Class A of this Part).

Class C
Permitted   C. The painting of the exterior of any building or work.
development

Development   C.1 Development is not permitted by Class C where the painting
not permitted   is for the purpose of advertisement, announcement or direction.
Interpretation   C.2 In Class C, 'painting' includes any application of colour.
of Class C

PART 3
CHANGES OF USE

Class A
Permitted   A. Development consisting of a change of the use of a build-
development   ing to a use falling within Class A1 (shops) of the Schedule to the Use Classes Order from a use falling within Class A3 (food and drink) of that Schedule or from a use for the sale, or display for sale, of motor vehicles.

Class B
Permitted   B. Development consisting of a change of the use of a build-
development   ing—
    (a) to a use for any purpose falling within Class B1 (business) of the Schedule to the Use Classes Order from any use failing within Class B2 (general industrial) or B8 (storage and distribution) of that Schedule;
    (b) to a use for any purpose failing within Class B8 (storage and distribution) of that Schedule from any use falling within Class B1 (business) or B2 (general industrial).

Development   Development is not permitted by Class B where the change is to or
not permitted   from a use failing within Class B8 of that Schedule, if the change of use relates to more than 235 square metres of floor space in the building.

Class C
Permitted   C. Development consisting of a change of use to a use falling
development   within Class A2 (financial and professional services) of the Schedule to the Use Classes Order from a use falling within Class A3 (food and drink) of that Schedule.

Class D
Permitted   D. Development consisting of a change of use of any prem-
development   ises with a display window at ground floor level to a use falling within Class A1 (shops) of the Schedule to the Use Classes Order from a use falling within Class A2 (financial and professional services) of that Schedule.

Class E
Permitted   E. Development consisting of a change of the use of a build-
development   ing or other land from a use permitted by planning permission granted on an application, to another use which that permission would have specifically authorised when it was granted.

Development   E.1 Development is not permitted by Class E if—
not permitted   (a) the application for planning permission referred to was made before the 5th December 1988;
     (b) it would be carried out more than 10 years after the grant of planning permission; or

(c) it would result in the breach of any condition, limitation or specification contained in that planning permission in relation to the use in question.

Class F
Permitted development

F. Development consisting of a change of the use of a building—

(a) to a mixed use for any purpose within Class A1 (shops) of the Schedule to the Use Classes Order and as a single flat, from a use for any purpose within Class A1 of that Schedule;

(b) to a mixed use for any purpose within Clan A2 (financial and professional services) of the Schedule to the Use Classes Order and as a single flat, from a use for any purpose within Class A2 of that Schedule;

(c) where that building has a display window at ground floor level, to a mixed use for any purpose within Class A1 (shops) of the Schedule to the Use Classes Order and as a single flat, from a use for any purpose within Class A2 (financial and professional services) of that Schedule.

Conditions

F.1 Development permitted by Class F is subject to the following conditions—

(a) some or all of the parts of the building used for any purposes within Class A1 or Class A2, as the case may be, of the Schedule to the Use Classes Order shall be situated on a floor below the part of the building used as a single flat;

(b) where the development consists of a change of use of any building with a display window at ground floor level, the ground floor shall not be used in whole or in part as the single flat;

(c) the single flat shall not be used otherwise than as a dwelling (whether or not as a sole or main residence)—

(i) by a single person or by people living together as a family, or

(ii) by not more than six residents living together as a single household (including a household where care is provided for residents).

Interpretation of Class F

F.2 For the purposes of Class F—

'care' means personal care for people in need of such care by reason of old age, disablement, past or present dependence on alcohol or drugs or past or present mental disorder.

Class G
Permitted development

G. Development consisting of a change of the use of a building—

(a) to a use for any purpose within Class A1 (shops) of the Schedule to the Use Classes Order from a mixed use for any purpose within Class A1 of that Schedule and as a single flat;

(b) to a use for any purpose within Class A2 (financial and professional services) of the Schedule to the Use Classes Order from a mixed use for any purpose within Class A2 of that Schedule and as a single flat;

(c) where that building has a display window at ground floor level, to a use for any purpose within Class A1 (shops) of the Schedule to the Use Classes Order from a mixed use for any purpose within Class A2 (financial and professional services) of that Schedule and as a single flat.

Development not permitted
G.1 Development is not permitted by Class G unless the part of the building used as a single flat was immediately prior to being so used used for any purpose within Class A1 or Class A2 of the Schedule to the Use Classes Order.

PART 4
TEMPORARY BUILDINGS AND USES

Class A
Permitted development
A. The provision on land of buildings, moveable structures, works, plant or machinery required temporarily in connection with and for the duration of operations being or to be carried out on, in, under or over that land or on land adjoining that land.

Development not permitted
A.1 Development is not permitted by Class A if—
  (a) the operations referred to are mining operations, or
  (b) planning permission is required for those operations but is not granted or deemed to be granted.

Conditions
A.2 Development is permitted by Class A subject to the conditions that, when the operations have been carried out—
  (a) any building, structure, works, plant or machinery permitted by Class A shall be removed, and
  (b) any adjoining land on which development permitted by Class A has been carried out shall, as soon as reasonably practicable, be reinstated to its condition before that development was carried out.

Class B
Permitted development
B. The use of any land for any purpose for not more than 28 days in total in any calendar year, of which not more than 14 days in total may be for the purposes referred to in paragraph B.2, and the provision on the land of any moveable structure for the purposes of the permitted use.

Development not permitted
B.1 Development is not permitted by Class B if—
  (a) the land in question is a building or is within the curtilage of a building,
  (b) the use of the land is for a caravan site,
  (c) the land is, or is within, a site of special scientific interest and the use of the land is for—
    (i) a purpose referred to in paragraph B.2(b) or other motor sports;
    (ii) clay pigeon shooting; or
    (iii) any war game,
  or
  (d) the use of the land is for the display of an advertisement.

Interpretation of Class B
B.2 The purposes mentioned in Class B above are—
  (a) the holding of a market;
  (b) motor car and motorcycle racing including trials of speed, and practising for these activities.

B.3 In Class B, 'war game' means an enacted, mock or imaginary battle conducted with weapons which are designed not to injure (including smoke bombs, or guns or grenades which fire or spray paint or are otherwise used to mark other participants), but excludes military activities or training exercises organised by or with the authority of the Secretary of State for Defence.

PART 5
CARAVAN SITES

Class A
Permitted development
A. The use of land, other than a building, as a caravan site in the circumstances referred to in paragraph A.2.

Condition
A.1 Development is permitted by Class A subject to the condition that the use shall be discontinued when the circumstances specified in paragraph A.2 cease to exist, and all caravans on the site shall be removed as soon as reasonably practicable.

Interpretation of Class A
A.2 The circumstances mentioned in Class A are those specified in paragraphs 2 to 10 of Schedule 1 to the 1960 Act (cases where a caravan site licence is not required), but in relation to those mentioned in paragraph 10 do not include use for winter quarters.

Class B
Permitted development
B. Development required by the conditions of a site licence for the time being in force under the 1960 Act.

PART 6
AGRICULTURAL BUILDINGS AND OPERATIONS

Class A   Development on units of 5 hectares or more

Permitted development
A. The carrying out on agricultural land comprised in an agricultural unit of 5 hectares or more in area of—
   (a) works for the erection, extension or alteration of a building; or
   (b) any excavation or engineering operations,
which are reasonably necessary for the purposes of agriculture within that unit.

Development not permitted
A.1 Development is not permitted by Class A if—
   (a) the development would be carried out on a separate parcel of land forming part of the unit which is less than 1 hectare in area;
   (b) it would consist of, or include, the erection, extension or alteration of a dwelling;
   (c) it would involve the provision of a building, structure or works not designed for agricultural purposes;
   (d) the ground area which would be covered by—
       (i) any works or structure (other than a fence) for accommodating livestock or any plant or machinery arising from engineering operations; or
       (ii) any building erected or extended or altered by virtue of Class A,
would exceed 465 square metres, calculated as described in paragraph D.2 below;
   (e) the height of any part of any building, structure or works within 3 kilometres of the perimeter of an aerodrome would exceed 3 metres;
   (f) the height of any part of any building, structure or works not within 3 kilometres of the perimeter of an aerodrome would exceed 12 metres;

(g) any part of the development would be within 25 metres of a metalled part of a trunk road or classified road;
(h) it would consist of, or include, the erection or construction of, or the carrying out of any works to, a building, structure or an excavation used or to be used for the accommodation of livestock or for the storage of slurry or sewage sludge where the building, structure or excavation is, or would be, within 400 metres of the curtilage of a protected building; or
(i) it would involve excavations or engineering operations on or over article 1(6) land which are connected with fish farming.

Conditions   A.2(1) Development is permitted by Class A subject to the following conditions—
(a) where development is carried out within 400 metres of the curtilage of a protected building, any building, structure, excavation or works resulting from the development shall not be used for the accommodation of livestock except in the circumstances described in paragraph D.3 below or for the storage of slurry or sewage sludge;
(b) where the development involves—
(i) the extraction of any mineral from the land (including removal from any disused railway embankment); or
(ii) the removal of any mineral from a mineral-working deposit,
the mineral shall not be moved off the unit;
(c) waste materials shall not be brought on to the land from elsewhere for deposit except for use in works described in Class A(a) or in the provision of a hard surface and any materials so brought shall be incorporated forthwith into the building or works in question.
(2) Subject to paragraph (3), development consisting of—
(a) the erection, extension or alteration of a building;
(b) the formation or alteration of a private way;
(c) the carrying out of excavations or the deposit of waste material (where the relevant area, as defined in paragraph D.4 below, exceeds 0.5 hectare); or
(d) the placing or assembly of a tank in any waters,
is permitted by Class A subject to the following conditions-
(i) the developer shall, before beginning the development, apply to the local planning authority for a determination as to whether the prior approval of the authority will be required to the siting, design and external appearance of the building, the siting and means of construction of the private way, the siting of the excavation or deposit or the siting and appearance of the tank, as the case may be;
(ii) the application shall be accompanied by a written description of the proposed development and of the materials to be used and a plan indicating the site together with any fee required to be paid;
(iii) the development shall not be begun before the occurrence of one of the following—
(aa) the receipt by the applicant from the local planning authority of a written notice of their determination that such prior approval is not required;
(bb) where the local planning authority give the applicant notice within 28 days following the date of receiving his application

of their determination that such prior approval is required, the giving of such approval; or

(cc) the expiry of 28 days following the date on which the application was received by the local planning authority without the local planning authority making any determination as to whether such approval is required or notifying the applicant of their determination;

(iv) (aa) where the local planning authority give the applicant notice that such prior approval is required the applicant shall display a site notice by site display on or near the land on which the proposed development is to be carried out, leaving the notice in position for not less than 21 days in the period of 28 days from the date on which the local planning authority gave the notice to the applicant;

(bb) where the site notice is, without any fault or intention of the applicant, removed, obscured or defaced before the period of 21 days referred to in sub-paragraph (aa) has elapsed, he shall be treated as having complied with the requirements of that sub-paragraph if he has taken reasonable steps for protection of the notice and, if need be, its replacement;

(v) the development shall, except to the extent that the local planning authority otherwise agree in writing, be carried out—

(aa) where prior approval is required, in accordance with the details approved;

(bb) where prior approval is not required, in accordance with the details submitted with the application; and

(vi) the development shall be carried out—

(aa) where approval has been given by the local planning authority, within a period of five years from the date on which approval was given;

(bb) in any other case, within a period of five years from the date on which the local planning authority were given the information referred to in sub-paragraph (d)(ii).

(3) The conditions in paragraph (2) do not apply to the extension or alteration of a building if the building is not on article 1(6) land except in the case of a significant extension or a significant alteration.

(4) Development consisting of the significant extension or the significant alteration of a building may only be carried out once by virtue of Class A(a).

Class B   Development on units of less than 5 hectares

Permitted development

B. The carrying out on agricultural land comprised in an agricultural unit of not less than 0.4 but less than 5 hectares in area of development consisting of—

(a) the extension or alteration of an agricultural building;

(b) the installation of additional or replacement plant or machinery;

(c) the provision, rearrangement or replacement of a sewer, main, pipe, cable or other apparatus;

(d) the provision, rearrangement or replacement of a private way;

(e) the provision of a hard surface;

The Town and Country Planning (General Permitted Development) Order 1995　　　355

    (f) the deposit of waste; or
    (g) the carrying out of any of the following operations in connection with fish farming, namely, repairing ponds and raceways; the installation of grading machinery, aeration equipment or flow meters and any associated channel; the dredging of ponds; and the replacement of tanks and nets, where the development is reasonably necessary for the purposes of agriculture within the unit.

Development not permitted
  B.1 Development is not permitted by Class B if—
    (a) the development would be carried out on a separate parcel of land forming part of the unit which is less than 0.4 hectare in area;
    (b) the external appearance of the premises would be materially affected;
    (c) any part of the development would be within 25 metres of a metalled part of a trunk road or classified road;
    (d) it would consist of, or involve, the carrying out of any works to a building or structure used or to be used for the accommodation of livestock or the storage of slurry or sewage sludge where the building or structure is within 400 metres of the curtilage of a protected building; or
    (e) it would relate to fish farming and would involve the placing or assembly of a tank on land or in any waters or the construction of a pond in which fish may be kept or an increase (otherwise than by the removal of silt) in the size of any tank or pond in which fish may be kept.
  B.2 Development is not permitted by Class B(a) if—
    (a) the height of any building would be increased;
    (b) the cubic content of the original building would be increased by more than 10%;
    (c) any part of any new building would be more than 30 metres from the original building;
    (d) the development would involve the extension, alteration or provision of a dwelling;
    (e) any part of the development would be carried out within 5 metres of any boundary of the unit; or
    (f) the ground area of any building extended by virtue of Class B(a) would exceed 465 square metres.
  B.3 Development is not permitted by Class B(b) if—
    (a) the height of any additional plant or machinery within 3 kilometres of the perimeter of an aerodrome would exceed 3 metres;
    (b) the height of any additional plant or machinery not within 3 kilometres of the perimeter of an aerodrome would exceed 12 metres;
    (c) the height of any replacement plant or machinery would exceed that of the plant or machinery being replaced; or
    (d) the area to be covered by the development would exceed 465 square metres calculated as described in paragraph D.2 below.
  B.4 Development is not permitted by Class B(e) if the area to be covered by the development would exceed 465 square metres calculated as described in paragraph D.2 below.

Conditions
  B.5 Development permitted by Class B and carried out within 400 metres of the curtilage of a protected building is subject to the condition that any building which is extended or altered, or any

works resulting from the development, shall not be used for the accommodation of livestock except in the circumstances described in paragraph D.3 below or for the storage of slurry or sewage sludge.

B.6 Development consisting of the extension or alteration of a building situated on article 1(6) land or the provision, rearrangement or replacement of a private way on such land is permitted subject to—

    (a) the condition that the developer shall, before beginning the development, apply to the local planning authority for a determination as to whether the prior approval of the authority will be required to the siting, design and external appearance of the building as extended or altered or the siting and means of construction of the private way; and

    (b) the conditions set out in paragraphs A.2(2)(ii) to (vi) above.

B.7 Development is permitted by Class B(f) subject to the following conditions—

    (a) that waste materials are not brought on to the land from elsewhere for deposit unless they are for use in works described in Class B(a), (d) or (e) and are incorporated forthwith into the building or works in question; and

    (b) that the height of the surface of the land will not be materially increased by the deposit.

Class C Mineral working for agricultural purposes

Permitted development

C. The winning and working on land held or occupied with land used for the purposes of agriculture of any minerals reasonably necessary for agricultural purposes within the agricultural unit of which it forms part.

Development not permitted

C.1 Development is not permitted by Class C if any excavation would be made within 25 metres of a metalled part of a trunk road or classified road.

Condition

C.2 Development is permitted by Class C subject to the condition that no mineral extracted during the course of the operation shall be moved to any place outside the land from which it was extracted, except to land which is held or occupied with that land and is used for the purposes of agriculture.

Interpretation of Part 6

D.1 For the purposes of Part 6—

'agricultural land' means land which, before development permitted by this Part is carried out, is land in use for agriculture and which is so used for the purposes of a trade or business, and excludes any dwellinghouse or garden;

'agricultural unit' means agricultural land which is occupied as a unit for the purposes of agriculture, including—

    (a) any dwelling or other building on that land occupied for the purpose of farming the land by the person who occupies the unit, or

    (b) any dwelling on that land occupied by a farmworker;

'building' does not include anything resulting from engineering operations;

'fish farming' means the breeding, rearing or keeping of fish or shellfish (which includes any kind of crustacean and mollusc);

'livestock' includes fish or shellfish which are farmed;

'protected building' means any permanent building which is normally occupied by people or would be so occupied, if it were in use for purposes for which it is apt; but does not include—
    (i)   a building within the agricultural unit; or
    (ii)   a dwelling or other building on another agricultural unit which is used for or in connection with agriculture;

'significant extension' and 'significant alteration' mean any extension or alteration of the building where the cubic content of the original building would be exceeded by more than 10% or the height of the building as extended or altered would exceed the height of the original building;

'slurry' means animal faeces and urine (whether or not water has been added for handling); and

'tank' includes any cage and any other structure for use in fish farming.

D.2 For the purposes of Part 6—
    (a)   an area calculated as described in this paragraph comprises the ground area which would be covered by the proposed development, together with the ground area of any building (other than a dwelling), or any structure, works, plant, machinery, ponds or tanks within the same unit which are being provided or have been provided within the preceding two years and any part of which would be within 90 metres of the proposed development;
    (b)   400 metres is to be measured along the ground.

D.3 The circumstances referred to in paragraphs A.2(1)(a) and B.5 are—
    (a)   that no other suitable building or structure, 400 metres or more from the curtilage of a protected building, is available to accommodate the livestock; and
    (b)   (i)   that the need to accommodate the livestock arises from—
        (aa)   quarantine requirements; or
        (bb)   an emergency due to another building or structure in which the livestock could otherwise be accommodated being unavailable because it has been damaged or destroyed by fire, flood or storm; or
    (ii)   in the case of animals normally kept out of doors, they require temporary accommodation in a building or other structure—
        (aa)   because they are sick or giving birth or newly born; or
        (bb)   to provide shelter against extreme weather conditions.

D.4 For the purposes of paragraph A.2(2)(c), the relevant area is the area of the proposed excavation or the area on which it is proposed to deposit waste together with the aggregate of the areas of all other excavations within the unit which have not been filled and of all other parts of the unit on or under which waste has been deposited and has not been removed.

D.5 In paragraph A.2(2)(iv), 'site notice' means a notice containing—
    (a)   the name of the applicant,
    (b)   the address or location of the proposed development,
    (c)   a description of the proposed development and of the materials to be used,

(d) a statement that the prior approval of the authority will be required to the siting, design and external appearance of the building, the siting and means of construction of the private way, the siting of the excavation or deposit or the siting and appearance of the tank, as the case may be,

(e) the name and address of the local planning authority,

and which is signed and dated by or on behalf of the applicant.

D.6 For the purposes of Class B—

(a) the erection of any additional building within the curtilage of another building is to be treated as the extension of that building and the additional building is not to be treated as an original building;

(b) where two or more original buildings are within the same curtilage and are used for the same undertaking they are to be treated as a single original building in making any measurement in connection with the extension or alteration of either of them.

D.7 In Class C, 'the purposes of agriculture' includes fertilising land used for the purposes of agriculture and the maintenance, improvement or alteration of any buildings, structures or works occupied or used for such purposes on land so used.

PART 7
FORESTRY BUILDINGS AND OPERATIONS

Class A
Permitted development

A. The carrying out on land used for the purposes of forestry, including afforestation, of development reasonably necessary for those purposes consisting of—

(a) works for the erection, extension or alteration of a building;

(b) the formation, alteration or maintenance of private ways;

(c) operations on that land, or on land held or occupied with that land, to obtain the materials required for the formation, alteration or maintenance of such ways;

(d) other operations (not including engineering or mining operations).

Development not permitted

A.1 Development is not permitted by Class A if—

(a) it would consist of or include the provision or alteration of a dwelling;

(b) the height of any building or works within 3 kilometres of the perimeter of an aerodrome would exceed 3 metres in height; or

(c) any part of the development would be within 25 metres of the metalled portion of a trunk road or classified road.

A.2(1) Subject to paragraph (3), development consisting of the erection of a building or the extension or alteration of a building or the formation or alteration of a private way is permitted by Class A subject to the following conditions—

(a) the developer shall, before beginning the development, apply to the local planning authority for a determination as to whether the prior approval of the authority will be required to the siting, design and external appearance of the building or, as the case may be, the siting and means of construction of the private way;

(b) the application shall be accompanied by a written description of the proposed development, the materials to be used and a plan indicating the site together with any fee required to be paid;

(c) the development shall not be begun before the occurrence of one of the following—

(i) the receipt by the applicant from the local planning authority of a written notice of their determination that such prior approval is not required;

(ii) where the local planning authority give the applicant notice within 28 days following the date of receiving his application of their determination that such prior approval is required, the giving of such approval;

(iii) the expiry of 28 days following the date on which the application was received by the local planning authority without the local planning authority making any determination as to whether such approval is required or notifying the applicant of their determination;

(d)(i) where the local planning authority give the applicant notice that such prior approval is required the applicant shall display a site notice by site display on or near the land on which the proposed development is to be carried out, leaving the notice in position for not less than 21 days in the period of 28 days from the date on which the local planning authority gave the notice to the applicant;

(ii) where the site notice is, without any fault or intention of the applicant, removed, obscured or defaced before the period of 21 days referred to in sub-paragraph (i) has elapsed, he shall be treated as having complied with the requirements of that sub-paragraph if he has taken reasonable steps for protection of the notice and, if need be, its replacement;

(e) the development shall, except to the extent that the local planning authority otherwise agree in writing, be carried out—

(i) where prior approval is required, in accordance with the details approved;

(ii) where prior approval is not required, in accordance with the details submitted with the application;

(f) the development shall be carried out—

(i) where approval has been given by the local planning authority, within a period of five years from the date on which approval was given,

(ii) in any other case, within a period of five years from the date on which the local planning authority were given the information referred to in sub-paragraph (b).

(2) In the case of development consisting of the significant extension or the significant alteration of the building such development may be carried out only once.

(3) Paragraph (1) does not preclude the extension or alteration of a building if the building is not on article 1(6) land except in the case of a significant extension or a significant alteration.

Interpretation of class A

A.3 For the purposes of Class A—

'significant extension' and 'significant alteration' mean any extension or alteration of the building where the cubic content of the original building would be exceeded by more than 10% or the height of the building as extended or altered would exceed the height of the original building; and

'site notice' means a notice containing—
(a) the name of the applicant,
(b) the address or location of the proposed development,
(c) a description of the proposed development and of the materials to be used,
(d) a statement that the prior approval of the authority will be required to the siting, design and external appearance of the building or, as the case may be, the siting and means of construction of the private way,
(e) the name and address of the local planning authority,
and which is signed and dated by or on behalf of the applicant.

PART 8
INDUSTRIAL AND WAREHOUSE DEVELOPMENT

Class A
Permitted development

A. **The extension or alteration of an industrial building or a warehouse.**

Development not permitted

A.1 Development is not permitted by Class A if—
(a) the building as extended or altered is to be used for purposes other than those of the undertaking concerned;
(b) the building is to be used for a purpose other than—
(i) in the case of an industrial building, the carrying out of an industrial process or the provision of employee facilities;
(ii) in the case of a warehouse, storage or distribution or the provision of employee facilities;
(c) the height of the building as extended or altered would exceed the height of the original building;
(d) the cubic content of the original building would be exceeded by more than—
(i) 10%, in respect of development on any article 1(5) land, or
(ii) 25%, in any other case;
(e) the floor space of the original building would be exceeded by more than—
(i) 500 square metres in respect of development on any article 1(5) land, or
(ii) 1,000 square metres in any other case;
(f) the external appearance of the premises of the undertaking concerned would be materially affected;
(g) any part of the development would be carried out within 5 metres of any boundary of the curtilage of the premises; or
(h) the development would lead to a reduction in the space available for the parking or turning of vehicles.

Conditions

A.2 Development is permitted by Class A subject to the conditions that any building extended or altered—
(a) shall only be used—
(i) in the case of an industrial building, for the carrying out of an industrial process for the purposes of the undertaking or the provision of employee facilities;
(ii) in the case of a warehouse, for storage or distribution for the purposes of the undertaking or the provision of employee facilities;

(b) shall not be used to provide employee facilities between 7.00 p.m. and 6.30 a.m. for employees other than those present at the premises of the undertaking for the purpose of their employment;

(c) shall not be used to provide employee facilities if a notifiable quantity of a hazardous substance is present at the premises of the undertaking.

Interpretation of Class A
A.3 For the purposes of Class A—
(a) the erection of any additional building within the curtilage of another building (whether by virtue of Class A or otherwise) and used in connection with it is to be treated as the extension of that building, and the additional building is not to be treated as an original building;

(b) where two or more original buildings are within the same curtilage and are used for the same undertaking, they are to be treated as a single original building in making any measurement;

(c) 'employee facilities' means social, care or recreational facilities provided for employees of the undertaking, including creche facilities provided for the children of such employees.

Class B Permitted development
B. Development carried out on industrial land for the purposes of an industrial process consisting of—
(a) the installation of additional or replacement plant or machinery,
(b) the provision, rearrangement or replacement of a sewer, main, pipe, cable or other apparatus, or
(c) the provision, rearrangement or replacement of a private way, private railway, siding or conveyor.

Development not permitted
B.1 Development described in Class B(a) is not permitted if—
(a) it would materially affect the external appearance of the premises of the undertaking concerned, or
(b) any plant or machinery would exceed a height of 15 metres above ground level or the height of anything replaced, whichever is the greater.

Interpretation of Class B
B.2 In Class B, 'industrial land' means land used for the carrying out of an industrial process, including land used for the purposes of an industrial undertaking as a dock, harbour or quay, but does not include land in or adjacent to and occupied together with a mine.

Class C Permitted development
C. The provision of a hard surface within the curtilage of an industrial building or warehouse to be used for the purpose of the undertaking concerned.

Class D Permitted development
D. The deposit of waste material resulting from an industrial process on any land comprised in a site which was used for that purpose on 1st July 1948 whether or not the superficial area or the height of the deposit is extended as a result.

Development not permitted
D.1 Development is not permitted by Class D if—
(a) the waste material is or includes material resulting from the winning and working of minerals, or
(b) the use on 1st July 1948 was for the deposit of material resulting from the winning and working of minerals.

Interpretation of Part 8	E. For the purposes of Part 8, in Classes A and C— 'industrial building' means a building used for the carrying out of an industrial process and includes a building used for the carrying out of such a process on land used as a dock, harbour or quay for the purposes of an industrial undertaking but does not include a building on land in or adjacent to and occupied together with a mine; and 'warehouse' means a building used for any purpose within Class B8 (storage or distribution) of the Schedule to the Use Classes Order but does not include a building on land in or adjacent to and occupied together with a mine.

PART 9
REPAIRS TO UNADOPTED STREETS AND PRIVATE WAYS

Class A Permitted development	**A. The carrying out on land within the boundaries of an unadopted street or private way of works required for the maintenance or improvement of the street or way.**
Interpretation of Class A	A.1 For the purposes of Class A— 'unadopted street' means a street not being a highway maintainable at the public expense within the meaning of the Highways Act 1980.

PART 10
REPAIRS TO SERVICES

Class A Permitted development	**The carrying out of any works for the purposes of inspecting, repairing or renewing any sewer, main, pipe, cable or other apparatus, including breaking open any land for that purpose.**

PART 11
DEVELOPMENT UNDER LOCAL OR PRIVATE ACTS OR ORDERS

Class A Permitted development	**A. Development authorised by—** **(a) a local or private Act of Parliament,** **(b) an order approved by both Houses of Parliament, or** **(c) an order under section 14 or 16 of the Harbours Act 1964 (orders for securing harbour efficiency etc., and orders conferring powers for improvement, construction etc. of harbours)** **which designates specifically the nature of the development authorised and the land upon which it may be carried out.**
Condition	A.1 Development is not permitted by Class A if it consists of or includes— (a) the erection, construction, alteration or extension of any building, bridge, aqueduct, pier or dam, or (b) the formation, laying out or alteration of a means of access to any highway used by vehicular traffic, unless the prior approval of the appropriate authority to the detailed plans and specifications is first obtained.

Prior approvals	A.2 The prior approval referred to in paragraph A.1 is not to be refused by the appropriate authority nor are conditions to be imposed unless they are satisfied that—
(a) the development (other than the provision of or works carried out to a dam) ought to be and could reasonably be carried out elsewhere on the land; or
(b) the design or exteral appearance of any building, bridge, aqueduct, pier or dam would injure the amenity of the neighbourhood and is reasonably capable of modification to avoid such injury.
Interpretation of Class A	A. 3 In Class A, 'appropriate authority' means—
(a) in Greater London or a metropolitan county, the local planning authority,
(b) in a National Park, outside a metropolitan county, the county planning authority,
(c) in any other case, the district planning authority.

PART 12
DEVELOPMENT BY LOCAL AUTHORITIES

Class A Permitted development	**A. The erection or construction and the maintenance, improvement or other alteration by a local authority or by an urban development corporation of—**
(a) any small ancillary building, works or equipment on land belonging to or maintained by them required for the purposes of any function exercised by them on that land otherwise than as statutory undertakers;
(b) lamp standards, information kiosks, passenger shelters, public shelters and seats, telephone boxes, fire alarms, public drinking fountains, horse troughs, refuse bins or baskets, barriers for the control of people waiting to enter public service vehicles, and similar structures or works required in connection with the operation of any public service administered by them.
Interpretation of Class A	A.1 For the purposes of Class A—
'urban development corporation' has the same meaning as in Part XVI of the Local Government, Planning and Land Act 1980 (urban development).
A.2 The reference in Class A to any small ancillary building, works or equipment is a reference to any ancillary building, works or equipment not exceeding 4 metres in height or 200 cubic metres in capacity.
Class B Permitted development	**B. The deposit by a local authority of waste material on any land comprised in a site which was used for that purpose on 1st July 1948 whether or not the superficial area or the height of the deposit is extended as a result.**
Development not permitted	B.1 Development is not permitted by Class B if the waste material is or includes material resulting from the winning and working of minerals.
Interpretation of Part 12	C. For the purposes of Part 12—
local authority' includes a parish or community council.

PART 13
DEVELOPMENT BY LOCAL HIGHWAY AUTHORITIES

Class A
Permitted development

A. **The carrying out by a local highway authority on land outside but adjoining the boundary of an existing highway of works required for or incidental to the maintenance or improvement of the highway.**

PART 14
DEVELOPMENT BY DRAINAGE BODIES

Class A
Permitted development

A. **Development by a drainage body in, on or under any watercourse or land drainage works and required in connection with the improvement, maintenance or repair of that watercourse or those works.**

Interpretation of Class A

A.1 For the purposes of Class A—
'drainage body' has the same meaning as in section 72(1) of the Land Drainage Act 1991 (interpretation) other than the National Rivers Authority.

PART 15
DEVELOPMENT BY THE NATIONAL RIVERS AUTHORITY

Class A
Permitted development

A. **Development by the National Rivers Authority, for the purposes of their functions, consisting of—**

    (a) **development not above ground level required in connection with conserving, redistributing or augmenting water resources,**

    (b) **development in, on or under any watercourse or land drainage works and required in connection with the improvement, maintenance or repair of that watercourse or those works,**

    (c) **the provision of a building, plant, machinery or apparatus in, on, over or under land for the purpose of survey or investigation,**

    (d) **the maintenance, improvement or repair of works for measuring the flow in any watercourse or channel,**

    (e) **any works authorised by or required in connection with an order made under section 73 of the Water Resources Act 1991 (power to make ordinary and emergency drought orders),**

    (f) **any other development in, on, over or under their operational land, other than the provision of a building but including the extension or alteration of a building.**

Development not permitted

A.1 Development is not permitted by Class A if—
(a) in the case of any Class A(a) development, it would include the construction of a reservoir,
(b) in the case of any Class A(f) development, it would consist of or include the extension or alteration of a building so that—
    (i) its design or external appearance would be materially affected,

(ii) the height of the original building would be exceeded, or the cubic content of the original building would be exceeded by more than 25%, or

(iii) the floor space of the original building would be exceeded by more than 1,000 square metres,

or

(c) in the case of any Class A(f) development, it would consist of the installation or erection of any plant or machinery exceeding 15 metres in height or the height of anything it replaces, whichever is the greater.

Condition A.2 Development is permitted by Class A(c) subject to the condition that, on completion of the survey or investigation, or at the expiration of six months from the commencement of the development concerned, whichever is the sooner, all such operations shall cease and all such buildings, plant, machinery and apparatus shall be removed and the land restored as soon as reasonably practicable to its former condition (or to any other condition which may be agreed with the local planning authority).

PART 16
DEVELOPMENT BY OR ON BEHALF OF SEWERAGE UNDERTAKERS

Class A
Permitted development **A. Development by or on behalf of a sewerage undertaker consisting of—**

(a) development not above ground level required in connection with the provision, improvement, maintenance or repair of a sewer, outfall pipe, sludge main or associated apparatus;

(b) the provision of a building, plant, machinery or apparatus in, on, over or under land for the purpose of survey or investigation;

(c) the maintenance, improvement or repair of works for measuring the flow in any watercourse or channel;

(d) any works authorised by or required in connection with an order made under section 73 of the Water Resources Act 1991 (power to make ordinary and emergency drought orders);

(e) any other development in, on, over or under their operational land, other than the provision of a building but including the extension or alteration of a building.

Development not permitted A.1 Development is not permitted by Class A(e) if—

(a) it would consist of or include the extension or alteration of a building so that—

(i) its design or external appearance would be materially affected;

(ii) the height of the original building would be exceeded, or the cubic content of the original building would be exceeded, by more than 25%; or

(iii) the floor space of the original building would be exceeded by more than 1,000 square metres;

or

(b) it would consist of the installation or erection of any plant or machinery exceeding 15 metres in height or the height of anything it replaces, whichever is the greater.

Condition	A.2 Development is permitted by Class A(b) subject to the condition that, on completion of the survey or investigation, or at the expiration of 6 months from the commencement of the development concerned, whichever is the sooner, all such operations shall cease and all such buildings, plant, machinery and apparatus shall be removed and the land restored as soon as reasonably practicable to its former condition (or to any other condition which may be agreed with the local planning authority).
Interpretation of Class A	A.3 For the purposes of Class A— 'associated apparatus', in relation to any sewer, main or pipe, means pumps, machinery or apparatus associated with the relevant sewer, main or pipe; 'sludge main' means a pipe or system of pipes (together with any pumps or other machinery or apparatus associated with it) for the conveyance of the residue of water or sewage treated in a water or sewage treatment works as the case may be, including final effluent or the products of the dewatering or incineration of such residue, or partly for any of those purposes and partly for the conveyance of trade effluent or its residue.

PART 17
DEVELOPMENT BY STATUTORY UNDERTAKERS

Class A Railway or light railway undertakings

Permitted development	**A. Development by railway undertakers on their operational land, required in connection with the movement of traffic by rail.**
Development not permitted	A.1 Development is not permitted by Class A if it consists of or includes— (a) the construction of a railway, (b) the construction or erection of a hotel, railway station or bridge, or (c) the construction or erection otherwise than wholly within a railway station of— (i) an office, residential or educational building, or a building used for an industrial process, or (ii) a car park, shop, restaurant, garage, petrol filling station or other building or structure provided under transport legislation.
Interpretation of Class A	A.2 For the purposes of Class A, references to the construction or erection of any building or structure include references to the reconstruction or alteration of a building or structure where its design or external appearance would be materially affected.

Class B Dock, pier, harbour, water transport, canal or inland navigation undertakings

Permitted development	**B. Development on operational land by statutory undertakers or their lessees in respect of dock, pier, harbour, water transport, or canal or inland navigation undertakings, required—** **(a) for the purposes of shipping, or** **(b) in connection with the embarking, disembarking, loading, discharging or transport of passengers, livestock or goods at a dock, pier or harbour, or with the movement of traffic by canal or inland navigation or by any railway forming part of the undertaking.**

Development not permitted	B.1 Development is not permitted by Class B if it consists of or includes—
	(a) the construction or erection of a hotel, or of a bridge or other building not required in connection with the handling of traffic,
	(b) the construction or erection otherwise than wholly within the limits of a dock, pier or harbour of—
	  (i) an educational building, or
	  (ii) a car park, shop, restaurant, garage, petrol filling station or other building provided under transport legislation.

Interpretation of Class B	B.2 For the purposes of Class B, references to the construction or erection of any building or structure include references to the reconstruction or alteration of a building or structure where its design or external appearance would be materially affected, and the reference to operational land includes land designated by an order made under section 14 or 16 of the Harbours Act 1964 (orders for securing harbour efficiency etc., and orders conferring powers for improvement, construction etc. of harbours), and which has come into force, whether or not the order was subject to the provisions of the Statutory Orders (Special Procedure) Act 1945.

Class C Works to inland waterways

Permitted development	C. **The improvement, maintenance or repair of an inland waterway (other than a commercial waterway or cruising waterway) to which section 104 of the Transport Act 1968 (classification of the Board's waterways) applies, and the repair or maintenance of a culvert, weir, lock, aqueduct, sluice, reservoir, let-off valve or other work used in connection with the control and operation of such a waterway.**

Class D Dredgings

Permitted development	D. **The use of any land by statutory undertakers in respect of dock, pier, harbour, water transport, canal or inland navigation undertakings for the spreading of any dredged material.**

Class E Water or hydraulic power undertakings

Permitted development	E. **Development for the purposes of their undertaking by statutory undertakers for the supply of water or hydraulic power consisting of—** (a) **development not above ground level required in connection with the supply of water or for conserving, redistributing or augmenting water resources, or for the conveyance of water treatment sludge,** (b) **development in, on or under any watercourse and required in connection with the improvement or maintenance of that watercourse,** (c) **the provision of a building, plant, machinery or apparatus in, on, over or under land for the purpose of survey or investigation,** (d) **the maintenance, improvement or repair of works for measuring the flow in any watercourse or channel,** (e) **the installation in a water distribution system of a booster station, valve house, meter or switch-gear house,** (f) **any works authorised by or required in connection with an order made under section 73 of the Water Resources**

Act 1991 (power to make ordinary and emergency drought orders),

(g) any other development in, on, over or under operational land other than the provision of a building but including the extension or alteration of a building.

Development not permitted
E.1 Development is not permitted by Class E if—
(a) in the case of any Class E(a) development, it would include the construction of a reservoir,
(b) in the case of any Class E(e) development involving the installation of a station or house exceeding 29 cubic metres in capacity, that installation is carried out at or above ground level or under a highway used by vehicular traffic,
(c) in the case of any Class E(g) development, it would consist of or include the extension or alteration of a building so that—
  (i) its design or external appearance would be materially affected;
  (ii) the height of the original building would be exceeded, or the cubic content of the original building would be exceeded by more than 25%, or
  (iii) the floor space of the original building would be exceeded by more than 1,000 square metres, or
(d) in the case of any Class E(g) development, it would consist of the installation or erection of any plant or machinery exceeding 15 metres in height or the height of anything it replaces, whichever is the greater.

Condition
E.2 Development is permitted by Class E(c) subject to the condition that, on completion of the survey or investigation, or at the expiration of six months from the commencement of the development, whichever is the sooner, all such operations shall cease and all such buildings, plant, machinery and apparatus shall be removed and the land restored as soon as reasonably practicable to its former condition (or to any other condition which may be agreed with the local planning authority).

Class F Gas suppliers

Permitted development
F. **Development by a public gas supplier required for the purposes of its undertaking consisting of—**
(a) **the laying underground of mains, pipes or other apparatus;**
(b) **the installation in a gas distribution system of apparatus for measuring, recording, controlling or varying the pressure, flow or volume of gas, and structures for housing such apparatus;**
(c) **the construction in any storage area or protective area specified in an order made under section 4 of the Gas Act 1965 (storage authorisation orders), of boreholes, and the erection or construction in any such area of any plant or machinery required in connection with the construction of such boreholes;**
(d) **the placing and storage on land of pipes and other apparatus to be included in a main or pipe which is being or is about to be laid or constructed in pursuance of planning permission granted or deemed to be granted under Part III of the Act (control over development);**

(e) the erection on operational land of the public gas supplier of a building solely for the protection of plant or machinery;

(f) any other development carried out in, on, over or under the operational land of the public gas supplier.

Development not permitted

F.1 Development is not permitted by Class F if—

(a) in the case of any Class F(b) development involving the installation of a structure for housing apparatus exceeding 29 cubic metres in capacity, that installation would be carried out at or above ground level, or under a highway used by vehicular traffic,

(b) in the case of any Class F(c) development—

(i) the borehole is shown in an order approved by the Secretary of State for Trade and Industry for the purpose of section 4(6) of the Gas Act 1965; or

(ii) any plant or machinery would exceed 6 metres in height, or

(c) in the case of any Class F(e) development, the building would exceed 15 metres in height, or

(d) in the case of any Class F(f) development—

(i) it would consist of or include the erection of a building, or the reconstruction or alteration of a building where its design or external appearance would be materially affected;

(ii) it would involve the installation of plant or machinery exceeding 15 metres in height, or capable without the carrying out of additional works of being extended to a height exceeding 15 metres; or

(iii) it would consist of or include the replacement of any plant or machinery, by plant or machinery exceeding 15 metres in height or exceeding the height of the plant or machinery replaced, whichever is the greater.

Conditions

F.2 Development is permitted by Class F subject to the following conditions—

(a) in the case of any Class F(a) development, not less than eight weeks before the beginning of operations to lay a notifiable pipe-line, the public gas supplier shall give notice in writing to the local planning authority of its intention to carry out that development, identifying the land under which the pipe-line is to be laid,

(b) in the case of any Class F(d) development, on completion of the laying or construction of the main or pipe, or at the expiry of a period of nine months from the beginning of the development, whichever is the sooner, any pipes or other apparatus still stored on the land shall be removed and the land restored as soon as reasonably practicable to its condition before the development took place (or to any other condition which may be agreed with the local planning authority),

(c) in the case of any Class F(e) development, approval of the details of the design and external appearance of the building shall be obtained, before the development is begun, from—

(i) in Greater London or a metropolitan county, the local planning authority,

(ii) in a National Park, outside a metropolitan county, the county planning authority,

(iii) in any other case, the district planning authority.

Class G   Electricity undertakings

Permitted development

G. Development by statutory undertakers for the generation, transmission or supply of electricity for the purposes of their undertaking consisting of—

(a) the installation or replacement in, on, over or under land of an electric line and the construction of shafts and tunnels and the installation or replacement of feeder or service pillars or transforming or switching stations or chambers reasonably necessary in connection with an electric line;

(b) the installation or replacement of any telecommunications line which connects any part of an electric line to any electrical plant or building, and the installation or replacement of any support for any such line;

(c) the sinking of boreholes to ascertain the nature of the subsoil and the installation of any plant or machinery reasonably necessary in connection with such boreholes;

(d) the extension or alteration of buildings on operational land;

(e) the erection on operational land of the undertaking or a building solely for the protection of plant or machinery;

(f) any other development carried out in, on, over or under the operational land of the undertaking.

Development not permitted

G.1   Development is not permitted by Class G if—

(a) in the case of any Class G(a) development—

(i) it would consist of or include the installation or replacement of an electric line to which section 37(1) of the Electricity Act 1989 (consent required for overhead lines) applies; or

(ii) it would consist of or include the installation or replacement at or above ground level or under a highway used by vehicular traffic, of a chamber for housing apparatus and the chamber would exceed 29 cubic metres in capacity;

(b) in the case of any Class G(b) development—

(i) the development would take place in a National Park, an area of outstanding natural beauty, or a site of special scientific interest;

(ii) the height of any support would exceed 15 metres; or

(iii) the telecommunications line would exceed 1,000 metres in length;

(c) in the case of any Class G(d) development—

(i) the height of the original building would be exceeded;

(ii) the cubic content of the original building would be exceeded by more than 25% or, in the case of any building on article 1(5) land, by more than 10%, or

(iii) the floor space of the original building would be exceeded by more than 1,000 square metres or, in the case of any building on article 1(5) land, by more than 500 square metres;

(d) in the case of any Class G(e) development, the building would exceed 15 metres in height, or

(e) in the case of any Class G(f) development, it would consist of or include—

(i) the erection of a building, or the reconstruction or alteration of a building where its design or external appearance would be materially affected, or

(ii) the installation or erection by way of addition or replacement of any plant or machinery exceeding 15 metres in height or the height of any plant or machinery replaced, whichever is the greater.

Conditions G.2 Development is permitted by Class G subject to the following conditions—

(a) in the case of any Class G(a) development consisting of or including the replacement of an existing electric line, compliance with any conditions contained in a planning permission relating to the height, design or position of the existing electric line which are capable of being applied to the replacement line;

(b) in the case of any Class G(a) development consisting of or including the installation of a temporary electric line providing a diversion for an existing electric line, on the ending of the diversion or at the end of a period of six months from the completion of the installation (whichever is the sooner) the temporary electric line shall be removed and the land on which any operations have been carried out to install that line shall be restored as soon as reasonably practicable to its condition before the installation took place;

(c) in the case of any Class G(c) development, on the completion of that development, or at the end of a period of six months from the beginning of that development (whichever is the sooner) any plant or machinery installed shall be removed and the land shall be restored as soon as reasonably practicable to its condition before the development took place;

(d) in the case of any Class G(e) development, approval of details of the design and external appearance of the buildings shall be obtained, before development is begun, from—

(i) in Greater London or a metropolitan county, the local planning authority,

(ii) in a National Park, outside a metropolitan county, the county planning authority,

(iii) in any other case, the district planning authority.

Interpretation of Class G G.3 For the purposes of Class G(a), 'electric line' has the meaning assigned to that term by section 64(1) of the Electricity Act 1989 (interpretation etc. of Part 1).

G.4 For the purposes of Class G(b), 'electrical plant' has the meaning assigned to that term by the said section 64(1) and 'telecommunications line' means a wire or cable (including its casing or coating) which forms part of a telecommunication apparatus within the meaning assigned to that term by paragraph 1 of Schedule 2 to the Telecommunications Act 1984 (the telecommunications code).

G.5 For the purposes of Class G(d), (e) and (0, the land of the holder of a licence under section 6(2) of the Electricity Act 1989 (licences authorising supply etc.) shall be treated as operational land if it would be operational land within section 263 of the Act (meaning of 'operational land') if such licence holders were statutory undertakers for the purpose of that section.

Class H Tramway or road transport undertakings

Permitted development H. **Development required for the purposes of the carrying on of any tramway or road transport undertaking consisting of—**

(a) the installation of posts, overhead wires, underground cables, feeder pillars or transformer boxes in, on, over

or adjacent to a highway for the purpose of supplying current to public service vehicles;

(b) the installation of tramway tracks, and conduits, drains and pipes in connection with such tracks for the working of tramways;

(c) the installation of telephone cables and apparatus, huts, stop posts and signs required in connection with the operation of public service vehicles;

(d) the erection or construction and the maintenance, improvement or other alteration of passenger shelters and barriers for the control of people waiting to enter public service vehicles;

(e) any other development on operational land of the undertaking.

Development not permitted
H.1 Development is not permitted by Class H if it would consist of—

(a) in the case of any Class H(a) development, the installation of a structure exceeding 17 cubic metres in capacity,

(b) in the case of any Class H(e) development—

(i) the erection of a building or the reconstruction or alteration of a building where its design or external appearance would be materially affected,

(ii) the installation or erection by way of addition or replacement of any plant or machinery which would exceed 15 metres in height or the height of any plant or machinery it replaces, whichever is the greater,

(iii) development, not wholly within a bus or tramway station, in pursuance of powers contained in transport legislation.

Class I Lighthouse undertakings

Permitted development
I. Development required for the purposes of the functions of a general or local lighthouse authority under the Merchant Shipping Act 1894 and any other statutory provision made with respect to a local lighthouse authority, or in the exercise by a local lighthouse authority of rights, powers or duties acquired by usage prior to the 1894 Act.

Development not permitted
I.1 Development is not permitted by Class I if it consists of or includes the erection of offices, or the reconstruction or alteration of offices where their design or external appearance would be materially affected.

Class J Post Office

Permitted development
J. Development required for the purposes of the Post Office consisting of—

(a) the installation of posting boxes or self-service machines,

(b) any other development carried out in, on, over or under the operational land of the undertaking.

Development not permitted
J.1 Development is not permitted by Class J if—

(a) it would consist of or include the erection of a building, or the reconstruction or alteration of a building where its design or external appearance would be materially affected, or

(b) it would consist of or include the installation or erection by way of addition or replacement of any plant or machinery which would exceed 15 metres in height or the height of any existing plant or machinery, whichever is the greater.

Interpretation of Part 17

K. For the purposes of Part 17—
'transport legislation' means section 14(1)(d) of the Transport Act 1962 (supplemental provisions relating to the Board's powers) or section 10(1)(x) of the Transport Act 1968 (general powers of Passenger Transport Executive).

PART 18
AVIATION DEVELOPMENT

Class A Development at an airport

Permitted development

A. The carrying out on operational land by a relevant airport operator or its agent of development (including the erection or alteration of an operational building) in connection with the provision of services and facilities at a relevant airport.

Development not permitted

A.1 Development is not permitted by Class A if it would consist of or include—
    (a) the construction or extension of a runway;
    (b) the construction of a passenger terminal the floor space of which would exceed 500 square metres;
    (c) the extension or alteration of a passenger terminal, where the floor space of the building as existing at 5th December 1988 or, if built after that date, of the building as built, would be exceeded by more than 15%;
    d) the erection of a building other than an operational building;
    (e) the alteration or reconstruction of a building other than an operational building, where its design or external appearance would be materially affected.

Condition

A.2 Development is permitted by Class A subject to the condition that the relevant airport operator consults the local planning authority before carrying out any development, unless that development falls within the description in paragraph A.4.

Interpretation of Class A

A.3 For the purposes of paragraph A.1, floor space shall be calculated by external measurement and without taking account of the floor space in any pier or satellite.

A.4 Development falls within this paragraph if—
    (a) it is urgently required for the efficient running of the airport, and
    (b) it consists of the carrying out of works, or the erection or construction of a structure or of an ancillary building, or the placing on land of equipment, and the works, structure, building, or equipment do not exceed 4 metres in height or 200 cubic metres in capacity.

Class B Air navigation development at an airport

Permitted development

B. The carrying out on operational land within the perimeter of a relevant airport by a relevant airport operator or its agent of development in connection with—
    (a) the provision of air traffic control services,
    (b) the navigation of aircraft using the airport, or
    (c) the monitoring of the movement of aircraft using the airport.

Class C Air navigation development near an airport

Permitted development
C. The carrying out on operational land outside but within 8 kilometres of the perimeter of a relevant airport, by a relevant airport operator or its agent, of development in connection with—
    (a) the provision of air traffic control services,
    (b) the navigation of aircraft using the airport, or
    (c) the monitoring of the movement of aircraft using the airport.

Development not permitted
C.1 Development is not permitted by Class C if—
    (a) any building erected would be used for a purpose other than housing equipment used in connection with the provision of air traffic control services, with assisting the navigation of aircraft, or with monitoring the movement of aircraft using the airport;
    (b) any building erected would exceed a height of 4 metres;
    (c) it would consist of the installation or erection of any radar or radio mast, antenna or other apparatus which would exceed 15 metres in height, or, where an existing mast, antenna or apparatus is replaced, the height of that mast, antenna or apparatus, if greater.

Class D Development by Civil Aviation Authority within an airport

Permitted development
D. The carrying out by the Civil Aviation Authority or its agents, within the perimeter of an airport at which the Authority provides air traffic control services, of development in connection with—
    (a) the provision of air traffic control services,
    (b) the navigation of aircraft using the airport, or
    (c) the monitoring of the movement of aircraft using the airport.

Class E Development by the Civil Aviation Authority for air traffic control and navigation

Permitted development
E. The carrying out on operational land of the Civil Aviation Authority by the Authority or its agents of development in connection with—
    (a) the provision of air traffic control services,
    (b) the navigation of aircraft, or
    (c) monitoring the movement of aircraft.

Development
E.1 Development is not permitted by Class E if—
    (a) any building erected would be used for a purpose other than housing equipment used in connection with the provision of air traffic control services, assisting the navigation of aircraft or monitoring the movement of aircraft;
    (b) any building erected would exceed a height of 4 metres; or
    (c) it would consist of the installation or erection of any radar or radio mast, antenna or other apparatus which would exceed 15 metres in height, or, where an existing mast, antenna or apparatus is replaced, the height of that mast, antenna or apparatus, if greater.

Class F Development by the Civil Aviation Authority in an emergency

Permitted development
F. The use of land by or on behalf of the Civil Aviation Authority in an emergency to station moveable apparatus replacing unserviceable apparatus.

Condition	F.1 Development is permitted by Class F subject to the condition that on or before the expiry of a period of six months beginning with the date on which the use began, the use shall cease, and any apparatus shall be removed, and the land shall be restored to its condition before the development took place, or to any other condition as may be agreed in writing between the local planning authority and the developer.

Class G Development by the Civil Aviation Authority for air traffic control etc.

Permitted development	**G. The use of land by or on behalf of the Civil Aviation Authority to provide services and facilities in connection with—** **(a) the provision of air traffic control services,** **(b) the navigation of aircraft, or** **(c) the monitoring of aircraft,** **and the erection or placing of moveable structures on the land for the purpose of that use.**
Condition	G.1 Development is permitted by Class G subject to the condition that, on or before the expiry of the period of six months beginning with the date on which the use began, the use shall cease, and any structure shall be removed, and the land shall be restored to its condition before the development took place, or to any other condition as may be agreed in writing between the local planning authority and the developer.

Class H Development by the Civil Aviation Authority for surveys etc.

Permitted development	**H. The use of land by or on behalf of the Civil Aviation Authority for the stationing and operation of apparatus in connection with the carrying out of surveys or investigations.**
Condition	H.1 Development is permitted by Class H subject to the condition that on or before the expiry of the period of six months beginning with the date on which the use began, the use shall cease, and any apparatus shall be removed, and the land shall be restored to its condition before the development took place, or to any other condition as may be agreed in writing between the local planning authority and the developer.

Class I Use of airport buildings managed by relevant airport operators

Permitted development	**I. The use of buildings within the perimeter of an airport managed by a relevant airport operator for purposes connected with air transport services or other flying activities at that airport.**
Interpretation of Part 18	J. For the purposes of Part 18— 'operational building' means a building, other than a hotel, required in connection with the movement or maintenance of aircraft, or with the embarking, disembarking, loading, discharge or transport of passengers, livestock or goods at a relevant airport; 'relevant airport' means an airport to which Part V of the Airports Act 1986 (status of certain airports as statutory undertakers etc.) applies; and 'relevant airport operator' means a relevant airport operator within the meaning of section 57 of the Airports Act 1986 (scope of Part V).

PART 19
DEVELOPMENT ANCILLARY TO MINING OPERATIONS

Class A
Permitted development

A. The carrying out of operations for the erection, extension, installation, rearrangement, replacement, repair or other alteration of any—
    (a) plant or machinery,
    (b) buildings,
    (c) private ways or private railways or sidings, or
    (d) sewers, mains, pipes, cables or other similar apparatus,
on land used as a mine.

Development not permitted

A.1 Development is not permitted by Class A—
    (a) in relation to land at an underground mine—
        (i) on land which is not an approved site; or
        (ii) on land to which the description in paragraph D.1(b) applies, unless a plan of that land was deposited with the mineral planning authority before 5th June 1989;
    (b) if the principal purpose of the development would be any purpose other than—
        (i) purposes in connection with the winning and working of minerals at that mine or of minerals brought to the surface at that mine; or
        (ii) the treatment, storage or removal from the mine of such minerals or waste materials derived from them;
    (c) if the external appearance of the mine would be materially affected;
    (d) if the height of any building, plant or machinery which is not in an excavation would exceed—
        (i) 15 metres above ground level; or
        (ii) the height of the building, plant or machinery, if any, which is being rearranged, replaced or repaired or otherwise altered,
whichever is the greater;
    (e) if the height of any building, plant or machinery in an excavation would exceed—
        (i) 15 metres above the excavated ground level; or
        (ii) 15 metres above the lowest point of the unexcavated ground immediately adjacent to the excavation; or
        (iii) the height of the building, plant or machinery, if any, which is being rearranged, replaced or repaired or otherwise altered,
whichever is the greatest;
    (f) if any building erected (other than a replacement building) would have a floor space exceeding 1,000 square metres; or
    (g) if the cubic content of any replaced, extended or altered building would exceed by more than 25% the cubic content of the building replaced, extended or altered or the floor space would exceed by more than 1,000 square metres the floor space of that building.

Condition

A.2 Development is permitted by Class A subject to the condition that before the end of the period of 24 months from the date when the mining operations have permanently ceased, or any longer period which the mineral planning authority agree in writing—

The Town and Country Planning (General Development Procedure) Order 1995   409

(2) Subject to paragraph (3), if the local planning authority have failed to satisfy the requirements of article 8 in respect of an application for planning permission at the time the application is referred to the Secretary of State under section 77 of the Act (reference of applications to Secretary of State), or any appeal to the Secretary of State is made under section 78 of the Act, article 8 shall continue to apply, as if such referral or appeal to the Secretary of State had not been made.

(3) Where paragraph (2) applies, when the local planning authority have satisfied the requirements of article 8, they shall inform the Secretary of State that they have done so.

10. Consultations before the grant of permission

(1) Before granting planning permission for development which, in their opinion, falls within a category set out in the table below, a local planning authority shall consult the authority or person mentioned in relation to that category, except where—

    (i) the local planning authority are the authority so mentioned;
    (ii) the local planning authority are required to consult the authority so mentioned under articles 11 or 12; or
    (iii) the authority or person so mentioned has advised the local planning authority that they do not wish to be consulted.

TABLE

Para	Description of Development	Consultee
(a)	Development likely to affect land in Greater London or in a metropolitan county	The local planning authority concerned
(b)	Development likely to affect land in a non-metropolitan county, other than land in a National Park	The district planning authority concerned
(c)	Development likely to affect land in a National Park	The county planning authority concerned
(d)	Development within an area which has been notified to the local planning authority by the Health and Safety Executive for the purpose of this provision because of the presence within the vicinity of toxic, highly reactive, explosive or inflammable substances and which involves the provision of— (i) residential accommodation; (ii) more than 250 square metres of retail floor space; (iii) more than 500 square metres of office floor space; or (iv) more than 750 square metres of floor space to be used for an industrial process, or which is otherwise likely to result in a material increase in the number of persons working within or visiting the notified area	The Health and Safety Executive
(e)	Development likely to result in a material increase in the volume or a material change in the character of traffic—	

	(i) entering or leaving a trunk road; or	In England, the Secretary of State for Transport and, in Wales, the Secretary of State for Wales
	(ii) using a level crossing over a railway	The operator of the network which includes or consists of the railway in question, and in England, the Secretary of State for Transport and, in Wales, the Secretary of State for Wales
(f)	Development likely to result in a material increase in the volume or a material change in the character of traffic entering or leaving a classified road or proposed highway	The local highway authority concerned
(g)	Development likely to prejudice the improvement or construction of a classified road or proposed highway	The local highway authority concerned
(h)	Development involving— (i) the formation, laying out or alteration of any means of access to a highway (other than a trunk road); or	The local highway authority concerned
	(ii) the construction of a highway or private means of access to premises affording access to a road in relation to which a toll order is in force	The local highway autority concerned, and in the case of a road subject to a concession, the concessionare
(i)	Development which consists of or includes the laying out or construction of a new street	The local highway authority
(j)	Development which involves the provision of a building or pipe-line in an area of coal working notified by the Coal Authority to the local planning authority	The Coal Authority
(k)	Development involving or including mining operations	The National Rivers Authority
(l)	Development within three kilometres of Windsor Castle, Windsor Great Park, or Windsor Home Park, or within 800 metres of any other royal palace or park, which might affect the amenities (including security) of that palace or park	The Secretary of State for National Heritage
(m)	Development of land in Greater London involving the demolition, in whole or part, or the material alteration of a listed building	The Historic Buildings and Monuments Commission for England

(n)	Development likely to affect the site of a scheduled monument	In England, the Historic Buildings and Monuments Commission for England and, in Wales, the Secretary of State for Wales
(o)	Development likely to affect any garden or park of special historic interest which is registered in accordance with section 8C of the Historic Buildings and Ancient Monuments Act 1953 (register of gardens) and which is classified as Grade I or Grade II*.	The Historic Buildings and Monuments Commission for England
(p)	Development involving the carrying out of works or operations in the bed of or on the banks of a river or stream	The National Rivers Authority
(q)	Development for the purpose of refining or storing mineral oils and their derivatives	The National Rivers Authority
(r)	Development involving the use of land for the deposit of refuse or waste	The National Rivers Authority
(s)	Development relating to the retention, treatment or disposal of sewage, trade-waste, slurry or sludge (other than the laying of sewers, the construction of pumphouses in a line of sewers, the construction of septic tanks and cesspools serving single dwellinghouses or single caravans or single buildings in which not more than ten people will normally reside, work or congregate, and works ancillary thereto)	The National Rivers Authority
(t)	Development relating to the use of land as a cemetery	The National Rivers Authority
(u)	Development— (i) in or likely to affect a site of special scientific interest of which notification has been given, or has effect as if given, to the local planning authority by the Nature Conservancy Council for England or the Countryside Council for Wales, in accordance with section 28 of the Wildlife and Countryside Act 1981 (areas of special scientific interest); or (ii) within an area which has been notified to the local planning authority by the Nature Conservancy Council for England or the Countryside Council for Wales, and which is within two kilometres of a site of special scientific interest of which notification has been given or has effect as if given as aforesaid	The Council which gave, or is to be regarded as having given, the notice

(v)	Development involving any land on which there is a theatre	The Theatres Trust
(w)	Development which is not for agricultural purposes and is not in accordance with the provisions of a development plan and involves— (i) the loss of not less than 20 hectares of grades 1, 2 or 3a agricultural land which is for the time being used (or was last used) for agricultural purposes; or (ii) the loss of less than 20 hectares of grades 1, 2 or 3a agricultural land which is for the time being used (or was last used) for agricultural purposes, in circumstances in which the development is likely to lead to a further loss of agricultural land amounting cumulatively to 20 hectares or more	In England, the Minister of Agriculture, Fisheries and Food and, in Wales, the Secretary of State for Wales
(x)	Development within 250 metres of land which— (i) is or has, at any time in the 30 years before the relevant application, been used for the deposit of refuse or waste; and (ii) has been notified to the local planning authority by the waste regulation authority for the purposes of this provision	The waste regulation authority concerned
(y)	Development for the purposes of fish farming	The National Rivers Authority

(2) In the above table—
 (a) in paragraph (d)(iv), 'industrial process' means a process for or incidental to any of the following purposes—
  (i) the making of any article or part of any article (including a ship or vessel, or a film, video or sound recording);
  (ii) the altering, repairing, maintaining, ornamenting, finishing, cleaning, washing, packing, canning, adapting for sale, breaking up or demolition of any article; or
  (iii) the getting, dressing or treatment of minerals in the course of any trade or business other than agriculture, and other than a process carried out on land used as a mine or adjacent to and occupied together with a mine (and in this sub-paragraph, 'mine' means any site on which mining operations are carried out),
 (b) in paragraph (e)(ii), 'network' and 'operator' have the same meaning as in Part I of the Railways Act 1993 (the provision of railway services);
 (c) in paragraphs (f) and (g), 'classified road' means a highway or proposed highway which—
  (i) is a classified road or a principal road by virtue of section 12(1) of the Highways Act 1980 (general provision as to principal and classified roads); or
  (ii) is classified for the purposes of any enactment by the Secretary of State by virtue of section 12(3) of that Act;
 (d) in paragraph (h), 'concessionaire', 'road subject to a concession' and 'toll order' have the same meaning as in Part I of the New Roads and Street Works Act 1991 (new roads in England and Wales);
 (e) in paragraph (i), 'street' has the same meaning as in section 48(1) of the New Roads and Street Works Act 1991 (streets, street works and undertakers), and 'new street' includes a continuation of an existing street;

(f) in paragraph (m), 'listed building' has the same meaning as in section 1 of the Planning (Listed Buildings and Conservation Areas) Act 1990 (listing of buildings of special architectural or historic interest);

(g) in paragraph (n), 'scheduled monument' has the same meaning as in section 1(11) of the Ancient Monuments and Archaeological Areas Act 1979 (schedule of monuments);

(h) in paragraph (s), 'slurry' means animal faeces and urine (whether or not water has been added for handling), and 'caravan' has the same meaning as for the purposes of Part I of the Caravan Sites and Control of Development Act 1960 (caravan sites);

(i) in paragraph (u), 'site of special scientific interest' means land to which section 28(1) of the Wildlife and Countryside Act 1981 (areas of special scientific interest) applies;

(j) in paragraph (v), 'theatre' has the same meaning as in section 5 of the Theatres Trust Act 1976 (interpretation); and

(k) in paragraph (x), 'waste regulation authority' has the same meaning as in section 30(1) of the Environmental Protection Act 1990 (authorities for purposes of Part II).

(3) The Secretary of State may give directions to a local planning authority requiring that authority to consult any person or body named in the directions, in any case or class of case specified in the directions.

(4) Where, by or under this article, a local planning authority are required to consult any person or body ('the consultee') before granting planning permission—

(a) they shall, unless an applicant has served a copy of an application for planning permission on the consultee, give notice of the application to the consultee; and

(b) they shall not determine the application until at least 14 days after the date on which notice is given under paragraph (a) or, if earlier, 14 days after the date of service of a copy of the application on the consultee by the applicant.

(5) The local planning authority shall, in determining the application, take into account any representations received from a consultee.

11. Consultation with county planning authority

Where a district planning authority are required by paragraph 7 of Schedule 1 to the Act (local planning authorities — distribution of functions) to consult the county planning authority before determining an application for planning permission, they shall not determine the application until the expiry of at least 14 days after the date of the notice given to the county planning authority in accordance with sub-paragraph (6)(b) of that paragraph.

12. Applications relating to county matters

(1) A county planning authority shall, before determining—

(a) an application for planning permission under Part III of the Act (control over development);

(b) an application for a certificate of lawful use or development under section 191 or 192 of the Act (certificates of lawfulness of existing or proposed use or development); or

(c) an application for approval of reserved matters,

give the district planning authority, if any, for the area in which the relevant land lies a period of at least 14 days, from the date of receipt of the application by the district authority, within which to make recommendations about the manner in which the application shall be determined; and shall take any such recommendations into account.

(2) A county planning authority shall—
(a) on determining an application of a kind mentioned in paragraph (1), as soon as reasonably practicable notify the district planning authority, if any, of the terms of their decision; or
(b) if any such application is referred to the Secretary of State, inform the district planning authority, if any, of the date when it was so referred and, when notified to them, of the terms of the decision.

13. Notice to parish and community councils

(1) Where the council of a parish or community are given information in relation to an application pursuant to paragraph 8(1) of Schedule 1 to the Act (local planning authorities — distribution of functions), they shall, as soon as practicable, notify the local planning authority who are determining the application whether they propose to make any representations about the manner in which the application should be determined, and shall make any representations to that authority within 14 days of the notification to them of the application.

(2) A local planning authority shall not determine any application in respect of which a parish or community are required to be given information before—
(a) the council of the parish or community inform them that they do not propose to make any representations;
(b) representations are made by that council; or
(c) the period of 14 days mentioned in paragraph (1) has elapsed,
whichever shall first occur; and in determining the application the authority shall take into account any representations received from the council of the parish or community.

(3) The district planning authority (or, in a metropolitan county, the local planning authority) shall notify the council of the parish or community of the terms of the decision on any such application or, where the application is referred to the Secretary of State, of the date when it was so referred and, when notified to them, of the terms of his decision—

14. Directions by the Secretary of State

(1) The Secretary of State may give directions restricting the grant of permission by a local planning authority, either indefinitely or during such a period as may be specified in the directions, in respect of any development or in respect of development of any class so specified.

(2) The Secretary of State may give directions—
(a) that particular proposed development of a description set out in Schedule 1 or Schedule 2 to the Town and Country Planning (Assessment of Environmental Effects) Regulations 1988 (descriptions of development) is exempted from the application of those Regulations, in accordance with Article 2(3) of Council Directive 85/337/EEC;
(b) as to whether particular proposed development is or is not development in respect of which those Regulations require the consideration of environmental information (as defined in those Regulations) before planning permission can be granted; or
(c) that development of any class described in the direction is development in respect of which those Regulations require the consideration of such information before such permission can be granted.

(3) A local planning authority shall deal with applications for planning permission for development to which a direction given under this article applies in such manner as to give effect to the direction.

15. Special provisions as to permission for development affecting certain existing and proposed highways

(1) Where an application is made to a local planning authority for planning permission for development which consists of or includes—

(a) the formation, laying out or alteration of any access to or from any part of a trunk road which is either a special road or, if not a special road, a road subject to a speed limit exceeding 40 miles per hour; or

(b) any development of land within 67 metres (or such other distance as may be specified in a direction given by the Secretary of State under this article) from the middle of—

(i) any highway (other than a trunk road) which the Secretary of State has provided, or is authorised to provide, in pursuance of an order under Part II of the Highways Act 1980 (trunk roads, classified roads, metropolitan roads, special roads) and which has not for the time being been transferred to any other highway authority;

(ii) any highway which he proposes to improve under Part V of that Act (improvement of highways) and in respect of which notice has been given to the local planning authority;

(iii) any highway to which he proposes to carry out improvements in pursuance of an order under Part II of that Act; or

(iv) any highway which he proposes to construct, the route of which is shown on the development plan or in respect of which he has given notice in writing to the relevant local planning authority together with maps or plans sufficient to identify the route of the highway,

the local planning authority shall notify the Secretary of State by sending him a copy of the application and any accompanying plans and drawings.

(2) An application referred to in paragraph (1) above shall not be determined unless—

(a) the local planning authority receive a direction given under article 14 of this Order (and in accordance with the terms of that direction);

(b) they receive notification by or on behalf of the Secretary of State that he does not propose to give any such direction in respect of the development to which the application relates; or

(c) a period of 28 days (or such longer period as may be agreed in writing between the local planning authority and the Secretary of State) from the date when notification was given to the Secretary of State has elapsed without receipt of such a direction.

(3) The Secretary of State may, in respect of any case or any class or description of cases, give a direction specifying a different distance for the purposes of paragraph 1(b) above.

16. Notification of mineral applications

(1) Where notice has been given for the purposes of this article to a mineral planning authority as respects land which is in their area and specified in the notice—

(a) by the Coal Authority that the land contains coal;

(b) by the Secretary of State for Trade and Industry that it contains gas or oil; or

(c) by the Crown Estates Commissioners that it contains silver or gold,

the mineral planning authority shall not determine any application for planning permission to win and work any mineral on that land, without first notifying the body or person who gave the notice that an application has been made.

(2) In this article, 'coal' means coal other than that—

(a) won or worked during the course of operations which are carried on exclusively for the purpose of exploring for coal; or

(b) which it is necessary to dig or carry away in the course of activities carried on for purposes which do not include the getting of coal or any product of coal.

17. Development not in accordance with the development plan

A local planning authority may in such cases and subject to such conditions as may be prescribed by directions given by the Secretary of State under this Order grant permission for development which does not accord with the provisions of the development plan in force in the area in which the land to which the application relates is situated.

18. Notice of reference of applications to the Secretary of State

On referring any application to the Secretary of State under section 77 of the Act (reference of applications to Secretary of State) pursuant to a direction in that behalf, a local planning authority shall serve on the applicant a notice—

(a) setting out the terms of the direction and any reasons given by the Secretary of State for issuing it;

(b) stating that the application has been referred to the Secretary of State; and

(c) containing a statement that the Secretary of State will, if the applicant so desires, afford to him an opportunity of appearing before and being heard by a person appointed by the Secretary of State for the purpose, and that the decision of the Secretary of State on the application will be final.

19. Representations to be taken into account

(1) A local planning authority shall, in determining an application for planning permission, take into account any representations made, where any notice of the application has been—

(a) given by site display under article 6 or 8, within 21 days beginning with the date when the notice was first displayed by site display;

(b) served on—

   (i) an owner of the land or a tenant of an agricultural holding under article 6, or

   (ii) an adjoining owner or occupier under article 8,

within 21 days beginning with the date when the notice was served on that person, provided that the representations are made by any person who satisfies them that he is such an owner, tenant or occupier; or

(c) given by local advertisement under article 6 or 8, within 14 days beginning with the date on which the notice was published,

and the representations and periods in this article are representations and periods prescribed for the purposes of section 71(2)(a) of the Act (consultations in connection with determinations under section 70).

(2) A local planning authority shall give notice of their decision to every person who has made representations which they were required to take into account in accordance with paragraph (1)(b)(i), and such notice is notice prescribed for the purposes of section 71(2)(b) of the Act.

(3) Paragraphs (1) and (2) of this article apply to applications referred to the Secretary of State under section 77 of the Act (reference of applications to Secretary of State) and paragraphs (1)(b) and (2) apply to appeals to the Secretary of State made under section 78 of the Act (right to appeal against planning decisions and failure to take such decisions), as if the references to—

(a) a local planning authority were to the Secretary of State, and

(b) determining an application for planning permission were to determining such application or appeal, as the case may be.

20. Time periods for decision

(1) Subject to paragraph (5), where a valid application under article 4 or regulation 3 of the 1988 Regulations (applications for planning permission) has been received by a local planning authority, they shall within the period specified in

paragraph (2) give the applicant notice of their decision or determination or notice that the application has been referred to the Secretary of State.

(2) The period specified in this paragraph is—
   (a) a period of eight weeks beginning with the date when the application was received by a local planning authority;
   (b) except where the applicant has already given notice of appeal to the Secretary of State, such extended period as may be agreed in writing between the applicant and the local planning authority by whom the application falls to be determined; or
   (c) where a fee due in respect of an application has been paid by a cheque which is subsequently dishonoured, the appropriate period specified in (a) or (b) above calculated without regard to any time between the date when the authority sent the applicant written notice of the dishonouring of the cheque and the date when the authority are satisfied that they have received the full amount of the fee.

(3) For the purposes of this article, the date when the application was received shall be taken to be the date when each of the following events has occurred—
   (a) the application form or application in writing has been lodged with the authority mentioned in article 5(1);
   (b) any certificate or documents required by the Act or this Order has been lodged with that authority; and
   (c) any fee required to be paid in respect of the application has been paid to that authority and, for this purpose, lodging a cheque for the amount of a fee is to be taken as payment.

(4) A local planning authority shall provide such information about applications made under article 4 or regulation 3 of the 1988 Regulations (including information as to the manner in which any such application has been dealt with) as the Secretary of State may by direction require; and any such direction may include provision as to the persons to be informed and the manner in which the information is to be provided.

(5) Subject to paragraph (6), a local planning authority shall not determine an application for planning permission, where any notice of the application has been—
   (a) given by site display under article 6 or 8, before the end of the period of 21 days beginning with the date when the notice was first displayed by site display;
   (b) served on—
      (i) an owner of the land or a tenant of an agricultural holding under article 6, or
      (ii) an adjoining owner or occupier under article 8
before the end of the period of 21 days beginning with the date when the notice was served on that person;
   (c) given by local advertisement under article 6 or 8, before the end of the period of 14 days beginning with the date on which the notice was published,
and the periods in this paragraph are periods prescribed for the purposes of section 71(1) of the Act (consultations in connection with determinations under section 70).

(6) Where, under paragraph (5), more than one of the prescribed periods applies, the local planning authority shall not determine the application before the end of the later or latest of such periods.

21. Applications made under planning condition

Where an application has been made to a local planning authority for any consent, agreement or approval required by a condition or limitation attached to a grant of planning permission (other than an application for approval of reserved matters or an application for approval under Part 24 of Schedule 2 to the Town and Country Planning (General Permitted Development) Order 1995 (development by telecommunications code system operators)) the authority shall give notice to the applicant of their decision on the application within a period of eight weeks from the date when the application was received by the authority, or such longer period as may be agreed by the applicant and the authority in writing.

22. Written notice of decision or determination relating to a planning application

(1) When the local planning authority give notice of a decision or determination on an application for planning permission or for approval of reserved matters, and a permission or approval is granted subject to conditions or the application is refused, the notice shall—

(a) state clearly and precisely their full reasons for the refusal or for any condition imposed; and

(b) where the Secretary of State has given a direction restricting the grant of permission for the development for which application is made or where he or a Government Department has expressed the view that the permission should not be granted (either wholly or in part) or should be granted subject to conditions, give details of the direction or of the view expressed,

and shall be accompanied by a notification in the terms (or substantially in the terms) set out in Part 2 of Schedule 1 to this Order.

(2) Where—

(a) the applicant for planning permission has submitted an environmental statement; and

(b) the local planning authority have decided (having taken environmental information into consideration) to grant permission (whether unconditionally or subject to conditions),

the notice given to the applicant in accordance with article 20(1) shall include a statement that environmental information has been taken into consideration by the authority.

23. Appeals

(1) An applicant who wishes to appeal to the Secretary of State under section 78 of the Act (right to appeal against planning decisions and failure to take such decisions) shall give notice of appeal to the Secretary of State by—

(a) serving on him, within the time limit specified in paragraph (2), a form obtained from him, together with such of the documents specified in paragraph (3) as are relevant to the appeal; and

(b) serving on the local planning authority a copy of the form mentioned in paragraph (a), as soon as reasonably practicable, together with a copy of any relevant documents mentioned in paragraph (3)(e).

(2) The time limit mentioned in paragraph (1) is six months from—

(a) the date of the notice of the decision or determination giving rise to the appeal;

(b) the expiry of the period specified in article 20 or, as the case may be, article 21; or

(c) In a case in which the authority have served a notice on the applicant in accordance with article 3(2) that they require further information, and he has not provided the information, the date of service of that notice,

or such longer period as the Secretary of State may, at any time, allow.

(3) The documents mentioned in paragraph (1) are—

(a) the application made to the local planning authority which has occasioned the appeal;

(b) all plans, drawings and documents sent to the authority in connection with the application;

(c) all correspondence with the authority relating to the application;

(d) any certificate provided to the authority under article 7;
(e) any other plans, documents or drawings relating to the application which were not sent to the authority;
(f) the notice of the decision or determination, if any;
(g) if the appeal relates to an application for approval of certain matters in accordance with a condition on a planning permission, the application for that permission, the plans submitted with that application and the planning permission granted.

24. Certificate of lawful use or development

(1) An application for a certificate under section 191(1) or 192(1) of the Act (certificates of lawfulness of existing or proposed use or development) shall be in writing and shall, in addition to specifying the land and describing the use, operations or other matter in question in accordance with those sections, include the following information—

(a) the paragraph of section 191(1) or, as the case may be, section 192(1), under which the application is made;

(b) in the case of an application under section 191(1), the date on which the use, operations or other matter began or, in the case of operations carried out without planning permission, the date on which the operations were substantially completed;

(c) in the case of an application under section 191(1)(a), the name of any use class specified in an order under section 55(2)(f) of the Act (meaning of 'development') which the applicant considers applicable to the use existing at the date of the application;

(d) in the case of an application under section 191(1)(c), sufficient details of the planning permission to enable it to be identified;

(e) in the case of an application under section 192(1)(a), the use of the land at the date of the application (or, when the land is not in use at that date, the purpose for which it was last used) and the name of any use class specified in an order under section 55(2)(f) of the Act which the applicant considers applicable to the proposed use;

(f) the applicant's reasons, if any, for regarding the use, operations or other matter described in the application as lawful; and

(g) such other information as the applicant considers to be relevant to the application.

(2) An application to which paragraph (1) applies shall be accompanied by—

(a) a plan identifying the land to which the application relates;

(b) such evidence verifying the information included in the application as the applicant can provide; and

(c) a statement setting out the applicant's interest in the land, the name and address of any other person known to the applicant to have an interest in the land and whether any such other person has been notified of the application.

(2A) Where, by virtue of section 299(2) of the Act, an application for a certificate under section 192(1) of the Act is made in respect of Crown land, it shall, in addition to the documents required by paragraph (2), be accompanied by—

(a) a statement that the application is made, by virtue of section 299(2) of the Act, in respect of Crown land; and

(b) where the application is made by a person authorised in writing by the appropriate authority, a copy of that authorisation.

(3) Where such an application specifies two or more uses, operations or other matters, the plan which accompanies the application shall indicate to which part of the land each such use, operation or matter relates.

(4) Articles 5(1) and 20(4) shall apply to an application for a certificate to which paragraph (1) applies as they apply to an application for planning permission.

(5) When the local planning authority receive an application to which paragraph (1) applies and any fee required to be paid in respect of the application, they shall, as soon as reasonably practicable, send to the applicant an acknowledgement of the application in the terms (or substantially in the terms) set out in Part 1 of Schedule 1.

(6) Where, after sending an acknowledgement as required by paragraph (5), the local planning authority consider that the application is invalid by reason of the failure to comply with the preceding paragraphs of this article or any other statutory requirement, they shall, as soon as practicable, notify the applicant that his application is invalid.

(7) The local planning authority may by notice in writing require the applicant to provide such further information as may be specified to enable them to deal with the application.

(8) The local planning authority shall give the applicant written notice of their decision within a period of eight weeks beginning with the date of receipt by the authority of the application and any fee required to be paid in respect of the application or, except where the applicant has already given notice of appeal to the Secretary of State, within such extended period as may be agreed upon in writing between the applicant and the authority.

(9) For the purpose of calculating the appropriate period specified in paragraph (8), where any fee required has been paid by a cheque which is subsequently dishonoured, the time between the date when the authority send the applicant written notice of the dishonouring of the cheque and the date when the authority receive the full amount of the fee shall not be taken into account.

(10) Where an application is refused, in whole or in part (including a case in which the authority modify the description of the use, operations or other matter in the application or substitute an alternative description for that description), the notice of decision shall state clearly and precisely the authority's full reasons for their decision and shall include a statement to the effect that if the applicant is aggrieved by the decision he may appeal to the Secretary of State under section 195 of the Act (appeals against refusal or failure to give decision on application).

(11) A certificate under section 191 or 192 of the Act shall be in the form set out in Schedule 4, or in a form substantially to the like effect.

(12) Where a local planning authority propose to revoke a certificate issued under section 191 or 192 of the Act in accordance with section 193(7) of the Act (certificates under sections 191 and 192: supplementary provisions), they shall, before they revoke the certificate, give notice of that proposal to—

(a) the owner of the land affected;
(b) the occupier of the land affected;
(c) any other person who will in their opinion be affected by the revocation; and
(d) in the case of a certificate issued by the Secretary of State under section 195 of the Act, the Secretary of State.

(13) A notice issued under paragraph (12) shall invite the person on whom the notice is served to make representations on the proposal to the authority within 14 days of service of the notice and the authority shall not revoke the certificate until all such periods allowed for making representations have expired.

(14) An authority shall give written notice of any revocation under section 193(7) of the Act to every person on whom notice of the proposed revocation was served under paragraph (12).

25. Register of applications

(1) In this article and in article 26, 'the local planning register authority' means—

(a) in Greater London or a metropolitan county, the local planning authority (and references to the area of the local planning register authority are, in this case, to the area of the local planning authority);

(b) in relation to land in a National Park (except in a metropolitan county), the county planning authority (and references to the area of the local planning register authority are, in this case, to the area of the county planning authority within a National Park);

(c) in relation to any other land, the district planning authority (and references to the area of the local planning register authority are, in this case, to the area of the district planning authority, other than any part of their area failing within a National Park).

(2) Each local planning register authority shall keep, in two parts, a register of every application for planning permission relating to their area.

(3) Part I of the register shall contain a copy of each such application, and a copy of any application for approval of reserved matters made in respect of an outline planning permission granted on such an application, made or sent to the local planning register authority and not finally disposed of, together with any accompanying plans and drawings.

(4) Part II of the register shall contain, in respect of every application for planning permission relating to the local planning register authority's area—

(a) a copy (which may be photographic) of the application and of plans and drawings submitted in relation thereto;

(b) particulars of any direction given under the Act or this Order in respect of the application;

(c) the decision, if any, of the local planning authority in respect of the application, including details of any conditions subject to which permission was granted, the date of such decision and the name of the local planning authority;

(d) the reference number, the date and effect of any decision of the Secretary of State in respect of the application, whether on appeal or on a reference under section 77 of the Act (reference of applications to Secretary of State);

(e) the date of any subsequent approval (whether approval of reserved matters or any other approval required) given in relation to the application.

(5) Where, on any appeal to the Secretary of State under section 174 of the Act (appeal against enforcement notices), the appellant is deemed to have made an application for planning permission and the Secretary of State has granted permission, the local planning register authority shall, on receipt of notification of the Secretary of State's decision, enter into Part II of the register referred to in paragraph (2) particulars of the development concerned, the land on which it was carried out, and the date and effect of the Secretary of State's decision.

(6) The register kept by the local planning register authority shall also contain the following information in respect of every application for a certificate under section 191 or 192 of the Act (certificates of lawfulness of existing or proposed use or development) relating to the authority's area—

(a) the name and address of the applicant;

(b) the date of the application;

(c) the address or location of the land to which the application relates;

(d) the description of the use, operations or other matter included in the application;

(e) the decision, if any, of the local planning authority in respect of the application and the date of such decision; and

(f) the reference number, date and effect of any decision of the Secretary of State on an appeal in respect of the application.

(7) The register shall contain the following information about simplified planning zone schemes in the area of the authority—

(a) brief particulars of any action taken by the authority or the Secretary of State in accordance with section 83 of or Schedule 7 to the Act (making of simplified planning zone schemes etc.) to establish or approve any simplified planning zone scheme, including the date of adoption or approval, the date on which the scheme or alteration becomes operative and the date on which it ceases to be operative;

    (b) a copy of any simplified planning zone scheme, or alteration to an existing scheme, including any diagrams, illustrations, descriptive matter or any other prescribed material which has been made available for inspection under Schedule 7 to the Act;

    (c) an index map showing the boundary of any operative or proposed simplified planning zone schemes, including alterations to existing schemes where appropriate, together with a reference to the entries in the register under sub-paragraph (a) and (b) above.

  (8) To enable any person to trace any entry in the register, every register shall include an index together with a separate index of applications for development involving mining operations or the creation of mineral working deposits.

  (9) Every entry in the register shall be made within 14 days of the receipt of an application, or of the giving or making of the relevant direction, decision or approval as the case may be.

  (10) The register shall either be kept at the principal office of the local planning register authority or that part of the register which relates to land in part of that authority's area shall be kept at a place within or convenient to that part.

  (11) For the purposes of paragraph (3) of this article, an application shall not be treated as finally disposed of unless—

    (a) it has been decided by the authority (or the appropriate period allowed under article 20(2) of this Order has expired without their giving a decision) and the period of six months specified in article 23 of this Order has expired without any appeal having been made to the Secretary of State;

    (b) if it has been referred to the Secretary of State under section 77 of the Act. (reference of applications to Secretary of State) or an appeal has been made to the Secretary of State under section 78 of the Act (right to appeal against planning decisions and failure to take such decisions), the Secretary of State has issued his decision and the period of six weeks specified in section 288 of the Act (proceedings for questioning the validity of certain orders, decisions and directions) has expired without any application having been made to the High Court under that section;

    (c) an application has been made to the High Court under section 288 of the Act and the matter has been finally determined, either by final dismissal of the application by a court or by the quashing of the Secretary of State's decision and the issue of a fresh decision (without a further application under the said section 288); or

    (d) it has been withdrawn before being decided by the authority or the Secretary of State, as the case may be, or an appeal has been withdrawn before the Secretary of State has issued his decision.

26. Register of enforcement and stop notices

  (1) Subject to paragraph (2) of this article, the register under section 188 of the Act (register of enforcement and stop notices) shall contain the following information with respect to every enforcement notice issued in relation to land in the area of the authority maintaining the register—

    (a) the address of the land to which the notice relates or a plan by reference to which its situation can be ascertained;

    (b) the name of the issuing authority;

    (c) the date of issue of the notice;

    (d) the date of service of copies of the notice;

    (e) a statement or summary of the breach of planning control alleged and the requirements of the notice, including the period within which any required steps are to be taken;

(f) the date specified in the notice as the date on which it is to take effect;

(g) information on any postponement of the date specified as the date on which the notice will take effect by reason of section 175(4) of the Act (appeals: supplementary provisions) and the date of the final determination or withdrawal of any appeal;

(h) the date of service and, if applicable, of withdrawal of any stop notice referring to the enforcement notice, together with a statement or summary of the activity prohibited by any such stop notice;

(i) the date, if any, on which the local planning authority are satisfied that steps required by the notice for a purpose mentioned in section 173(4)(b) of the Act (remedying any injury to amenity) have been taken.

(2) That register shall also contain the following information with respect to every breach of condition notice served in relation to land in the area of the authority maintaining the register—

(a) the address of the land to which the notice relates or a plan by reference to which its situation can be ascertained;

(b) the name of the serving authority;

(c) the date of service of the notice;

(d) details of the relevant planning permission sufficient to enable it to be identified;

(e) a statement or summary of the condition which has not been complied with and the requirements of the notice, including the period allowed for compliance.

(3) All entries relating to an enforcement notice, stop notice or breach of condition notice shall be removed from the register if—

(a) in the case of an enforcement notice or stop notice, the relevant enforcement notice is quashed by the Secretary of State;

(b) in the case of a breach of condition notice, the notice is quashed by a court;

(c) in any case, the relevant notice is withdrawn.

(4) Every register shall include an index for enabling a person to trace any entry in the register by reference to the address of the land to which the notice relates.

(5) Where a county planning authority issue an enforcement notice or serve a stop notice or a breach of condition notice, they shall supply the information specified in paragraph (1) or (2) of this article, as the case may be, in relation to the notice to the district planning authority in whose area the land to which the notice relates is situated and shall inform that authority if the notice is withdrawn or the relevant enforcement notice or breach of condition notice is quashed.

(6) The information prescribed in paragraphs (1) and (2) of this article shall be entered in the register as soon as practicable and in any event within 14 days of the occurrence to which it relates, and information shall be so supplied under paragraph (5) that entries may be made within the said period of 14 days.

(7) The register shall either be kept at the principal office of the local planning register authority or that part of the register which relates to land in part of that authority's area shall be kept at a place within or convenient to that part.

27. Directions

Any power conferred by this Order to give a direction includes power to cancel or vary the direction by a subsequent direction.

28. Revocations, transitionals and savings

(1) Subject to paragraphs (2) to (5) of this article, the statutory instruments specified in Schedule 5 are revoked to the extent not already revoked.

(2) Where an area of coal working has been notified to the local planning authority for the purposes of paragraph (i) of the table in article 18 of the Town and Country Planning General Development Order 1988 (consultations before the grant of permission) before the date of the coming into force of this Order, such notification

shall be treated as if it had been made for the purposes of paragraph (j) of the table in article 10 of this Order by the Coal Authority on or after that date; and, in relation to a particular application for planning permission made before 31st October 1994, the local planning authority are not required to consult the Coal Authority if they have already consulted the British Coal Corporation.

(3) Any notice given for the purposes of article 13 of the Town and Country Planning General Development Order 1988 (notification of mineral applications) before the date of the coming into force of this Order, shall be treated as if it had been given for the purposes of article 16 of this Order by the Coal Authority on or after that date; and, in relation to a particular application for planning permission made before 31st October 1994, the mineral planning authority are not required to notify the Coal Authority, before determining the application, if they have already notified the British Coal Corporation that that application has been made.

(4) The relevant provisions of the Town and Country Planning General Development Order 1988, in the form in which they were in force immediately before 27th July 1992, shall continue to apply with respect to applications made under section 64 of the Act (applications to determine whether planning permission required) before 27th July 1992.

(5) The relevant provisions of the Town and Country Planning General Development Order 1988, in the form in which they were in force immediately before 27th July 1992, shall continue to apply with respect to applications for established use certificates made under section 192 of the Act (applications for established use certificates), as originally enacted, before 27th July 1992.

SCHEDULE 1

Articles 5, 22 and 24

PART 1
TOWN AND COUNTRY PLANNING ACT 1990

Letter to be sent by a local planning authority when they receive an application for planning permission or for a certificate of lawful use or development.

Thank you for your application dated ....
which I received on ....
I am still examining your application form and the accompanying plans and documents to see whether they comply with the law.*
If I find that your application is invalid because it does not comply with the statutory requirements then I shall write to you again as soon as I can.*
If, by (*insert date at end of period of eight weeks beginning with the date when the application was received*) ....
- you have not been told that your application is invalid; or
- you have not been told that your fee cheque has been dishonoured; or
- you have not been given a decision in writing; or
- you have not agreed in writing to extend the period in which the decision may be given,

then you can appeal to the Secretary of State for the Environment/Wales* under section 78/ section 195* of the Town and Country Planning Act 1990. You should appeal within six months and you must use a form which you can get from the Planning Inspectorate at Tollgate House, Houlton Street, Bristol BS2 9DJ/Cathays Park, Cardiff CF1 3NQ*. This does not apply if your application has already been referred to the Secretary of State for the Environment/Wales*.

*Delete where inappropriate

PART 2
TOWN AND COUNTRY PLANNING ACT 1990

Notification to be sent to an applicant when a local planning authority refuse planning permission or grant it subject to conditions (*To be endorsed on notices of decision*)

Appeals to the Secretary of State

- If you are aggrieved by the decision of your local planning authority to refuse permission for the proposed development or to grant it subject to conditions, then you can appeal to the Secretary of State for the Environment/Wales* under section 78 of the Town and Country Planning Act 1990.
- If you want to appeal, then you must do so within six months of the date of this notice, using a form which you can get from the Planning Inspectorate at Tollgate House, Houlton Street, Bristol BS2 9DJ/Cathays Park, Cardiff CF1 3NQ*.
- The Secretary of State can allow a longer period for giving notice of an appeal, but he will not normally be prepared to use this power unless there are special circumstances which excuse the delay in giving notice of appeal.
- The Secretary of State need not consider an appeal if it seems to him that the local planning authority could not have granted planning permission for the proposed development or could not have granted it without the conditions they imposed, having regard to the statutory requirements, to the provisions of any development order and to any directions given under a development order.
- In practice, the Secretary of State does not refuse to consider appeals solely because the local planning authority based their decision on a direction given by him.

Purchase Notices

- If either the local planning authority or the Secretary of State for the Environment/Wales* refuses permission to develop land or grants it subject to conditions, the owner may claim that he can neither put the land to a reasonably beneficial use in its existing state nor render the land capable of a reasonably beneficial use by the carrying out of any development which has been or would be permitted.
- In these circumstances, the owner may serve a purchase notice on the Council (District Council, London Borough Council or Common Council of the City of London) in whose area the land is situated. This notice will require the Council to purchase his interest in the land in accordance with the provisions of Part VI of the Town and Country Planning Act 1990.

*Delete where inappropriate

SCHEDULE 2   Articles 6, 7 and 9

PART 1

Town and Country Planning (General Development Procedure) Order 1995

NOTICE UNDER ARTICLE 6 OF APPLICATION FOR PLANNING PERMISSION

(to be published in a newspaper or to be served on an owner* or a tenant**)

Proposed development at *(a)* ....
I give notice that *(b)* ....
is applying to the *(c)* .... Council
for planning permission to *(d)* ....
Any owner* of the land or tenant** who wishes to make representations about this application should write to the Council at *(e)* ....
by *(f)* ....

* 'owner' means a person having a freehold interest or a leasehold interest the unexpired term of which is not less than seven years, or, in the case of development consisting of the winning or working of minerals, a person entitled to an interest in a mineral in the land (other than oil, gas, coal, gold or silver).

** 'tenant' means a tenant of an agricultural holding any part of which is comprised in the land.

Signed ....
†On behalf of ....
Date ....

Statement of owners' rights

The grant of planning permission does not affect owners' rights to retain or dispose of their property, unless there is some provision to the contrary in an agreement or in a lease.

Statement of agricultural tenants' rights

The grant of planning permission for non-agricultural development may affect agricultural tenants' security of tenure.

†delete where inappropriate

Insert:
(a) address or location of the proposed development
(b) applicant's name
(c) name of Council
(d) description of the proposed development
(e) address of the Council
(f) date giving a period of 21 days beginning with the date of service, or 14 days beginning with the date of publication, of the notice (as the case may be)

Town and Country Planning (General Development Procedure) Order 1995

NOTICE UNDER ARTICLE 6 OF APPLICATION FOR PLANNING PERMISSION

(to be posted in the case of an application for planning permission for development consisting of the winning and working of minerals by underground operations (in addition to the service or publication of any other requisite notices in this Schedule))

Proposed development at *(a)* ....
I give notice that *(b)* ....
is applying to the *(c)* .... Council
for planning permission to *(d)* ....
Members of the public may inspect copies of:
- the application
- the plans
- and other documents submitted with it

at *(e)* ....
during all reasonable hours until *(f)* ....
Anyone who wishes to make representations about this application should write to the Council at *(g)* ....
.... by *(f)* ....
          Signed ....
          †On behalf of ....
          Date ....

†Delete where inappropriate

Insert:
(a) address or location of the proposed development
(b) applicant's name
(c) name of Council
(d) description of the proposed development
(e) address at which the application may be inspected (the applicant is responsible for making the application available for inspection within the area of the local planning authority)
(f) date giving a period of 21 days, beginning with the date when the notice is posted
(g) address of Council

Town and Country Planning (General Development Procedure) Order 1995
NOTICE UNDER ARTICLES 6 AND 9(1) OF APPEAL
(to be published in a newspaper or to be served on an owner* or a tenant**)

Proposed development at *(a)* ....
I give notice that *(b)* ....
having applied to the *(c)* .... Council
to *(d)* ....
is appealing to the Secretary of State for the Environment/Secretary of State for Wales†
    against the decision of the Council†
    on the failure of the Council to give notice of a decision†
Any owner* of the land or tenant** who wishes to make representations about this appeal should write to the Secretary of State for the Environment/Wales† at the Department of the Environment at Tollgate House, Houlton Street, Bristol BS2 9DJ/Welsh Office at Planning Division, Cathays Park, Cardiff CFI 3NQ†, by *(e)* ....
* 'owner' means a person having a freehold interest or a leasehold interest the unexpired term of which is not less than seven years, or, in the case of development consisting of the winning or working of minerals, a person entitled to an interest in a mineral in the land (other than oil, gas, coal, gold or silver).
** 'tenant' means a tenant of an agricultural holding any part of which is comprised in the land.

                                          Signed ....
                                          †On behalf of ....
                                          Date ....

Statement of owners' rights
    The grant of planning permission does not affect owners' rights to retain or dispose of their property, unless there is some provision to the contrary in an agreement or in a lease.

Statement of agricultural tenants' rights
    The grant of planning permission for non-agricultural development may affect agricultural tenants' security of tenure.

†delete where inappropriate

Insert:
(a) address or location of the proposed development
(b) applicant's name
(c) name of Council
(d) description of the proposed development
(e) date giving a period of 21 days beginning with the date of service, or 14 days beginning with the date of publication, of the notice (as the case may be)

Town and Country Planning (General Development Procedure) Order 1995
NOTICE UNDER ARTICLES 6 AND 9(1) OF APPEAL
(to be posted in the case of an application for planning permission for development consisting of the winning and working of minerals by underground operations (in addition to the service or publication of any other requisite notices in this Schedule))

Proposed development at *(a)* ....
I give notice that *(b)* ....
having applied to the *(c)* .... Council
to *(d)* ....
is appealing to the Secretary of State for the Environment/Secretary of State for Wales*
   against the decision of the Council*
   on the failure of the Council to give notice of a decision*
Members of the public may inspect copies of:
- the application
- the plans
- and other documents submitted with it

at *(e)* .... during all reasonable hours until *(f)* ....
Anyone who wishes to make representations about this appeal should write to the Secretary of State for the Environment/Wales* at the Department of the Environment at Tollgate House, Houlton Street, Bristol BS2 9DJ/Welsh Office at Planning Division, Cathays Park, Cardiff CFI 3NQ* by *(f)* ....
....

                           Signed ....
                           *On behalf of ....
                           Date ....

*delete where inappropriate

Insert:
(a)   address or location of the proposed development
(b)   applicant's name
(c)   name of Council
(d)   description of the proposed development
(e)   address of Council
(f)   date giving a period of 21 days, beginning with the date when the notice is posted

PART 2
Town and Country Planning (General Development Procedure) Order 1995
CERTIFICATE UNDER ARTICLE 7

Certificate A*(a)*
I certify that:
on the day 21 days before the date of the accompanying application/appeal*
nobody, except the applicant/appellant*, was the owner*(b)* of any part of the land
to which the application/appeal* relates.

Signed ....
*On behalf of ....
Date ....

*delete where inappropriate

(a) This Certificate is for use with applications and appeals for planning permission (articles 7 and 9(1) of the Order). One of Certificates A, B, C or D (or the appropriate certificate in the case of certain minerals applications) must be completed, together with the Agricultural Holdings Certificate.

(b) 'owner' means a person having a freehold interest or a leasehold interest the unexpired term of which is not less than seven years, or, in the case of development consisting of the winning and working of minerals, a person entitled to an interest in a mineral in the land (other than oil, gas, coal, gold or silver).

Town and Country Planning (General Development Procedure) Order 1995
CERTIFICATE UNDER ARTICLE 7
Certificate B *(a)*

I certify that:
I have/The applicant has/The appellant has* given the requisite notice to everyone else who, on the day 21 days before the date of the accompanying application/appeal*, was the owner *(b)* of any part of the land to which the application/appeal* relates, as listed below.

Owner's *(b)* name	Address at which notice was served	Date on which notice was served

Signed ....
*On behalf of ....
Date ....

*delete where inappropriate

(a) This Certificate is for use with applications and appeals for planning permission (articles 7 and 9(1) of the Order). One of Certificates A, B, C or D (or the appropriate certificate in the case of certain minerals applications) must be completed, together with the Agricultural Holdings Certificate.

(b) 'owner' means a person having a freehold interest or a leasehold interest the unexpired term of which is not less than seven years, or, in the case of development consisting of the winning and working of minerals, a person entitled to an interest in a mineral in the land (other than oil, gas, coal, gold or silver).

Town and Country Planning (General Development Procedure) Order 1995
CERTIFICATE UNDER ARTICLE 7
Certificate C*(a)*
I certify that:
- I/The applicant/The appellant* cannot issue a Certificate A or B in respect of the accompanying application/appeal*.
- I have/The applicant has/The appellant has* given the requisite notice to the persons specified below, being persons who on the day 21 days before the date of the application/ appeal*, were owners*(b)* of any part of the land to which the application/appeal* relates.

Owner's*(b)* name	Address at which notice was served	Date on which notice was served

- I have/The applicant has/The appellant has* taken all reasonable steps open to me/him/her* to find out the names and addresses of the other owners*(b)* of the land, or of a part of it, but have/has* been unable to do so. These steps were as follows: *(c)* ....
....
- Notice of the application/appeal*, as attached to this Certificate, has been published in the*(d)* ....
....
on*(e)* ....

Signed ....
*On behalf of ....
Date ....

*delete where inappropriate

(a) This Certificate is for use with applications and appeals for planning permission (articles 7 and 9(1) of the Order). One of Certificates A, B, C or D (or the appropriate certificate in the case of certain minerals applications) must be completed, together with the Agricultural Holdings Certificate.
(b) 'owner' means a person having a freehold interest or a leasehold interest the unexpired term of which is not less than seven years, or, in the case of development consisting of the winning and working of minerals, a person entitled to an interest in a mineral in the land (other than oil, gas, coal, gold or silver).

Insert:
(c) description of steps taken
(d) name of newspaper circulating in the area where the land is situated
(e) date of publication (which must be not earlier than the day 21 days before the date of the application or appeal)

Town and Country Planning (General Development Procedure) Order 1995
CERTIFICATE UNDER ARTICLE 7
Certificate D(a)
I certify that:
- I/The applicant/The appellant* cannot issue a Certificate A in respect of the accompanying application/appeal*.
- I/The applicant/The appellant* have/has* taken all reasonable steps open to me/him/her* to find out the names and addresses of everyone else who, on the day 21 days before the date of the application/appeal*, was the owner(b) of any part of the land to which the application/appeal* relates, but have/has* been unable to do so. These steps were as follows:
  (c) ....
  ....
- Notice of the application/appeal*, as attached to this certificate, has been published in the (d) ....
  ....
  on (e) ....

          Signed ....
          *On behalf of ....
          Date ....

*delete where inappropriate

(a) This Certificate is for use with applications and appeals for planning permission (articles 7 and 9(1) of the Order). One of Certificates A, B, C or D (or the appropriate certificate in the case of certain minerals applications) must be completed, together with the Agricultural Holdings Certificate.

(b) 'owner' means a person having a freehold interest or a leasehold interest the unexpired term of which is not less than seven years, or, in the case of development consisting of the winning and working of minerals, a person entitled to an interest in a mineral in the land (other than oil, gas, coal, gold or silver).

Insert:
(c) description of steps taken
(d) name of newspaper circulating in the area where the land is situated
(e) date of publication (which must be not earlier than the day 21 days before the date of the application or appeal)

Town and Country Planning (General Development Procedure) Order 1995
CERTIFICATE UNDER ARTICLE 7
Agricultural Holdings Certificate *(a)*

Whichever is appropriate of the following alternatives must form part of Certificates A, B, C or D. If the applicant is the sole agricultural tenant he or she must delete the first alternative and insert 'not applicable' as the information required by the second alternative.

• None of the land to which the application/appeal relates is, or is part of, an agricultural holding.

or

• I have/The applicant has/The appellant has given the requisite notice to every person other than my/him/her* self who, on the day 21 days before the date of the application/ appeal*, was a tenant of an agricultural holding on all or part of the land to which the application/appeal* relates, as follows:

Tenant's name	Address at which notice was served	Date on which notice was served

Signed ....
*On behalf of ....
Date ....

*delete where inappropriate

(a) This Certificate is for use with applications and appeals for planning permission (articles 7 and 9(1) of the Order). One of Certificates A, B, C or D (or the appropriate certificate in the case of certain minerals applications) must be completed together with the Agricultural Holdings Certificate.

Town and Country Planning (General Development Procedure) Order 1995
CERTIFICATE UNDER ARTICLE 7
(for use with applications and appeals for planning permission for development consisting of the winning and working of minerals by underground operations)

I certify that:
- I have/The applicant has/The appellant has* given the requisite notice to the persons specified below being persons who, on the day 21 days before the date of the accompanying application/appeal, were owners*(a)* of any part of the land to which the application/appeal relates.

Owner's *(a)* name	Address at which notice was served	Date on which notice was served

- There is no person (other than me/the applicant/the appellant*) who, on the day 21 days before the date of the accompanying application/appeal*, was the owner*(a)* of any part of the land to which this application/appeal* relates, whom I/the applicant/the appellant* know/s* to be such a person and whose name and address is known to me/the applicant/the appellant* but to whom I have/the applicant/the appellant has* not given the requisite notice.
- I have/The applicant/The appellant has* posted the requisite notice, sited and displayed in such a way as to be easily visible and legible by members of the public, in at least one place in every parish or community within which there is situated any part of the land to which the accompanying application/appeal* relates, as listed below.

  Parish/Community   Location of notice   Date posted

- Save as specified below* this/these* notice/s* was/were* left in position for not less than seven days in the period of 21 days immediately preceding the making of the application/ appeal*.

** The following notice/s* was/were*, however, left in position for less than seven days in the period of not more than 21 days immediately preceding the making of the application/appeal*.

  Parish/Community   Location of notice   Date posted

  This happened because it/they* was/were* removed/obscured/defaced* before seven days had passed during the period of 21 days mentioned above. This was not my/the applicant's/ the appellant's* fault or intent.
  I/The applicant/The appellant* took the following steps to protect and replace the notice:
  (b) ....
  ....

- Notice of the application/appeal*, as attached to this certificate, has been published in the *(c)* ....
  ....
  on *(d)* ....

Agricultural Holdings Certificate

Whichever is appropriate of the following alternatives must form part of this certificate. If the applicant is the sole agricultural tenant he or she must delete the first alternative and insert 'not applicable' as the information required by the second alternative.

- None of the land to which the application/appeal* relates is, or is part of, an agricultural holding.

or

- I have/The applicant has/The appellant has* given the requisite notice to every person other than my/him/her* self who, on the day 21 days before the date of the application/ appeal*, was a tenant of an agricultural holding on all or part of the land to which the application/appeal* relates, as follows:

Tenant's name	Address at which notice was served	Date on which notice was served

Signed ....
*On behalf of ....
Date ....

*delete where inappropriate

(a) 'owner' means a person having a freehold interest or a leasehold interest the unexpired term of which is not less than seven years or a person entitled to an interest in a mineral in the land (other than oil, gas, coal, gold or silver).

Insert:
(b) description of steps taken
(c) name of newspaper circulating in the area where the land is situated
(d) date of publication (which must be not earlier than the day 21 days before the date of the application or appeal)

Article 8 SCHEDULE 3

Town and Country Planning (General Development Procedure) Order 1995

NOTICE UNDER ARTICLE 8

(to be published in a newspaper, displayed on or near the site, or served on owners and/or occupiers of adjoining land)

Proposed development at *(a)* ....
I give notice that *(b)* ....
is applying to the *(c)* .... Council
for planning permission to *(d)* ....
The proposed development does not accord with the provisions of the development plan in force in the area in which the land to which the application relates is situated*
Members of the public may inspect copies of:
- the application
- the plans
- and other documents submitted with it

at *(e)* .... during
all reasonable hours until *(f)* ....
Anyone who wishes to make representations about this application should write to the Council at *(g)* ....
.... by *(f)* ....

Signed ....
....
(Council's authorised officer)
On behalf of .... Council
Date ....

*delete where inappropriate

Insert:
(a) address or location of the proposed development
(b) applicant's name
(c) name of Council
(d) description of the proposed development
(e) address at which the application may be inspected
(f) date giving a period of 21 days, beginning with the date when the notice is first displayed on or near the site or served on an owner and/or occupier of adjoining land, or a period of 14 days, beginning with the date when the notice is published in a newspaper (as the case may be)
(g) address of Council

NOTICE OF APPLICATION FOR PLANNING PERMISSION
Town and Country Planning (General Development Procedure) Order 1995
NOTICE UNDER ARTICLE 8 OF APPLICATION FOR PLANNING PERMISSION ACCOMPANIED BY AN ENVIRONMENTAL STATEMENT

(to be published in a newspaper and displayed on or near the site)
Proposed development at *(a)* ....
I give notice that *(b)* ....
is applying to the *(c)* .... Council
for planning permission to *(d)* ....
and that the application is accompanied by an environmental statement
The proposed development does not accord with the provisions of the development plan in force in the area in which the land to which the application relates is situated*
Members of the public may inspect copies of:
- the application
- the plans
- the environmental statement
- and other documents submitted with the application

at *(e)* .... during all reasonable hours until *(f)* ....
Members of the public may obtain copies of the environmental statement from *(g)* . ...
so long as stocks last, at a charge of *(h)* ....
Anyone who wishes to make representations about this application should write to the Council at *(i)* ....
.... by *(f)* ....

                      Signed ....
                      ....
                      (Council's authorised officer)
                      On behalf of .... Council
                      Date ....

*delete where inappropriate

Insert:
- *(a)* address or location of the proposed development
- *(b)* applicant's name
- *(c)* name of Council
- *(d)* description of the proposed development
- *(e)* address at which the application may be inspected
- *(f)* date giving a period of 21 days, beginning with the date when the notice is first displayed on or near the site, or a period of 14 days, beginning with the date when the notice is published in a newspaper (as the case may be)
- *(g)* address from where copies of the environmental statement may be obtained (whether or not the same as *(e)*)
- *(h)* amount of charge, if any
- *(i)* address of Council

SCHEDULE 4 Article 24

TOWN AND COUNTRY PLANNING ACT 1990: SECTIONS 191 AND 192 (as amended by section 10 of the Planning and Compensation Act 1991)

TOWN AND COUNTRY PLANNING (GENERAL DEVELOPMENT PROCEDURE) ORDER 1995: ARTICLE 24

CERTIFICATE OF LAWFUL USE OR DEVELOPMENT

The *(a)* .... Council hereby certify that on *(b)* .... the use*/operations*/matter* described in the First Schedule to this certificate in respect of the land specified in the Second Schedule to this certificate and edged*/hatched*/coloured* *(c)* .... on the plan attached to this certificate, was*/were*/would have been* lawful within the meaning of section 191 of the Town and Country Planning Act 1990 (as amended), for the following reason(s):

....
....
....

Signed .... (Council's authorised officer)
On behalf of *(a)* .... Council
Date ....
First Schedule
(d)
Second Schedule
(e)

Notes
1 This certificate is issued solely for the purpose of section 191*/192* of the Town and Country Planning Act 1990 (as amended).
2 It certifies that the use*/operations*/matter* specified in the First Schedule taking place on the land described in the Second Schedule was*/were*/would have been* lawful, on the specified date and, thus, was not*/were not*/would not have been* liable to enforcement action under section 172 of the 1990 Act on that date.
3 This certificate applies only to the extent of the use*/operations*/matter* described in the First Schedule and to the land specified in the Second Schedule and identified on the attached plan. Any use*/operations*/matter* which is*/are* materially different from that*/those* described or which relate/s* to other land may render the owner or occupier liable to enforcement action.
*4 The effect of the certificate is also qualified by the proviso in section 192(4) of the 1990 Act, as amended, which states that the lawfulness of a described use or operation is only conclusively presumed where there has been no material change, before the use is instituted or the operations begun, in any of the matters relevant to determining such lawfulness.

*delete where inappropriate

Insert:
(a)   name of Council
(b)   date of application to the Council
(c)   colour used on the plan
(d)   full description of use, operations or other matter, if necessary, by reference to details in the application or submitted plans, including a reference to the use class, if any, specified in an order under section 55(2)(f) of the 1990 Act, within which the certificated use falls
(e)   address or location of the site

SCHEDULE 5   Article 28
[omitted]

TOWN AND COUNTRY PLANNING (USE CLASSES) ORDER 1987 (SI 1987, No. 764)

(as amended by: SI 1991 No. 1567; SI 1992 No. 610; SI 1992 No. 657; SI 1994 No. 724; SI 1995 No. 297)

The Secretary of State for the Environment, as respects England, and the Secretary of State for Wales, as respects Wales, in exercise of the powers conferred on them by sections 55(2)(f) and 333(7) of the Town and Country Planning Act 1990 and all other powers enabling them in that behalf, hereby make the following Order—

1. Citation and commencement
This Order may be cited as the Town and Country Planning (Use Classes) Order 1987 and shall come into force on 1st June 1987.

2. Interpretation
In this Order, unless the context otherwise requires:—
'care' means personal care for people in need of such care by reason of old age, disablement, past or present dependence on alcohol or drugs or past or present mental disorder, and in class C2 also includes the personal care of children and medical care and treatment;
'day centre' means premises which are visited during the day for social or recreational purposes or for the purposes of rehabilitation or occupational training, at which care is also provided;
'industrial process' means a process for or incidental to any of the following purposes:—
    (a) the making of any article or part of any article (including a ship or vessel, or a film, video or sound recording);
    (b) the altering, repairing, maintaining, ornamenting, finishing, cleaning, washing, packing, canning, adapting for sale, breaking up or demolition of any article; or
    (c) the getting, dressing or treatment of minerals;
in the course of any trade or business other than agriculture, and other than a use carried out in or adjacent to a mine or quarry;
'Schedule' means the Schedule to this Order;
'site' means the whole area of land within a single unit of occupation.

3. Use Classes
(1) Subject to the provisions of this Order, where a building or other land is used for a purpose of any class specified in the Schedule, the use of that building or that other land for any other purpose of the same class shall not be taken to involve development of the land.
(2) References in paragraph (1) to a building include references to land occupied with the building and used for the same purposes.
(3) A use which is included in and ordinarily incidental to any use in a class specified in the Schedule is not excluded from the use to which it is incidental merely because it is specified in the Schedule as a separate use.
(4) Where land on a single site or on adjacent sites used as parts of a single undertaking is used for purposes consisting of or including purposes falling within classes B1 and B2 in the Schedule, those classes may be treated as a single class in considering the use of that land for the purposes of this Order, so long as the area used for a purpose falling within class B2 is not substantially increased as a result.

(5) [repealed]
(6) No class specified in the Schedule includes use—
   (a) as a theatre,
   (b) as an amusement arcade or centre, or a funfair,
   (c) as a launderette,
   (d) for the sale of fuel for motor vehicles,
   (e) for the sale or display for sale of motor vehicles,
   (f) for a taxi business or business for the hire of motor vehicles,
   (g) as a scrapyard, or a yard for the storage or distribution of minerals or the breaking of motor vehicles,
   (h) for any work registrable under the Alkali, etc. Works Regulation Act 1906,
   (i) as a hostel.

4. Change of use of part of building or land

In the case of a building used for a purpose within class C3 (dwellinghouses) in the Schedule, the use as a separate dwellinghouse of any part of the building or of any land occupied with and used for the same purposes as the building is not, by virtue of this Order, to be taken as not amounting to development.

5. Revocation

The Town and Country Planning (Use Classes) Order 1972 and the Town and Country Planning (Use Classes) (Amendment) Order 1983 are hereby revoked.

SCHEDULE
PART A

Class A1. Shops

Use for all or any of the following purposes—
   (a) for the retail sale of goods other than hot food,
   (b) as a post office,
   (c) for the sale of tickets or as a travel agency,
   (d) for the sale of sandwiches or other cold food for consumption off the premises,
   (e) for hairdressing,
   (f) for the direction of funerals,
   (g) for the display of goods for sale,
   (h) for the hiring out of domestic or personal goods or articles,
   (i) for the washing or cleaning of clothes or fabrics on the premises,
   (j) for the reception of goods to be washed, cleaned or repaired,
where the sale, display or service is to visiting members of the public.

Class A2. Financial and professional services

Use for the provision of—
   (a) financial services, or
   (b) professional services (other than health or medical services), or
   (c) any other services (including use as a betting office) which it is appropriate to provide in a shopping area.
where the services are provided principally to visiting members of the public.

Class A3. Food and drink

Use for the sale of food or drink for consumption on the premises or of hot food for consumption off the premises.

PART B

Class B1. Business

Use for all or any of the following purposes—

(a) as an office other than a use within class A2 (financial and professional services),
(b) for research and development of products or processes, or
(c) for any industrial process,

being a use which can be carried out in any residential area without detriment to the amenity of that area by reason of noise, vibration, smell, fumes, smoke, soot, ash, dust or grit.

Class B2. General industrial
Use for the carrying on of an industrial process other than one falling within class B1 above.

Classes B3 to B7. [repealed]

Class B8. Storage or distribution
Use for storage or as a distribution centre.

PART C

Class C1. Hotels
Use as a hotel or as a boarding or guest house where, in each case, no significant element of care is provided.

Class C2. Residential institutions
Use for the provision of residential accommodation and care to people in need of care (other than a use within class C3 (dwelling houses)).
Use as a hospital or nursing home.
Use as a residential school, college or training centre.

Class C3. Dwellinghouses
Use as a dwellinghouse (whether or not as a sole or main residence)—
(a) by a single person or by people living together as a family, or
(b) by not more than 6 residents living together as a single household (including a household where care is provided for residents).

PART D

Class D1. Non-residential institutions
Any use not including a residential use—
(a) for the provision of any medical or health services except the use of premises attached to the residence of the consultant or practitioner,
(b) as a crèche, day nursery or day centre,
(c) for the provision of education,
(d) for the display of works of art (otherwise than for sale or hire),
(e) as a museum,
(f) as a public library or public reading room,
(g) as a public hall or exhibition hall,
(h) for, or in connection with, public worship or religious instruction.

Class D2. Assembly and leisure
Use as—
(a) a cinema,
(b) a concert hall,
(c) a bingo hall or casino,
(d) a dance hall,
(e) a swimming bath, skating rink, gymnasium or area for other indoor or outdoor sports or recreations, not involving motorised vehicles or firearms.

TOWN AND COUNTRY PLANNING (ASSESSMENT OF ENVIRONMENTAL EFFECTS) REGULATIONS 1988 (SI 1988, No. 1199)

(as amended by: SI 1992 No. 1494
SI 1994 No. 677.)

The Secretary of State for the Environment as respects England and the Secretary of State for Wales as respects Wales, being designated Ministers for the purposes of section 2(2) of the European Communities Act 1972 in relation to measures relating to the requirement for an assessment of the impact on the environment of projects likely to have significant effects on the environment, in exercise of the powers conferred upon them by the said section 2 hereby make the following Regulations, a draft of which has been laid before and approved by a resolution of each House of Parliament:—

1. **Citation, commencement and application**
   (1) These Regulations may be cited as the Town and Country Planning (Assessment of Environmental Effects) Regulations 1988.
   (2) These Regulations shall come into force on the third day after the day on which they are made.
   (3) Subject to paragraph (4), these Regulations apply throughout England and Wales.
   (4) Paragraphs (2) and (5)(a) of regulation 13 shall not apply to the Isles of Scilly and, in relation to the Isles of Scilly, the reference in paragraph (6) of that regulation to paragraph (5) of that regulation shall be construed as a reference to paragraph (5)(b).
   (5) These regulations apply to local authority applications mentioned in paragraph (1) of regulation 25A in accordance with the modifications set out in that paragraph.

2. **Interpretation**
   (1) In these Regulations, unless the contrary intention appears—
   'the Act' means the Town and Country Planning Act 1990 references to sections are references to sections of that Act and expressions used in that Act and these Regulations have the meaning they have in the Act save that, in relation to an appeal, references to the Secretary of State shall not be construed as references to an inspector;
   'aerodrome' means a defined area on land or water (including any buildings and other installations) intended to be used either wholly or in part for the arrival, departure and surface movement of aircraft;
   'controlled waste' has the meaning assigned to it by section 30(1) of the Control of Pollution Act 1974;
   'documents' include photographs, drawings, maps and plans;
   'environmental information' means the environmental statement prepared by the applicant or appellant, any representations made by any body required by these Regulations to be invited to make representations or to be consulted and any representations duly made by any other person about the likely environmental effects of the proposed development;
   'environmental statement' means such a statement as is described in Schedule 3;
   'exempt development' means particular proposed development which is the subject of a direction by the Secretary of State that these Regulations do not apply in relation to it;
   'the General Development Order' means the Town and Country Planning General Development Order 1988;

'inspector' means a person appointed by the Secretary of State pursuant to Schedule 6 to the Act to determine an appeal;
'the land' means the land on which proposed development would be carried out;
'local planning authority' means the body to whom it falls or would but for a direction under section 77 fall, to determine an application for planning permission, or to whom it would fall (but for any such direction) to determine a proposed application;
'principal council' has the meaning assigned to that term by section 270(1) of the Local Government Act 1972;
'register' means a register kept pursuant to section 69 and 'appropriate register' means the register on which particulars of an application for planning permission for the relevant development would fall to be placed when such an application is made;
'Schedule' means a Schedule to these Regulations;
'Schedule 1 application' means an application for planning permission (other than an application made pursuant to section 73 or section 63 for the carrying out of development of any description mentioned in Schedule 1, which is not exempt development;
'Schedule 2 application' means, subject to paragraph (2), an application for planning permission (other than an application made pursuant to section 73 or section 63) for the carrying out of development of any description mentioned in Schedule 2, which is not exempt development and which would be likely to have significant effects on the environment by virtue of factors such as its nature, size or location;
'special road' means, any road which for the purposes of Part I of the New Roads and Street Works Act 1991 is a road subject to a concession and any other road authorised by a scheme made by a local highway authority under section 16 of the Highways Act 1980 for the use of traffic within Classes I and II of Schedule 4 to that Act; and
'special waste' means waste to which that term is applied by regulation 2 of the Control of Pollution (Special Waste) Regulations 1980.

(2) Where the Secretary of State gives a direction which includes a statement that in his opinion proposed development would be likely, or would not be likely, to have significant effects on the environment by virtue of factors such as its nature, size or location, or includes such a statement in a notification under regulation 10(1), that statement shall determine whether an application for planning permission for that development is, or is not, a Schedule 2 application by reason of the effects the development would be likely to have; and references in these Regulations to a Schedule 2 application shall be interpreted accordingly.

3. Extension of the power to provide in a development order for the giving of directions as respects the manner in which planning applications are dealt with

The provisions enabling the Secretary of State to give directions which may be included in a development order by virtue of section 31 shall include provisions enabling him to direct—

(a) that particular proposed development of a description set out in Schedule 1 or 2 is exempt development to which these Regulations do not apply in accordance with Article 2(3) of Council Directive 85/337/EEC;

(b) that particular proposed development is not development in respect of which the consideration of environmental information is required before planning permission can be granted;

(c) that particular proposed development or development of any class is development in respect of which such consideration is required.

4. Prohibition on the grant of planning permission without consideration of environmental information

(1) This regulation applies to any Schedule 1 or Schedule 2 application received by the authority with whom it is lodged on or after 15th July 1988.

For the purposes of this paragraph, the date of receipt of an application by an authority shall be determined in accordance with article 10 of the General Development Order.

(2) The local planning authority or the Secretary of State or an inspector shall not grant planning permission pursuant to an application to which this regulation applies unless they have first taken the environmental information into consideration and state in their decision that they have done so.

(3) Subject to any direction of the Secretary of State, the occurrence of an event mentioned in paragraph (4) shall determine in the case of an application for planning permission for development, other than exempt development, that, for the purposes of this regulation, the application is a Schedule 1 or 2 application.

(4) The events referred to in paragraph (3) are—

   (i) the submission by the applicant of an environmental statement expressed to be for the purposes of these Regulations;

   (ii) a failure by the applicant to apply to the Secretary of State for a direction where the local planning authority have given such an opinion as is mentioned in regulation 5(6)(a); and

   (iii) the making to that authority by the applicant of a written statement agreeing or conceding that the submission of an environmental statement is required.

5. Opinion as to whether an application will be a Schedule 1 or 2 application

(1) A person who is minded to apply for planning permission may ask the local planning authority to state in writing whether in their opinion the proposed development would be within a description mentioned in Schedule 1 or 2 and, if so,—

   (a) within which such description; and

   (b) if it falls within a description in Schedule 2, whether its likely effects would be such that regulation 4 would apply.

(2) A request made pursuant to paragraph (1) shall be accompanied by—

   (a) a plan sufficient to identify the land;

   (b) a brief description of the nature and purpose of the proposed development and of its possible effects on the environment;

   (c) such other information or representations as the person making the request may wish to provide or make.

(3) An authority receiving a request under paragraph (1) shall, if they consider that they have not been provided with sufficient information to give an opinion on the questions raised, notify the person making the request of the particular points on which they require further information.

(4) An authority shall respond to a request under paragraph (1) within 3 weeks beginning with the date of receipt of the request or such longer period as may be agreed in writing with the person making the request; and if they express an opinion to the effect that the consideration of environmental information would be required before planning permission could be granted for the proposed development, they shall provide with the opinion a written statement giving clearly and precisely their full reasons for their conclusion.

(5) An authority shall make a copy of any opinion given pursuant to a request under paragraph (1), and any accompanying statement of reasons and a copy of the relevant request and the accompanying documents available for public inspection at any reasonable hour at the place where the appropriate register (or relevant section of

that register) is kept until such time, if any, as a copy of that opinion is required by regulation 7 to be placed on Part I of that register.
(6) Where an authority—
  (a) give an opinion to the effect mentioned in paragraph (4); or
  (b) fail to give an opinion within the relevant period mentioned in paragraph (4),
the person who requested the opinion may apply in accordance with regulation 6 to the Secretary of State for a direction on the matter.
(7) Paragraph (6)(b) applies notwithstanding that the authority may not have received further information which they have sought under paragraph (3).

6. Pre-application directions

(1) A person applying to the Secretary of State for a direction pursuant to regulation 5(6) shall submit with his application—
  (a) a copy of his request under regulation 5(1) to the local planning authority and the documents which accompanied it;
  (b) a copy of any notification under regulation 5(3) which he has received and of any response;
  (c) a copy of any opinion given by the authority and of the accompanying statement of reasons; and
  (d) any representations he wishes to make.
(2) A person applying as aforesaid shall, when he makes the application, send the local planning authority a copy of the application and of any representations he makes to the Secretary of State.
(3) The Secretary of State shall notify an applicant in writing of any points on which he considers the information provided pursuant to paragraph (1) is insufficient to enable him to give a direction; and may request the local planning authority to provide such information as they can on any of those points.
(4) The Secretary of State shall issue a direction within 3 weeks beginning with the date of receipt of the application or such longer period as he may reasonably require.
(5) The Secretary of State shall upon giving a direction send a copy to the applicant and the local planning authority; and where he gives a direction that the proposed application would be a Schedule 1 or Schedule 2 application, he shall at the same time send them a written statement giving his full reasons for his conclusion clearly and precisely.

7. Availability of directions etc. for inspection

(1) Where particulars of a planning application are placed on Part I of the register, the local planning authority shall take steps to secure that there is also placed on that Part a copy of any direction which the Secretary of State has given as to whether the application is, or is not, a Schedule 1 or 2 application; and of any relevant opinion given pursuant to regulation 5.
(2) Where the Secretary of State gives any such direction as is mentioned in paragraph (1) after particulars of the relevant application have been placed on Part I of the register or sends the applicant a notification under regulation 10, the local planning authority shall take steps to secure that a copy of that direction or notification is also placed on that Part of the register.
(3) Where the local planning authority notify an applicant under regulation 9 that they consider his application cannot be granted unless he submits an environmental statement, they shall take steps to secure that a copy of that notification is placed on Part I of the register.
(4) Where the Secretary of State gives, otherwise than pursuant to regulation 6, a direction as to whether the consideration of environmental information is

required before planning permission can be granted for a particular proposed development he shall forthwith send a copy of the direction to the local planning authority and to such other persons as he considers it desirable to send a copy together, where necessary, with documents sufficient to identify the land and the development.

(5) Where a copy of a direction is received by the local planning authority before application is made for planning permission for the development in question, the authority shall take steps to secure that a copy of the direction and any documents sent with it are available for public inspection at all reasonable hours at the place where the appropriate register (or section of that register) is kept.

8. Procedure to facilitate preparation of environmental statements

(1) A prospective applicant may give the local planning authority notice in writing that he intends to make a Schedule 1 or Schedule 2 application and to submit an environmental statement with his application.

(2) A notice under paragraph (1) shall include the information necessary to identify, or be accompanied by documents identifying, the land and the nature and purpose of the proposed development, and shall indicate the main environmental consequences to which the prospective applicant proposes to refer in his environmental statement.

(3) Paragraph (4) applies where—
  (a) the local planning authority receive in relation to a proposed planning application—
    (i) such a notice as is mentioned in paragraph (1); or
    (ii) such a statement as is mentioned in regulation 4(4)(iii); or
    (iii) a copy of a direction by the Secretary of State under regulation 6 that a proposed application would be a Schedule 1 or Schedule 2 application;

(4) Where this paragraph applies, the authority in question shall—
  (a) notify the bodies mentioned in paragraph (5) in writing of the name and address of the prospective applicant and of the duty imposed upon them by regulation 22 to make information available to the prospective applicant;
  (b) inform the prospective applicant in writing of the names and addresses of the bodies so notified.

(5) The bodies referred to in paragraph (4) are—
  (a) any body which the local planning authority would be required by article 18 of the General Development Order or any direction under that article to consult if the application were before them;
  (b) the following bodies if not referred to in subparagraph (a),—
    (i) any principal council for the area where the land is situated, if not the local planning authority;
    (ii) the Countryside Commission;
    (iii) the Nature Conservancy Council; for Wales: The Countryside Commission for Wales;
  (c) where the proposed development is a development of a description referred to in Paragraph (6) the chief inspector for England and Wales appointed under Part I of the Environmental Protection Act 1990.

(6) The development referred to in paragraph (5)(c) is any development which in the opinion of the local planning authority will—
  (a) involve mining operations, or manufacturing industry or the disposal of waste; and
  (b) is likely either—
    (i) to give rise to waste, the disposal of which requires an authorisation under the Radioactive Substances Act 1960, or to discharges (other than of domestic

sewage) which are controlled waste or special waste or are likely to require the licence or consent of a water authority; or

(ii) to involve works specified in Schedule 1 to the Health and Safety (Emissions to the Atmosphere) Regulations 1983.

(7) Paragraph (4) shall apply (but subject to the modifications mentioned in paragraph (8)) where a Schedule 1 or Schedule 2 application has been made without an environmental statement and—

(i) the Secretary of State has given a direction to the effect that the consideration of environmental information is required before planning permission can be granted; or

(ii) the applicant has informed the local planning authority or, where the application has been referred to the Secretary of State or is the subject of an appeal, the Secretary of State, that he proposes to submit an environmental statement.

(8) In its application by virtue of paragraph (7), paragraph (4) shall have effect—

(a) as if references to the prospective applicant were references to the applicant or appellant, as appropriate; and

(b) where the application has been referred to the Secretary of State or is the subject of an appeal, as if references to the local planning authority in paragraphs (4) and (6) were references to the Secretary of State and regulation (5)(a) referred to such bodies as the Secretary of State considers would be required to be consulted by or under article 18 of the General Development Order if the case were before the local planning authority.

9. Application made to a planning authority without an environmental statement

(1) Where it appears to the local planning authority that an application for planning permission is a Schedule 1 or a Schedule 2 application, and it is not accompanied by an environmental statement, they shall (unless the application is the subject of a direction under section 77 within 3 weeks beginning with the date of receipt of the application, or such longer period as they may agree with the applicant in writing, notify the applicant in writing that they consider the submission of such a statement is required, giving their full reasons for their view clearly and precisely.

(2) An applicant receiving a notification pursuant to paragraph (1) may within 3 weeks beginning with the date of the notification write to the authority to inform them that he—

(i) accepts their view and is providing an environmental statement; or

(ii) is applying in writing to the Secretary of State for his direction on the matter.

(3) If the applicant does not write in accordance with paragraph (2), the permission sought shall be deemed to be refused at the end of the 3 week period; but no appeal shall lie to the Secretary of State by virtue of Section 78.

The deemed refusal shall be treated as a decision of the authority for the purposes of article 27(2)(c) of the General Development Order.

(4) Except where the Secretary of State gives a direction to the effect that regulation 4 does not apply, an authority which has given a notification in accordance with paragraph (1) shall determine the relevant application only by refusing planning permission if the applicant does not submit an environmental statement and comply with regulation 13(5).

(5) A person applying to the Secretary of State for a direction pursuant to paragraph (2) shall send with his application copies of—

(a) his application for planning permission;

(b) all documents sent to the authority as part of the application; and

(c) all correspondence with the authority relating to the development proposed, and paragraphs (2) to (5) of regulation 6 shall apply in relation to the application.

10. Application referred to the Secretary of State without an environmental statement

(1) Where it appears to the Secretary of State that an application for planning permission which has been referred to him for determination is a Schedule 1 or a Schedule 2 application, and it is not accompanied by an environmental statement, he shall within 3 weeks beginning with the date he received the application, or such longer period as he may reasonably require, notify the applicant in writing that the submission of an environmental statement is required, giving his full reasons for his view clearly and precisely.

(2) An applicant receiving a notification pursuant to paragraph (1) may within 3 weeks beginning with the date of the notification write to the Secretary of State to inform him that he proposes to provide an environmental statement.

(3) If the applicant does not write in accordance with paragraph (2), the Secretary of State shall be under no duty to deal with the application: and at the end of the 3 week period he shall inform the applicant in writing that no further action is being taken on the application.

(4) Where the Secretary of State has given a notification in accordance with paragraph (1), he shall determine the relevant application only by refusing planning permission if the applicant does not submit an environmental statement and comply with regulation 13(5).

(5) The Secretary of State shall send a copy of any notification under paragraph (1) to the local planning authority.

11. Appeal to the Secretary of State without an environmental statement

(1) Where the Secretary of State on consideration of an appeal under section 78 forms the view that the relevant application is a Schedule 1 or a Schedule 2 application, and the documents sent to him for the purposes of the appeal do not include a copy of an environmental statement, regulation 10 shall apply subject to any necessary modifications.

(2) Where an inspector is dealing with an appeal and any question arises as to whether the relevant application is a Schedule 1 or a Schedule 2 application and it appears to the inspector that it may be such an application and no environmental statement has been submitted, the inspector shall refer the matter to the Secretary of State.

(3) Where a question is referred pursuant to paragraph (2), the Secretary of State shall direct whether or not the application is a Schedule 1 or Schedule 2 application; and the inspector shall not determine the appeal, except by refusing planning permission, before he receives a direction.

(4) Where the Secretary of State directs as aforesaid, he shall forthwith send copies of the direction to the appellant, the local planning authority and the inspector, and to any other person he considers desirable, and where he directs that the application is a Schedule 1 or Schedule 2 application he shall at the same time send those persons a written statement giving his full reasons for his conclusions clearly and precisely.

(5) Where the Secretary of State directs that the application is a Schedule 1 or Schedule 2 application, the appellant may within 3 weeks beginning with the date of the direction write to the Secretary of State to inform him that he proposes to provide an environmental statement.

(6) If the appellant does not write in accordance with paragraph (5), the inspector shall be under no duty to deal with the appeal; and at the end of the 3 week period he shall inform the appellant that no further action is being taken on the appeal.

(7) Where the Secretary of State has directed that the relevant application is a Schedule 1 or Schedule 2 application, the inspector shall determine the appeal only

by refusing planning permission if the appellant does not submit an environmental statement and comply with regulation 13(5).

12. [repealed]

13. Publicity where an environmental statement is submitted in course of planning procedures

(1) Where a Schedule 1 or a Schedule 2 application has been made without an environmental statement and the applicant proposes to submit one, he shall before submitting it, comply with paragraphs (2) to (5).

(2) The applicant shall publish in a local newspaper circulating in the locality in which the land is situated (hereinafter referred to as 'the locality') a notice stating—

   (a) his name and that he is the applicant for planning permission and the name and address of the local planning authority;

   (b) the date on which the application was made and, if it be the case, that it has been referred to the Secretary of State for determination or is the subject of an appeal to him;

   (c) the address or location and the nature of the proposed development;

   (d) that a copy of the application and of the plans and other documents submitted with it together with a copy of the environmental statement may be inspected by members of the public at all reasonable hours;

   (e) an address in the locality at which those documents may be inspected, and the latest date on which they will be available for inspection (being a date not less than 20 days later than the date on which the notice is published);

   (f) an address in the locality (whether or not the same as that given pursuant to sub-paragraph (e)) at which copies of the environmental statement may be obtained;

   (g) that copies may be obtained there so long as stocks last;

   (h) if a charge is to be made for a copy, the amount of the charge; and

   (i) that any person wishing to make representations about the application should make them in writing, before the date named in accordance with sub-paragraph (e), to the local planning authority or (in the case of an application referred to the Secretary of State or an appeal) to the Secretary of State.

(3) The applicant shall, unless he has not, and was not reasonably able to acquire, such rights as would enable him to do so, post on the land a notice containing the information specified in paragraph (2), except that the date named as the latest date on which the documents will be available for inspection shall be not less than 20 days later than the date on which the notice is first posted.

(4) The notice mentioned in paragraph (3) must—

   (a) be left in position for not less than 7 days in the month immediately preceding the date of the submission of the environmental statement; and

   (b) be affixed firmly to some object on the land and sited and displayed in such a way as to be easily visible to, and readable by, members of the public without going on to the land.

(5) The environmental statement, when submitted, shall be accompanied by—

   (a) a copy of the notice mentioned in paragraph (2) certified by or on behalf of the applicant as having been published in a named newspaper on a date specified in the certificate; and

   (b) a certificate by or on behalf of the applicant which states either—

      (i) that he has posted a notice on the land in compliance with this regulation and when he did so, and that the notice was left in position for not less than 7 days in the month immediately preceding the date of the submission of the statement, or that, without any fault or intention on his part, it was removed, obscured or defaced before 7 days had elapsed and he took reasonable steps for its protection or replacement, specifying the steps taken; or

(ii) that the applicant was unable to comply with paragraphs (3) and (4) above because he did not have the necessary rights to do so; that he has taken such reasonable steps as are open to him to acquire those rights; and has been unable to do so, specifying the steps taken.

(6) Where an applicant proposes to provide an environmental statement in the circumstances mentioned in paragraph (1), the local planning authority, the Secretary of State or the inspector, as the case may be, shall (unless disposed to refuse the permission sought) suspend consideration of the application or appeal until receipt of the statement and the other documents mentioned in paragraph (5); and shall not determine it during the period of 21 days beginning with the date of receipt of the statement and the other documents so mentioned.

(7) If any person issues a certificate which purports to comply with the requirements of paragraph (5)(b) and which contains a statement which he knows to be false or misleading in a material particular, or recklessly issues a certificate which purports to comply with those requirements and which contains a statement which is false or misleading in a material particular, he shall be guilty of an offence and liable on summary conviction to a fine not exceeding level 3 on the standard scale.

(8) The reference in paragraph (7) to a fine not exceeding level 3 on the standard scale shall be construed in accordance with section 37 (standard scale of fines for summary offences) of the Criminal Justice Act 1982.

(9) Where it is proposed to submit an environmental statement in connection with an appeal, this regulation applies with the substitution, except in paragraph 2(a), of references to the appellant for references to the applicant.

14. Procedure where the planning authority receive an environmental statement

(1) When an applicant making a Schedule 1 or Schedule 2 application submits an environmental statement to the local planning authority he shall provide the authority with three additional copies of the statement for transmission to the Secretary of State and, if at the same time he serves a copy of the statement or of a part of it on any other body, he shall—

   (a) serve with it a copy of the application and any plan submitted with it (unless he has already served these documents on the body in question);

   (b) inform the body that representations may be made to the local planning authority;

   (c) inform the authority of the name of every body whom he has so served, of the date of service and, where he has not served a copy of the whole of the statement, of the part of which a copy was served.

(2) When a local planning authority receive an environmental statement in connection with a Schedule 1 or Schedule 2 application the authority shall—

   (a) take steps to secure that a copy of the statement is placed on Part I of the register with the application;

   (b) send to the Secretary of State three copies of the statement and a copy of the relevant application and of any documents submitted with the application;

   (c) advise any body mentioned in regulation 8(5) on whom the applicant has not served a copy of the statement or a part of it, that a statement will be taken into consideration in determining the application, elicit whether they wish to receive a copy of the statement or any part of it and inform them that they may make representations;

   (d) inform the applicant of the copies required by those bodies and of the names and addresses of the bodies concerned and enquire of him whether he proposes to serve the required copy on each of those bodies or send the required copies to the authority for service;

   (e) serve on the relevant body any copy sent to them by the applicant for service.

(3) The applicant shall inform the authority which of the courses mentioned in paragraph 2(d) he proposes to follow and shall serve copies of the environmental statement or a part of it on each body on whom he has said he will serve a copy or send the necessary copies to the authority, as the case may be. Where the applicant elects to send copies to the bodies directly he shall inform the authority as mentioned in paragraph (1)(c).

(4) The local planning authority shall not determine the application until the expiry of 14 days from the last date on which a copy of the environmental statement or a part of it was served in accordance with this regulation.

15. Procedure where the Secretary of State receives an environmental statement

(1) This regulation applies where an applicant submits to the Secretary of State an environmental statement relating to a Schedule 1 or Schedule 2 application which is before the Secretary of State for determination or is the subject of an appeal to him.

(2) The applicant shall submit four copies of the statement to the Secretary of State who shall transmit one copy to the local planning authority.

(3) The local planning authority shall take steps to secure that the copy so transmitted is placed on the register.

(4) If at the same time as he submits a statement to the Secretary of State the applicant serves a copy of it or a part of it on any other body, the applicant shall comply with regulation 14(1)(a) and (b) and inform the Secretary of State of the matters mentioned in regulation 14(1)(c).

(5) The Secretary of State shall comply with regulation 14(2)(c) to (e) and the applicant with regulation 14(3) as if—

    (a) references in any of those provisions and regulation 8(6) to the local planning authority were references to the Secretary of State; and

    (b) regulation 8(5)(a) referred to such bodies as the Secretary of State considers would be required to be consulted by or under article 18 of the General Development Order if the matter were before the local planning authority;

and the Secretary of State or the inspector shall comply with regulation 14(4) as if it referred to him instead of to the local planning authority.

(6) [repealed]

(7) In this regulation, references to the applicant include references to an appellant.

16. Extension of the period for an authority's decision on a planning application

(1) In determining for the purposes of section 78(2) (appeal in default of planning decision) the time which has elapsed without the local planning authority giving notice to the applicant of their decision in a case where—

    (a) the authority have notified an applicant in accordance with regulation 9(1) that the submission of an environmental statement is required; and

    (b) the Secretary of State has given a direction in the matter, no account shall be taken of any period before the issue of the direction.

(2) Where it falls to an authority determining an application for planning permission to take environmental information into consideration, article 23 of the Town and Country Planning General Development Order 1988 shall have effect as if—

    (a) for the reference in paragraph (2)(a) of that article to a period of 8 weeks there was substituted a reference to a period of 16 weeks:

    (b) after paragraph (3)(b) of that article there was inserted—

        '(ba) the environmental statement required to be submitted in respect of the application has been submitted, together with the documents required to accompany that statement; and'

17. [repealed]

18. Availability of copies of an environmental statement

An applicant for planning permission or an appellant who submits an environmental statement in connection with his application or appeal shall ensure that a reasonable number of copies of the statement are available at the address named in the notices published or posted pursuant to regulation article 12B of the Town and Country Planning General Development Order 1988 or regulation 13 as the address at which such copies may be obtained.

19. Provision of a copy of an environmental statement for the Secretary of State

Where an applicant for planning permission has submitted an environmental statement in connection with his application and the application—

(a) is directed to be referred to the Secretary of State under section 77; or

(b) occasions an appeal under section 78,

the applicant shall supply the Secretary of State with three copies of the statement unless, in the case of a referred application, the local planning authority have done so when referring the application to him.

20. Charges

(1) A reasonable charge reflecting printing and distribution costs may be made to a member of the public for a copy of an environmental statement made available in accordance with regulation 18 and for any copy, in excess of one, of the whole or part of a statement supplied to a body pursuant to regulation 14 or 15.

(2) A reasonable charge reflecting the cost of making the relevant information available may be made by a body supplying in accordance with regulation 22(1) information sought by an applicant or appellant.

21. Further information and evidence respecting environmental statements

(1) The local planning authority or the Secretary of State or an inspector, when dealing with an application or appeal in relation to which an environmental statement has been provided, may in writing require the applicant or appellant to provide such further information as may be specified concerning any matter which is required to be, or may be, dealt with in the statement; and where in the opinion of the authority or the Secretary of State or the inspector—

(a) the applicant or appellant could (having regard in particular to current knowledge and methods of assessment) provide further information about any matter mentioned in paragraph 3 of Schedule 3; and

(b) that further information is reasonably required to give proper consideration to the likely environmental effects of the proposed development,

they or he shall notify the applicant or appellant in writing accordingly, and the applicant or appellant shall provide that further information.

(2) Paragraphs (3) to (9) shall apply in relation to further information required of an applicant or appellant after those paragraphs come into force except in so far as such further information is required to be provided for the purposes of a local inquiry held under the Act and the request for such further information states that it is to be provided for such purposes.

(3) The recipient of the further information shall publish in a local newspaper circulating in the locality in which the land is situated (hereinafter referred to as 'the locality') a notice stating—

(a) the name of the applicant for planning permission or the appellant (as the case may be) and the name and address of the local planning authority;

(b) the date on which the application was made and, if it be the case, that it has been referred to the Secretary of State for determination or is the subject of an appeal to him;

(c) the address or location and the nature of the proposed development;
(d) that further information is available in relation to an environmental statement which has already been provided;
(e) that a copy of the further information may be inspected by members of the public at all reasonable hours;
(f) an address in the locality at which the further information may be inspected and the latest date on which it will be available for inspection (being a date not less than 20 days later than the date on which the notice is published);
(g) an address in the locality (whether or not the same as that given pursuant to sub-paragraph (f)) at which copies of the further information may be obtained;
(h) that copies may be obtained there so long as stocks last;
(i) if a charge is to be made for a copy, the amount of the charge; and
(j) that any person wishing to make representations about the further information should make them in writing, before the date specified in accordance with sub-paragraph (f), to the local planning authority, the Secretary of State or the inspector (as the case may be).

(4) The recipient of the further information shall send a copy of it to each person to whom the environmental statement to which it relates was sent.

(5) Where the recipient of the further information is a local planning authority they shall—
(a) take steps to secure that a copy of the further information is placed on Part I of the register with the application and the environmental statement; and
(b) send to the Secretary of State three copies of the further information.

(6) The recipient of the further information may by notice in writing require the applicant or appellant to provide such number of copies of the further information as is specified in the notice (being the number required for the purposes of paragraph (4) or (5)).

(7) Where further information is required to be provided, the local planning authority, the Secretary of State or the inspector, as the case may be, shall suspend determination of the application or appeal; and shall not determine it before the expiry of 14 days after the date on which the further information was sent to all persons to whom the environmental statement was sent or the expiry of 21 days after the date that notice of it was published in a local newspaper, whichever is the later.

(8) The applicant or appellant who provides further information in accordance with paragraph (1) shall ensure that a reasonable number of copies of the information is available at the address named in the notice published pursuant to paragraph (3) as the address at which such copies may be obtained.

(9) A reasonable charge reflecting printing and distribution costs may be made to a member of the public for a copy of the further information made available in accordance with paragraph (8) and for any copy, in excess of one, of the whole or part of the further information supplied to a person pursuant to paragraph (4).

(10) The local planning authority or the Secretary of State or an inspector may in writing require an applicant or appellant to produce such evidence as they may reasonably call for to verify any information in his environmental statement.

22. Provision of information

(1) Subject to paragraph (2), the local planning authority and any body notified in accordance with these Regulations that a person has made or is proposing to make a Schedule 1 or Schedule 2 application, shall, if requested by the applicant (or prospective applicant) or may without such a request, enter into consultation with him to determine whether the body has in its possession any information which he or they consider relevant to the preparation of an environmental statement and, if they have, the body shall make any such information available to him.

(2) Paragraph (1) shall not require the disclosure by a body of confidential information.

23. Duty to inform the Secretary of State
Where, after environmental information has been taken into consideration, a local planning authority determine an application for planning permission, they shall inform the Secretary of State of the decision taken and provide details of any conditions subject to which any planning permission was granted.

24. Service of notices etc.
Any notice or other document to be sent, served or given under these Regulations may be served or given in a manner specified in section 283(1).

25. Application to the High Court
For the purposes of Part XII of the Act (validity of certain decisions), the reference in section 245 to action of the Secretary of State which is not within the powers of the Act shall be taken to extend to a grant of planning permission in contravention of regulation 4 of these Regulations.

25A. Local authority applications
(1) In the application of these Regulations to a Schedule 1 or Schedule 2 application (or proposed application) where the local planning authority is also (or would also be) the applicant (whether alone or jointly with any other person), the following modifications shall apply—
    (a) regulations 5 and 6 shall not apply;
    (b) regulation 8(1) to (3) shall not apply but regulation 8(4)(a) shall apply where an authority proposes to make a Schedule 1 or Schedule 2 application and to submit an environmental statement with that application;
    (c) regulation 9 shall not apply;
    (d) regulation 10(5) shall not apply;
    (e) save for the purposes of regulation 15(4) and (5), regulation 14 shall apply as if—
        (i) in paragraph (1), for 'When an applicant' to 'other body, he shall' was substituted 'When an applicant making a Schedule 1 or Schedule 2 application submits an environmental statement and at the same time serves a copy of the statement or of a part of it on any other body, he shall' and subparagraph (c) was omitted;
        (ii) in paragraph (2), for subparagraphs (d) and (e) was substituted—
            '(d) serve on any such body that has expressed a wish to receive a copy of the statement or any part of it such a copy.';
        (iii) paragraph (3) was omitted;
    (f) regulation 15 shall apply as if—
        (i) paragraph (2) was omitted;
        (ii) for paragraph (3) was substituted—
            '(3) The local planning authority shall take steps to secure that a copy of the environmental statement is placed on the register.'

(2) An authority which is minded to make a planning application in relation to which it would be the local planning authority may request the Secretary of State in writing for a direction as to whether the proposed application would be a Schedule 1 or a Schedule 2 application.

(3) A request made pursuant to paragraph (2) shall be accompanied by—
    (a) a plan sufficient to identify the land;
    (b) a brief description of the nature and purpose of the proposed development and of its possible effects on the environment;
    (c) such other information or representations as the authority may wish to provide or make.

(4) An authority making a request under paragraph (2) shall send to the Secretary of State any further information he may request in writing to enable him to give a direction.

26. [repealed]

Regulation 2(1)   SCHEDULE 1
DESCRIPTIONS OF DEVELOPMENT

(1) The carrying out of building or other operations, or the change of use of buildings or other land (where a material change) to provide any of the following—
 1. A crude-oil refinery (excluding an undertaking manufacturing only lubricants from crude oil) or an installation for the gasification and liquefaction of 500 tonnes or more of coal or bituminous shale per day.
 2. A thermal power station or other combustion installation with a heat output of 300 megawatts or more, other than a nuclear power station or other nuclear reactor.
 3. An installation designed solely for the permanent storage or final disposal of radioactive waste.
 4. An integrated works for the initial melting of cast-iron and steel.
 5. An installation for the extraction of asbestos or for the processing and transformation of asbestos or products containing asbestos:—
  (a) where the installation produces asbestos-cement products, with an annual production of more than 20,000 tonnes of finished products; or
  (b) where the installation produces friction material, with an annual production of more than 50 tonnes of finished products; or
  (c) in other cases, where the installation will utilise more than 200 tonnes of asbestos per year.
 6. An integrated chemical installation, that is to say, an industrial installation or group of installations where two or more linked chemical or physical processes are employed for the manufacture of olefins from petroleum products, or of sulphuric acid, nitric acid, hydrofluoric acid, chlorine or fluorine.
 7. A special road; a line for long-distance railway traffic; or an aerodrome with a basic runway length of 2,100m or more.
 8. A trading port, an inland waterway which permits the passage of vessels of over 1,350 tonnes or a port for inland waterway traffic capable of handling such vessels.
 9. A waste-disposal installation for the incineration or chemical treatment of special waste.
(2) The carrying out of operations whereby land is filled with special waste, or the change of use of land (where a material change) to use for the deposit of such waste.

Regulation 2(1)   SCHEDULE 2
DESCRIPTIONS OF DEVELOPMENT

Development for any of the following purposes—

1. **Agriculture**
   (a) water-management for agriculture;
   (b) poultry-rearing;
   (c) pig-rearing;
   (d) a salmon hatchery;
   (e) an installation for the rearing of salmon;
   (f) the reclamation of land from the sea.

2. **Extractive industry**
   (a) extracting peat;
   (b) deep drilling, including in particular—

(i) geothermal drilling;
(ii) drilling for the storage of nuclear waste material;
(iii) drilling for water supplies;
but excluding drilling to investigate the stability of the soil;
    (c) extracting minerals (other than metalliferous and energy-producing minerals) such as marble, sand, gravel, shale, salt, phosphates and potash;
    (d) extracting coal or lignite by underground or open-cast mining;
    (e) extracting petroleum;
    (f) extracting natural gas;
    (g) extracting ores;
    (h) extracting bituminous shale;
    (i) extracting minerals (other than metalliferous and energy-producing minerals) by open-cast mining;
    (j) a surface industrial installation for the extraction of coal, petroleum, natural gas or ores or bituminous shale;
    (k) a coke oven (dry distillation of coal);
    (l) an installation for the manufacture of cement.

3. Energy industry

    (a) a non-nuclear thermal power station, not being an installation falling within Schedule 1, or an installation for the production of electricity, steam and hot water;
    (b) an industrial installation for carrying gas, steam or hot water; or the transmission of electrical energy by overhead cables;
    (c) the surface storage of natural gas;
    (d) the underground storage of combustible gases;
    (e) the surface storage of fossil fuels;
    (f) the industrial briquetting of coal or lignite;
    (g) an installation for the production or enrichment of nuclear fuels;
    (h) an installation for the reprocessing of irradiated nuclear fuels;
    (i) an installation for the collection or processing of radioactive waste, not being an installation falling within Schedule 1;
    (j) an installation for hydroelectric energy production;
    (k) a wind generator.

4. Processing of metals

    (a) an ironworks or steelworks including a foundry, forge, drawing plant or rolling mill (not being a works falling within Schedule 1);
    (b) an installation for the production (including smelting, refining, drawing and rolling) of non-ferrous metals, other than precious metals;
    (c) the pressing, drawing or stamping of large castings;
    (d) the surface treatment and coating of metals;
    (e) boilermaking or manufacturing reservoirs, tanks and other sheet-metal containers;
    (f) manufacturing or assembling motor vehicles or manufacturing motor-vehicle engines;
    (g) a shipyard;
    (h) an installation for the construction or repair of aircraft;
    (i) the manufacture of railway equipment;
    (j) swaging by explosives;
    (k) an installation for the roasting or sintering of metallic ores.

5. Glass making

    The manufacture of glass.

6. Chemical industry
   (a) the treatment of intermediate products and production of chemicals, other than development falling within Schedule 1;
   (b) the production of pesticides or pharmaceutical products, paints or varnishes, elastomers or peroxides;
   (c) the storage of petroleum or petrochemical or chemical products.

7. Food industry
   (a) the manufacture of vegetable or animal oils or fats;
   (b) the packing or canning of animal or vegetable products;
   (c) the manufacture of dairy products;
   (d) brewing or malting;
   (e) confectionery or syrup manufacture;
   (f) an installation for the slaughter of animals;
   (g) an industrial starch manufacturing installation;
   (h) a fish-meal or fish-oil factory;
   (i) a sugar factory.

8. Textile, leather, wood and paper industries
   (a) a wool scouring, degreasing and bleaching factory;
   (b) the manufacture of fibre board, particle board or plywood;
   (c) the manufacture of pulp, paper or board;
   (d) a fibre-dyeing factory;
   (e) a cellulose-processing and production installation;
   (f) a tannery or a leather dressing factory.

9. Rubber industry
The manufacture and treatment of elastomer-based products.

10. Infrastructure projects
   (a) an industrial estate development project;
   (b) an urban development project;
   (c) a ski-lift or cable-car;
   (d) the construction of a road, or a harbour, including a fishing harbour, or an aerodrome, not being development falling within Schedule 1;
   (e) canalisation or flood-relief works;
   (f) a dam or other installation designed to hold water or store it on a long-term basis;
   (g) a tramway, elevated or underground railway, suspended line or similar line, exclusively or mainly for passenger transport;
   (h) an oil or gas pipeline installation;
   (i) a long-distance aqueduct;
   (j) a yacht marina;
   (k) a motorway service area;
   (l) coast protection works.

11. Other projects
   (a) a holiday village or hotel complex;
   (b) a permanent racing or test track for cars or motor cycles;
   (c) an installation for the disposal of controlled waste or waste from mines and quarries, not being an installation falling within Schedule 1;
   (d) a waste water treatment plant;
   (e) a site for depositing sludge;
   (f) the storage of scrap iron;
   (g) a test bench for engines, turbines or reactors;

(h) the manufacture of artificial mineral fibres;
(i) the manufacture, packing, loading or placing in cartridges of gunpowder or other explosives;
(j) a knackers' yard.

12. The modification of a development which has been carried out, where that development is within a description mentioned in Schedule 1.

13. Development within a description mentioned in Schedule 1, where it is exclusively or mainly for the development and testing of new methods or products and will not be permitted for longer than one year.

Regulation 2(1) SCHEDULE 3

1. An environmental statement comprises a document or series of documents providing for the purpose of assessing the likely impact upon the environment of the development proposed to be carried out, the information specified in paragraph 2 (referred to in this Schedule as 'the specified information').

2. The specified information is—
   (a). a description of the development proposed, comprising information about the site and the design and size or scale of the development;
   (b) the data necessary to identify and assess the main effects which that development is likely to have on the environment;
   (c) a description of the likely significant effects, direct and indirect, on the environment of the development, explained by reference to its possible impact on—
   human beings;
   flora;
   fauna;
   soil;
   water;
   air;
   climate;
   the landscape;
   the inter-action between any of the foregoing;
   material assets;
   the cultural heritage;
   (d) where significant adverse effects are identified with respect to any of the foregoing, a description of the measures envisaged in order to avoid, reduce or remedy those effects; and
   (e) a summary in non-technical language of the information specified above.

3. An environmental statement may include, by way of explanation or amplification of any specified information, further information on any of the following matters—
   (a) the physical characteristics of the proposed development, and the land-use requirements during the construction and operational phases;
   (b) the main characteristics of the production processes proposed, including the nature and quality of the materials to be used;
   (c) the estimated type and quantity of expected residues and emissions (including pollutants of water, air or soil, noise, vibration, light, heat and radiation) resulting from the proposed development when in operation;
   (d) (in outline) the main alternatives (if any) studied by the applicant, appellant or authority and an indication of the main reasons for choosing the development proposed, taking into account the environmental effects;
   (e) the likely significant direct and indirect effects on the environment of the development proposed which may result from—

(i) the use of natural resources;
(ii) the emission of pollutants, the creation of nuisances, and the elimination of waste;
(f) the forecasting methods used to assess any effects on the environment about which information is given under subparagraph (e); and
(g) any difficulties, such as technical deficiencies or lack of know-how, encountered in compiling any specified information.

In paragraph (e), 'effects' includes secondary, cumulative, short, medium and long term, permanent, temporary, positive and negative effects.

4. Where further information is included in an environmental statement pursuant to paragraph 3, a non-technical summary of that information shall also be provided.

TOWN AND COUNTRY PLANNING (DEVELOPMENT PLAN) REGULATIONS 1991
(SI 1991, No. 2794)

The Secretary of State for the Environment, as respects England, and the Secretary of State for Wales, as respects Wales, in exercise of the powers conferred on them by sections 12, 13, 26, 31, 33, 36, 37(4), 38(5), 40, 46, 53 and 336(1) of, and paragraph 4 of Part I and paragraph 17 of Part II of Schedule 2 to, the Town and Country Planning Act 1990 and paragraphs 40, 41(2), 45(1), 46(1) and 47(7) of Schedule 4 to the Planning and Compensation Act 1991 and of all other powers enabling them in that behalf hereby make the following regulations—

PART 1
GENERAL

1. Citation and commencement
These Regulations may be cited as the Town and Country Planning (Development Plan) Regulations 1991 and shall come into force on 10th February 1992.

2. Interpretation
(1) In these Regulations—
'the 1990 Act' means the Town and Country Planning Act 1990;
'the 1991 Act' means the Planning and Compensation Act 1991;
'by advertisement' means by publication in the London Gazette and by local advertisement;
'by local advertisement' means by publication on at least one occasion in two successive weeks in a local newspaper circulating in the area of the local planning authority;
'statutory plan' means a unitary development plan, structure plan, local plan, minerals local plan or waste local plan.
(2) In these Regulations—
(a) a reference to the section of an Act is a reference to that section of the 1990 Act;
(b) a reference to a numbered form is a reference to the correspondingly numbered form in the Schedule to these Regulations;
(c) in relation to the making, alteration or replacement of a statutory plan by two or more local planning authorities jointly, a reference to a local planning authority shall be read as a reference to all of the local planning authorities making, altering or replacing the plan.
(3) Part 8 of these Regulations shall be interpreted in accordance with regulation 38.

3. Application

These Regulations apply with respect to—

(a) the form and content of unitary development plans and the procedure to be followed in connection with the making, alteration and replacement of such plans under Chapter I of Part II of the 1990 Act;

(b) the form and content of structure plans and the procedure to be followed in connection with the alteration and replacement of such plans under Chapter II of Part II of the 1990 Act;

(c) the form and content of local plans, minerals local plans and waste local plans and the procedure to be followed in connection with the making, alteration and replacement of such plans under Chapter II of Part II of the 1990 Act.

PART 2
FORM AND CONTENT OF STATUTORY PLANS

4. Title

(1) The title of a statutory plan shall consist of the name of the area of the local planning authority followed by 'unitary development plan', 'structure plan', 'local plan', 'minerals local plan' or 'waste local plan', as the case may be.

(2) Where policies in respect of development consisting of the winning and working of minerals or involving the depositing of mineral waste ('mineral policies') are included in a local plan or waste policies are included in a local plan or a minerals local plan, the local plan or minerals local plan including such policies shall have a sub-title consisting of the words 'including mineral policies', 'including waste policies' or 'including mineral and waste policies', as the case may be.

5. Structure plan diagrams

(1) A structure plan shall contain a diagram, called the key diagram, illustrating the general policies formulated in the plan's written statement.

(2) A structure plan may also contain a diagram, called an inset diagram, drawn to a larger scale than the key diagram, and illustrating the application of the general policies to part of the area covered by the structure plan.

(3) Where an inset diagram is included in a structure plan, the area covered by the inset diagram shall be identified on the key diagram and the application of the general policies to that area shall be illustrated on that inset diagram only.

(4) No key diagram or inset diagram contained in a structure plan shall be on a map base.

(5) The title of a structure plan shall be set out on the key diagram and on any inset diagram contained in the plan and the key diagram and any inset diagram shall include an explanation of any symbol or notation used in the diagram.

6. Maps

(1) The map required by section 12(4)(b) to be included in a unitary development plan, and by section 36(6)(a) to be included in a local plan, a minerals local plan and a waste local plan, shall be called the proposals map and shall be a map of the authority's area reproduced from, or based upon, an Ordnance Survey map and shall show National Grid lines and reference numbers.

(2) Policies for any part of the authority's area may be illustrated on a separate map on a larger scale than the proposals map, called an inset map.

(3) Where an inset map is included in a plan, the area covered by the inset map shall be identified on the proposals map and the policies for that area shall be illustrated on that inset map only.

(4) The title (and any sub-title) of a statutory plan mentioned in paragraph (1) shall be set out on the proposals map and any inset map contained in the plan and

the proposals map and any inset map shall show the scale to which it has been prepared and include an explanation of any symbol or notation used in the map.

7. Reasoned justification
(1) A local plan, minerals local plan and waste local plan shall contain a reasoned justification of the policies formulated in the plan.

(2) The reasoned justification shall be set out so as to be readily distinguishable from the other contents of the plan.

PART 3
ACTION AREAS

8. Action areas: prescribed period
The period prescribed for the purpose of section 12(8) and 36(7) (period for the commencement of comprehensive treatment of an action area) is a period of 10 years beginning with the date on which the relevant plan is first made available for inspection in accordance with section 13(2)(a) or 40(2)(a), as the case may be.

PART 4
PROCEDURE

9. Regard to be had to certain matters and statement of regard
(1) In formulating their general policies in Part I of a unitary development plan or in a structure plan, the local planning authority shall, in addition to the matters specified in section 12(6), in the case of a unitary development plan, and in section 31(6), in the case of a structure plan, have regard to—
  (a) social and economic considerations;
  (b) environmental considerations; and
  (c) any policies and proposals of an urban development corporation which affects or may be expected to affect, their area.

(2) In formulating their waste policies in Part II of a unitary development plan, or in a waste local plan, or in a local plan or minerals local plan containing waste policies, a local planning authority shall have regard to any waste disposal plan for their area under section 50 of the Environmental Protection Act 1990

(3) The reasoned justification of the general policies in Part I and of the policies in Part II of a unitary development plan shall contain a statement of—
  (a) the regard which the local planning authority have had in formulating their general policies in Part I to the matters specified in section 12(6) and paragraph (1);
  (b) the regard which the authority have had in formulating their waste policies in Part II to any waste disposal plan for their area and the reason for any inconsistency between their waste policies and the waste disposal plan; and
  (c) the account which the authority have taken of any enterprise zone scheme in their area.

(4) The explanatory memorandum accompanying proposals for the alteration or replacement of a structure plan shall contain a statement of the regard which the local planning authority have had in formulating their general policies to the matters specified in section 31(6) and paragraph (1).

(5) The reasoned justification of the policies formulated in a local plan, minerals local plan or waste local plan shall contain a statement of—
  (a) in the case of a local plan, the regard which the local planning authority have had in formulating their policies to any enterprise zone scheme in their area;
  (b) in the case of a waste local plan, or a local plan or a minerals local plan containing waste policies, the regard which the local planning authority have had in formulating their waste policies to any waste disposal plan and the reason for any inconsistency between their waste policies and the waste disposal plan.

10. Pre-deposit consultation

(1) When preparing proposals for a statutory plan or for the alteration or replacement of such a plan under section 13(1), 33(1) or 40(1), and before finally determining the contents of the proposals, the local planning authority shall consult—

(a) the Secretary of State for the Environment and the Secretary of State for Transport, in England, or the Secretary of State for Wales, in Wales;

(b) any other local planning authority for the area covered by the proposals;

(c) any local planning authority for an area adjacent to the area covered by the proposals;

(d) except in the case of structure plan proposals, the council of any parish or community for the area covered by the proposals;

(e) the National Rivers Authority;

(f) the Countryside Commission and the Nature Conservancy Council for England, in England, or the Countryside Council for Wales, in Wales;

(g) the Historic Buildings and Monuments Commission for England, in England.

(2) The local planning authority shall consider any representations made by the consultees before finally determining the contents of the proposals.

(3) The local planning authority shall prepare a statement of any other persons they have consulted when preparing their proposals, in addition to those listed in paragraph (1), and of any steps they have taken to publicise their proposals and to provide persons with an opportunity of making representations in respect of those proposals.

11. Deposit of proposals

(1) A local planning authority making proposals for a statutory plan or for the alteration or replacement of a statutory plan available for inspection in accordance with section 13(2)(a), 33(2)(a) or 40(2)(a), shall—

(a) make the proposals available at their principal office and at such other places within their area as they consider appropriate;

(b) give notice by advertisement in Form 1; and

(c) give notice in similar form to any consultee under regulation 10(1) and to any other person whom they consider should be given notice.

(2) Proposals made available for inspection shall be accompanied by—

(a) the statement prepared pursuant to regulation 10(3);

(b) in the case of local plan, minerals local plan or waste local plan proposals made available in accordance with section 40(2)(a), any statement supplied under section 46(2);

(c) in the case of structure plan proposals made available in accordance with section 33(2)(a), the explanatory memorandum.

(3) The local planning authority shall send 4 copies of the documents made available for inspection to the Secretary of State.

12. Objections and representations

(1) The period within which objections and representations may be made to the local planning authority with respect to proposals for a statutory plan, or for the alteration or replacement of such a plan, made available for inspection under section 13(2)(a), 33(2)(a) or 40(2)(a), shall be six weeks beginning with the date on which a notice given pursuant to regulation 11(1)(b) is first published in a local newspaper.

(2) Objections and representations shall be made in writing and addressed to the local planning authority in accordance with the details given in the published notice.

(3) In addition to the requirement to consider objections imposed by sections 13(6), 33(6) or 40(7), as the case may be, the local planning authority shall also consider any representations made in accordance with this regulation.

Town and Country Planning (Development Plan) Regulations 1991 465

(4) In the case of deposited proposals for a statutory plan or for the replacement of a statutory plan, a representation that matters relating to the development and use of land not included in the deposited proposals ought to have been so included shall be treated as an objection made to the proposals in accordance with the regulations for the purpose of
  (a) regulation 17;
  (b) in the case of statutory plan proposals other than structure plan proposals, regulation 14 and sections 16 and 42,
if the representation is made within the time and in the manner required by this regulation.

13. Withdrawal of proposals

(1) On the withdrawal of proposals for a local plan, minerals local plan or waste local plan, or for the alteration or replacement of such a plan, the local planning authority shall—
  (a) withdraw the copies of the proposals made available for inspection under section 40(2)(a); and
  (b) give notice that the proposals have been withdrawn to every person who has made an objection or representation with respect to the proposals.

(2) On the withdrawal of proposals for a unitary development plan, or for the alteration or replacement of a unitary development plan or a structure plan, the local planning authority shall, in addition to the persons specified in section 14(2)(b), in the case of unitary development plan proposals, or in section 34(2)(b), in the case of structure plan proposals, give notice of the withdrawal to every person who has made a representation with respect to the proposals.

(3) A local planning authority withdrawing proposals for a statutory plan, or for the alteration or replacement of such a plan, shall also give notice by advertisement.

(4) The notice of withdrawal required by sections 14(2)(b), 34(2)(b) and by this regulation shall be in Form 2.

14. Local inquiry or other hearing

(1) A local planning authority shall, at least six weeks before the opening of any local inquiry or other hearing which they cause to be held to consider objections to proposals for a statutory plan or for the alteration or replacement of a statutory plan made available for inspection under section 13(2) or 40(2)—
  (a) give any person who has objected to, or made a representation in respect of, the proposals in accordance with these regulations and not withdrawn the objection or representation, notice of the time and place at which the inquiry or other hearing is to be held, the name of the person appointed to hold it, and its purpose; and
  (b) in the case of a local inquiry, give notice of that information by local advertisement.

(2) A local inquiry referred to in paragraph (1) shall be held in public.

15. Examination in public

(1) A local planning authority shall, at least six weeks before the opening of an examination in public which they cause to be held of matters affecting the consideration of proposals for the alteration or replacement of a structure plan—
  (a) make available for inspection at any place at which the plan proposals have been made available for inspection a list of the matters with which the examination in public will be concerned and the persons who have been invited to take part in it;
  (b) give any person who has objected to, or made a representation in respect of, the proposals in accordance with these regulations and not withdrawn the objection or representation, notice of the time and place at which the examination in public is to be held, the name of the person or persons appointed to hold it and its purpose, and the availability for inspection of the list mentioned in sub-paragraph (a); and

(c) give notice of that information by local advertisement.

(2) Any notice given under paragraph (1) shall invite representations to be made to the local planning authority on the list referred to in paragraph (1)(a) within 28 days of the date on which the notice is first published in a local newspaper.

16. Consideration of proposals following a local inquiry or other hearing or examination in public

(1) Where a local planning authority cause a local inquiry or other hearing to be held for a purpose mentioned in regulation 14(1), or an examination in public to be held for a purpose mentioned in regulation 15, the authority shall, after considering the report of the person holding the inquiry, other hearing, or examination in public, as the case may be, prepare a statement of—

(a) the decisions they have reached in the light of the report and any recommendations contained in the report; and

(b) the reasons for those decisions.

(2) Where a list of proposed modifications to the statutory plan proposals is made available for inspection under regulation 18(1) after the statement of decisions and reasons is prepared, the report mentioned in paragraph (1) and that statement shall be made available for inspection from the date on which, and at the places at which, the list is made available for inspection.

(3) Where such a list is not made available for inspection under regulation 18(1) after the statement of decisions and reasons is prepared, the local planning authority shall—

(a) give notice by local advertisement in Form 3;

(b) serve a notice in similar form on any person who has objected to, or made a representation in respect of, the plan proposals in accordance with these regulations and not withdrawn the objection or representation; and

(c) make copies of the report mentioned in paragraph (1) and the statement of decisions and reasons available for inspection at any place at which the plan proposals have been made available for inspection.

(4) Where the report of the person holding the inquiry, other hearing, or examination in public, as the case may be, contains recommendations that the statutory plan proposals should be modified in a manner specified in the report and the local planning authority intend not to accept one or more of those recommendations—

(a) the authority shall make a list of the recommendations that they do not intend to accept available for inspection from the date on which, and at the places at which, the report is made available for inspection;

(b) the notice given in Form 3, or in Form 4, as the case may be, shall record the authority's intention not to accept those recommendations and invite objections and representations to be made in respect of that intention within six weeks of the date on which the notice is first published in a local newspaper;

(c) paragraphs (3) and (4) of regulation 18 shall apply to any objection and representation made in respect of that intention as they apply to objections and representations made in respect of proposed modifications;

(d) where a local inquiry or other hearing is held to consider objections made to that intention, regulation 14 shall apply, and where an examination in public is held to consider matters in connection with that intention, regulation 15 shall apply, as those regulations apply in the case of statutory plan proposals, and this regulation shall apply following such a local inquiry or other hearing or examination in public as it applies to a local inquiry or other hearing or examination in public mentioned in paragraph (1); and

(e) where objections have been made to that intention in accordance with these regulations and not withdrawn and the local planning authority do not cause a local inquiry or other hearing or examination in public to be held, regulation 17 shall apply to the consideration of the objections as it applies to the consideration of objections to statutory plan proposals.

(5) Where notice is given in Form 3 and paragraph (4) does not apply, the notice shall give 28 days notice of the local planning authority's intention to adopt the statutory plan proposals.

17. Consideration of objections without a local inquiry or other hearing or examination in public

(1) Where objections have been made to statutory plan proposals in accordance with these regulations and not withdrawn and the local planning authority do not cause a local inquiry or other hearing or examination in public to be held, the authority shall prepare a statement of their decisions as respects all the objections and their reasons for each decision.

(2) Paragraphs (2), (3) and (5) of regulation 16 shall apply where a statement is prepared pursuant to paragraph (1) as they apply where a statement is prepared pursuant to regulation 16(1).

18. Modification of proposals

(1) Subject to paragraph (7), a local planning authority proposing to modify proposals for a statutory plan or for the alteration or replacement of a statutory plan (whether to comply with a direction given by the Secretary of State or on their own initiative) shall, unless they are satisfied that the modifications they intend to make will not materially affect the content of the proposals—
    (a) prepare a list of the modifications with their reasons for proposing them;
    (b) make copies of that list available for inspection at any place at which the plan proposals have been made available for inspection;
    (c) give notice by local advertisement in Form 4; and
    (d) serve a notice in similar form on any person who has objected to, or made a representation in respect of, the plan proposals in accordance with these regulations and not withdrawn the objection or representation.

(2) The period within which objections and representations may be made to the local planning authority in respect of proposed modifications is six weeks beginning with the date on which a notice given pursuant to paragraph (1) is first published in a local newspaper.

(3) Objections and representations shall be made in writing and addressed in accordance with the details given in the notice.

(4) An objection to, or representation in respect of, proposed modifications, made in accordance with this regulation, shall be treated as an objection made in accordance with the regulations for the purpose of section 13(6), in the case of unitary development plan proposals, section 33(6), in the case of structure plan proposals, and section 40(7), in the case of local plan, minerals local plan or waste local plan proposals.

(5) Where a local inquiry or other hearing is held to consider objections made to proposed modifications, regulation 14 shall apply, and where an examination in public is held to consider matters in connection with proposed modifications, regulation 15 shall apply, as those regulations apply in the case of statutory plan proposals, and regulation 16 shall apply following such a local inquiry or other hearing or examination in public as it applies to a local inquiry or other hearing or examination in public mentioned in paragraph (1) of that regulation.

(6) Where objections have been made to proposed modifications in accordance with this regulation and not withdrawn and the local planning authority do not cause a local inquiry or other hearing or examination in public to be held, regulation 17 shall apply to the consideration of the objections as it applies to the consideration of objections to statutory plan proposals.

(7) Unless a list of proposed modifications contains only modifications proposed by the local planning authority in order to comply with a direction given by the Secretary of State under section 17(1), 35(2) or 43(4), it shall not be made available for inspection, and the notice referred to in paragraph (1) shall not be given or served, until after—

(a) the period for objecting to the statutory plan proposals after they have been made available for inspection has expired, or, in the case of a second or subsequent list of proposed modifications, the period for objecting to the previous list of proposed modifications has expired; and

(b) any statement (or further statement) required by regulation 16(1) or 17(1), as the case may be, has been prepared.

19. Notice of intention to adopt

Without prejudice to sections 13(6), 32(7) and 40(7), proposals for a statutory plan or for the alteration or replacement of such a plan shall not be adopted by a local planning authority until the period given by the authority in their notice of intention to adopt in Form 1, or where the authority has also given notice of their intention to adopt in Form 3 or Form 4, the period in the last such notice to be given by the authority, has expired.

20. Adoption

(1) When a local planning authority adopt proposals for a statutory plan or for the alteration or replacement of a statutory plan they shall—

(a) give notice by advertisement in Form 5; and

(b) serve notice in similar form on any person who has asked to be notified of the adoption.

(2) A copy of the notice given pursuant to paragraph (1) and of the adopted proposals shall be made available for inspection at any place at which the proposals were made available for inspection under regulation 11(1)(a).

(3) The local planning authority shall, not later than the date on which notice is first given by advertisement pursuant to paragraph (1), send 4 copies of the adopted proposals to the Secretary of State.

PART 5
INTERVENTION BY THE SECRETARY OF STATE

21. Documents to be supplied to the Secretary of State

A local planning authority shall supply the Secretary of State with a copy of every notice published by the authority in accordance with these Regulations when the notice is first published, together with a copy of every document made available for inspection in accordance with these regulations.

22. Direction to modify proposals

(1) Where the Secretary of State directs a local planning authority to modify their proposals under section 17(1), 35(2) or 43(4) the authority shall make a copy of the direction available for inspection with any subsequent list of modifications made so available pursuant to regulation 18(1), and that list shall indicate—

(a) which modifications have been proposed to comply with the direction; or

(b) where modifications have not been proposed to comply, or to comply fully, with the direction, the authority's reasons for not doing so.

(2) Any notice of adoption of the proposals given pursuant to regulation 20(1) shall state that the local planning authority have satisfied the Secretary of State that they have made the modifications necessary to conform with the direction to modify or that the direction has been withdrawn, as the case may be.

(3) A copy of any notification by the Secretary of State that he is satisfied with the modifications made or that the direction is withdrawn shall be made available for

Town and Country Planning (Development Plan) Regulations 1991 469

inspection from the date on which, and at the places at which, the adopted proposals are made available for inspection.

23. Direction not to adopt proposals

If, before the local planning authority have adopted proposals for a statutory plan or for the alteration or replacement of such a plan, the Secretary of State directs them not to adopt the proposals until he has decided whether to give them a direction under section 18(1), 35A(1) or 44(1), as the case may be, they shall not adopt the proposals until he has notified them of his decision.

24. Called-in proposals

(1) Where the Secretary of State is minded to approve with modifications proposals for a statutory plan or for the alteration or replacement of a statutory plan submitted to him for his approval, he shall, unless, in his opinion, the proposed modifications will not materially affect the content of the plan proposals, send a list of the proposed modifications to the local planning authority, and the authority shall, upon receipt of the list—

 (a) make copies of the list available for inspection at any place at which the plan proposals have been made available for inspection;

 (b) give notice by local advertisement in Form 6; and

 (c) serve notice in similar form on any person who has objected to, or made a representation in respect of, the plan in accordance with these regulations and not withdrawn the objection or representation and on any other person on whom the Secretary of State directs them to serve such a notice.

(2) The period within which objections or representations may be made to the Secretary of State in respect of the proposed modifications is six weeks beginning with the date on which a notice given pursuant to paragraph (1) is first published in a local newspaper.

(3) Objections and representations shall be made in writing and addressed in accordance with the details given in the notice.

(4) Where the Secretary of State causes a local inquiry or other hearing to be held for the purpose of considering objections to statutory plan proposals submitted to him for his approval, or to modifications which he proposes to make to such proposals, he shall give such notice as the local planning authority would be required to give by regulation 14(1) if they were proposing to hold an inquiry or other hearing.

(5) Where the Secretary of State causes an examination in public to be held under section 20(4) or 35B(2) of matters affecting his consideration of proposals submitted to him for his approval, or modifications which he proposes to make to such proposals, he shall—

 (a) send a list of the matters with which the examination in public will be concerned and the persons who have been invited to take part in it to the local planning authority; and

 (b) give such notice as the local planning authority would be required to give by regulation 15 if they were proposing to hold an examination in public.

(6) The local planning authority shall, on receipt of a list sent to them pursuant to paragraph (5), make that list available for inspection at any place at which the plan proposals have been made available for inspection.

(7) The local planning authority shall, on being notified by the Secretary of State of his decision on statutory plan proposals submitted to him for his approval—

 (a) give notice by advertisement in Form 7;

 (b) serve a notice in similar form on any person who has asked to be notified of the decision reached on the proposals and on any other person on whom the Secretary of State directs them to serve such a notice; and

 (c) make a copy of the Secretary of State's notification and of the approved or rejected proposals available for inspection at any place at which the proposals were made available for inspection under regulation 11(1)(a).

25. Making, alteration and replacement of statutory plans by the Secretary of State

(1) These Regulations apply, so far as practicable and with any necessary modifications, to the making, alteration and replacement of a statutory plan by the Secretary of State as they apply to the making, alteration or replacement of a statutory plan by a local planning authority.

(2) When a statutory plan or alteration made by the Secretary of State becomes operative, the local planning authority entitled to prepare proposals for the alteration or replacement of the plan made or altered by the Secretary of State shall comply with regulation 27 in respect of that plan.

PART 6
AVAILABILITY OF DOCUMENTS AND INDEX

26. Availability of documents for inspection

(1) Subject to paragraph (3), documents made available for inspection pursuant to Part II of the 1990 Act or these Regulations by a local planning authority making, altering or replacing a statutory plan shall be made so available at the place and time specified by the authority when giving notice of their availability for inspection, and shall, unless the statutory plan proposals are withdrawn, remain so available until the expiration of six weeks from the date of publication of the notice of adoption, approval or rejection of the proposals.

(2) The local planning authority shall, on request and on payment of a reasonable charge, provide, as soon as practicable, a copy of any document made available for inspection mentioned in paragraph (1).

(3) Adopted proposals made available for inspection under regulation 20(2) and approved proposals made available for inspection under regulation 24(7)(c) shall remain so available until printed copies of the proposals are made available for inspection under regulation 27(1).

27. Availability of plans after adoption or approval

(1) As soon as practicable after proposals for a statutory plan or for the alteration or replacement of a statutory plan have been adopted or approved, the local planning authority which prepared the proposals shall secure that printed copies of the statutory plan, the statutory plan as altered, or the replacement plan, as the case may be, are available for inspection during normal office hours at their principal office and at such other places within their area as they consider appropriate and, on payment of a reasonable charge, for purchase.

(2) A local planning authority shall continue to make printed copies of a statutory plan, altered statutory plan, or replacement plan made available for inspection and purchase under paragraph (1) so available until the relevant plan is altered, further altered, or replaced, as the case may be.

28. Index

(1) A local planning authority shall keep an index containing the following information in respect of the development plan for their area—

    (a) the title of any plan forming part of or constituting the development plan for their area;

    (b) the date on which that plan was adopted or approved;

    (c) the title and date of adoption or approval of any alteration to that plan;

    (d) the date of the first publication of any notice given under these Regulations in respect of proposals for the making of a plan which will form part of or constitute the development plan for their area or for the alteration or replacement of such a plan; and

    (e) the places at which any plan, alteration or notice listed in the index may be inspected.

(2) In a non-metropolitan area, the index kept by the local planning authority shall also contain the date of any statement supplied under section 35C or paragraph 47 of Schedule 4 to the 1991 Act, or prepared under regulations 30 or 36, in relation to a plan listed in the index and shall identify the places at which the statement may be inspected.

(3) A local planning authority shall also keep a map showing the boundary of any plan listed in their index.

(4) The index and map kept in accordance with this regulation shall be made available for inspection during normal office hours at the local planning authority's principal office and at such other places within their area as they consider appropriate.

PART 7
CONFORMITY AND CONFLICT

29. Statement of conformity of proposals with structure plan: prescribed period

The prescribed period for the purpose of section 46(1)(b) is 28 days.

30. Statement of conformity on adoption or approval of structure plan

(1) An authority responsible for a structure plan shall, where any proposals of theirs for the alteration or replacement of a structure plan are adopted or approved, prepare a statement in respect of any local plan for which the authority is responsible, and any minerals local plan and waste local plan for their area, stating whether the plan is, or as the case may be, is not, in general conformity with the altered or new structure plan.

(2) A statement prepared under paragraph (1) stating that a local plan, minerals local plan or waste local plan is not in general conformity with a structure plan shall specify the respects in which it is not in such conformity.

(3) A local planning authority which makes available for inspection a plan to which a statement under section 35C or paragraph (1) relates, shall make a copy of the statement available for inspection at any place at which the plan is made available for inspection.

(4) In this regulation, references to an authority responsible for a structure plan or a local plan shall be construed in accordance with section 35C(5).

31. Conflict between structure plans and local plans, minerals local plans and waste local plans

The provisions of a local plan prevail for all purposes over any conflicting provisions in a structure plan made by the same authority, and the provisions of a minerals local plan and of a waste local plan prevail for all purposes over any conflicting provisions in a structure plan, unless the local plan, minerals local plan or waste local plan is one—

(a) stated under regulation 30(1) not to be in general conformity with the structure plan; and

(b) neither altered nor replaced after the statement was prepared.

32. Conflict between local plans and mineral local plans or waste local plans

Where there is a conflict between provisions in a local plan and provisions in a minerals local plan or waste local plan, the more recently adopted or approved provisions prevail.

33. Conflict within statutory plans

Where there is a conflict between the written statement of a statutory plan and any other document forming part of the plan, the provisions of the written statement prevail.

PART 8
TRANSITIONAL PROVISIONS

34. Unitary development plan proposals deposited under the old law

(1) This regulation applies to proposals for a unitary development plan treated as if made available for inspection under section 13(2) by virtue of paragraph 41(1) of Schedule 4 to the 1991 Act.

(2) Where this regulation applies and the six week period afforded under the old law for making objections to the unitary development plan proposals made available for inspection under section 13(3) of the old law has not expired at commencement—

(a) the local planning authority which made the proposals available for inspection under the old law shall, as soon as practicable, give notice by advertisement that objections may be made under the new law to any policy contained in the proposals, including local plan policies incorporated into the proposals under the old law, and that the period given for making objections to the proposals is to be treated as expiring six weeks after the date on which the notice is first published in a local newspaper; and

(b) the period for making objections to the proposals shall be so treated for all purposes.

35. Existing policy statement

(1) An existing policy statement shall be made in Form 8.

(2) A local planning authority intending to publish an existing policy statement shall—

(a) make copies of their existing policy statement available for inspection at any place at which the statutory plan proposals are made available for inspection for the purpose of regulation 11(1)(a);

(b) where the statutory plan proposals are first made available for inspection on or after commencement, publish the statement with the notice of deposit of those proposals on each occasion on which that notice is published pursuant to regulation 11(1)(b) and include a copy of the statement with any notice given pursuant to regulation 11(1)(c);

(c) where the statutory plan proposals were made available for inspection under the old law and the authority is required to give notice by regulation 34(2)(a), publish the statement with that notice on each occasion on which that notice is published pursuant to that regulation.

(5) In this regulation 'existing policy statement' means a statement made for the purpose of paragraph 4 of Part I or paragraph 17 of Part II of Schedule 2 to the 1990 Act or paragraphs 41(2), 45(1), or 46(1) of Schedule 4 to the 1991 Act.

36. Conflict between structure plans and saved local plans

(1) Where proposals for the alteration or replacement of a structure plan are adopted or approved and the local planning authority concerned are the only local planning authority in their area, that authority shall prepare a statement that any saved local plan in operation in the area is, or, as the case may be, is not, in general conformity with the altered or new structure plan.

(2) A statement prepared under paragraph (1) stating that a saved local plan is not in general conformity with a structure plan shall specify the respects in which it is not in such conformity.

(3) A local planning authority which make available for inspection a saved local plan to which a statement under paragraph 47(2) of Schedule 4 to the 1991 Act or paragraph (1) relates, shall make a copy of the statement available for inspection at any place at which the plan is made available for inspection.

(4) The provisions of a saved local plan mentioned in paragraph (1) prevail for all purposes over any conflicting provisions in the structure plan unless the saved local

plan is one stated under that paragraph not to be in general conformity with the structure plan.

(5) In this regulation, the references to a saved local plan do not include a reference to a saved local plan to which paragraph 44(2) of Schedule 4 to the 1991 Act applies.

37. Availability of plans adopted or approved before commencement

Where, immediately before commencement, a local planning authority are making a plan forming part of or constituting the development plan for their area available for inspection, that authority shall continue to make that plan available for inspection until the plan ceases to have effect in relation to the authority's area.

38. Interpretation of Part 8

In this Part, 'commencement', 'the old law' and 'the new law' have the meaning given to those expressions by paragraph 40 of Schedule 4 to the 1991 Act.

PART 9
REVOCATION AND SAVINGS

39. Revocation and savings
[omitted]

SCHEDULE
PRESCRIBED FORMS

Regulation 11   FORM 1:

NOTICE OF DEPOSIT OF PROPOSALS FOR A STATUTORY PLAN OR FOR THE ALTERATION OR REPLACEMENT OF A STATUTORY PLAN.

Town and Country Planning Act 1990
Notice of Deposit of Proposals for [the [Alteration] [Replacement] of] a [Unitary Development Plan] [Structure Plan] [Local Plan] [Minerals Local Plan] [Waste Local Plan]
(Title of plan)

(1) have prepared proposals for [the [alteration] [replacement] of] the above plan. Copies of the proposals are available for public inspection at (2) free of charge on (3).

Objections to, and representations in respect of, the proposals should be sent in writing to (4) before (5). Objections and representations should specify the matters to which they relate and the grounds on which they are made, and may be accompanied by a request to be notified at a specified address of the withdrawal, adoption, approval or rejection of the proposals.

Only objectors whose objections are made in writing and sent to the address specified above within the six week period ending on (5) will have a right to have their objections considered at a local inquiry.

Notice of Intention to Adopt Proposals
If no objections are received during the period given for making objections (1) intend to adopt the proposals on the expiry of that period.

Notes
1. Omit any expression within square brackets which is inappropriate.
2. Insert:
   (1) the name of the local planning authority;
   (2) the address of the local planning authority's principal office and of any other places at which the documents are available for inspection;
   (3) the days on which, and hours between which, the documents are available for inspection;

(4) the name or title of the officer to whom objections and representations should be sent and the address to which they are to be sent;
(5) the date which provides a period of six weeks beginning with the date on which the notice is first published in a local newspaper for the making of objections and representations.

Regulation 13 FORM 2:

NOTICE OF WITHDRAWAL OF PROPOSALS FOR A STATUTORY PLAN OR FOR THE ALTERATION OR REPLACEMENT OF A STATUTORY PLAN.

Town and Country Planning Act 1990
Notice of Withdrawal of Proposals for [the [Alteration] [Replacement] of] a [Unitary Development Plan] [Structure Plan] [Local Plan] [Minerals Local plan] [Waste Local Plan]
(Title of plan)

Copies of these proposals made available for inspection by (1) have been withdrawn because (2)

Notes
1. Omit any expression within square brackets which is inappropriate.
2. Insert:
    (1) the name of the local planning authority;
    (2) the reasons why the proposals have been withdrawn.

Regulations 16 and 17 FORM 3:

NOTICE OF INTENTION TO ADOPT PROPOSALS FOR A STATUTORY PLAN OR FOR THE ALTERATION OR REPLACEMENT OF A STATUTORY PLAN WITHOUT PROPOSING MODIFICATIONS OR FURTHER MODIFICATIONS.

Town and Country Planning Act 1990
Notice of Intention to Adopt Proposals for [the [Alteration] [Replacement] of] a [Unitary Development Plan] [Structure Plan] [Local Plan] [Minerals Local Plan] [Waste Local Plan]
(Title of plan)

(1) propose to adopt these plan proposals without proposing any [further] modifications. Copies of the plan proposals [, the report of the person who held the [local inquiry] [hearing] [examination in public] and the authority's statement of reasons and decisions in the light of the report] [and the authority's statement of reasons and decisions as respects objections to the plan proposals] are available for inspection at (2) on (3).
[The authority do not intend to accept the recommendations in the report that the proposals should be modified. A list of the recommendations which the authority do not intend to accept is available for inspection with the above documents. Objections to, and representations in respect of, the intention not to modify the plan proposals in accordance with the recommendations in the report should be sent in writing to (4) before (5). Objections and representations should specify the matters to which they relate and the grounds on which they are made, and may be accompanied by a request to be notified at a specified address of the withdrawal, adoption, approval or rejection of the plan proposals. (1) will adopt the proposals after that date if no objections are received.]
[(1) will adopt the proposals after (6)]

Notes
1. Omit any expression within square brackets which is inappropriate.
2. Insert—
    (1) the name of the local planning authority;

(2) the address of the local planning authority's principal office and of any other places at which the documents are available for inspection;
(3) the days on which, and hours between which, the documents are available for inspection;
(4) the name or title of the officer to whom objections and representations should be sent and the address to which they are to be sent;
(5) the date which provides a period of six weeks beginning with the date on which the notice is first published in a local newspaper for the making of objections and representations;
(6) the date which is 28 days after the date on which the notice is first published in a local newspaper.

Regulation 18 FORM 4:

NOTICE OF PROPOSED MODIFICATIONS TO PROPOSALS FOR A STATUTORY PLAN OR FOR THE ALTERATION OR REPLACEMENT OF A STATUTORY PLAN

Town and Country Planning Act 1990
Notice of Proposed Modifications to Proposals for [the Alteration] [Replacement] of] a [Unitary Development Plan] [Structure Plan] [Local Plan] [Minerals Local Plan] [Waste Local Plan]
(Title of plan)

(1) propose to modify these plan proposals.
A list of the proposed modifications (other than modifications which the authority are satisfied will not materially affect the content of the plan proposals) with the authority's reasons for proposing them are available for inspection at (2) on (3). Copies of the plan proposals [, a direction from the Secretary of State directing the authority to modify the plan proposals,] [, the report of the person who held the [local inquiry] [hearing] [examination in public] and the authority's statement of reasons and decisions in the light of the report] [and the authority's statement of reasons and decisions as respects objections to the plan proposals] are similarly available for inspection.
[The authority do not intend to accept all of the recommendations in the report. A list of the recommendations which the authority do not intend to accept is available for inspection with the above documents.]
Objections to, and representations in respect of, the proposed modifications [and to the intention not to modify the plan proposals in accordance with certain of the recommendations in the report] should be sent in writing to (4) before (5). Objections and representations should specify the matters to which they relate and the grounds on which they are made, and may be accompanied by a request to be notified at a specified address of the withdrawal, adoption, approval or rejection of the plan proposals.

Notice of Intention to Adopt Proposals
If no objections are received during the period given for making objections [and the Secretary of State is satisfied that the modifications proposed conform with his direction or the direction is withdrawn] (1) intend to adopt the proposals on the expiry of that period.

Notes
1. Omit any expression within square brackets which is inappropriate.
2. Insert—
    (1) the name of the local planning authority;
    (2) the address of the local planning authority's principal office and of any other places at which the documents are available for inspection;

(3) the days on which, and hours between which, the documents are available for inspection;

(4) the name or title of the officer to whom objections and representations should be sent and the address to which they are to be sent;

(5) the date which provides a period of six weeks beginning with the date on which the notice is first published in a local newspaper for the making of objections and representations.

Regulation 20   FORM 5:

NOTICE OF PROPOSED ADOPTION OF PROPOSALS FOR A STATUTORY PLAN OR FOR THE ALTERATION OR REPLACEMENT OF A STATUTORY PLAN

Town and Country Planning Act 1990
Notice of Proposed Modifications to Proposals for [the [Alteration] [Replacement] of] a [Unitary Development Plan] [Structure Plan] [Local Plan] [Minerals Local Plan] [Waste Local Plan]

On (1) (2) adopted these plan proposals [with modifications]. [The Secretary of State [was satisfied that the necessary modifications had been made to comply with] [withdrew] his direction to the authority to modify the proposals].

Copies of the adopted proposals [and of the Secretary of State's notification [that he was satisfied with the modifications made to comply with] [withdrawing] his direction] are available for inspection at (3) on (4).

The proposals became operative on their adoption, but any person aggrieved by the proposals who desires to question their validity on the ground that they are not within the powers conferred by Part II of the Town and Country Planning Act 1990 or that any requirement of that Act or of any regulation made under it has not been complied with in relation to the adoption of the proposals, may, within six weeks from (5), make an application to the High Court under section 287 of the 1990 Act.

Notes
1. Omit any expression within square brackets which is inappropriate.
2. Insert—
   (1) the date on which the proposals were adopted;
   (2) the name of the local planning authority;
   (3) the address of the local planning authority's principal office and of any other place at which the documents are available for inspection;
   (4) the days on which, and hours between which, the documents are available for inspection;
   (5) the date on which this notice is first published.

Regulation 24   FORM 6:

NOTICE OF PROPOSED MODIFICATIONS BY THE SECRETARY OF STATE TO PROPOSALS FOR A STATUTORY PLAN OR THE ALTERATION OR REPLACEMENT OF A STATUTORY PLAN SUBMITTED TO HIM FOR HIS APPROVAL

Town and Country Planning Act 1990
Notice of Proposed Modifications to Proposals for [the [Alteration] [Replacement] of] a [Unitary Development Plan] [Structure Plan] [Local Plan] [Minerals Local Plan] [Waste Local Plan]
(Title of plan)

The Secretary of State for [the Environment] [Wales] proposes to modify these plan proposals prepared by (1) and submitted to the Secretary of State for his approval.

A copy of the plan proposals and a list of the proposed modifications (other than modifications which the Secretary of State is satisfied will not materially affect the content of the plan proposals) are available for inspection at (2) on (3).

Objections to, and representations in respect of, the proposed modifications should be sent in writing to (4) before (5) and may be accompanied by a request to be notified at a specified address of the approval or rejection of the plan proposals.

Notes
1. Omit any expression within square brackets which is inappropriate.
2. Insert—
    (1) the name of the local planning authority;
    (2) the address of the local authority's principal office and of any other places at which the documents are available for inspection;
    (3) the days on which, and hours between which, the documents are available for inspection;
    (4) the name and address of the appropriate Regional Director of the Department of the Environment or the Welsh Office to whom such objections and representations should be sent;
    (5) the date which provides a period of six weeks beginning with the date on which the notice is first published in a local newspaper for the making of objections and representations.

Regulation 24   FORM 7:
NOTICE OF APPROVAL OR REJECTION BY THE SECRETARY OF STATE OF PROPOSALS FOR A STATUTORY PLAN OR THE ALTERATION OR REPLACEMENT OF A STATUTORY PLAN SUBMITTED TO HIM FOR HIS APPROVAL

Town and Country Planning Act 1990
Notice of [Approval] [Rejection] by the Secretary of State of Proposals for [the Alteration] [Replacement] of] a [Unitary Development Plan] [Structure Plan] [Local Plan] [Minerals Local Plan] [Waste Local Plan]
(Title of plan)

The Secretary of State for [the Environment] [Wales] [approved] [rejected] these plan proposals prepared by (1) [in part] [and] [with modifications] [and] [with reservations].

Copies of the proposals and of the Secretary of State's letter notifying his decision are available for inspection at (2) on (3).

[The proposals [became] [become] operative on (4), but any person aggrieved by the proposals who desires to question their validity on the ground that they are not within the powers conferred by Part II of the Town and Country Planning Act 1990 or that any requirement of that Act or of any regulation made under it has not been complied with in relation to the approval of the proposals, may, within six weeks from (5), make an application to the High Court under section 287 of the 1990 Act.]

Notes
1. Omit any expression within square brackets which is inappropriate.
2. Insert—
    (1) the name of the local planning authority;
    (2) the address of the local planning authority's principal office and of any other place at which the documents are available for inspection;
    (3) the days on which, and hours between which, the documents are available for inspection;
    (4) the appropriate date;
    (5) the date on which this notice is first published.

Regulation 35 FORM 8:

EXISTING POLICY STATEMENT

Town and Country Planning Act 1990
Planning and Compensation Act 1991
Statement Identifying Policies in Proposals for [the Alteration] [Replacement] of] a [Unitary Development Plan] [Local Plan] [Minerals Local Plan] [Waste Local Plan] as Policies Previously Contained in a Local Plan
(Title of plan)

The proposals for [the [alteration] [replacement] of] the above plan, made available for inspection by (1) at (2), include policies which were, in the opinion of the authority, previously contained in a local plan for the area ('existing policies'). A list of the policies contained in the proposals which have been identified by the authority as existing policies is set out below.

[Objections may be made to these policies at the same time and in the same manner as objections may be made to the other policies in the proposals.] [The period for objecting to the above proposals set out in the notice of deposit first published locally on (3) is extended and such objections, including objections to policies identified as existing policies, should be sent in writing to (4) before (5).] However, the person holding any local inquiry or other hearing need not allow a person who objects to a policy which has been identified as an existing policy to appear at the local inquiry or other hearing if he is satisfied that the policy so identified is an existing policy and that there has been no significant change in circumstances affecting the existing policy since it first formed part of the local plan.

(List of policies identified by the authority as existing policies)

Notes
1. Omit any expression within square brackets which is inappropriate.
2. Insert—
    (1) the name of the local planning authority;
    (2) the address of the local planning authority's principal office and of any other place at which the documents are available for inspection;
    (3) the date on which the notice of deposit was first published in a local newspaper;
    (4) the name or title of the officer to whom objections should be sent and the address to which they are to be sent;
    (5) the date which provides a period of six weeks beginning with the date on which the notice is first published in a local newspaper for the making of objections.

TOWN AND COUNTRY PLANNING (INQUIRIES PROCEDURE) RULES 1992
(SI 1992, No. 2038)

The Lord Chancellor, in exercise of the powers conferred on him by section 11 of the Tribunals and Inquiries Act 1971, and all other powers enabling him in that behalf, and after consultation with the Council on Tribunals, hereby makes the following Rules:

1. Citation and Commencement

These Rules may be cited as the Town and Country Planning (Inquiries Procedure) Rules 1992 and shall come into force on 30th September 1992.

2. Interpretation

In these Rules, unless the context otherwise requires—

'applicant', in the case of an appeal, means the appellant;
'assessor' means a person appointed by the Secretary of State to sit with an inspector at an inquiry or re-opened inquiry to advise the inspector on such matters arising as the Secretary of State may specify;
'the Commission' means the Historic Buildings and Monuments Commission for England;
'conservation area consent' has the meaning given in section 74(1) of the Listed Buildings Act;
'development order' has the meaning given in section 59 of the Planning Act;
'document' includes a photograph, map or plan;
'inquiry' means a local inquiry in relation to which these Rules apply;
'inspector' means a person appointed by the Secretary of State to hold an inquiry or a re-opened inquiry;
'land' means the land, tree or building to which an inquiry relates;
'the Listed Building Act' means the Planning (Listed Buildings and Conservation Areas) Act 1990;
'listed building consent' has the meaning given in section 8(7) of the Listed Buildings Act;
'local planning authority' means—
  (i) in relation to a referred application, the body who would otherwise have dealt with the application;
  (ii) in relation to an appeal, the body who were responsible for dealing with the application occasioning the appeal;
'outline statement' means a written statement of the principal submissions which a person proposes to put forward at an inquiry;
'the Planning Act' means the Town and Country Planning Act 1990;
'pre-inquiry meeting' means a meeting held before an inquiry to consider what may be done with a view to securing that the inquiry is conducted efficiently and expeditiously, and where two or more such meetings are held references to the conclusion of a pre-inquiry meeting are references to the conclusion of the final meeting;
'referred application' means an application of any description mentioned in rule 3(1) which is referred to the Secretary of State for determination;
'relevant date' means the date of the Secretary of State's written notice to the applicant and the local planning authority of his intention to cause an inquiry to be held, and 'relevant notice' means that notice;
'the 1988 Rules' means the Town and Country Planning (Inquiries Procedure) Rules 1988;
'statement of case' means, and is comprised of, a written statement which contains full particulars of the case which a person proposes to put forward at an inquiry, and a list of any documents which that person intends to refer to or put in evidence;
'statutory party' means—
  (a) a person mentioned in paragraph (1)(b)(i) of article 22A of the Town and Country Planning General Development Order 1988 whose representations the Secretary of State is required by paragraph (3) of that article to take into account in determining the referred application or appeal to which an inquiry relates; and, in the case of an appeal, such a person whose representations the local planning authority were required by paragraph (1) of that article to take into account in determining the application occasioning the appeal; and
  (b) a person whose representations the Secretary of State is required by paragraphs (3)(b) and (5) of regulation 6 of the Planning (Listed Buildings and Conservation Areas) Regulations 1990 to take into account in determining the

referred application or appeal to which an inquiry relates, and, in the case of an appeal, a person whose representations the local planning authority were required by paragraph (3)(b) of that regulation to take into account in determining the application occasioning the appeal.

'tree preservation order' has the meaning given in section 198 of the Planning Act.

3. Application of Rules

(1) These Rules apply in relation to any local inquiry caused by the Secretary of State to be held in England or Wales before he determines—

(a) an application in relation to planning permission referred to him under section 77, or an appeal to him under section 78, of the Planning Act;

(b) an application for consent referred to him under a tree preservation order or an appeal to him under such an order, with the exceptions that rule 4(1) shall not apply and the references to a statutory party shall be omitted;

(c) an application for listed building consent referred to him under section 12, or for variation or discharge of conditions referred to him under that section as applied by section 19, or an appeal to him under section 20, of the Listed Buildings Act;

(d) an application for conservation area consent referred to him under section 12 (including an application to which that section is applied by section 19), or an appeal to him under section 20, of the Listed Buildings Act as those sections are applied by virtue of section 74(3) of that Act,

but do not apply to any local inquiry by reason of the application of any provision mentioned in this paragraph by any other enactment.

(2) Where these Rules apply in relation to an appeal which at some time fell to be disposed of in accordance with the Town and Country Planning Appeals (Determination by Inspectors) (Inquiries Procedure) Rules 1992 or Rules superseded by those Rules, any step taken or thing done under those Rules which could have been done under any corresponding provision of these Rules shall have effect as if it had been taken or done under that corresponding provision.

4. Preliminary information to be supplied by local planning authority

(1) The local planning authority shall, on receipt of a notice from the Secretary of State of his intention to cause an inquiry to be held ('the relevant notice', forthwith inform him and the applicant in writing of the name and address of any statutory party who has made representations to them; and the Secretary of State shall as soon as practicable thereafter inform the applicant and the local planning authority in writing of the name and address of any statutory party who has made representations to him.

(2) This paragraph applies where—

(a) the Secretary of State has given to the local planning authority a direction restricting the grant of planning permission for which application was made; or

(b) in a case relating to listed building consent, the Commission has given a direction to the local planning authority pursuant to section 14(2) of the Listed Buildings Act as to how the application is to be determined; or

(c) the Secretary of State or any other Minister of the Crown or any government department, or any body falling within rule 11(1)(c), has expressed in writing to the local planning authority the view that the application should not be granted either wholly or in part, or should be granted only subject to conditions, or, in the case of an application for consent under a tree preservation order, should be granted together with a direction requiring replanting; or

(d) any authority or person consulted in pursuance of a development order has made representations to the local planning authority about the application.

(3) Where paragraph (2) applies, the local planning authority shall forthwith after the date of the relevant notice ('the relevant date') inform the person or body concerned of the inquiry and, unless they have already done so, that person or body

shall thereupon give the local planning authority a written statement of the reasons for making the direction, expressing the view or making the representations, as the case may be.

5. Procedure where Secretary of State causes pre-inquiry meeting to be held

(1) The Secretary of State may cause a pre-inquiry meeting to be held if it appears to him desirable and where he does so the following paragraphs apply.

(2) The Secretary of State shall serve with the relevant notice a notification of his intention to cause a meeting to be held and a statement of the matters about which he particularly wishes to be informed for the purposes of his consideration of the application or appeal in question, and where another Minister of the Crown or a government department has expressed in writing to the Secretary of State a view which is mentioned in rule 4(2)(c), the Secretary of State shall set this out in his statement and shall supply a copy of the statement to the Minister or government department concerned.

(3) The local planning authority shall cause to be published in a newspaper circulating in the locality in which the land is situated a notice of the Secretaryf of State's intention to cause a meeting to be held and of the statement served in accordance with paragraph (2).

(4) The applicant and the local planning authority shall, not later than 8 weeks after the relevant date, each serve an outline statement on the other and on the Secretary of State.

(5) Where rule 4(2) applies, the local planning authority shall—
  (a) include in their outline statement the terms of—
    (i) any direction given together with a statement of the reasons therefor, and
    (ii) any view expressed or representation made on which they intend to rely
in their submissions at the inquiry; and
  (b) within the period mentioned in paragraph (4), supply a copy of their statement to the person or body concerned.

(6) The Secretary of State may in writing require any other person who has notified him of an intention or a wish to appear at the inquiry to serve, within 4 weeks of being so required, an outline statement on him, the applicant and the local lanning authority.

(7) The meeting (or, where there is more than one, the first meeting) shall be held not later than 16 weeks after the relevant date.

(8) The Secretary of State shall give not less than 3 weeks written notice of the meeting to the applicant, the local planning authority, any person known at the date of the notice to be entitled to appear at the inquiry and any other person whose presence at the meeting seems to him to be desirable; and he may require the local planning authority to take in relation to notification of the meeting, one or more of the steps which he may under rule 10(6) require them to take in relation to notification of the inquiry.

(9) The inspector shall preside at the meeting and shall determine the matters to be discussed and the procedure to be followed, and he may require any person present at the meeting who, in his opinion, is behaving in a disruptive manner to leave and may refuse to permit that person to return or to attend any further meeting, or may permit him to return or attend only on such conditions as he may specify.

(10) Where a pre-inquiry meeting has been held pursuant to paragraph (1), the inspector may hold a further meeting. He shall arrange for such notice to be given of a further meeting as appears to him necessary; and paragraph (9) shall apply to such a meeting.

6. Service of statements of case etc.

(1) Subject to paragraph (4), the local planning authority shall, not later than—
  (a) 6 weeks after the relevant date, or

(b) where a pre-inquiry meeting is held pursuant to rule 5, 4 weeks after the conclusion of that meeting,
serve a statement of case on the Secretary of State, the applicant and any statutory party.

(2) Where rule 4(2) applies, the local planning authority shall, unless they have already done so in an outline statement, include in their statement of case the matters mentioned in rule 5(5)(a) and shall supply a copy of the statement to the person or body concerned.

(3) Subject to paragraph (4), the applicant shall, not later than—
   (a) in the case of a referred application where no pre-inquiry meeting is held pursuant to rule 5, 6 weeks after the relevant date, or
   (b) in the case of an appeal where no such meeting is held, 9 weeks after the relevant date, or
   (c) in any case where a pre-inquiry meeting is held pursuant to rule 5, 4 weeks after the conclusion of that meeting,
serve a statement of case on the Secretary of State, the local planning authority and any statutory party.

(4) The statement of case mentioned in paragraph (1) or, as the case may be, paragraph (3) shall be served no later than the day which is 4 weeks before the date fixed for the holding of the inquiry, where that day falls within whichever of the periods mentioned in either of those paragraphs is applicable to the case.

(5) The applicant and the local planning authority may each require the other to send to them a copy of any document, or of the relevant part of any document, referred to in the list of documents comprised in that party's statement of case; and any such document, or relevant part, shall be sent as soon as practicable to the party who required it.

(6) The Secretary of State may in writing require any other person who has notified him of an intention or a wish to appear at an inquiry to serve a statement of case, within 4 weeks of being so required, on the applicant, the local planning authority, the Secretary of State and any (or any other) statutory party.

(7) The Secretary of State shall supply any person from whom he requires a statement of case in accordance with paragraph (6) with a copy of the applicant's and the local planning authority's statement of case and shall inform that person of the name and address of every person on whom his statement of case is required to be served.

(8) The Secretary of State or an inspector may require any person who has served a statement of case in accordance with this rule to provide such further information about the matters contained in the statement as he may specify; and a person so required shall provide the Secretary of State, or as the case may be, the inspector, with that information in writing and shall, at the same time, send a copy to any other person on whom the statement of case has been served.

(9) Any person other than the applicant who serves a statement of case on the local planning authority shall serve with it a copy of any document, or of the relevant part of any document, referred to in the list comprised in that statement, unless a copy of the document or part of the document in question is already available for inspection pursuant to paragraph (11).

(10) Unless he has already done so, the Secretary of State shall in the case of a referred application, and may in the case of an appeal, not later than 12 weeks from the relevant date serve a written statement of the matters referred to in rule 5(2) on the applicant, the local planning authority, any statutory party and any person from whom he has required a statement of case.

(11) The local planning authority shall afford to any person who so requests a reasonable opportunity to inspect and, where practicable, take copies of any statement

of case or other document which, or a copy of which, has been served on them in accordance with this rule, and of their statement of case together with a copy of any document, or of the relevant part of any document, referred to in the list comprised in that statement or otherwise served by them pursuant to this rule; and shall specify in their statement of case the time and place at which the opportunity will be afforded.

7. Further power of inspector to hold pre-inquiry meetings

(1) Where no pre-inquiry meeting is held pursuant to rule 5, an inspector may hold one if he thinks it desirable.

(2) An inspector shall arrange for not less than 2 weeks written notice of a meeting he proposes to hold under paragraph (1) to be given to the applicant, the local planning authority, any person known at the date of the notice to be entitled to appear at the inquiry and any other person whose presence at the meeting appears to him to be desirable.

(3) Rule 5(9) shall apply to a meeting held under this rule.

8. Inquiry time-table

(1) Where a pre-inquiry meeting is held pursuant to rule 5 an inspector shall, and in any other case may, arrange a time-table for the proceedings at, or at part of, an inquiry and may at any time vary the time-table.

(2) An inspector may specify in a time-table arranged pursuant to this rule a date by which any proof of evidence and summary required by rule 13(1) to be sent to him shall be so sent.

9. Notification of appointment of assessor

Where the Secretary of State appoints an assessor, he shall notify every person entitled to appear at the inquiry of the name of the assessor and of the matters on which he is to advise the inspector.

10. Date and notification of inquiry

(1) The date fixed by the Secretary of State for the holding of an inquiry shall be, unless he considers such a date impracticable, not later than—

　(a)　2 weeks after the relevant date; or

　(b)　in a case where a pre-inquiry meeting is held pursuant to rule 5, 8 weeks after the conclusion of that meeting.

(2) Where the Secretary of State considers it impracticable to fix a date in accordance with paragraph (1), the date fixed shall be the earliest date after the end of the relevant period mentioned in that paragraph which he considers to be practicable.

(3) Unless the Secretary of State agrees a lesser period of notice with the applicant and the local planning authority, he shall give not less than 4 weeks written notice of the date, time and place fixed by him for the holding of an inquiry to every person entitled to appear at the inquiry.

(4) The Secretary of State may vary the date fixed for the holding of an inquiry, whether or not the date as varied is within the relevant period mentioned in paragraph (1); and paragraph (3) shall apply to a variation of a date as it applied to the date originally fixed.

(5) The Secretary of State may vary the time or place for the holding of an inquiry and shall give such notice of any such variation as appears to him to be reasonable.

(6) The Secretary of State may require the local planning authority to take one or more of the following steps—

　(a)　not less than 2 weeks before the date fixed for the holding of an inquiry, to publish a notice of the inquiry in one or more newspapers circulating in the locality in which the land is situated;

(b) to serve a notice of the inquiry on such persons or classes of persons as he may specify, within such period as he may specify;

(c) to post a notice of the inquiry in a conspicuous place near to the land, within such period as he may specify.

(7) Where the land is under the control of the applicant he shall, if so required by the Secretary of State, affix a notice of the inquiry firmly to the land or to some object on or near the land, in such manner as to be readily visible to and legible by members of the public; and he shall not remove the notice, or cause or permit it to be removed, for such period before the inquiry as the Secretary of State may specify.

(8) Every notice of inquiry published, served or posted pursuant to paragraph (6), or affixed pursuant to paragraph (7), shall contain—

(a) a clear statement of the date, time and place of the inquiry and of the powers enabling the Secretary of State to determine the application or appeal in question;

(b) a written description of the land sufficient to identify approximately its location; and

(c) a brief description of the subject matter of the application or appeal.

11. Appearances at inquiry

(1) The persons entitled to appear at an inquiry are—

(a) the applicant;

(b) the local planning authority;

(c) any of the following bodies if the land is situated in their area and they are not the local planning authority—

(i) a county or district council;

(ii) a National Park Committee within the meaning of paragraph 5 of Schedule 17 to the Local Government Act 1972;

(iii) a joint planning board constituted under section 2(1) of the Planning Act or a joint planning board or special planning board reconstituted under Part I of Schedule 17 to the Local Government Act 1972;

(iv) an urban development corporation established under section 135 of the Local Government, Planning and Land Act 1980;

(v) an enterprise zone authority designated under Schedule 32 to the Local Government, Planning and Land Act 1980;

(vi) the Broads Authority, within the meaning of the Norfolk and Suffolk Broads Act 1988;

(vii) a housing action trust specified in an order made under section 67(1) of the Housing Act 1988;

(d) where the land is in an area designated as a new town, the development corporation for the new town or the Commission for the New Towns as its successor;

(e) a statutory party;

(f) the council of the parish or community in which the land is situated, if that council made representations to the local planning authority in respect of the application in pursuance of a provision of a development order;

(g) where the application was required to be notified to the Commission under section 14 of the Listed Buildings Act, the Commission;

(h) any other person who has served a statement of case in accordance with rule 6(6) or who has served an outline statement in accordance with rule 5(6).

(2) Nothing in paragraph (1) shall prevent the inspector from permitting any other person to appear at an inquiry, and such permission shall not be unreasonably withheld.

(3) Any person entitled or permitted to appear may do so on his own behalf or be represented by counsel, solicitor or any other person.

12. Representative of government departments and other authorities at inquiry

(1) Where—
   (a) the Secretary of State or the Commission has given a direction such as is described in rule 4(2)(a) or (b); or
   (b) the Secretary of State or any other Minister of the Crown or any government department, or any body falling within rule 11(1)(c), has expressed a view such as is described in rule 4(2)(c) and the local planning authority have included the terms of the expression of view in a statement served in accordance with rule 5(4) or 6(1); or
   (c) another Minister of the Crown or any government department has expressed a view such as is described in rule 4(2)(c) and the Secretary of State has included its terms in a statement served in accordance with rule 5(2) or 6(10),
the applicant may, not later than 2 weeks before the date of an inquiry, apply in writing to the Secretary of State for a representative of the Secretary of State or of the other Minister, department or body concerned to be made available at the inquiry.

(2) Where an application is made in accordance with paragraph (1), the Secretary of State shall make a representative available to attend the inquiry or, as the case may be, transmit the application to the other Minister, department or body concerned, who shall make a representative available to attend the inquiry.

(3) A person attending an inquiry as a representative in pursuance of this rule shall state the reasons for the direction or expressed view and shall give evidence and be subject to cross-examination to the same extent as any other witness.

(4) Nothing in paragraph (3) shall require a representative of a Minister or a government department to answer any question which in the opinion of the inspector is directed to the merits of government policy.

13. Proof of evidence

(1) A person entitled to appear at an inquiry who proposes to give, or to call another person to give, evidence at the inquiry by reading a proof of evidence shall send a copy of the proof to the inspector together with, subject to paragraph (2), a written summary.

(2) No written summary shall be required where the proof of evidence proposed to be read contains no more than 1500 words.

(3) The proof and any summary shall be sent to the inspector not later than—
   (a) 3 weeks before the date fixed for the holding of the inquiry, or
   (b) where a time-table has been arranged pursuant to rule 8 which specifies a date by which the proof and any summary shall be sent to the inspector, that date.

(4) Where the applicant or the local planning authority send a copy of a proof to an inspector in accordance with paragraph (1), with or without a summary, they shall at the same time send a copy of that proof and any summary to the other party, and to any statutory party; and where any other party so sends a copy of such documents he shall at the same time send a copy to the applicant, the local planning authority and any (or any other) statutory party.

(5) Where a written summary is provided in accordance with paragraph (1), only that summary shall be read at the inquiry, unless the inspector permits or requires otherwise.

(6) Any person required by this rule to send a copy of a proof to any other person shall send with it a copy of the whole, or the relevant part, of any document referred to in it, unless a copy of the document or part of the document in question is already available for inspection pursuant to rule 6(11).

(7) The local planning authority shall afford to any person who so requests a reasonable opportunity to inspect and, where practicable, take copies of any document sent to or by them in accordance with this rule.

14. Procedure at inquiry

(1) Except as otherwise provided in these Rules, the inspector shall determine the procedure at an inquiry.

(2) Unless in any particular case the inspector with the consent of the applicant otherwise determines, the applicant shall begin and shall have the right of final reply; and the other persons entitled or permitted to appear shall be heard in such order as the inspector may determine.

(3) A person entitled to appear at an inquiry shall be entitled to call evidence and the applicant, the local planning authority and a statutory party shall be entitled to cross-examine persons giving evidence, but, subject to the foregoing and paragraphs (4) and (5), the calling of evidence and the cross-examination of persons giving evidence shall otherwise be at the inspector's discretion.

(4) The inspector may refuse to permit—
    (a) the giving or production of evidence,
    (b) the cross-examination of persons giving evidence, or
    (c) the presentation of any other matter,
which he considers to be irrelevant or repetitious; but where he refuses to permit the giving of oral evidence, the person wishing to give the evidence may submit to him any evidence or other matter in writing before the close of the inquiry.

(5) Where a person gives evidence at an inquiry by reading a summary of his evidence in accordance with rule 13(5), the proof of evidence referred to in rule 13(1) shall, unless the person required to provide the summary notifies the inspector that he now wishes to rely on the contents of that summary only, be treated as tendered in evidence, and the person whose evidence the proof contains shall then be subject to cross-examination on it to the same extent as if it were evidence he had given orally.

(6) The inspector may direct that facilities shall be afforded to any person appearing at an inquiry to take or obtain copies of documentary evidence open to public inspection.

(7) The inspector may require any person appearing or present at an inquiry who, in his opinion, is behaving in a disruptive manner to leave and may refuse to permit that person to return, or may permit him to return only on such conditions as he may specify; but any such person may submit to him any evidence or other matter in writing before the close of the inquiry.

(8) The inspector may allow any person to alter or add to a statement of case served under rule 6 so far as may be necessary for the purposes of the inquiry; but he shall (if necessary by adjourning the inquiry) give every other person entitled to appear who is appearing at the inquiry an adequate opportunity of considering any fresh matter or document.

(9) The inspector may proceed with an inquiry in the absence of any person entitled to appear at it.

(10) The inspector may take into account any written representation or evidence or any other document received by him from any person before an inquiry opens or during the inquiry provided that he discloses it at the inquiry.

(11) The inspector may from time to time adjourn an inquiry and, if the date, time and place of the adjourned inquiry are announced at the inquiry before the adjournment, no furthr notice shall be required.

15. Site inspections

(1) The inspector may make an unaccompanied inspection of the land before or during an inquiry without giving notice of his intention to the persons entitled to appear at the inquiry.

(2) The inspector may, during an inquiry or after its close, inspect the land in the company of the applicant, the local planning authority and any statutory party; and

he shall make such an inspection if so requested by the applicant or the local planning authority before or during an inquiry.

(3) In all cases where the inspector intends to make an inspection of the kind referred to in paragraph (2) he shall announce during the inquiry the date and time at which he proposes to make it.

(4) The inspector shall not be bound to defer an inspection of the kind referred to in paragraph (2) where any person mentioned in that paragraph is not present at the time appointed.

16. Procedure after inquiry

(1) After the close of an inquiry, the inspector shall make a report in writing to the Secretary of State which shall include his conclusions and his recommendations or his reasons for not making any recommendations.

(2) Where an assessor has been appointed, he may, after the close of the inquiry, make a report in writing to the inspector in respect of the matters on which he was appointed to advise.

(3) Where an assessor makes a report in accordance with paragraph (2), the inspector shall append it to his own report and shall state in his own report how far he agrees or disagrees with the assessor's report and, where he disagrees with the assessor, his reasons for that disagreement.

(4) If, after the close of an inquiry, the Secretary of State—

(a) differs from the inspector on any matter of fact mentioned in, or appearing to him to be material to, a conclusion reached by the inspector, or

(b) takes into consideration any new evidence or new matter of fact (not being a matter of government policy),

and is for that reason disposed to disagree with a recommendation made by the inspector, he shall not come to a decision which is at variance with that recommendation without first notifying the persons entitled to appear at the inquiry who appeared at it of his disagreement and the reasons for it; and affording to them an opportunity of making written representations to him within 3 weeks of the date of the notification, or (if the Secretary of State has taken into consideration any new evidence or new matter of fact, not being a matter of government policy) of asking within that period for the re-opening of the inquiry.

(5) The Secretary of State may, as he thinks fit, cause an inquiry to be re-opened, and he shall do so if asked by the applicant or the local planning authority in the circumstances and within the period mentioned in paragraph (4); and where an inquiry is re-opened (whether by the same or a different inspector)—

(a) the Secretary of State shall send to the persons entitled to appear at the inquiry who appeared at it a written statement of the matters with respect to which further evidence is invited; and

(b) paragraphs (3) to (8) of rule 10 shall apply as if the references to an inquiry were references to a re-opened inquiry.

17. Notification of decision

(1) The Secretary of State shall notify his decision on an application or appeal, and his reasons for it, in writing to all persons entitled to appear at the inquiry who did appear, and to any other person who, having appeared at the inquiry, has asked to be notified of the decision.

(2) Where a copy of the inspector's report is not sent with the notification of the decision, the notification shall be accompanied by a statement of his conclusions and of any recommendations made by him; and if a person entitled to be notified of the decision has not received a copy of that report, he shall be supplied with a copy of it on written application made to the Secretary of State within 4 weeks of the date of the decision.

(3) In this rule 'report' includes any assessor's report appended to the inspector's report but does not include any other documents so appended, but any person who has received a copy of the report may apply to the Secretary of State in writing, within 6 weeks of the date of the Secretary of State's decision, for an opportunity of inspecting any such documents and the Secretary of State shall afford him that opportunity.

18. Procedure following quashing of decision

Where a decision of the Secretary of State on an application or appeal in respect of which an inquiry has been held is quashed in proceedings before any court, the Secretary of State—

(a) shall send to the persons entitled to appear at the inquiry who appeared at it a written statement of the matters with respect to which further representations are invited for the purposes of his further consideration of the application or appeal; and

(b) shall afford to those persons the opportunity of making, within 3 weeks of the date of the written statement, written representations to him in respect of those matters or of asking for the re-opening of the inquiry; and

(c) may, as he thinks fit, cause the inquiry to be reopened (whether by the same or a different inspector) and if he does so paragraphs (3) to (8) of rule 10 shall apply as if the references to an inquiry were references to a re-opened inquiry.

19. Allowing further time

The Secretary of State may at any time in any particular case allow further time for the taking of any step which is required or enabled to be taken by virtue of these Rules, and references in these Rules to a day by which, or a period within which, any step is required or enabled to be taken shall be construed accordingly.

20. Service of notices by post

Notices or documents required or authorised to be served or sent under these Rules may be sent by post.

21. Revocation, savings and transitional

(1) Subject to paragraph (2), the Town and Country Planning (Inquiries Procedure) Rules 1988 are hereby revoked except rule 21 of those Rules so far as it makes provision for the continued application of the Town and Country Planning (Inquiries Procedure) Rules 1974.

(2) Any application or appeal to which the 1988 Rules applied which has not been determined on the date when these Rules come into force ('the commencement date') shall be continued under these Rules, but—

(a) rule 13 and 14(5) of the 1988 Rules shall continue to apply, and rules 8(2), 13 and 14(5) of these Rules shall not apply in a case where at the commencement date—

(i) an inquiry has been opened but not closed; or

(ii) a date has been fixed for the holding of an inquiry which is less than 6 weeks after the commencement date; and

(b) persons who were section 29(3) parties under the 1988 Rules shall be treated as statutory parties.

TOWN AND COUNTRY PLANNING APPEALS (DETERMINATION BY INSPECTORS) (INQUIRIES PROCEDURE) RULES 1992
(SI 1992, No. 2039)

The Lord Chancellor, in exercise of the powers conferred on him by section 11 of the Tribunals and Inquiries Act 1971, and all other powers enabling him in that behalf, and after consultation with the Council on Tribunals, hereby makes the following Rules:

1. Citation and commencement

These Rules may be cited as the Town and Country Planning Appeals (Determination by Inspectors) (Inquiries Procedure) Rules 1992 and shall come into force on 30th September 1992.

2. Interpretation

In these Rules, unless the context otherwise requires—

'assessor' means a person appointed by the Secretary of State to sit with an inspector at an inquiry or re-opened inquiry to advise the inspector on such matters arising as the Secretary of State may specify;

'the Commission' means the Historic Buildings and Monuments Commission for England;

'conservation area consent' has the meaning given in section 74(1) of the Listed Buildings Act;

'development order' has the meaning given in section 59 of the Planning Act:

'document' includes a photograph, map or plan;

'inquiry' means a local inquiry in relation to which these Rules apply;

'inspector' means a person appointed by the Secretary of State under Schedule 6 to the Planning Act or, as the case may be, Schedule 3 to the Listed Buildings Act to determine an appeal;

'land' means the land or building to which an inquiry relates;

'the Listed Buildings Act' means the Planning (Listed Buildings and Conservation Areas) Act 1990

'listed building consent' has the meaning given in section 8(7) of the Listed Buildings Act;

'local planning authority' means the body who were responsible for dealing with the application occasioning the appeal;

'the Planning Act' means the Town and Country Planning Act 1990

'pre-inquiry meeting' means a meeting held before an inquiry to consider what may be done with a view to securing that the inquiry is conducted efficiently and expeditiously;

'relevant date' means the date of the written notice informing the appellant and the local planning authority that an inquiry is to be held, and 'relevant notice' means that notice;

'the 1988 Rules' means the Town and Country Planning Appeals (Determination by Inspectors) (Inquiries Procedure) Rules 1988;

'statement of case' means, and is comprised of, a written statement which contains full particulars of the case which a person proposes to put forward at an inquiry, and a list of any documents which that person intends to refer to or put in evidence.

'statutory party' means

(a) a person mentioned in paragraph (1)(b)(i) of article 22A of the Town and Country Planning General Development Order 1988 whose representations the inspector is required by paragraph (3) of that article to take into account in determining the appeal to which an inquiry relates, and such a person whose representations the local planning authority were required by paragraph (1) of that article to take into account in determining the application occasioning the appeal; and

(b) a person whose representations the inspector is required by paragraphs (3)(b) and (5) of regulation 6 of the Planning (Listed Buildings and Conservation Areas) Regulations 1990 to take into account in determining the appeal to which an inquiry relates, and a person whose representations the local planning authority were required by paragraph (3)(b) of that regulation to take into account in determining the application occasioning the appeal.

3. Application of Rules

(1) These Rules apply in relation to any local inquiry held in England or Wales by an inspector before he determines—

(a) an appeal to the Secretary of State in relation to planning permission under section 78 of the Planning Act;

(b) an appeal to the Secretary of State in relation to listed building consent under section 20 of the Listed Buildings Act, or in relation to conservation area consent under that section as applied by virtue of section 74(3) of that Act,

but do not apply to any local inquiry by reason of the application of any provision mentioned in this paragraph by any other enactment.

(2) Where these Rules apply in relation to an appeal which at some time fell to be disposed of in accordance with the Town and Country Planning (Inquiries Procedure) Rules 1992 or Rules superseded by those Rules, any step taken or thing done under those Rules which could have been done under any corresponding provision of these Rules shall have effect as if it had been taken or done under that corresponding provision.

4. Preliminary information to be supplied by local planning authority

(1) The local planning authority shall, on receipt of a notice informing them that an inquiry is to be held ('the relevant notice'), forthwith inform the Secretary of State and the appellant in writing of the name and address of any statutory party who has made representations to them; and the Secretary of State shall as soon as practicable thereafter inform the appellant and the local planning authority of the name and address of any statutory party who has made representations to him.

(2) This paragraph applies where—

(a) the Secretary of State has given to the local planning authority a direction restricting the grant of planning permission for which application was made; or

(b) in a case relating to listed building consent, the Commission has given a direction to the local planning authority pursuant to section 14(2) of the Listed Buildings Act as to how the application is to be determined; or

(c) the Secretary of State or any other Minister of the Crown or any government department, or any body falling within rule 11(1)(c), has expressed in writing to the local planning authority the view that the application should not be granted either wholly or in part, or should be granted only subject to conditions; or

(d) any authority or person consulted in pursuance of a development order has made representations to the local planning authority about the application.

(3) Where paragraph (2) applies, the local planning authority shall forthwith after the date of the relevant notice ('the relevant date') inform the person or body concerned of the inquiry and, unless they have already done so, that person or body shall thereupon give the local planning authority a written statement of the reasons for making the direction, expressing the view or making the representations, as the case may be.

5. Notification of identity of inspector

(1) Subject to paragraph (2), the Secretary of State shall notify the name of the inspector to every person entitled to appear at the inquiry.

(2) Where the Secretary of State appoints another inspector instead of the person previously appointed and it is not practicable to notify the new appointment before the inquiry is held, the inspector holding the inquiry shall, at its commencement, announce his name and the fact of his appointment.

6. Service of statements of case etc.

(1) Subject to paragraph (4), the local planning authority shall, not later than 6 weeks after the relevant date, serve a statement of case on the Secretary of State, the appellant and any statutory party.

(2) Where rule 4(2) applies, the local planning authority shall—
  (a) include in their statement of case the terms of—
    (i) any direction given together with a statement of the reasons therefor; and
    (ii) any view expressed or representation made on which they intend to rely in their submissions at the inquiry; and
  (b) within the period mentioned in paragraph (1) supply a copy of their statement to the person or body concerned.

(3) Subject to paragraph (4), the appellant shall, not later than 9 weeks after the relevant date, serve a statement of case on the Secretary of State, the local planning authority and any statutory party.

(4) The statement of case mentioned in paragraph (1) or, as the case may be, paragraph (3) shall be served no later than the day which is 4 weeks before the date fixed for the holding of the inquiry, where that day falls within the period mentioned in whichever of those paragraphs is applicable to the case.

(5) The appellant and the local planning authority may each require the other to send them a copy of any document, or of the relevant part of any document, referred to in the list of documents comprised in that party's statement of case; and any such document, or relevant part, shall be sent as soon as practicable to the party who required it.

(6) The Secretary of State may in writing require any other person who has notified him of an intention or a wish to appear at an inquiry to serve a statement of case, within 4 weeks of being so required, on the appellant, the local planning authority, the Secretary of State and any (or any other) statutory party.

(7) The Secretary of State shall supply any person from whom he requires a statement of case in accordance with paragraph (6) with a copy of the appellant's and the local planning authority's statement of case and shall inform that person of the name and address of every person on whom his statement of case is required to be served.

(8) The Secretary of State may require any person who has served a statement of case in accordance with this rule to provide such further information about the matters contained in the statement as he may specify; and a person so required shall provide the Secretary of State with that information in writing and shall, at the same time, send a copy to any other person on whom the statement of case has been served.

(9) Any person other than the appellant who serves a statement of case on the local planning authority shall serve with it a copy of any document, or of the relevant part of any document, referred to in the list comprised in that statement, unless a copy of the document or part of the document in question is already available for inspection pursuant to paragraph (11).

(10) The Secretary of State shall transmit any statement of case served on him in accordance with this rule to the inspector.

(11) The local planning authority shall afford to any person who so requests a reasonable opportunity to inspect and, where practicable, take copies of any statement of case or other document which, or a copy of which, has been served on them in accordance with this rule, and of their statement of case together with a copy of any document, or of the relevant part of any document, referred to in the list comprised in that statement or otherwise served by them pursuant to this rule; and shall specify in their statement of case the time and place at which the opportunity will be afforded.

7. Statements of matters and pre-inquiry meetings

(1) An inspector may, not later than 12 weeks after the relevant date, cause to be served on the appellant, the local planning authority and any statutory party a written statement of the matters about which he particularly wishes to be informed for the purposes of his consideration of the appeal.

(2) An inspector may hold a pre-inquiry meeting where he considers it desirable and shall arrange for not less than 2 weeks written notice of it to be given to the appellant, the local planning authority, any statutory party, any other person known to be entitled to appear at the inquiry and any other person whose presence at the meeting appears to him to be desirable.

(3) The inspector shall preside at the pre-inquiry meeting and shall determine the matters to be discussed and the procedure to be followed, and he may require any person present at the meeting who, in his opinion, is behaving in a disruptive manner to leave and may refuse to permit that person to return or to attend any further meeting, or may permit him to return or attend only on such conditions as he may specify.

8. Inquiry time-table

(1) An inspector may at any time arrange a time-table for the proceedings at, or at part of, an inquiry and may at any time vary the time-table.

(2) An inspector may specify in a time-table arranged pursuant to this rule a date by which any proof of evidence and summary required by rule 14(1) to be sent to him shall be so sent.

9. Notification of appointment of assessor

Where the Secretary of State appoints an assessor, he shall notify every person entitled to appear at the inquiry of the name of the assessor and of the matters on which he is to advise the inspector.

10. Date and notification of inquiry

(1) The date fixed by the Secretary of State for the holding of an inquiry shall be, unless he considers such a date impracticable, not later than 20 weeks after the relevant date: and where he considers it impracticable to fix a date in accordance with the preceding provisions of this paragraph, the date fixed shall be the earliest date after the end of the period mentioned which he considers to be practicable.

(2) Unless the Secretary of State agrees a lesser period of notice with the appellant and the local planning authority, he shall give not less than 4 weeks written notice of the date, time and place for the holding of an inquiry to every person entitled to appear at the inquiry.

(3) The Secretary of State may vary the date fixed for the holding of an inquiry, whether or not the date as varied is within the period of 20 weeks mentioned in paragraph (1); and paragraph (2) shall apply to the variation of a date as it applied to the date originally fixed.

(4) The Secretary of State may vary the time or place for the holding of an inquiry and shall give such notice of any such variation as appears to him to be reasonable.

(5) The Secretary of State may require the local planning authority to take one or more of the following steps—

(a) not less than 2 weeks before the date fixed for the holding of an inquiry, to publish a notice of the inquiry in one or more newspapers circulating in the locality in which the land is situated;

(b) to serve a notice of the inquiry on such persons or classes of persons as he may specify, within such period as he may specify;

(c) to post a notice of the inquiry in a conspicuous place near to the land, within such period as he may specify.

(6) Where the land is under the control of the appellant he shall, if so required by the Secretary of State, affix a notice of the inquiry firmly to the land or to some object on or near the land, in such manner as to be readily visible to and legible by members of the public: and he shall not remove the notice, or cause or permit it to be removed, for such period before the inquiry as the Secretary of State may specify.

TCP Appeals (Determination by Inspectors) (Inquiries Procedure) Rules 1992   493

(7) Every notice of inquiry published, served or posted pursuant to paragraph (5), or affixed pursuant to paragraph (6), shall contain—
    (a) a clear statement of the date, time and place of the inquiry and of the powers enabling the inspector to determine the appeal in question;
    (b) a written description of the land sufficient to identify approximately its location: and
    (c) a brief description of the subject matter of the appeal.

11. Appearances at inquiry

(1) The persons entitled to appear at an inquiry are—
    (a) the appellant;
    (b) the local planning authority;
    (c) any of the following bodies if the land is situated in their area and they are not the local planning authority—
        (i) a county or district council;
        (ii) a National Park Committee within the meaning of paragraph 5 of Schedule 17 to the Local Government Act 1972;
        (iii) a joint planning board constituted under section 2(1) of the Planning Act or a joint planning board or special planning board reconstituted under Part I of Schedule 17 to the Local Government Act 1972;
        (iv) an urban development corporation established under section 135 of the Local Government, Planning and Land Act 1980;
        (v) an enterprise zone authority designated under Schedule 32 to the Local Government, Planning and Land Act 1980;
        (vi) the Broads Authority, within the meaning of the Norfolk and Suffolk Broads Act 1988;
        (vii) a housing action trust specified in an order made under section 67(1) of the Housing Act 1988;
    (d) where the land is in an area designated as a new town, the development corporation for the new town or the Commission for the New Towns as its successor;
    (e) a statutory party;
    (f) the council of the parish or community in which the land is situated, if that council made representations to the local planning authority in respect of the application in pursuance of a provision of a development order;
    (g) where the application was required to be notified to the Commission under section 14 of the Listed Buildings Act, the Commission;
    (h) any other person who has served a statement of case in accordance with rule 6(6).

(2) Nothing in paragraph (1) shall prevent the inspector from permitting any other person to appear at an inquiry, and such permission shall not be unreasonably withheld.

(3) Any person entitled or permitted to appear may do so on his own behalf or be represented by counsel, solicitor or any other person.

12. Representatives of government departments and other authorities at inquiry

(1) Where—
    (a) the Secretary of State or the Commission has given a direction such as is described in rule 4(2)(a) or (b): or
    (b) the Secretary of State or any other Minister of the Crown or any government department, or any body falling within rule 11(1)(c), has expressed a view such as is described in rule 4(2)(c) and the local planning authority have included its terms in a statement served in accordance with rule 6(1),

the appellant may, not later than 2 weeks before the date of an inquiry, apply in writing to the Secretary of State for a representative of the Secretary of State or of the other Minister, department or body concerned to be made available at the inquiry.

(2) Where an application is made in accordance with paragraph (1), the Secretary of State shall make a representative available to attend the inquiry or, as the case may be, transmit the application to the other Minister, department or body concerned who shall make a representative available to attend the inquiry.

(3) A person attending an inquiry as a representative in pursuance of this rule shall state the reasons for the direction or expressed view and shall give evidence and be subject to cross-examination to the same extent as any other witness.

(4) Nothing in paragraph (3) shall require a representative of a Minister or a government department to answer any question which in the opinion of the inspector is directed to the merits of government policy.

13. Inspector may act in place of Secretary of State

An inspector may in place of the Secretary of State take such steps as the Secretary of State is required or enabled to take under or by virtue of rule 6(6) to (8), rule 10, rule 12(1) or (2) or rule 20: and where an inspector requires further information pursuant to rule 6(8), that information shall be sent to him.

14. Proofs of evidence

(1) A person entitled to appear at an inquiry who proposes to give, or to call another person to give, evidence at the inquiry by reading a proof of evidence shall send a copy of the proof to the inspector together with, subject to paragraph (2), a written summary.

(2) No written summary shall be required where the proof of evidence proposed to be read contains no more than 1500 words.

(3) The proof and any summary shall be sent to the inspector not later than—
   (a) 3 weeks before the date fixed for the holding of the inquiry, or
   (b) where a time-table has been arranged pursuant to rule 8 which specifies a date by which the proof and any summary shall be sent to the inspector, that date.

(4) Where the appellant or the local planning authority send a copy of a proof to an inspector in accordance with paragraph (1), with or without a summary, they shall at the same time send a copy of that proof and any summary to the other party, and to any statutory party; and where any other party so sends a copy of such documents he shall at the same time send a copy to the appellant, the local planning authority and any (or any other) statutory party.

(5) Where a written summary is provided in accordance with paragraph (1), only that summary shall be read at the inquiry, unless the inspector permits or requires otherwise.

(6) Any person required by this rule to send a copy of a proof to any other person shall send with it a copy of the whole, or the relevant part, of any document referred to in it, unless a copy of the document or part of the document in question is already available for inspection pursuant to rule 6(11).

(7) The local planning authority shall afford to any person who so requests a reasonable opportunity to inspect and, where practicable, take copies of any document sent to or by them in accordance with this rule.

15. Procedure at inquiry

(1) Except as otherwise provided in these Rules, the inspector shall determine the procedure at an inquiry.

(2) Unless in any particular case the inspector with the consent of the appellant otherwise determines, the appellant shall begin and shall have the right of final reply;

and the other persons entitled or permitted to appear shall be heard in such order as the inspector may determine.

(3) A person entitled to appear at an inquiry shall be entitled to call evidence and the appellant, the local planning authority and any statutory party shall be entitled to cross-examine persons giving evidence, but, subject to the foregoing and paragraphs (4) and (5), the calling of evidence and the cross-examination of persons giving evidence shall otherwise be at the inspector's discretion.

(4) The inspector may refuse to permit—
   (a) the giving or production of evidence,
   (b) the cross-examination of persons giving evidence, or
   (c) the presentation of any other matter,

which he considers to be irrelevant or repetitious; but where he refuses to permit the giving of oral evidence, the person wishing to give the evidence may submit to him any evidence or other matter in writing before the close of the inquiry.

(5) Where a person gives evidence at an inquiry by reading a summary of his evidence in accordance with rule 14(5), the proof of evidence referred to in rule 14(1) shall, unless the person required to provide the summary notifies the inspector that he now wishes to rely on the contents of the summary alone, be treated as tendered in evidence, and the person whose evidence the proof contains shall then be subject to cross-examination on it to the same extent as if it were evidence he had given orally.

(6) The inspector may direct that facilities shall be afforded to any person appearing at an inquiry to take or obtain copies of documentary evidence open to public inspection.

(7) The inspector may require any person appearing or present at an inquiry who, in his opinion, is behaving in a disruptive manner to leave and may refuse to permit that person to return, or may permit him to return only on such conditions as he may specify; but any such person may submit to him any evidence or other matter in writing before the close of the inquiry.

(8) The inspector may allow any person to alter or add to a statement of case served under rule 6 so far as may be necessary for the purposes of the inquiry; but he shall (if necessary by adjourning the inquiry) give every other person entitled to appear who is appearing at the inquiry an adequate opportunity of considering any fresh matter or document.

(9) The inspector may proceed with an inquiry in the absence of any person entitled to appear at it.

(10) The inspector may take into account any written representation or evidence or any other document received by him from any person before an inquiry opens or during the inquiry provided that he discloses it at the inquiry.

(11) The inspector may from time to time adjourn an inquiry and, if the date, time and place of the adjourned inquiry are announced before the adjournment, no further notice shall be required.

16. Site inspections

(1) The inspector may make an unaccompanied inspection of the land before or during an inquiry without giving notice of his intention to the persons entitled to appear at the inquiry.

(2) The inspector may, during an inquiry or after its close, inspect the land in the company of the appellant, the local planning authority and any statutory party: and he shall make such an inspection if so requested by the appellant or the local planning authority before or during an inquiry.

(3) In all cases where the inspector intends to make an inspection of the kind referred to in paragraph (2) he shall announce during the inquiry the date and time at which he proposes to make it.

(4) The inspector shall not be bound to defer an inspection of the kind referred to in paragraph (2) where any person mentioned in that paragraph is not present at the time appointed.

17. Procedure after inquiry

(1) Where an assessor has been appointed, he may, after the close of the inquiry, make a report in writing to the inspector in respect of the matters on which he was appointed to advise, and where he does so the inspector shall state in his notification of his decision pursuant to rule 18 that such a report was made.

(2) If after the close of an inquiry, an inspector proposes to take into consideration any new evidence or any new matter of fact (not being a matter of government policy) which was not raised at the inquiry and which he considers to be material to his decision, he shall not come to a decision without first—

(a) notifying the persons entitled to appear at the inquiry who appeared at it of the matter in question: and

(b) affording to them an opportunity of making written representations to him with respect to it within 3 weeks of the date of the notification or of asking within that period for the re-opening of the inquiry.

(3) An inspector may, as he thinks fit, cause an inquiry to be re-opened, and he shall do so if asked by the appellant or the local planning authority in the circumstances and within the period mentioned in paragraph (2); and where an inquiry is re-opened—

(a) the inspector shall send to the persons entitled to appear at the inquiry who appeared at it a written statement of the matters with respect to which further evidence is invited; and

(b) paragraphs (2) to (7) of rule 10 shall apply as if the references to an inquiry were references to a re-opened inquiry.

18. Notification of decision

(1) An inspector shall notify his decision on an appeal, and his reasons for it, in writing to all persons entitled to appear at the inquiry who did appear, and to any other person who, having appeared at the inquiry, has asked to be notified of the decision.

(2) Any person entitled to be notified of the inspector's decision under paragraph (1) may apply to the Secretary of State in writing, within 6 weeks of the date of the Secretary of State's decision, for an opportunity of inspecting any such documents listed in the notification and any report made by an assessor and the Secretary of State shall afford him that opportunity.

19. Procedure following quashing of decision

Where a decision of an inspector on an appeal in respect of which an inquiry has been held is quashed in proceedings before any court, the Secretary of State—

(a) shall send to the persons entitled to appear at the inquiry who appeared at it a written statement of the matters with respect to which further representations are invited for the purposes of the further consideration of the appeal; and

(b) shall afford to those persons the opportunity of making, within 3 weeks of the date of the written statement, written representations to him in respect of those matters or of asking for the re-opening of the inquiry; and

(c) may, as he thinks fit, direct that the inquiry be re-opened, and if he does so paragraphs (2) to (7) of rule 10 shall apply as if the references to an inquiry were references to a re-opened inquiry.

20. Allowing further time

The Secretary of State may at any time in any particular case allow further time for the taking of any step which is required or enabled to be taken by virtue of these Rules, and references in these Rules to a day by which, or a period within which, any step is required or enabled to be taken shall be construed accordingly.

21. Service of notices by post
Notices or documents required or authorised to be served or sent under these Rules may be sent by post.

Rule 22 deals with revocation of the previous rules, SI 1988 No. 945 and SI 1988 No 944, savings and transitional matters.

CONSERVATION (NATURAL HABITATS, & c.) REGULATIONS 1994
(SI 1994 No. 2716)

. . .

10. Meaning of 'European site' in these Regulations
(1) In these Regulations a 'European site' means—
   (a) a special area of conservation.
   (b) a site of Community importance which has been placed on the list referred to in the third sub-paragraph of Article 4(2) of the Habitats Directive.
   (c) a site hosting a priority natural habitat type or priority species in respect of which consultation has been initiated under Article 5(1) of the Habitats Directive, during the consultation period or pending a decision of the Council under Article 5(3), or
   (d) an area classified pursuant to Article 4(1) or (2) of the Wild Birds Directive.

(2) Sites which are European sites by virtue only of paragraph (1)(c) are not within regulations 20(1) and (2), 24 and 48 (which relate to the approval of certain plans and projects); but this is without prejudice to their protection under other provisions of these Regulations.

. . .

PART IV
ADAPTATION OF PLANNING AND OTHER CONTROLS
Introductory

47. Application of provisions of this Part
(1) The requirements of—
   (a) regulations 48 and 49 (requirement to consider effect on European sites). and
   (b) regulations 50 and 51 (requirement to review certain existing decisions and consents, &c.).
apply, subject to and in accordance with the provisions of regulations 54 to 85, in relation to the matters specified in those provisions.

(2) Supplementary provision is made by—
   (a) regulation 52 (co-ordination where more than one competent authority involved), and
   (b) regulation 53 (compensatory measures where plan or project is agreed to notwithstanding a negative assessment of the implications for a European site).

General provisions for protection of European sites

48. Assessment of implications for European site
(1) A competent authority, before deciding to undertake, or give any consent, permission or other authorisation for, a plan or project which—
   (a) is likely to have a significant effect on a European site in Great Britain (either alone or in combination with other plans or projects), and

(b) is not directly connected with or necessary to the management of the site, shall make an appropriate assessment of the implications for the site in view of that site's conservation objectives.

(2) A person applying for any such consent, permission or other authorisation shall provide such information as the competent authority may reasonably require for the purposes of the assessment.

(3) The competent authority shall for the purposes of the assessment consult the appropriate nature conservation body and have regard to any representations made by that body within such reasonable time as the authority may specify.

(4) They shall also, if they consider it appropriate, take the opinion of the general public; and if they do so, they shall take such steps for that purpose as they consider appropriate.

(5) In the light of the conclusions of the assessment, and subject to regulation 49, the authority shall agree to the plan or project only after having ascertained that it will not adversely affect the integrity of the European site.

(6) In considering whether a plan or project will adversely affect the integrity of the site, the authority shall have regard to the manner in which it is proposed to be carried out or to any conditions or restrictions subject to which they propose that the consent, permission or other authorisation should be given.

(7) This regulation does not apply in relation to a site which is a European site by reason only of regulation 10(1)(c) (site protected in accordance with Article 5(4)).

49. Considerations of overriding public interest

(1) If they are satisfied that, there being no alternative solutions, the plan or project must be carried out for imperative reasons of overriding public interest (which, subject to paragraph (2), may be of a social or economic nature), the competent authority may agree to the plan or project notwithstanding a negative assessment of the implications for the site.

(2) Where the site concerned hosts a priority natural habitat type or a priority species, the reasons referred to in paragraph (1) must be either—

(a) reasons relating to human health, public safety or beneficial consequences of primary importance to the environment, or

(b) other reasons which in the opinion of the European Commission are imperative reasons of overriding public interest.

(3) Where a competent authority other than the Secretary of State desire to obtain the opinion of the European Commission as to whether reasons are to be considered imperative reasons of overriding public interest, they shall submit a written request to the Secretary of State—

(a) identifying the matter on which an opinion is sought, and

(b) accompanied by any documents or information which may be required.

(4) The Secretary of State may thereupon, if he thinks fit, seek the opinion of the Commission; and if he does so, he shall upon receiving the Commission's opinion transmit it to the authority.

(5) Where an authority other than the Secretary of State propose to agree to a plan or project under this regulation notwithstanding a negative assessment of the implications for a European site, they shall notify the Secretary of State.

Having notified the Secretary of State they shall not agree to the plan or project before the end of the period of 21 days beginning with the day notified to them by the Secretary of State as that on which their notification was received by him, unless the Secretary of State notifies them that they may do so.

(6) In any such case the Secretary of State may give directions to the authority prohibiting them from agreeing to the plan or project, either indefinitely or during such period as may be specified in the direction.

This power is without prejudice to any other power of the Secretary of State in relation to the decision in question.

50. Review of existing decisions and consents, &c

(1) Where before the date on which a site becomes a European site or, if later, the commencement of these Regulations, a competent authority have decided to undertake, or have given any consent, permission or other authorisation for, a plan or project to which regulation 48(1) would apply if it were to be reconsidered as of that date, the authority shall as soon as reasonably practicable, review their decision or, as the case may be, the consent, permission or other authorisation, and shall affirm, modify or revoke it.

(2) They shall for that purpose make an appropriate assessment of the implications for the site in view of that site's conservation objectives; and the provisions of regulation 48(2) to (4) shall apply, with the appropriate modifications in relation to such a review.

(3) Subject to the following provisions of this Part, any review required by this regulation shall be carried out under existing statutory procedures where such procedures exist, and if none exist the Secretary of State may give directions as to the procedure to be followed.

(4) Nothing in this regulation shall affect anything done in pursuance of the decision, or the consent, permission or other authorisation, before the date mentioned in paragraph (1).

51. Consideration on review

(1) The following provisions apply where a decision, or a consent, permission or other authorisation falls to be reviewed under regulation 50.

(2) Subject as follows, the provisions of regulation 48(5) and (6) and regulation 49 shall apply, with the appropriate modifications, in relation to the decision on the review.

(3) The decision, or the consent, permission or other authorisation, may be affirmed if it appears to the authority reviewing it that other action taken or to be taken by them, or by another authority, will secure that the plan or project does not adversely affect the integrity of the site.

Where that object may be attained in a number of ways, the authority or authorities concerned shall seek to secure that the action taken is the least onerous to those affected.

(4) The Secretary of State may issue guidance to authorities for the purposes of paragraph (3) as to the manner of determining which of different ways should be adopted for securing that the plan or project does not have any such effect, and in particular—

    (a) the order of application of different controls, and

    (b) the extent to which account should be taken of the possible exercise of other powers;

and the authorities concerned shall have regard to any guidance so issued in discharging their functions under that paragraph.

(5) Any modification or revocation effected in pursuance of this regulation shall be carried out under existing statutory procedures where such procedures exist.

If none exist, the Secretary of State may give directions as to the procedure to be followed.

52. Co-ordination where more than one competent authority involved

(1) The following provisions apply where a plan or project—

    (a) is undertaken by more than one competent authority,

    (b) requires the consent, permission or other authorisation of more than one competent authority, or

(c) is undertaken by one or more competent authorities and requires the consent, permission or other authorisation of one or more other competent authorities.

(2) Nothing in regulation 48(1) or 50(2) requires a competent authority to assess any implications of a plan or project which would be more appropriately assessed under that provision by another competent authority.

(3) The Secretary of State may issue guidance to authorities for the purposes of regulations 48 to 51 as to the circumstances in which an authority may or should adopt the reasoning or conclusions of another competent authority as to whether a plan or project—
 (a) is likely to have a significant effect on a European site, or
 (b) will adversely affect the integrity of a European site;
and the authorities involved shall have regard to any guidance so issued in discharging their functions under those regulations.

(4) In determining whether a plan or project should be agreed to under regulation 49(1) (considerations of overriding public interest) a competent authority other than the Secretary of State shall seek and have regard to the views of the other competent authority or authorities involved.

53. Compensatory measures

Where in accordance with regulation 49 (considerations of overriding public interest)—
 (a) a plan or project is agreed to, notwithstanding a negative assessment of the implications for a European site, or
 (b) a decision, or a consent, permission or other authorisation, is affirmed on review, notwithstanding such an assessment,
the Secretary of State shall secure that any necessary compensatory measures are taken to ensure that the overall coherence of Natura 2000 is protected.
(Natura 2000 is a European network of special areas of conservation and special protection areas which exists under the EU's Wild Birds and Habitats Directives.)

Planning

54. Grant of planning permission

(1) Regulations 48 and 49 (requirement to consider effect on European site) apply in England and Wales, in relation to—
 (a) granting planning permission on an application under Part III of the Town and Country Planning Act 1990;
 (b) granting planning permission, or upholding a decision of the local planning authority to grant planning permission (whether or not subject to the same conditions and limitations as those imposed by the local planning authority), on determining an appeal under section 78 of that Act in respect of such an application;
 (c) granting planning permission under—
  (i) section 141(2)(a) of that Act (action by Secretary of State in relation to purchase notice),
  (ii) section 177(1)(a) of that Act (powers of Secretary of State on appeal against enforcement notice), or
  (iii) section 196(5) of that Act as originally enacted (powers of Secretary of State on reference or appeal as to established use certificate);
 (d) directing under section 90(1), (2) or (2A) of that Act (development with government authorisation), or under section 5(1) of the Pipe-lines Act 1962, that planning permission shall be deemed to be granted;
 (e) making—
  (i) an order under section 102 of that Act (order requiring discontinuance of use or removal of buildings or works), including an order made under that section

by virtue of section 104 (powers of Secretary of State), which grants planning permission, or

(ii) an order under paragraph 1 of Schedule 9 to that Act (order requiring discontinuance of mineral working), including an order made under that paragraph by virtue of paragraph 11 of that Schedule (default powers of Secretary of State), which grants planning permission,
or confirming any such order under section 103 of that Act;

(f) directing under—
(i) section 141(3) of that Act (action by Secretary of State in relation to purchase notice), or
(ii) section 35(5) of the Planning (Listed Buildings and Conservation Areas) Act 1990 (action by Secretary of State in relation to listed building purchase notice), that if an application is made for planning permission it shall be granted.

(2) [omitted]

(3) Where regulations 48 and 49 apply, the competent authority may, if they consider that any adverse effects of the plan or project on the integrity of a European site would be avoided if the planning permission were subject to conditions or limitations, grant planning permission or, as the case may be, take action which results in planning permission being granted or deemed to be granted subject to those conditions or limitations.

(4) Where regulations 48 and 49 apply, outline planning permission shall not be granted unless the competent authority are satisfied (whether by reason of the conditions and limitations to which the outline planning permission is to be made subject, or otherwise) that no development likely adversely to affect the integrity of a European site could be carried out under the permission, whether before or after obtaining approval of any reserved matters.

In this paragraph 'outline planning permission' and 'reserved matters' have the same meaning as in section 92 of the Town and Country Planning Act 1990 or section 39 of the Town and Country Planning (Scotland) Act 1972.

55. Planning permission: duty to review

(1) Subject to the following provisions of this regulation, regulations 50 and 51 (requirement to review certain decisions and consents, &c.) apply to any planning permission or deemed planning permission, unless—

(a) the development to which it related has been completed, or
(b) it was granted subject to a condition as to the time within which the development to which it related was to be begun and that time has expired without the development having been begun, or
(c) it was granted for a limited period and that period has expired.

(2) Regulations 50 and 51 do not apply to planning permission granted or deemed to have been granted—

(a) by a development order (but see regulations 60 to 64 below);
(b) by virtue of the adoption of a simplified planning zone scheme or of alterations to such a scheme (but see regulation 65 below);
(c) by virtue of the taking effect of an order designating an enterprise zone under Schedule 32 to the Local Government, Planning and Land Act 1980 or by virtue of the approval of a modified enterprise zone scheme (but see regulation 66 below).

(3) Planning permission deemed to be granted by virtue of—

(a) a direction under section 90(1) of the Town and Country Planning Act 1990 or section 37(1) of the Town and Country Planning (Scotland) Act 1972 in respect of development for which an authorisation has been granted under section 1 or 3 of the Pipe-lines Act 1962,
(b) a direction under section 5(1) of the Pipe-lines Act 1962,

(c) a direction under section 90(1) of the Town and Country Planning Act 1990 or section 37(1) of the Town and Country Planning (Scotland) Act 1972 in respect of development for which a consent has been given under section 36 or 37 of the Electricity Act 1989,

(d) a direction under section 90(2) of the Town and Country Planning Act 1990 or paragraph 7 of Schedule 8 to the Electricity Act 1989, or

(e) a direction under section 90(2A) of the Town and Country Planning Act 1990 (which relates to development in pursuance of an order under section 1 or 3 of the Transport and Works Act 1992),

shall be reviewed in accordance with the following provisions of this Part in conjunction with the review of the underlying authorisation, consent or order.

(4) In the case of planning permission deemed to have been granted in any other case by a direction under section 90(1) of the Town and Country Planning Act 1990 or section 37(1) of the Town and Country Planning (Scotland) Act 1972, the local planning authority shall—

(a) identify any such permission which they consider falls to be reviewed under regulations 50 and 51, and

(b) refer the matter to the government department which made the direction;

and the department shall, if it agrees that the planning permission does fall to be so reviewed, thereupon review the direction in accordance with those regulations.

(5) Save as otherwise expressly provided, regulations 50 and 51 do not apply to planning permission granted or deemed to be granted by a public general Act of Parliament.

(6) Subject to paragraphs (3) and (4), where planning permission granted by the Secretary of State falls to be reviewed under regulations 50 and 51—

(a) it shall be reviewed by the local planning authority, and

(b) the power conferred by section 97 of the Town and Country Planning Act 1990 or section 42 of the Town and Country Planning (Scotland) Act 1972 (revocation or modification of planning permission) shall be exercisable by that authority as in relation to planning permission granted on an application under Part III of that Act.

In a non-metropolitan county in England and Wales the function of reviewing any such planning permission shall be exercised by the district planning authority unless it relates to a county matter (within the meaning of Schedule 1 to the Town and Country Planning Act 1990) in which case it shall be exercised by the county planning authority.

56. Planning permission: consideration on review

(1) In reviewing any planning permission or deemed planning permission in pursuance of regulations 50 and 51, the competent authority shall, in England and Wales—

(a) consider whether any adverse effects could be overcome by planning obligations under section 106 of the Town and Country Planning Act 1990 being entered into, and

(b) if they consider that those effects could be so overcome, invite those concerned to enter into such obligations;

and so far as the adverse effects are not thus overcome the authority shall make such order under section 97 of that Act (power to revoke or modify planning permission), or under section 102 of or paragraph 1 of Schedule 9 to that Act (order requiring discontinuance of use, &c.), as may be required.

(2) [omitted]

(3) Where the authority ascertain that the carrying out or, as the case may be, the continuation of the development would adversely affect the integrity of a European

site, they nevertheless need not proceed under regulations 50 and 51 if and so long as they consider that there is no likelihood of the development being carried out or continued.

57. Effect of orders made on review: England and Wales

(1) An order under section 97 of the Town and Country Planning Act 1990 (power to revoke or modify planning permission) made pursuant to regulation 55 shall take effect upon service of the notices required by section 98(2) of that Act or, where there is more than one such notice and those notices are served at different times, upon the service of the last such notice to be served.

(2) Where the Secretary of State determines not to confirm such an order, the order shall cease to have effect from the time of that determination, and the permission revoked or modified by the order shall thereafter have effect as if the order had never been made, and—

(a) any period specified in the permission for the taking of any action, being a period which had not expired prior to the date upon which the order took effect under paragraph (1) above, shall be extended by a period equal to that during which the order had effect; and

(b) there shall be substituted for any date specified in the permission as being a date by which any action should be taken, not being a date falling prior to the date upon which the order took effect under paragraph (1) above, such date as post-dates the specified date by a period equal to that during which the order had effect.

(3) An order under section 102 of, or under paragraph 1 of Schedule 9 to, the Town and Country Planning Act 1990 (order requiring discontinuance of use, &c.) made pursuant to regulation 55 shall insofar as it requires the discontinuance of a use of land or imposes conditions upon the continuance of a use of land, take effect upon service of the notices required by section 103(3) or, where there is more than one such notice and those notices are served at different times, upon service of the last such notice to be served.

(4) Where the Secretary of State determines not to confirm any such order, the order shall cease to have effect from the time of that determination and the use which by the order was discontinued or upon whose continuance conditions were imposed—

(a) may thereafter be continued as if the order had never been made, and

(b) shall be treated for the purposes of the Town and Country Planning Act 1990 as if it had continued without interruption or modification throughout the period during which the order had effect.

(5) An order under section 97 of that Act (power to revoke or modify planning permission) made in pursuance of regulation 55 shall not affect so much of the development authorised by the permission as was carried out prior to the order taking effect.

(6) An order under section 102 of, or under paragraph 1 of Schedule 9 to, that Act (order requiring discontinuance of use, &c.) made in pursuance of regulation 55 shall not affect anything done prior to the site becoming a European site or, if later, the commencement of these Regulations.

58. [omitted]

59. Planning permission: supplementary provisions as to compensation

(1) Where the Secretary of State determines not to confirm—

(a) an order under section 97 of the Town and Country Planning Act 1990 (revocation or modification of planning permission) which has taken effect under regulation 57(1), or

(b) [omitted]

any claim for compensation under section 107 of the Act of 1990 or section 153 of the Act of 1972 shall be limited to any loss or damage directly attributable to the permission being suspended or temporarily modified for the duration of the period between the order so taking effect and the Secretary of State determining not to confirm the order.

(2) Where the Secretary of State determines not to confirm—

(a) an order under section 102 of the Town and Country Planning Act 1990 (order requiring discontinuance of use, &c.) which has taken effect under regulation 57(3) above, or

(b) [omitted]

any claim for compensation under section 115 of the Act of 1990 or section 159 of the Act of 1972 shall be limited to any loss or damage directly attributable to any right to continue a use of the land being, by virtue of the order, suspended or subject to conditions for the duration of the period between the order so taking effect and the Secretary of State determining not to confirm the order.

(3) Where compensation is payable in respect of—

(a) an order under section 97 of the Town and Country Planning Act 1990, or

(b) any order mentioned in section 115(1) of that Act (compensation in respect of orders under s.102, &c.), or to which that section applies by virtue of section 115(5),

and the order has been made pursuant to regulation 50, the question as to the amount of the compensation shall be referred, by the authority liable to pay the compensation, to and be determined by the Lands Tribunal unless and to the extent that in any particular case the Secretary of State has indicated in writing that such a reference and determination may be dispensed with.

(4) [omitted]

60. General development orders

(1) It shall be a condition of any planning permission granted by a general development order, whether made before or after the commencement of these Regulations, that development which—

(a) is likely to have a significant effect on a European site in Great Britain (either alone or in combination with other plans or projects), and

(b) is not directly connected with or necessary to the management of the site, shall not be begun until the developer has received written notification of the approval of the local planning authority under regulation 62.

(2) It shall be a condition of any planning permission granted by a general development order made before the commencement of these Regulations that development which—

(a) is likely to have a significant effect on a European site in Great Britain (either alone or in combination with other plans or projects), and

(b) is not directly connected with or necessary to the management of the site, and which was begun but not completed before the commencement of these Regulations, shall not be continued until the developer has received written notification of the approval of the local planning authority under regulation 62.

(3) Nothing in this regulation shall affect anything done before the commencement of these Regulations.

61. General development orders: opinion of appropriate nature conservation body

(1) Where it is intended to carry out development in reliance on the permission granted by a general development order, application may be made in writing to the appropriate nature conservation body for their opinion whether the development is likely to have such an effect as is mentioned in regulation 60(1)(a) or (2)(a).

The application shall give details of the development which is intended to be carried out.

(2) On receiving such an application, the appropriate nature conservation body shall consider whether the development is likely to have such an effect.

(3) Where they consider that they have sufficient information to conclude that the development will, or will not, have such an effect, they shall in writing notify the applicant and the local planning authority of their opinion.

(4) If they consider that they have insufficient information to reach either of those conclusions, they shall notify the applicant in writing indicating in what respects they consider the information insufficient; and the applicant may supply further information with a view to enabling them to reach a decision on the application.

(5) The opinion of the appropriate nature conservation body, notified in accordance with paragraph (3), that the development is not likely to have such an effect as is mentioned in regulation 60(1)(a) or (2)(a) shall be conclusive of that question for the purpose of reliance on the planning permission granted by a general development order.

62. General development orders: approval of local planning authority

(1) Where it is intended to carry out development in reliance upon the permission granted by a general development order, application may be made in writing to the local planning authority for their approval.

(2) The application shall—
  (a) give details of the development which is intended to be carried out; and
  (b) be accompanied by—
    (i) a copy of any relevant notification by the appropriate nature conservation body under regulation 61, and
    (ii) any fee required to be paid.

(3) For the purposes of their consideration of the application the local planning authority shall assume that the development is likely to have such an effect as is mentioned in regulation 60(1)(a) or (2)(a).

(4) The authority shall send a copy of the application to the appropriate nature conservation body and shall take account of any representations made by them.

(5) If in their representations the appropriate nature conservation body state their opinion that the development is not likely to have such an effect as is mentioned in regulation 60(1)(a) or (2)(a), the local planning authority shall send a copy of the representations to the applicant; and the sending of that copy shall have the same effect as a notification by the appropriate nature conservation body of its opinion under regulation 61(3).

(6) In any other case the local planning authority shall, taking account of any representations made by the appropriate nature conservation body, make an appropriate assessment of the implications of the development for the European site in view of that site's conservation objectives.

In the light of the conclusions of the assessment the authority shall approve the development only after having ascertained that it will not adversely affect the integrity of the site.

63. General development orders: supplementary

(1) The local planning authority for the purposes of regulations 60 to 62 shall be the authority to whom an application for approval under regulation 62 would fall to be made if it were an application for planning permission.

(2) The fee payable in connection with an application for such approval is—
  (a) £25 in the case of applications made before 3rd January 1995, and
  (b) £30 in the case of applications made on or after that date.

(3) Approval required by regulation 60 shall be treated—
  (a) for the purposes of the provisions of the Town and Country Planning Act 1990, or the Town and Country Planning (Scotland) Act 1972, relating to appeals, as approval required by a condition imposed on a grant of planning permission; and

(b) for the purposes of the provisions of any general development order relating to the time within which notice of a decision should be made, as approval required by a condition attached to a grant of planning permission.

64. Special development orders

(1) A special development order made after the commencement of these Regulations may not grant planning permission for development which—

  (a) is likely to have a significant effect on a European site in Great Britain (either alone or in combination with other plans or projects), and

  (b) is not directly connected with or necessary to the management of the site;

and any such order made before the commencement of these Regulations shall, on and after that date, cease to have effect to grant such permission, whether or not the development authorised by the permission has been begun.

(2) Nothing in this regulation shall affect anything done before the commencement of these Regulations.

65. Simplified planning zones

The adoption or approval of a simplified planning zone scheme after the commencement of these Regulations shall not have effect to grant planning permission for development which—

  (a) is likely to have a significant effect on a European site in Great Britain (either alone or in combination with other plans or projects), and

  (b) is not directly connected with or necessary to the management of the site; and every simplified planning zone scheme already in force shall cease to have effect to grant such permission, whether or not the development authorised by the permission has been begun.

66. Enterprise zones

An order designating an enterprise zone, or the approval of a modified scheme, if made or given after the commencement of these Regulations, shall not have effect to grant planning permission for development which—

  (a) is likely to have a significant effect on a European site in Great Britain (either alone or in combination with other plans or projects), and

  (b) is not directly connected with or necessary to the management of the site;

and where the order or approval was made or given before that date, the permission granted by virtue of the taking effect of the order or the modifications shall, from that date, cease to have effect to grant planning permission for such development, whether or not the development authorised by the permission has been begun.

67. Simplified planning zones and enterprise zones: supplementary provisions as to compensation

(1) Where in England and Wales—

  (a) planning permission is withdrawn by regulation 65 or 66, and

  (b) development authorised by the permission had been begun but not completed before the commencement of these Regulations, and

  (c) on an application made under Part III of the Town and Country Planning Act 1990 before the end of the period of 12 months beginning with the date of commencement of these Regulations, planning permission for the development is refused or is granted subject to conditions other than those imposed by the scheme, section 107(1)(a) of that Act (compensation in respect of abortive expenditure) shall apply as if the permission granted by the scheme had been granted by the local planning authority under Part III of that Act and had been revoked or modified by an order under section 97 of that Act.

(2) [omitted]

(3) Paragraphs (1) and (2) above do not apply in relation to planning permission for the development of operational land by statutory undertakers.

68. Construction as one with planning legislation
Regulations 54 to 67 shall be construed as one—
  (a) in England and Wales, with the Town and Country Planning Act 1990; and
  (b) [omitted]

TOWN AND COUNTRY PLANNING (DEMOLITION — DESCRIPTION OF BUILDINGS) DIRECTION 1995

The Secretary of State for the Environment, as respects England, and the Secretary of State for Wales, as respects Wales, in exercise of the powers conferred on them by section 55(2)(g) of the Town and Country Planning Act 1990 and of all other powers enabling them in that behalf, hereby give the following direction:

1. This direction shall come into force on 3 June 1995.

2.—(1) Subject to sub-paragraph (2), the demolition of the following descriptions of building shall not be taken, for the purposes of the Town and Country Planning Act 1990, to involve development of land:
  (a) any building which is a listed building as defined in section 1(5) of the Planning (Listed Buildings and Conservation Areas) Act 1990;
  (b) any building in a conservation area;
  (c) any building which is a scheduled monument as defined in section 1(11) of the Ancient Monuments and Archaeological Areas Act 1979;
  (d) subject to sub-paragraph (3), any building other than a dwellinghouse or a building adjoining a dwellinghouse;
  (e) any building the cubic content of which, measured externally, does not exceed 50 cubic metres;
  (f) the whole or any part of any gate, fence, wall or other means of enclosure.

(2) The descriptions of building in sub-paragraph (1) do not include the whole or any part of any gate, fence, wall or other means of enclosure in a conservation area.

(3) A building is not to be regarded as a dwellinghouse for the purpose of sub-paragraph (1)(d) if the use of that building, or part of that building, as a dwellinghouse is ancillary to any non-residential use of that building or other buildings on the same site.

3. In this direction—
'building' does not include part of a building, except—
  (a) for the purposes of paragraph 2(1)(f); and
  (b) in paragraphs 2(2) and (3);
and each house in a pair of semi-detached houses, and every house in a row of terrace houses (whether or not, in either case, the house is in residential use), is to be regarded as a building;
'conservation area' has the same meaning as in section 91(1) of the Planning (Listed Buildings and Conservation Areas) Act 1990;
'dwellinghouse' includes—
  (a) a residential home or hostel, and
  (b) a building containing a flat;
'flat' means a separate and self-contained set of premises constructed or adapted for use for the purpose of a dwelling and forming part of a building from some other part of which it is divided horizontally; and
'site' means the whole area of land within a single unit of occupation.

4. The Town and Country Planning (Demolition — Description of Buildings) Direction 1994 is hereby cancelled.

INDEX

Conservation (Natural Habitats, & c.) Regulations 1994
 regs 10, 47–57, 59–68 *497–507*

Environment Act 1995
 s. 96, Schs 9, 13, 14 *304–328*

Planning (Listed Buildings & Conservation Areas) Act 1990
 ss. 1–44, *44A*, 45–88, *88A, 88B*, 89–94, Schs 1–4 *249–304*

Town and Country Planning Act 1990
 ss. 1–4, 4A, 5–8, *8A*, 9, 10, 10A, 11, 12, *12A*, 13–23, *23A, 23B, 23C*, 24–27, *27A*, 28, 28A, 29–35, *35A, 35B, 35C*, 36–46, 49–51, *51A*, 52–54, *54A*, 55–70, *70A*, 71, *71A*, 72–73, *73A*, 74–106, *106A, 106B*, 107–147, 147A, 148–171, *171A, 171B, 171C, 171D*, 172–173, *173A*, 174–187, *187A, 187B*, 188–196, *196A, 196B, 196C*, 197–214, *214A, 214B, 214C, 214D*, 215–244, *244A*, 245–299, *299A*, 300–316, *316A*, 317–322, *322A*, 323–337, Schs 1, 1A–17 *1–248*

Town and Country Planning Appeals (Determination by Inspectors) (Inquiries Procedure) Rules 1992
 rr. 1–21 *488–497*

Town and Country Planning (Assessment of Environmental Effects) Regulations 1988
 regs 1–25, *25A*, 26, Schs 1–3 *444–461*

Town and Country Planning (Demolition — Description of Buildings) Direction 1995 *507*

Town and Country Planning (Development Plan) Regulations 1991
 rr. 1–39, Sch *461–478*

Town and Country Planning (Environmental Assessment and Permitted Development) Regulations 1995
 rr. 1–6 *328–331*

Town and Country Planning (General Development Procedure) Order 1995
 rr. 1–28, Schs 1–4 *332–402*

Town and Country Planning (General Permitted Development) Order 1995
 rr. 1–9, Schs 1–2 *403–441*

Town and Country Planning (Inquiries Procedure) Rules 1992 *478–488*

Town and Country Planning (Use Classes) Order 1987
 rr. 1–5, Sch *441–443*

BLACKSTONE'S STATUTES

TITLES IN THE SERIES

Contract, Tort and Restitution Statutes
Public Law Statutes
Employment Law Statutes
Criminal Law Statutes
Evidence Statutes
Family Law Statutes
Property Law Statutes
Commercial and Consumer Law Statutes
English Legal System Statutes
EC Legislation
International Law Documents
Landlord and Tenant Statutes
Medical Law Statutes
Planning Law Statutes
Intellectual Property Statutes
Environmental Law Statutes
International Human Rights Documents